THE
PUBLIC GENERAL ACTS
AND GENERAL SYNOD MEASURES
1979

[IN THREE PARTS]

PART I
(Chapters 1–27)

with
Lists of the Public General Acts,
Local Acts and an Index

LONDON
HER MAJESTY'S STATIONERY OFFICE
£60 net

HMSO
£60.00
11.80

ISBN 0 11 840194 7*

c

THIS PUBLICATION
relates to
the Public General Acts
and General Synod Measures
which received the Royal Assent in 1979
in which year ended the TWENTY-SEVENTH
and began the TWENTY-EIGHTH Year
of the Reign of HER MAJESTY
QUEEN ELIZABETH THE SECOND
That year comprised
the end of the Fifth Session of the
Forty-Seventh Parliament
and
the beginning of the First Session
of the Forty-Eighth Parliament
of the United Kingdom of Great Britain
and Northern Ireland

d

Printed by BERNARD M. THIMONT,
Controller of Her Majesty's Stationery Office and
Queen's Printer of Acts of Parliament

e

CONTENTS

PART I

PART II

PART III

TABLE I

Alphabetical List of
the Public General Acts of 1979

TABLE II

Chronological List of the Public General Acts of 1979

* Consolidation Act.

---

* Consolidation Act.

TABLE III

Alphabetical List of
the Local and Personal Acts of 1979

TABLE IV

Chronological List of
the General Synod Measures of 1979

There were no Measures passed by the General Synod of the
Church of England during the year 1979

Price Commission (Amendment) Act 1979

1979 CHAPTER 1

An Act to limit the application of section 9 of the Price Commission Act 1977.   [12th February 1979]

BE IT ENACTED by the Queen's most Excellent Majesty, by and with the advice and consent of the Lords Spiritual and Temporal, and Commons, in this present Parliament assembled, and by the authority of the same, as follows:—

1.—(1) Section 9 of the Price Commission Act 1977 (safeguard for basic profits) shall cease to apply except as regards the profits which persons are not to be prevented from earning by virtue of any such notice as is mentioned in section 13(1) of that Act (enforcement of orders made in consequence of reports on examinations); and accordingly that Act shall be amended as provided in the following provisions of this section.

Amendment of Price Commission Act 1977.
1977 c. 33.

(2) Section 4(5)(*b*) and (ii) (duty of the Price Commission to give a variation notice to the relevant person in cases where it appears to them that, apart from section 4(5), his profit would, in consequence of a notification under section 4(1), be kept below the profit determined in his case in pursuance of the said section 9) shall cease to have effect.

(3) In section 4(5)—

   (*a*) after paragraph (*a*) there shall be inserted—

      " (*aa*) that the whole or part of the increase ought not to be so restricted because of an increase in the costs of imported raw materials,";

Part I   A

(*b*) after paragraph (*i*) there shall be inserted—

" (*ia*) it shall be the duty of the Commission, in a case falling within paragraph (*aa*) of this sub-section, to give to the relevant person a variation notice allowing so much of the increase as they consider ought not to be restricted for the reason mentioned in that paragraph.".

(4) In section 5(4) (application of section 4(5) in relation to notifications in respect of prices) for the words " and for any other reference to the increase there were substituted a reference to the price " there shall be substituted the words " and as if—

(i) in paragraph (*aa*), for the words from " the whole " to " restricted " there were substituted the words " a particular increase in the price ought not to be restricted by virtue of section 5(3) of this Act ";

(ii) in paragraph (*ia*), for the words from " so " to " as " there were substituted the words " the increase in the price which "; and

(iii) for any reference to the increase (except those in para-graphs (*a*), (*aa*) and (*ia*)) there were substituted a reference to the price; ".

(5) In section 7 (restrictions, undertakings and orders in con-sequence of reports on investigations) there shall be omitted—

(*a*) in subsection (1), the words " and subject to section 9 of this Act ";

(*b*) in subsection (5)(*a*)(ii), the words " except by virtue of section 9 of this Act " ;

(*c*) subsection (7)(*b*) and the word " and " preceding it ; and

(*d*) in subsection (8), the words " apart from section 9 of this Act ".

(6) In section 9 (safeguard for basic profits)—

(*a*) subsection (1)(*a*) (which provides for the making of regulations as to the profits which are relevant for the purposes of section 4(5)(*b*)) shall be omitted ; and

(*b*) in subsection (1)(*b*), for the words " any provision of section 7 of this Act " there shall be substituted the words " any such notice as is mentioned in section 13(1) of this Act ".

(7) In section 13 (enforcement of orders and supervision of undertakings in consequence of reports on examinations) there shall be omitted—

(*a*) in subsection (1)(*b*), the words " by virtue of subsection (6) of this section " ; and (*b*) in subsection (6), the words from "and section 9(1)" onwards.

(8) The enactments mentioned in the Schedule to this Act are hereby repealed to the extent specified in the third column of that Schedule.

(9) The preceding provisions of this section shall not apply in relation to any increase of which notice was given to the Price Commission as mentioned in section 4(1) of the Price 1977 c. 33. Commission Act 1977 before 17th January 1979; but as from the passing of this Act the regulations then in force under section 9 of that Act shall apply in relation to any such increase only so far as they were made in pursuance of subsection (1)(*a*) of the said section 9.

2.—(1) As from the end of the relevant period the Price Com- Duration of mission Act 1977 shall have effect as it would if the following Act. provisions of this Act, namely section 1 and the Schedule, had not been enacted, but without prejudice to the operation of those provisions during that period.

(2) Subject to subsection (3), the relevant period for the purposes of this section is the period of one year beginning with the date on which this Act is passed.

(3) Her Majesty may by Order in Council extend or further extend the relevant period for the purposes of this section; but the extension effected by any particular Order under this subsection shall not exceed 12 months.

(4) An Order under subsection (3) shall not be made unless a draft of the Order has been laid before Parliament and approved by a resolution of each House of Parliament.

3. This Act may be cited as the Price Commission (Amend- Short title. ment) Act 1979.

A 2

SCHEDULE

REPEALS

Chapter	Short title	Extent of repeal

1977 c. 33.	Price Commission Act 1977.	Section 4(5)(*b*) and (ii).
		In section 7—
		  (*a*) in subsection (1), the words "and subject to section 9 of this Act";
		  (*b*) in subsection (5)(*a*)(ii), the words "except by virtue of section 9 of this Act";
		  (*c*) subsection (7)(*b*) and the word "and" preceding it; and
		  (*d*) in subsection (8), the words "apart from section 9 of this Act".
		Section 9(1)(*a*).
		In section 13—
		  (*a*) in subsection (1)(*b*), the words "by virtue of subsection (6) of this section"; and
		  (*b*) in subsection (6), the words from "and section 9(1)" onwards.

Customs and Excise Management Act 1979

1979 CHAPTER 2

An Act to consolidate the enactments relating to the collection and management of the revenues of customs and excise and in some cases to other matters in relation to which the Commissioners of Customs and Excise for the time being perform functions, with amendments to give effect to recommendations of the Law Commission and the Scottish Law Commission. [22nd February 1979]

BE IT ENACTED by the Queen's most Excellent Majesty, by and with the advice and consent of the Lords Spiritual and Temporal, and Commons, in this present Parliament assembled, and by the authority of the same, as follows:—

PART I

PRELIMINARY

1.—(1) In this Act, unless the context otherwise requires—   Interpretation.

" aerodrome " means any area of land or water designed, equipped, set apart or commonly used for affording facilities for the landing and departure of aircraft;

" approved route " has the meaning given by section 26 below;

" approved wharf " has the meaning given by section 20 below;

" armed forces " means the Royal Navy, the Royal Marines, the regular army and the regular air force, and any reserve or auxiliary force of any of those services which has been called out on permanent service, or called into actual service, or embodied;

A3

" assigned matter " means any matter in relation to which the Commissioners are for the time being required in pursuance of any enactment to perform any duties;

" boarding station " means a boarding station for the time being appointed under section 19 below;

" boundary " means the land boundary of Northern Ireland;

" British ship " means a British ship within the meaning of the Merchant Shipping Act 1894, so, however, as not to include a ship registered in any country other than the United Kingdom, the Channel Islands, the Isle of Man or a colony within the meaning of the British Nationality Act 1948;

" claimant ", in relation to proceedings for the condemnation of any thing as being forfeited, means a person claiming that the thing is not liable to forfeiture;

" coasting ship " has the meaning given by section 69 below;

" commander ", in relation to an aircraft, includes any person having or taking the charge or command of the aircraft;

" the Commissioners " means the Commissioners of Customs and Excise;

" Community transit goods "—

    (*a*) in relation to imported goods, means—

        (i) goods which have been imported under the internal or external Community transit procedure for transit through the United Kingdom with a view to exportation where the importation was and the transit and exportation are to be part of one Community transit operation; or

        (ii) goods which have, at the port or airport at which they were imported, been placed under the internal or external Community transit procedure for transit through the United Kingdom with a view to exportation where the transit and exportation are to be part of one Community transit operation;

    (*b*) in relation to goods for exportation, means—

        (i) goods which have been imported as mentioned in paragraph (*a*)(i) of this definition and are to be exported as part of the Community transit operation in the course of which they were imported; or

        (ii) goods which have, under the internal or external Community transit procedure,

1894 c. 60.

1948 c. 56.

transited the United Kingdom from the
port or airport at which they were imported
and are to be exported as part of the Community transit operation which commenced
at that port or airport ;

" container " includes any bundle or package and any box,
cask or other receptacle whatsoever ;

" the customs and excise Acts " means the Customs and
Excise Acts 1979 and any other enactment for the time
being in force relating to customs or excise ;

" the Customs and Excise Acts 1979 " means—
this Act,
the Customs and Excise Duties (General Reliefs) Act 1979 c. 3.
1979,
the Alcoholic Liquor Duties Act 1979, 1979 c. 4.
the Hydrocarbon Oil Duties Act 1979, 1979 c. 5.
the Matches and Mechanical Lighters Duties Act 1979, 1979 c. 6.
and
the Tobacco Products Duty Act 1979 ; 1979 c. 7.

" customs warehouse " means a place of security approved
by the Commissioners under subsection (2) (whether or
not it is also approved under subsection (1)) of section
92 below ;

" customs and excise airport " has the meaning given by
section 21(7) below ;

" customs and excise station " has the meaning given by
section 26 below ;

" drawback goods " means goods in the case of which a
claim for drawback has been or is to be made ;

" dutiable goods ", except in the expression " dutiable or
restricted goods ", means goods of a class or description subject to any duty of customs or excise, whether
or not those goods are in fact chargeable with that
duty, and whether or not that duty has been paid
thereon ;

" dutiable or restricted goods " has the meaning given by
section 52 below ;

" examination station " has the meaning given by section
22 below ;

" excise licence trade " means, subject to subsection (5)
below, a trade or business for the carrying on of which
an excise licence is required ;

" excise warehouse " means a place of security approved by
the Commissioners under subsection (1) (whether or not

it is also approved under subsection (2)) of section 92 below, and, except in that section, also includes a distiller's warehouse ;

" exporter ", in relation to goods for exportation or for use as stores, includes the shipper of the goods and any person performing in relation to an aircraft functions corresponding with those of a shipper ;

" goods " includes stores and baggage ;

" holiday ", in relation to any part of the United Kingdom, means any day that is a bank holiday in that part of the United Kingdom under the Banking and Financial Dealings Act 1971, Christmas Day, Good Friday and the day appointed for the purposes of customs and excise for the celebration of Her Majesty's birthday ;

1971 c. 80.

" hovercraft " means a hovercraft within the meaning of the Hovercraft Act 1968 ;

1968 c. 59.

" importer ", in relation to any goods at any time between their importation and the time when they are delivered out of charge, includes any owner or other person for the time being possessed of or beneficially interested in the goods and, in relation to goods imported by means of a pipe-line, includes the owner of the pipe-line ;

" justice " and " justice of the peace " in Scotland includes a sheriff and in Northern Ireland, in relation to any powers and duties which can under any enactment for the time being in force be exercised and performed only by a resident magistrate, means a resident magistrate ;

" land " and " landing ", in relation to aircraft, include alighting on water ;

" law officer of the Crown " means the Attorney General or in Scotland the Lord Advocate or in Northern Ireland the Attorney General for Northern Ireland ;

" licence year ", in relation to an excise licence issuable annually, means the period of 12 months ending on the date on which that licence expires in any year ;

" master ", in relation to a ship, includes any person having or taking the charge or command of the ship ;

" nautical mile " means a distance of 1,852 metres ;

" night " means the period between 11 pm and 5 am ;

" occupier ", in relation to any bonded premises, means the person who has given security to the Crown in respect of those premises ;

" officer " means, subject to section 8(2) below, a person commissioned by the Commissioners ;

" owner ", in relation to an aircraft, includes the operator of the aircraft ;

" owner ", in relation to a pipe-line, means (except in the case of a pipe-line vested in the Crown which in pursuance of arrangements in that behalf is operated by another) the person in whom the line is vested and, in the said excepted case, means the person operating the line ;

" perfect entry " means an entry made in accordance with section 37 below or warehousing regulations, as the case may require ;

" pipe-line " has the meaning given by section 65 of the Pipe-lines Act 1962 (that Act being taken, for the purposes of this definition, to extend to Northern Ireland) ;

" port " means a port appointed by the Commissioners under section 19 below ;

" prescribed area " means such an area in Northern Ireland adjoining the boundary as the Commissioners may by regulations prescribe ;

" prescribed sum ", in relation to the penalty provided for an offence, has the meaning given by section 171(2) below ;

" prohibited or restricted goods " means goods of a class or description of which the importation, exportation or carriage coastwise is for the time being prohibited or restricted under or by virtue of any enactment ;

" proper ", in relation to the person by, with or to whom, or the place at which, anything is to be done, means the person or place appointed or authorised in that behalf by the Commissioners ;

" proprietor ", in relation to any goods, includes any owner, importer, exporter, shipper or other person for the time being possessed of or beneficially interested in those goods ;

" Queen's warehouse " means any place provided by the Crown or appointed by the Commissioners for the deposit of goods for security thereof and of the duties chargeable thereon ;

" the revenue trade provisions of the customs and excise Acts " means—

    (a) the provisions of the customs and excise Acts relating to the protection, security, collection or management of the revenues derived from the duties of excise on goods produced or manufactured in the United Kingdom ;

(*b*) the provisions of the customs and excise Acts relating to any activity or facility for the carrying on or provision of which an excise licence is required ; and

(*c*) the provisions of the Betting and Gaming Duties Act 1972 (so far as not included in paragraph (*b*) above) ;

" revenue trader " means any person carrying on a trade or business subject to any of the revenue trade provisions of the customs and excise Acts, whether or not that trade or business is an excise licence trade, and includes a registered club ;

" ship " and " vessel " include any boat or other vessel whatsoever (and, to the extent provided in section 2 below, any hovercraft) ;

" shipment " includes loading into an aircraft, and " shipped " and cognate expressions shall be construed accordingly ;

" stores " means, subject to subsection (4) below, goods for use in a ship or aircraft and includes fuel and spare parts and other articles of equipment, whether or not for immediate fitting ;

" tons register " means the tons of a ship's net tonnage as ascertained and registered according to the tonnage regulations of the Merchant Shipping Act 1894 or, in the case of a ship which is not registered under that Act, ascertained in like manner as if it were to be so registered ;

" transit goods ", except in the expression " Community transit goods ", means imported goods entered on importation for transit or transhipment ;

" transit or transhipment ", in relation to the entry of goods, means transit through the United Kingdom or transhipment with a view to the re-exportation of the goods in question ;

" transit shed " has the meaning given by section 25 below ;

" vehicle " includes a railway vehicle ;

" warehouse ", except in the expressions " Queen's warehouse " and " distiller's warehouse ", means a place of security approved by the Commissioners under subsection (1) or (2) or subsections (1) and (2) of section 92 below and, except in that section, also includes a distiller's warehouse ; and " warehoused " and cognate expressions shall, subject to subsection (4) of that section, be construed accordingly ;

" warehousing regulations " means regulations under section 93 below.

(2) This Act and the other Acts included in the Customs and Excise Acts 1979 shall be construed as one Act but where a provision of this Act refers to this Act that reference is not to be construed as including a reference to any of the others.

(3) Any expression used in this Act or in any instrument made under this Act to which a meaning is given by any other Act included in the Customs and Excise Acts 1979 has, except where the context otherwise requires, the same meaning in this Act or any such instrument as in that Act; and for ease of reference the Table below indicates the expressions used in this Act to which a meaning is given by any other such Act—

Alcoholic Liquor Duties Act 1979

" beer "
" brewer " and " brewer for sale "
" cider "
" compounder "
" distiller "
" distiller's warehouse "
" dutiable alcoholic liquor "
" licensed ", in relation to producers of wine or made-wine
" made-wine "
" producer of made-wine "
" producer of wine "
" proof "
" rectifier "
" registered club "
" spirits "
" wine "

Hydrocarbon Oil Duties Act 1979

" rebate "
" refinery "

Tobacco Products Duty Act 1979

" tobacco products "

(4) Subject to section 12 of the Customs and Excise Duties 1979 c. 3. (General Reliefs) Act 1979 (by which goods for use in naval ships or establishments may be required to be treated as exported), any goods for use in a ship or aircraft as merchandise for sale by retail to persons carried therein shall be treated for the purposes of the customs and excise Acts as stores, and any reference in those Acts to the consumption of stores shall, in relation to goods so treated, be construed as referring to the sale thereof as aforesaid.

(5) A person who deals in or sells tobacco products in the course of a trade or business carried on by him shall be deemed for the purposes of this Act to be carrying on an excise licence trade (and to be a revenue trader) notwithstanding that no excise licence is required for carrying on that trade or business.

Part I

(6) In computing for the purposes of this Act any period expressed therein as a period of clear days no account shall be taken of the day of the event from which the period is computed or of any Sunday or holiday.

(7) The provisions of this Act in so far as they relate to customs duties apply, notwithstanding that any duties are imposed for the benefit of the Communities, as if the revenue from duties so imposed remained part of the revenues of the Crown.

Application to hovercraft.

2.—(1) This Part, Parts III to VII and Parts X to XII of this Act shall apply as if references to ships or vessels included references to hovercraft, and the said Parts III to VII shall apply in relation to an approved wharf or transit shed which is not in a port as if it were in a port.

(2) All other provisions of the customs and excise Acts shall apply as if references (however expressed) to goods or passengers carried in or moved by ships or vessels included references to goods or passengers carried in or moved by hovercraft.

(3) In all the provisions of the customs and excise Acts " landed ", " loaded ", " master ", " shipped ", " shipped as stores ", " transhipment ", voyage ", " waterborne " and cognate expressions shall be construed in accordance with subsections (1) and (2) above.

(4) References in the customs and excise Acts to goods imported or exported by land, or conveyed into or out of Northern Ireland by land, include references to goods imported, exported or conveyed across any part of the boundary of Northern Ireland ; and it is hereby declared that in those Acts references to vehicles include references to hovercraft proceeding over land or water or partly over land and partly over water.

(5) Any power of making regulations or other instruments relating to the importation or exportation of goods conferred by the customs and excise Acts may be exercised so as to make provision for the importation or exportation of goods by hovercraft which is different from the provision made for the importation or exportation of goods by other means.

Application to pipe-lines.

3.—(1) In the customs and excise Acts " shipping " and " loading " and cognate expressions, where used in relation to importation or exportation, include, in relation to importation or exportation by means of a pipe-line, the conveyance of goods by means of the pipe-line and the charging and discharging of goods into and from the pipe-line, but subject to any necessary modifications.

(2) In the customs and excise Acts " importer ", in relation to goods imported by means of a pipe-line, includes the owner of the pipe-line.

(3) Any power of making regulations or other instruments relating to the importation or exportation of goods conferred by the customs and excise Acts may be exercised so as to make provision for the importation or exportation of goods by means of a pipe-line which is different from the provision made for the importation or exportation of goods by other means.

4.—(1) The provisions of the Customs and Excise Acts 1979 relating to aircraft shall apply in relation to any aircraft belonging to or employed in the service of Her Majesty other than a military aircraft.

(2) In this section " military aircraft " includes naval and air force aircraft and any aircraft commanded by a person in naval, military or air force service detailed for the purpose of such command.

5.—(1) The provisions of this section shall have effect for the purposes of the customs and excise Acts.

(2) Subject to subsections (3) and (6) below, the time of importation of any goods shall be deemed to be—

(a) where the goods are brought by sea, the time when the ship carrying them comes within the limits of a port ;

(b) where the goods are brought by air, the time when the aircraft carrying them lands in the United Kingdom or the time when the goods are unloaded in the United Kingdom, whichever is the earlier ;

(c) where the goods are brought by land, the time when the goods are brought across the boundary into Northern Ireland.

(3) In the case of goods brought by sea of which entry is not required under section 37 below, the time of importation shall be deemed to be the time when the ship carrying them came within the limits of the port at which the goods are discharged.

(4) Subject to subsections (5) and (7) below, the time of exportation of any goods from the United Kingdom shall be deemed to be—

(a) where the goods are exported by sea or air, the time when the goods are shipped for exportation ;

(b) where the goods are exported by land, the time when they are cleared by the proper officer at the last customs and excise station on their way to the boundary.

(5) In the case of goods of a class or description with respect to the exportation of which any prohibition or restriction is for the time being in force under or by virtue of any enactment which are exported by sea or air, the time of exportation shall be deemed to be the time when the exporting ship or aircraft

PART I

departs from the last port or customs and excise airport at which it is cleared before departing for a destination outside the United Kingdom.

(6) Goods imported by means of a pipe-line shall be treated as imported at the time when they are brought within the limits of a port or brought across the boundary into Northern Ireland.

(7) Goods exported by means of a pipe-line shall be treated as exported at the time when they are charged into that pipe-line for exportation.

(8) A ship shall be deemed to have arrived at or departed from a port at the time when the ship comes within or, as the case may be, leaves the limits of that port.

PART II

ADMINISTRATION

Appointment and duties of Commissioners, officers, etc.

Appointment and general duties of Commissioners, etc.

6.—(1) Her Majesty may from time to time, under the Great Seal of the United Kingdom, appoint persons to be Commissioners of Customs and Excise, and any person so appointed shall hold office during Her Majesty's pleasure and may be paid such remuneration and allowances as the Minister for the Civil Service may determine.

(2) In addition to the duties conferred on them by or under any other enactment, the Commissioners shall, subject to the general control of the Treasury, be charged with the duty of collecting and accounting for, and otherwise managing, the revenues of customs and excise.

(3) The Commissioners may commission such officers and appoint or authorise such other persons to discharge any duties in relation to any assigned matter on such terms and conditions, and may pay to them such remuneration and allowances, as the Commissioners may with the sanction of the Minister for the Civil Service determine.

(4) The Commissioners may at their pleasure suspend, reduce, discharge or restore any officer or person so commissioned, appointed or authorised.

(5) The days on which and the hours between which offices of customs and excise are to be open or officers are to be available for the performance of particular duties shall be such as the Commissioners may direct.

Privileges of Commissioners, etc.

7.—(1) Save as expressly provided by or under any enactment, no sum granted by way of remuneration or superannuation allowance to any person as being or having been a Commissioner, officer or person appointed by the Commissioners to discharge any duty relating to customs or excise shall before payment thereof to or for the use of that person be capable of assignment or be liable to be taken under or by virtue of any legal process.

(2) The benefits and advantages arising from membership of the Customs Annuity and Benevolent Fund shall be available to and in respect of the Commissioners, all officers and all persons appointed by the Commissioners to discharge any duty relating to any assigned matter.

8.—(1) Any act or thing required or authorised by or under any enactment to be done by the Commissioners or any of them may be done—

> (*a*) by any one or more of the Commissioners ; or
>
> (*b*) if the Commissioners so authorise, by a secretary or assistant secretary to the Commissioners ; or
>
> (*c*) by any other person authorised generally or specially in that behalf in writing by the Commissioners.

(2) Any person, whether an officer or not, engaged by the orders or with the concurrence of the Commissioners (whether previously or subsequently expressed) in the performance of any act or duty relating to an assigned matter which is by law required or authorised to be performed by or with an officer, shall be deemed to be the proper officer by or with whom that act or duty is to be performed.

(3) Any person deemed by virtue of subsection (2) above to be the proper officer shall have all the powers of an officer in relation to the act or duty performed or to be performed by him as mentioned in that subsection.

9. For the purpose of implementing Community obligations the Commissioners shall co-operate with other customs services on matters of mutual concern, and (without prejudice to the foregoing) may for that purpose—

> (*a*) give effect, in accordance with such arrangements as they may direct or by regulations prescribe, to any Community requirement or practice as to the movement of goods between countries, including any rules requiring payment to be made in connection with the exportation of goods to compensate for any relief from customs duty allowed or to be allowed (and may recover any such payment as if it were an amount of customs duty unpaid) ; and
>
> (*b*) give effect to any reciprocal arrangements made between member States (with or without other countries or territories) for securing, by the exchange of information or

otherwise, the due administration of their customs laws and the prevention or detection of fraud or evasion.

Disclosure by Commissioners of certain information as to imported goods.

10.—(1) On being notified at any time by the Treasury that they are satisfied that it is in the national interest that the information in question should be disclosed to persons other than the Commissioners, the Commissioners may disclose through such person as may be specified in the notification such information to which this section applies, in respect of imported goods of such descriptions, as may be so specified.

(2) The information to which this section applies is information contained in any document with which the Commissioners have been provided in pursuance of the Customs and Excise Acts 1979 for the purpose of making entry of any goods on their importation, being information of the following descriptions only, namely—

(a) the description of the goods, including any maker's catalogue number ;

(b) the quantities of the goods imported in a particular period, so, however, that if any quantity is given by value it shall not also be given in any other form ;

(c) the name of the maker of the goods ;

(d) the country of origin of the goods ;

(e) the country from which the goods were consigned.

(3) Without prejudice to paragraph 10 of Schedule 7 to this Act, this section also applies to information of any of those descriptions contained in any document with which the Commissioners have been provided for that purpose after 7th March 1967 in pursuance of the Customs and Excise Act 1952.

1952 c. 44.

(4) The Treasury may by order add to the descriptions of information to which this section applies any further description of information contained in any document such as is mentioned in subsection (2) or (3) above other than the price of the goods or the name of the importer of the goods.

(5) The power to make orders under subsection (4) above shall be exercisable by statutory instrument subject to annulment in pursuance of a resolution of either House of Parliament.

Assistance to be rendered by police, etc.

11. It shall be the duty of every constable and every member of Her Majesty's armed forces or coastguard to assist in the enforcement of the law relating to any assigned matter.

Power to hold inquiries.

12.—(1) The Commissioners may hold or cause to be held such inquiries as they consider necessary or desirable for the purposes of any assigned matter, including inquiries into the conduct of any officer or of any person appointed by them.

(2) The person holding any such inquiry—

    (a) may require any person, subject to the tender of the reasonable expenses of his attendance, to attend as a witness and give evidence or to produce any document in his possession or control which relates to any matter in question at the inquiry and is such as would be subject to production in a court of law ; and

    (b) may require evidence to be given on oath, and for that purpose shall have power to administer oaths.

(3) If any person fails without reasonable excuse to comply with any such requirement as aforesaid, he shall be liable on summary conviction to a penalty of £25.

(4) Subject to the foregoing provisions of this section, the procedure and conduct of any inquiry under this section shall be such as the Commissioners may direct.

Offences in connection with Commissioners, officers, etc.

13. If, for the purpose of obtaining admission to any house or other place, or of doing or procuring to be done any act which he would not be entitled to do or procure to be done of his own authority, or for any other unlawful purpose, any person falsely assumes the name, designation or character of a Commissioner or officer or of a person appointed by the Commissioners he may be detained and shall, in addition to any other punishment to which he may have rendered himself liable, be liable— *Unlawful assumption of character of officer, etc.*

    (a) on summary conviction, to a penalty of the prescribed sum, or to imprisonment for a term not exceeding 3 months, or to both ; or

    (b) on conviction on indictment, to a penalty of any amount, or to imprisonment for a term not exceeding 2 years, or to both.

14.—(1) If any person to whom a commission or other written authority has been issued by the Commissioners is required by the Commissioners to deliver up or account to their satisfaction for that commission or authority and fails to comply within such period as may be specified in the requirement, he shall be liable on summary conviction to a penalty of £20. *Failure to surrender commission, etc.*

(2) If the failure continues after he is convicted thereof he shall be guilty of a further offence and be liable on summary conviction to a penalty of £5 for every day on which the failure has so continued.

15.—(1) If any Commissioner or officer or any person appointed or authorised by the Commissioners to discharge any duty relating to an assigned matter—

   (a) directly or indirectly asks for or takes in connection with any of his duties any payment or other reward whatsoever, whether pecuniary or other, or any promise or security for any such payment or reward, not being a payment or reward which he is lawfully entitled to claim or receive ; or

   (b) enters into or acquiesces in any agreement to do, abstain from doing, permit, conceal or connive at any act or thing whereby Her Majesty is or may be defrauded or which is otherwise unlawful, being an act or thing relating to an assigned matter,

he shall be guilty of an offence under this section.

   (2) If any person—

   (a) directly or indirectly offers or gives to any Commissioner or officer or to any person appointed or authorised by the Commissioners as aforesaid any payment or other reward whatsoever, whether pecuniary or other, or any promise or security for any such payment or reward ; or

   (b) proposes or enters into any agreement with any Commissioner, officer or person appointed or authorised as aforesaid,

in order to induce him to do, abstain from doing, permit, conceal or connive at any act or thing whereby Her Majesty is or may be defrauded or which is otherwise unlawful, being an act or thing relating to an assigned matter, or otherwise to take any course contrary to his duty, he shall be guilty of an offence under this section.

   (3) Any person committing an offence under this section shall be liable on summary conviction to a penalty of £500 and may be detained.

16.—(1) Any person who—

   (a) obstructs, hinders, molests or assaults any person duly engaged in the performance of any duty or the exercise of any power imposed or conferred on him by or under any enactment relating to an assigned matter, or any person acting in his aid ; or

   (b) does anything which impedes or is calculated to impede the carrying out of any search for any thing liable to forfeiture under any such enactment or the detention, seizure or removal of any such thing ; or

(c) rescues, damages or destroys any thing so liable to forfeiture or does anything calculated to prevent the procuring or giving of evidence as to whether or not any thing is so liable to forfeiture ; or

(d) prevents the detention of any person by a person duly engaged or acting as aforesaid or rescues any person so detained,

or who attempts to do any of the aforementioned things, shall be guilty of an offence under this section.

(2) A person guilty of an offence under this section shall be liable—

(a) on summary conviction, to a penalty of the prescribed sum, or to imprisonment for a term not exceeding 3 months, or to both ; or

(b) on conviction on indictment, to a penalty of any amount, or to imprisonment for a term not exceeding 2 years, or to both.

(3) Any person committing an offence under this section and any person aiding or abetting the commission of such an offence may be detained.

Commissioners' receipts and expenses

17.—(1) Save for such sums as may be required for any disbursements permitted by section 10 of the Exchequer and Audit Departments Act 1866, all money and securities for money collected or received in Great Britain for or on account of customs or excise shall be paid or remitted to and accounted for by the Bank of England in such manner as the Commissioners may with the approval of the Treasury direct, and shall be placed to the account in the books of the Bank entitled " the General Account of the Commissioners of Customs and Excise ".

(2) The Bank shall deliver to the Commissioners each day a statement in writing of the money or securities for money, if any, received on that day from or on account of the Commissioners, and every statement so delivered shall be deemed to be a sufficient acknowledgement by the Bank of the receipt of the money and securities specified therein.

(3) Any money and securities for money standing to the credit of the General Account shall be dealt with as provided in section 10 of the Exchequer and Audit Departments Act 1866 subject, however, to payment to the Government of the Isle of Man of the amounts mentioned in section 2(1) of the Isle of Man Act 1958 (payments of Isle of Man share of equal duties).

(4) All money and securities for money collected or received in Northern Ireland for or on account of—

> (a) duties of customs or excise on goods imported into or manufactured or produced in Northern Ireland; or

> (b) any duties of excise specified in any order of the Treasury for the time being in force under section 37(3) of the Northern Ireland Constitution Act 1973,

1973 c. 36.

1866 c. 39.

shall be dealt with as provided in section 10 of the Exchequer and Audit Departments Act 1866.

(5) Notwithstanding anything in section 10 of the Exchequer and Audit Departments Act 1866 or in subsection (1) above as to the disbursements which may be made out of money collected or received for or on account of customs or excise—

> (a) any sum required for the purpose of such disbursements in the Port of London shall be paid out of the General Account; and

> (b) no repayment of sums overpaid in error shall be made unless the claim thereto is made and evidence in support thereof is submitted to the Commissioners within 6 years of the date of the overpayment and the claim is established to the satisfaction of the Commissioners.

(6) Any reference in this section to money and securities for money collected or received for or on account of customs or excise or of any duties thereof includes a reference to any sums received under or by virtue of any enactment relating to customs or excise or to those duties by way of pecuniary penalties or the pecuniary proceeds of any forfeiture, costs, or otherwise howsoever.

Remuneration and expenses of Commissioners.

18. Any remuneration and allowances payable to the Commissioners under this Act and any expenses of the Commissioners under the Customs and Excise Acts 1979 shall be defrayed out of money provided by Parliament.

PART III

CUSTOMS AND EXCISE CONTROL AREAS

Appointment of ports, etc.

19.—(1) The Commissioners may by order made by statutory instrument appoint and name as a port for the purposes of customs and excise any area in the United Kingdom specified in the order.

(2) The appointment of any port for those purposes made before 1st August 1952 may be revoked, and the name or limits of any such port may be altered, by an order under subsection

(1) above as if the appointment had been made by an order under that subsection.

(3) The Commissioners may in any port from time to time appoint boarding stations for the purpose of the boarding of or disembarkation from ships by officers.

20.—(1) The Commissioners may approve, for such periods and subject to such conditions and restrictions as they think fit, places for the loading or unloading of goods or of any class or description of goods; and any place so approved is referred to in this Act as an " approved wharf ".

(2) The Commissioners may at any time for reasonable cause revoke or vary the terms of any approval given under this section.

(3) Any person contravening or failing to comply with any condition or restriction imposed by the Commissioners under this section shall be liable on summary conviction to a penalty of £100.

21.—(1) Save as permitted by the Commissioners, the commander of an aircraft entering the United Kingdom from a place outside the United Kingdom shall not cause or permit the aircraft to land—

(a) for the first time after its arrival in the United Kingdom; or

(b) at any time while it is carrying passengers or goods brought in that aircraft from a place outside the United Kingdom and not yet cleared,

at any place other than a customs and excise airport.

(2) Save as permitted by the Commissioners, no person importing or concerned in importing any goods in any aircraft shall bring the goods into the United Kingdom at any place other than a customs and excise airport.

(3) Save as permitted by the Commissioners—

(a) no person shall depart on a flight to a place or area outside the United Kingdom from any place in the United Kingdom other than a customs and excise airport; and

(b) the commander of any aircraft engaged in a flight from a customs and excise airport to a place or area outside the United Kingdom shall not cause or permit it to land at any place in the United Kingdom other than a customs and excise airport specified in the application for clearance for that flight.

(4) Subsections (1) to (3) above shall not apply in relation to any aircraft flying from or to any place or area outside the United Kingdom to or from any place in the United Kingdom which is required by or under any enactment relating to air navigation, or is compelled by accident, stress of weather or other unavoidable cause, to land at a place other than a customs and excise airport ; but, subject to subsection (5) below,—

(*a*) the commander of any such aircraft—

(i) shall immediately report the landing to an officer or constable and shall on demand produce to him the journey log book belonging to the aircraft,

(ii) shall not without the consent of an officer permit any goods carried in the aircraft to be unloaded from, or any of the crew or passengers to depart from the vicinity of, the aircraft, and

(iii) shall comply with any directions given by an officer with respect to any such goods ; and

(*b*) no passenger or member of the crew shall without the consent of an officer or constable leave the immediate vicinity of any such aircraft.

(5) Nothing in subsection (4) above shall prohibit—

(*a*) the departure of passengers or crew from the vicinity of an aircraft ; or

(*b*) the removal of goods from an aircraft,

where that departure or removal is necessary for reasons of health, safety or the preservation of life or property.

(6) Any person contravening or failing to comply with any provision of this section shall be liable on summary conviction to a penalty of £200, or to imprisonment for a term not exceeding 3 months, or to both.

(7) In this Act " customs and excise airport " means an aerodrome for the time being designated as a place for the landing or departure of aircraft for the purposes of the customs and excise Acts by an order made by the Secretary of State with the concurrence of the Commissioners which is in force under 1949 c. 67. an Order in Council made in pursuance of section 8 of the Civil Aviation Act 1949.

Approval of examination stations at customs and excise airports.

22.—(1) The Commissioners may, in any customs and excise airport, approve for such periods and subject to such conditions and restrictions as they think fit a part of, or a place at, that airport for the loading and unloading of goods and the embarkation and disembarkation of passengers; and any such part or place so approved is referred to in this Act as an " examination station ".

(2) The Commissioners may at any time for reasonable cause revoke or vary the terms of any approval given under this section.

(3) Any person contravening or failing to comply with any condition or restriction imposed by the Commissioners under this section shall be liable on summary conviction to a penalty of £100.

23.—(1) The Commissioners may by regulations impose conditions and restrictions as respects the movement of hovercraft and the carriage of goods by hovercraft, and in particular—

    (*a*) may prescribe the procedure to be followed by hovercraft proceeding to or from a port or any customs and excise airport or customs and excise station, and authorise the proper officer to give directions as to their routes ; and

    (*b*) may make provision for cases where by reason of accident, or in any other circumstance, it is impracticable to comply with any conditions or restrictions imposed or directions given as respects hovercraft.

(2) Subsection (1) above shall apply to hovercraft proceeding to or from any approved wharf or transit shed which is not in a port as if it were a port.

(3) If any person contravenes or fails to comply with any regulation made under subsection (1) above, or with any direction given by the Commissioners or the proper officer in pursuance of any such regulation, he shall be liable on summary conviction to a penalty of £100 and any goods in respect of which the offence was committed shall be liable to forfeiture.

24.—(1) Goods shall not be imported or exported by means of a pipe-line that is not for the time being approved by the Commissioners for the purposes of this section.

(2) Uncleared goods, that is to say—

    (*a*) imported goods, whether or not chargeable with duty, which have not been cleared out of charge, and in particular goods which are, or are to be, moved under section 30 below ; or (*b*) dutiable goods moved from warehouse without payment of duty,

shall not be moved by means of a pipe-line that is not for the time being approved by the Commissioners for the purposes of this section.

(3) The Commissioners may give their approval under this section for such period and subject to such conditions as they think fit, and may at any time for reasonable cause—

    (*a*) vary the terms of their approval ; and

    (*b*) (if they have given to the owner of the pipe-line not less than 3 months' written notice of their intention so to do) revoke their approval.

(4) Section 49 of the Pipe-lines Act 1962 (procedure for service of documents under that Act) shall apply to a notice required by subsection (3)(*b*) above to be served on the owner of a pipe-line as it applies to a document required by that Act to be so served.

(5) A person who—

    (*a*) contravenes subsection (1) or (2) above, or contravenes or fails to comply with a condition imposed by the Commissioners under subsection (3) above ; or

    (*b*) except with the authority of the proper officer or for just and sufficient cause, obtains access to goods which are in, or in course of conveyance by, a pipe-line approved under this section,

shall be guilty of an offence under this section and may be detained ; and any goods in respect of which the offence was committed shall be liable to forfeiture.

(6) A person guilty of an offence under this section shall be liable—

    (*a*) on summary conviction, to a penalty of the prescribed sum, or to imprisonment for a term not exceeding 6 months, or to both ; or

    (*b*) on conviction on indictment, to a penalty of any amount, or to imprisonment for a term not exceeding 2 years, or to both.

(7) In the application of subsection (4) above to Northern Ireland, the reference to the Pipe-lines Act 1962 shall have effect as if that Act extended to Northern Ireland.

25.—(1) The Commissioners may approve, for such periods and subject to such conditions and restrictions as they see fit, places for the deposit of goods imported and not yet cleared out of charge, including goods not yet reported and entered under this Act ; and any place so approved is referred to in this Act as a " transit shed ".

(2) Where, by any local Act, provision is made for the landing of goods without entry for deposit in transit sheds authorised thereunder, the provisions of this Act relating to goods deposited in transit sheds approved under this section shall have effect in relation to goods deposited in transit sheds authorised under that Act.

(3) The Commissioners may at any time for reasonable cause revoke or vary the terms of any approval given under subsection (1) above.

(4) Any person contravening or failing to comply with any condition or restriction imposed by the Commissioners under subsection (1) above shall be liable on summary conviction to a penalty of £100.

26.—(1) The Commissioners may, for the purpose of safeguarding the revenue and for the better enforcement of any prohibition or restriction for the time being in force under or by virtue of any enactment with respect to the importation or exportation of any goods, make regulations— *Power to regulate movements of goods into and out of Northern Ireland by land.*

   (a) prohibiting the importation or exportation by land of all goods or of any class or description of goods except within such hours and by such routes within Northern Ireland (referred to in this Act as " approved routes ") as may be prescribed by the regulations ;

   (b) appointing places for the examination and entry of and payment of any duty chargeable on any goods being imported or exported by land (referred to in this Act as " customs and excise stations ").

(2) If any person contravenes or fails to comply with any regulation made under subsection (1) above he shall be liable on summary conviction to a penalty of £100, and any goods in respect of which the offence was committed shall be liable to forfeiture.

27.—(1) At any time while a ship is within the limits of a port, or an aircraft is at a customs and excise airport, or a vehicle is on an approved route, any officer and any other person duly engaged in the prevention of smuggling may board the ship, aircraft or vehicle and remain therein and rummage and search any part thereof. *Officers power of boarding.*

(2) The Commissioners may station officers in any ship at any time while it is within the limits of a port, and if the master of any ship neglects or refuses to provide—

   (a) reasonable accommodation below decks for any officer stationed therein ; or (*b*) means of safe access to and egress from the ship in accordance with the requirements of any such officer,

the master shall be liable on summary conviction to a penalty of £50.

28.—(1) Without prejudice to section 27 above, the proper officer shall have free access to every part of any ship or aircraft at a port or customs and excise airport and of any vehicle brought to a customs and excise station, and may—

(*a*) cause any goods to be marked before they are unloaded from that ship, aircraft or vehicle ;

(*b*) lock up, seal, mark or otherwise secure any goods carried in the ship, aircraft or vehicle or any place or container in which they are so carried ; and

(*c*) break open any place or container which is locked and of which the keys are withheld.

(2) Any goods found concealed on board any such ship, aircraft or vehicle shall be liable to forfeiture.

29.—(1) Where, in the case of a ship, aircraft or vehicle of which due report has been made under section 35 below, any goods are still on board that ship, aircraft or vehicle at the expiration of the relevant period, the proper officer may detain that ship, aircraft or vehicle until there have been repaid to the Commissioners—

(*a*) any expenses properly incurred in watching and guarding the goods beyond the relevant period, except, in the case of a ship or aircraft, in respect of the day of clearance inwards ; and

(*b*) where the goods are removed by virtue of any provision of the Customs and Excise Acts 1979 from the ship, aircraft or vehicle to a Queen's warehouse, the expenses of that removal.

(2) In subsection (1) above, " the relevant period " means—

(*a*) in the case of a ship or vehicle, 21 clear days from the date of making due report of the ship or vehicle under section 35 below or such longer period as the Commissioners may in any case allow ;

(*b*) in the case of an aircraft, 7 clear days from the date of making due report of the aircraft under that section or such longer period as the Commissioners may in any case allow.

(3) Where, in the case of—

(*a*) any derelict or other ship or aircraft coming, driven or brought into the United Kingdom under legal process, by stress of weather or for safety ; or

(*b*) any vehicle in Northern Ireland which suffers any
    mishap,

it is necessary for the protection of the revenue to station any
officer in charge thereof, whether on board or otherwise, the
proper officer may detain that ship, aircraft or vehicle until any
expenses thereby incurred by the Commissioners have been
repaid.

30.—(1) The Commissioners may from time to time give
general or special directions as to the manner in which, and the
conditions under which, goods to which this section applies, or
any class or description of such goods, may be moved within the
limits of any port or customs and excise airport or between
any port or customs and excise airport and any other place.

Control of
movement
of uncleared
goods within
or between
port or
airport and
other places.

(2) This section applies to goods chargeable with any duty
which has not been paid, to drawback goods, and to any other
goods which have not been cleared out of charge.

(3) Any directions under subsection (1) above may require
that any goods to which this section applies shall be moved
only—

(*a*) by persons licensed by the Commissioners for that
    purpose ;

(*b*) in such ships, aircraft or vehicles or by such other means
    as may be approved by the Commissioners for that
    purpose ;

and any such licence or approval may be granted for such period
and subject to such conditions and restrictions as the Commissioners think fit and may be revoked at any time by the
Commissioners.

(4) Any person contravening or failing to comply with any
direction given or condition or restriction imposed, or the terms
of any licence granted, by the Commissioners under this section
shall be liable on summary conviction to a penalty of £50.

31.—(1) The Commissioners may by regulations impose conditions and restrictions as respects—

Control of
movement of
goods to and
from inland
clearance
depot, etc.

(*a*) the movement of imported goods between the place of
    importation and a place approved by the Commis-
    sioners for the clearance out of charge of such goods ;
    and

(*b*) the movement of goods intended for export between a
    place approved by the Commissioners for the examina-
    tion of such goods and the place of exportation.

PART III

(2) Regulations under subsection (1) above may in particular—

   (a) require the goods to be moved within such period and by such route as may be specified by or under the regulations ;

   (b) require the goods to be carried in a vehicle or container complying with such requirements and secured in such manner as may be so specified ;

   (c) prohibit, except in such circumstances as may be so specified, any unloading or loading of the vehicle or container or any interference with its security.

(3) If any person contravenes or fails to comply with any regulation under subsection (1) above or any requirement imposed by or under any such regulation, that person and the person then in charge of the goods shall each be liable on summary conviction to a penalty of £500 and any goods in respect of which the offence was committed shall be liable to forfeiture.

Penalty for carrying away officers.

32.—(1) If any ship or aircraft departs from any place, or any vehicle crosses the boundary out of Northern Ireland, carrying on board without his consent any officer of customs and excise or other Government officer, including an officer of the Government of Northern Ireland, the master of the ship or commander of the aircraft or the person in charge of the vehicle shall be liable on summary conviction to a penalty of £100.

(2) Without prejudice to the liability of any person under subsection (1) above, the amount of any expenses incurred by the Commissioners or by any Government department, including a department of the Government of Northern Ireland, by reason of the carrying away of any officer may be recovered summarily as a civil debt from that person or from the owner of the ship, aircraft or vehicle concerned.

(3) For the purposes of this section, the guard of a railway train shall be deemed to be the person in charge of any vehicle forming part of that train.

Power to inspect aircraft, aerodromes, records, etc.

33.—(1) The commander of an aircraft shall permit an officer at any time to board the aircraft and inspect—

   (a) the aircraft and any goods loaded therein ; and

   (b) all documents relating to the aircraft or to goods or persons carried therein ;

and an officer shall have the right of access at any time to any place to which access is required for the purpose of any such inspection.

(2) The person in control of any aerodrome shall permit an officer at any time to enter upon and inspect the aerodrome and all buildings and goods thereon.

(3) The person in control of an aerodrome licensed under any enactment relating to air navigation and, if so required by the Commissioners, the person in control of any other aerodrome shall—

(a) keep a record in such form and manner as the Commissioners may approve of all aircraft arriving at or departing from the aerodrome ;

(b) keep that record available and produce it on demand to any officer, together with all other documents kept on the aerodrome which relate to the movement of aircraft ; and

(c) permit any officer to make copies of and take extracts from any such record or document.

(4) If any person contravenes or fails to comply with any of the provisions of this section he shall be liable on summary conviction to a penalty of £200 or to imprisonment for a term not exceeding 3 months, or to both.

34.—(1) If it appears to any officer or constable that an aircraft is intended or likely to depart for a destination outside the United Kingdom from—

(a) any place other than a customs and excise airport ; or

(b) a customs and excise airport before clearance outwards is given,

he may give such instructions and take such steps by way of detention of the aircraft or otherwise as appear to him necessary in order to prevent the flight.

(2) Any person who contravenes any instructions given under subsection (1) above shall be liable on summary conviction to a penalty of £200, or to imprisonment for a term not exceeding 3 months, or to both.

(3) If an aircraft flies in contravention of any instruction given under subsection (1) above or notwithstanding any steps taken to prevent the flight, the owner and the commander thereof shall, without prejudice to the liability of any other person under subsection (2) above, each be liable on summary conviction to a penalty of £200, or to imprisonment for a term not exceeding 3 months, or to both, unless he proves that the flight took place without his consent or connivance.

PART IV

CONTROL OF IMPORTATION

Inward entry and clearance

Report
inwards.

35.—(1) Report shall be made in such form and manner and containing such particulars as the Commissioners may direct of every ship and aircraft to which this section applies, of every vehicle entering Northern Ireland by land, and of all goods otherwise conveyed into Northern Ireland by land.

(2) This section applies to every ship arriving at a port—

(*a*) from any place outside the United Kingdom ; or

(*b*) carrying any goods brought in that ship from some place outside the United Kingdom and not yet cleared on importation.

(3) This section applies to every aircraft arriving at any place in the United Kingdom—

(*a*) from any place or area outside the United Kingdom ; or

(*b*) carrying passengers or goods taken on board that aircraft at a place outside the United Kingdom, being passengers or goods either—

(i) bound for a destination in the United Kingdom and not already cleared at a customs and excise airport ; or

(ii) bound for a destination outside the United Kingdom.

(4) The Commissioners may make regulations prescribing the procedure for making report under this section.

(5) If the person by whom the report should be made fails to make report as required by or under this section—

(*a*) he shall be liable on summary conviction to a penalty of £100 ; and

(*b*) any goods required to be reported which are not duly reported may be detained by any officer until so reported or until the omission is explained to the satisfaction of the Commissioners, and may in the meantime be deposited in a Queen's warehouse.

(6) The person making the report shall at the time of making it answer all such questions relating to the ship, aircraft or vehicle, to the goods carried therein, to the crew and to the voyage, flight or journey as may be put to him by the proper officer ; and if he refuses to answer he shall be liable on summary conviction to a penalty of £100.

(7) If at any time after a ship or aircraft carrying goods brought therein from any place outside the United Kingdom arrives within 12 nautical miles of the coast of the United Kingdom, or after a vehicle crosses the boundary into Northern Ireland, and before report has been made in accordance with this section—

> (a) bulk is broken ; or
>
> (b) any alteration is made in the stowage of any goods carried so as to facilitate the unloading of any part thereof before due report has been made ; or
>
> (c) any part of the goods is staved, destroyed or thrown overboard or any container is opened,

and the matter is not explained to the satisfaction of the Commissioners, the master of the ship or commander of the aircraft or the person in charge of the vehicle shall be liable on summary conviction to a penalty of £100.

(8) For the purposes of subsection (7) above, the guard of a railway train shall be deemed to be the person in charge of any vehicle forming part of that train.

36.—(1) The person in command of any ship having a commission from Her Majesty or any foreign State which has on board any goods loaded in any place outside the United Kingdom shall, before any such goods are unloaded, or at any time when called upon to do so by the proper officer, deliver to the proper officer an account of the goods in accordance with subsection (2) below, and if he fails so to do he shall be liable on summary conviction to a penalty of £100.

Provisions as to Her Majesty's ships, etc.

(2) An account of goods under subsection (1) above shall be in such form, and shall contain to the best of the knowledge of the person delivering the account such particulars, and shall be delivered in such manner, as the Commissioners may direct.

(3) The person delivering such an account shall when delivering it answer all such questions relating to the goods as may be put to him by the proper officer and if he refuses to answer he shall be liable on summary conviction to a penalty of £100.

(4) Subject in the case of ships having a commission from Her Majesty to any regulations made by the Treasury, the provisions of Parts III to VII of this Act as to the boarding and search of ships shall have effect in relation to such a ship as aforesaid as they have effect in relation to any other ship, and any officer may remove to a Queen's warehouse any goods loaded as aforesaid found on board the ship.

PART IV
Entry of
goods on
importation.

37.—(1) The importer of any goods, other than goods which are exempt from the requirements of this section, shall deliver to the proper officer an entry thereof in such form and manner and containing such particulars as the Commissioners may direct.

(2) The following goods are exempt from the requirements of this section—

   (*a*) whales and fresh fish (including shell-fish) of British taking brought by British ships ;

   (*b*) passengers' baggage ; and

   (*c*) Community transit goods.

(3) Subject to subsections (4) and (5) below, goods may be entered under this section—

   (*a*) for home use, if so eligible ; or

   (*b*) for warehousing ; or

   (*c*) for transit or transhipment ; or

   (*d*) for inward processing ; or

   (*e*) in such cases as the Commissioners may permit, for temporary retention with a view to subsequent re-exportation.

(4) All goods imported by means of a pipe-line and chargeable with duty shall be entered for warehousing.

(5) The Commissioners may—

   (*a*) refuse to accept an entry of any goods if they are not satisfied that those goods were imported before the time of the delivery of the entry ;

   (*b*) subject to subsection (4) above, direct that goods of any class or description specified in the direction shall not be permitted to be entered for warehousing.

(6) If, in the case of any goods which are not dutiable goods, any such entry as aforesaid is inaccurate in any particular, the importer shall, within 14 clear days of the delivery of the entry or such longer period as the Commissioners may in any case allow, deliver to the proper officer a full and accurate account of the goods.

(7) If an account of the goods is delivered in accordance with subsection (6) above and the Commissioners are satisfied that the inaccuracy was inadvertent and immaterial except for statistical purposes, then notwithstanding anything in the Customs and Excise Acts 1979 or in any instrument made thereunder the goods shall not be liable to forfeiture, or the importer to any penalty, by reason only of the inaccuracy of the entry.

38.—(1) Without prejudice to section 37 above, where on the importation of any goods the importer is unable for want of full information to make immediately perfect entry thereof, he may, subject to subsection (2) below, on making a signed declaration to that effect before the proper officer, deliver to that officer an entry of the goods by bill of sight in such form and manner and containing such particulars as the Commissioners may direct.

(2) Notwithstanding subsection (1) above, the Commissioners may refuse to accept an entry by bill of sight of any goods if they are not satisfied that those goods were imported before the delivery of the entry.

(3) An entry of any goods by bill of sight under subsection (1) above when signed by the proper officer shall be the warrant for the examination of the goods by the importer in the presence of the proper officer with a view to making perfect entry thereof.

(4) If within such period from the date of the entry of any goods by bill of sight as the Commissioners may allow, no entry purporting to be a perfect entry has been made of those goods, the proper officer may cause the goods to be deposited in a Queen's warehouse; and, without prejudice to section 99(3) below, if any goods so deposited are not cleared within one month from the date of deposit the Commissioners may sell them.

39.—(1) With the permission of the proper officer, surplus stores of any ship or aircraft—

(*a*) if intended for private use and in quantities which do not appear to him to be excessive, may be entered and otherwise treated as if they were goods imported in the ship or aircraft; or

(*b*) in any other case may, subject to subsection (2) below, be entered for warehousing notwithstanding that they could not lawfully be imported as merchandise.

(2) Goods entered for warehousing by virtue of subsection (1)(*b*) above shall not, except with the sanction of the Commissioners, be further entered, or be removed from the warehouse, otherwise than for use as stores.

40.—(1) Where in the case of any imported goods—

(*a*) entry has not been made thereof by the expiration of the relevant period; or

(*b*) at the expiration of 21 clear days from the relevant date, entry having been made of the goods, they have not been unloaded from the importing ship or aircraft or, in the case of goods which have been unloaded or which have been imported by land, have not been produced for examination and clearance ; or

(*c*) being goods imported by sea and not being in large quantity, they are at any time after the arrival of the importing ship at the port at which they are to be unloaded the only goods remaining to be unloaded from that ship at that port,

the proper officer may cause the goods to be deposited in a Queen's warehouse.

(2) Where any small package or consignment of goods is imported, the proper officer may at any time after the relevant date cause that package or consignment to be deposited in a Queen's warehouse to await entry.

(3) Without prejudice to section 99(3) below, if any goods deposited in a Queen's warehouse by the proper officer under this section are not cleared by the importer thereof—

(*a*) in the case of goods which are in the opinion of the Commissioners of a perishable nature, forthwith ; or

(*b*) in any other case, within 3 months after they have been so deposited or such longer time as the Commissioners may in any case allow,

the Commissioners may sell them.

(4) In this section—

(*a*) " the relevant period " means a period of, in the case of goods imported by air, 7 or, in any other case, 14 clear days from the relevant date ; and

(*b*) " the relevant date " means, subject to subsection (5) below, the date when report was made of the importing ship, aircraft or vehicle or of the goods under section 35 above, or, where no such report was made, the date when it should properly have been made.

(5) Where any restriction is placed upon the unloading of goods from any ship or aircraft by virtue of any enactment relating to the prevention of epidemic and infectious diseases, then, in relation to that ship or aircraft, " the relevant date " in this section means the date of the removal of the restriction.

Failure to comply with provisions as to entry.

41. Without prejudice to any liability under any other provision of the Customs and Excise Acts 1979, any person making entry of goods on their importation who fails to comply with any of the requirements of this Part of this Act in connection with that entry shall be liable on summary conviction to a penalty of £50, and the goods in question shall be liable to forfeiture.

42.—(1) The Commissioners may make regulations—

    (*a*) prescribing the procedure to be followed by a ship arriving at a port, an aircraft arriving at a customs and excise airport, or a person conveying goods into Northern Ireland by land ;

    (*b*) regulating the unloading, landing, movement and removal of goods on their importation ;

and different regulations may be made with respect to importation by sea, air or land respectively.

(2) If any person contravenes or fails to comply with any regulation made under this section or with any direction given by the Commissioners or the proper officer in pursuance of any such regulation, he shall be liable on summary conviction to a penalty of £100 and any goods in respect of which the offence was committed shall be liable to forfeiture.

Provisions as to duty on imported goods

43.—(1) Save as permitted by or under the customs and excise Acts or section 2(2) of the European Communities Act 1972 or any Community regulation or other instrument having the force of law, no imported goods shall be delivered or removed on importation until the importer has paid to the proper officer any duty chargeable thereon, and that duty shall, in the case of goods of which entry is made, be paid on making the entry.

(2) The duties of customs or excise and the rates thereof chargeable on imported goods—

    (*a*) if entry is made thereof, except where the entry or, in the case of an entry by bill of sight, the perfect entry is for warehousing, shall be those in force with respect to such goods at the time of the delivery of the entry ;

    (*b*) if entry or, in the case of goods entered by bill of sight, perfect entry is made thereof for warehousing, shall be ascertained in accordance with warehousing regulations ;

    (*c*) if no entry is made thereof, shall be those in force with respect to such goods at the time of their importation.

(3) Any goods brought or coming into the United Kingdom by sea otherwise than as cargo, stores or baggage carried in a ship shall be chargeable with the like duty, if any, as would be applicable to those goods if they had been imported as merchandise ; and if any question arises as to the origin of the goods they shall, unless that question is determined under section

120 below, section 14 of the Customs and Excise Duties (General Reliefs) Act 1979 (produce of the sea or continental shelf) or under a Community regulation or other instrument having the force of law, be deemed to be the produce of such country as the Commissioners may on investigation determine.

(4) Where, in accordance with approval given by the Commissioners, entry of goods is made by any method involving the use of a computer, subsection (2) above shall have effect as if the reference in paragraph (*a*) to the time of the delivery of the entry were a reference to the time when particulars contained in the entry are accepted by the computer.

(5) Subject to sections 10 and 11 of the Customs and Excise Duties (General Reliefs) Act 1979 (reliefs for re-imported goods) and save as provided by or under any such enactments or instruments as are mentioned in subsection (1) above, any goods which are re-imported into the United Kingdom after exportation therefrom, whether they were manufactured or produced in or outside the United Kingdom and whether or not any duty was paid thereon at a previous importation, shall be treated for the purpose of charging duty—

(*a*) as if they were being imported for the first time ; and

(*b*) in the case of goods manufactured or produced in the United Kingdom, as if they had not been so manufactured or produced.

Exclusion of s. 43(1) for importers etc. keeping standing deposits.

44. Where the Commissioners so direct, section 43(1) above shall not apply if and so long as the importer or his agent pays to, and keeps deposited with, the Commissioners a sum by way of standing deposit sufficient in their opinion to cover any duty which may become payable in respect of goods entered by that importer or agent, and if the importer or agent complies with such other conditions as the Commissioners may impose.

Deferred payment of customs duty.

45.—(1) The Commissioners may by regulations provide for the payment of customs duty to be deferred in such cases as may be specified by the regulations and subject to such conditions as may be imposed by or under the regulations ; and duty of which payment is deferred under the regulations shall be treated, for such purposes as may be specified thereby, as if it had been paid.

(2) Regulations under this section may make different provision for goods of different descriptions or for goods of the same description in different circumstances.

Goods to be warehoused without payment of duty.

46. Any goods which are on their importation permitted to be entered for warehousing shall be allowed, subject to such conditions or restrictions as may be imposed by or under warehousing regulations, to be warehoused without payment of duty.

47. Where any goods are entered for transit or transhipment, the Commissioners may allow the goods to be removed for that purpose, subject to such conditions and restrictions as they see fit, without payment of duty.

PART IV
Relief from payment of duty of goods entered for transit or transhipment.

48. In such cases as the Commissioners may by regulations prescribe, where the Commissioners are satisfied that goods are imported only temporarily with a view to subsequent re-exportation, they may permit the goods to be delivered on importation, subject to such conditions as they see fit to impose, without payment of duty.

Relief from payment of duty of goods temporarily imported.

Forfeiture, offences, etc. in connection with importation

49.—(1) Where—

Forfeiture of goods improperly imported.

   (a) except as provided by or under the Customs and Excise Acts 1979, any imported goods, being goods chargeable on their importation with customs or excise duty, are, without payment of that duty—

      (i) unshipped in any port,

      (ii) unloaded from any aircraft in the United Kingdom,

      (iii) unloaded from any vehicle in, or otherwise brought across the boundary into, Northern Ireland, or

      (iv) removed from their place of importation or from any approved wharf, examination station or transit shed ; or

   (b) any goods are imported, landed or unloaded contrary to any prohibition or restriction for the time being in force with respect thereto under or by virtue of any enactment ; or

   (c) any goods, being goods chargeable with any duty or goods the importation of which is for the time being prohibited or restricted by or under any enactment, are found, whether before or after the unloading thereof, to have been concealed in any manner on board any ship or aircraft or, while in Northern Ireland, in any vehicle ; or

   (d) any goods are imported concealed in a container holding goods of a different description ; or

   (e) any imported goods are found, whether before or after delivery, not to correspond with the entry made thereof ; or

   (f) any imported goods are concealed or packed in any manner appearing to be intended to deceive an officer,

PART IV those goods shall, subject to subsection (2) below, be liable to forfeiture.

(2) Where any goods, the importation of which is for the time being prohibited or restricted by or under any enactment, are on their importation either—

(a) reported as intended for exportation in the same ship, aircraft or vehicle ; or

(b) entered for transit or transhipment ; or

(c) entered to be warehoused for exportation or for use as stores,

the Commissioners may, if they see fit, permit the goods to be dealt with accordingly.

Penalty for improper importation of goods.

50.—(1) Subsection (2) below applies to goods of the following descriptions, that is to say—

(a) goods chargeable with a duty which has not been paid ; and

(b) goods the importation, landing or unloading of which is for the time being prohibited or restricted by or under any enactment.

(2) If any person with intent to defraud Her Majesty of any such duty or to evade any such prohibition or restriction as is mentioned in subsection (1) above—

(a) unships or lands in any port or unloads from any aircraft in the United Kingdom or from any vehicle in Northern Ireland any goods to which this subsection applies, or assists or is otherwise concerned in such unshipping, landing or unloading ; or

(b) removes from their place of importation or from any approved wharf, examination station, transit shed or customs and excise station any goods to which this subsection applies or assists or is otherwise concerned in such removal,

he shall be guilty of an offence under this subsection and may be detained.

(3) If any person imports or is concerned in importing any goods contrary to any prohibition or restriction for the time being in force under or by virtue of any enactment with respect to those goods, whether or not the goods are unloaded, and does so with intent to evade the prohibition or restriction, he shall be guilty of an offence under this subsection and may be detained.

(4) Subject to subsection (5) below, a person guilty of an offence under subsection (2) or (3) above shall be liable—

(a) on summary conviction, to a penalty of the prescribed sum or of three times the value of the goods, whichever is the greater, or to imprisonment for a term not exceeding 6 months, or to both ; or

(b) on conviction on indictment, to a penalty of any amount, or to imprisonment for a term not exceeding 2 years, or to both.

(5) In the case of an offence under subsection (2) or (3) above in connection with a prohibition or restriction on importation having effect by virtue of section 3 of the Misuse of Drugs Act 1971, subsection (4) above shall have effect subject to the modifications specified in Schedule 1 to this Act.

1971 c. 38.

(6) If any person—

(a) imports or causes to be imported any goods concealed in a container holding goods of a different description ; or

(b) directly or indirectly imports or causes to be imported or entered any goods found, whether before or after delivery, not to correspond with the entry made thereof,

he shall be liable on summary conviction to a penalty of three times the value of the goods or £100, whichever is the greater.

(7) In any case where a person would, apart from this subsection, be guilty of—

(a) an offence under this section in connection with the importation of goods contrary to a prohibition or restriction ; and

(b) a corresponding offence under the enactment or other instrument imposing the prohibition or restriction, being an offence for which a fine or other penalty is expressly provided by that enactment or other instrument,

he shall not be guilty of the offence mentioned in paragraph (a) of this subsection.

51.—(1) If goods of any class or description chargeable with duty on their importation from the Republic of Ireland are found in the possession or control of any person within the prescribed area in Northern Ireland, any officer or any person having by law in Northern Ireland the powers of an officer may require that person to furnish proof that the goods have not been imported from the Republic of Ireland or that the duty chargeable on their importation has been paid.

Special provisions as to proof in Northern Ireland.

(2) If proof of any matter is required to be furnished in relation to any goods under subsection (1) above but is not

B4

furnished to the satisfaction of the Commissioners, the goods shall, for the purposes of proceedings under the customs and excise Acts, be deemed to have been unlawfully imported from the Republic of Ireland without payment of duty, unless the contrary is proved.

PART V

CONTROL OF EXPORTATION

Outward entry and clearance of goods

Meaning for this Part of "dutiable or restricted goods".

52. For the purposes of this Part of this Act "dutiable or restricted goods" are goods of the following descriptions, that is to say—

(a) goods from warehouse, other than goods which have been kept, without being warehoused, in a warehouse by virtue of section 92(4) below ;

(b) transit goods ;

(c) any other goods chargeable with any duty which has not been paid ;

(d) drawback goods ;

(e) goods with respect to the exportation of which any restriction is for the time being in force under or by virtue of any enactment ;

(f) any goods required by or under any provision of this Act other than a provision of this Part or by or under a provision of any other Act to be entered before exportation or before shipment for exportation or as stores.

Entry outwards of dutiable or restricted goods.

53.—(1) Where any dutiable or restricted goods, not being Community transit goods, are to be shipped for exportation or as stores for use on a voyage or flight to an eventual destination outside the United Kingdom or are brought to any customs and excise station for exportation, the exporter shall, subject to subsection (3) below and section 56 below—

(a) deliver to the proper officer an entry outwards of the goods under this section in such form and manner and containing such particulars as the Commissioners may direct ; and

(b) give security to the satisfaction of the Commissioners that the goods will be duly shipped or exported and discharged at the destination for which they are entered outwards within such time as the Commissioners consider reasonable, or, in the case of goods for use as stores, will be duly so used, or that they will be otherwise accounted for to the satisfaction of the Commissioners.

(2) Directions under this section may, if the Commissioners think fit, contain provisions authorising the delivery in circumstances specified in the directions of provisional entries under this section, and imposing requirements on persons delivering such entries as to the subsequent delivery of perfected entries, and the obtaining and retention for a specified period of receipts for perfected entries.

This subsection shall not come into force until such day as the Commissioners may appoint by order made by statutory instrument.

(3) The Commissioners may relax all or any of the requirements imposed by or under subsection (1) or (2) above as they think fit in relation to any goods.

(4) If any goods of which entry is required under this section are shipped for exportation or as stores or are waterborne for such shipment before entry thereof has been duly made, the goods shall be liable to forfeiture and, where the shipping or making waterborne is done with fraudulent intent, any person concerned therein with knowledge of that intent shall be guilty of an offence under this subsection and may be detained.

(5) A person guilty of an offence under subsection (4) above shall be liable—

    (a) on summary conviction, to a penalty of the prescribed sum or of three times the value of the goods, whichever is the greater, or to imprisonment for a term not exceeding 6 months, or to both ; or

    (b) on conviction on indictment, to a penalty of any amount, or to imprisonment for a term not exceeding 2 years, or to both.

(6) Any person who, being required by directions given under subsection (2) above to obtain and retain for a specified period a receipt for any entry, fails to produce a receipt complying with the directions on demand made by the proper officer at any time during that period shall be liable on summary conviction to a penalty of £100.

(7) Any person who contravenes or fails to comply with any directions given under subsection (2) above shall be liable on summary conviction to a penalty of £100.

(8) If any goods are found not to correspond with any entry thereof made under this section, they shall be liable to forfeiture.

54.—(1) Subject to subsection (6) below and to section 56 below, before any goods which are not dutiable or restricted goods are exported or shipped for exportation, the exporter shall, unless the goods are Community transit goods, deliver to the proper officer an entry outwards of the goods under this section.

Entry outwards of goods which are not dutiable or restricted goods.

PART V   (2) The form of entries under this section, the particulars to be contained therein and the manner of their delivery shall be such as the Commissioners may from time to time direct.

(3) Directions under this section may, if the Commissioners think fit, contain provisions authorising the delivery in circumstances specified in the directions of provisional entries under this section, and imposing requirements on persons delivering such entries as to the subsequent delivery of perfected entries, and the obtaining and retention for a specified period of receipts for perfected entries.

(4) Where the particulars contained in any entry delivered under this section are in any way incorrect or inaccurate, the person delivering it shall notify the proper officer of any necessary correction within a period of 14 days beginning with the day of delivery.

(5) The Commissioners may give directions under this section imposing on persons specified in the directions requirements as to the giving of information with respect to, and the furnishing of documents in connection with, goods which have been entered under this section but are not exported or shipped for exportation within a specified period beginning with the day of delivery of the entry.

(6) The Commissioners may relax any requirement imposed by or under this section as they think fit in relation to any goods.

(7) If any goods of which entry is required under this section are exported or shipped for exportation before delivery of an entry in respect thereof, the exporter shall be liable on summary conviction to a penalty of £100.

(8) Any person who fails to comply with subsection (4) above in the case of any entry shall be liable on summary conviction to a penalty of £10.

(9) Any person who, being required by directions given under this section to obtain and retain for a specified period a receipt for any entry, fails to produce a receipt complying with the directions on demand made by the proper officer at any time during that period shall be liable on summary conviction to a penalty of £100.

(10) Any person who contravenes or fails to comply with any directions given under this section shall be liable on summary conviction to a penalty of £100.

Register of
exporters and
assignment of
identifying
numbers.
55.—(1) The Commissioners shall have power—

    (*a*) to maintain a register of exporters ;

    (*b*) to enter therein any person applying for registration and appearing to them to be concerned in the exportation of goods and to satisfy such requirements for registration as they may think fit to impose ;

(c) to give directions imposing requirements on registered persons (and, in particular, requirements as to the keeping of records and accounts and the giving of access thereto) as a condition of their remaining on the register ;

(d) to assign to registered persons numbers for use for export purposes ; and

(e) to cancel the registration of any person if it appears to them that he has failed to comply with any direction under this section or that there is other reasonable cause for cancellation.

(2) The Commissioners may relax any requirement imposed under this section as they think fit in relation to any goods.

56.—(1) If the Commissioners think fit so to direct—

(a) dutiable or restricted goods falling within paragraph (c) or (d) of section 52 above may be shipped for exportation without entry under section 53 above ; and

(b) goods which are not dutiable or restricted goods may be shipped for exportation without entry under section 54 above,

if, before shipment, a number assigned under section 55 above to a person concerned in the exportation of the goods, together with such particulars of the goods and other information relating thereto as the directions may require, is furnished in accordance with the directions to a person specified therein.

(2) Directions under this section may contain provision enabling the Commissioners to exclude shipments of goods from their operation in particular cases by giving notice to that effect in accordance with the directions.

(3) The Commissioners may relax any requirement imposed under this section as they think fit in relation to any goods.

(4) If any person, for the purpose of enabling any goods to be shipped without entry by virtue of directions given under this section, furnishes a number other than one for the time being assigned to him under section 55 above, then, unless the number is one for the time being assigned to another person under that section and is furnished with that person's consent, he shall be liable on summary conviction to a penalty of £100.

57.—(1) Subject to subsection (2) below and section 58 below, in any of the following events, that is to say—

(a) where any dutiable or restricted goods are, by virtue of section 53(3) or 56 above, exported without entry under section 53 above, shipped for exportation without such an entry or shipped as stores for use on a voyage or flight to an eventual destination outside the United Kingdom without such an entry ; or

(b) where any goods which are not dutiable or restricted goods are, by virtue of section 56 above, shipped for exportation without entry under section 54 above,

the exporter of the goods shall deliver to the proper officer a specification of the goods in accordance with this section.

(2) No specification need be delivered as required by subsection (1) above in the case of Community transit goods or in the case of goods shipped as stores where the shipment as stores is permitted by the Commissioners and such conditions as they see fit to impose are complied with.

(3) A specification of goods under this section shall—

(a) be in such form and contain such particulars as the Commissioners may direct ; and

(b) be delivered in such manner as they may direct within a period of 14 days or such longer period as they may direct—

(i) after the clearance outwards of the ship or aircraft from the place of loading ; or

(ii) in the case of goods exported by land, after the goods have been exported.

(4) Where any goods are shipped for exportation without entry by virtue of directions given under section 56 above, the person whose number was furnished in relation to the goods for the purpose of their shipment without entry shall, if it was so furnished with his consent, be the exporter of the goods for the purposes of this section.

(5) For the purposes of this section, any ship built, or aircraft manufactured, in the United Kingdom departing for the first time for a voyage or flight to a place outside the United Kingdom for the purpose of its delivery to a consignee outside the United Kingdom shall be treated both as goods shipped for exportation and as the exporting ship or aircraft, and the owner of the ship or aircraft or, where the owner is outside the United Kingdom, the builder of the ship or the manufacturer of the aircraft shall be deemed to be the exporter.

(6) For goods exported by means of a pipe-line the period for delivery of a specification of the goods under this section shall be 14 days from the time when the goods are charged into the pipe-line for exportation or such longer period as the Commissioners may direct.

(7) Where any goods in respect of which a specification is required under this section are shipped as stores on board any ship which has touched at a port for the purpose only of

shipping those goods and then departing for a place outside the
United Kingdom, and which is permitted by the Commissioners
to depart without being cleared outwards from that port, this
section shall have effect as if for the reference in subsection (3)
above to the clearance outwards of the ship there were substituted a reference to the shipping of the goods.

(8) The Commissioners may give a direction under this subsection requiring any person delivering a specification under
this section in relation to goods shipped for exportation to obtain
a receipt therefor in accordance with the direction and to retain
it for a period specified therein.

The Commissioners may relax any requirement imposed under
this subsection as they think fit in relation to any goods.

(9) If in the case of any such goods as are mentioned in
subsection (1) above no specification is delivered in accordance
with this section, the exporter of the goods shall be liable on
summary conviction to a penalty of £100.

(10) If, when a specification has been delivered under this
section, any goods to which it relates have not in fact been
exported or shipped as stores or the particulars contained therein
are in any other way incorrect or inaccurate, the person signing
the specification and the exporter of the goods shall each be
liable on summary conviction to a penalty of £10 unless one of
them notifies the proper officer of any necessary correction within
a period of 14 days beginning with the day of delivery.

(11) Any person who contravenes or fails to comply with
any direction given under subsection (8) above shall be liable
on summary conviction to a penalty of £100.

(12) Any person who, being required by a direction given
under subsection (8) above to obtain and retain for a specified
period a receipt for a specification under this section, fails to
produce a receipt complying with the direction on demand made
by the proper officer at any time during that period shall be
liable on summary conviction to a penalty of £100.

58.—(1) In connection with any arrangements approved by
the Commissioners for recording particulars of exported goods
by computer they may relax the requirements of section 57 above
by suspending the obligation to deliver the specifications there
mentioned on condition that— *Relaxation of requirements of s. 57 where particulars of goods recorded by computer.*

  (a) the particulars which should otherwise be contained
      in the specifications, or such of those particulars as the
      Commissioners may specify, are recorded by computer
      in accordance with the arrangements ; and

    (*b*) the particulars so recorded are subsequently delivered to the proper officer within such time as the Commissioners may specify;

and subject to such other conditions as they may impose.

(2) If under subsection (1) above particulars are recorded by computer, and any goods to which the particulars relate have not in fact been exported or shipped as stores, or the particulars are in any other way incorrect or inaccurate, the exporter of the goods and any other person who caused the incorrect or inaccurate particulars to be recorded shall each be liable on summary conviction to a penalty of £5 unless one of them, either himself or by an agent, corrects the particulars within the period mentioned in section 57(3) above.

Restrictions
on putting
export goods
alongside for
oading.

59.—(1) This section applies to all goods which are required to be entered outwards before shipment for exportation, whether under section 53 or section 54 above.

(2) The Commissioners may make regulations—

    (*a*) prohibiting, as from such date as is specified in the regulations, the putting of any goods to which this section applies alongside any ship or aircraft for loading for exportation, except under a written authority in that behalf obtained in accordance with, and in such form as is specified in, the regulations; and

    (*b*) requiring any person putting goods alongside a ship or aircraft under one or more such authorities to endorse the authority or each of the authorities with such particulars as are specified in the regulations, and to deliver the endorsed authority or authorities, together with a written statement of the number of authorities delivered, to the proper officer within such period as is so specified.

(3) Regulations under subsection (2) above may make different provision for different circumstances.

(4) Without prejudice to section 3 above, subsection (2) above shall apply to the charging of goods into a pipe-line for exportation as it applies to the putting of goods alongside a ship or aircraft for loading for exportation.

(5) The Commissioners may relax any requirement imposed under subsection (2) above as they think fit in relation to any goods.

(6) Any person who contravenes or fails to comply with any regulation under subsection (2) above shall be liable on summary conviction to a penalty of £100.

(7) This section shall not come into force until such day as the Commissioners may appoint by order made by statutory instrument.

60.—(1) No person shall export any dutiable or restricted goods falling within paragraphs (*a*) to (*d*) of section 52 above, or enter any such goods for exportation, in any ship of less than 40 tons register.

(2) Subsection (1) above shall not apply to hovercraft, but dutiable or restricted goods shall only be exported in a hovercraft if it is of a class or description for the time being approved by the Commissioners and subject to such conditions and restrictions as they may impose.

(3) Any goods shipped or entered contrary to subsection (1) or (2) above shall be liable to forfeiture.

(4) A person contravening or failing to comply with subsection (2) above, or with any condition or restriction imposed thereunder, shall be liable on summary conviction to a penalty of three times the value of the goods or £100, whichever is the greater.

(5) If any goods which have been entered at any port, customs and excise airport or customs and excise station under section 53 above have not been duly shipped before the clearance from that port or airport of the ship or aircraft for which they were entered or, as the case may be, have not been duly exported by land, the goods shall be liable to forfeiture unless notice of the failure to ship or export is given to the proper officer immediately after that clearance has been given.

(6) Subject to subsection (7) below, if any goods entered but not shipped or exported as mentioned in subsection (5) above have not, at the expiration of a period of 14 days after the clearance of the ship or aircraft as mentioned in that subsection or, in the case of goods entered for exportation by land, after the date of the entry, been either—

(*a*) warehoused ; or

(*b*) again entered for exportation or for use as stores ; or

(*c*) otherwise accounted for to the satisfaction of the Commissioners,

the person by whom the entry was made shall be liable on summary conviction to a penalty of £25.

(7) Subsection (6) above shall not apply where, before the expiration of the said period, the goods have been seized by virtue of subsection (5) above.

61.—(1) The Commissioners may give directions—

    (*a*) as to the quantity of any goods which may be carried in any ship or aircraft as stores for use on a voyage or flight to an eventual destination outside the United Kingdom ;

    (*b*) as to the authorisation to be obtained for the supply and carriage of, and the procedure to be followed in supplying, any goods as stores for use as mentioned in paragraph (*a*) above, whether or not any duty is chargeable or has been paid, or any drawback is payable, in respect of those goods.

1979 c. 5.

(2) Save as provided in subsection (3) below and in section 18 of the Hydrocarbon Oil Duties Act 1979 (relief for fuel for ships in home waters) and notwithstanding anything in the customs and excise Acts, goods shall not be permitted to be shipped as stores without payment of duty or on drawback except in a ship of not less than 40 tons register or in an aircraft departing for a voyage or flight to some place outside the United Kingdom.

(3) The Commissioners may, in such cases and subject to such conditions and restrictions as they see fit, permit goods to be shipped as mentioned in subsection (2) above in any ship of less than 40 tons register which is departing for a place or area outside the United Kingdom.

(4) For the purposes of subsections (2) and (3) above, all hovercraft (of whatever size) shall be treated as ships of less than 40 tons register.

(5) If any goods shipped or carried as stores for use on a voyage or flight to an eventual destination outside the United Kingdom are without the authority of the proper officer landed or unloaded at any place in the United Kingdom—

    (*a*) the goods shall be liable to forfeiture ; and

    (*b*) the master or commander and the owner of the ship or aircraft shall each be liable on summary conviction to a penalty of three times the value of the goods or £100, whichever is the greater.

(6) The proper officer may lock up, mark, seal or otherwise secure any goods entered, shipped or carried as stores for use as mentioned in subsection (5) above or any place or container in which such goods are kept or held.

(7) If any ship or aircraft which has departed from any port or customs and excise airport for a destination outside the United Kingdom carrying stores fails to reach the destination for which it was cleared outwards and returns to any place within the United Kingdom, then—

(a) if the failure was not due to stress of weather, mechanical defect or any other unavoidable cause and any deficiency is discovered in the said goods ; or

(b) if the failure was due to any such cause as is mentioned in paragraph (a) above and any deficiency is discovered in the said goods which, in the opinion of the Commissioners, exceeds the quantity which might fairly have been consumed having regard to the length of time between the ship's or aircraft's departure and return as aforesaid,

the master of the ship or the commander of the aircraft shall be liable on summary conviction to a penalty of £50, and shall also pay on the deficiency or, as the case may be, on the excess deficiency any duty chargeable on the importation of such goods.

(8) Any duty payable under subsection (7) above shall be recoverable summarily as a civil debt.

62.—(1) The Commissioners may give directions under this subsection imposing on persons specified in the directions requirements as to the giving of information with respect to, or the furnishing of documents in connection with, goods exported, or intended to be exported, in any such vehicle or container as is specified in the directions, or by such other means, or in accordance with any such commercial procedure, as is so specified.

Information documentation, etc. as to export goods.

(2) The Commissioners may give directions under this subsection providing that, before any goods are shipped for exportation, a number identifying the goods in compliance with the directions is to be given in accordance with the directions by and to such persons as are specified in the directions.

This subsection shall not come into force until such day as the Commissioners may appoint by order made by statutory instrument.

(3) The Commissioners may relax any requirement imposed under subsection (1) or (2) above as they think fit in relation to any goods.

(4) Any person who contravenes or fails to comply with any direction given under subsection (1) or (2) above shall be liable on summary conviction to a penalty of £100.

Outward entry and clearance of ships, etc.

63.—(1) Where a ship is to load any goods at a port for exportation or as stores for use on a voyage to an eventual destination outside the United Kingdom, the master of the ship shall, before any goods are taken on board that ship at that port, other than goods for exportation loaded in accordance

Entry outwards of exporting ships.

with a stiffening order issued by the proper officer, deliver to the proper officer—

    (a) an entry outwards of the ship in such form and manner and containing such particulars as the Commissioners may direct ; and

    (b) a certificate from the proper officer of the clearance inwards or coastwise of the ship of her last voyage with cargo ; and

    (c) if the ship has already loaded goods at some other port for exportation or as stores for use as aforesaid or has been cleared in ballast from some other port, the clearance outwards of the ship from that other port.

(2) If, on the arrival at any port of a ship carrying goods coastwise from one place in the United Kingdom to another such place, it is desired that the ship shall proceed with those goods or any of them to a place outside the United Kingdom, entry outwards shall be made of that ship (whether or not any other goods are to be loaded at that port) and of any of those goods which are duitable or restricted goods as if the goods were to be loaded for exportation at that port, but any such entry may, subject to such conditions as the Commissioners see fit to impose, be made without the goods being first discharged.

(3) A ship may, subject to subsection (4) below, be entered outwards from a port under this section notwithstanding that before departing for any place outside the United Kingdom the ship is to go to another port.

(4) A ship carrying cargo brought in that ship from some place outside the United Kingdom and intended to be discharged in the United Kingdom may only be entered outwards by virtue of subsection (3) above subject to such conditions as the Commissioners see fit to impose.

(5) If, when a ship is required by this section to be entered outwards from any port, any goods are taken on board that ship at that port, except in accordance with such a stiffening order as is mentioned in subsection (1) above, before the ship is so entered, the goods shall be liable to forfeiture and the master of the ship shall be liable on summary conviction to a penalty of £100.

(6) Where goods are taken on board a ship as mentioned in subsection (5) above or made waterborne for that purpose with fraudulent intent, any person concerned therein with knowledge of that intent may be detained and shall be liable—

    (a) on summary conviction, to a penalty of the prescribed sum or of three times the value of the goods, whichever is the greater, or to imprisonment for a term not exceeding 6 months, or to both ; or

(b) on conviction on indictment, to a penalty of any amount, or to imprisonment for a term not exceeding 2 years, or to both.

64.—(1) Save as permitted by the Commissioners, no ship or aircraft shall depart from any port or customs and excise airport from which it commences, or at which it touches during, a voyage or flight to an eventual destination outside the United Kingdom until clearance of the ship or aircraft for that departure has been obtained from the proper officer at that port or airport.

(2) The Commissioners may give directions—

(a) as to the procedure for obtaining clearance under this section ;

(b) as to the documents to be produced and the information to be furnished by any person applying for such clearance.

(3) Where clearance is sought under this section for any ship which is in ballast or has on board no goods other than stores, the baggage of passengers carried in that ship, chalk, slate, or empty returned containers upon which no freight or profit is earned, the proper officer in granting clearance thereof shall, on the application of the master, clear the ship as in ballast.

(4) Any officer may board any ship which is cleared outwards from a port at any time while the ship is within the limits of a port or within 3 nautical miles of the coast of the United Kingdom and require the production of the ship's clearance, and if the master refuses to produce it or to answer such questions as the officer may put to him concerning the ship, cargo and intended voyage, he shall be liable on summary conviction to a penalty of £25.

(5) Every ship departing from a port shall, if so required for the purpose of disembarking an officer or of further examination, bring to at the boarding station, and if any ship fails to comply with any such requirement the master shall be liable on summary conviction to a penalty of £50.

(6) If any ship or aircraft required to be cleared under this section departs from any port or customs and excise airport without a valid clearance, the master or commander shall be liable on summary conviction to a penalty of £100.

(7) If, where any aircraft is required to obtain clearance from any customs and excise airport under this section, any goods are loaded, or are waterborne for loading, into that aircraft at that airport before application for clearance has been made, the goods shall be liable to forfeiture and, where the loading or making waterborne is done with fraudulent intent, any person concerned

therein with knowledge of that intent shall be guilty of an offence under this subsection and may be detained.

(8) A person guilty of an offence under subsection (7) above shall be liable—

    (*a*) on summary conviction, to a penalty of the prescribed sum or of three times the value of the goods, whichever is the greater, or to imprisonment for a term not exceeding 6 months, or to both ; or

    (*b*) on conviction on indictment, to a penalty of any amount, or to imprisonment for a term not exceeding 2 years, or to both.

Power to refuse or cancel clearance of ship or aircraft.

65.—(1) For the purpose of the detention thereof in pursuance of any power or duty conferred or imposed by or under any enactment, or for the purpose of securing compliance with any provision of the Customs and Excise Acts 1979 or of any other enactment or of any instrument made thereunder, being a provision relating to the importation or exportation of goods—

    (*a*) the proper officer may at any time refuse clearance of any ship or aircraft ; and

    (*b*) where clearance has been granted to a ship or aircraft, any officer may at any time while the ship is within the limits of any port or the aircraft is at any customs and excise airport demand that the clearance shall be returned to him.

(2) Any such demand may be made either orally or in writing on the master of the ship or commander of the aircraft, and if made in writing may be served—

    (*a*) by delivering it to him personally ; or

    (*b*) by leaving it at his last known place of abode ; or

    (*c*) by leaving it on board the ship or aircraft with the person appearing to be in charge or command thereof.

(3) Where a demand for the return of a clearance is made as aforesaid—

    (*a*) the clearance shall forthwith become void ; and

    (*b*) if the demand is not complied with, the master of the ship or the commander of the aircraft shall be liable on summary conviction to a penalty of £100.

General regulation of exportation, etc.

Power to make regulations as to exportation, etc.

66.—(1) The Commissioners may make regulations—

    (*a*) regulating with respect to ships and aircraft respectively the loading and making waterborne for loading of goods for exportation or as stores and the embarking of passengers for a destination outside the United Kingdom ;

(b) prescribing the procedure to be followed and the documents to be produced and information to be furnished by any person conveying goods out of Northern Ireland by land ;

(c) requiring delivery of a manifest containing such particulars as the Commissioners may direct of all cargo carried in an exporting ship and, if the Commissioners so direct, such other documents relating to the cargo as are specified in the direction ;

(d) requiring delivery of a certificate of the fuel shipped in any ship departing from a port for a place outside the United Kingdom.

(2) If any person contravenes or fails to comply with any regulation made under this section, he shall be liable on summary conviction to a penalty of £100 and any goods in respect of which the offence was committed shall be liable to forfeiture.

Offences in relation to exportation

67.—(1) If any goods which have been loaded or retained on board any ship or aircraft for exportation are not exported to and discharged at a place outside the United Kingdom but are unloaded in the United Kingdom, then, unless—

Offences in relation to exportation of goods.

(a) the unloading was authorised by the proper officer ; and

(b) except where that officer otherwise permits, any duty chargeable and unpaid on the goods is paid and any drawback or allowance paid in respect thereof is repaid,

the master of the ship or the commander of the aircraft and any person concerned in the unshipping, relanding, landing, unloading or carrying of the goods from the ship or aircraft without such authority, payment or repayment shall each be guilty of an offence under this section.

(2) The Commissioners may impose such conditions as they see fit with respect to any goods loaded or retained as mentioned in subsection (1) above which are permitted to be unloaded in the United Kingdom.

(3) If any person contravenes or fails to comply with, or is concerned in any contravention of or failure to comply with, any condition imposed under subsection (2) above he shall be guilty of an offence under this section.

(4) Where any goods loaded or retained as mentioned in subsection (1) above or brought to a customs and excise station for exportation by land are—

(a) goods from warehouse, other than goods which have been kept, without being warehoused, in a warehouse by virtue of section 92(4) below ;

   (*b*) transit goods ;

   (*c*) other goods chargeable with a duty which has not been paid ; or

   (*d*) drawback goods,

then if any container in which the goods are held is without the authority of the proper officer opened, or any mark, letter or device on any such container or on any lot of the goods is without that authority cancelled, obliterated or altered, every person concerned in the opening, cancellation, obliteration or alteration shall be guilty of an offence under this section.

(5) Any goods in respect of which an offence under this section is committed shall be liable to forfeiture and any person guilty of an offence under this section shall be liable on summary conviction to a penalty of three times the value of the goods or £100, whichever is the greater.

68.—(1) If any goods are—

   (*a*) exported or shipped as stores ; or

   (*b*) brought to any place in the United Kingdom for the purpose of being exported or shipped as stores,

and the exportation or shipment is or would be contrary to any prohibition or restriction for the time being in force with respect to those goods under or by virtue of any enactment, the goods shall be liable to forfeiture and the exporter or intending exporter of the goods and any agent of his concerned in the exportation or shipment or intended exportation or shipment shall each be liable on summary conviction to a penalty of three times the value of the goods or £100, whichever is the greater.

(2) Any person knowingly concerned in the exportation or shipment as stores, or in the attempted exportation or shipment as stores, of any goods with intent to evade any such prohibition or restriction as is mentioned in subsection (1) above shall be guilty of an offence under this subsection and may be detained.

(3) Subject to subsection (4) below, a person guilty of an offence under subsection (2) above shall be liable—

   (*a*) on summary conviction, to a penalty of the prescribed sum or of three times the value of the goods, whichever is the greater, or to imprisonment for a term not exceeding 6 months, or to both ; or

   (*b*) on conviction on indictment, to a penalty of any amount, or to imprisonment for a term not exceeding 2 years, or to both.

(4) In the case of an offence under subsection (2) above in connection with a prohibition or restriction on exportation

having effect by virtue of section 3 of the Misuse of Drugs Act 1971, subsection (3) above shall have effect subject to the modifications specified in Schedule 1 to this Act.

(5) If by virtue of any such restriction as is mentioned in subsection (1) above any goods may be exported only when consigned to a particular place or person and any goods so consigned are delivered to some other place or person, the ship, aircraft or vehicle in which they were exported shall be liable to forfeiture unless it is proved to the satisfaction of the Commissioners that both the owner of the ship, aircraft or vehicle and the master of the ship, commander of the aircraft or person in charge of the vehicle—

(a) took all reasonable steps to secure that the goods were delivered to the particular place to which or person to whom they were consigned ; and

(b) did not connive at or, except under duress, consent to the delivery of the goods to that other place or person.

(6) In any case where a person would, apart from this subsection, be guilty of—

(a) an offence under subsection (1) or (2) above ; and

(b) a corresponding offence under the enactment or instrument imposing the prohibition or restriction in question, being an offence for which a fine or other penalty is expressly provided by that enactment or other instrument,

he shall not be guilty of the offence mentioned in paragraph (a) of this subsection.

PART VI

CONTROL OF COASTWISE TRAFFIC

69.—(1) Subject to section 70 below, any ship for the time Coasting being engaged in the trade of carrying goods coastwise between trade. places in the United Kingdom shall for the purposes of the Customs and Excise Acts 1979 be a coasting ship.

(2) Subject to that section, no goods not yet entered on importation and no goods for exportation shall be carried in a ship engaged in the trade of carrying goods coastwise.

(3) The Commissioners may from time to time give directions as to what trade by water between places in the United Kingdom is or is not to be deemed to be carrying goods coastwise.

70.—(1) The Commissioners may, subject to such conditions Coasting and restrictions as they see fit to impose, permit a ship to carry trade— goods coastwise notwithstanding that the ship is carrying goods exceptional brought therein from some place outside the United Kingdom provisions.

and not yet entered on importation ; but a ship so permitted to carry goods coastwise shall not for the purposes of the Customs and Excise Acts 1979 be a coasting ship.

(2) The Commissioners may, subject to such conditions and restrictions as they see fit to impose, permit goods brought by an importing ship to some place in the United Kingdom but consigned to and intended to be delivered at some other such place to be transhipped before due entry of the goods has been made to another ship for carriage coastwise to that other place.

(3) Where any ship has begun to load goods at any place in the United Kingdom for exportation or as stores for use on a voyage to an eventual destination outside the United Kingdom and is to go to any other such place to complete loading, the Commissioners may, subject to such conditions as they see fit to impose, permit that ship to carry other goods coastwise until she has completed her loading.

(4) If, where any goods are permitted to be carried coastwise in any ship under this section, the goods are loaded, unloaded, carried or otherwise dealt with contrary to any condition or restriction imposed by the Commissioners, the goods shall be liable to forfeiture and the master of the ship shall be liable on summary conviction to a penalty of £50.

Clearance of coasting ship and transire.
71.—(1) Subject to the provisions of this section and save as permitted by the Commissioners, before any coasting ship departs from any port the master thereof shall deliver to the proper officer an account in such form and manner and containing such particulars as the Commissioners may direct ; and that account when signed by the proper officer shall be the transire, that is to say, the clearance of the ship from that port and the pass for any goods to which the account relates.

(2) The Commissioners may, subject to such conditions as they see fit to impose, grant a general transire in respect of any coasting ship and any goods carried therein.

(3) Any such general transire may be revoked by the proper officer by notice in writing delivered to the master or the owner of the ship or to any member of the crew on board the ship.

(4) If a coasting ship departs from any port without a correct account having been delivered, except as permitted by the Commissioners or under and in compliance with any conditions imposed on the grant of a general transire, the master shall be liable on summary conviction to a penalty of £50.

72.—(1) The proper officer may examine any goods carried or to be carried in a coasting ship—

PART VI
Additional
powers of
officers in
relation to
coasting
ships.

    (*a*) at any time while they are on board the ship ; or

    (*b*) at any place in the United Kingdom to which the goods have been brought for shipment in, or at which they have been unloaded from, the ship.

(2) For the purpose of examining any goods in pursuance of subsection (1) above, the proper officer may require any container to be opened or unpacked ; and any such opening or unpacking and any repacking shall be done by or at the expense of the proprietor of the goods.

(3) The proper officer—

    (*a*) may board and search a coasting ship at any time during its voyage ;

    (*b*) may at any time require any document which should properly be on board a coasting ship to be produced or brought to him for examination ;

and if the master of the ship fails to produce or bring any such document to the proper officer when required, he shall be liable on summary conviction to a penalty of £50.

73.—(1) The Commissioners may make regulations as to the carriage of goods coastwise—

Power to make
regulations as
to carriage
of goods
coastwise,
etc.

    (*a*) regulating the loading and unloading and the making waterborne for loading of the goods ;

    (*b*) requiring the keeping and production by the master of a coasting ship of such record of the cargo carried in that ship as may be prescribed by the regulations.

(2) If any person contravenes or fails to comply with any regulation made under this section, he shall be liable on summary conviction to a penalty of £50 and any goods in respect of which the offence was committed shall be liable to forfeiture.

74.—(1) If in the case of any coasting ship—

    (*a*) any goods are taken on board or removed therefrom at sea or at any place outside the United Kingdom ; or

    (*b*) except for some unavoidable cause, the ship touches at any place outside the United Kingdom or deviates from her voyage ; or

    (*c*) the ship touches at any place outside the United Kingdom and the master does not report that fact in writing to the proper officer at the first port at which the ship arrives thereafter,

the master of the ship shall be liable on summary conviction to a penalty of £100.

(2) Any goods which are shipped and carried coastwise, or which, having been carried coastwise, are unloaded in any place in the United Kingdom, otherwise than in accordance with the provisions of sections 69 to 71 above or of any regulations made under section 73 above, or which are brought to any place for the purpose of being so shipped and carried coastwise, shall be liable to forfeiture.

(3) If any goods—

    (*a*) are carried coastwise or shipped as stores in a coasting ship contrary to any prohibition or restriction for the time being in force with respect thereto under or by virtue of any enactment ; or

    (*b*) are brought to any place in the United Kingdom for the purpose of being so carried or shipped,

then those goods shall be liable to forfeiture and the shipper or intending shipper of the goods shall be liable on summary conviction to a penalty of £100.

(4) In any case where a person would, apart from this subsection, be guilty of—

    (*a*) an offence under subsection (3) above ; and

    (*b*) a corresponding offence under the enactment or other instrument imposing the prohibition or restriction in question, being an offence for which a fine or other penalty is expressly provided by that enactment or other instrument,

he shall not be guilty of the offence mentioned in paragraph (*a*) of this subsection.

PART VII

CUSTOMS AND EXCISE CONTROL: SUPPLEMENTARY PROVISIONS

Special requirements as to movement of certain goods

Explosives.
1875 c. 17.
75.—(1) No goods which are explosives within the meaning of the Explosives Act 1875 shall be loaded into any ship or aircraft for exportation, exported by land or shipped for carriage coastwise as cargo, until due entry has been made of the goods in such form and manner and containing such particulars as the Commissioners may direct.

(2) Without prejudice to sections 53 and 60 above, any goods required to be entered under this section which are loaded, exported or shipped as mentioned in subsection (1) above without being entered under this section shall be liable to forfeiture, and the exporter or, as the case may be, shipper shall be liable on summary conviction to a penalty of £100.

76.—(1) Without prejudice to any other requirement of this Act as to the entry or clearance of goods, the Commissioners may, where they are satisfied that it is expedient in the public interest, by order made by statutory instrument require with respect to any goods entry and clearance of the goods in such manner as the Commissioners may direct before their exportation or shipment for exportation, for carriage coastwise or as stores.

(2) Without prejudice to sections 53 and 60 above, if any person required by virtue of an order made under this section to make entry or obtain clearance of any goods, ships or exports, or attempts to ship or export, those goods without such entry or clearance or otherwise contrary to the order, he shall be liable on summary conviction to a penalty of £100.

Additional provisions as to information

77.—(1) An officer may require any person—

  (a) concerned with the importation, exportation or shipment for carriage coastwise of goods of which an entry or specification is required for that purpose by or under this Act; or

  (b) concerned in the carriage, unloading, landing or loading of goods which are being or have been imported or exported,

to furnish in such form as the officer may require any information relating to the goods and to produce and allow the officer to inspect and take extracts from or make copies of any invoice, bill of lading or other book or document whatsoever relating to the goods.

(2) If any person without reasonable cause fails to comply with a requirement imposed on him under subsection (1) above he shall be liable on summary conviction to a penalty of £50.

(3) Where any prohibition or restriction to which this subsection applies, that is to say, any prohibition or restriction under or by virtue of any enactment with respect to—

  (a) the exportation of goods to any particular destination; or

  (b) the exportation of goods of any particular class or description to any particular destination,

is for the time being in force, then, if any person about to ship for exportation or to export any goods or, as the case may be, any goods of that class or description, in the course of making entry thereof before shipment or exportation makes a declaration as to the ultimate destination thereof, and the Commissioners have reason to suspect that the declaration is untrue in any material particular, the goods may be detained until the

Commissioners are satisfied as to the truth of the declaration, and if they are not so satisfied the goods shall be liable to forfeiture.

(4) Any person concerned in the exportation of any goods which are subject to any prohibition or restriction to which subsection (3) above applies shall, if so required by the Commissioners, satisfy the Commissioners that those goods have not reached any destination other than that mentioned in the entry delivered in respect of the goods.

(5) If any person required under subsection (4) above to satisfy the Commissioners as mentioned in that subsection fails to do so, then, unless he proves—

(a) that he did not consent to or connive at the goods reaching any destination other than that mentioned in the entry delivered in respect of the goods ; and

(b) that he took all reasonable steps to secure that the ultimate destination of the goods was not other than that so mentioned,

he shall be liable on summary conviction to a penalty of three times the value of the goods or £100, whichever is the greater.

Customs and excise control of persons entering or leaving the United Kingdom.

78.—(1) Any person entering the United Kingdom shall, at such place and in such manner as the Commissioners may direct, declare any thing contained in his baggage or carried with him which—

(a) he has obtained outside the United Kingdom ; or

(b) being dutiable goods or chargeable goods, he has obtained in the United Kingdom without payment of duty or tax,

1979 c. 3. and in respect of which he is not entitled to exemption from duty and tax by virtue of any order under section 13 of the Customs and Excise Duties (General Reliefs) Act 1979 (personal reliefs).

In this subsection " chargeable goods " means goods on the importation of which value added tax is chargeable or goods obtained in the United Kingdom before 1st April 1973 which 1963 c. 9. are chargeable goods within the meaning of the Purchase Tax Act 1963 ; and " tax " means value added tax or purchase tax.

(2) Any person entering or leaving the United Kingdom shall answer such questions as the proper officer may put to him with respect to his baggage and any thing contained therein or carried with him, and shall, if required by the proper officer, produce that baggage and any such thing for examination at such place as the Commissioners may direct.

(3) Any person failing to declare any thing or to produce any baggage or thing as required by this section shall be liable on summary conviction to a penalty of three times the value of the

thing not declared or of the baggage or thing not produced, as the case may be, or £100, whichever is the greater.

(4) Any thing chargeable with any duty or tax which is found concealed, or is not declared, and any thing which is being taken into or out of the United Kingdom contrary to any prohibition or restriction for the time being in force with respect thereto under or by virtue of any enactment, shall be liable to forfeiture.

79.—(1) The Commissioners may, if they consider it neces- Power to sary, require evidence to be produced to their satisfaction in require support of any information required by or under Parts III to evidence in VII of this Act to be provided in respect of goods imported or support of exported. information.

(2) Without prejudice to subsection (1) above, where any question as to the duties chargeable on any imported goods, or the operation of any prohibition or restriction on importation, depends on any question as to the place from which the goods were consigned, or any question where they or other goods are to be treated as grown, manufactured or produced, or any question as to payments made on relief from duty allowed in any country or territory, then—

(a) the Commissioners may require the importer of the goods to furnish to them, in such form as they may prescribe, proof of—

(i) any statement made to them as to any fact necessary to determine that question, or

(ii) the accuracy of any certificate or other document furnished in connection with the importation of the goods and relating to the matter in issue,

and if such proof is not furnished to their satisfaction, the question may be determined without regard to that statement or to that certificate or document; and

(b) if in any proceedings relating to the goods or to the duty chargeable thereon the accuracy of any such certificate or document comes in question, it shall be for the person relying on it to furnish proof of its accuracy.

80.—(1) Where on the exportation of any goods from the Power to United Kingdom there has been furnished for the purpose of any require Community requirement or practice any certificate or other information evidence as to the origin of those goods, or as to payments or production made or relief from duty allowed in any country or territory, of documents then, for the purpose of verifying or investigating that certificate where origin or evidence, the Commissioners or an officer may require the of goods exporter, or any other person appearing to the Commissioners exported is or officer to have been concerned in any way with the goods, evidenced or with any goods from which, directly or indirectly, they have under Community law or practice.

PART VII

been produced or manufactured, or to have been concerned with the obtaining or furnishing of the certificate or evidence,—

    (*a*) to furnish such information, in such form and within such time, as the Commissioners or officer may specify in the requirement ; or

    (*b*) to produce for inspection, and to allow the taking of copies or extracts from, such invoices, bills of lading, books or documents as may be so specified.

(2) Any person who, without reasonable cause, fails to comply with a requirement imposed on him under subsection (1) above shall be liable on summary conviction to a penalty of £50.

Prevention of smuggling

Power to regulate small craft.

81.—(1) In this section " small ships " means—

    (*a*) ships not exceeding 100 tons register ; and

    (*b*) hovercraft, of whatever size.

(2) The Commissioners may make general regulations with respect to small ships and any such regulations may in particular make provision as to the purposes for which and the limits within which such ships may be used.

(3) Different provision may be made by regulations under this section for different classes or descriptions of small ships.

(4) The Commissioners may, in respect of any small ship, grant a licence exempting that ship from all or any of the provisions of any regulations made under this section.

(5) Any such licence may be granted for such period, for such purposes and subject to such conditions and restrictions as the Commissioners see fit, and may be revoked at any time by the Commissioners.

(6) Any small ship which, except under and in accordance with the terms of a licence granted under this section, is used contrary to any regulation made under this section, and any ship granted such a licence which is found not to have that licence on board, shall be liable to forfeiture.

1894 c. 60.

(7) Every boat belonging to a British ship and every other vessel not exceeding 100 tons register, not being a fishing boat entered in the fishing boat register under the Merchant Shipping Act 1894, and every hovercraft, shall be marked in such manner as the Commissioners may direct, and any such boat, vessel or hovercraft which is not so marked shall be liable to forfeiture.

82.—(1) The person in command or charge of any vessel in the service of Her Majesty which is engaged in the prevention of smuggling—

(*a*) may haul up and leave that vessel on any part of the coast or of the shore or bank of any river or creek ; and

(*b*) may moor that vessel at any place below high water mark on any part of the coast or of any such shore or bank.

(2) Any officer and any person acting in aid of an officer or otherwise duly engaged in the prevention of smuggling may for that purpose patrol upon and pass freely along and over any part of the coast or of the shore or bank of any river or creek, over any railway or aerodrome or land adjoining any aerodrome, and over any land in Northern Ireland within the prescribed area.

(3) Nothing in this section shall authorise the use of or entry into any garden or pleasure ground.

83.—(1) Where, in pursuance of any power conferred by the customs and excise Acts or of any requirement imposed by or under those Acts, a seal, lock or mark is used to secure or identify any goods for any of the purposes of those Acts and—

(*a*) at any time while the goods are in the United Kingdom or within the limits of any port or on passage between ports in the United Kingdom, the seal, lock or mark is wilfully and prematurely removed or tampered with by any person ; or

(*b*) at any time before the seal, lock or mark is lawfully removed, any of the goods are wilfully removed by any person,

that person and the person then in charge of the goods shall each be liable on summary conviction to a penalty of £500.

(2) For the purposes of subsection (1) above, goods in a ship or aircraft shall be deemed to be in the charge of the master of the ship or commander of the aircraft.

(3) Where, in pursuance of any Community requirement or practice which relates to the movement of goods between countries or of any international agreement to which the United Kingdom is a party and which so relates,—

(*a*) a seal, lock or mark is used (whether in the United Kingdom or elsewhere) to secure or identify any goods for customs or excise purposes ; and

(*b*) at any time while the goods are in the United Kingdom, the seal, lock or mark is wilfuly and prematurely removed or tampered with by any person, that person and the person then in charge of the goods shall each be liable on summary conviction to a penalty of £500.

Penalty for signalling to smugglers.

84.—(1) In this section references to a " prohibited signal " or a " prohibited message " are references to a signal or message connected with the smuggling or intended smuggling of goods into or out of the United Kingdom.

(2) Any person who by any means makes any prohibited signal or transmits any prohibited message from any part of the United Kingdom or from any ship or aircraft for the information of a person in any ship or aircraft or across the boundary shall be liable on summary conviction to a penalty of £100, or to imprisonment for a term not exceeding 6 months, or to both, and may be detained ; and any equipment or apparatus used for sending the signal or message shall be liable to forfeiture.

(3) Subsection (2) above applies whether or not the person for whom the signal or message is intended is in a position to receive it or is actually engaged at the time in smuggling goods.

(4) If, in any proceedings under subsection (2) above, any question arises as to whether any signal or message was a prohibited signal or message, the burden of proof shall lie upon the defendant or claimant.

(5) If any officer or constable or any member of Her Majesty's armed forces or coastguard has reasonable grounds for suspecting that any prohibited signal or message is being or is about to be made or transmitted from any ship, aircraft, vehicle, house or place, he may board or enter that ship, aircraft, vehicle, house or place and take such steps as are reasonably necessary to stop or prevent the sending of the signal or message.

Penalty for interfering with revenue vessels, etc.

85.—(1) Any person who save for just and sufficient cause interferes in any way with any ship, aircraft, vehicle, buoy, anchor, chain, rope or mark which is being used for the purposes of any functions of the Commissioners under Parts III to VII of this Act shall be liable on summary conviction to a penalty of £25.

(2) Any person who fires upon any vessel, aircraft or vehicle in the service of Her Majesty while that vessel, aircraft or vehicle is engaged in the prevention of smuggling shall be liable on conviction on indictment to imprisonment for a term not exceeding 5 years.

Special penalty where offender armed or disguised.

86. Any person concerned in the movement, carriage or concealment of goods—

> (*a*) contrary to or for the purpose of contravening any pro-
> hibition or restriction for the time being in force under

or by virtue of any enactment with respect to the importation or exportation thereof ; or

(*b*) without payment having been made of or security given for any duty payable thereon,

who, while so concerned, is armed with any offensive weapon or disguised in any way, and any person so armed for disguised found in the United Kingdom in possession of any goods liable to forfeiture under any provision of the customs and excise Acts relating to imported goods or prohibited or restricted goods, shall be liable on conviction on indictment to imprisonment for a term not exceeding 3 years and may be detained.

87. If any person offers any goods for sale as having been imported without payment of duty, or as having been otherwise unlawfully imported, then, whether or not the goods were so imported or were in fact chargeable with duty, the goods shall be liable to forfeiture and the person so offering them for sale shall be liable on summary conviction to a penalty of three times the value of the goods or £100, whichever is the greater, and may be detained.

Penalty for offering goods for sale as smuggled goods.

Forfeiture of ships, etc. for certain offences

88. Where—

(*a*) a ship is or has been within the limits of any port or within 3 or, being a British ship, 12 nautical miles of the coast of the United Kingdom ; or

(*b*) an aircraft is or has been at any place, whether on land or on water, in the United Kingdom ; or

(*c*) a vehicle is or has been within the limits of any port or at any aerodrome or, while in Northern Ireland, within the prescribed area,

while constructed, adapted, altered or fitted in any manner for the purpose of concealing goods, that ship, aircraft or vehicle shall be liable to forfeiture.

Forfeiture of ship, aircraft or vehicle constructed, etc. for concealing goods.

89.—(1) If any part of the cargo of a ship is thrown overboard or is staved or destroyed to prevent seizure—

(*a*) while the ship is within 3 nautical miles of the coast of the United Kingdom ; or

(*b*) where the ship, having been properly summoned to bring to by any vessel in the service of Her Majesty, fails so to do and chase is given, at any time during the chase,

the ship shall be liable to forfeiture.

Forfeiture of ship jettisoning cargo, etc.

Part I

C

(2) For the purposes of this section a ship shall be deemed to have been properly summoned to bring to—

    (*a*) if the vessel making the summons did so by means of an international signal code or other recognised means and while flying her proper ensign; and

    (*b*) in the case of a ship which is not a British ship, if at the time when the summons was made the ship was within 3 nautical miles of the coast of the United Kingdom.

Forfeiture of ship or aircraft unable to account for missing cargo.

90. Where a ship has been within the limits of any port, or an aircraft has been in the United Kingdom, with a cargo on board and a substantial part of that cargo is afterwards found to be missing, then, if the master of the ship or commander of the aircraft fails to account therefor to the satisfaction of the Commissioners, the ship or aircraft shall be liable to forfeiture.

Ships failing to bring to.

91.—(1) If, save for just and sufficient cause, any ship which is liable to forfeiture or examination under or by virtue of any provision of the Customs and Excise Acts 1979 does not bring to when required to do so, the master of the ship shall be liable on summary conviction to a penalty of £50.

(2) Where any ship liable to forfeiture or examination as aforesaid has failed to bring to when required to do so and chase has been given thereto by any vessel in the service of Her Majesty and, after the commander of that vessel has hoisted the proper ensign and caused a gun to be fired as a signal, the ship still fails to bring to, the ship may be fired upon.

PART VIII

WAREHOUSES AND QUEEN'S WAREHOUSES AND RELATED PROVISIONS ABOUT PIPE-LINES

Approval of warehouses.

92.—(1) The Commissioners may approve, for such periods and subject to such conditions as they think fit, places of security for the deposit, keeping and securing—

    (*a*) of imported goods chargeable as such with excise duty (whether or not also chargeable with customs duty) without payment of the excise duty;

    (*b*) of goods for exportation or for use as stores, being goods not eligible for home use;

    (*c*) of goods manufactured or produced in the United Kingdom and permitted by or under the customs and excise Acts to be warehoused without payment of any duty of excise chargeable thereon;

    (*d*) of goods imported into or manufactured or produced in the United Kingdom and permitted by or under the customs and excise Acts to be warehoused on drawback,

subject to and in accordance with warehousing regulations; and any place of security so approved is referred to in this Act as an " excise warehouse ".

(2) The Commissioners may approve, for such periods and subject to such conditions as they think fit, places of security for the deposit, keeping and securing—

    (*a*) of imported goods chargeable with customs duty or otherwise not for the time being in free circulation in member States (whether or not also chargeable with excise duty) without payment of the customs duty;

    (*b*) of such other goods as the Commissioners may allow to be warehoused for exportation or for use as stores in cases where relief from or repayment of any customs duty or other payment is conditional on their exportation or use as stores,

subject to and in accordance with warehousing regulations; and any place of security so approved is referred to in this Act as a " customs warehouse ".

(3) The same place may be approved under this section both as a customs and as an excise warehouse.

(4) Notwithstanding subsection (2) above and the terms of the approval of the warehouse but subject to directions under subsection (5) below, goods of the following descriptions, not being goods chargeable with excise duty which has not been paid, that is to say—

    (*a*) goods originating in member States;

    (*b*) goods which are in free circulation in member States; and

    (*c*) goods placed on importation under a customs procedure (other than warehousing) involving the suspension of, or the giving of relief from, customs duties,

may be kept, without being warehoused, in a customs warehouse.

(5) The Commissioners may from time to time give directions—

    (*a*) as to the goods which may or may not be deposited in any particular warehouse or class of warehouse;

    (*b*) as to the part of any warehouse in which any class or description of goods may be kept or secured.

(6) If, after the approval of a warehouse as an excise warehouse, the occupier thereof makes without the previous consent of the Commissioners any alteration therein or addition thereto, he shall be liable on summary conviction to a penalty of £200.

(7) The Commissioners may at any time for reasonable cause revoke or vary the terms of their approval of any warehouse under this section.

(8) Any person contravening or failing to comply with any condition imposed or direction given by the Commissioners under this section shall be liable on summary conviction to a penalty of £100.

Regulation of warehouses and ware-housed goods.

93.—(1) The Commissioners may by regulations under this section (referred to in this Act as " warehousing regulations ") regulate the deposit, keeping, securing and treatment of goods in and the removal of goods from warehouse.

(2) Warehousing regulations may, without prejudice to the generality of subsection (1) above, include provisions—

(*a*) imposing or providing for the imposition under the regulations of conditions and restrictions subject to which goods may be deposited in, kept in or removed from warehouse or made available there to their owner for any prescribed purpose ;

(*b*) requiring goods deposited in warehouse to be produced to or made available for inspection by an officer on request by him ;

(*c*) permitting the carrying out on warehoused goods of such operations (other than operations consisting of the mixing of spirits with wine or made-wine) as may be prescribed by or allowed under the regulations in such manner and subject to such conditions and restrictions as may be imposed by or under the regulations ;

(*d*) for determining, for the purpose of charging or securing the payment of duty, the duties of customs or excise and the rates thereof to be applied to warehoused goods (other than goods falling within section 92(2)(*b*) above) and in that connection—

(i) for determining the time by reference to which warehoused goods are to be classified ;

(ii) for determining the time at which warehoused goods are to be treated as having been removed from warehouse ;

(iii) for ascertaining the quantity which is to be taken as the quantity of warehoused goods ;

(e) enabling the Commissioners to allow goods to be removed from warehouse without payment of duty in such circumstances and subject to such conditions as they may determine ;

(f) permitting goods to be destroyed or abandoned to the Commissioners without payment of customs duty in such circumstances and subject to such conditions as they may determine,

and may contain such incidental or supplementary provisions as the Commissioners think necessary or expedient for the protection of the revenue.

(3) Warehousing regulations may make different provision for warehouses or parts of warehouses of different descriptions or for goods of different classes or descriptions or of the same class or description in different circumstances.

(4) Warehousing regulations may make provision about the removal of goods from one warehouse to another or from one part of a warehouse to another part or for treating goods remaining in a warehouse as if, for all or any prescribed purposes of the customs and excise Acts, they had been so removed ; and regulations about the removal of goods may, for all or any prescribed purposes of those Acts, include provision for treating the goods as having been warehoused or removed from warehouse (where they would not otherwise be so treated).

(5) Warehousing regulations made by virtue of paragraph (a) or (c) of subsection (2) above may also provide for the forfeiture of goods in the event of non-compliance with any condition or restriction imposed by virtue of that paragraph or in the event of the carrying out of any operation on warehoused goods which is not by virtue of the said paragraph (c) permitted to be carried out in warehouse.

(6) If any person fails to comply with any warehousing regulation or with any condition or restriction imposed under a warehousing regulation he shall be liable on summary conviction to a penalty of £100.

(7) In this section " prescribed " means prescribed by warehousing regulations.

94.—(1) Subject to subsection (2) below, this section applies where goods have been warehoused and, before they are lawfully removed from warehouse in accordance with a proper clearance thereof, they are found to be missing or deficient.

Deficiency in warehoused goods.

(2) This section shall not apply in relation to a deficiency in goods entered and cleared from warehouse for exportation or

shipment as stores unless the proper officer has reasonable grounds to suppose that the whole or part of the deficiency has arisen from unlawful abstraction.

(3) In any case where this section applies, unless it is shown to the satisfaction of the Commissioners that the absence of or deficiency in the goods can be accounted for by natural waste or other legitimate cause, the Commissioners may require the occupier of the warehouse or the proprietor of the goods to pay immediately in respect of the missing goods or of the whole or any part of the deficiency, as they see fit, the duty chargeable or deemed under warehousing regulations to be chargeable on such goods or, in the case of goods warehoused on drawback which could not lawfully be entered for home use, an amount equal to the drawback and any allowance paid in respect of the goods.

(4) If, on the written demand of an officer, the occupier of the warehouse or the proprietor of the goods refuses to pay any sum which he is required to pay under subsection (3) above he shall in addition be liable on summary conviction to a penalty of double that sum.

(5) This section has effect without prejudice to any penalty or forfeiture incurred under any other provision of the customs and excise Acts.

Deficiency in goods occurring in course of removal from warehouse without payment of duty.

95.—(1) Where any goods have been lawfully permitted to be taken from a warehouse without payment of duty for removal to another warehouse or to some other place, section 94 above shall, subject to subsection (2) below, have effect in relation to those goods in the course of that removal as if those goods were still in warehouse.

(2) In its application in relation to any goods by virtue of subsection (1) above, section 94 above shall have effect as if the following provisions were omitted, namely—

(a) subsection (2), and the reference to that subsection in subsection (1) ; and

(b) the references in subsections (3) and (4) to the occupier of the warehouse.

Deficiency in certain goods moved by pipe-line.

96.—(1) This section applies where goods of any of the following descriptions, that is to say—

(a) goods which are chargeable with a duty which has not been paid ;

(b) goods on which duty has been repaid or remitted in whole or in part ; and

(c) goods on which drawback has been paid,

are moved by pipe-line, or notified to the proper officer as being goods to be moved by pipe-line, and are at any time thereafter found to be missing or deficient.

(2) In any case where this section applies, unless it is shown to the satisfaction of the Commissioners that the absence of or deficiency in the goods can be accounted for by natural waste or other legitimate cause, the Commissioners may require the owner of the pipe-line or the proprietor of the goods to pay immediately in respect of the missing goods, or in respect of the whole or any part of the deficiency, as they see fit, the amount of the duty unpaid or repaid thereon or, as the case may be, an amount equal to the drawback paid thereon.

(3) If, on the written demand of an officer, any person refuses to pay any sum which he is required to pay under subsection (2) above he shall in addition be liable on summary conviction to a penalty of double that sum.

(4) For the purposes of this section any absence or deficiency in the case of goods marked by a pipe-line used for the importation or exportation of goods shall be deemed to have taken place within the United Kingdom unless the contrary is shown.

(5) This section has effect without prejudice to any penalty or forfeiture incurred under any other provision of the customs and excise Acts.

97.—(1) This section applies to—

    (*a*) any loss or damage caused to goods while in a warehouse or pipe-line ; and

    (*b*) any unlawful removal of goods from a warehouse or pipe-line.

(2) Subject to subsection (3) below, no compensation shall be payable by, and no action shall lie against, the Commissioners or any officer acting in the execution of his duty for any loss or damage to which this section applies or for any unlawful removal to which this section applies.

(3) If any goods in a warehouse or pipe-line are destroyed, stolen or unlawfully removed by or with the assistance or connivance of an officer and that officer is convicted of the offence, then, except where the proprietor of the goods or the occupier of the warehouse or, as the case may be, the owner of the pipe-line was a party to the offence, the Commissioners shall pay compensation for any loss caused by any such destruction, theft or removal.

(4) Where compensation is payable by virtue of subsection (3) above then, notwithstanding any provision of the Customs and Excise Acts 1979, no duty shall be payable on the goods by the

proprietor of the goods or by the occupier of the warehouse or, as the case may be, the owner of the pipe-line, and any sum paid by way of duty on those goods by any of those persons before the conviction shall be repaid.

98.—(1) Where the Commissioners intend to revoke or not to renew their approval of a warehouse, they shall, not later than the beginning of the prescribed period ending with the date when the revocation is to take effect or the approval is due to expire, as the case may be, give notice of their intention, specifying therein the said date.

(2) The notice shall be given in writing and shall be deemed to have been served on all persons interested in any goods then deposited in that warehouse, or permitted under the Customs and Excise Acts 1979 to be so deposited between the date of the giving of the notice and the date specified therein, if addressed to the occupier of, and left at, the warehouse.

(3) If, after the date specified in the notice or such later date as the Commissioners may in any case allow, any goods not duly cleared still remain in the warehouse they may be taken by an officer to a Queen's warehouse and, without prejudice to section 99(3) below, if they are not cleared therefrom within one month may be sold.

(4) In this section " the prescribed period " means—

    (*a*) in the case of a warehouse which is a customs warehouse but not also an excise warehouse, such period as may be prescribed by warehousing regulations ;

    (*b*) in the case of a warehouse which is or is also an excise warehouse, 3 months.

99.—(1) The following provisions of this section shall have effect in relation to any goods which are deposited in a Queen's warehouse under or by virtue of any provision of the Customs and Excise Acts 1979.

(2) Such rent shall be payable while the goods are deposited as may be fixed by the Commissioners.

(3) If the goods are of a combustible or inflammable nature or otherwise of such a character as to require special care or treatment—

    (*a*) they shall, in addition to any other charges payable thereon, be chargeable with such expenses for securing, watching and guarding them as the Commissioners see fit ;

    (*b*) neither the Commissioners nor any officer shall be liable to make good any damage which the goods may have sustained ; and

(c) if the proprietor of the goods has not cleared them within a period of 14 days from the date of deposit, they may be sold by the Commissioners;

but, in the case of goods deposited by virtue of section 40(2) above, paragraph (c) above shall only apply if the goods are of a combustible or inflammable nature.

(4) Save as permitted by or under the Customs and Excise Acts 1979, the goods shall not be removed from the warehouse until—

(a) any duty chargeable thereon; and

(b) any charges in respect thereof—

    (i) for their removal to the warehouse, and

    (ii) under subsections (2) and (3) above,

have been paid and, in the case of goods requiring entry and not yet entered, until entry has been made thereof.

(5) The officer having the custody of the goods may refuse to allow them to be removed until it is shown to his satisfaction that any freight charges due thereon have been paid.

(6) If the goods are sold under or by virtue of any provision of the Customs and Excise Acts 1979, the proceeds of sale shall be applied—

(a) first, in paying any duty chargeable on the goods;

(b) secondly, in defraying any such charges as are mentioned in subsection (4) above; and

(c) thirdly, in defraying any charges for freight;

and if the person who was immediately before the sale the proprietor of the goods makes application in that behalf the remainder, if any, shall be paid over to him.

(7) When the goods are authorised to be sold under or by virtue of any provision of the Customs and Excise Acts 1979 but cannot be sold—

(a) if the goods are to be exported, for a sum sufficient to make the payment mentioned in paragraph (b) of subsection (6) above; or

(b) in any other case, for a sum sufficient to make the payments mentioned in paragraphs (a) and (b) of that subsection,

the Commissioners may destroy the goods.

100.—(1) Any person who, except with the authority of the proper officer or for just and sufficient cause, opens any of the doors or locks of a warehouse or Queen's warehouse or makes or obtains access to any such warehouse or to any goods warehoused therein shall be liable on summary conviction to a penalty of £500 and may be detained.

(2) Where—

(a) any goods which have been entered for warehousing are taken into the warehouse without the authority of, or otherwise than in accordance with any directions given by, the proper officer ; or

(b) save as permitted by the Customs and Excise Acts 1979 or by or under warehousing regulations, any goods which have been entered for warehousing are removed without being duly warehoused or are otherwise not duly warehoused ; or

(c) any goods which have been deposited in a warehouse or Queen's warehouse are unlawfully removed therefrom or are unlawfully loaded into any ship, aircraft or vehicle for removal or for exportation or use as stores ; or

(d) any goods entered for warehousing are concealed either before or after they have been warehoused ; or

(e) any goods which have been lawfully permitted to be removed from a warehouse or Queen's warehouse without payment of duty for any purpose are not duly delivered at the destination to which they should have been taken in accordance with that permission,

those goods shall be liable to forfeiture.

(3) If any person who took, removed, loaded or concealed any goods as mentioned in subsection (2) above did so with intent to defraud Her Majesty of any duty chargeable thereon or to evade any prohibition or restriction for the time being in force with respect thereto under or by virtue of any enactment, he shall be guilty of an offence under this subsection and may be detained.

(4) A person guilty of an offence under subsection (3) above shall be liable—

(a) on summary conviction, to a penalty of the prescribed sum or of three times the value of the goods, whichever is the greater, or to imprisonment for a term not exceeding 6 months, or to both ; or

(b) on conviction on indictment, to a penalty of any amount, or to imprisonment for a term not exceeding 2 years, or to both.

PART IX

CONTROL OF EXCISE LICENCE TRADES AND REVENUE TRADERS

Excise licences—general provisions

Excise licences.

101.—(1) An excise licence shall be in such form and contain such particulars as the Commissioners may direct and, subject to the provisions of any enactment relating to the licence or Part IX trade in question, may be granted by the proper officer on payment of the appropriate duty.

(2) An excise licence for the carrying on of a trade shall be granted in respect of one set of premises only, but a licence for the same trade may be granted to the same person in respect of each of two or more sets of premises.

(3) Where an excise licence trade is carried on at any set of premises by two or more persons in partnership, then, subject to the provisions of any enactment relating to the licence or trade in question, not more than one licence shall be required to be taken out by those persons in respect of those premises in any one licence year.

(4) Without prejudice to any other requirement as to the production of licences contained in the Customs and Excise Acts 1979, if any person who is the holder of an excise licence to carry on any trade or to manufacture or sell any goods fails to produce his licence for examination within a reasonable time after being so requested by an officer he shall be liable on summary conviction to a penalty of £50.

102.—(1) Any government department or local authority Payment having power to grant an excise licence may, if they think fit, for excise grant the licence upon receipt of a cheque for the amount of licences the duty payable thereon. by cheque.

(2) Where a licence is granted to any person on receipt of a cheque and the cheque is subsequently dishonoured, the licence shall be void as from the time when it was granted, and the department or authority who granted it shall send to that person, by letter sent by registered post or the recorded delivery service and addressed to him at the address given by him when applying for the licence, a notice requiring him to deliver up the licence within the period of 7 days from the date when the notice was posted.

(3) If a person who has been required under subsection (2) above to deliver up a licence fails to comply with the requirement within the period mentioned in that subsection he shall be liable on summary conviction to a penalty of the following amount, that is to say—

    (*a*) where the licence is a gaming licence or a gaming machine licence, a penalty of £500 ;

    (*b*) in any other case, a penalty of £50.

103.—(1) Subject to subsection (2) below, where a person who Renewal has taken out an excise licence issuable annually in respect of of excise any trade takes out a fresh licence in respect of that trade for licences.

PART IX

the next following licence year, then, subject to the provisions of any enactment relating to the licence or trade in question, the fresh licence shall bear the date of the day immediately following that on which the previous licence expires.

(2) Where an application for the fresh licence is made after the day on which the previous licence expires or such later day as the Commissioners may in any case allow, the licence shall bear the date of the day when the application is made.

Transfer and removal of excise licence trades and licences.

104.—(1) Subject to any provision of the Customs and Excise Acts 1979 or of any other enactment relating to the licence or trade in question, where the holder of an excise licence to carry on any trade dies, or where the holder of such a licence in respect of premises specified therein leaves those premises, the proper officer may transfer that licence in such manner as the Commissioners may direct, without any additional payment, to some other person for the remainder of the period for which the licence was granted.

(2) Subject to any such provision as aforesaid, where any person who holds an excise licence in respect of any premises removes his trade to other premises on which it may be lawfully carried on, the proper officer may authorise in such manner as the Commissioners may direct the carrying on, without any additional payment other than any required to be paid by subsection (3) below, of that trade on those other premises for the remainder of the period for which the licence was granted.

(3) Where, in a case falling within subsection (2) above, the amount of the duty payable on the grant of the licence was determined by reference to the annual value of the premises in respect of which it was granted and would have been greater if the licence had originally been granted in respect of the premises to which the trade is removed, such additional sum shall be payable as bears the same proportion to the difference as the remainder of the period for which the licence was granted bears to a year.

(4) Notwithstanding anything in subsections (1) to (3) above, where by any other enactment relating to the licence or trade in question the authorisation of any court or other authority or the production of any certificate is required for such a transfer or removal of an excise licence trade as is mentioned in this section, no transfer or removal of an excise licence to carry on that trade shall be granted unless it is shown to the satisfaction of the proper officer that the authorisation or certificate has been granted.

105.—(1) Where any imported goods are on importation
warehoused without payment of duty, then, notwithstanding
that they are goods for the sale of which an excise licence is
required, a licence shall not be required for a sale of those goods
at any time before they are delivered for home use if the sale
is made to one person or to persons carrying on trade or business
in partnership and—

>   (*a*) is of not less than one complete container or lot of the
>   goods ; and

>   (*b*) if it is a sale of wine or a sale of spirits, is of not less
>   than 100 gallons.

(2) Any person may sell by auction by sample in any place
any goods for the sale of which an excise licence is required
without holding such a licence if the proprietor of the goods
holds a licence for the sale of such goods granted in respect of
premises in the same locality.

(3) The Commissioners may if they see fit authorise any
person to sell by auction any goods for the sale of which an
excise licence is required without holding such a licence where
they are satisfied that the goods are the property of a private
person and are not being sold for profit or by way of trade.

106.—(1) If any person holding an excise licence for the
sale of any goods contravenes the terms of that licence, or sells
otherwise than as he is authorised by the licence, or contravenes or fails to comply with any provision of the Customs and
Excise Acts 1979 or any other Act applicable to the licence,
then, if he does not thereby commit an offence under any other
enactment, he shall be liable on summary conviction to a penalty
of £50.

(2) Subject to subsection (3) below, if in the case of any
goods for the sale of which an excise licence is required, any
person solicits or takes any order for any such goods otherwise
than under the authority of the appropriate licence for their
sale granted in respect of the premises at which the order is
solicited or taken, he shall be liable on summary conviction to
the same penalty as a person selling those goods without that
licence.

(3) Subsection (2) above shall not apply—

>   (*a*) in relation to a sale of goods in warehouse for which
>   an excise licence is by virtue of section 105 above
>   not required ; or

>   (*b*) to a bona fide traveller taking orders for goods which
>   his employer is duly licensed to sell.

PART IX

Power to
require person
carrying on
excise licence
trade to
display sign.

107.—(1) The Commissioners may require any person holding an excise licence to carry on any trade to affix to and maintain on the premises in respect of which the licence is granted, in such form and manner and containing such particulars as they may direct, a notification of the person to whom and the purpose for which the licence is granted.

(2) If any person contravenes or fails to comply with any requirement made or direction given under this section he shall be liable on summary conviction to a penalty of £50.

(3) If any person not duly licensed to carry on an excise licence trade affixes to any premises any sign or notice purporting to show that he is so licensed he shall be liable on summary conviction to a penalty of £50.

General provisions as to entries of premises, etc.

Making of
entries.

108.—(1) Where by or under the revenue trade provisions of the customs and excise Acts any person is required to make entry of any premises or article—

> (*a*) the entry shall be made in such form and manner and contain such particulars ; and
>
> (*b*) the premises or article shall be, and be kept, marked in such manner,

as the Commissioners may direct.

(2) No entry shall be valid unless the person by whom it was made—

> (*a*) had at the time of its making attained the age of 18 years ; and
>
> (*b*) was at that time and is for the time being a true and real owner of the trade in respect of which the entry was made.

(3) Where any person required to make entry is a body corporate—

> (*a*) the entry shall be signed by a director, general manager, secretary or other similar officer of the body and, except where authority for that person to sign has been given under the seal of the body, shall be made under that seal ; and
>
> (*b*) both the body corporate and the person by whom the entry is signed shall be liable for all duties charged in respect of the trade to which the entry relates.

(4) If any person making entry of any premises or article contravenes or fails to comply with any direction of the Commissioners given under this section with respect thereto, he shall be liable on summary conviction to a penalty of £100.

109.—(1) The Commissioners may at any time, by notice in writing to the person by whom any existing entry was signed addressed to him at any premises entered by him, require a new entry to be made of any premises or article to which the existing entry relates, and the existing entry shall, without prejudice to any liability incurred, become void at the expiration of 14 days from the delivery of the notice.

(2) Save as permitted by the Commissioners and subject to such conditions as they may impose, no premises or article of which entry has been made by any person shall, while that entry remains in force, be entered by any other person for any purpose of the revenue trade provisions of the customs and excise Acts, and any entry made in contravention of this subsection shall be void.

(3) Where the person by whom entry has been made of any premises absconds or quits possession of the premises and discontinues the trade in respect of which the entry was made, and the Commissioners permit a further entry to be made of the premises by some other person, the former entry shall be deemed to have been withdrawn and shall be void.

110. For the purpose of any proceedings before any court, if any question arises as to whether or not entry under the revenue trade provisions of the customs and excise Acts has been made by any person, or of any premises or article, or for any purpose, then—

    (*a*) if a document purporting to be an original entry made by the person, or of the premises or article, or for the purpose, in question is produced to the court by an officer, that document shall, until the contrary is proved, be sufficient evidence that the entry was so made ; and

    (*b*) if the officer in whose custody any such entry, if made, would be gives evidence that the original entries produced by him to the court constitute all those in his custody and that no such entry as is in question is among them, it shall be deemed, until the contrary is proved, that no such entry has been made.

111.—(1) If any person uses for any purpose of his trade any premises or article required by or under the revenue trade provisions of the customs and excise Acts to be entered for that purpose without entry having been duly made thereof, he shall be liable on summary conviction to a penalty of £200, and any such article and any goods found on any such premises or in any such article shall be liable to forfeiture.

(2) If any person who has made entry of any premises or article fraudulently uses those premises or that article for any

PART IX

purpose other than that for which entry was made thereof he shall be liable on summary conviction to a penalty of £100.

General provisions as to revenue traders

Power of entry upon premises, etc. of revenue traders.

112.—(1) An officer may, subject to subsection (2) below, at any time enter upon any premises of which entry is made, or is required by or under the revenue trade provisions of the customs and excise Acts to be made, or any other premises owned or used by a revenue trader for the purposes of his trade and may inspect the premises and search for, examine and take account of any machinery, vessels, utensils, goods or materials belonging to or in any way connected with that trade.

(2) Except in the case of such traders as are mentioned in subsection (3) below, no officer shall exercise the powers conferred on him by subsection (1) above by night unless he is accompanied by a constable.

(3) Where any such premises as are mentioned in subsection (1) above are those of a distiller, rectifier, compounder, brewer for sale, producer of wine, producer of made-wine or maker of cider, and an officer, after having demanded admission into the premises and declared his name and business at the entrance thereof, is not immediately admitted, that officer and any person acting in his aid may, subject to subsection (4) below, break open any door or window of the premises or break through any wall thereof for the purpose of obtaining admission.

(4) No officer or person acting in his aid shall exercise the powers conferred on him by subsection (3) above by night unless he is accompanied by a constable.

(5) Subsection (1) above applies to vehicles, vessels, aircraft, hovercraft or structures in or from which tobacco products are sold or dealt in or dutiable alcoholic liquors are sold by retail as it applies to premises.

(6) This section applies to the occupier of a refinery as it applies to a distiller, whether or not the occupier is a revenue trader.

Power to search for concealed pipes, etc.

113.—(1) If an officer has reasonable grounds to suspect that any secret pipe or other means of conveyance, cock, vessel or utensil is kept or used by a revenue trader to whom this section applies, that officer may, subject to subsection (2) below, at any time, break open any part of the premises of that trader and forcibly enter thereon and so far as is reasonably necessary break up the ground in or adjoining those premises or any wall thereof to search for that pipe or other means of conveyance, cock, vessel or utensil.

(2) No officer shall exercise the powers conferred on him by subsection (1) above by night unless he is accompanied by a constable.

(3) If the officer finds any such pipe or other form of conveyance leading to or from the trader's premises, he may enter any other premises from or into which it leads, and so far as is reasonably necessary break up any part of those other premises to trace its course, and may cut it away and turn any cock thereon, and examine whether it conveys or conceals any goods chargeable with a duty of excise, or any materials used in the manufacture of such goods, in such manner as to prevent a true account thereof from being taken.

(4) Every such pipe or other means of conveyance, cock, vessel or utensil as aforesaid, and all goods chargeable with a duty of excise or materials for the manufacture of such goods found therein, shall be liable to forfeiture, and the trader shall be liable on summary conviction to a penalty of £100.

(5) If any damage is done in any such search as aforesaid and the search is unsuccessful, the Commissioners shall make good the damage.

(6) The revenue traders to whom this section applies are distillers, rectifiers, compounders, brewers for sale, producers of wine, producers of made-wine and makers of cider.

(7) This section also applies to the occupier of a refinery as it applies to the traders mentioned in subsection (6) above, whether or not the occupier is a revenue trader.

114.—(1) If it appears to the satisfaction of the Commissioners that any substance or liquor is used, or is capable of being used, in the manufacture or preparation for sale of any goods chargeable, as goods manufactured or produced in the United Kingdom, with a duty of excise, and that that substance or liquor is of a noxious or detrimental nature or, being a chemical or artificial extract or product, may affect prejudicially the interests of the revenue, the Commissioners may by regulations prohibit the use of that substance or liquor in the manufacture or preparation for sale of any goods specified in the regulations.

Power to prohibit use of certain substances in exciseable goods.

(2) If while any such regulations are in force any person knowingly uses a substance or liquor thereby prohibited in the manufacture or preparation for sale of any goods specified in the regulations he shall be liable on summary conviction to a penalty of £50.

(3) Any substance or liquor the use of which is for the time being prohibited by any such regulations found in the possession

PART IX

of any person licensed for the manufacture or sale of any goods specified in the regulations, and any goods in the manufacture or preparation of which any substance or liquid has been used contrary to any such prohibition, shall be liable to forfeiture.

Power to keep specimen on premises of revenue traders.

115.—(1) The proper officer may place and leave on the premises of a revenue trader a specimen, that is to say, a document in which may be entered any particulars relating to the trader's trade from time to time recorded by that or any other officer.

(2) Any such specimen shall be deposited at some place on premises entered by the trader where convenient access may be had thereto at any time by the trader and by any officer, and any officer may at any time remove the specimen and deposit a new one in its place.

(3) Where any charge of duty made by an officer upon a trader is not recorded in a specimen, the officer shall, if so required in writing by the trader at the time when the officer takes his account for the purpose of charging duty, give to the trader a copy of the charge in writing under his hand.

(4) If any person other than an officer removes, conceals, withholds, damages or destroys a specimen, or alters, defaces, or obliterates any entry therein, he shall be liable on summary conviction to a penalty of £200.

Payment of excise duty by revenue traders.

116.—(1) Every revenue trader shall pay any duty of excise payable in respect of his trade at or within such time, at such place and to such person as the Commissioners may direct, whether or not payment of that duty has been secured by bond or otherwise.

(2) If any duty payable is not paid in accordance with subsection (1) above, it shall be paid on demand made by the Commissioners either to the trader personally or by delivering the demand in writing at his place of abode or business.

(3) If any duty is not paid on demand made under subsection (2) above the trader shall in addition be liable on summary conviction to a penalty of double the amount due.

Execution and distress against revenue traders.

117.—(1) Where any sum is owing by a revenue trader in respect of any relevant excise duty or of any relevant penalty, all the following things which are in the possession or custody of that trader or of any agent of his or of any other person on his behalf shall be liable to be taken in execution in default of the payment of that sum, that is to say—

(a) all goods liable to a relevant excise duty, whether or not that duty has been paid ;

(b) all materials for manufacturing or producing any such goods ; and

(c) all apparatus, equipment, machinery, tools, vessels and utensils for, or for preparing any such materials for, such manufacture or production, or by which the trade in respect of which the duty is imposed is carried on.

(2) Subsection (1) above shall also apply in relation to things falling within paragraph (a), (b) or (c) of that subsection which, although they are not still in the possession or custody of the trader, an agent of his or other person on his behalf, were in such possession or custody—

(a) at the time when the relevant excise duty was charged or became chargeable or at any time while it was owing ; or

(b) at the time of the commission of the offence for which the penalty was incurred.

(3) Notwithstanding anything in subsection (1) or (2) above, but subject to subsection (4) below, where the proper officer has taken account of and charged any goods chargeable with a relevant excise duty and those goods are in the ordinary course of trade sold for full and valuable consideration to a bona fide purchaser and delivered into his possession before the issue of any warrant or process for distress or seizure of the goods, those goods shall not be liable to be seized under this section.

(4) Where any goods have been seized under this section, the burden of proof that the goods are by virtue of subsection (3) above not liable to be so seized shall lie upon the person claiming that they are not so liable.

(5) Where any relevant excise duty payable by a revenue trader remains unpaid after the time within which it is payable, the proper officer may by warrant signed by him empower any person to distrain any thing liable to be taken in execution under this section and, subject to subsection (6) below, to sell any thing so distrained by public auction after giving 6 days' notice of the sale.

(6) Where, under subsection (5) above, any thing has been distrained in respect of duty payable by a distiller, brewer, licensed producer of wine, licensed producer of made-wine or registered maker of cider he may, subject in the case of a distiller to the requirements of section 27(3) and (4) of the Alcoholic 1979 c. 4. Liquor Duties Act 1979 in connection with the sending out or other removal of spirits, at any time before the day appointed for the sale remove the whole or part of any products of or materials for his manufacture which have been so distrained upon paying to the proper officer in or towards payment of the duty the true value of those products or materials.

(7) The proceeds of any sale under subsection (5) above shall be applied in or towards payment of the costs and expenses of the distress and sale and in or towards payment of the duty due from the trader, and the surplus (if any) shall be paid to the trader.

(8) In this section—

"relevant excise duty" means excise duty other than duty chargeable on imported goods ; and

"relevant penalty" means a penalty incurred under the revenue trade provisions of the customs and excise Acts.

(9) In the application of this section to Scotland any reference to distress or seizure shall be construed as a reference to poinding.

Liability of ostensible owner or principal manager.

118. Any person who acts ostensibly as the owner or who is a principal manager of the business of a revenue trader in respect of which entry of any premises or article has been made or who occupies or uses any entered premises or article shall, notwithstanding that he is under full age, be liable in like manner as the real and true owner of the business for all duties charged and all penalties incurred in respect of that business.

PART X

DUTIES AND DRAWBACKS—GENERAL PROVISIONS

General provisions relating to imported goods

Delivery of imported goods on giving of security for duty.

119.—(1) Where it is impracticable immediately to ascertain whether any or what duty is payable in respect of any imported goods which are entered for home use, whether on importation or from warehouse, the Commissioners may, if they think fit and notwithstanding any other provision of the Customs and Excise Acts 1979, allow those goods to be delivered upon the importer giving security by deposit of money or otherwise to their satisfaction for payment of any amount unpaid which may be payable by way of duty.

(2) The Commissioners may for the purposes of subsection (1) above treat goods as entered for home use notwithstanding that the entry does not contain all the particulars required for perfect entry if it contains as many of those particulars as are then known to the importer, and in that event the importer shall supply the remaining particulars as soon as may be to the Commissioners.

(3) Where goods are allowed to be delivered under this section, the Commissioners shall, when they have determined the amount of duty which in their opinion is payable, give to the importer a notice specifying that amount.

(4) On the giving of a notice under subsection (3) above the amount specified in the notice or, where any amount has been deposited under subsection (1) above, any difference between those amounts shall forthwith be paid or repaid as the case may require.

(5) Subject to subsection (6) below, if the importer disputes the correctness of the amount specified in a notice given to him under subsection (3) above he may at any time within 3 months of the date of the notice make such a requirement for reference to arbitration or such an application to the court as is provided for by section 127 below, and that section shall have effect accordingly.

(6) No requirement or application shall be made by virtue of subsection (5) above until any sum falling to be paid by the importer under subsection (4) above has been paid, and where any sum so falls to be paid no interest shall be paid under section 127(2) below in respect of any period before that sum is paid.

120.—(1) The Secretary of State may by regulations make provision for determining, for the purposes of any duty of customs or excise, the origin of any goods in cases where it does not fall to be determined under a Community regulation or any Act or other instrument having the force of law. *Regulations for determining origin of goods.*

(2) Regulations under this section may—

    (a) make provision as to the evidence which is to be required or is to be sufficient for the purpose of showing that goods are of a particular origin ; and

    (b) make different provision for different purposes and in relation to goods of different descriptions.

(3) Subject to the provisions of any regulations under this section, where in connection with a duty of customs or excise chargeable on any goods any question arises as to the origin of the goods, the Commissioners may require the importer of the goods to furnish to them, in such form as they may prescribe, proof of any statement made to them as to any fact necessary to determine that question ; and if such proof is not furnished to their satisfaction, the question may be determined without regard to that statement.

PART X
Power to
impose
restrictions
where duty
depends on
certain matters
other than
use.

121. Where any question as to the duties of customs or excise chargeable on any imported goods depends on any matter (other than the use to be made of the goods) not reasonably ascertainable from an examination of the goods, and that question is not in law conclusively determined by the production of any certificate or other document, then, on the importation of those goods, the Commissioners may impose such conditions as they see fit for the prevention of abuse or the protection of the revenue (including conditions requiring security for the observance of any conditions so imposed).

Regulations
where customs
duty depends
on use.

122.—(1) The Commissioners may, in accordance with subsection (2) below, make regulations applying in cases where any question as to the duties of customs chargeable on any goods depends on the use to be made of them.

(2) In cases in which a Community instrument makes provision for the purpose of securing that the relevant use is made of the goods, regulations under this section may make provision for any matter which under the instrument is required or authorised to be dealt with by the authorities of member States or which otherwise arises out of the instrument; and in other cases regulations under this section may make such provision for that purpose as appears to the Commissioners to be necessary or expedient.

Repayment of
duty where
goods
returned or
destroyed
by importer.

123.—(1) Subject to such conditions as the Commissioners see fit to impose, where it is shown to the satisfaction of the Commissioners—

   (a) that goods were imported in pursuance of a contract of sale and that the description, quality, state or condition of the goods was not in accordance with the contract or that the goods were damaged in transit; and

   (b) that the importer with the consent of the seller either—

      (i) returned the goods unused to the seller and for that purpose complied with the provisions of section 53 above as to entry in like manner as if they had been dutiable or restricted goods for the purposes of Part V of this Act; or

      (ii) destroyed the goods unused,

the importer shall be entitled to obtain from the Commissioners repayment of any duty of customs or excise paid on the importation of the goods.

(2) Nothing in this section shall apply to goods imported on approval, or on sale or return, or on other similar terms.

124.—(1) Where——

   (*a*) any imported goods have been relieved from customs or excise duty chargeable on their importation or have been charged with duty at a reduced rate ; and

   (*b*) any condition or other obligation required to be complied with in connection with the relief or with the charge of duty at that rate is not complied with,

the goods shall be liable to forfeiture.

(2) The provisions of this section shall apply whether or not any undertaking or security has been given for compliance with the condition or obligation or for the payment of the duty payable apart therefrom, and the forfeiture of any goods under this section shall not affect any liability of any person who has given any such undertaking or security.

125.—(1) For the purposes of any duty for the time being chargeable on any imported goods by reference to their value (whether a Community customs duty or not), the value of the goods shall, subject to subsection (2) below, be taken according to the rules applicable in the case of Community customs duties, and duty shall be paid on that value.

(2) In relation to an importation in the course of trade within the Communities the value of any imported goods for the purposes mentioned in subsection (1) above shall be determined on the basis of a delivery to the buyer at the port or place of importation into the United Kingdom.

(3) The Commissioners may make regulations for the purpose of giving effect to the foregoing provisions of this section, and in particular for requiring any importer or other person concerned with the importation of goods—

   (*a*) to furnish to the Commissioners in such form as they may require, such information as is in their opinion necessary for a proper valuation of the goods ; and

   (*b*) to produce any books of account or other documents of whatever nature relating to the purchase, importation or sale of the goods by that person.

(4) If any person contravenes or fails to comply with any regulation made under subsection (3) above he shall be liable on summary conviction to a penalty of £50.

126.—(1) Subject to subsections (2) to (4) below, if any imported goods contain as a part or ingredient thereof any article chargeable with excise duty, excise duty shall be chargeable on the goods in respect of each such article according to the quantity thereof appearing to the Commissioners to be used in the manufacture or preparation of the goods.

(2) Where, in the opinion of the Treasury, it is necessary for the protection of the revenue, such imported goods shall be chargeable with the amount of excise duty with which they would be chargeable if they consisted wholly of the chargeable article or, if the goods contain more than one such article, of that one of the chargeable articles which will yield the highest amount of excise duty.

(3) Schedule 2 to this Act shall have effect with respect to the excise duties to be charged, and the excise drawbacks to be allowed, on imported composite goods containing a dutiable part or ingredient and with respect to rebates and drawbacks of excise duties charged in accordance with that Schedule.

(4) Subsections (1) and (2) above do not apply where other provision is made by any other enactment relating to excise duties on imported goods.

(5) Any rebate which can be allowed by law on any article when separately charged shall be allowed in charging goods under subsection (1) or (2) above in respect of any quantity of that article used in the manufacture or preparation of the goods.

Determination of disputes as to duties on imported goods.

127.—(1) If, before the delivery of any imported goods out of charge, any dispute arises as to whether any or what duty is payable on those goods, the importer shall pay the amount demanded by the proper officer but may, not later than 3 months after the date of the payment—

   (*a*) if the dispute is in relation to the value of the goods, require the question to be referred to the arbitration of a referee appointed by the Lord Chancellor (not being an official of any government department), whose decision shall be final and conclusive ; or

   (*b*) in any other case, apply to the High Court or, in Scotland, to the Court of Session for a declaration as to the amount of duty, if any, properly payable on the goods.

(2) If on any such reference or application the referee or court determines that a lesser or no amount was properly payable in respect of duty on the goods, the amount overpaid shall be repaid by the Commissioners, together with interest thereon from the date of the overpayment at such rate as the referee or court may determine ; and any sum so repaid shall be accepted by the importer in satisfaction of all claims in respect of the importation of the goods in question and the duty payable thereon and of all damages and expenses incidental to the dispute other than the costs of the proceedings.

(3) The procedure on any reference to a referee under this section shall be such as may be determined by the referee.

General provisions relating to charge of duty on and delivery of goods

128.—(1) During any period not exceeding 3 months specified at any time by order of the Commissioners for the purposes of this section, the Commissioners may refuse to allow the removal for home use on payment of duty, or the sending out for home use after the charging of duty, of goods of any class or description chargeable with a duty of customs or excise, notwithstanding payment of that duty, in quantities exceeding those which appear to the Commissioners to be reasonable in the circumstances.

(2) Where the Commissioners have during any such period exercised their powers under this section with respect to goods of any class or description, then, in the case of any such goods which are removed or sent out for home use after the end of that period, the duties of customs or excise and the rates thereof chargeable on those goods shall, notwithstanding any other provision of the customs and excise Acts relating to the determination of those duties and rates, be those in force at the date of the removal or sending out of the goods.

129.—(1) Subject to subsection (2) below, where any goods—

    (a) which have been imported but not yet cleared for any purpose for which they may be entered on importation ; or

    (b) which are warehoused,

have by reason of their state or condition ceased to be worth the full duty chargeable thereon and have been denatured in such manner as the Commissioners may direct and in accordance with such conditions as they see fit to impose, the Commissioners may remit or repay the whole or part of any duty chargeable or paid thereon, or waive repayment of the whole or part of any drawback paid on their warehousing, upon the delivery of the goods for use for such purposes as the Commissioners may allow.

(2) Subsection (1) above does not apply in relation to spirits.

(3) Where, whether under subsection (1) above or otherwise, any goods chargeable with duty have gone into home use after having been denatured by mixture with some other substance, any person who separates the goods from that other substance shall be guilty of an offence under this subsection and may be detained, and the goods shall be liable to forfeiture.

(4) A person guilty of an offence under subsection (3) above shall be liable—

    (a) on summary conviction, to a penalty of the prescribed sum or of three times the value of the goods, whichever

PART X

    is the greater, or to imprisonment for a term not exceeding 6 months, or to both ; or

    (*b*) on conviction on indictment, to a penalty of any amount, or to imprisonment for a term not exceeding 2 years, or to both.

Power to remit or repay duty on goods lost or destroyed, etc.

130.—(1) Where it is shown to the satisfaction of the Commissioners that any goods chargeable with any duty have been lost or destroyed by unavoidable accident—

    (*a*) after importation but before clearance for any purpose for which they might be entered on importation ; or

    (*b*) in the case of goods chargeable with a duty of excise on their manufacture or production or on their removal from the place of their manufacture or production, at any time before their removal from that place ; or

    (*c*) while in a warehouse or Queen's warehouse ; or

    (*d*) at any time while that duty is otherwise lawfully unpaid, except when payment of that duty has become due but has been allowed by the Commissioners to be deferred ; or

    (*e*) at any time after drawback of that duty has been paid,

the Commissioners may remit or repay any duty chargeable or paid thereon or waive repayment of any drawback paid on their warehousing.

(2) The Commissioners may, at the request of the proprietor of the goods in question and subject to compliance with such conditions as the Commissioners see fit to impose, permit the destruction of, and waive payment of duty or repayment of drawback on—

    (*a*) any part of any warehoused goods which becomes damaged or surplus by reason of the carrying out of any permitted operation on those goods in warehouse, and any refuse resulting from any such operation ; and

    (*b*) any imported goods not yet cleared for any purpose for which they might be entered on importation or any warehoused goods, being in either case goods which have by reason of their state or condition ceased to be worth the full duty chargeable thereon.

Enforcement of bond in respect of goods removed without payment of duty.

131. If any goods which have been lawfully permitted to be removed for any purpose without payment of duty are unlawfully taken from any ship, aircraft, vehicle or place before that purpose is accomplished, the Commissioners may if they see fit enforce any bond given in respect thereof notwithstanding that any time prescribed in the bond for accomplishing that purpose has not expired.

Drawback, allowances, duties, etc.—general

132.—(1) Without prejudice to any other provision of the Customs and Excise Acts 1979 or any other Act, where draw- back is allowable on the shipment of any goods as stores, the like drawback shall, subject to such conditions and restrictions as the Commissioners see fit to impose, be allowed on the warehousing in an excise warehouse of those goods for use as stores.

(2) Without prejudice to any other provision of the Customs and Excise Acts 1979 or any other Act, where drawback would be payable on the exportation of any goods, or on the warehousing of any goods for exportation, then, subject to such conditions and restrictions as the Commissioners see fit, the like drawback shall be payable on the shipment of any such goods as stores or, as the case may be, on their warehousing in an excise warehouse for use as stores.

133.—(1) Any claim for drawback shall be made in such form and manner and contain such particulars as the Com- missioners may direct.

(2) Where drawback has been claimed in the case of any goods subsections (3) to (6) below shall apply in relation to the claim.

(3) No drawback shall be payable unless it is shown to the satisfaction of the Commissioners that duty in respect of the goods or of the article contained therein or used in the manufacture or preparation thereof in respect of which the claim is made has been duly paid and has not been drawn back.

(4) No drawback shall be paid until the person entitled thereto or his agent has made a declaration in such form and manner and containing such particulars as the Commissioners may direct that the conditions on which the drawback is payable have been fulfilled.

(5) The Commissioners may require any person who has been concerned at any stage with the goods or article—

    (*a*) to furnish such information as may be reasonably necessary to enable the Commissioners to determine whether duty has been duly paid and not drawn back and for enabling a calculation to be made of the amount of drawback payable ; and

    (*b*) to produce any book of account or other document of whatever nature relating to the goods or article.

(6) If any person fails to comply with any requirement made under subsection (5) above, he shall be liable on summary conviction to a penalty of £50.

PART X
Drawback and
allowance on
goods damaged
or destroyed
after shipment.

134.—(1) Where it is proved to the satisfaction of the Commissioners that any goods after being duly shipped for exportation have been destroyed by accident on board the exporting ship or aircraft, any amount payable in respect of the goods by way of drawback, allowance or repayment of duty shall be payable in the same manner as if the goods had been exported to their destination.

(2) Where it is proved to the satisfaction of the Commissioners that any goods, after being duly shipped for exportation, have been materially damaged by accident on board the exporting ship or aircraft, and the goods are with the consent of and in accordance with any conditions imposed by the Commissioners relanded or unloaded again in or brought back into the United Kingdom and either abandoned to the Commissioners or destroyed, any amount payable in respect of the goods by way of drawback, allowance or repayment of duty shall be paid as if they had been duly exported and not so relanded, unloaded or brought back.

(3) Notwithstanding any provision of the Customs and Excise Acts 1979 or any other Act relating to the reimportation of exported goods, the person to whom any amount is payable or has been paid under subsection (2) above shall not be required to pay any duty in respect of any goods relanded, unloaded or brought back under that subsection.

Time limit on
payment of
drawback or
allowance.

135. No payment shall be made in respect of any drawback or allowance unless the debenture or other document authorising payment is presented for payment within 2 years from the date of the event on the happening of which the drawback or allowance became payable.

Offences in
connection
with claims for
drawback, etc.

136.—(1) If any person obtains or attempts to obtain, or does anything whereby there might be obtained by any person, any amount by way of drawback, allowance, remission or repayment of, or any rebate from, any duty in respect of any goods which is not lawfully payable or allowable in respect thereof or which is greater than the amount so payable or allowable, he shall be guilty of an offence under this subsection.

(2) A person guilty of an offence under subsection (1) above shall be liable on summary conviction—

(a) if the offence was committed with intent to defraud Her Majesty, to a penalty of three times the value of the goods or £200, whichever is the greater;

(b) in any other case, to a penalty of three times the amount improperly obtained or allowed or which might have been improperly obtained or allowed or £100, whichever is the greater.

(3) Any goods in respect of which an offence under subsection (1) above is committed shall be liable to forfeiture; but in the case of a claim for drawback, the Commissioners may, if they see fit, instead of seizing the goods either refuse to allow any drawback thereon or allow only such drawback as they consider proper.

(4) Without prejudice to the foregoing provisions of this section, if, in the case of any goods upon which a claim for drawback, allowance, remission or repayment of duty has been made, it is found that those goods do not correspond with any entry made thereof in connection with that claim, the goods shall be liable to forfeiture and any person by whom any such entry or claim was made shall be liable on summary conviction to a penalty of three times the amount claimed or £100, whichever is the greater.

(5) Subsection (4) above applies in the case of any goods upon which a claim for drawback, allowance, remission or repayment of duty has been made where it is found that the goods, if sold for home use, would realise less than the amount claimed as it applies where the finding specified in that subsection is made except that it does not apply by virtue of this subsection to any claim under—

(a) section 123 or 134(2) above; or

(b) section 46, 61 or 64 of the Alcoholic Liquor Duties Act 1979 (remission or repayment of duty on certain spoilt liquors).

1979 c. 4.

137.—(1) Without prejudice to any other provision of the Customs and Excise Acts 1979, any amount due by way of customs or excise duty may be recovered as a debt due to the Crown.

Recovery of duties and calculation of duties, drawbacks, etc.

(2) Any duty, drawback, allowance or rebate the rate of which is expressed by reference to a specified quantity or weight of any goods shall, subject to subsection (3) below, be chargeable or allowable on any fraction of that quantity or weight of the goods, and the amount payable or allowable on any such fraction shall be calculated proportionately.

(3) The Commissioners may for the purposes of subsection (2) above determine the fractions to be taken into account in the case of any weight or quantity.

(4) For the purpose of calculating any amount due from or to any person under the customs and excise Acts by way of duty, drawback, allowance, repayment or rebate any fraction of a penny in that amount shall be disregarded.

Part XI

Detention of Persons, Forfeiture and Legal Proceedings

Detention of persons

Provisions as to detention of persons.

138.—(1) Any person who has committed, or whom there are reasonable grounds to suspect of having committed, any offence for which he is liable to be detained under the customs and excise Acts may be detained by any officer or constable or any member of Her Majesty's armed forces or coastguard at any time within 3 years from the date of the commission of the offence.

(2) Where it was not practicable to detain any person so liable at the time of the commission of the offence, or where any such person having been then or subsequently detained for that offence has escaped, he may be detained by any officer or constable or any member of Her Majesty's armed forces or coastguard at any time and may be proceeded against in like manner as if the offence had been committed at the date when he was finally detained.

(3) Where any person who is a member of the crew of any ship in Her Majesty's employment or service is detained by an officer for an offence under the customs and excise Acts, the commanding officer of the ship shall, if so required by the detaining officer, keep that person secured on board that ship until he can be brought before a court and shall then deliver him up to the proper officer.

(4) Where any person has been detained by virtue of this section otherwise than by an officer, the person detaining him shall give notice of the detention to an officer at the nearest convenient office of customs and excise.

Forfeiture

Provisions as to detention, seizure and condemnation of goods, etc.

139.—(1) Any thing liable to forfeiture under the customs and excise Acts may be seized or detained by any officer or constable or any member of Her Majesty's armed forces or coastguard.

(2) Where any thing is seized or detained as liable to forfeiture under the customs and excise Acts by a person other than an officer, that person shall, subject to subsection (3) below, either—

    (a) deliver that thing to the nearest convenient office of customs and excise ; or

    (b) if such delivery is not practicable, give to the Commissioners at the nearest convenient office of customs and excise notice in writing of the seizure or detention with full particulars of the thing seized or detained.

(3) Where the person seizing or detaining any thing as liable to forfeiture under the customs and excise Acts is a constable and that thing is or may be required for use in connection with any proceedings to be brought otherwise than under those Acts it may, subject to subsection (4) below, be retained in the custody of the police until either those proceedings are completed or it is decided that no such proceedings shall be brought.

(4) The following provisions apply in relation to things retained in the custody of the police by virtue of subsection (3) above, that is to say—

(a) notice in writing of the seizure or detention and of the intention to retain the thing in question in the custody of the police, together with full particulars as to that thing, shall be given to the Commissioners at the nearest convenient office of customs and excise ;

(b) any officer shall be permitted to examine that thing and take account thereof at any time while it remains in the custody of the police ;

(c) nothing in the Police (Property) Act 1897 shall apply in relation to that thing. 1897 c. 30.

(5) Subject to subsections (3) and (4) above and to Schedule 3 to this Act, any thing seized or detained under the customs and excise Acts shall, pending the determination as to its forfeiture or disposal, be dealt with, and, if condemned or deemed to have been condemned or forfeited, shall be disposed of in such manner as the Commissioners may direct.

(6) Schedule 3 to this Act shall have effect for the purpose of forfeitures, and of proceedings for the condemnation of any thing as being forfeited, under the customs and excise Acts.

(7) If any person, not being an officer, by whom any thing is seized or detained or who has custody thereof after its seizure or detention, fails to comply with any requirement of this section or with any direction of the Commissioners given thereunder, he shall be liable on summary conviction to a penalty of £50.

(8) Subsections (2) to (7) above shall apply in relation to any dutiable goods seized or detained by any person other than an officer notwithstanding that they were not so seized as liable to forfeiture under the customs and excise Acts.

140. Where, by any provision of, or of any instrument made under, the Customs and Excise Acts 1979, any spirits become liable to forfeiture by reason of some offence committed by a revenue trader, then— Forfeiture of spirits.

(a) where that provision specifies the quantity of those spirits but does not specify the spirits so liable, the

Commissioners may seize the equivalent of that quantity computed at proof from any spirits in the stock of that trader ; and

(b) where that provision specifies the spirits so liable the Commissioners may, if they think fit, seize instead of the spirits so specified an equivalent quantity computed at proof of any other spirits in the stock of that trader.

Forfeiture of ships, etc. used in connection with goods liable to forfeiture.

141.—(1) Without prejudice to any other provision of the Customs and Excise Acts 1979, where any thing has become liable to forfeiture under the customs and excise Acts—

(a) any ship, aircraft, vehicle, animal, container (including any article of passengers' baggage) or other thing whatsoever which has been used for the carriage, handling, deposit or concealment of the thing so liable to forfeiture, either at a time when it was so liable or for the purposes of the commission of the offence for which it later became so liable ; and

(b) any other thing mixed, packed or found with the thing so liable,

shall also be liable to forfeiture.

(2) Where any ship, aircraft, vehicle or animal has become liable to forfeiture under the customs and excise Acts, whether by virtue of subsection (1) above or otherwise, all tackle, apparel or furniture thereof shall also be liable to forfeiture.

(3) Where any of the following, that is to say—

(a) any ship not exceeding 100 tons register ;

(b) any aircraft ; or

(c) any hovercraft,

becomes liable to forfeiture under this section by reason of having been used in the importation, exportation or carriage of goods contrary to or for the purpose of contravening any prohibition or restriction for the time being in force with respect to those goods, or without payment having been made of, or security given for, any duty payable thereon, the owner and the master or commander shall each be liable on summary conviction to a penalty equal to the value of the ship, aircraft or hovercraft or £500, whichever is the less.

Special provision as to forfeiture of larger ships.

142.—(1) Notwithstanding any other provision of the Customs and Excise Acts 1979, a ship of 250 or more tons register shall not be liable to forfeiture under or by virtue of any provision of the Customs and Excise Acts 1979, except under section 88

above, unless the offence in respect of or in connection with
which the forfeiture is claimed—

(a) was substantially the object of the voyage during which
the offence was committed ; or

(b) was committed while the ship was under chase by a
vessel in the service of Her Majesty after failing to
bring to when properly summoned to do so by that
vessel.

(2) For the purposes of this section, a ship shall be deemed
to have been properly summoned to bring to—

(a) if the vessel making the summons did so by means of
an international signal code or other recognised means
and while flying her proper ensign ; and

(b) in the case of a ship which is not a British ship, if at
the time when the summons was made the ship was
within 3 nautical miles of the coast of the United
Kingdom.

(3) For the purposes of this section, all hovercraft (of whatever size) shall be treated as ships of less than 250 tons register.

(4) The exemption from forfeiture of any ship under this
section shall not affect any liability to forfeiture of goods carried
therein.

143.—(1) Where any ship of 250 or more tons register would, Penalty
but for section 142 above, be liable to forfeiture for or in in lieu of
connection with any offence under the customs and excise Acts forfeiture of
and, in the opinion of the Commissioners, a responsible officer larger ship
of the ship is implicated either by his own act or by neglect where
in that offence, the Commissioners may fine that ship such responsible officer
sum not exceeding £50 as they see fit. implicated in offence.

(2) For the purposes of this section, all hovercraft (of whatever size) shall be treated as ships of less than 250 tons register.

(3) Where any ship is liable to a fine under subsection (1)
above but the Commissioners consider that fine an inadequate
penalty for the offence, they may take proceedings in accordance
with Schedule 3 to this Act, in like manner as they might but
for section 142 above have taken proceedings for the condemnation of the ship if notice of claim had been given in respect
thereof, for the condemnation of the ship in such sum not
exceeding £500 as the court may see fit.

(4) Where any fine is to be imposed or any proceedings are
to be taken under this section, the Commissioners may require
such sum as they see fit, not exceeding £50 or, as the case may
be, £500, to be deposited with them to await their final decision

or, as the case may be, the decision of the court, and may detain the ship until that sum has been so deposited.

(5) No claim shall lie against the Commissioners for damages in respect of the payment of any deposit or the detention of any ship under this section.

(6) For the purposes of this section—

(a) " responsible officer ", in relation to any ship, means the master, a mate or an engineer of the ship and, in the case of a ship carrying a passenger certificate, the purser or chief steward and, in the case of a ship manned wholly or partly by Asiatic seamen, the serang or other leading Asiatic officer of the ship ;

(b) without prejudice to any other grounds upon which a responsible officer of any ship may be held to be implicated by neglect, he may be so held if goods not owned to by any member of the crew are discovered in a place under that officer's supervision in which they could not reasonably have been put if he had exercised proper care at the time of the loading of the ship or subsequently.

Protection of officers, etc. in relation to seizure and detention of goods, etc.

144.—(1) Where, in any proceedings for the condemnation of any thing seized as liable to forfeiture under the customs and excise Acts, judgment is given for the claimant, the court may, if it sees fit, certify that there were reasonable grounds for the seizure.

(2) Where any proceedings, whether civil or criminal, are brought against the Commissioners, a law officer of the Crown or any person authorised by or under the Customs and Excise Acts 1979 to seize or detain any thing liable to forfeiture under the customs and excise Acts on account of the seizure or detention of any thing, and judgment is given for the plaintiff or prosecutor, then if either—

(a) a certificate relating to the seizure has been granted under subsection (1) above ; or

(b) the court is satisfied that there were reasonable grounds for seizing or detaining that thing under the customs and excise Acts,

the plaintiff or prosecutor shall not be entitled to recover any damages or costs and the defendant shall not be liable to any punishment.

(3) Nothing in subsection (2) above shall affect any right of any person to the return of the thing seized or detained or to compensation in respect of any damage to the thing or in respect of the destruction thereof.

(4) Any certificate under subsection (1) above may be proved
by the production of either the original certificate or a certified
copy thereof purporting to be signed by an officer of the court
by which it was granted.

General provisions as to legal proceedings

145.—(1) Subject to the following provisions of this section, Institution of
no proceedings for an offence under the customs and excise Acts proceedings.
or for condemnation under Schedule 3 to this Act shall be
instituted except by order of the Commissioners.

(2) Subject to the following provisions of this section, any
proceedings under the customs and excise Acts instituted in a
magistrates' court, and any such proceedings instituted in a
court of summary jurisdiction in Northern Ireland, shall be
commenced in the name of an officer.

(3) Subsections (1) and (2) above shall not apply to proceedings on indictment in Scotland.

(4) In the case of the death, removal, discharge or absence
of the officer in whose name any proceedings were commenced
under subsection (2) above, those proceedings may be continued
by any officer authorised in that behalf by the Commissioners.

(5) Nothing in the foregoing provisions of this section shall
prevent the institution of proceedings for an offence under the
customs and excise Acts by order and in the name of a law
officer of the Crown in any case in which he thinks it proper
that proceedings should be so instituted.

(6) Notwithstanding anything in the foregoing provisions of
this section, where any person has been detained for any offence
for which he is liable to be detained under the customs and
excise Acts, any court before which he is brought may proceed
to deal with the case although the proceedings have not been
instituted by order of the Commissioners or have not been commenced in the name of an officer.

146.—(1) Any summons or other process issued anywhere in Service of
the United Kingdom for the purpose of any proceedings under process.
the customs and excise Acts may be served on the person to
whom it is addressed in any part of the United Kingdom without any further endorsement, and shall be deemed to have been
duly served—

    (a) if delivered to him personally ; or

    (b) if left at his last known place of abode or business or,
       in the case of a body corporate, at their registered or
       principal office ; or

(c) if left on board any vessel or aircraft to which he may belong or have lately belonged.

(2) Any summons, notice, order or other document issued for the purposes of any proceedings under the customs and excise Acts, or of any appeal from the decision of the court in any such proceedings, may be served by an officer.

In this subsection "appeal" includes an appeal by way of case stated.

(3) This section shall not apply in relation to proceedings instituted in the High Court or Court of Session.

147.—(1) Save as otherwise expressly provided in the customs and excise Acts and notwithstanding anything in any other enactment, any proceedings for an offence under those Acts—

> (a) may be commenced at any time within 3 years from the date of the commission of the offence ; and
>
> (b) shall not be commenced later than 3 years from that date.

(2) Where, in England or Wales, a magistrates' court has begun to inquire into an information charging a person with an offence under the customs and excise Acts as examining justices the court shall not proceed under section 25(3) of the Criminal Law Act 1977 to try the information summarily without the consent of—

> (a) the Attorney General, in a case where the proceedings were instituted by his order and in his name ; or
>
> (b) the Commissioners, in any other case.

(3) In the case of proceedings in England or Wales, without prejudice to any right to require the statement of a case for the opinion of the High Court, the prosecutor may appeal to the Crown Court against any decision of a magistrates' court in proceedings for an offence under the customs and excise Acts.

(4) In the case of proceedings in Northern Ireland, without prejudice to any right to require the statement of a case for the opinion of the High Court, the prosecutor may appeal to the county court against any decision of a court of summary jurisdiction in proceedings for an offence under the customs and excise Acts.

(5) In the application of the customs and excise Acts to Scotland, and subject to any express provision made by the enactment in question, any offence which is made punishable on summary conviction—

> (a) shall if prosecuted summarily be prosecuted in the sheriff court ;
>
> (b) may be also prosecuted by any other method.

148.—(1) Proceedings for an offence under the customs and
excise Acts may be commenced—

(a) in any court having jurisdiction in the place where the
    person charged with the offence resides or is found;
    or

(b) if any thing was detained or seized in connection with
    the offence, in any court having jurisdiction in the place
    where that thing was so detained or seized or was found
    or condemned as forfeited; or

(c) in any court having jurisdiction anywhere in that part
    of the United Kingdom, namely—

    (i) England and Wales,

    (ii) Scotland, or

    (iii) Northern Ireland,

    in which the place where the offence was committed
    is situated.

(2) Where any such offence was committed at some place
outside the area of any commission of the peace, the place of
the commission of the offence shall, for the purposes of the jurisdiction of any court, be deemed to be any place in the United
Kingdom where the offender is found or to which he is first
brought after the commission of the offence.

(3) The jurisdiction under subsection (2) above shall be in
addition to and not in derogation of any jurisdiction or power
of any court under any other enactment.

149.—(1) Where, in any proceedings for an offence under
the customs and excise Acts, a magistrates' court in England or
Wales or a court of summary jurisdiction in Scotland, in addition to ordering the person convicted to pay a penalty for the
offence—

(a) orders him to be imprisoned for a term in respect of the
    same offence; and

(b) further (whether at the same time or subsequently)
    orders him to be imprisoned for a term in respect of
    non-payment of that penalty or default of a sufficient
    distress to satisfy the amount of that penalty,

the aggregate of the terms for which he is so ordered to be
imprisoned shall not exceed 15 months.

(2) Where the sum adjudged to be paid by the conviction
of a court of summary jurisdiction in Scotland under the
customs and excise Acts (including any expenses adjudged to be
paid by the conviction whose amount is ascertained by the
conviction) exceeds £50 the maximum period of imprisonment
that may be imposed in respect of the non-payment of that sum

shall, notwithstanding anything in section 199 of the Criminal Procedure (Scotland) Act 1975, be fixed in accordance with the following scale, that is to say—

Where the amount of the sum adjudged to be paid by the conviction—	The said period shall be a period not exceeding—
exceeds £50 but does not exceed £100 ...	90 days
exceeds £100 but does not exceed £250 ...	6 months
exceeds £250 but does not exceed £500 ...	9 months
exceeds £500	12 months.

(3) Where, under any enactment for the time being in force in Northern Ireland, a court of summary jurisdiction has power to order a person to be imprisoned in respect of the non-payment of a penalty, or of the default of a sufficient distress to satisfy the amount of that penalty, for a term in addition and succession to a term of imprisonment imposed for the same offence as the penalty, then in relation to a sentence for an offence under the customs and excise Acts the aggregate of those terms of imprisonment may, notwithstanding anything in any such enactment, be any period not exceeding 15 months.

150.—(1) Where liability for any offence under the customs and excise Acts is incurred by two or more persons jointly, those persons shall each be liable for the full amount of any pecuniary penalty and may be proceeded against jointly or severally as the Commissioners may see fit.

(2) In any proceedings for an offence under the customs and excise Acts instituted in England, Wales or Northern Ireland, any court by whom the matter is considered may mitigate any pecuniary penalty as they see fit.

(3) In any proceedings for an offence or for the condemnation of any thing as being forfeited under the customs and excise Acts, the fact that security has been given by bond or otherwise for the payment of any duty or for compliance with any condition in respect of the non-payment of which or non-compliance with which the proceedings are instituted shall not be a defence.

151. The balance of any sum paid or recovered on account of any penalty imposed under the customs and excise Acts, after paying any such compensation or costs as are mentioned in section 114 of the Magistrates' Courts Act 1952 to persons other than the Commissioners shall, notwithstanding any local or other special right or privilege of whatever origin, be accounted for and paid to the Commissioners or as they direct.

152. The Commissioners may, as they see fit—

    (*a*) stay, sist or compound any proceedings for an offence or for the condemnation of any thing as being forfeited under the customs and excise Acts ; or

    (*b*) restore, subject to such conditions (if any) as they think proper, any thing forfeited or seized under those Acts ; or

    (*c*) after judgment, mitigate or remit any pecuniary penalty imposed under those Acts ; or

    (*d*) order any person who has been imprisoned to be discharged before the expiration of his term of imprisonment, being a person imprisoned for any offence under those Acts or in respect of the non-payment of a penalty or other sum adjudged to be paid or awarded in relation to such an offence or in respect of the default of a sufficient distress to satisfy such a sum ;

but paragraph (*a*) above shall not apply to proceedings on indictment in Scotland.

PART XI

Power of Commissioners to mitigate penalties, etc.

153.—(1) Any document purporting to be signed either by one or more of the Commissioners, or by their order, or by any other person with their authority, shall, until the contrary is proved, be deemed to have been so signed and to be made and issued by the Commissioners, and may be proved by the production of a copy thereof purporting to be so signed.

Proof of certain documents.

(2) Without prejudice to subsection (1) above, the Documentary Evidence Act 1868 shall apply in relation to—

1868 c. 37.

    (*a*) any document issued by the Commissioners ;

    (*b*) any document issued before 1st April 1909, by the Commissioners of Customs or the Commissioners of Customs and the Commissioners of Inland Revenue jointly ;

    (*c*) any document issued before that date in relation to the revenue of excise by the Commissioners of Inland Revenue,

as it applies in relation to the documents mentioned in that Act.

(3) That Act shall, as applied by subsection (2) above, have effect as if the persons mentioned in paragraphs (*a*) to (*c*) of that subsection were included in the first column of the Schedule to that Act, and any of the Commissioners or any secretary or assistant secretary to the Commissioners were specified in the second column of that Schedule in connection with those persons.

D4

154.—(1) An averment in any process in proceedings under the customs and excise Acts—

    (a) that those proceedings were instituted by the order of the Commissioners ; or

    (b) that any person is or was a Commissioner, officer or constable, or a member of Her Majesty's armed forces or coastguard ; or

    (c) that any person is or was appointed or authorised by the Commissioners to discharge, or was engaged by the orders or with the concurrence of the Commissioners in the discharge of, any duty ; or

    (d) that the Commissioners have or have not been satisfied as to any matter as to which they are required by any provision of those Acts to be satisfied ; or

    (e) that any ship is a British ship ; or

    (f) that any goods thrown overboard, staved or destroyed were so dealt with in order to prevent or avoid the seizure of those goods,

shall, until the contrary is proved, be sufficient evidence of the matter in question.

(2) Where in any proceedings relating to customs or excise any question arises as to the place from which any goods have been brought or as to whether or not—

    (a) any duty has been paid or secured in respect of any goods ; or

    (b) any goods or other things whatsoever are of the description or nature alleged in the information, writ or other process ; or

    (c) any goods have been lawfully imported or lawfully unloaded from any ship or aircraft ; or

    (d) any goods have been lawfully loaded into any ship or aircraft or lawfully exported or were lawfully waterborne ; or

    (e) any goods were lawfully brought to any place for the purpose of being loaded into any ship or aircraft or exported ; or

    (f) any goods are or were subject to any prohibition of or restriction on their importation or exportation,

then, where those proceedings are brought by or against the Commissioners, a law officer of the Crown or an officer, or against any other person in respect of anything purporting to have been done in pursuance of any power or duty conferred or imposed on him by or under the customs and excise Acts, the burden of proof shall lie upon the other party to the proceedings.

155.—(1) Any officer or any other person authorised in that PART XI
behalf by the Commissioners may, although he is not a barrister, Persons who
advocate or solicitor, conduct any proceedings before any may conduct
magistrates' court in England or Wales or court of summary proceedings.
jurisdiction in Scotland or Northern Ireland or before any
examining justices, being proceedings under any enactment
relating to an assigned matter or proceedings arising out of the
same circumstances as any proceedings commenced under any
such enactment, whether or not the last mentioned proceedings
are persisted in.

(2) Any person who has been admitted as a solicitor and is
employed by the Commissioners may act as a solicitor in any
proceedings in England, Wales or Northern Ireland relating to
any assigned matter notwithstanding that he does not hold a
current practising certificate.

*Saving for outlying enactments of certain general provisions as
to offences*

156.—(1) In subsections (2), (3) and (4) below (which re- Saving for
produce certain enactments not required as general provisions outlying
for the purposes of the enactments re-enacted in the Customs enactments
and Excise Acts 1979) " the outlying provisions of the customs of certain
and excise Acts " means— general
provisions as
    (*a*) the Betting and Gaming Duties Act 1972, as for the to offences.
        time being amended ; and 1972 c. 25.

    (*b*) all other provisions of the customs and excise Acts, as
        for the time being amended, which were passed
        before the commencement of this Act and are not
        re-enacted in the Customs and Excise Acts 1979.

(2) It is hereby declared that any act or omission in respect
of which a pecuniary penalty (however described) is imposed
by any of the outlying provisions of the customs and excise
Acts is an offence under that provision ; and accordingly in
this Part of this Act any reference to an offence under the
customs and excise Acts includes a reference to such an act or
omission.

(3) Subject to any express provision made by the enactment
in question, an offence under any of the outlying provisions of the
customs and excise Acts—

    (*a*) where it is punishable with imprisonment for a term of
        2 years, with or without a pecuniary penalty, shall be
        punishable either on summary conviction or on con-
        viction on indictment ;

    (*b*) in any other case, shall be punishable on summary con-
        viction.

This subsection does not apply to Scotland.

PART XI

(4) Without prejudice to any other method of prosecution and subject to any express provision made by the enactment in question, it shall be competent in Scotland to prosecute an offence under any of the outlying provisions of the customs and excise Acts summarily in the sheriff court; but no sentence of the sheriff court on summary conviction shall impose any term of imprisonment exceeding 6 months.

PART XII

GENERAL AND MISCELLANEOUS

General powers, etc.

Bonds and security.

157.—(1) Without prejudice to any express requirement as to security contained in the customs and excise Acts, the Commissioners may, if they see fit, require any person to give security by bond or otherwise for the observance of any condition in connection with customs or excise.

(2) Any bond taken for the purposes of any assigned matter—

 (*a*) shall be taken on behalf of Her Majesty; and

 (*b*) shall be valid notwithstanding that it is entered into by a person under full age; and

 (*c*) may be cancelled at any time by or by order of the Commissioners.

Power to require provision of facilities.

158.—(1) A person to whom this section applies, that is to say, a revenue trader and any person required by the Commissioners under the Customs and Excise Acts 1979 to give security in respect of any premises or place to be used for the examination of goods by an officer, shall—

 (*a*) provide and maintain such appliances and afford such other facilities reasonably necessary to enable an officer to take any account or make any examination or search or to perform any other of his duties on the premises of that trader or at the bonded premises or place as the Commissioners may direct;

 (*b*) keep any appliances so provided in a convenient place approved by the proper officer for that purpose; and

 (*c*) allow the proper officer at any time to use anything so provided and give him any assistance necessary for the performance of his duties.

(2) Any person who contravenes or fails to comply with any provision of subsection (1) above shall be liable on summary conviction to a penalty of £100.

(3) A person to whom this section applies shall provide and maintain any fitting required for the purpose of affixing any

lock which the proper officer may require to affix to the premises
of that person or any part thereof or to any vessel, utensil or
other apparatus whatsoever kept thereon, and in default—

   (a) the fitting may be provided or any work necessary for
       its maintenance may be carried out by the proper
       officer, and any expenses so incurred shall be paid on
       demand by that person ; and
   (b) if that person fails to pay those expenses on demand,
       he shall in addition be liable on summary conviction
       to a penalty of £100.

(4) If any person to whom this section applies or any servant
of his—

   (a) wilfully destroys or damages any such fitting as is
       mentioned in subsection (3) above or any lock or key
       provided for use therewith, or any label or seal placed
       on any such lock ; or
   (b) improperly obtains access to any place or article
       secured by any such lock ; or
   (c) has any such fitting or any article intended to be
       secured by means thereof so constructed that that
       intention is defeated,

he shall be liable on summary conviction to a penalty of £500
and may be detained.

159.—(1) Without prejudice to any other power conferred   Power to
by the Customs and Excise Acts 1979, an officer may examine   examine and
and take account of any goods—   take account
                                                               of goods.
   (a) which are imported ; or
   (b) which are in a warehouse or Queen's warehouse ; or
   (c) which have been loaded into any ship or aircraft at
       any place in the United Kingdom ; or
   (d) which are entered for exportation or for use as stores ;
       or
   (e) which are brought to any place in the United Kingdom
       for exportation or for shipment for exportation or as
       stores ; or
   (f) in the case of which any claim for drawback, allowance,
       rebate, remission or repayment of duty is made ;

and may for that purpose require any container to be opened
or unpacked.

(2) Any examination of goods by an officer under the Customs
and Excise Acts 1979 shall be made at such place as the Commissioners appoint for the purpose.

(3) In the case of such goods as the Commissioners may
direct, and subject to such conditions as they see fit to impose,

an officer may permit goods to be skipped on the quay or bulked, sorted, lotted, packed or repacked before account is taken thereof.

(4) Any opening, unpacking, weighing, measuring, repacking, bulking, sorting, lotting, marking, numbering, loading, unloading, carrying or landing of goods or their containers for the purposes of, or incidental to, the examination by an officer, removal or warehousing thereof shall be done, and any facilities or assistance required for any such examination shall be provided, by or at the expense of the proprietor of the goods.

(5) If any imported goods which an officer has power under the Customs and Excise Acts 1979 to examine are without the authority of the proper officer removed from customs and excise charge before they have been examined, those goods shall be liable to forfeiture.

(6) If any goods falling within subsection (5) above are removed by a person with intent to defraud Her Majesty of any duty chargeable thereon or to evade any prohibition or restriction for the time being in force with respect thereto under or by virtue of any enactment, that person shall be guilty of an offence under this subsection and may be detained.

(7) A person guilty of an offence under subsection (6) above shall be liable—

    (a) on summary conviction, to a penalty of the prescribed sum or of three times the value of the goods, whichever is the greater, or to imprisonment for a term not exceeding 6 months, or to both ; or

    (b) on conviction on indictment, to a penalty of any amount, or to imprisonment for a term not exceeding 2 years, or to both.

(8) Without prejudice to the foregoing provisions of this section, where by this section or by or under any other provision of the Customs and Excise Acts 1979 an account is authorised or required to be taken of any goods for any purpose by an officer, the Commissioners may, with the consent of the proprietor of the goods, accept as the account of those goods for that purpose an account taken by such other person as may be approved in that behalf by both the Commissioners and the proprietor of the goods.

Power to take samples.

160.—(1) An officer may at any time take samples of any goods—

    (a) which he is empowered by the Customs and Excise Acts 1979 to examine ; or

(b) which are on premises where goods chargeable with any duty are manufactured, prepared or subjected to any process ; or

(c) which, being dutiable goods, are held by any person as stock for his business or as materials for manufacture or processing.

(2) Where an officer takes from any vessel, pipe or utensil on the premises of any of the following revenue traders, that is to say, a distiller, brewer for sale, producer of wine, producer of made-wine or maker of cider, a sample of any product of, or of any materials for, the manufacture of that trader—

(a) the trader may, if he wishes, stir up and mix together the contents of that vessel, pipe or utensil before the sample is taken ; and

(b) the sample taken by the officer shall be deemed to be representative of the whole contents of that vessel, pipe or utensil.

(3) Any sample taken under this section shall be disposed of and accounted for in such manner as the Commissioners may direct.

(4) Where any sample is taken under this section from any goods chargeable with a duty of customs or excise after that duty has been paid, other than—

(a) a sample taken when goods are first entered on importation ; or

(b) a sample taken from goods in respect of which a claim for drawback, allowance, rebate, remission or repayment of that duty is being made,

and the sample so taken is to be retained, the officer taking it shall, if so required by the person in possession of the goods, pay for the sample on behalf of the Commissioners such sum as reasonably represents the wholesale value thereof.

161.—(1) Without prejudice to any other power conferred Power to by the Customs and Excise Acts 1979 but subject to subsection search (2) below, where there are reasonable grounds to suspect that premises. any thing liable to forfeiture under the customs and excise Acts is kept or concealed in any building or place, any officer having a writ of assistance may—

(a) enter that building or place at any time, whether by day or night, on any day, and search for, seize, and detain or remove any such thing ; and

(b) so far as is reasonably necessary for the purpose of such entry, search, seizure, detention or removal, break open any door, window or container and force and remove any other impediment or obstruction.

(2) No officer shall exercise the power of entry conferred on him by subsection (1) above by night unless he is accompanied by a constable.

(3) Without prejudice to subsection (1) above or to any other power conferred by the Customs and Excise Acts 1979, if a justice of the peace is satisfied by information upon oath given by an officer that there are reasonable grounds to suspect that any thing liable to forfeiture under the customs and excise Acts is kept or concealed in any building or place, he may by warrant under his hand given on any day authorise that officer or any other person named in the warrant to enter and search any building or place so named.

(4) An officer or person named in a warrant under subsection (3) above shall thereupon have the like powers in relation to the building or place named in the warrant, subject to the like conditions as to entry by night, as if he were an officer having a writ of assistance and acting upon reasonable grounds of suspicion.

(5) Where there are reasonable grounds to suspect that any still, vessel, utensil, spirits or materials for the manufacture of spirits is or are unlawfully kept or deposited in any building or place, subsections (3) and (4) above shall apply in relation to any constable as they would apply in relation to an officer.

(6) A writ of assistance shall continue in force during the reign in which it is issued and for 6 months thereafter.

Power to enter land for or in connection with access to pipe-lines.

162. Where any thing conveyed by a pipe-line is chargeable with a duty of customs or excise which has not been paid, an officer may enter any land adjacent to the pipe-line in order to get to the pipe-line for the purpose of exercising in relation to that thing any power conferred by or under the Customs and Excise Acts 1979 or to get from the pipe-line after an exercise of any such power.

This section does not extend to Northern Ireland.

Power to search vehicles or vessels.

163.—(1) Without prejudice to any other power conferred by the Customs and Excise Acts 1979, where there are reasonable grounds to suspect that any vehicle or vessel is or may be carrying any goods which are—

(a) chargeable with any duty which has not been paid or secured ; or

(b) in the course of being unlawfully removed from or to any place ; or

(c) otherwise liable to forfeiture under the customs and excise Acts,

any officer or constable or member of Her Majesty's armed forces or coastguard may stop and search that vehicle or vessel.

(2) If when so required by any such officer, constable or member the person in charge of any such vehicle or vessel refuses to stop or to permit the vehicle or vessel to be searched, he shall be liable on summary conviction to a penalty of £100.

164.—(1) Where there are reasonable grounds to suspect that Power to any person to whom this section applies is carrying any article— search

(*a*) which is chargeable with any duty which has not been persons. paid or secured ; or

(*b*) with respect to the importation or exportation of which any prohibition or restriction is for the time being in force under or by virtue of any enactment,

any officer or any person acting under the directions of an officer may, subject to subsections (2) and (3) below, search him and any article he has with him.

(2) A person who is to be searched in pursuance of this section may require to be taken before a justice of the peace or a superior of the officer or other person concerned, and the justice or superior shall consider the grounds for suspicion and direct accordingly whether or not the search is to take place.

(3) No woman or girl shall be searched in pursuance of this section except by a woman.

(4) This section applies to the following persons, namely—

(*a*) any person who is on board or has landed from any ship or aircraft ;

(*b*) any person entering or about to leave the United Kingdom ;

(*c*) any person within the dock area of a port ;

(*d*) any person at a customs and excise airport ;

(*e*) any person in, entering or leaving any approved wharf or transit shed which is not in a port ;

(*f*) in Northern Ireland, any person travelling from or to any place which is on or beyond the boundary.

165. Subject to any directions of the Treasury as to amount, Power to pay the Commissioners may at their discretion pay rewards in respect rewards. of any service which appears to them to merit reward rendered to them by any person in relation to any assigned matter.

166.—(1) If any person requests an officer or a person Agents. appointed by the Commissioners to transact any business relating to an assigned matter with him on behalf of another person, the officer or person so appointed may refuse to transact that business with him unless written authority from that other person is produced in such form as the Commissioners may direct.

(2) Subject to subsection (1) above, anything required by the Customs and Excise Acts 1979 to be done by the importer or exporter of any goods may, except where the Commissioners otherwise require, be done on his behalf by an agent.

General offences

167.—(1) If any person either knowingly or recklessly—

(a) makes or signs, or causes to be made or signed, or delivers or causes to be delivered to the Commissioners or an officer, any declaration, notice, certificate or other document whatsoever ; or

(b) makes any statement in answer to any question put to him by an officer which he is required by or under any enactment to answer,

being a document or statement produced or made for any purpose of any assigned matter, which is untrue in any material particular, he shall be guilty of an offence under this subsection and may be detained ; and any goods in relation to which the document or statement was made shall be liable to forfeiture.

(2) Without prejudice to subsection (4) below, a person who commits an offence under subsection (1) above shall be liable—

(a) on summary conviction, to a penalty of the prescribed sum, or to imprisonment for a term not exceeding 6 months, or to both ; or

(b) on conviction on indictment, to a penalty of any amount, or to imprisonment for a term not exceeding 2 years, or to both.

(3) If any person—

(a) makes or signs, or causes to be made or signed, or delivers or causes to be delivered to the Commissioners or an officer, any declaration, notice, certificate or other document whatsoever ; or

(b) makes any statement in answer to any question put to him by an officer which he is required by or under any enactment to answer,

being a document or statement produced or made for any purpose of any assigned matter, which is untrue in any material particular, then, without prejudice to subsection (4) below, he shall be liable on summary conviction to a penalty of £300.

(4) Where by reason of any such document or statement as is mentioned in subsection (1) or (3) above the full amount of any duty payable is not paid or any overpayment is made in respect of any drawback, allowance, rebate or repayment of duty, the amount of the duty unpaid or of the overpayment shall

be recoverable as a debt due to the Crown or may be summarily
recovered as a civil debt.

168.—(1) If any person—   Counterfeiting
    documents,
(a) counterfeits or falsifies any document which is required etc.
    by or under any enactment relating to an assigned
    matter or which is used in the transaction of any
    business relating to an assigned matter ; or

(b) knowingly accepts, receives or uses any such document
    so counterfeited or falsified ; or

(c) alters any such document after it is officially issued ;
    or

(d) counterfeits any seal, signature, initials or other mark
    of, or used by, any officer for the verification of such
    a document or for the security of goods or for any
    other purpose relating to an assigned matter,

he shall be guilty of an offence under this section and may be
detained.

(2) A person guilty of an offence under this section shall be
liable—

(a) on summary conviction, to a penalty of the prescribed
    sum, or to imprisonment for a term not exceeding 6
    months, or to both ; or

(b) on conviction on indictment, to a penalty of any amount,
    or to imprisonment for a term not exceeding 2 years,
    or to both.

169.—(1) If any person required by or under the customs and False scales,
excise Acts to provide scales for any purpose of those Acts etc.
provides, uses or permits to be used any scales which are false
or unjust he shall be guilty of an offence under this section.

(2) Where any article is or is to be weighed, counted, gauged
or measured for the purposes of the taking of an account or the
making of an examination by an officer, then if—

(a) any such person as is mentioned in subsection (1) above ;
    or

(b) any person by whom or on whose behalf the article is
    weighed, counted, gauged or measured,

does anything whereby the officer is or might be prevented from,
or hindered or deceived in, taking a true and just account or
making a due examination, he shall be guilty of an offence under
this section.

This subsection applies whether the thing is done before, during or after the weighing, counting, gauging or measuring of
the article in question.

(3) Any person committing an offence under this section shall be liable on summary conviction to a penalty of £200 and any false or unjust scales, and any article in connection with which the offence was committed, shall be liable to forfeiture.

(4) In this section " scales " includes weights, measures and weighing or measuring machines or instruments.

Penalty for
fraudulent
evasion of
duty, etc.

170.—(1) Without prejudice to any other provision of the Customs and Excise Acts 1979, if any person—

    (*a*) knowingly acquires possession of any of the following goods, that is to say—

        (i) goods which have been unlawfully removed from a warehouse or Queen's warehouse ;

        (ii) goods which are chargeable with a duty which has not been paid ;

        (iii) goods with respect to the importation or exportation of which any prohibition or restriction is for the time being in force under or by virtue of any enactment ; or

    (*b*) is in any way knowingly concerned in carrying, removing, depositing, harbouring, keeping or concealing or in any manner dealing with any such goods,

and does so with intent to defraud Her Majesty of any duty payable on the goods or to evade any such prohibition or restriction with respect to the goods he shall be guilty of an offence under this section and may be detained.

(2) Without prejudice to any other provision of the Customs and Excise Acts 1979, if any person is, in relation to any goods, in any way knowingly concerned in any fraudulent evasion or attempt at evasion—

    (*a*) of any duty chargeable on the goods ;

    (*b*) of any prohibition or restriction for the time being in force with respect to the goods under or by virtue of any enactment ; or

    (*c*) of any provision of the Customs and Excise Acts 1979 applicable to the goods,

he shall be guilty of an offence under this section and may be detained.

(3) Subject to subsection (4) below, a person guilty of an offence under this section shall be liable—

    (*a*) on summary conviction, to a penalty of the prescribed sum or of three times the value of the goods, whichever is the greater, or to imprisonment for a term not exceeding 6 months, or to both ; or

(b) on conviction on indictment, to a penalty of any amount,
or to imprisonment for a term not exceeding 2 years,
or to both.

(4) In the case of an offence under this section in connection
with a prohibition or restriction on importation or exportation
having effect by virtue of section 3 of the Misuse of Drugs Act 1971 c. 38.
1971, subsection (3) above shall have effect subject to the modifications specified in Schedule 1 to this Act.

(5) In any case where a person would, apart from this subsection, be guilty of—

(a) an offence under this section in connection with a
prohibition or restriction ; and

(b) a corresponding offence under the enactment or other
instrument imposing the prohibition or restriction,
being an offence for which a fine or other penalty is
expressly provided by that enactment or other instrument,

he shall not be guilty of the offence mentioned in paragraph (a)
of this subsection.

171.—(1) Where—   General
provisions as

(a) by any provision of any enactment relating to an to offences and
assigned matter a punishment is prescribed for any penalties.
offence thereunder or for any contravention of or
failure to comply with any regulation, direction, condition or requirement made, given or imposed thereunder ; and

(b) any person is convicted in the same proceedings of more
than one such offence, contravention or failure,

that person shall be liable to that punishment for each such
offence, contravention or failure of which he is so convicted.

(2) In this Act the " prescribed sum ", in relation to the
penalty provided for an offence, means—

(a) if the offence was committed in England, Wales or
Northern Ireland, the prescribed sum within the meaning of section 28 of the Criminal Law Act 1977 (£1,000 1977 c. 45.
or other sum substituted by order under section 61(1)
of that Act) ;

(b) if the offence was committed in Scotland, the prescribed
sum within the meaning of section 289B of the Criminal 1975 c. 21.
Procedure (Scotland) Act 1975 (£1,000 or other sum
substituted by order under section 289D(1) of that
Act) ;

and in subsection (1)(a) above, the reference to a provision by
which a punishment is prescribed includes a reference to a

provision which makes a person liable to a penalty of the prescribed sum within the meaning of this subsection.

(3) Where a penalty for an offence under any enactment relating to an assigned matter is required to be fixed by reference to the value of any goods, that value shall be taken as the price which those goods might reasonably be expected to have fetched, after payment of any duty or tax chargeable thereon, if they had been sold in the open market at or about the date of the commission of the offence for which the penalty is imposed.

(4) Where an offence under any enactment relating to an assigned matter which has been committed by a body corporate is proved to have been committed with the consent or connivance of, or to be attributable to any neglect on the part of, any director, manager, secretary or other similar officer of the body corporate or any person purporting to act in any such capacity, he as well as the body corporate shall be guilty of that offence and shall be liable to be proceeded against and punished accordingly.

In this subsection " director ", in relation to any body corporate established by or under any enactment for the purpose of carrying on under national ownership any industry or part of an industry or undertaking, being a body corporate whose affairs are managed by the members thereof, means a member of that body corporate.

(5) Where in any proceedings for an offence under the customs and excise Acts any question arises as to the duty or the rate thereof chargeable on any imported goods, and it is not possible to ascertain the relevant time specified in section 43 above, that duty or rate shall be determined as if the goods had been imported without entry at the time when the proceedings were commenced.

Miscellaneous

Regulations.   **172.**—(1) Any power to make regulations under this Act shall be exercisable by statutory instrument.

(2) Subject to subsection (3) below, a statutory instrument containing regulations made under this Act shall be subject to annulment in pursuance of a resolution of either House of Parliament.

(3) A statutory instrument containing regulations made under section 120 above shall be subject to annulment in pursuance of a resolution of the House of Commons.

173. Directions given under any provision of this Act may make different provision for different circumstances and may be varied or revoked by subsequent directions thereunder.

174.—(1) For the purposes of the customs and excise Acts, subject to section 6(2) and (3) of the Customs and Excise Duties (General Reliefs) Act 1979 and subsection (2) below, goods removed into the United Kingdom from the Isle of Man shall be deemed not to be imported into the United Kingdom.

(2) Subsection (1) above shall not apply to the removal of—

(a) any explosives within the meaning of the Explosives Act 1875 on the unloading or landing of which any restriction is for the time being in force under or by virtue of that Act ; or

(b) copies of copyright works to which section 22 of the Copyright Act 1956 applies.

(3) For the purposes of the customs and excise Acts, subject to subsection (4) below, goods removed from the United Kingdom to the Isle of Man shall be deemed not to be exported from the United Kingdom.

(4) Any enactment relating to the allowance of drawback of any excise duty on the exportation from the United Kingdom of any goods shall have effect, subject to such conditions and modifications as the Commissioners may by regulations prescribe, as if the removal of such goods to the Isle of Man were the exportation of the goods.

175.—(1) In the application of this Act to Scotland—

(a) any reference to costs shall be construed as a reference to expenses ;

(b) any provision that any amount shall be recoverable summarily as a civil debt shall be construed as if the word " summarily " were omitted ;

(c) any reference to a plaintiff shall be construed as a reference to a pursuer ;

(d) any reference to a magistrates' court shall be construed as a reference to the sheriff court.

(2) No Commissioner or officer and no person appointed by the Commissioners to discharge any duty relating to customs or excise shall be compelled to serve on any jury in Scotland whatsoever.

Part XII
Game
licences.
S.R. & O.
1908/844.
1908 c. 16.

176.—(1) Subject to the following provisions of this section, and save as expressly provided in section 102 above, the provisions of this Act relating to excise shall not apply in relation to the excise duties on licences to kill game and on licences to deal in game (which, by virtue of the Order in Council made under section 6 of the Finance Act 1908, are leviable by local authorities).

(2) The Treasury may by order provide that, subject to such modifications, if any, as may be specified in the order, any provision of this Act so specified which confers or imposes powers, duties or liabilities with respect to excise duties and to the issue and cancellation of excise licences on which those duties are imposed and to other matters relating to excise duties and licences shall have effect in relation to a local authority and their officers with respect to the duties and licences referred to in subsection (1) above as they have effect in relation to the Commissioners and officers with respect to other excise duties and licences ; and those provisions and, subject as aforesaid, any provisions relating to punishments and penalties in connection therewith shall have effect accordingly.

(3) Any order under this section shall be made by statutory instrument and may amend the Order in Council made under section 6 of the Finance Act 1908.

(4) Notwithstanding anything in section 145 above as applied under subsection (2) above, a local authority may authorise the bringing by any constable of proceedings, or any particular proceedings, for an offence under this or any other Act relating to the duties referred to in subsection (1) above.

(5) A document purporting to be a copy of a resolution authorising the bringing of proceedings in accordance with subsection (4) above and to be signed by an officer of the local authority shall be evidence, until the contrary is shown, that the bringing of the proceedings was duly authorised.

(6) This section extends to England and Wales only.

Consequential
amendments,
repeals and
saving and
transitional
provisions.
1972 c. 41.

177.—(1) The enactments specified in Schedule 4 to this Act shall be amended in accordance with the provisions of that Schedule.

(2) The enactments specified in Schedule 5 to this Act (which relate to purchase tax and whose repeal by virtue of section 54(8) of and Part II of Schedule 28 to the Finance Act 1972 has not yet taken effect) shall be amended in accordance with the provisions of that Schedule ; and accordingly the following entry shall be inserted at the end of Part II of the said Schedule 28—

" 1979 c. 2   The Customs and Excise   Schedule 5."
Management Act 1979.

(3) The enactments specified in Schedule 6 to this Act are hereby repealed to the extent specified in the third column of that Schedule.

(4) The saving and transitional provisions contained in Schedule 7 to this Act shall have effect.

(5) The provisions of Schedules 4, 5 and 7 to this Act shall not be taken as prejudicing the operation of sections 15 to 17 of the Interpretation Act 1978 (which relate to the effect of repeals). 1978 c. 30.

178.—(1) This Act may be cited as the Customs and Excise Management Act 1979.

Citation and commence-ment.

(2) This Act, the Customs and Excise Duties (General Reliefs) Act 1979, the Alcoholic Liquor Duties Act 1979, the Hydrocarbon Oil Duties Act 1979, the Matches and Mechanical Lighters Duties Act 1979 and the Tobacco Products Duty Act 1979 may be cited together as the Customs and Excise Acts 1979.

1979 c. 3.
1979 c. 4.
1979 c. 5.
1979 c. 6.
1979 c. 7.

(3) This Act shall come into operation on 1st April 1979.

SCHEDULES

SCHEDULE 1

Sections 50(5), 68(4) and 170(4).

CONTROLLED DRUGS: VARIATION OF PUNISHMENTS FOR CERTAIN OFFENCES UNDER THIS ACT

1. Section 50(4), 68(3) and 170(3) of this Act shall have effect in a case where the goods in respect of which the offence referred to in that subsection was committed were a Class A drug or a Class B drug as if for the words from " shall be liable " onwards there were substituted the following words, that is to say—

" shall be liable—

    (a) on summary conviction, to a penalty of the prescribed sum or of three times the value of the goods, whichever is the greater, or to imprisonment for a term not exceeding 6 months, or to both ;

    (b) on conviction on indictment, to a penalty of any amount, or to imprisonment for a term not exceeding 14 years, or to both.".

2. Section 50(4), 68(3) and 170(3) of this Act shall have effect in a case where the goods in respect of which the offence referred to in that subsection was committed were a Class C drug as if for the words from " shall be liable " onwards there were substituted the following words, that is to say—

" shall be liable—

    (a) on summary conviction in Great Britain, to a penalty of three times the value of the goods or £500, whichever is the greater, or to imprisonment for a term not exceeding 3 months, or to both ;

    (b) on summary conviction in Northern Ireland, to a penalty of three times the value of the goods or £100, whichever is the greater, or to imprisonment for a term not exceeding 6 months, or to both ;

    (c) on conviction on indictment, to a penalty of any amount, or to imprisonment for a term not exceeding 5 years, or to both.".

1971 c. 38.

3. In this Schedule " Class A drug ", " Class B drug " and " Class C drug " have the same meanings as in the Misuse of Drugs Act 1971.

SCHEDULE 2

Section 126(3).

COMPOSITE GOODS:

SUPPLEMENTARY PROVISIONS AS TO EXCISE DUTIES AND DRAWBACKS

Duties

1.—(1) Where under subsection (1) of the principal section imported goods of any class or description are chargeable with a duty of excise in respect of any article contained in the goods as a part or ingredient of them and it appears to the Treasury on the recommendation of the Commissioners that to charge the duty according to the quantity of the article used in the manufacture or preparation of the goods (as provided by the principal section) is inconvenient and of no material advantage to the revenue or to importers of goods of that class or description, then the Treasury may by order give a direction in relation to goods of that class or description under and in accordance with this paragraph.

(2) An order under this paragraph may direct that in the case of goods of the class or description to which it applies the duty chargeable shall be calculated in such of the following ways as may be provided by the order, that is to say—

(a) at a rate specified in the order by reference to the weight, quantity or value of the goods ; or

(b) by reference to a quantity so specified of the article, and (where material) on the basis that the article is of such value, type or quality as may be so specified.

(3) If it appears to the Treasury on the recommendation of the Commissioners that, in the case of goods of any class or description, the net amounts payable in the absence of any direction under this paragraph are insignificant, the order may direct that any such goods shall be treated for the purpose of the duty as not containing the article in respect of which the duty is chargeable.

(4) If it appears to the Treasury on the recommendation of the Commissioners that goods of any class or description are substantially of the same nature and use as if they consisted wholly of the article in respect of which the duty is chargeable, the order may direct that any such goods shall be treated for the purpose of the duty as consisting wholly of that article.

(5) In making an order under this paragraph the Treasury shall have regard to the quantity and (where material) the type or quality of the article in question appearing to them, on the advice of the Commissioners, to be ordinarily used in the manufacture or preparation of goods of the class or description to which the order applies which are imported into the United Kingdom.

2. Where a direction given by virtue of paragraph 1 above is in force as regards goods of any class or description and any article contained in them, and goods of that class or description are imported into the United Kingdom containing a quantity of that article such as, in the opinion of the Commissioners, to suggest that advantage is being taken of the direction for the purpose of evading duty on the article, the Commissioners may, notwithstanding the direction, require that on those goods the duty in question shall be calculated as if they consisted wholly of that article or (if the Commissioners see fit) shall be calculated according to the quantity of the article actually contained in the goods.

3. Nothing in paragraphs 1 and 2 above shall affect the powers of the Treasury under subsection (2) of the principal section ; and

any goods as regards which a direction under that subsection is for the time being in force shall be deemed to be excepted from any order under paragraph 1 above.

Drawbacks

4. Where a direction is given by virtue of paragraph 1 above as regards imported goods of any class or description, the Treasury may by order provide that for the purpose of allowing any drawback of excise duties there shall, in such cases and subject to such conditions (if any) as may be specified in the order, be treated as paid on imported goods of that class or description the same duties as would be chargeable apart from the direction.

5.—(1) Where, in the case of imported goods of any class or description which contain as a part or ingredient any article chargeable with a duty of excise, drawback of the duty may be allowed in respect of the article according to the quantity contained in the goods or the quantity used in their preparation or manufacture, and it appears to the Treasury on the recommendation of the Commissioners that to allow the drawback according to that quantity is inconvenient and of no material advantage to the revenue or to the persons entitled to the drawback, then the Treasury may by order give the like directions as to the manner in which the drawback is to be calculated, or in which the goods are to be treated for the purposes of the drawback, as by virtue of paragraph 1 above they may give in relation to charging duty.

(2) For the purposes of this paragraph, the reference in paragraph 1(5) above to goods imported into the United Kingdom shall be taken as a reference to goods in the case of which the drawback may be allowed.

Supplementary

6. Where any order under paragraph 1 or 5 above directs that, for the purpose of any duty or of any drawback, goods are to be treated as not containing or as consisting wholly of a particular article, the goods shall be so treated also for the purpose of determining whether any other duty is chargeable or any other drawback may be allowed, as the case may be ; but any duty or drawback which is charged or allowed shall, notwithstanding the direction, be calculated by reference to the actual quantity and value of the goods and, except for the duty or drawback to which the direction relates, by reference to their actual composition.

7. Where a resolution passed by the House of Commons has statutory effect under the Provisional Collection of Taxes Act 1968 in relation to any duty of excise charged on imported goods, and any provision about that duty contained in an order under paragraph 1 above is expressed to be made in view of the resolution, then that provision may be varied or revoked retrospectively by an order made not later than one month after the resolution ceases to have statutory effect, and that order may include provision for repayment of any

duty overpaid or for other matters arising from its having retrospective effect ; but no such order shall have retrospective effect for the
purpose of increasing the duty chargeable on any goods.

8. The power to make orders under this Schedule shall be exercisable by statutory instrument subject to annulment in pursuance
of a resolution of the House of Commons.

Interpretation

9. In this Schedule " the principal section " means section 126 of
this Act.

SCHEDULE 3

PROVISIONS RELATING TO FORFEITURE

Notice of seizure

1.—(1) The Commissioners shall, except as provided in sub-
paragraph (2) below, give notice of the seizure of any thing as liable
to forfeiture and of the grounds therefor to any person who to their
knowledge was at the time of the seizure the owner or one of the
owners thereof.

(2) Notice need not be given under this paragraph if the seizure
was made in the presence of—

> (a) the person whose offence or suspected offence occasioned
> the seizure ; or
> (b) the owner or any of the owners of the thing seized or any
> servant or agent of his ; or
> (c) in the case of any thing seized in any ship or aircraft, the
> master or commander.

2. Notice under paragraph 1 above shall be given in writing and
shall be deemed to have been duly served on the person concerned—

> (a) if delivered to him personally ; or
> (b) if addressed to him and left or forwarded by post to him at
> his usual or last known place of abode or business or, in
> the case of a body corporate, at their registered or principal
> office ; or
> (c) where he has no address within the United Kingdom, or his
> address is unknown, by publication of notice of the seizure
> in the London, Edinburgh or Belfast Gazette.

Notice of claim

3. Any person claiming that any thing seized as liable to forfeiture
is not so liable shall, within one month of the date of the notice of
seizure or, where no such notice has been served on him, within one
month of the date of the seizure, give notice of his claim in writing
to the Commissioners at any office of customs and excise.

4.—(1) Any notice under paragraph 3 above shall specify the name and address of the claimant and, in the case of a claimant who is outside the United Kingdom, shall specify the name and address of a solicitor in the United Kingdom who is authorised to accept service of process and to act on behalf of the claimant.

(2) Service of process upon a solicitor so specified shall be deemed to be proper service upon the claimant.

Condemnation

5. If on the expiration of the relevant period under paragraph 3 above for the giving of notice of claim in respect of any thing no such notice has been given to the Commissioners, or if, in the case of any such notice given, any requirement of paragraph 4 above is not complied with, the thing in question shall be deemed to have been duly condemned as forfeited.

6. Where notice of claim in respect of any thing is duly given in accordance with paragraphs 3 and 4 above, the Commissioners shall take proceedings for the condemnation of that thing by the court, and if the court finds that the thing was at the time of seizure liable to forfeiture the court shall condemn it as forfeited.

7. Where any thing is in accordance with either of paragraphs 5 or 6 above condemned or deemed to have been condemned as forfeited, then, without prejudice to any delivery up or sale of the thing by the Commissioners under paragraph 16 below, the forfeiture shall have effect as from the date when the liability to forfeiture arose.

Proceedings for condemnation by court

8. Proceedings for condemnation shall be civil proceedings and may be instituted—

    (a) in England or Wales either in the High Court or in a magistrates' court ;

    (b) in Scotland either in the Court of Session or in the sheriff court ;

    (c) in Northern Ireland either in the High Court or in a court of summary jurisdiction.

9. Proceedings for the condemnation of any thing instituted in a magistrates' court in England or Wales, in the sheriff court in Scotland or in a court of summary jurisdiction in Northern Ireland may be so instituted—

    (a) in any such court having jurisdiction in the place where any offence in connection with that thing was committed or where any proceedings for such an offence are instituted ; or

    (b) in any such court having jurisdiction in the place where the claimant resides or, if the claimant has specified a solicitor under paragraph 4 above, in the place where that solicitor has his office ; or

    (c) in any such court having jurisdiction in the place where that thing was found, detained or seized or to which it is first brought after being found, detained or seized.

10.—(1) In any proceedings for condemnation instituted in England, Wales or Northern Ireland, the claimant or his solicitor shall make oath that the thing seized was, or was to the best of his knowledge and belief, the property of the claimant at the time of the seizure.

(2) In any such proceedings instituted in the High Court, the claimant shall give such security for the costs of the proceedings as may be determined by the Court.

(3) If any requirement of this paragraph is not complied with, the court shall give judgment for the Commissioners.

11.—(1) In the case of any proceedings for condemnation instituted in a magistrates' court in England or Wales, without prejudice to any right to require the statement of a case for the opinion of the High Court, either party may appeal against the decision of that court to the Crown Court.

(2) In the case of any proceedings for condemnation instituted in a court of summary jurisdiction in Northern Ireland, without prejudice to any right to require the statement of a case for the opinion of the High Court, either party may appeal against the decision of that court to the county court.

12. Where an appeal, including an appeal by way of case stated, has been made against the decision of the court in any proceedings for the condemnation of any thing, that thing shall, pending the final determination of the matter, be left with the Commissioners or at any convenient office of customs and excise.

Provisions as to proof

13. In any proceedings arising out of the seizure of any thing, the fact, form and manner of the seizure shall be taken to have been as set forth in the process without any further evidence thereof, unless the contrary is proved.

14. In any proceedings, the condemnation by a court of any thing as forfeited may be proved by the production either of the order or certificate of condemnation or of a certified copy thereof purporting to be signed by an officer of the court by which the order or certificate was made or granted.

Special provisions as to certain claimants

15. For the purposes of any claim to, or proceedings for the condemnation of, any thing, where that thing is at the time of seizure the property of a body corporate, of two or more partners or of any number of persons exceeding five, the oath required by paragraph 10 above to be taken and any other thing required by this Schedule or by any rules of the court to be done by, or by any person authorised by, the claimant or owner may be taken or done by, or by any other person authorised by, the following persons respectively, that is to say—

    (a) where the owner is a body corporate, the secretary or some duly authorised officer of that body ;

(b) where the owners are in partnership, any one of those owners ;

(c) where the owners are any number of persons exceeding five not being in partnership, any two of those persons on behalf of themselves and their co-owners.

Power to deal with seizures before condemnation, etc.

16. Where any thing has been seized as liable to forfeiture the Commissioners may at any time if they see fit and notwithstanding that the thing has not yet been condemned, or is not yet deemed to have been condemned, as forfeited—

(a) deliver it up to any claimant upon his paying to the Commissioners such sum as they think proper, being a sum not exceeding that which in their opinion represents the value of the thing, including any duty or tax chargeable thereon which has not been paid ;

(b) if the thing seized is a living creature or is in the opinion of the Commissioners of a perishable nature, sell or destroy it.

17.—(1) If, where any thing is delivered up, sold or destroyed under paragraph 16 above, it is held in proceedings taken under this Schedule that the thing was not liable to forfeiture at the time of its seizure, the Commissioners shall, subject to any deduction allowed under sub-paragraph (2) below, on demand by the claimant tender to him—

(a) an amount equal to any sum paid by him under sub-paragraph (a) of that paragraph ; or

(b) where they have sold the thing, an amount equal to the proceeds of sale ; or

(c) where they have destroyed the thing, an amount equal to the market value of the thing at the time of its seizure.

(2) Where the amount to be tendered under sub-paragraph (1)(a), (b) or (c) above includes any sum on account of any duty or tax chargeable on the thing which had not been paid before its seizure the Commissioners may deduct so much of that amount as represents that duty or tax.

(3) If the claimant accepts any amount tendered to him under sub-paragraph (1) above, he shall not be entitled to maintain any action on account of the seizure, detention, sale or destruction of the thing.

(4) For the purposes of sub-paragraph (1)(c) above, the market value of any thing at the time of its seizure shall be taken to be such amount as the Commissioners and the claimant may agree or, in default of agreement, as may be determined by a referee appointed by the Lord Chancellor (not being an official of any government department), whose decision shall be final and conclusive ; and the procedure on any reference to a referee shall be such as may be determined by the referee.

SCHEDULE 4

CONSEQUENTIAL AMENDMENTS

*Construction of references in Acts passed before 1st April 1909
and in instruments made thereunder*

1. Save where the context otherwise requires, any reference in, or in any instrument made under, any enactment relating to customs or excise passed before 1st April 1909 to any of the persons mentioned in column 1 of the following Table shall be construed as a reference to the persons respectively specified in relation thereto in column 2.

TABLE

Original reference	*To be construed as reference to—*
Commissioners of Customs Commissioners of Inland Revenue Commissioners of Excise	Commissioners of Customs and Excise.
Solicitor for the Customs Solicitor of Inland Revenue	Solicitor for the Customs and Excise.
Secretary for the Customs Secretary of the Commissioners of Inland Revenue	Secretary to the Commissioners of Customs and Excise.
Accountant and Comptroller General of Customs Accountant and Comptroller General of Inland Revenue	Accountant and Comptroller General of the Customs and Excise.
Collector of Customs Collector of Inland Revenue Collector of Excise	Collector of Customs and Excise.
Officer of Customs Officer of Inland Revenue Officer of Excise	Officer of Customs and Excise.

Isle of Man Act 1958

2. In section 2(1) of the Isle of Man Act 1958 the words from 1958 c. 11. " shall not be paid " to " but " shall be omitted.

Diplomatic Privileges Act 1964

3. In section 2 of the Diplomatic Privileges Act 1964, after sub- 1964 c. 81. section (5) there shall be inserted the following subsection—

" (5A) The reference in Article 36 to customs duties shall be construed as including a reference to excise duties chargeable on goods imported into the United Kingdom."

Provisional Collection of Taxes Act 1964

4. In section 3 of the Provisional Collection of Taxes Act 1968, 1968 c. 2. after subsection (2) there shall be inserted the following subsection—

" (2A) Subsection (2) above shall apply for the purposes of a duty of excise imposed as mentioned in subsection (1) above to the extent that the duty is charged on goods imported into the United Kingdom, as it applies for the purposes of a duty of customs so imposed.".

5. In section 3(3) of the Provisional Collection of Taxes Act 1968, after the words " duty of excise " there shall be inserted the words " then—

> (a) where it is a duty of excise charged otherwise than on goods ; or
>
> (b) where it is a duty of excise charged on goods, to the extent that it is charged on goods produced or manufactured in the United Kingdom ; ".

Consular Relations Act 1968

6. In section 1 of the Consular Relations Act 1968, after subsection (8) there shall be inserted the following subsection—

> " (8A) The references in Articles 50 and 62 to customs duties shall be construed as including references to excise duties chargeable on goods imported into the United Kingdom."

7. In section 5 of the Consular Relations Act 1968, after subsection (1) there shall be inserted the following subsection—

> " (1A) In subsection (1)(b) of this section the expression " the law relating to customs ", to the extent that it refers to the law relating to duties on goods, refers to the law relating to duties (whether of customs or excise) for the time being chargeable on goods imported into the United Kingdom."

Misuse of Drugs Act 1971

8. In section 12(1)(b) of the Misuse of Drugs Act 1971, after the words " the Customs and Excise Act 1952 " there shall be inserted the words " or under section 50, 68 or 170 of the Customs and Excise Management Act 1979 ".

Finance Act 1972

9. In section 17 of the Finance Act 1972, after subsection (1) there shall be inserted the following subsection—

> "(1A) Section 125(3) of the Customs and Excise Management Act 1979 shall have effect in its application by virtue of subsection (1) of this section as if the reference to subsections (1) and (2) of that section included a reference to section 11 of this Act."

10. In section 17 of the Finance Act 1972, for subsection (2) there shall be substituted the following subsection—

> " (2) The following provisions of the Customs and Excise Management Act 1979 shall be excepted from the enactments which are to have effect as mentioned in subsection (1) of this section, that is to say—
>
> (a) section 43(5) (re-importation) ;
>
> (b) section 125(1) and (2) (valuation of goods imported) ;
>
> (c) section 126 (charge of duty on manufactured or composite imported articles) ;
>
> (d) section 127(1)(b) (declaration as to duty payable) ; and
>
> (e) section 174 (Isle of Man)."

11. In section 27 of the Finance Act 1972, for subsection (1) (as originally enacted) there shall be substituted the following subsection—

" (1) Where imported goods subject to a duty of customs or excise or a duty of customs and a duty of excise are supplied while warehoused, the supply shall be disregarded for the purposes of this Part of this Act if the goods are supplied before payment of the duty to which they are subject or, where they are subject to a duty of customs and a duty of excise, of the duty of excise."

Table of textual amendments

12. In the enactments specified in the following Table, for so much of the provision in column 1 as is specified in column 2 there shall be substituted the words in column 3.

TABLE

PART I

ENACTMENTS OF THE PARLIAMENT OF THE UNITED KINGDOM

Section or Schedule	Words or provision replaced	Replacement
CROWN DEBTS AND JUDGMENTS ACT 1860 c. 115		
Section 1 (as amended by the Customs and Excise Act 1952).	From " the Customs " to " 1952 ".	" customs and excise contained in subsection (2) of section 157 of the Customs and Excise Management Act 1979 ".
	" sections ".	" subsection ".
NAVAL PRIZE ACT 1864 c. 25		
Section 47.	" duties of Customs ".	" duties chargeable on imported goods (whether of customs or excise) ".
Sections 48 and 48A.	" the Customs " (twice).	" customs or excise ".
	" relating to the Customs ".	" relating to customs or excise ".
Section 49.	" duties of Customs ".	" duties (whether of customs or excise) chargeable on imported goods ".
EXPLOSIVES ACT 1875 c. 17		
Section 40(9)(e).	" the Customs " (twice).	" customs or excise ".
Section 43.	" the Customs " (twice).	" customs or excise ".
CUSTOMS AND INLAND REVENUE ACT 1879 c. 21		
Section 5 (as originally enacted).	From the beginning to " following ".	" The importation of the following goods is prohibited, that is to say ".
STAMP DUTIES MANAGEMENT ACT 1891 c. 38		
Section 23.	" duty of excise ".	" duty of excise other than a duty of excise chargeable on goods imported into the United Kingdom ".
MERCHANT SHIPPING ACT 1894 c. 60		
Section 492.	" customs laws " (twice).	" customs or excise laws ".
FOREIGN PRISON-MADE GOODS ACT 1897 c. 63		
Section 1 (as originally enacted).	From the beginning to " following ".	" The importation of the following goods is prohibited ".

Part I

E

Section or Schedule	Words or provision replaced	Replacement
REVENUE ACT 1898 c. 46		
Section 1 (as originally enacted).	From the beginning to " following ".	" The importation of the following articles is prohibited ".
FINANCE ACT 1901 c. 7		
Section 10.	" customs import duty " (in three places).	" customs duty ".
SEAL FISHERIES (NORTH PACIFIC) ACT 1912 c. 10		
Section 4 (as originally enacted).	From " shall " onwards.	" are hereby prohibited to be imported ".
PILOTAGE ACT 1913 (2 & 3 Geo. 5) c. 31		
Section 48(3).	" relating to Customs ".	" relating to customs or excise ".
PUBLIC HEALTH ACT 1936 c. 49		
Section 2(1).	" relating to the Customs ".	" for the time being in force relating to customs or excise".
DISEASES OF FISH ACT 1937 c. 33		
Section 1(2).	" the Customs Acts ".	" the enactments for the time being in force relating to customs or excise ".
TRADE MARKS ACT 1938 c. 22		
Section 64A(5).	" section 11 of the Customs and Excise Act 1952 ". " customs ".	" section 17 of the Customs and Excise Management Act 1979 ". " duties (whether of customs or excise) charged on imported goods "
IMPORT, EXPORT AND CUSTOMS POWERS (DEFENCE) ACT 1939 c. 69		
Sections 1(4) and 3(1).	" enactments relating to customs ".	" enactments for the time being in force relating to customs or excise ".
Section 1(5) (as originally enacted).	" section eleven of the Customs and Inland Revenue Act 1879 ".	" section 145 of the Customs and Excise Management Act 1979 ".
Section 9(2).	" Customs Consolidation Act 1876, and the enactments amending that Act ".	" Customs and Excise Management Act 1979 ".
EXCHANGE CONTROL ACT 1947 c. 14		
Schedule 5, Part III, paragraph 1(1) and (2).	" enactments relating to customs ".	" enactments for the time being in force relating to customs or excise ".
Schedule 5, Part III, paragraph 2 (as originally enacted).	" section one hundred and sixty-eight of the Customs Consolidation Act 1876 ".	" section 167 of the Customs and Excise Management Act 1979 ".
RADIOACTIVE SUBSTANCES ACT 1948 c. 37		
Section 2(2).	" enactments relating to customs ".	" enactments for the time being in force relating to customs or excise ".

Section or Schedule	Words or provision replaced	Replacement
	RADIOACTIVE SUBSTANCES ACT 1948 c. 37 — *continued*	
Section 2(3).	" Customs Consolidation Act 1876, and the enactments amending that Act ".	" Customs and Excise Management Act 1979 ".
	MERCHANT SHIPPING (SAFETY CONVENTION) ACT 1949 c. 43	
Section 24(5).	" the Customs Consolidation Act 1876 ".	" section 35 of the Customs and Excise Management Act 1979 ".
	CIVIL AVIATION ACT 1949 c. 67	
Section 8(2)(*m*).	" relating to customs ".	" for the time being in force relating to customs or excise".
	DISEASES OF ANIMALS ACT 1950 c. 36	
Section 24(6).	" section 79(2) of the Customs and Excise Act 1952 ". " that Act ".	" section 5(2) of the Customs and Excise Management Act 1979 ". " the customs and excise Acts ".
Section 73(4A)(*a*).	" the Customs and Excise Act 1952, or at a customs airport ".	" the Customs and Excise Management Act 1979, or at a customs and excise airport ".
	POST OFFICE ACT 1953 c. 36	
Section 16(1). Section 17(1).	" customs ". " customs duty ".	" customs or excise ". " duty charged on imported goods (whether a customs or an excise duty) ".
	PROTECTION OF BIRDS ACT 1954 c. 30	
Section 7(3).	" the Customs and Excise Act 1952, the Seventh Schedule ".	" the Customs and Excise Management Act 1979, Schedule 3 ".
Section 14(1) (in the definition of " importation ").	" the Customs and Excise Act 1952 ".	" the Customs and Excise Management Act 1979 ".
	FOOD AND DRUGS ACT 1955 (4 Eliz. 2) c. 16	
Section 135(1) (in the definition of " importation ").	" the Customs and Excise Act 1952 ".	" the Customs and Excise Management Act 1979 ".
	FOOD AND DRUGS (SCOTLAND) ACT 1956 c. 30	
Section 58(1) (in the definition of " importation ").	" the Customs and Excise Act 1952 ".	" the Customs and Excise Management Act 1979 ".
	COPYRIGHT ACT 1956 c. 74	
Section 22(6).	" section eleven of the Customs and Excise Act 1952 ". " customs ".	" section 17 of the Customs and Excise Management Act 1979 ". " duties (whether of customs or excise) charged on imported goods ".
Section 22(7).	" the Customs and Excise Act 1952 ".	" the Customs and Excise Management Act 1979 ".

Section or Schedule	Words or provision replaced	Replacement
	CINEMATOGRAPH FILMS ACT 1957 c. 21	
Section 4(5).	" section three hundred and one of the Customs and Excise Act 1952 ".	" section 167 of the Customs and Excise Management Act 1979 ".
	ISLE OF MAN ACT 1958 c. 11	
Section 2(4).	" duties of customs " (in four places).	" duties of customs or excise ".
	DOG LICENCES ACT 1959 c. 55	
Section 15(1).	From " section three hundred and thirteen " to " dog licences) ".	" section 176(2) of the Customs and Excise Management Act 1979 (which makes provision for the application of certain provisions of that Act to game licences and duties thereon and is applied by section 16(5) below) ".
Section 16(5).	From the beginning to " the said section three hundred and thirteen ".	" Subsections (1) to (3) of section 176 of the Customs and Excise Management Act 1979 (which make provision for the application of certain provisions of that Act to game licences and duties thereon), and any order made by the Treasury under that section,".
	From " duties transferred under section six " to " the said Act of 1908 ".	" duties on licences to kill and to deal in game and to local authorities and their officers with respect to those duties and licences, and the reference in the said subsection (3) to the Order in Council made under section 6 of the Finance Act 1908 ".
	FINANCE ACT 1961 c. 36	
Section 37(3).	" the Customs and Excise Act 1952 ".	" the Customs and Excise Management Act 1979 ".
	WEIGHTS AND MEASURES ACT 1963 c. 31	
Section 21(5)(*b*)(ii).	" the Customs and Excise Act 1952 ".	" the Customs and Excise Management Act 1979 ".
	LICENSING ACT 1964 c. 26	
Section 87(1).	" section 16 of the Customs and Excise Act 1952 ".	" section 22 of the Customs and Excise Management Act 1979 ".
	AGRICULTURE AND HORTICULTURE ACT 1964 c. 28	
Section 1(12).	" enactments relating to customs ".	" enactments for the time being in force relating to customs or excise ".
	" duties of customs ".	" duties (whether of customs or excise) charged on imported goods ".

Section or Schedule	Words or provision replaced	Replacement
	AGRICULTURE AND HORTICULTURE ACT 1964 c. 28—*continued*	
Schedule, paragraph 1(1).	From " the Customs and Excise Act 1952 " to " customs generally ".	" the Customs and Excise Management Act 1979 (as for the time being amended) and any other statutory provisions for the time being in force and relating to customs or excise generally ".
	" duties of customs ".	" duties (whether of customs or excise) charged on imported goods ".
Schedule, paragraph 1(2).	" customs generally ".	" customs or excise generally ".
	From " section 259 " to " 1952 ".	" section 126 of the Customs and Excise Management Act 1979 ".
Schedule, paragraph 1(3)(*a*).	" section 46 of the Customs and Excise Act 1952 ".	" section 51 of the Customs and Excise Management Act 1979 ".
	DIPLOMATIC PRIVILEGES ACT 1964 c. 81	
Section 7(1)(*b*).	" customs duties ".	" duties (whether of customs or excise) chargeable on imported goods ".
	FINANCE (No. 2) ACT 1964 c. 92	
Section 7(11).	" customs station ".	" customs and excise station ".
Section 9(5).	" the Customs and Excise Act 1952 ".	" the Customs and Excise Management Act 1979 ".
	" that Act ".	" the Customs and Excise Acts 1979 ".
	" section 270 ".	" section 135 ".
	" section 271(1) ".	" section 136(1) and (2) ".
	" section 301(2) ".	" section 167(4) ".
Section 9(6).	" section 11 of the Customs and Excise Act 1952 ".	" section 17 of the Customs and Excise Management Act 1979 ".
Section 10(2).	" the Customs and Excise Act 1952 ".	" the Customs and Excise Management Act 1979 ".
	FINANCE ACT 1966 c. 18	
Section 2(13)(*b*).	" section 11 of the Act of 1952 ".	" section 17 of the Customs and Excise Management Act 1979 ".
Section 53(2).	From " Customs and Excise Act 1952 " to " that Act ".	" Customs and Excise Management Act 1979 ".
Schedule 1, paragraph 4.	"Act of 1952 ".	" Customs and Excise Management Act 1979 ".
	" that Act ".	" the Customs and Excise Acts 1979 ".
	" section 270 ".	" section 135 ".
	" section 271(1) ".	" section 136(1) and (2) ".
	" section 301(2) ".	" section 167(4) ".

Section or Schedule	Words or provision replaced	Replacement
	PLANT HEALTH ACT 1967 c. 8	
Section 2(2).	" the Customs and Excise Act 1952 ".	" the Customs and Excise Management Act 1979 ".
	FINANCE ACT 1967 c. 54	
Section 7(8)(*b*).	" sections 281 and 287 of the Act of 1952 ".	" sections 145 and 151 of the Customs and Excise Management Act 1979 ".
	" the excise Acts " (twice).	" the customs and excise Acts ".
Section 45(3)(*a*).	From " Customs and Excise Act 1952 " to " that Act ".	" Customs and Excise Management Act 1979 ".
	WIRELESS TELEGRAPHY ACT 1967 c. 72	
Section 7(5).	" the Customs and Excise Act 1952 ".	" the Customs and Excise Management Act 1979 ".
Section 7(6).	" 1952 ".	" 1979 ".
	PROVISIONAL COLLECTION OF TAXES ACT 1968 c. 2	
Section 3(3).	" the excise Acts ".	" the revenue trade provisions of the customs and excise Acts ".
Section 3(5).	" the Customs and Excise Act 1952 ".	" the Customs and Excise Management Act 1979 ".
Section 4.	" duty of customs or excise ".	" duty of excise ".
	CONSULAR RELATIONS ACT 1968 c. 18	
Section 8(1).	From " customs duty " to " which are ".	" duty (whether of customs or excise) paid on imported hydrocarbon oil (within the meaning of the Hydrocarbon Oil Duties Act 1979) or value added tax paid on the importation of such oil which is ".
Section 8(1)(*b*).	" they ".	" it ".
	" customs duty "	" duty ".
	FIREARMS ACT 1968 c. 27	
Section 45(2)(*b*).	" enactments relating to customs ".	" enactments for the time being in force relating to customs or excise ".
	TRADE DESCRIPTIONS ACT 1968 c. 29	
Section 32(*b*)	" Customs and Excise Act 1952 ".	" Customs and Excise Management Act 1979 ".

Section or Schedule	Words or provision replaced	Replacement
	INTERNATIONAL ORGANISATIONS ACT 1968 c. 48	
Section 9. Schedule 1, paragraphs 3(1), 4, 9, 10, 16 and 17.	" customs duty ". " customs duties ".	" duty ". " duties (whether of customs or excise) ".
Schedule 1, paragraphs 6 and 12.	From " customs duty " to " which are ".	" duty (whether of customs or excise) paid on imported hydrocarbon oil (within the meaning of the Hydrocarbon Oil Duties Act 1979) or value added tax paid on the importation of such oil which is ".
	CIVIL AVIATION ACT 1968 c. 61	
Section 14(5)(*a*).	" customs duty ".	" duty (whether of customs or excise) chargeable on imported goods ".
	MEDICINES ACT 1968 c. 67	
Section 116(1).	" section 44 of the Customs and Excise Act 1952 ".	" section 49 of the Customs and Excise Management Act 1979 ".
Section 116(2).	" section 56 of the Customs and Excise Act 1952 ".	" section 68 of the Customs and Excise Management Act 1979 ".
	CUSTOMS DUTIES (DUMPING AND SUBSIDIES) ACT 1969 c. 16	
Section 9(2).	" the Customs and Excise Act 1952 ". " the customs Acts ".	" the Customs and Excise Management Act 1979 ". " the enactments for the time being in force relating to customs or excise ".
	" section 255 of the Customs and Excise Act 1952 ".	" section 119 of the Customs and Excise Management Act 1979 ".
Section 10(1).	" duty of customs " and " customs duty ".	" duty (whether of customs or excise) ".
Section 17 (in the definition of " importer ").	" customs charge ".	" charge ".
	FINANCE ACT 1969 c. 32	
Section 61(3)(*a*).	" the Customs and Excise Act 1952 ".	" the Customs and Excise Acts 1979 ".
	POST OFFICE ACT 1969 c. 48	
Schedule 4, paragraph 2(5).	" of customs ".	" (whether of customs or excise) charged on imported goods ".

Section or Schedule	Words or provision replaced	Replacement
	VEHICLES (EXCISE) ACT 1971 c. 10	
Section 3(2).	From " and to the issue " onwards.	" (other than duties on imported goods) and to the issue and cancellation of licences on which duties of excise are imposed and to other matters (not being matters relating only to duties on imported goods) under the Acts relating to duties of excise and excise licences; and, subject to those provisions and in particular to section 28 or 29 and to section 35(3) of this Act, all enactments relating to those duties and to punishments and penalties in connection therewith (other than enactments relating only to duties on imported goods) shall apply accordingly.".
Section 28(5).	" Section 281 of the Customs and Excise Act 1952 ". " section 283(1) ".	" Section 145 of the Customs and Excise Management Act 1979 ". " section 147(1) ".
Section 35(3).	" Section 287 of the Customs and Excise Act 1952 ".	" Section 151 of the Customs and Excise Management Act 1979 ".
	MISUSE OF DRUGS ACT 1971 c. 38	
Section 22(a)(ii).	" the Customs and Excise Act 1952, that is to say sections 45(1), 56(2) and 304 ".	" the Customs and Excise Act 1979, that is to say, sections 50(1) to (4), 68(2) and (3) and 170 ".
	MINERAL WORKINGS (OFFSHORE INSTALLATIONS) ACT 1971 c. 61	
Section 10(2).	Paragraph (b).	" (b) the Customs and Excise Acts 1979, or any enactment to be construed as one with those Acts or any of them; ".
	DIPLOMATIC AND OTHER PRIVILEGES ACT 1971 c. 64	
Section 1(1).	From " customs duty " to " 1971) ".	" duty (whether of customs or excise) paid on imported hydrocarbon oil (within the meaning of the Hydrocarbon Oil Duties Act 1979) or value added tax paid on the importation of such oil ".
Section 1(1)(b).	" customs duty ".	" duty ".

Section or Schedule	Words or provision replaced	Replacement
Betting and Gaming Duties Act 1972 c. 25		
Sections 15(4) and 20(3).	" the excise Acts ".	" the customs and excise Acts ".
Section 30(2).	" the Customs and Excise Act 1952 ".	" the Customs and Excise Management Act 1979 ".
Finance Act 1972 c. 41		
Section 1(3)(*a*).	" section 11 of the Customs and Excise Act 1952 ".	" section 17 of the Customs and Excise Management Act 1979 ".
Section 12(8).	" the Customs and Excise Act 1952 ".	" the Customs and Excise Management Act 1979 ".
Section 17(1).	" the Customs and Excise Act 1952 ".	" the Customs and Excise Acts 1979 ".
	" to customs generally ".	" generally to customs or excise duties on imported goods ".
	" duties of customs ".	" duties (whether of customs or excise) ".
Section 27(2).	From the beginning to " customs ".	" Where goods produced or manufactured in the United Kingdom subject to a duty of excise or such goods mixed with imported goods subject to a duty (whether of customs or excise) ".
Section 38(8).	" Sections 281 to 291 of the Customs and Excise Act 1952 ".	" Sections 145 to 155 of the Customs and Excise Management Act 1979 ".
	" section 290(2) ".	" section 154(2) ".
Section 40(5).	" section 260 of the Customs and Excise Act 1952 ".	" section 127 of the Customs and Excise Management Act 1979 ".
Section 47(2).	" section 79 of the Customs and Excise Act 1952 ".	" section 5 of the Customs and Excise Management Act 1979 ".
	" section 28 of the Customs and Excise Act 1952 ".	" section 37 of the Customs and Excise Management Act 1979 ".
Schedule 4, Group 10, Items 6(*a*) and (*b*) and 12(*a*).	" customs airport ".	" customs and excise airport ".
Schedule 4, Group 10, Note (1).	From " customs airport " onwards.	" ' customs and excise airport ' have the same meanings as in the Customs and Excise Management Act 1979.".
Schedule 4, Group 15, Item 1.	" section 28 of the Customs and Excise Act 1952 ".	" section 37 of the Customs and Excise Management Act 1979 ".
Schedule 7, paragraph 2(2)(*a*).	" section 11 of the Customs and Excise Act 1952 ".	" section 17 of the Customs and Excise Management Act 1979 ".
Schedule 7, paragraph 22(5).	" Sections 281 to 291 of the Customs and Excise Act 1952 ".	" Sections 145 to 155 of the Customs and Excise Management Act 1979 ".
Schedule 7, paragraph 22(6).	" Section 290(2) of the Customs and Excise Act 1952 ".	" Section 154(2) of the Customs and Excise Management Act 1979 ".
Schedule 7, paragraph 23.	" the Customs and Excise Act 1952 ".	" the Customs and Excise Management Act 1979 ".

Section or Schedule	Words or provision replaced	Replacement
European Communities Act 1972 c. 68		
Section 6(5).	Paragraph (*a*).	" (*a*) the Customs and Excise Management Act 1979 (as for the time being amended by any later Act) and any other statutory provisions for the time being in force relating generally to customs or excise duties on imported goods; and ".
	From " section 267 " to " customs duties ".	" section 133 (except subsection (3) and the reference to that subsection in subsection (2)) and section 159 of the Customs and Excise Management Act 1979 shall apply as they apply in relation to a drawback of excise duties ".
Section 6(6).	" section 259 of the Customs and Excise Act 1952 ".	" section 126 of the Customs and Excise Management Act 1979 ".
Powers of Criminal Courts Act 1973 c. 62		
Sections 31(7) and 32(2).	" section 285 of the Customs and Excise Act 1952 ".	" section 149(1) of the Customs and Excise Management Act 1979 ".
Health and Safety at Work etc. Act 1974 c. 37		
Schedule 3, paragraph 2(2).	" the Customs and Excise Act 1952 ".	" the Customs and Excise Acts 1979 ".
Merchant Shipping Act 1974 c. 43		
Section 2(9) (in the definition of "importer").	" customs purposes ".	" customs or excise purposes ".
Schedule 4, paragraph 1(3).	" Section 53 of the Customs and Excise Act 1952 ".	" Section 65 of the Customs and Excise Management Act 1979 ".
Schedule 4, paragraph 2(1)(*c*).	" customs Acts which relate to duties of customs ".	" enactments for the time being in force relating to duties (whether of customs or excise) chargeable on goods imported into the United Kingdom ".
Salmon and Freshwater Fisheries Act 1975 c. 51		
Schedule 4, paragraph 6.	" Schedule 7 to the Customs and Excise Act 1952 ".	" Schedule 3 to the Customs and Excise Management Act 1979 ".
	Paragraph (*a*).	" (*a*) paragraphs 1(2) and 5 shall be omitted; ".
Licensing (Scotland) Act 1976 c. 66		
Section 63(2).	" section 16 of the Customs and Excise Act 1952 ".	" section 22 of the Customs and Excise Management Act 1979 ".

Section or Schedule	Words or provision replaced	Replacement

ENDANGERED SPECIES (IMPORT AND EXPORT) ACT 1976 c. 72

Section or Schedule	Words or provision replaced	Replacement
Section 1(8).	" the Customs and Excise Act 1952 ".	" the Customs and Excise Management Act 1979 ".
Section 4(8).	" section 45 or 304 of the Customs and Excise Act 1952 ".	" section 50 or 170 of the Customs and Excise Management Act 1979 ".
Section 5(4) (in the definition of " airport ").	From " customs airport " to " 1952 ".	" customs and excise airport as mentioned in section 21(7) of the Customs and Excise Management Act 1979 ".
Section 5(4) (in the definition of " port ").	" section 13(1) ".	" section 19(1) ".

FINANCE ACT 1977 c. 36

Section or Schedule	Words or provision replaced	Replacement
Section 10(5).	" made by the Commissioners ".	" made by statutory instrument by the Commissioners which shall be subject to annulment in pursuance of a resolution of either House of Parliament ".
Section 59(3)(a).	" the Customs and Excise Act 1952 ".	" such of the Customs and Excise Acts 1979 as the provision in question requires ".

FINANCE ACT 1978 c. 42

Section or Schedule	Words or provision replaced	Replacement
Section 80(3)(a).	" the Customs and Excise Act 1952 ".	" the Customs and Excise Management Act 1979 ".

PART II

ENACTMENTS OF THE PARLIAMENT OF NORTHERN IRELAND

CONTROL OF FERTILISERS ACT (NORTHERN IRELAND) 1953 c. 33

Section or Schedule	Words or provision replaced	Replacement
Section 8(2).	" section four of the Customs and Excise Act 1952 ".	" section 8 of the Customs and Excise Management Act 1979 ".

DISEASES OF ANIMALS ACT (NORTHERN IRELAND) 1958 c. 13

Section or Schedule	Words or provision replaced	Replacement
Section 52(2) (in the definition of " the Customs Acts ").	" the Customs and Excise Act 1952 ".	" the Customs and Excise Management Act 1979 ".

MAGISTRATES' COURTS ACT (NORTHERN IRELAND) 1964 c. 21

Section or Schedule	Words or provision replaced	Replacement
Section 62(3).	" section 286(2) of the Customs and Excise Act 1952 ".	" section 150(2) of the Customs and Excise Management Act 1979 ".
Section 64(3).	" section 285(3) of the Customs and Excise Act 1952 ".	" section 149(3) of the Customs and Excise Management Act 1979 ".

WEIGHTS AND MEASURES ACT (NORTHERN IRELAND) 1967 c. 6

Section or Schedule	Words or provision replaced	Replacement
Section 15(5)(b).	" the Customs and Excise Act 1952 ".	" the Customs and Excise Management Act 1979 ".

PLANT HEALTH ACT (NORTHERN IRELAND) 1967 c. 28

Section or Schedule	Words or provision replaced	Replacement
Section 2(2).	" the Customs and Excise Act 1952 ".	" the Customs and Excise Management Act 1979 ".

MISCELLANEOUS TRANSFERRED EXCISE DUTIES ACT (NORTHERN IRELAND) 1972 c. 11

Section or Schedule	Words or provision replaced	Replacement
Section 73.	" the Customs and Excise Act 1952 ".	" the Customs and Excise Management Act 1979 ".

Section 177(2).

SCHEDULE 5

TRANSITORY CONSEQUENTIAL AMENDMENTS OF ENACTMENTS
RELATING TO PURCHASE TAX

Purchase Tax Act 1963

1963 c. 9.

1. In section 1(3)(*a*) of the Purchase Tax Act 1963 (in this Schedule referred to as "the 1963 Act") for the words "section 11 of the Customs and Excise Act 1952" there shall be substituted the words "section 17 of the Customs and Excise Management Act 1979".

2.—(1) In section 25 of the 1963 Act the amendments specified in this paragraph shall be made.

(2) In subsection (1)—

(*a*) for the words "the Customs and Excise Act 1952" there shall be substituted the words "the Customs and Excise Management Act 1979"; and

(*b*) after the word "customs", in each place where it occurs, there shall be inserted the words "or excise".

(3) In subsection (2)—

(*a*) the words "of the Customs and Excise Act 1952" shall be omitted;

(*b*) in paragraph (*a*), for the words "section 34(4), 35 and 36" there shall be substituted the words "section 43(5) of the Customs and Excise Management Act 1979, and sections 10 and 11 of the Customs and Excise Duties (General Reliefs) Act 1979";

(*c*) in paragraph (*b*), for the words "section 37" there shall be substituted the words "section 5 of the Customs and Excise Duties (General Reliefs) Act 1979";

(*d*) in paragraph (*c*), for the words "section 259" there shall be substituted the words "section 5 of the Customs and Excise Excise Management Act 1979"; and

(*e*) in paragraph (*d*), for the words "section 272" there shall be substituted the words "section 12 of the Customs and Excise Duties (General Reliefs) Act 1979".

(4) In subsection (3)—

(*a*) for the words "section 258 of the Customs and Excise Act 1952" there shall be substituted the words "section 125 of the Customs and Excise Management Act 1979"; and

(*b*) for the words "section 260" there shall be substituted the words "section 127".

(5) In subsection (4), for the words "Section 46 of the Customs and Excise Act 1952" there shall be substituted the words "Section 51 of the Customs and Excise Management Act 1979".

3.—(1) In section 34 of the 1963 Act the amendments specified in this paragraph shall be made.

(2) In subsection (1) for the words "the Customs and Excise Act 1952" and "the said Act of 1952" there shall be substituted the words "the Customs and Excise Management Act 1979".

(3) In subsection (2)—

(a) for the words "Sections 290(2) and 301(2) of the Customs and Excise Act 1952" there shall be substituted the words "Sections 154(2) and 167(4) of the Customs and Excise Management Act 1979"; and

(b) after the words "duty of excise" there shall be inserted the words "for the time being chargeable on goods produced or manufactured in the United Kingdom".

(4) For subsection (3) there shall be substituted the following subsection—

"(3) Section 156 of the Customs and Excise Management Act 1979 shall apply to this Act as it applies to the outlying provisions of the customs and excise Acts within the meaning of that section; and the reference in subsection (2) of that section to Part XI of that Act includes a reference to that Part as applied in relation to penalties under this Act by subsection (1) of this section."

4. In Schedule 2 to the 1963 Act, in paragraph 2 (b) for the words "duties of customs" there shall be substituted the words "duties (whether of customs or excise)".

Finance Act 1964

5. In section 10(2)(b) of the Finance Act 1964—

(a) for the words "subsection (1) above" there shall be substituted the words "section 1(4) of the Customs and Excise Management Act 1979"; and

(b) for the words "section 307 of the Act of 1952" there shall be substituted the words "section 1(1) of that Act".

Finance Act 1967

6. In section 9(1) of the Finance Act 1967 for the words "the Act of 1952" there shall be substituted the words "the Customs and Excise Management Act 1979".

SCHEDULE 6

REPEALS

PART I

ENACTMENTS OF THE PARLIAMENT OF THE UNITED KINGDOM

Chapter	Short Title	Extent of Repeal
15 & 16 Geo. 6 & 1 Eliz. 2. c. 44.	The Customs and Excise Act 1952.	Parts I, II, III, IX, X, XI and XII except the following provisions, that is to say— sections 35 to 37, 41 to 43, 237, 241 to 243, 263(3) to (5), in the proviso to section 271(3), paragraph (i), section 272, so much of section 307(1) as is repealed by the Alcoholic Liquor Duties Act 1979, sections 309(1), (3) and (4) and 310 and section 315(c) and (d). Schedule 7. Schedule 10, except paragraph 15.
1 & 2 Eliz. 2. c. 34.	The Finance Act 1953.	Sections 33(1) and 35(2).
5 & 6 Eliz. 2. c. 49.	The Finance Act 1957.	Sections 5 and 42(2)(a). Schedule 2.
6 & 7 Eliz. 2. c. 11.	The Isle of Man Act 1958.	In section 2(1), the words from "shall not be paid" to "but".
6 & 7 Eliz. 2. c. 56.	The Finance Act 1958.	Section 40(2)(b).
7 & 8 Eliz. 2. c. 58.	The Finance Act 1959.	Section 37(2)(a).
8 & 9 Eliz. 2. c. 44.	The Finance Act 1960.	In section 79, subsections (2) and (3)(a) and, in subsection (6), the words from "or any tobacco dealer's licence" onwards.
9 & 10 Eliz. 2. c. 36.	The Finance Act 1961.	Sections 11 and 37(2).
10 & 11 Eliz. 2. c. 44.	The Finance Act 1962.	In section 34, in subsection (2) the words from "Part I" to " 1952 and ".
10 & 11 Eliz. 2. c. 58.	The Pipe-lines Act 1962.	Section 56.
1963 c. 25.	The Finance Act 1963.	Section 7. In section 73, subsection (3) and, in subsection (4), the words from " Part I " to " 1952 and ".
1964 c. 49.	The Finance Act 1964.	Sections 10(1) and 26(2) and (3).
1966 c. 18.	The Finance Act 1966.	Sections 10 and 11. In Schedule 2, paragraph 1, except the words from ''section 107(1)'' to " spirits) ".

Chapter	Short Title	Extent of Repeal
1967 c. 54.	The Finance Act 1967.	Section 3. In section 4(5), paragraph (*a*)(i) and (v). In section 5, in subsection (1), paragraphs (*a*) and (*b*) and subsection (2). In Schedule 6, paragraphs 5, 6, and 12. In Schedule 9, paragraph 7.
1967 c. 80.	The Criminal Justice Act 1967.	Section 93(4). In section 106(2)(*b*) the words "and (4)".
1968 c. 44.	The Finance Act 1968.	Sections 6 and 61(3).
1968 c. 59.	The Hovercraft Act 1968.	In the Schedule, paragraph 4(*c*).
1969 c. 39.	The Age of Majority (Scotland) Act 1969.	In Schedule 1, the entry relating to the Customs and Excise Act 1952.
1969 c. 46.	The Family Law Reform Act 1969.	In Schedule 1, the entry relating to the Customs and Excise Act 1952.
1970 c. 24.	The Finance Act 1970.	Section 5. Section 7(5) and (8). Section 36(3). In Schedule 2, paragraph 5.
1971 c. 12.	The Hydrocarbon Oil (Customs & Excise) Act 1971.	Section 22. In Schedule 6, paragraph 1.
1971 c. 23.	The Courts Act 1971.	In Schedule 9, the entry relating to the Customs and Excise Act 1952.
1971 c. 38.	The Misuse of Drugs Act 1971.	Section 26.
1971 c. 68.	The Finance Act 1971.	Section 11. In section 69(3), the words from "sections 3" to "1952". Schedule 1.
1972 c. 25.	The Betting and Gaming Duties Act 1972.	In Schedule 2, paragraph 7. In Schedule 4, paragraph 10.
1972 c. 41.	The Finance Act 1972.	Section 17(5). Section 55(4). Section 134(3)(*a*).
1972 c. 68.	The European Communities Act 1972.	Section 5(4) and (7) to (9). In Schedule 4, paragraph 2.
1973 c. 51.	The Finance Act 1973.	Section 2. Section 59(3)(*a*).
1974 c. 30.	The Finance Act 1974.	Section 1(7) and (8). In section 57(3)(*a*), the words from "except so far" to "1952 and".
1975 c. 7.	The Finance Act 1975.	Section 4.
1975 c. 45.	The Finance (No. 2) Act 1975.	Section 1(7) and (8). Sections 8 and 16. In section 75, in subsection (2), the words from "and in Part I" onwards and subsection (3)(*a*).

SCH. 6

Chapter	Short title	Extent of repeal
1975 c. 45. (*cont.*).	The Finance (No. 2) Act 1975.—(*cont.*).	In Schedule 3, paragraphs 1, 14, 23, 39 to 41, 43 and, in paragraph 44, sub-paragraph (*c*). In Schedule 6, paragraphs 1 to 4.
1976 c. 40.	The Finance Act 1976.	Section 15. Section 132(3)(*a*). In Schedule 3, paragraphs 2 to 4 and 6.
1977 c. 36.	The Finance Act 1977.	Sections 8 and 9. In Schedule 6, paragraph 21.
1977 c. 45.	The Criminal Law Act 1977.	In Schedule 5, in paragraph 1, sub-paragraphs (1)(*a*) and (2)(*c*).
1978 c. 42.	The Finance Act 1978.	Sections 3 to 5 and 79. In Schedule 12, paragraphs 7(1), 11 to 14, 16 to 19 (except paragraph 19(7)(*d*)) and 21 to 24.

PART II

ENACTMENTS OF THE PARLIAMENT OF NORTHERN IRELAND

1954 c. 8 (N.I.).	The Excise (Amendment) Act (Northern Ireland) 1954.	Sections 1 and 3.
1969 c. 28 (N.I.).	The Age of Majority Act (Northern Ireland) 1969.	In Schedule 1, the entry relating to the Customs and Excise Act 1952.

Section 177(4).

SCHEDULE 7

SAVING AND TRANSITIONAL PROVISIONS

1952 c. 44.
1970 s. 24.
1972 c. 68.

1. Notwithstanding the repeal by this Act of section 258 of the Customs and Excise Act 1952, of paragraph 5 of Schedule 2 to the Finance Act 1970, and of paragraph 2(8) of Schedule 4 to the European Communities Act 1972, that section (together with Schedule 6) as it had effect immediately before the entry date within the meaning of the said Act of 1972, shall continue to have effect for cases in which the value of goods falls to be determined as at a time before that date.

1972 c. 41.

2. Notwithstanding the repeal by this Act of subsections (2) and (5) of section 283 of the Customs and Excise Act 1952, those subsections shall continue to have effect in relation to offences under Part I of, and paragraph 22 of Schedule 7 to, the Finance Act 1972 ; and, accordingly, in section 38(8) of, and paragraph 22(5) of Schedule 7 to, that Act (as amended by Schedule 4 to this Act) the reference in that section and in that paragraph to sections 145 to 155 of this Act shall be construed as including a reference to the said section 283(2) and (5).

3. Notwithstanding the repeal by this Act of section 308(3) of the Customs and Excise Act 1952, section 277 of the Customs Consolida- tion Act 1876 does not apply in relation to any Act passed after 1st January 1953.

4. Nothing in the repeal by this Act of paragraph 1 of Schedule 3 to the Finance (No. 2) Act 1975 shall affect the operation of section 1(3) of the Isle of Man Act 1958 in relation to provisions which fell to be construed immediately before the commencement of this Act as provided in that paragraph.

5. The repeal by this Act of section 5(4) of the European Com- munities Act 1972 (which, so far as it relates to enactments con- tained in this Act, is re-enacted by section 1(7) of this Act) shall not affect the application of any law not contained in this Act which relates to customs duties.

6. The repeal by this Act of any enactment already repealed by section 75(5) of the Finance (No. 2) Act 1975 and specified in Part I of Schedule 14 to that Act shall not affect the operation of the saving in paragraph 2 in that Part in relation to that enactment.

7. The repeal by this Act of section 8(4) of the Finance (No. 2) Act 1975 and the repeal by any of the Customs and Excise Acts 1979 of any provision of Part I of Schedule 3 to that Act shall not affect the right to any drawback or other relief under any enactment amended by that provision in respect of customs duty charged before the end of 1975.

8. Any such reference as is specified in paragraph 1 of Schedule 3 to the Finance (No. 2) Act 1975 (" customs duty ", " excise duty " and associated references), being a reference in—

(*a*) any instrument of a legislative character made under the customs and excise Acts which was in force at the end of 1975 ; or

(*b*) any local and personal or private Act which was then in force,

shall continue to be construed as provided by that paragraph not- withstanding the repeal of that paragraph by this Act.

9. Any such reference as is specified in sub-paragraph (2), (6) or (8) of paragraph 19 of Schedule 12 to the Finance Act 1978 (" customs Acts ", " excise Acts ", " excise trade ", " excise trader ", " customs airport " and " customs station "), being a reference in—

(*a*) any instrument in force immediately before the commence- ment of this Act ; or

(*b*) any local and personal or private Act then in force,

shall continue to be construed as provided by the said sub-paragraph (2), (6) or (8), as the case may be, notwithstanding the repeal of that sub-paragraph by this Act.

10.—(1) Any provision of this Act relating to anything done or required or authorised to be done under or in pursuance of the

Customs and Excise Acts 1979 shall have effect as if any reference to those Acts included a reference to the Customs and Excise Act 1952.

(2) Any provision of this Act relating to anything done or required or authorised to be done under, in pursuance of or by reference to that provision or any other provision of this Act shall have effect as if any reference to that provision, or that other provision, as the case may be, included a reference to the corresponding provision of the enactments repealed by this Act.

11. Any functions which, immediately before the commencement of this Act, fall to be performed on behalf of any other person by the Commissioners or by officers or by any person appointed by the Commissioners shall continue to be so performed by them unless and until other arrangements are made, notwithstanding that those functions are not expressly mentioned in this Act.

12.—(1) The repeal by this Act of subsection (4) of section 316 of the Customs and Excise Act 1952 shall not affect any such right or privilege as is referred to in that subsection.

(2) Where by any enactment, grant or other instrument, any right or privilege not relating to customs or excise has at any time been granted by reference to the then existing limits of any port or approved wharf appointed or approved for the purposes of customs and excise, then, subject to any provision contained in that instrument, nothing in any order made or other thing done under section 19 or 20 of this Act shall affect that right or privilege.

Customs and Excise Duties (General Reliefs) Act 1979

1979 CHAPTER 3

An Act to consolidate certain enactments relating to reliefs and exemptions from customs and excise duties, section 7 of the Finance Act 1968 and certain other related enactments. [22nd February 1979]

BE IT ENACTED by the Queen's most Excellent Majesty, by and with the advice and consent of the Lords Spiritual and Temporal, and Commons, in this present Parliament assembled, and by the authority of the same, as follows:—

Principal reliefs from customs duties

1.—(1) The Secretary of State may, in accordance with subsections (2) to (6) below, by order provide for relieving goods from the whole or part of any customs duty chargeable on goods imported into the United Kingdom.

(2) Goods of any description may be relieved from customs duty if and in so far as the relief appears to the Secretary of State to be necessary or expedient with a view to—

    (*a*) conforming with any Community obligations ; or

    (*b*) otherwise affording relief provided for by or under the Community Treaties or any decisions of the representatives of the governments of the member States of the Coal and Steel Community meeting in Council.

Reliefs from customs duty for conformity with Community obligations and other international obligations, etc.

(3) Goods of any description may be relieved from customs duty if and in so far as the relief appears to the Secretary of State to be necessary or expedient with a view to conforming with an international agreement relating to matters other than commercial relations.

(4) Exposed cinematograph film may be relieved from customs duty if certified as provided by the order to be of an educational character.

(5) Relief given by virtue of subsection (4) above may be restricted with a view to securing reciprocity in countries or territories outside the United Kingdom.

(6) Articles recorded with sound, other than exposed cinematograph film, may be relieved from customs duty (other than duty chargeable on similar articles not so recorded) if the articles are not produced in quantity for general sale as so recorded.

Reliefs from customs duty referable to Community practices.

2.—(1) The Secretary of State may by regulations make such provision as regards reliefs from customs duty chargeable on goods imported into the United Kingdom as appears to him to be expedient having regard to the practices adopted or to be adopted in other member States, whether by law or administrative action and whether or not for conformity with Community obligations.

(2) Regulations under this section may amend or repeal accordingly any of sections 1, 3, 4 and 15 of this Act.

Power to exempt particular importations of certain goods from customs duty.

3.—(1) Subject to the provisions of this section, the Secretary of State may direct that payment shall not be required of the whole or part of any customs duty which is chargeable on any goods imported or proposed to be imported into the United Kingdom if he is satisfied—

> (a) that the goods qualify for relief under this section ; and
>
> (b) that in all the circumstances it is expedient for the relief to be given.

(2) The following goods qualify for relief under this section, that is to say, articles intended and reasonably required—

> (a) for the purpose of subjecting the articles, or any material or component in the articles, to examination or tests with a view to promoting or improving the manufacture in the United Kingdom of goods similar to those articles or to that material or component, as the case may be ; or

(*b*) for the purpose of subjecting goods capable of use with those or similar articles (including goods which might be used as materials or components in such articles or in which such articles might be used as materials or components) to examination or tests with a view to promoting or improving the manufacture in the United Kingdom of those or similar goods.

(3) Any direction of the Secretary of State under this section may be given subject to such conditions as he thinks fit.

(4) Where a direction given by the Secretary of State under this section is subject to any conditions, and it is proposed to use or dispose of the goods in any manner for which the consent of the Secretary of State is required by the conditions, the Secretary of State may consent to the goods being so used or disposed of subject to payment of the duty which would have been payable but for the direction or such part of the duty as the Secretary of State thinks appropriate in the circumstances.

(5) The Secretary of State shall not give a direction under this section except on a written application made by the importer, and a direction under this section shall have effect to such extent (if any) as the Commissioners may allow if the goods have been released from customs and excise control without the importer having given to the Commissioners notice of the direction or of his application or intention to apply for it.

(6) Any notice to the Commissioners under subsection (5) above shall be in such form as they may require, and the Commissioners on receiving any such notice or at any time afterwards may impose any such conditions as they see fit for the protection of the revenue (including conditions requiring security for the observance of any conditions subject to which relief is granted.

(7) A direction of the Secretary of State under this section shall have effect only if and so long as any conditions of the relief, including any conditions imposed by the Commissioners under subsection (6) above, are complied with; but where any customs duty is paid on the importation of any goods, and the Commissioners are satisfied that by virtue of a direction subsequently given and having effect under this section payment of the duty is not required, then the duty shall be repaid.

4.—(1) The Secretary of State may by order make provision for the administration of any relief under section 1 above or for the implementation or administration of any like relief provided for by any Community instrument.

(2) An order under this section may in particular—

(*a*) impose or authorise the imposition of conditions for securing that goods relieved from duty as being imported for a particular purpose are used for that purpose or such other conditions as appear expedient to secure the object or prevent abuse of the relief ;

(*b*) where the relief is limited to a quota of imported goods, provide for determining the allocation of the quota or for enabling it to be determined by the issue of certificates or licences or otherwise ;

(*c*) confer on a government department or any other authority or person functions in connection with the administration of the relief or the enforcement of any condition of relief ;

(*d*) authorise any government department having any such functions to make payments (whether for remuneration or for expenses) to persons advising the department or otherwise acting in the administration of the relief ;

(*e*) require the payment of fees by persons applying for the relief or applying for the registration of any person or premises in connection with the relief ;

(*f*) authorise articles for which relief is claimed to be sold or otherwise disposed of if the relief is not allowed and duty is not paid.

(3) Any expenses incurred by a government department by virtue of any order under this section shall be defrayed out of money provided by Parliament, and any fees received by a government department by virtue of any such order shall be paid into the Consolidated Fund.

Reliefs from duties for Channel Islands or Isle of Man goods

5.—(1) Subject to subsection (2) below, any goods which are the produce or growth of any of the Channel Islands or which have been manufactured in any of those islands from—

(*a*) materials which are such produce or growth ; or

(*b*) materials not chargeable with any duty in the United Kingdom ; or

(*c*) materials so chargeable upon which that duty has been paid and not drawn back,

may be imported without payment of any customs duty chargeable thereon.

(2) Subsection (1) above shall not apply in relation to any goods unless the master of the ship or commander of the aircraft in which the goods are imported produces to the proper officer at the place of importation a certificate from the Lieutenant-Governor or other proper authority of the island from which the goods are imported that a declaration in such form and containing such particulars as the Commissioners may direct has been made before a magistrate of that island by the person exporting the goods therefrom that the goods are goods to which this section applies.

(3) Directions under subsection (2) above may make different provision for different circumstances and may be varied or revoked by subsequent directions thereunder.

6.—(1) Without prejudice to section 174(1) of the Customs and Excise Management Act 1979 but subject to the provisions of this section, goods removed into the United Kingdom from the Isle of Man shall be deemed, for the purposes of any charge of duty on goods imported into the United Kingdom, not to be imported.

Relief from duty of certain goods from Isle of Man and supplementary provisions.
1979 c. 2.

(2) Where in the case of any goods which are the produce or growth of the Isle of Man, or which have been manufactured in that island from materials which are such produce or growth, a duty of excise is chargeable on like goods or materials manufactured or produced in the United Kingdom, a like duty of excise shall be payable on the removal of those goods into the United Kingdom from the Isle of Man.

(3) Any goods manufactured in the Isle of Man wholly or partly from imported materials, being materials—

> (a) which, if they had been imported into the United Kingdom, would have been chargeable with customs or excise duty ; and

> (b) which on their importation into the Isle of Man either were not charged with customs or excise duty or were charged with a lower amount by way of customs or excise duty than would have been payable on their importation into the United Kingdom,

shall on their removal into the United Kingdom from the Isle of Man be chargeable with customs or excise duty as if they were being imported.

(4) Schedule 1 to this Act shall have effect for the purpose of restricting the removal into the United Kingdom of certain dutiable goods imported into or removed to the Isle of Man.

Miscellaneous reliefs from customs and excise duties

Relief from
customs or
excise duty on
imported
legacies.

7. Where it is shown to the satisfaction of the Commissioners that—

(*a*) any imported goods were chattels or corporeal moveables belonging to or in the possession of a deceased person which had been used before his death and were not at the time of his death used or held by him for business purposes ; and

(*b*) the importation thereof is by or for a person resident in the United Kingdom who upon that death becomes entitled thereto bv virtue of anv testamentary disposition or intestacy,

the Commissioners may remit or repay any customs or excise duty which would otherwise be payable or which has been paid on the importation thereof.

Relief from
customs or
excise duty on
trade samples,
labels, etc.

8. The Commissioners may allow the delivery without payment of customs or excise duty on importation, subject to such conditions and restrictions as they see fit—

(*a*) of trade samples of such goods as they see fit, whether imported as samples or drawn from the goods on their importation :

(*b*) of labels or other articles supplied without charge for the purpose of being re-exported with goods manufactured or produced in, and to be exported from, the United Kingdom.

Relief from
customs or
excise duty on
antiques,
prizes, etc.

9. The Commissioners may allow the delivery without payment of customs or excise duty on importation—

(*a*) of any goods (other than spirits or wine) which are proved to the satisfaction of the Commissioners to have been manufactured or produced more than 100 years before the date of importation ;

(*b*) of articles which are shown to the satisfaction of the Commissioners to have been awarded abroad to any person for distinction in art, literature, science or sport, or for public service, or otherwise as a record of meritorious achievement or conduct, and to be imported by or on behalf of that person.

Reliefs from excise duties

Relief from
excise duty on
certain United
Kingdom
goods
re-imported.

10.—(1) Without prejudice to any other enactment relating to excise, the following provisions of this section shall have effect in relation to goods manufactured or produced in the United Kingdom which are re-imported into the United Kingdom after exportation therefrom.

(2) If the goods are at the date of their re-importation excise goods, they may on re-importation be delivered for home use without payment of excise duty if it is shown to the satisfaction of the Commissioners—

(a) that at the date of their exportation the goods were not excise goods or, if they were then excise goods, that the excise duty had been paid before their exportation ; and

(b) that no drawback in respect of the excise duty and no allowance has been paid on their exportation or that any such drawback or allowance so paid has been repaid to the Consolidated Fund ; and

(c) that the goods have not undergone any process outside the United Kingdom since their exportation.

(3) If the goods both are at the date of their re-importation and were at the date of their exportation excise goods, but they were exported without the excise duty having been paid from a warehouse or from the place where they were manufactured or produced, then, where the following conditions are satisfied, that is to say—

(a) it is shown to the satisfaction of the Commissioners that they have not undergone any process outside the United Kingdom since their exportation ; and

(b) any allowance paid on their exportation is repaid to the Consolidated Fund,

the goods may on their re-importation, subject to such conditions and restrictions as the Commissioners may impose, be entered and removed without payment of excise duty for re-warehousing or for return to the place where they were manufactured or produced, as the case may be.

(4) Nothing in this section shall authorise the delivery for home use of any goods not otherwise eligible therefor.

(5) In this section—

" excise goods " means goods—

(a) of a class or description chargeable at the time in question with a duty of excise ; or

(b) in the manufacture or preparation of which any goods of such a class or description have been used ;

" the excise duty " means the duty by virtue of which the goods are or were at the time in question excise goods.

Relief from
excise duty on
certain foreign
goods
re-imported.

11.—(1) Without prejudice to any other enactment relating to excise but subject to subsection (2) below, goods manufactured or produced outside the United Kingdom which are re-imported into the United Kingdom after exportation therefrom may on their re-importation be delivered without payment of excise duty for home use, where so eligible, if it is shown to the satisfaction of the Commissioners—

(*a*) that no excise duty was chargeable thereon at their previous importation or that any excise duty so chargeable was then paid ; and

(*b*) that no drawback has been paid or excise duty refunded on their exportation or that any drawback so paid or excise duty so refunded has been repaid to the Consolidated Fund ; and

(*c*) that the goods have not undergone any process outside the United Kingdom since their exportation.

(2) For the purposes of this section goods which on their previous importation were entered for transit or transhipment or were permitted to be delivered without payment of excise duty as being imported only temporarily with a view to subsequent re-exportation and which were re-exported accordingly shall on their re-importation be deemed not to have been previously imported.

Relief for goods for Her Majesty's ships

Supply of
duty-free
goods to
Her Majesty's
ships.

12.—(1) The Treasury may by regulations provide that, subject to any prescribed conditions, goods of any description specified in the regulations which are supplied either—

(*a*) to any ship of the Royal Navy in commission of a description so specified, for the use of persons serving in that ship, being persons borne on the books of that or some other ship of the Royal Navy or a naval establishment ; or

(*b*) to the Secretary of State, for the use of persons serving in ships of the Royal Navy or naval establishments,

shall for all or any purposes of any excise duty or drawback in respect of those goods be treated as exported, and a person supplying or intending to supply goods as mentioned in paragraph (*a*) or (*b*) above shall be treated accordingly as exporting or intending to export them.

(2) Regulations made under this section with respect to goods of any description may regulate or provide for regulating the quantity allowed to any ship or establishment, the manner in which they are to be obtained and their use or distribution.

(3) The regulations may—

(*a*) contain such other incidental or supplementary provisions as appear to the Treasury to be necessary for the purposes of this section, including any adaptations of the customs and excise Acts ; and

(*b*) make different provision in relation to different cases, and in particular in relation to different classes or descriptions of goods or of ships or establishments.

(4) In subsection (1) above " prescribed " means prescribed by regulations under this section or, in pursuance of any such regulations, by the Commissioners after consultation with the Secretary of State.

(5) Before making any regulations under this section, the Treasury shall consult with the Secretary of State and with the Commissioners.

(6) The powers conferred by this section shall apply for the purposes of customs duty as they apply for the purposes of excise duty but shall not so apply after such day as the Commissioners may by order appoint.

Personal reliefs

13.—(1) The Commissioners may by order make provision for conferring on persons entering the United Kingdom reliefs from duty and value added tax ; and any such relief may take the form either of an exemption from payment of duty and tax or of a provision whereby the sum payable by way of duty or tax is less than it would otherwise be.

Power to provide, in relation to persons entering the United Kingdom, for reliefs from duty and value added tax and for simplified computation of duty and tax.

(2) Without prejudice to subsection (1) above, the Commissioners may by order make provision whereby, in such cases and to such extent as may be specified in the order, a sum calculated at a rate specified in the order is treated as the aggregate amount payable by way of duty and tax in respect of goods imported by a person entering the United Kingdom ; but any order making such provision shall enable the person concerned to elect that duty and tax shall be charged on the goods in question at the rate which would be applicable apart from that provision.

(3) An order under this section—

(*a*) may make any relief for which it provides subject to conditions, including conditions which are to be complied with after the importation of the goods to which the relief applies ;

(*b*) may contain such incidental and supplementary provisions as the Commissioners think necessary or expedient, including provisions for the forfeiture of goods in the event of non-compliance with any condition subject to which they have been relieved from duty or tax ; and

(*c*) may make different provision for different cases.

(4) In this section—

" duty " means customs or excise duty chargeable on goods imported into the United Kingdom and, in the case of excise duty, includes any addition thereto by virtue of section 1 of the Excise Duties (Surcharges or Rebates) Act 1979 ; and

1979 c. 8.

" value added tax " or " tax " means value added tax chargeable on the importation of goods.

(5) Nothing in any order under this section shall be construed as authorising any person to import any thing in contravention of any prohibition or restriction for the time being in force with respect thereto under or by virtue of any enactment.

Produce of the sea or continental shelf

Produce of the sea or continental shelf.

14.—(1) Fish, whales or other natural produce of the sea, or goods produced or manufactured therefrom at sea, if brought direct to the United Kingdom, shall—

(a) in the case of goods which, under any enactment or instrument having the force of law, are to be treated as originating in the United Kingdom, be deemed for the purposes of any charge to customs duty not to be imported ; and

(b) in the case of goods which, under any enactment or instrument having the force of law, are to be treated as originating in any other country or territory, be deemed to be consigned to the United Kingdom from that country.

(2) Any goods brought into the United Kingdom which are shown to the satisfaction of the Commissioners to have been grown, produced or manufactured in any area for the time being designated under section 1(7) of the Continental Shelf Act 1964 and to have been so brought direct from that area shall be deemed for the purposes of any charge to customs duty not to be imported.

1964 c. 29.

(3) The Secretary of State may by regulations prescribe cases in which, with a view to exempting any goods from any duty, or charging any goods with duty at a reduced or preferential rate, under any of the enactments relating to duties of customs the continental shelf of any country prescribed by the regulations, or of any country of a class of countries so prescribed, shall be treated for the purposes of such of those enactments or of any instruments made thereunder as may be so prescribed as if that shelf formed part of that country and any goods brought from that shelf were consigned from that country.

(4) In subsection (3) above "continental shelf", in relation to any country means—

   (a) if that country is the United Kingdom, any area for the time being designated under section 1(7) of the Continental Shelf Act 1964 ; 1964 c. 29.

   (b) in any other case, the seabed and sub-soil of the submarine areas adjacent to the coast, but outside the seaward limits of the territorial waters, of that country over which the exercise by that country of sovereign rights in accordance with international law is recognised or authorised by Her Majesty's Government in the United Kingdom.

False statements etc. in connection with reliefs from customs duties

15.—(1) If a person— False statements etc. in connection with reliefs from customs duties.

   (a) for the purpose of an application for relief from customs duty under section 1 or 3 above or under a Community instrument ; or

   (b) for the purpose of an application for an authorisation under regulations made under section 2 above,

makes any statement or furnishes any document which is false in a material particular to any government department or to any authority or person on whom functions are conferred by or under section 1, 3 or 4 above or a Community instrument, then—

   (i) any decision allowing the relief or granting the authorisation applied for shall be of no effect ; and

   (ii) if the statement was made or the document was furnished knowingly or recklessly, that person shall be guilty of an offence under this section.

(2) A person guilty of an offence under this section shall be liable—

   (a) on summary conviction, to a fine not exceeding the prescribed sum, or to imprisonment for a term not exceeding 3 months, or to both ; or

   (b) on conviction on indictment, to a fine of any amount or to imprisonment for a term not exceeding 2 years, or to both.

(3) In subsection (2)(a) above " the prescribed sum " means—

   (a) if the offence was committed in England, Wales or Northern Ireland, the prescribed sum within the meaning of section 28 of the Criminal Law Act 1977 (£1,000 or other sum substituted by order under section 61(1) of that Act) ; 1977 c. 45.

(*b*) if the offence was committed in Scotland, the prescribed sum within the meaning of section 289B of the Criminal Procedure (Scotland) Act 1975 (£1,000 or other sum substituted by order under section 289D(1) of that Act).

(4) References in Parts XI and XII of the Customs and Excise Management Act 1979 to an offence under the customs and excise Acts shall not apply to an offence under this section.

Supplementary provisions

16. As soon as may be after the end of each financial year the Secretary of State shall lay before each House of Parliament a report on the exercise during that year of the powers conferred by sections 1, 3 and 4 above with respect to the allowance of exemptions and reliefs from customs duties (including the power to amend or revoke orders providing for any exemption or relief from customs duties).

17.—(1) Any power to make orders or regulations under this Act shall be exercisable by statutory instrument.

(2) Any statutory instrument containing regulations under section 2 or 12 above shall be subject to annulment in pursuance of a resolution of either House of Parliament except where, in the case of regulations under section 2, a draft of the regulations has been approved by resolution of each House of Parliament.

(3) Any statutory instrument containing an order under section 1, 4 or 13 above or regulations under section 14(3) above shall be subject to annulment in pursuance of a resolution of the House of Commons except in a case falling within subsection (4) below.

(4) Subject to subsection (5) below, where an order under section 1, 4 or 13 above restricts any relief from duty or tax the statutory instrument containing the order shall be laid before the House of Commons after being made and, unless the order is approved by that House before the end of the period of 28 days beginning with the day on which it was made, it shall cease to have effect at the end of that period but without prejudice to anything previously done under the order or to the making of a new order.

In reckoning the said period of 28 days no account shall be taken of any time during which Parliament is dissolved or prorogued or during which the House of Commons is adjourned for more than 4 days.

(5) Subsection (4) above does not apply in the case of an instrument containing an order under section 1 or 4 above which states that it does not restrict any relief otherwise than in pursuance of a Community obligation.

(6) For the purposes of this section restricting any relief includes removing or reducing any relief previously conferred.

18.—(1) This Act and the other Acts included in the Customs and Excise Acts 1979 shall be construed as one Act but where a provision of this Act refers to this Act that reference is not to be construed as including a reference to any of the others.

Interpretation.

(2) Any expression used in this Act or in any instrument made under this Act to which a meaning is given by any other Act included in the Customs and Excise Acts 1979 has, except where the context otherwise requires, the same meaning in this Act or in any such instrument as in that Act; and for ease of reference the Table below indicates the expressions used in this Act to which a meaning is given by any other such Act—

Customs and Excise Management Act 1979
" the Commissioners "
" the Customs and Excise Acts 1979 "
" the customs and excise Acts "
" customs and excise airport "
" goods "
" hovercraft "
" importer "
" master "
" officer " and " proper " in relation to an officer
" port "
" ship "
" transit and transhipment "
" warehouse "

Alcoholic Liquor Duties Act 1979
" spirits "
" wine "

(3) This Act applies as if references to ships included references to hovercraft.

19.—(1) The enactments specified in Schedule 2 to this Act shall be amended in accordance with the provisions of that Schedule.

Consequential amendments, repeals and transitional provision.

(2) The enactments specified in Part I of Schedule 3 to this Act are hereby repealed to the extent specified in the third column of that Schedule and the regulations specified in Part II of that Schedule are hereby revoked to the extent so specified.

(3) References to import duties in instruments in force at the commencement of this Act shall, on and after that commencement, be construed—

1958 c. 6.

1972 c. 68.

(*a*) in the case of references in orders under section 5 or directions under section 6 of the Import Duties Act 1958, as references to customs duties charged under section 5(1) or (2) of the European Communities Act 1972 ;

(*b*) in the case of references in such orders or directions made by virtue of section 5(1A) of the said Act of 1958 or in regulations under section 5(6) of the European Communities Act 1972, as references to customs duties (whether so charged or charged under the

1969 c. 16.

1978 c. 42.

Customs Duties (Dumping and Subsidies) Act 1969 or section 6(1) of the Finance Act 1978).

Citation and commence-ment.

20.—(1) This Act may be cited as the Customs and Excise Duties (General Reliefs) Act 1979 and is included in the Acts which may be cited as the Customs and Excise Acts 1979.

(2) This Act shall come into operation on 1st April 1979.

SCHEDULES

SCHEDULE 1

Section 6(4).

RESTRICTIONS ON REMOVAL OF GOODS INTO UNITED KINGDOM FROM
ISLE OF MAN

1. Where any goods which, if they were imported into the United
Kingdom, would be chargeable with customs or excise duty are
imported into the Isle of Man and on that importation either are
not charged with any customs or excise duty or are charged with a
lower amount by way of customs or excise duty than would have
been payable on their importation into the United Kingdom, then—

  (*a*) if the goods are cleared out of charge in the Isle of Man
       for home use or to be dealt with in any other manner in
       the Isle of Man, they shall not thereafter be removed into
       the United Kingdom ;

  (*b*) in any other case, the goods shall not be removed from the
       Isle of Man into the United Kingdom until they have been
       cleared for that purpose by the proper officer and, except in
       the case of goods reported on arrival for removal into the
       United Kingdom in the same ship or aircraft and in con-
       tinuance of the same voyage or flight, until security has
       been given to the satisfaction of the Commissioners for the
       due delivery thereof at some port or customs and excise
       airport in the United Kingdom.

2. Where any goods—

  (*a*) manufactured or produced in the United Kingdom and
       chargeable with a duty of excise on being so manufactured
       or produced or on being sent out from the premises of the
       manufacturer ; or

  (*b*) imported into the United Kingdom and chargeable on that
       importation with a duty of customs or excise,

have been removed from the United Kingdom into the Isle of Man
without payment of that duty or on drawback of the excise duty,
then, save with the permission of the Commissioners and subject
to such conditions as they see fit to impose, neither those goods
nor any other goods in the manufacture or preparation of which
those goods have been used shall thereafter be removed from the
Isle of Man into the United Kingdom.

3. Any goods removed into the United Kingdom contrary to paragraph 1 or 2 above shall be liable to forfeiture, and any person
concerned in the removal of the goods shall be liable on summary
conviction to a penalty of three times the value of the goods or £100,
whichever is the greater.

SCHEDULE 2

CONSEQUENTIAL AMENDMENTS

Agriculture and Horticulture Act 1964

1. At the end of paragraph 1(2) of the Schedule to the Agriculture and Horticulture Act 1964 there shall be added the words " nor the operation of sections 1 to 4 and 14 to 16 of the Customs and Excise Duties (General Reliefs) Act 1979 ".

Finance Act 1972

2. In section 17 of the Finance Act 1972, after the subsection (2)
inserted by paragraph 10 of Schedule 4 to the Customs and Excise Management Act 1979 there shall be inserted the following subsection—

" (2A) The provisions of the Customs and Excise Duties (General Reliefs) Act 1979 other than sections 7, 8 and 9(*b*) (various reliefs for imported goods other than legacies, trade samples and prizes) shall also be excepted from the enactments which are to have effect as mentioned in subsection (1) of this section."

European Communities Act 1972

3. For section 5(3) of the European Communities Act 1972 (in this Schedule referred to as " the Act of 1972 ") there shall be substituted the following subsection—

" (3) Schedule 2 to this Act shall also have effect in connection with the powers to make orders conferred by subsections (1) and (2) above.".

4. In section 6(5) of the Act of 1972, for paragraph (*b*), there shall be substituted the following paragraph—

" (*b*) sections 1, 3, 4, 5, 6 (including Schedule 1), 7, 8, 9, 12, 13, 15, 17 and 18 of the Customs and Excise Duties (General Reliefs) Act 1979 but so that—

(i) any references in sections 1, 3 and 4 to the Secretary of State shall include the Ministers ; and

(ii) the reference in section 15 to an application for an authorisation under regulations made under section 2 of that Act shall be read as a reference to an application for an authorisation under regulations made under section 2(2) of this Act ; ".

5. In Schedule 2 to the Act of 1972 there shall be added at the end the following paragraphs—

" 4.—(1) The power to make orders under section 5(1) or (2) of this Act shall be exercisable in accordance with the following provisions of this paragraph.

(2) The power to make such orders shall be exercisable by statutory instrument and includes power to amend or revoke any such order made in the exercise of that power.

(3) Any statutory instrument containing any such order shall be subject to annulment in pursuance of a resolution of the House of Commons except in a case falling within sub-paragraph (4) below.

(4) Subject to sub-paragraph (6) below, where an order imposes or increases any customs duty, or restricts any relief from customs duty under the said section 5, the statutory instrument containing the order shall be laid before the House of Commons after being made and, unless the order is approved by that House before the end of the period of 28 days beginning with the day on which it was made, it shall cease to have effect at the end of that period, but without prejudice to anything previously done under the order or to the making of a new order.

In reckoning the said period of 28 days no account shall be taken of any time during which Parliament is dissolved or prorogued or during which the House of Commons is adjourned for more than 4 days.

(5) Where an order has the effect of altering the rate of duty on any goods in such a way that the new rate is not directly comparable with the old, it shall not be treated for the purposes of sub-paragraph (4) above as increasing the duty on those goods if it declares the opinion of the Treasury to be that, in the circumstances existing at the date of the order, the alteration is not calculated to raise the general level of duty on the goods.

(6) Sub-paragraph (4) above does not apply in the case of an instrument containing an order which states that it does not impose or increase any customs duty or restrict any relief from customs duty otherwise than in pursuance of a Community obligation.

5. As soon as may be after the end of each financial year the Secretary of State shall lay before each House of Parliament a report on the exercise during that year of the powers conferred by section 5(1) and (2) of this Act with respect to the imposition of customs duties and the allowance of exemptions and reliefs from duties so imposed (including the power to amend or revoke orders imposing customs duties or providing for any exemption or relief from duties so imposed).".

Finance Act 1977

6. In section 10(4) of the Finance Act 1977, for the words "those sections" there shall be substituted the words "the said section 6"

1977 c. 36.

SCHEDULE 3
REPEALS AND REVOCATIONS
PART I
ENACTMENTS REPEALED

Chapter	Short Title	Extent of Repeal
15 & 16 Geo. 6 & 1 Eliz. 2. c. 44.	The Customs and Excise Act 1952.	Sections 35 to 37 and 41 to 43. Section 272. Sections 309(1), (3) and (4) and 310.
6 & 7 Eliz. 2. c. 6.	The Import Duties Act 1958.	Sections 4, 5 and 6. Section 10(1). Sections 12(4) and 13. Sections 15 and 16. In Schedule 3, paragraphs 4, 5 and 8. In Schedule 4, paragraph 2.
8 & 9 Eliz. 2. c. 44.	The Finance Act 1960.	Section 10(1).
1967 c. 54.	The Finance Act 1967.	Section 2.
1968 c. 44.	The Finance Act 1968.	Section 7.
1969 c. 32.	The Finance Act 1969.	Section 54.
1972 c. 41.	The Finance Act 1972.	Section 55(2) and (3).
1972 c. 68.	The European Communities Act 1972.	In section 5, subsections (5), (6) and (6A). In Schedule 4, paragraph 1.
1975 c. 45.	The Finance (No. 2) Act 1975.	In Schedule 3, paragraphs 10, 11 and 13.
1977 c. 36.	The Finance Act 1977.	Section 12.
1978 c. 42.	The Finance Act 1978.	Section 6(8). In Schedule 12, paragraphs 9, 10, 15, 19(7)(*d*), 20, 25 and 26.

PART II
REGULATIONS REVOKED

Year and Number	Title	Extent of Revocation
1976/2130.	The Customs Duties (ECSC) Relief Regulations 1976.	All the regulations.
1977/910.	The Inward Processing Relief Regulations 1977.	Regulation 7(1).
1977/1785.	The Customs and Excise (Relief for Returned Goods) Regulations 1977.	All the regulations.
1978/1148.	The Customs Duties (Inward and Outward Processing Relief) Regulations 1978.	Regulation 2.

Alcoholic Liquor Duties Act 1979

1979 CHAPTER 4

An Act to consolidate the enactments relating to the excise duties on spirits, beer, wine, made-wine and cider together with certain other enactments relating to excise.   [22nd February 1979]

BE IT ENACTED by the Queen's most Excellent Majesty, by and with the advice and consent of the Lords Spiritual and Temporal, and Commons, in this present Parliament assembled, and by the authority of the same, as follows:—

PART I

PRELIMINARY

1.—(1) Subsections (2) to (8) below define for the purposes of this Act the alcoholic liquors which are subject to excise duty under this Act, that is to say—

    (*a*) spirits,

    (*b*) beer,

    (*c*) wine,

    (*d*) made-wine, and

    (*e*) cider ;

and in this Act " dutiable alcoholic liquor " means any of those liquors and " duty " means excise duty.

(2) " Spirits " means, subject to subsections (7) and (8) below, spirits of any description and includes all liquors mixed with spirits and all mixtures, compounds or preparations made with spirits but does not include methylated spirits.

(3) " Beer " includes ale, porter, stout and any other description of beer, and any liquor which is made or sold as a description of beer or as a substitute for beer and which on analysis

The alcoholic liquors dutiable under this Act.

F3

PART I of a sample thereof at any time is found to be of a strength exceeding 2° of proof, but does not include—

    (a) black beer the worts whereof before fermentation were of a specific gravity of 1200° or more ; or

    (b) liquor made elsewhere than upon the licensed premises of a brewer for sale which on analysis of a sample at any time is found to be of an original gravity not exceeding 1016° and to be of a strength not exceeding 2° of proof.

(4) " Wine " means any liquor obtained from the alcoholic fermentation of fresh grapes or of the must of fresh grapes, whether or not the liquor is fortified with spirits or flavoured with aromatic extracts.

(5) " Made-wine " means any liquor obtained from the alcoholic fermentation of any substance or by mixing a liquor so obtained or derived from a liquor so obtained with any other liquor or substance but does not include wine, beer, black beer, spirits or cider.

(6) " Cider " means cider (or perry) of a strength less than 8·7 per cent. of alcohol by volume (at a temperature of 20°C) obtained from the fermentation of apple or pear juice without the addition at any time of any alcoholic liquor or of any liquor or substance which communicates colour or flavour other than such as the Commissioners may allow as appearing to them to be necessary to make cider (or perry).

(7) Angostura bitters, that is to say, the aromatic flavouring essence commonly known as angostura bitters, shall be deemed not to be spirits, but this subsection does not apply for the purposes of sections 2, 5, 6 and 27 to 30 below.

(8) Methyl alcohol, notwithstanding that it is so purified or prepared as to be drinkable, shall not be deemed to be spirits nor shall naptha or any mixture or preparation containing naphtha or methyl alcohol and not containing spirits as defined in subsection (2) above.

Ascertainment of strength, weight and volume of spirits and other liquors. **2.**—(1) For the purposes of the Customs and Excise Acts 1979, the strength, weight or volume of any spirits shall be ascertained in accordance with the following provisions of this section.

(2) Spirits shall be deemed to be at proof if the volume of the ethyl alcohol contained therein made up to the volume of the spirits with distilled water has a weight equal to that of twelve-thirteenths of a volume of distilled water equal to the volume of the spirits, the volume of each liquid being computed as at 51°F.

(3) " Degree of proof ", " degree over proof " and " degree under proof " shall be construed by reference to a scale on which 100° denotes the strength of spirits at proof and—

(a) 101°, or 1 degree over proof, denotes the strength of spirits which would be at proof if there were added thereto such quantity of distilled water as would increase by 1 per cent. the volume of the spirits computed as at 50°F ;

(b) 99°, or 1 degree under proof, denotes the strength of spirits which would be at proof if there were removed therefrom such quantity of distilled water as would reduce by 1 per cent. the volume of the spirits computed as at 50°F ;

and so in proportion for any other number of degrees.

(4) The equivalent at proof of any spirits not at proof shall for the purposes of the Customs and Excise Acts 1979 be deemed to be their volume—

(a) multiplied by the number of degrees of proof representing their strength ; and

(b) divided by 100.

(5) The Commissioners may make regulations prescribing the means to be used for ascertaining for any purpose the strength, weight or volume of spirits, and any such regulations may provide that in ascertaining for any purpose the strength of any spirits any substance contained therein which is not ethyl alcohol or distilled water may be treated as if it were.

(6) Different regulations may be made under subsection (5) above for different purposes.

(7) This section shall apply to methylated spirits and to any fermented liquor as it applies to spirits but, in relation to wine, made-wine or cider shall not apply so as to prevent the strength, weight or volume of wine, made-wine or cider from being ascertained for the purpose of charging duty thereon by methods other than that provided in this section.

3.—(1) For the purposes of the Customs and Excise Acts 1979—

Meaning of and method of ascertaining gravity of liquids.

(a) " gravity ", in relation to any liquid, means the ratio of the weight of a volume of the liquid to the weight of an equal volume of distilled water, the volume of each liquid being computed as at 60°F ;

(b) where the gravity of any liquid is expressed as a number of degrees that number shall be the said ratio multiplied by 1,000 ; and (*c*) " original gravity ", in relation to any liquid in which fermentation has taken place, means its gravity before fermentation.

(2) The gravity of any liquid at any time shall be ascertained by such means as the Commissioners may approve, and the gravity so ascertained shall be deemed to be the true gravity of the liquid.

(3) Subject to subsection (5) below, where for any purposes of the Customs and Excise Acts 1979 it is necessary to ascertain the original gravity of worts in which fermentation has commenced or of any liquid produced from such worts, that gravity shall be determined in such manner as the Commissioners may by regulations prescribe.

(4) Different regulations may be made under subsection (3) above in relation to different liquids.

(5) Where the original gravity of any worts has been determined in accordance with regulations made under subsection (3) above for the purpose of charging duty under section 38 below by reference to the quantity and original gravity of worts produced, a deduction of $\frac{3}{4}°$ shall be allowed from the original gravity so determined, so however as not to reduce the original gravity by reference to which the duty is charged below the gravity of the worts as ascertained by the proper officer in accordance with subsection (2) above.

Interpretation. **4.**—(1) In this Act, unless the context otherwise requires,—
" authorised methylator " means a person authorised to methylate spirits under section 75(1) below ;
" beer " has the meaning given by section 1 above ;
" black beer " means beer of the description called or similar to black beer, mum, spruce beer or Berlin white beer, and any other preparation (whether fermented or not) of a similar character ;
" brewer " and " brewer for sale " have the meanings given by section 47 below ;
" British compounded spirits " means spirits which have, in the United Kingdom, had any flavour communicated thereto or ingredient or material mixed therewith, not being methylated spirits ;
" case ", in relation to dutiable alcoholic liquor, means 1 dozen units each consisting of a container holding not less than 23 nor more than 28 fluid ounces, or the equivalent of that number of such units made up wholly or partly of containers of a larger or smaller size ;
" cider " has the meaning given by section 1 above ;

" compounder " means a person holding a licence as a compounder under section 18 below ;

" distiller ", means a person holding a distiller's licence under section 12 below ;

" distiller's licence " has the meaning given by section 12(1) below ;

" distiller's warehouse " means a place of security provided by a distiller and approved by the Commissioners under section 15(1) below ;

" distillery " means premises where spirits are manufactured, whether by distillation of a fermented liquor or by any other process ;

" dutiable alcoholic liquor " has the meaning given by section 1(1) above ;

" duty " has the meaning given by section 1(1) above and " duty-paid ", " duty-free " and references to drawback shall be construed accordingly ;

" gravity " and " original gravity " have the meanings given by section 3 above ;

" justices' licence " and " justices on-licence "—

    (*a*) in the application of this Act to England and 1964 c. 26. Wales have the meanings respectively given to them by sections 1(1) and 1(2)(*a*) of the Licensing Act 1964 and in both cases include a canteen licence granted under Part X and an occasional licence granted under section 180 of that Act ;

    (*b*) in the application of this Act to Northern Ireland mean a licence corresponding to the relevant licence such as is mentioned in paragraph (*a*) of this definition ;

" licensed ", in relation to a producer of wine or of made-wine, means a producer who holds a licence to produce wine or made-wine respectively under subsection (2) of section 54 or 55 below ;

" licensed methylator " means a person holding a licence under section 75(2) below ;

" limited licence to brew beer " has the meaning given by section 47(2) below ;

" made-wine " has the meaning given by section 1 above ;

" the Management Act " means the Customs and Excise 1979 c. 2. Management Act 1979 ;

" methylated spirits " means spirits mixed in the United Kingdom with some other substance in accordance with regulations made under section 77 below :

" the prescribed sum ", in relation to the penalty provided for an offence, means—

    (a) if the offence was committed in England or Wales or in Northern Ireland, the prescribed sum within the meaning of section 28 of the Criminal Law Act 1977 (£1,000 or other sum substituted by order under section 61(1) of that Act) ;

    (b) if the offence was committed in Scotland, the prescribed sum within the meaning of section 289B of the Criminal Procedure (Scotland) Act 1975 (£1,000 or other sum substituted by order under section 289D(1) of that Act) ;

" producer of made-wine " includes a person who renders made-wine sparkling, and " produce ", in relation to made-wine, shall be construed accordingly ;

" producer of wine " includes a person who renders wine sparkling, and " produce ", in relation to wine, shall be construed accordingly ;

" proof ", in relation to the strength of spirits, has the meaning given by section 2 above ;

" rectifier " means a person holding a licence as a rectifier under section 18 below ;

" registered club " means a club which is for the time being registered within the meaning of the Licensing Act 1964 or which is for the time being a registered club within the meaning of the Licensing (Scotland) Act 1976 or which is for the time being a registered club within the meaning of the Registration of Clubs Act (Northern Ireland) 1967 ;

" retailer " means—

    (a) in relation to dutiable alcoholic liquor, a person who sells such liquor by retail ;

    (b) in relation to methylated spirits, a person holding a licence under section 76 below ;

" Scottish licence " includes a licence of a type described in Schedule 1 to the Licensing (Scotland) Act 1976, (other than an off-sale licence), an occasional licence granted in terms of section 33 of the said Act, an occasional permission granted in terms of section 34 of the said Act, and a licence granted in terms of section 40 of the said Act ;

" spirits " has the meaning given by section 1 above ;

" spirits advice note " and " spirits consignment note " have the meanings given by section 27(5) below ;

" spirits of wine " means plain spirits of a strength of not less than 43° over proof manufactured in the United Kingdom ;

" wholesale ", in relation to dealing in dutiable alcoholic liquor, has the meaning given by section 65(8) below ;

" wholesaler " means a person holding a licence under section 65 below ;

" wine " has the meaning given by section 1 above.

(2) This Act and the other Acts included in the Customs and Excise Acts 1979 shall be construed as one Act but where a provision of this Act refers to this Act that reference is not to be construed as including a reference to any of the others.

(3) Any expression used in this Act or in any instrument made under this Act to which a meaning is given by any other Act included in the Customs and Excise Acts 1979 has, except where the context otherwise requires, the same meaning in this Act or in any such instrument as in that Act ; and for ease of reference the Table below indicates the expressions used in this Act to which a meaning is given by any other such Act—

Management Act

" the Commissioners "
" container "
" the Customs and Excise Acts 1979 "
" excise warehouse "
" goods "
" hovercraft "
" importer "
" licence year "
" nautical mile "
" night "
" occupier "
" officer " and " proper " in relation to an officer
" ship " and " British ship "
" shipped "
" shipment "
" stores "
" tons register "
" warehouse "
" warehousing regulations ".

(4) For the purposes of this Act, selling by retail, in relation to dutiable alcoholic liquor, means the sale at any one time to any one person of quantities not exceeding the following, that is to say—

(*a*) in the case of spirits, wine or made-wine, 2 gallons or 1 case ;

(*b*) in the case of beer or cider, 4½ gallons or 2 cases.

PART II

SPIRITS

Charge of excise duty

5. There shall be charged on spirits—

(*a*) imported into the United Kingdom ; or

(*b*) distilled, or manufactured by any other process whatsoever, in the United Kingdom.

Spirits: charge of excise duty.

PART II   a duty of excise at the rates shown in the following Table—

TABLE

Description of spirits	Rates of duty (per proof gallon) £
1. Spirits warehoused for 3 years or more ...	27·0900
2. Spirits not warehoused or warehoused for less than 3 years	27·1650

Reliefs from excise duty

Power to exempt angostura bitters from duty.

6. On the importation of the aromatic flavouring essence commonly known as angostura bitters, the Commissioners may, subject to such conditions as they see fit to impose, direct the bitters to be treated for the purposes of the charge of duty on spirits as not being spirits.

Exemption from duty of spirits in articles used for medical purposes.

7. Duty shall not be payable on any spirits contained in an article imported or delivered from warehouse which is recognised by the Commissioners as being used for medical purposes.

Repayment of duty in respect of spirits used for medical or scientific purposes.

8.—(1) If any person proves to the satisfaction of the Commissioners that any spirits on which duty has been paid have been delivered to him and have been used—

    (*a*) solely in the manufacture or preparation of any article recognised by the Commissioners as being used for medical purposes ; or

    (*b*) for scientific purposes,

he shall, subject to such conditions as the Commissioners may by regulations impose, be entitled to obtain from the Commissioners the repayment of the duty paid thereon.

(2) If any person contravenes or fails to comply with any regulation made under this section he shall be liable on summary conviction to a penalty of £100.

Remission of duty on spirits for methylation.

9. The Commissioners may, subject to such conditions as they see fit to impose, permit spirits to be delivered from warehouse for methylation without payment of the duty chargeable thereon.

Remission of duty on spirits for use in art or manufacture.

10.—(1) Where, in the case of any art or manufacture carried on by any person in which the use of spirits is required, it is proved to the satisfaction of the Commissioners that the use of methylated spirits is unsuitable or detrimental, the Commissioners may, if they think fit and subject to such conditions as they see fit to impose, authorise that person to receive, and permit the delivery from warehouse to that person of, spirits for use in that art or manufacture without payment of the duty chargeable thereon.

(2) If any person contravenes or fails to comply with any condition imposed under this section then, in addition to any other penalty he may have incurred, he shall be liable on summary conviction to a penalty of £50.

11. On the importation of goods not for human consumption Relief from containing spirits as a part or ingredient thereof, the Com- duty on missioners may, subject to such conditions as they may think imported fit to impose, direct the goods to be treated for the purposes for human of the charge of duty on spirits (and in particular the charge consumption under section 126 of the Management Act) as not containing containing spirits. spirits.

Manufacture of spirits

12.—(1) No person shall manufacture spirits, whether by dis- Licence to tillation of a fermented liquor or by any other process, unless he manufacture holds an excise licence for that purpose under this section spirits. (referred to in this Act as a " distiller's licence ").

(2) A licence granted under this section shall expire on the 30th September next after it is granted.

(3) On any licence granted under this section there shall be charged an excise licence duty of £15·75.

(4) The Commissioners may refuse to grant a distiller's licence in respect of any premises on which, from their situation with respect to premises used by a rectifier, brewer for sale or vinegar-maker, they think it inexpedient to allow the manufacture of spirits.

(5) Where the largest still to be used on any premises in respect of which a distiller's licence is sought for the manufacture of spirits by distillation of a fermented liquor is of less than 400 gallons capacity, the Commissioners may refuse to grant the licence or may grant it only subject to such conditions as they see fit to impose.

(6) The Commissioners may refuse to grant a distiller's licence in respect of any premises situated in an area where the Commissioners are not satisfied that convenient living accommodation for the officers to be placed in charge of the distillery can be found unless the distiller undertakes to provide to the satisfaction of the Commissioners lodgings for those officers which satisfy the conditions specified in subsections (7) and (8) below.

(7) The lodgings must be conveniently situated with respect to the distillery but must not form part of the distillery or of the distiller's dwelling house.

(8) The rent unfurnished of the lodgings must either be agreed between the distiller and the Commissioners or, in default of agreement, must be equal—

(a) if the lodgings are in England or Wales, to their gross value for the purposes of section 19 of the General 1967 c. 9. Rate Act 1967 ;

(b) if the lodgings are in Scotland, to their gross annual value ascertained in accordance with the provisions of section 6(2) to (4) of the Valuation and Rating (Scotland) Act 1956 for the purpose of making up the valuation roll;

(c) if the lodgings are in Northern Ireland, to their annual value ascertained in accordance with section 531 of the Income and Corporation Taxes Act 1970.

(9) If a distiller to whom a licence has been granted upon his giving the undertaking mentioned in subsection (6) above fails to provide lodgings in accordance with that undertaking or to keep those lodgings in repair, or if he in any way interferes with the use and enjoyment of those lodgings by the officer residing therein, the Commissioners may suspend or revoke the licence.

13.—(1) The Commissioners may, with a view to the protection of the revenue, make regulations—

(a) regulating the manufacture of spirits, whether by distillation of a fermented liquor or by any other process;

(b) for securing and collecting the duty on spirits manufactured in the United Kingdom; and

(c) regulating the removal of spirits from a distillery;

and different regulations may be made in respect of manufacture for different purposes or by different processes.

(2) Where—

(a) the Commissioners are satisfied that any process of manufacture carried on by any person involving the manufacture of spirits is primarily directed to the production of some article other than spirits; or

(b) the Commissioners see fit in the case of any person manufacturing spirits by any process other than distillation of a fermented liquor,

they may direct that, subject to compliance with such conditions as they think proper to impose, such of the provisions of this Act relating to the manufacture of, or manufacturers of, spirits or such of any regulations made under this section as may be specified in the direction shall not apply in the case of that person.

(3) If, save as provided in subsection (2) above, any person contravenes or fails to comply with any regulation made under subsection (1) above he shall, subject to subsection (4) below, be liable on summary conviction to a penalty of £1,000, and any spirits, and any vessels, utensils and materials used for distilling or otherwise manufacturing or for preparing spirits, in respect of which the offence was committed shall be liable to forfeiture.

(4) The Commissioners may by any regulation under subsection (1) above provide a penalty of an amount less than that specified in subsection (3) above for any contravention of or failure to comply with that regulation.

(5) If any person in whose case a direction is given by the Commissioners under subsection (2) above acts in contravention of or fails to comply with any condition imposed under that subsection which is applicable in his case, he shall be liable, on summary conviction to a penalty of £100, and any spirits in respect of which the offence was committed shall be liable to forfeiture.

14.—(1) In the case of a distillery where spirits are manufactured by distillation of a fermented liquor, the duty on spirits shall, in addition to being charged on the spirits distilled, be chargeable in respect of each distillation period in accordance with the following provisions of this section.

Duty on spirits— attenuation charge.

(2) There shall be calculated the quantity of spirits at proof capable of being produced from any wort and wash made at the distillery on the assumption that from every 100 gallons of wort and wash 1 gallon of spirits at proof will be produced for every 5 degrees of attenuation, that is to say, for every 5 degrees of difference between the highest gravity of the wort and the lowest gravity of the wash before distillation, and so in proportion for any less number of gallons of wort and wash or any less number of degrees of attenuation.

(3) The gravity of wort or wash for the purposes of subsection (2) above shall be taken as that declared by the distiller except that, if either gravity is found by the proper officer before distillation and the gravity so found is, in the case of wort, higher or, in the case of wash, lower than that declared by the distiller, the gravity to be taken shall be that so found by the proper officer.

(4) There shall be ascertained the quantity computed at proof of the spirits and feints produced at the distillery after deducting the feints remaining at the end of the last preceding distillation period.

(5) If the quantity calculated under subsection (2) above exceeds the quantity ascertained under subsection (4) above the duty on spirits shall, subject to subsection (6) below, be charged and become payable immediately on that excess.

(6) The Commissioners may make such allowance as in their opinion is reasonable from any charge under this section on proof to their satisfaction that the charge arises wholly or in

PART II   part on account of the removal of wash for the separation of
yeast or on account of the loss or destruction of wort or wash
by unavoidable accident.

(7) In this section, " distillation period " means the period
prescribed by regulations under section 13(1) above for the
purpose of taking account of feints and spirits produced.

Distiller's
warehouse.   **15.**—(1) A distiller may provide in association with his distillery a place of security for the deposit of spirits manufactured
at that distillery and, if that place is approved by the Commissioners and entry is made thereof by the distiller, may deposit
therein without payment of duty any spirits so manufactured.

(2) If the place of security so provided is outside the
distillery, the Commissioners may attach to their approval such
conditions as they see fit, and if those conditions are not for
the time being observed, that place shall be deemed not to
have been approved by the Commissioners.

(3) A place of security for the time being approved by the
Commissioners under subsection (1) above is referred to in
this Act as a " distiller's warehouse ".

(4) A distiller who provides a distiller's warehouse shall, to
the satisfaction of the Commissioners, provide accommodation
at the warehouse for the officer in charge thereof, and if he fails
so to do he shall be liable on summary conviction to a penalty
of £50 ; but nothing in this subsection shall prejudice any power
of the Commissioners to require the provision of accommodation
as a condition of their approval of any other premises or place
under the Customs and Excise Acts 1979.

(5) A distiller who, after the approval of a distiller's warehouse provided by him, makes without the previous consent
of the Commissioners any alteration therein or addition thereto
shall be liable on summary conviction to a penalty of £200.

(6) The Commissioners may make regulations—

(a) regulating the warehousing of spirits in a distiller's
warehouse ;

(b) permitting, in so far as it appears to them necessary in
order to meet the circumstances of any special case
and subject to such conditions as they see fit to impose,
the deposit by a distiller in his distiller's warehouse
without payment of duty of spirits other than spirits
manufactured at the distillery associated with that
warehouse :

(c) for securing the duties on spirits so warehoused ;

and subject to any such regulations, the provisions of Parts VIII and X of the Management Act, except sections 92 and 96, shall apply in relation to a distiller's warehouse and spirits warehoused therein as they apply in relation to an excise warehouse approved under subsection (1) of section 92 of that Act and goods warehoused therein.

(7) If any person contravenes or fails to comply with any regulation made under subsection (6) above he shall, subject to subsection (8) below, be liable on summary conviction to a penalty of £1,000, and any spirits in respect of which the offence was committed shall be liable to forfeiture.

(8) The Commissioners may by any regulation under subsection (6) above provide a penalty of an amount less than that specified in subsection (7) above for any contravention of or failure to comply with that regulation.

(9) The Commissioners may at any time for reasonable cause revoke or vary the terms of their approval of a distiller's warehouse.

16.—(1) The Commissioners may, with a view to the protection of the revenue, make regulations regulating the racking at a distillery of duty-paid spirits.

Racking of duty-paid spirits at distillery.

(2) If any person contravenes or fails to comply with any regulation made under this section, he shall be liable on summary conviction to a penalty of £50 and any spirits in respect of which the offence was committed shall be liable to forfeiture.

(3) If on an officer's taking stock of duty-paid spirits racked at a distillery, a greater quantity of spirits computed at proof is found at the place of racking than ought to be there according to any accounts required by regulations made under this section to be kept thereof, then—

    (a) duty shall be charged on the excess ; and

    (b) except as provided in subsection (4) below, if the excess amounts to more than 1 per cent. of the quantity of spirits computed at proof lawfully brought into the place of racking since stock was last taken, that excess shall be liable to forfeiture, and the distiller shall be liable on summary conviction to a penalty of double the duty so charged.

(4) Paragraph (b) of subsection (3) above shall not apply where the excess is less than 1 gallon at proof.

PART II
Offences in
connection
with removal
of spirits from
distillery, etc.

17.—(1) If any person—

(*a*) conceals in or without the consent of the proper officer removes from a distillery any wort, wash, low wines, feints or spirits ; or

(*b*) knowingly buys or receives any wort, wash, low wines, feints or spirits so concealed or removed ; or

(*c*) knowingly buys or receives or has in his possession any spirits which have been removed from the place where they ought to have been charged with duty before the duty payable thereon has been charged and either paid or secured, not being spirits which have been condemned or are deemed to have been condemned as forfeited,

he shall be guilty of an offence under this section and may be detained, and the goods shall be liable to forfeiture.

(2) A person guilty of an offence under this section shall be liable—

(*a*) on summary conviction, to a penalty of the prescribed sum or three times the value of the goods, whichever is the greater, or to imprisonment for a term not exceeding 6 months, or to both ; or

(*b*) on conviction on indictment, to a penalty of any amount, or to imprisonment for a term not exceeding 2 years, or to both.

Rectifying and compounding of spirits

Rectifier's and
compounder's
licences.

18.—(1) No person shall rectify or compound spirits and keep a still for that purpose unless he holds an excise licence under this section as a rectifier.

(2) Except as permitted by the Commissioners and subject to such conditions as they see fit to impose, no other person shall compound spirits unless he holds an excise licence under this section as a compounder.

(3) Any licence granted under this section shall expire on the 30th September next after it is granted.

(4) On any licence granted under this section there shall be charged an excise licence duty of £15·75.

(5) The Commissioners may refuse to grant any person a licence as a rectifier in respect of any premises on which, from their situation with respect to a distillery, they think it inexpedient to allow the keeping of a still for rectifying or compounding spirits.

(6) Without prejudice to section 25 below and except as provided by this section, if any person rectifies or compounds spirits otherwise than under and in accordance with an excise licence under this Act so authorising him, he shall be liable on summary conviction to a penalty of £500.

19.—(1) The Commissioners may, with a view to the protection of the revenue, make regulations—

(*a*) regulating the rectifying and compounding of spirits ;

(*b*) regulating the receipt, storage, removal and delivery of spirits by rectifiers and compounders ;

and different regulations may be made under this section for rectifiers and compounders.

(2) If any person contravenes or fails to comply with any regulation made under this section, he shall, subject to subsection (3) below, be liable on summary conviction to a penalty of £500, and any spirits and any other article in respect of which the offence was committed shall be liable to forfeiture.

(3) The Commissioners may by any regulation under this section provide a penalty of an amount less than that specified in subsection (2) above for any contravention of or failure to comply with that regulation.

20.—(1) If at any time when an account is taken by an officer and a balance struck of the spirits in the stock of a rectifier any excess is found, that excess shall be liable to forfeiture, and the rectifier shall be liable on summary conviction to a penalty of double the duty on a like quantity of plain spirits at proof charged at the highest rate.

(2) If at any time when an account is taken and a balance struck as mentioned in subsection (1) above any deficiency is found which cannot be accounted for to the satisfaction of the Commissioners and which when computed at proof exceeds 5 per cent. of the aggregate of—

(*a*) the balance so computed struck when an account was last taken ; and

(*b*) any quantity of spirits so computed since lawfully received by the rectifier,

the rectifier shall be liable on summary conviction to a penalty of double the duty on a quantity of plain spirits at proof charged at the highest rate equal to the quantity by which the deficiency exceeds the said 5 per cent.

(3) For the purposes of any such account and of this section—

(*a*) spirits used by a rectifier in warehouse in pursuance of warehousing regulations shall be deemed not to be spirits in his stock as a rectifier ; and (*b*) where a rectifier also carries on the trade of a wholesaler of spirits on the same premises, all spirits in his possession (other than spirits so used) shall be deemed to be spirits in his stock as a rectifier.

21.—(1) A rectifier shall not distil or extract feints or spirits from any other material than spirits on which duty has been duly paid.

(2) A rectifier shall not have in his possession—

(*a*) except for duty-paid spirits, any materials capable of being distilled into feints or spirits ;

(*b*) any spirits for which he has not received a proper spirits advice note or spirits consignment note.

(3) If a rectifier contravenes subsection (1) or (2) above, or if his still is found to contain any materials capable of being distilled as aforesaid other than duty-paid spirits, whether or not mixed with spirits on which duty has been duly paid, he shall be liable on summary conviction to a penalty of £500 or double the duty on a quantity of plain spirits at proof charged at the highest rate equal to the quantity of the materials or spirits in respect of which the offence was committed, whichever is the greater.

(4) If a rectifier is convicted more than once under this section, his licence shall become void and he shall be disqualified from holding a licence as a rectifier for a period of 3 years from the date of his latest conviction.

(5) Spirits used in warehouse in pursuance of warehousing regulations shall be treated for the purposes of this section as duty-paid spirits.

22.—(1) Subject to the provisions of this section and to such conditions and restrictions as the Commissioners may by regulations impose, a rectifier or compounder may warehouse in an excise warehouse on drawback any British compounded spirits or spirits of wine rectified or compounded by him from duty-paid spirits and not containing any methyl alcohol or any wine, made-wine or other fermented liquor.

(2) British compounded spirits may be warehoused under this section for exportation, for use in any permitted operation in warehouse, for use as stores or, except in the case of tinctures other than perfumed spirits, for home use.

(3) Spirits of wine may be warehoused under this section—

(*a*) for exportation, for use in any permitted operation in warehouse, or for use as stores ; or (*b*) if of a strength of not less than 50° over proof, for delivery for use in art or manufacture under section 10 above ; or

(*c*) if of a strength of not less than 74° over proof, for home use.

(4) The Commissioners may, subject to such conditions and restrictions as they may by regulations impose, allow drawback on tinctures or spirits of wine exported or, except in the case of spirits of wine, shipped as stores by a rectifier or compounder direct from his premises.

(5) Subject to subsection (6) below, the amount of any drawback payable under this section shall be calculated by reference to the quantity of the British compounded spirits or spirits of wine computed at proof and shall be an amount equal to the duty at the appropriate rate chargeable on a like quantity of spirits at the date when duty was paid on the spirits from which the British compounded spirits or spirits of wine were rectified or compounded.

(6) The Commissioners may, in the case of tinctures exported or shipped as stores by a rectifier or compounder direct from his premises, make such addition to the quantity of spirits as they see fit in respect of waste.

(7) No drawback shall be payable under this section in the case of medicinal spirits in respect of which a repayment of duty has been obtained under section 8 above.

(8) British compounded spirits warehoused under this section for home use shall upon delivery from warehouse for that purpose be chargeable with the same rate of duty as spirits warehoused by a distiller.

(9) If any person contravenes or fails to comply with any regulation made under this section then, in addition to any other penalty he may have incurred under the Customs and Excise Acts 1979, he shall be liable on summary conviction to a penalty of £100, and any article in respect of which the offence was committed shall be liable to forfeiture.

(10) In this section " tinctures " means medicinal spirits, flavouring essences, perfumed spirits and such other articles containing spirits as the Commissioners may by regulations specify as tinctures.

23.—(1) Where any British compounded spirits—

Allowance on British compounds.

(*a*) having been warehoused, are on removal from warehouse exported or shipped as stores ; or

(b) are permitted under section 22 above to be exported or shipped as stores on drawback direct from the premises of a rectifier or compounder ; or

(c) are used in warehouse for fortifying wine or for any other purpose for which spirits are permitted by or under this or any other Act to be used in warehouse,

there shall, subject to the provisions of this section and to such conditions as the Commissioners see fit to impose, be paid in respect of each gallon of those spirits computed at proof an allowance of £0·02.

(2) In the case of British compounded spirits of a strength exceeding 11° over proof which are deposited in a warehouse, the allowance mentioned in subsection (1) above may, subject as aforesaid, instead of being paid as provided in that subsection be paid on the warehousing of the spirits.

(3) No allowance shall be payable on any British compounded spirits under this section if those spirits were compounded in warehouse in pursuance of warehousing regulations or, in any other case, unless it is proved to the satisfaction of the Commissioners that the spirits have been distinctly altered in character by redistillation with or by the addition of flavouring or other matter.

(4) Any allowance on British compounded spirits under this section—

(a) when paid on their exportation or shipment as stores, shall be paid to the person by whom security is given for that exportation or shipment ;

(b) when paid on their use in warehouse, shall be paid to the person upon whose written request they are so used ;

(c) when paid on their warehousing, shall be paid to the person in whose name they are warehoused.

General provisions relating to manufacture of spirits and British compounds

Restriction on carrying on of other trades by distiller or rectifier.

24.—(1) A distiller or rectifier shall not—

(a) carry on upon his premises the trade of a brewer for sale, producer of wine or of made-wine, maker of cider, vinegar-maker, refiner of sugar, wholesaler or retailer of wine, made-wine or beer, or retailer of methylated spirits or cider ; or

(b) carry on the trade of a distiller or, as the case may be, rectifier on any premises communicating otherwise than by a public roadway with other premises on which any such trade as is mentioned in paragraph (*a*) above or that of a wholesaler of spirits is carried on.

(2) Save with the permission of the Commissioners and subject to compliance with such conditions as they see fit to impose, a distiller or rectifier shall not—

(*a*) carry on upon his premises the trade of a retailer of spirits ; or

(*b*) carry on the trade of a distiller or, as the case may be, rectifier on any premises communicating otherwise than by a public roadway with other premises on which the trade of retailer of spirits is carried on.

(3) Save with the permission of the Commissioners and subject to compliance with such conditions as they see fit to impose, a distiller or rectifier shall not be concerned or interested in the trade of a retailer of spirits carried on within 2 miles of his distillery or, as the case may be, rectifying house.

(4) If any person contravenes any provision of this section or contravenes or fails to comply with any condition imposed thereunder, he shall be liable on summary conviction to a penalty of £200.

25.—(1) Save as provided by or under this Act, any person who, otherwise than under and in accordance with an excise licence under this Act so authorising him— Penalty for unlawful manufacture of spirits, etc.

(*a*) manufactures spirits, whether by distillation of a fermented liquor or by any other process ; or

(*b*) has in his possession or uses a still for distilling, rectifying or compounding spirits ; or

(*c*) distils or has in his possession any low wines or feints ; or

(*d*) not being a vinegar-maker, brews or makes or has in his possession any wort or wash fit for distillation,

shall be liable on summary conviction to a penalty of £1,000.

(2) Where there is insufficient evidence to convict a person of an offence under subsection (1) above, but it is proved that such an offence has been committed on some part of premises belonging to or occupied by that person in such circumstances that it could not have been committed without his knowledge, that person shall be liable on summary conviction to a penalty of £100.

(3) Any person found on premises on which spirits are being unlawfully manufactured or on which a still is being unlawfully used for rectifying or compounding spirits may be detained.

(4) All spirits and stills, vessels, utensils, wort, wash and other materials for manufacturing, distilling or preparing spirits—

    (*a*) found in the possession of any person who commits an offence under subsection (1) above ; or

    (*b*) found on any premises on which such an offence has been committed,

shall be liable to forfeiture.

(5) Notwithstanding any other provision of the Customs and Excise Acts 1979 relating to goods seized as liable to forfeiture, any officer by whom any thing is seized as liable to forfeiture under subsection (4) above may at his discretion forthwith spill, break up or destroy that thing.

(6) Without prejudice to any other power conferred by the Customs and Excise Acts 1979, if any officer has reasonable grounds for suspecting that any thing liable to forfeiture under this section is in or upon any land or other premises in Northern Ireland, he may enter upon those premises, if need be by force, and search them and seize and remove any thing which he has reasonable grounds to believe to be so liable.

General provisions relating to spirits

Importation and exportation of spirits.

26.—(1) Save as permitted by the Commissioners, spirits shall not be imported—

    (*a*) in any ship of less than 40 tons register ; or

    (*b*) in containers of a capacity of less than 9 gallons each unless in bottles properly packed in cases.

(2) Save as permitted by the Commissioners, spirits other than bottled spirits shall not be exported, or be removed to the Isle of Man, or be brought to any place or be waterborne for exportation or for removal to the Isle of Man, in containers holding less than 9 gallons each.

(3) Any spirits imported, exported, removed, brought or waterborne contrary to this section shall be liable to forfeiture.

(4) Where any ship is or has been, in the case of a British ship, within 12 or, in any other case, within 3 nautical miles of the coast of the United Kingdom while having on board or attached in any manner thereto any spirits in containers other than such as are permitted by or under subsection (1) of this section, the ship and any such spirits found therein shall be liable to forfeiture.

(5) For the purposes of subsection (1) above, all hovercraft (of whatever size) shall be treated as ships of less than 40 tons register and subsection (4) above shall apply as if any reference to a ship included a reference to a hovercraft.

27.—(1) Where any spirits are sent out from the stock of a Spirits rectifier or compounder or, otherwise than in the circumstances consignment specified in subsection (2) below, are sent out from the stock of and spirits a wholesaler or retailer, the person sending them out shall, advice notes. subject to any dispensation granted by the Commissioners, send to the person to whom they are sent a spirits consignment note, and shall send it either with the spirits or so that it is either delivered or posted on the day on which the spirits are sent out.

(2) The circumstances referred to in subsection (1) above in relation to a wholesaler or retailer are that—

(a) in the case of spirits sent out from the stock of a wholesaler, the spirits are sent out in a quantity not exceeding 1 gallon at a time and are sold by him by retail to a person who is not a wholesaler or retailer of spirits ; and

(b) in the case of spirits sent out from the stock of a retailer, the spirits are sent out in a quantity not exceeding 1 gallon of the same denomination at a time for one person.

(3) The person by whom any spirits—

(a) are sent out from a distillery ; or

(b) are removed from a warehouse ; or

(c) not being spirits to which the requirement imposed by subsection (1) above to send a spirits consignment note applies, are otherwise removed from any place in the United Kingdom to any other such place in a quantity exceeding 1 gallon of the same denomination at a time for any one person,

shall, subject to any dispensation granted by the Commissioners, send to the person to whom the spirits are to be delivered a spirits advice note, and shall send that note either with the spirits or so that it is either delivered or posted on the day on which the spirits are sent out or removed.

(4) A distiller shall not send out from his distillery, or, save as permitted by the Commissioners in the case of samples, remove from a distiller's warehouse associated with his distillery, any spirits in a quantity of less than 9 gallons.

(5) In this Act—

" spirits advice note " means a document containing such particulars as the Commissioners may direct ;

" spirits consignment note " means a consignment note or similar document containing such particulars as the Commissioners may direct.

Regulations about the keeping and production of spirits advice and spirits consignment notes, etc.

28.—(1) As respects spirits in the case of which a requirement is imposed by this Act that a spirits advice note or a spirits consignment note shall be sent in connection with their removal, the Commissioners may make regulations requiring the keeping and production of such notes and copies thereof, and of stock books.

(2) If any person contravenes or fails to comply with any regulation made under this section he shall, except in the circumstances specified in subsection (3) below, be liable on summary conviction to a penalty of £200.

(3) No liability shall be incurred under subsection (2) above for failure to keep or produce a spirits advice note, spirits consignment note or copy of such a note in accordance with any such regulation if it is proved that the note or, as the case may be, the note and any copy thereof was or were lost or destroyed by accident.

Offences in connection with spirits advice and spirits consignment notes.

29.—(1) Where a spirits advice note or a spirits consignment note is required by this Act in connection with the removal of any spirits, then if any person—

(a) sends out or causes to be sent out, any spirits without the proper spirits advice note or spirits consignment note being duly sent ; or

(b) requests, obtains or uses, or causes or permits to be requested, obtained or used, a spirits advice note or a spirits consignment note for any purpose otherwise than in accordance with the terms thereof ; or

(c) in any manner uses or causes or permits the use of any spirits advice note or spirits consignment note so that the taking or checking of any account or the making of any examination by an officer is or may be frustrated or evaded ; or

(d) produces or causes or permits the production of any spirits advice note or spirits consignment note to an officer as having been received with or in connection with any spirits other than those to which it relates,

he shall, in addition to any other punishment to which he may have become liable, be liable on summary conviction to a

penalty of three times the value of any spirits in respect of which PART II
the offence was committed or £100, whichever is the greater.

(2) Any spirits—

   (*a*) in connection with the removal of which a spirits advice note is required by this Act which are found in the course of being, or to have been, sent out, removed or received—

      (i) without a proper spirits advice note having been duly sent, or

      (ii) in contravention of section 27(4) above ; or

   (*b*) in the case of which an altered or untrue spirits advice note has been sent,

shall be liable to forfeiture, and any person in whose possession any such spirits are found shall be liable on summary conviction to a penalty of three times the value of the goods or £100, whichever is the greater.

30.—(1) If in any proceedings under section 29 above, any question arises as to the accuracy of the description of any spirits in a spirits advice note or spirits consignment note— Special provisions as to spirits advice and spirits consignment notes.

   (*a*) the burden of proof that the spirits correspond with the description shall lie on the person claiming that the spirits so correspond, who shall furnish that proof by the evidence of two persons competent to decide by examination of the spirits ;

   (*b*) the description of spirits shall not be deemed to be inaccurate by reason only of the fact that they are of a strength differing from that specified in the spirits advice note or spirits consignment note where the actual strength is not more than 1° of proof above or 2° of proof below that so specified.

(2) If a distiller, rectifier or compounder or a wholesaler or retailer of spirits is convicted of an offence in relation to spirits under section 29 above, the Commissioners may revoke his licence and refuse to re-grant him a licence during the remainder of the period for which the revoked licence would have been in force.

31.—(1) No spirits shall be delivered for home use unless they have been warehoused for a period of at least 3 years or, in the case of rum, at least 2 years. But this subsection shall not apply— Restriction on delivery of immature spirits for home use.

   (*a*) to spirits delivered for any purpose for which they may for the time being be delivered without payment of duty ; or (*b*) to spirits delivered for methylation under section 9 above or for use in art or manufacture under section 10 above ; or

(*c*) to spirits which have been warehoused on drawback ; or

(*d*) to mixtures, compounds or preparations charged with duty on importation in respect of the spirits contained in them or used in their preparation or manufacture ; or

(*e*) subject to such conditions as the Commissioners may by regulations impose, to spirits delivered to a rectifier or compounder, a manufacturing chemist or a manufacturer of perfumes for use in his manufacture, or to such other persons for such purposes as the Commissioners see fit to authorise for the purposes of this paragraph ; or

(*f*) subject to such conditions as aforesaid, to spirits delivered for scientific purposes under section 8 above ; or

(*g*) subject to such conditions as aforesaid, to imported Geneva, perfumed spirits or liqueurs ; or

(*h*) to imported compounded spirits of any kind specified for the purposes of this paragraph in regulations made by the Commissioners ; or

(*i*) to the supply of spirits of wine for the purpose of making medicines to registered medical practitioners, hospitals and persons entitled to carry on the business of a chemist and druggist ; or

(*j*) to spirits compounded in warehouse in pursuance of warehousing regulations.

(2) For the purposes of this section, in the case of imported spirits, any period which is shown to the satisfaction of the Commissioners to have elapsed between the dates of manufacture and importation shall be treated as a period during which the spirits have been warehoused.

(3) If any person procures or attempts to procure the delivery of spirits in contravention of this section or contravenes or fails to comply with any regulation made thereunder, he shall be liable on summary conviction to a penalty of £100, and any spirits in respect of which the offence was committed shall be liable to forfeiture.

Restriction
on transfer
of British
spirits in
warehouse.

32.—(1) No spirits in a distiller's warehouse may be transferred to a purchaser until the distiller has given such security for the payment of duty as the Commissioners may require, and any spirits so transferred shall not again be transferred while those spirits remain in that warehouse.

(2) Spirits manufactured in the United Kingdom chargeable with duty which has not been paid which are in any warehouse other than a distiller's warehouse shall not be transferred into the name of a purchaser until the purchaser produces to the officer in charge of the warehouse a written order for the delivery of the spirits signed by the person in whose name they are warehoused and countersigned by the occupier of the warehouse or a servant of his acting for him at the warehouse.

(3) Any spirits duly transferred in accordance with the provisions of this section shall be discharged from any liability under the Customs and Excise Acts 1979 in respect of the nonpayment of any duty or penalty by the transferor.

33.—(1) If any person uses otherwise than for a medical or scientific purpose— Restrictions on use of certain goods relieved from spirits duty.

> (a) any mixture which has on importation been relieved to any extent of the duty chargeable in respect of the spirits contained in it or used in its preparation or manufacture by reason of being a mixture which is recognised by the Commissioners as being used for medical purposes ; or
>
> (b) any article containing spirits which were exempted from duty under section 7 above ; or
>
> (c) any article manufactured or prepared from spirits in respect of which repayment of duty has been obtained under section 8 above ; or
>
> (d) any article in respect of which he has paid or agreed to pay a price fixed on the assumption that a repayment of duty will be obtained as mentioned in paragraph (c) above,

he shall, unless he has complied with the requirements specified in subsection (2) below, be liable on summary conviction to a penalty of three times the value of the mixture or article so used or £100, whichever is the greater, and any article in his possession in the preparation or manufacture of which the mixture or article has been used shall be liable to forfeiture.

(2) The requirements with which a person must comply to avoid incurring liability under subsection (1) above are that—

> (a) he must obtain the consent of the Commissioners in writing to the use of the mixture or article otherwise than for a medical or scientific purpose ; and
>
> (b) he must pay to the Commissioners an amount equal to the difference between the duty charged on the mixture and the duty which would have been chargeable if it had not been a mixture recognised as mentioned in subsection (1)(a) above, or to the amount of the duty repaid or assumed to be repayable, as the case may be.

(3) The Commissioners may make regulations for the purpose of enforcing the provisions of this section.

(4) Regulations under subsection (3) above may in particular require any person carrying on any trade in which spirits, or mixtures or articles containing or prepared or manufactured with spirits, are in the opinion of the Commissioners likely to be or to have been used—

> (*a*) to give and verify particulars of the materials which he is using or has used and of any such mixtures or articles which he has sold ; and
>
> (*b*) to produce any books of account or other documents of whatever nature relating to any such materials, mixtures or articles.

(5) If any person contravenes or fails to comply with any regulation made under subsection (3) above he shall be liable on summary conviction to a penalty of £100.

(6) In this section " mixture " includes a preparation and a compound, and any reference to a mixture or article includes a reference to any part thereof.

Prohibition of grogging.

34.—(1) No person shall—

> (*a*) subject any cask to any process for the purpose of extracting any spirits absorbed in the wood thereof ; or
>
> (*b*) have on his premises any cask which is being subjected to any such process or any spirits extracted from the wood of any cask.

(2) Any person contravening any provision of this section shall be liable on summary conviction to a penalty of £50.

(3) All spirits extracted contrary to this section and every cask which is being subjected to any such process or which, being upon premises upon which spirits so extracted are found, has been subjected to any such process shall be liable to forfeiture.

Returns as to importation, manufacture, sale or use of alcohols.

35.—(1) The Commissioners may, in so far as it seems to them expedient so to do for the purposes of protecting the revenue arising from the duties on spirits, make regulations requiring importers, manufacturers, sellers or users of—

> (*a*) the following alcohols, that is to say, methyl, propyl, butyl or amyl alcohol, or
>
> (*b*) any of the isomeric forms of such alcohols,

to furnish returns containing such particulars as may be prescribed by the regulations in respect of the importation, manufacture, sale or use by any such persons of any of the articles specified in paragraphs (*a*) and (*b*) above.

(2) Provision may be made by any regulations under this section for requiring persons by whom and premises on which any such articles are manufactured to be registered.

(3) If any person contravenes or fails to comply with any regulation made under this section he shall be liable on summary conviction to a penalty of £25.

PART III

BEER

Charge of excise duty

36. There shall be charged on beer—

(a) imported into the United Kingdom ; or

(b) brewed in the United Kingdom,

a duty of excise at the rate of £17·4240 for every 36 gallons, that rate being, however, increased in the case of beer of an original gravity exceeding 1030° by £0·5808 for each additional degree.

Beer: charge of excise duty.

Computation of excise duty

37.—(1) The quantity of worts and the gravity thereof by reference to which the duty on beer brewed in the United Kingdom is charged shall, according as is provided in sections 38 and 39 below, be either—

(a) the quantity and the original gravity of the worts produced ; or

(b) the quantity of worts of an original gravity of 1055° deemed to have been brewed from the materials used.

Charge of duty on beer brewed in the United Kingdom: general.

(2) For the purpose of ascertaining the quantity of worts of an original gravity of 1055° deemed to have been brewed from the materials used, a brewer shall be deemed, subject to subsection (4) below, to have brewed 36 gallons of worts of that gravity for every unit of materials recorded by him in pursuance of regulations under section 49 or 53 below or used by him in any brewing.

(3) For the purposes of subsection (2) above " unit of materials " means—

(a) 84 pounds weight of malt or corn of any description ; or

(b) 56 pounds weight of sugar ; or

(*c*) a quantity of malt, corn and sugar, or of any two of those materials, which by relation to paragraph (*a*) and (*b*) above is the equivalent of either of the quantities mentioned in those paragraphs.

(4) In the case of a brewer for sale, where any materials used for brewing by the brewer are proved to the satisfaction of the Commissioners to be of such a description or nature that some deduction from the quantity deemed to have been brewed should be made, the Commissioners shall make such a deduction from that quantity as will in their opinion afford just relief to the brewer.

(5) In subsection (3) above " sugar " includes—

(*a*) any saccharine substance, extract or syrup ;

(*b*) rice ;

(*c*) flaked maize and any other description of corn which in the opinion of the Commissioners is prepared in a manner similar to flaked maize ;

(*d*) any other material capable of being used in brewing except malt or corn ;

and " corn " in that subsection means corn other than corn included in the foregoing definition of sugar.

(6) In the case of a brewer for sale, this section and section 38 below shall have effect as if priming and colouring solutions were worts.

Charge of duty on beer brewed in the United Kingdom: brewer for sale.

38.—(1) The duty on beer brewed by a brewer for sale shall be charged and paid in accordance with the following provisions of this section.

(2) In respect of each brewing, duty shall first be charged by reference to the quantity and original gravity of the worts produced, as recorded by the brewer in pursuance of regulations made under section 49 below or as ascertained by the proper officer, whichever quantity and whichever gravity is the greater, less 6 per cent. of that quantity.

(3) There shall be ascertained in respect of each brewing—

(*a*) the quantity of worts of an original gravity of 1055° which is the equivalent of the worts produced ; and

(*b*) the quantity of worts of that gravity deemed to have been brewed from the materials used in accordance with section 37(2) above ;

and if the quantity mentioned in paragraph (*b*) above, less 4 per cent., exceeds the quantity mentioned in paragraph (*a*) above duty shall in addition be charged on the excess, less 6 per cent. thereof.

(4) For the purposes of subsection (3)(*a*) above, the equivalent therein mentioned shall be taken to be the quantity of the worts produced—

    (*a*) multiplied by the number, less 1000, of the degrees representing their original gravity ; and

    (*b*) divided by 55.

(5) If at any time while any worts are in the collecting or fermenting vessels at a brewery the original gravity of the worts is found to exceed by 5° or more the gravity recorded by the brewer in pursuance of regulations made under section 49 below or that ascertained by the proper officer, those worts may be deemed to be the produce of a fresh brewing and be charged with duty accordingly.

(6) Where beer has been prepared by a process of mixing by a brewer for sale and the aggregate amount charged in respect of duty on the several constituents of the beer exceeds the amount which would have been so charged on the mixture, the Commissioners may, subject to such conditions as they see fit to impose, remit or repay the excess.

(7) The conditions which may be imposed under subsection (6) above include conditions as to the method of computing the amount which would have been charged in respect of duty on the mixture and of ascertaining any matter by reference to which that amount is to be computed.

(8) Subject to subsection (9) below, the amount payable in respect of duty shall become due immediately duty is charged by the proper officer.

(9) The Commissioners may cause the charge to be made up at the close of each month in respect of all the brewings during that month, and, in that case, the aggregate of the quantities of worts produced and the aggregate of the quantities of worts deemed to have been brewed from the materials used shall be treated as worts produced or deemed to have been brewed in one brewing, and, subject to subsection (10) below, the Commissioners may, if they think fit, allow payment of the duty to be deferred upon such terms as they see fit.

(10) Where the Commissioners allow payment of duty to be deferred under subsection (9) above the date of payment shall be—

    (*a*) in the case of worts of beer to which this paragraph applies, such date as may be so allowed, not being later than the twenty-fifth day of the twelfth month after the month in which the duty was charged ;

    (*b*) in any other case, such date as may be so allowed, not being later than the twenty-fifth day of the month next following that in which the duty was charged.

(11) Paragraph (*a*) of subsection (10) above applies to worts of beer of an original gravity of or exceeding 1070° and worts of lager beer, being in each case beer kept for a period of at least three months on the entered premises in which it is brewed, but does not apply to priming or colouring solutions.

Charge of
duty on
beer brewed
in the United
Kingdom:
private
brewer.

39.—(1) The duty on beer brewed by the holder of a limited licence to brew beer or of a corresponding licence in Northern Ireland shall be charged and paid in accordance with subsections (2) and (3) below.

(2) Duty shall be charged by reference to the quantity of worts of an original gravity of 1055° deemed to have been brewed from the materials used in accordance with section 37(2) above, less 6 per cent. of that quantity.

(3) The charge of duty shall be made up and the amount payable in respect thereof shall be paid at such times as the Commissioners may appoint.

Charge of
duty on
imported beer.

40.—(1) When any beer is imported or is removed into the United Kingdom from the Isle of Man, the importer of or person so removing the beer shall deliver to the proper officer in such form and manner as the Commissioners may direct a declaration of the original gravity thereof ; and, for the purpose of charging duty on the beer, the original gravity thereof shall be taken to be the original gravity stated in the declaration or the original gravity as ascertained by the proper officer, whichever is the higher.

(2) If the original gravity as ascertained by the proper officer exceeds by 2° or more that stated in the declaration, the beer shall be liable to forfeiture ; and if the original gravity as so ascertained exceeds by 5° or more that stated in the declaration, the importer of or person removing the beer, and any agent of his by whom the declaration was made, shall each be liable on summary conviction to a penalty of £100.

Reliefs from excise duty

Exemption
from duty
of beer
brewed for
private
consumption.

41. The duty on beer brewed in the United Kingdom shall not be chargeable on beer brewed by a person who—

(*a*) brews only for his own domestic use or for consumption by farm labourers employed by him in the actual course of their labour or employment ; and

(*b*) is not also a wholesaler or retailer of beer.

Drawback on
exportation,
removal to
warehouse,
shipment as
stores, etc.

42.—(1) This section applies to—

(*a*) beer which has been brewed by a brewer for sale ; and

(*b*) beer which has been imported, or which has been removed into the United Kingdom from the Isle of Man.

(2) Subject to the provisions of this section and to such conditions as the Commissioners see fit to impose, drawback shall be allowable—

(a) on the removal by any person of any beer to which this section applies to an excise warehouse on the premises of a licensed producer of made-wine ; or

(b) on the exportation or removal to the Isle of Man by any person of any such beer ; or

(c) on the shipment as stores by any person of any such beer ;

and shall also be allowable, subject as aforesaid, in the case of any beer to which this section applies which it is shown to the satisfaction of the Commissioners is being exported, removed or shipped as mentioned in paragraph (b) or (c) above as an ingredient of other goods.

(3) In the case of beer brewed in the United Kingdom, the person intending to remove, export or ship the beer shall produce to the proper officer a declaration made by the brewer in such form and manner as the Commissioners may direct stating the date upon which the beer was brewed and the original gravity thereof and that the proper duty has been charged thereon.

(4) In the case of beer brewed outside the United Kingdom, the person intending to remove, export or ship the beer shall produce to the proper officer in such form and manner as the Commissioners may direct a declaration that the proper duty has been charged and paid thereon.

(5) The amount of the drawback payable under this section in respect of any duty paid shall be calculated according to the rate of drawback applicable during the period of currency of the rate at which the duty was paid to like beer charged with that rate of duty during that period.

(6) Drawback under this section shall, where it is shown to the satisfaction of the Commissioners that duty has been paid, be allowed at the same rate as the rate at which the duty is charged ; but as respects beer of an original gravity of less than 1030° the amount of drawback allowable shall not exceed the amount of the duty shown to the satisfaction of the Commissioners to have been paid.

43.—(1) Subject to any regulations made by the Commissioners, a brewer for sale or a wholesaler of beer shall be entitled to warehouse in an excise warehouse for exportation or for use as stores any beer on which duty has been charged, and to add to the beer in warehouse finings for clarification or any other substance sanctioned by the Commissioners for the purpose of preparing the beer for exportation or for use as stores.

Warehousing of beer for exportation, etc.

PART III   (2) Subject to subsection (3) below, where the duty charged in respect of any beer warehoused under this section has been paid, drawback shall be allowed and paid as if the beer had been exported at the time of the warehousing.

(3) Subsections (3) to (5) of section 42 above shall apply in relation to beer warehoused on drawback under this section as if the beer were being exported at the date of its warehousing.

(4) Drawback under this section shall, where it is shown to the satisfaction of the Commissioners that duty has been paid, be allowed at the same rate as the rate at which the duty is charged ; but as respects beer of an original gravity of less than 1030° the amount of drawback allowable shall not exceed the amount of the duty shown to the satisfaction of the Commissioners to have been paid.

Remission or repayment of duty on beer used for purposes of research or experiment.

44.—(1) Where it is proved to the satisfaction of the Commissioners that any beer brewed in the United Kingdom which is chargeable with duty is to be used only for the purposes of research or of experiments in brewing, the Commissioners may, if they think fit and subject to such conditions as they see fit to impose, remit or repay the duty chargeable on that beer.

(2) If any person contravenes or fails to comply with any condition imposed under subsection (1) above, then, in addition to any other penalty he may have incurred, he shall be liable on summary conviction to a penalty of £50.

Repayment of duty on beer used in the production or manufacture of other beverages, etc.

45. The Commissioners may by regulations provide for duty charged on beer which is used as an ingredient in the production or manufacture of—

(a) any beverage of an alcoholic strength not exceeding 2° of proof ; or

(b) any such article (other than a beverage) as the Commissioners may determine having regard to the alcoholic content thereof,

to be repaid subject to such conditions as may be imposed by or under the regulations.

Remission or repayment of duty on spoilt beer.

46.—(1) Where it is proved to the satisfaction of the Commissioners in the case of any brewer for sale that—

(a) any materials upon which a charge of duty has been made, or

(b) any worts or beer (whether manufactured by him or not),

have been destroyed or become spoilt or otherwise unfit for use by unavoidable accident while on the entered premises of the brewer and, in the case of any such substances which have become spoilt or unfit for use, have been destroyed with the permission and in the presence of the proper officer, the Commissioners shall remit or repay any duty charged or paid in respect thereof.

(2) Where it is shown to the satisfaction of the Commissioners that any beer which has been removed from the entered premises of a brewer for sale has accidentally become spoilt or otherwise unfit for use and, in the case of beer delivered to another person, has been returned to the brewer as so spoilt or unfit, the Commissioners shall, subject to compliance with such conditions as they may by regulations impose, remit or repay any duty charged or paid in respect of the beer.

(3) If any person contravenes or fails to comply with any regulation made under subsection (2) above, he shall be liable on summary conviction to a penalty of £50.

Brewing of beer

47.—(1) No person shall brew beer unless he holds an excise Licences to licence under this section to brew beer or is exempted from brew beer. holding one by subsection (5) below.

(2) An excise licence under this section may—

> (a) authorise the person to whom it is granted to brew beer for sale ; or
>
> (b) authorise the person to whom it is granted to brew beer not for sale and only for his own domestic use or for consumption by any persons employed by him in the actual course of their employment ;

and in this Act—

> " brewer " means a person holding a licence under this section ;
>
> " brewer for sale " means a person holding a licence to brew beer for sale ; and
>
> " limited licence to brew beer " means a licence to brew beer as mentioned in paragraph (b) above.

(3) Any licence granted under this section shall expire on the 30th September next after it is granted.

(4) On every licence to brew beer there shall be charged an excise licence duty of the following amount, that is to say—

> (a) in the case of a licence to brew beer for sale, £15·75 ;
>
> (b) in the case of a limited licence to brew beer, £0·20.

(5) A licence to brew beer shall not be required—

(a) for the brewing of beer only for the brewer's own domestic use or for consumption by farm labourers employed by the brewer in the actual course of their labour or employment; or

(b) for the brewing of beer (with the authority of the Commissioners and subject to compliance with such conditions as they see fit to impose) solely for the purposes of research or of experiments in brewing;

but this subsection shall not exempt any person who is also a wholesaler or retailer of beer.

(6) The Commissioners may refuse to grant a licence under this section in respect of any premises on which, from the situation of those premises with respect to a distillery, they think it inexpedient to allow the brewing of beer.

(7) If any person, except as permitted by subsection (5) above, brews beer otherwise than under and in accordance with a licence under this section, he shall be liable on summary conviction to a penalty of £500 and all worts, beer and vessels, utensils and materials for brewing in his possession shall be liable to forfeiture.

Licence to use premises for adding solutions to beer.

48.—(1) A brewer for sale shall not use for the purpose of adding priming or colouring solutions to beer any premises other than premises entered by him for the brewing of beer or an excise warehouse unless he holds an excise licence for that purpose under this section.

(2) A licence granted under this section shall expire on the 30th September next after it is granted.

(3) On any licence granted under this section there shall be charged an excise licence duty of £15·75.

(4) If any brewer for sale uses any premises for the purpose mentioned in subsection (1) above contrary to this section or otherwise than in accordance with any licence granted to him in respect thereof under this section, he shall be liable on summary conviction to a penalty of £100.

Power to regulate manufacture of beer by brewers for sale.

49.—(1) The Commissioners may, with a view to the protection of the revenue, make regulations—

(a) regulating the manufacture of beer by brewers for sale;

(b) for securing the duties on beer brewed by brewers for sale;

(c) regulating with respect to brewers for sale the preparation, use, storage and removal of priming and colouring solutions;

(*d*) for enabling such solutions to be warehoused without
payment of the duty chargeable on beer ;

(*e*) regulating the addition of such solutions to beer at
premises in respect of which a licence has been granted
under section 48 above ;

(*f*) for applying to such solutions, subject to such modifications and exceptions as may be specified in the regulations, any provision of, or of any instrument made
under, any enactment relating to or containing provisions incidental to the duty on beer brewed in the
United Kingdom.

(2) Any person contravening or failing to comply with any
regulation made under this section shall be liable on summary
conviction to a penalty of £100, and any article in respect of
which the offence was committed shall be liable to forfeiture.

50.—(1) The Commissioners may make regulations as Regulations
respects—   as respects
                                                         sugar kept
(*a*) the receipt, storage, removal and disposal of sugar by by brewers
brewers for sale ;   for sale.

(*b*) the books and other documents relating to sugar to be
kept by brewers for sale ;

(*c*) the powers of officers to inspect and take copies of any
such book or other document and to take stock of the
sugar in the possession of any brewer for sale.

(2) If any brewer for sale contravenes or fails to comply with
any regulation made under this section he shall be liable on
summary conviction to a penalty of £50.

(3) If, on taking stock at any time, the proper officer finds
that the quantity of any description of sugar in the possession
of any brewer for sale differs from the quantity of that description which ought to be in his possession according to any book
or other document kept by him in pursuance of any regulations
made under this section, then—

(*a*) if the quantity in his possession exceeds the quantity
which ought to be in his possession, the excess shall be
liable to forfeiture ;

(*b*) if the quantity in his possession is less by more than
2 per cent. than the quantity which ought to be in his
possession, the deficiency above 2 per cent. shall, unless
accounted for to the satisfaction of the Commissioners,
be deemed to have been used in the brewing of beer
without particulars thereof having been recorded in
pursuance of regulations made under section 49 above,
and duty shall be charged in respect thereof
as if that deficiency had been so used.

PART III

(4) In this section " sugar " means sugar of any description and any saccharine substance, extract or syrup.

Power to require production of books by brewers for sale.

51.—(1) Where the Commissioners are satisfied that it is necessary for the purpose of securing the collection of the duty on beer brewed in the United Kingdom, any person specially authorised in writing in that behalf by the Commissioners may require any brewer for sale to produce to that person any book or document whatsoever relating to his business as a brewer.

(2) If any brewer for sale fails to comply with any requirement imposed under subsection (1) above within a period of one hour he shall, on summary conviction, be liable to a penalty of £100 and to a further penalty of £10 for every day or part of a day thereafter during which the failure continues.

Offences by brewers for sale.

52.—(1) If any brewer for sale conceals any worts or beer so as to prevent an officer from taking an account thereof, or after particulars of any worts or beer have been recorded by the brewer in pursuance of regulations made under section 49 above, mixes any sugar with those worts or with that beer so as to increase the quantity or the gravity or original gravity thereof, he shall be liable on summary conviction to a penalty of £100, and the worts or beer in respect of which the offence was committed shall be liable to forfeiture.

(2) If any brewer for sale adds to beer before it is delivered from his entered premises anything other than—

    (*a*) water ;

    (*b*) finings for the purpose of clarification ; or

    (*c*) such other substances as may be sanctioned by the Commissioners,

he shall be liable on summary conviction to a penalty of £50.

(3) If any beer to which anything other than any substance falling within paragraph (*a*), (*b*) or (*c*) of subsection (2) above has been added is found in the possession of a brewer for sale, he shall be liable on summary conviction to a penalty of £50 and the beer shall be liable to forfeiture.

(4) In this section " sugar " means sugar of any description and any saccharine substance, extract or syrup, and includes any material capable of being used in brewing except malt or corn.

Special provisions as to holders of limited licences to brew beer.

53.—(1) A limited licence to brew beer shall be granted in respect of one set of premises only, being premises occupied by the brewer.

For the purposes of this subsection the land and buildings within one curtilage, or any lands and buildings in Scotland with their parts and pertinents, shall be treated as one set of premises.

(2) A limited licence to brew beer granted to any person shall not be transferred to any other person except the widow, personal representatives, liquidator or trustee in bankruptcy of the person to whom the licence was granted.

(3) The Commissioners may make regulations prescribing the documents to be kept by holders of limited licences to brew beer and otherwise for securing any duty payable on, and safeguarding the revenue in connection with the brewing of, beer brewed by the holders of limited licences to brew beer.

(4) If any holder of a limited licence to brew beer—

(a) contravenes or fails to comply with any provision of this section or any regulation made thereunder ; or

(b) sells or offers for sale any beer brewed by him,

he shall be liable on summary conviction to a penalty of £25.

(5) An officer may at all reasonable times enter and inspect any premises used for the purposes of brewing by the holder of a limited licence to brew beer and examine the vessels and utensils used by him for the purposes of brewing, and take samples of any worts, beer or materials for brewing in the possession of the brewer.

PART IV

WINE AND MADE-WINE

54.—(1) There shall be charged on wine—

(a) imported into the United Kingdom ; or

(b) produced in the United Kingdom by a person who is required by subsection (2) below to be licensed to produce wine for sale,

Wine: charge of excise duty.

a duty of excise at the rates shown in Schedule 1 to this Act and the duty shall, in so far as it is chargeable on wine produced in the United Kingdom, be charged and paid in accordance with regulations under section 56 below.

(2) Subject to subsection (4) below, a person who, on any premises in the United Kingdom, produces wine for sale must hold an excise licence under this subsection in respect of those premises for that purpose.

(3) On any licence under subsection (2) above there shall be charged an excise licence duty at the rate of £5·25 per annum.

(4) A person who, in warehouse, produces wine for sale by rendering it sparkling in accordance with warehousing regula-

tions need not hold an excise licence under subsection (2) above in respect of those premises.

(5) If any person who is required by subsection (2) above to hold a licence under that subsection in respect of any premises produces wine on those premises without being the holder of a licence under that subsection in respect of those premises he shall be liable on summary conviction to a penalty of £500 and the wine and all vessels, utensils and materials for producing wine found in his possession shall be liable to forfeiture.

Made-wine: charge of excise duty.

55.—(1) There shall be charged on made-wine—

(a) imported into the United Kingdom ; or

(b) produced in the United Kingdom by a person who is required by subsection (2) below to be licensed to produce made-wine for sale,

a duty of excise at the rates shown in Schedule 2 to this Act and the duty shall, in so far as it is chargeable on made-wine produced in the United Kingdom, be charged and paid in accordance with regulations under section 56 below.

(2) Subject to subsections (4) and (5) below, a person who, on any premises in the United Kingdom, produces made-wine for sale must hold an excise licence under this subsection in respect of those premises for that purpose.

(3) On any licence under subsection (2) above there shall be charged an excise licence duty at the rate of £5·25 per annum.

(4) A person who, in warehouse, produces made-wine for sale by rendering it sparkling in accordance with warehousing regulations need not hold an excise licence under subsection (2) above in respect of those premises.

(5) A person need not hold an excise licence under subsection (2) above in respect of premises on which he produces made-wine for sale so long as all the following conditions are satisfied in relation to the production of made-wine by him on those premises, that is to say—

(a) the duty chargeable on each alcoholic ingredient used by him has become payable before he uses it ;

(b) the ingredients he uses do not include cider or black beer ;

(c) he does not increase by fermentation the alcoholic strength of any liquor or substance used by him ; and

(d) he does not render any made-wine sparkling.

(6) If any person who is required by subsection (2) above to hold a licence under that subsection in respect of any premises produces made-wine on those premises without being the holder of a licence under that subsection in respect of those premises he shall be liable on summary conviction to a penalty

of £500 and the made-wine and all vessels, utensils and materials PART IV
for producing made-wine found in his possession shall be liable
to forfeiture.

56.—(1) The Commissioners may with a view to managing Power to
the duties on wine and made-wine produced in the United regulate
Kingdom for sale make regulations— making of

    (a) regulating the production of wine and made-wine for wine and
made-wine
    sale, and the issue, renewal and cancellation of excise and provide
    licences therefor ; for charging

    (b) for determining the duty and the rates thereof and in duty thereon.
    that connection prescribing the method of charging the
    duty ;

    (c) prohibiting or restricting the use of wine in the produc-
    tion of made-wine ;

    (d) for securing and collecting the duty ;

    (e) for relieving wine or made-wine from the duty in such
    circumstances and to such extent as may be prescribed
    in the regulations.

(2) If any person contravenes or fails to comply with any
regulation made under this section, he shall be liable on summary conviction to a penalty of £50 and any article in respect
of which the offence was committed shall be liable to forfeiture.

57. The Commissioners may, subject to such conditions as they Mixing of
see fit to impose, permit the mixing in an excise warehouse made-wine
with made-wine (whether imported into or produced in the and spirits in
United Kingdom) of duty-free spirits in a proportion not exceed- warehouse.
ing 20 gallons of proof spirits to 100 gallons of made-wine, so,
however, that the mixture shall not by virtue of this section be
raised to a greater strength than 32° of proof.

58.—(1) The Commissioners may, subject to such conditions Mixing of
as they see fit to impose, permit the mixing in an excise ware- wine and
house with wine (whether imported into or produced in the United spirits in
Kingdom) of duty-free spirits in a proportion not exceeding 10 warehouse.
gallons of proof spirits to 100 gallons of wine, so, however,
that the mixture shall not, except as provided by subsection (2)
below, be raised to a greater strength than 40° of proof.

(2) If the Commissioners are satisfied that it is necessary for
the preservation of the wine, they may permit the fortification
of wine by virtue of this section for exportation only to a greater
strength than 40° of proof.

59.—(1) Neither imported wine nor imported made-wine shall Rendering
be rendered sparkling, whether by aeration, fermentation or imported
any other process, except in warehouse in accordance with wine or
warehousing regulations. made-wine
sparkling in
warehouse.

Part IV   (2) Any person who contravenes subsection (1) above and any person who is concerned in such a contravention shall be liable on summary conviction to a penalty of £100.

(3) All imported wine and imported made-wine rendered or being rendered sparkling in contravention of subsection (1) above, and all machinery, utensils, bottles and materials (including wine or made-wine) used or intended to be used in any process for rendering any wine or made-wine sparkling in contravention of that subsection shall be liable to forfeiture.

Repayment of duty on imported wine or made-wine used in the production or manufacture of other beverages, etc.

60.—(1) The Commissioners may by regulations provide for duty charged on imported wine or imported made-wine which is used as an ingredient in the production or manufacture of—

(a) any beverage of an alcoholic strength not exceeding 2° of proof ; or

(b) any such article (other than a beverage) as the Commissioners may determine having regard to the alcoholic content thereof,

to be repaid subject to such conditions as may be imposed by or under the regulations.

(2) The Commissioners may by regulations provide for duty charged on imported wine which is converted into vinegar to be repaid subject to such conditions as may be imposed by or under the regulations.

Remission or repayment of duty on spoilt wine or made-wine.

61.—(1) Where it is shown to the satisfaction of the Commissioners that any wine or made-wine which has been removed from the entered premises of a licensed producer of wine or of made-wine has accidentally become spoilt or otherwise unfit for use and, in the case of wine or made-wine delivered to another person, has been returned to the producer as so spoilt or unfit, the Commissioners shall, subject to compliance with such conditions as they may by regulations impose, remit or repay any duty charged or paid in respect of the wine or made-wine.

(2) If any person contravenes or fails to comply with any regulation made under subsection (1) above, he shall be liable on summary conviction to a penalty of £50.

Part V
Cider

Excise duty on cider.

62.—(1) There shall be charged on cider—

(a) imported into the United Kingdom ; or

(b) made in the United Kingdom by a person who is required by subsection (2) below to be registered as a maker of cider,

a duty of excise at the rate of £0.2420 a gallon.

(2) Subject to subsection (3) below, a person who, on any premises in the United Kingdom, makes cider for sale must be registered with the Commissioners in respect of those premises.

(3) The Treasury may by order made by statutory instrument provide for exempting from subsection (2) above makers of cider whose production does not exceed such limit as is specified in the order and who comply with such other conditions as may be so specified.

(4) If any person who is required by subsection (2) above to be registered in respect of any premises makes cider on those premises without being registered in respect of them, he shall be liable on summary conviction to a penalty of £500 and the cider and all vessels, utensils and materials for making cider found in his possession shall be liable to forfeiture.

(5) The Commissioners may with a view to managing the duty on cider made in the United Kingdom make regulations—

    (a) regulating the making of cider for sale and the registration and cancellation of registration of makers of cider ;

    (b) for determining the duty and the rate thereof and in that connection prescribing the method of charging the duty ;

    (c) for securing and collecting the duty ;

    (d) for relieving cider from the duty in such circumstances and to such extent as may be prescribed in the regulations.

(6) If any person contravenes or fails to comply with any regulation made under subsection (5) above, he shall be liable on summary conviction to a penalty of £50 and any article in respect of which the offence was committed shall be liable to forfeiture.

63. The Commissioners may by regulations provide for duty charged on imported cider which is used as an ingredient in the production or manufacture of— *Repayment of duty on imported cider used in the production or manufacture of other beverages, etc.*

    (a) any beverage of an alcoholic strength not exceeding 2° of proof ; or

    (b) any such article (other than a beverage) as the Commissioners may determine having regard to the alcoholic content thereof,

to be repaid subject to such conditions as may be imposed by or under the regulations.

64.—(1) Where it is shown to the satisfaction of the Commissioners that any cider which has been removed from the entered premises of a registered maker of cider has accidentally become spoilt or otherwise unfit for use and, in the case of cider delivered to another person, has been returned to the maker *Remission or repayment of duty on spoilt cider.*

as so spoilt or unfit, the Commissioners shall, subject to compliance with such conditions as they may by regulations impose, remit or repay any duty charged or paid in respect of the cider.

(2) If any person contravenes or fails to comply with any regulation made under subsection (1) above, he shall be liable on summary conviction to a penalty of £50.

PART VI

GENERAL CONTROL PROVISIONS

Sale of dutiable alcoholic liquors

Excise licence for dealing wholesale in certain alcoholic liquors.

65.—(1) Subject to the provisions of this section, no person shall deal wholesale in any of the alcoholic liquors to which this section applies, that is to say, spirits, beer, wine and made-wine, unless he holds an excise licence for that purpose under this section in respect of that liquor.

(2) A licence granted under this section shall expire on the 30th June next after it is granted.

(3) On any licence granted under this section there shall be charged an excise licence duty of £5.

(4) Subject in the case of a distiller to section 27(4) above, any alcoholic liquor to which this section applies which is the produce of a licensed manufacturer may be dealt in wholesale without an excise licence under this section—

(a) at the premises where it is manufactured ; or

(b) if the liquor is supplied to the purchaser direct from the premises where it is manufactured, at any other place by the manufacturer or a servant or agent of his.

In this subsection " licensed manufacturer " means a distiller, rectifier, compounder, brewer for sale or licensed producer of wine or of made-wine.

(5) Without prejudice to subsection (4) above, an excise licence under this section as a wholesale dealer in spirits shall not, except with the permission of the Commissioners and subject to such conditions as they see fit to impose, be granted to a distiller in respect of any premises within 2 miles of his distillery.

(6) A person holding a licence under this section in respect of wine may deal wholesale at his licensed premises in made-wine as well as wine without taking out a further licence under this section.

(7) If, save as permitted by this section, any person deals wholesale in any alcoholic liquor to which this section applies

otherwise than under and in accordance with a licence under this PART VI
Act so authorising him he shall be liable on summary conviction
to a penalty of £100.

(8) For the purposes of this section, dealing wholesale means
the sale at any one time to any one person of quantities not less
than the following, namely—
(a) in the case of spirits, wine or made-wine, 2 gallons or
1 case ; or
(b) in the case of beer, 4½ gallons or 2 cases.

66.—(1) Subject to subsection (2) below, an excise licence Excise
shall not be required for the sale wholesale of— licence not
(a) any liquor which, whether made on the premises of a required for
brewer for sale or elsewhere, is found on analysis of alcoholic
a sample thereof at any time to be of an original liquors.
gravity not exceeding 1016° and of a strength not
exceeding 2° of proof ;
(b) perfumes ;
(c) flavouring essences recognised by the Commissioners as
not being intended for consumption as or with dutiable
alcoholic liquor ;
(d) spirits, wine or made-wine so medicated as to be, in
the opinion of the Commissioners, intended for use
as a medicine and not as a beverage.

(2) Subsection (1)(a) above shall not apply to Northern Ireland.

67.—(1) The Commissioners may, with a view to the protec- Power to
tion of the revenue, make regulations regulating the keeping of regulate
spirits, beer, wine, made-wine or cider respectively by whole- keeping of
salers and retailers. dutiable
alcoholic
(2) If any person contravenes or fails to comply with any liquors by
regulation made under this section, he shall be liable on wholesalers
summary conviction to a penalty of £100, and any liquor, and retailers.
container or utensil in respect of which the offence was committed
shall be liable to forfeiture.

68. If at any time on the taking of an account by an officer Penalty for
of the spirits in the stock or possession of a wholesaler or retailer excess in
of spirits the quantity of those spirits computed at proof is found stock of
to exceed the quantity which ought to be in his possession wholesaler
according to any stock book required under this Act to be kept of spirits.
by the wholesaler or retailer, the excess shall be liable to forfeiture
and the wholesaler or retailer shall be liable on summary
conviction to a penalty of double the duty on a like quantity of
plain spirits at proof charged at the highest rate.

PART VI
Miscellaneous
provisions as
to wholesalers
and retailers
of spirits.

69.—(1) A wholesaler of spirits shall not carry on his business on any premises communicating otherwise than by a public roadway with any premises entered or used by a distiller or rectifier.

(2) Save with the permission of the Commissioners and subject to compliance with such conditions as they see fit to impose, a retailer of spirits shall not—

    (*a*) carry on his business on any premises which are entered or used by a distiller or rectifier or which communicate otherwise than by a public roadway with any such premises ; or

    (*b*) be concerned or interested in the business of a distiller or rectifier carried on upon any premises within 2 miles of any premises at which he sells spirits by retail.

(3) If any person contravenes or fails to comply with subsection (1) or (2) above or any condition imposed under subsection (2) above, he shall be liable on summary conviction to a penalty of £200.

(4) A retailer of spirits shall not, unless he is also a wholesaler of spirits, sell or send out spirits to a rectifier or to a wholesaler or retailer of spirits, nor shall he buy or receive spirits from another such retailer who is not also such a wholesaler ; and if he contravenes or fails to comply with this subsection he shall be liable on summary conviction to a penalty of £50.

70.—(1) If any person hawks spirits or, save as permitted by the Customs and Excise Acts 1979 or some other Act, sells or exposes for sale any spirits otherwise than on premises in respect of which he holds an excise licence as a wholesaler of spirits or a justice's licence (or in Scotland, a Scottish licence) authorising him to sell spirits, the spirits shall be liable to forfeiture and he shall be liable on summary conviction to a penalty of £100 and may be detained.

(2) If any person knowingly sells or delivers or causes to be sold or delivered any spirits in order that they may be unlawfully consumed or brought into home use, then, in addition to any other punishment he may have incurred, he shall be liable on summary conviction to a penalty of £100.

(3) If any person receives, buys or procures any spirits from a person not authorised to sell or deliver them, he shall be liable on summary conviction to a penalty of £100.

(4) If any spirits delivered in bottle from a warehouse for home use are sold by a wholesaler or retailer of spirits at a strength lower than that by reference to which the duty chargeable thereon was computed, he shall be liable on summary conviction to a penalty of £50.

(5) For the purposes of this section "Scottish licence" includes an off-licence in terms of Schedule 1 to the Licensing (Scotland) Act 1976.

71.—(1) If any person—

(a) for the purpose of selling any liquor, describes the liquor (whether in any notice or advertisement or on any label or wrapper, or in any other manner whatsoever) by any name or words such as to indicate that the liquor is, or is a substitute for, or bears any resemblance to, any description of spirits, or that the liquor is wine fortified or mixed with spirits or any description of spirits ; or

(b) sells, offers for sale, or has in his possession for the purpose of sale, any liquor so described,

that person shall be guilty of an offence under this section unless he proves that the duty chargeable on spirits has been paid in respect of not less than 97½ per cent. of the liquor.

(2) Notwithstanding anything in this section—

(a) the name " port " or " sherry " or the name of any other description of genuine wine ; or

(b) a name which, before 4th May 1932, was used to describe a liquor containing vermouth and spirits, the quantity of vermouth being not less than the quantity of spirits computed at proof,

shall not, for the purposes of this section, be treated as being in itself such a description as to give such an indication as is mentioned in subsection (1)(a) above.

(3) Notwithstanding anything in this section, a person who has sold, offered for sale, or had in his possession for the purpose of sale, any liquor described only by any such name as is mentioned in subsection (2)(a) above shall not be guilty of an offence under this section by reason that the liquor has been described by some other person (not being the agent or servant of the first mentioned person) by that name in association with some other description such as to give such an indication as is mentioned in subsection (1)(a) above.

(4) Any person guilty of an offence under this section shall be liable on summary conviction to a penalty of £100 ; and on the conviction of a person under this section the court may direct that any liquor and other article by means of or in relation to which the offence has been committed shall be forfeited, and any liquor or other article so directed to be forfeited shall be destroyed or otherwise disposed of as the court may direct.

(5) Nothing in this section as it applies to England and Wales or Northern Ireland shall apply to any liquor which is prepared—

    (*a*) on any premises in respect of which a justices' on-licence is in force ; or

    (*b*) in any registered club ; or

    (*c*) on any premises, or on board any aircraft, vessel or vehicle in the case of which, by virtue of section 199(*c*)
        or (*d*) of the Licensing Act 1964, a justices' licence is not required,

for immediate consumption on those premises, in that club or on board that aircraft, vessel or vehicle, as the case may be.

(6) Nothing in this section as it applies to Scotland shall apply to any liquor which is prepared—

    (*a*) on any premises in respect of which a Scottish licence is in force ; or

    (*b*) in any registered club ; or

    (*c*) in any theatre, or on board any aircraft, vessel or vehicle in the case of which, by virtue of section 138(1)(*b*) or
        (*c*) of the Licensing (Scotland) Act 1976, a Scottish licence is not required,

for immediate consumption on those premises, in that club, at that theatre or on board that aircraft, vessel or vehicle, as the case may be.

Offences by wholesaler or retailer of beer.   **72.**—(1) If any wholesaler or retailer of beer dilutes any beer or adds anything to beer other than finings for the purpose of clarification he shall be liable on summary conviction to a penalty of £50.

(2) If any beer which has been diluted or to which anything other than finings for the purpose of clarification has been added is found in the possession of a wholesaler or retailer of beer he shall be liable on summary conviction to a penalty of £50 and the beer shall be liable to forfeiture.

(3) Subject to subsection (4) below, if a wholesaler or retailer of beer receives or has in his custody or possession any sugar of any description or any saccharine substance, extract or syrup, except such as he proves to be for domestic use, or any preparation for increasing the gravity of beer, he shall be liable on summary conviction to a penalty of £50 and the article in question shall be liable to forfeiture.

(4) Where a wholesaler or retailer of beer carries on upon the same premises the trade of a brewer for sale or of a grocer, subsection (3) above shall not apply to sugar and other preparations duly held by him in accordance with regulations made

under section 50 above as a brewer for sale, or to sugar or syrup kept by him for sale in the ordinary course of his trade as a grocer.

73.—(1) If any person—

(a) for the purpose of selling any substance, describes the substance (whether in any notice or advertisement, or on any label, or in any other manner whatsoever) by any name or words such as to indicate that the substance is, or is a substitute for, or bears any resemblance to, beer or any description of beer ; or

(b) sells, offers for sale or has in his possession for the purpose of sale any substance so described,

that person shall be guilty of an offence under this section unless he proves that the duty chargeable on beer has been paid in respect of the whole of the substance.

(2) Black beer the worts whereof before fermentation were of a specific gravity of 1200° or more is not a substance to which this section applies ; and for the purposes of this section the name " black beer " shall not in itself be taken to be such a description as to give such an indication as is mentioned in subsection (1)(a) above.

(3) For the purposes of this section the name " ginger beer " or " ginger ale " shall not in itself be taken to be such a description as to give such an indication as is mentioned in subsection (1)(a) above.

(4) Any person guilty of an offence under this section shall be liable on summary conviction to a penalty of £100 ; and on the conviction of a person under this section the court may order that any article by means of or in relation to which the offence has been committed shall be forfeited, and any article so directed to be forfeited shall be destroyed or otherwise disposed of as the court may direct.

74. For the purposes of this Act, as against any person selling or offering for sale the liquor in question—

(a) any liquor sold or offered for sale as wine or under the name by which any wine is usually designated or known shall be deemed to be wine ; and

(b) any fermented liquor which is of a strength exceeding 40° of proof, not being imported wine delivered for home use in that state on which the appropriate duty has been duly paid, shall be deemed to be spirits.

Paragraph (a) above is without prejudice to any liability under section 71 above.

Licence or
authority to
manufacture
and deal
wholesale in
methylated
spirits.

Methylated spirits

75.—(1) The Commissioners may authorise any distiller, rectifier or compounder to methylate spirits, and any person so authorised is referred to in this Act as an " authorised methylator ".

(2) No person other than an authorised methylator shall methylate spirits or deal wholesale in methylated spirits unless he holds an excise licence as a methylator under this section.

(3) A licence granted under this section shall expire on the 30th September next after it is granted.

(4) On any licence granted under this section there shall be charged an excise licence duty of £10·50.

(5) Any person who, not being an authorised methylator, methylates spirits otherwise than under and in accordance with a licence under this section shall be liable on summary conviction to a penalty of £50.

(6) The Commissioners may at any time revoke or suspend any authorisation or licence granted under this section.

(7) For the purposes of this section, dealing wholesale means the sale at any one time to any one person of a quantity of methylated spirits of not less than 5 gallons or such smaller quantity as the Commissioners may by regulations specify.

Licence
to retail
methylated
spirits.

76.—(1) No person shall sell methylated spirits by retail unless he holds an excise licence for that purpose under this section.

(2) A licence granted under this section shall expire on the 30th September next after it is granted.

(3) On any licence granted under this section there shall be charged an excise licence duty of £0·50.

(4) A licence under this section shall not be granted—

(*a*) to a distiller, rectifier or compounder ; or

(*b*) in England, Wales or Northern Ireland, to a person holding a justice's on-licence in respect of spirits, beer, wine or made-wine ; or

(*c*) in Scotland—

(i) to a person holding a Scottish licence in respect of spirits, beer, wine or made-wine, or

(ii) to any other person except in accordance with the Methylated Spirits (Sale by Retail) (Scotland) Act 1937.

1937 c. 48.

(5) For the purposes of this section, sale by retail means the sale at any one time to any one person of a quantity of methylated spirits not exceeding 4 gallons.

77.—(1) The Commissioners may with a view to the protection of the revenue make regulations—

Power
to make
regulations
relating to
methylated
spirits.

    (*a*) regulating the methylation of spirits and the supply,
storage, removal, sale, delivery, receipt, use and
exportation or shipment as stores of methylated
spirits ;

    (*b*) prescribing the spirits which may be used, and the sub-
stances which may be mixed therewith, for methylation ;

    (*c*) permitting spirits to be methylated in warehouse ;

    (*d*) permitting the sale without a licence of such methylated
spirits as may be specified in the regulations ;

    (*e*) regulating the importation, receipt, removal, storage and
use of spirits for methylation ;

    (*f*) regulating the storage and removal of substances to be
used in methylating spirits ;

    (*g*) prescribing the manner in which account is to be kept
of stocks of methylated spirits in the possession of
authorised or licensed methylators and of retailers of
methylated spirits ;

    (*h*) for securing any duty chargeable in respect of methylated
spirits of any class.

(2) Different regulations may be made under this section with
respect to different classes of methylated spirits or different kinds
of methylated spirits of any class.

(3) If any person contravenes or fails to comply with any
regulation under this section, he shall be liable on summary
conviction to a penalty of £100.

(4) If, save as permitted by any regulation under this section,
any person sells methylated spirits otherwise than under and in
accordance with a licence under section 75 or 76 above, he shall
be liable on summary conviction to a penalty of £50.

(5) Any spirits or methylated spirits in respect of which an
offence under subsection (3) or (4) above is committed shall be
liable to forfeiture.

(6) Nothing in any regulations made under this section shall
prejudice the operation of the Methylated Spirits (Sale by Retail)
(Scotland) Act 1937.

78.—(1) If, at any time when an account is taken and a
balance struck of the quantity of any kind of methylated spirits
in the possession of an authorised or licensed methylator, that
quantity computed at proof differs from the quantity so computed which ought to be in his possession according to any

accounts required by regulations made under section 77 above to be kept thereof, then, subject to subsection (2) below—

(*a*) if the former quantity exceeds the latter, the excess, or such part thereof as the Commissioners may determine, shall be liable to forfeiture ;

(*b*) if the former quantity is less than the latter, the methylator shall on demand by the Commissioners pay on the deficiency or such part thereof as the Commissioners may specify the duty payable on spirits.

(2) Subsection (1) above shall not apply if the excess is not more than 1 per cent. or the deficiency is not more than 2 per cent. of the aggregate computed at proof of—

(*a*) the balance struck when an account was last taken ; and

(*b*) any quantity which has since been lawfully added to the methylator's stock.

(3) If any person authorised by regulations made under section 77 above to supply any kind of methylated spirits knowingly supplies such spirits to any person not authorised by those regulations to receive them, he shall, without prejudice to any penalty he may have incurred, pay thereon the duty payable on spirits.

(4) If any person other than an authorised or licensed methylator has in his possession any methylated spirits obtained otherwise than from a person authorised by regulations under the said section 77 to supply those spirits, he shall be liable on summary conviction to a penalty of £100 and the methylated spirits shall be liable to forfeiture.

Inspection of premises, etc.

79. Without prejudice to any other power conferred by the Customs and Excise Acts 1979, an officer may in the daytime enter and inspect the premises of any person authorised by regulations made under section 77 above to receive methylated spirits, and may inspect and examine any methylated spirits thereon and take samples of any methylated spirits or of any goods containing methylated spirits, paying a reasonable price for each sample.

Prohibition of use of methylated spirits, etc. as a beverage or medicine.

80.—(1) If any person—

(*a*) prepares or attempts to prepare any liquor to which this section applies for use as a beverage or as a mixture with a beverage ; or

(*b*) sells any such liquor, whether so prepared or not, as a beverage or mixed with a beverage ; or

(c) uses any such liquor or any derivative thereof in the preparation of any article capable of being used wholly or partially as a beverage or internally as a medicine ; or

(d) sells or has in his possession any such article in the preparation of which any such liquor or any derivative thereof has been used ; or

(e) except as permitted by the Commissioners and in accordance with any conditions imposed by them, purifies or attempts to purify any such liquor or, after any such liquor has once been used, recovers or attempts to recover the spirit or alcohol contained therein by distillation or condensation or in any other manner,

he shall be liable on summary conviction to a penalty of £100 and the liquor in respect of which the offence was committed shall be liable to forfeiture.

(2) Nothing in this section shall prohibit the use of any liquor to which this section applies or any derivative thereof—

(a) in the preparation for use as a medicine of sulphuric ether, chloroform, or any other article which the Commissioners may by order specify ; or

(b) in the making for external use only of any article sold or supplied in accordance with regulations made by the Commissioners under section 77 above ; or

(c) in any art or manufacture,

or the sale or possession of any article permitted to be prepared or made by virtue of paragraph (a) or (b) above where the article is sold or possessed for use as mentioned in that paragraph.

(3) The liquors to which this section applies are methylated spirits, methyl alcohol, and any mixture containing methylated spirits or methyl alcohol.

Still licences

81.—(1) Subject to the provisions of this section, no person shall keep or use a still otherwise than as a distiller, rectifier, or compounder unless he holds an excise licence for that purpose under this section.

Licence for keeping still otherwise than as a distiller, etc.

(2) A licence granted under this section shall expire on the 5th July next after it is granted.

PART VI

(3) On any licence granted under this section there shall be charged an excise licence duty of £0·50.

(4) The Commissioners may permit, subject to such conditions as they see fit to impose, the keeping and use without a licence under this section of a still—

    (a) kept by a person who makes or keeps stills solely for the purpose of sale ; or

    (b) kept or used for experimental, analytical or scientific purposes ; or

    (c) kept or used for the manufacture of any article other than spirits.

(5) If any person required to hold a licence under this section keeps or uses a still otherwise than under and in accordance with such a licence, he shall be liable on summary conviction to a penalty of £100 and the still shall be liable to forfeiture.

(6) If any person holding a licence under this section is convicted of any offence whatever in relation to methylated spirits, the Commissioners may suspend or revoke his licence.

Power to make regulations with respect to stills.

82.—(1) The Commissioners may, with a view to the protection of the revenue, make regulations—

    (a) regulating the keeping and use of stills by persons other than distillers or rectifiers ;

    (b) regulating the manufacture of stills ;

    (c) prohibiting, except in such cases and upon such conditions as may be prescribed by the regulations, the keeping or use by persons other than distillers or rectifiers of stills of greater capacity than 50 gallons ;

    (d) regulating the removal of stills or parts thereof.

(2) If any person contravenes or fails to comply with any regulation made under this section he shall be liable on summary conviction to a penalty of £100 and any still or part thereof in respect of which the offence was committed shall be liable to forfeiture.

Power of entry on premises of person keeping or using still.

83.—(1) Without prejudice to any other power conferred by the Customs and Excise Acts 1979, an officer may, subject to subsection (2) below, at any time enter upon the premises of any person licensed or permitted to keep a still under section 81 above and examine any still or retort kept or used by that person.

(2) No officer shall exercise the powers conferred on him by subsection (1) above by night unless he is accompanied by a constable.

Relief from, and payment by instalments of, liquor licence duties PART VI

84.—(1) Any manufacturing or wholesale chemist and druggist who—

(a) requires an excise licence for the purposes only of selling spirits of wine wholesale for medicinal purposes to registered medical practitioners, duly registered pharmaceutical chemists, chemists and druggists or persons requiring the spirits for use for scientific purposes in any laboratory ; and

(b) undertakes not to sell spirits otherwise than for those purposes and to those persons,

may obtain that licence on payment of a reduced excise licence duty of £2.

(2) The Commissioners may attach such conditions to any licence granted on payment of a reduced duty under this section as they think expedient for the protection of the revenue.

(3) If any person holding a licence granted on payment of a reduced duty under this section sells spirits in any manner contrary to his undertaking or to the conditions attached to his licence he shall be liable on summary conviction to a penalty of £50.

Reduced duty on excise licence for sale of spirits for medical purposes, etc.

85.—(1) This section applies to any excise licence under this Act other than—

(a) a licence to which section 86 below applies ; and

(b) a limited licence to brew beer.

(2) Where an excise licence to which this section applies is granted after the commencement of the licence year—

(a) to a person who has not within the 2 years immediately preceding held a similar licence ; or

(b) in respect of premises in respect of which the person to whom the licence is granted has not within that period held a similar licence,

the proper officer may grant the licence on payment of such sum as bears to the duty payable thereon apart from this section the same proportion as the period for which the licence will be in force bears to a year.

Reduced duty on part-year licences generally.

86.—(1) This section applies to an excise licence granted under the following provisions of this Act for the following purposes respectively, that is to say—

(a) under section 65, to deal wholesale in any alcoholic liquor to which that section applies ;

(b) under section 75, to manufacture and deal wholesale in methylated spirits ;

Reduced duty on certain part-year licences.

(c) under section 76, to sell methylated spirits by retail;

(d) under section 81, to keep or use a still.

(2) Subject to subsection (3) below, where any licence to which this section applies is granted more than 3 months after the commencement of the licence year—

> (a) to a person who has not within the 2 years immediately preceding held a similar licence ; or
>
> (b) in respect of premises in respect of which the person to whom the licence is granted has not within that period held a similar licence,

the proper officer may grant the licence upon payment of such proportion of the full duty chargeable thereon as is specified in the following table in relation to the month during which the licence is taken out, that is to say—

Month from the commencement of the licence year	*Proportion of full duty*
4th to 6th	$\frac{3}{4}$
7th to 9th	$\frac{1}{2}$
10th to 12th	$\frac{1}{4}$

(3) In its application to a wholesaler who has been granted relief under section 87(3) below on his trade being temporarily discontinued, subsection (2) above shall apply as respects the grant, on his first resuming his trade thereafter, of his new licence as a wholesaler as if paragraphs (a) and (b) thereof were omitted.

Relief from duty on discontinuance of trade.

87.—(1) Where a distiller, rectifier, compounder, brewer for sale, beer-primer, producer of wine or of made-wine or a wholesaler satisfies the Commissioners that his trade has been permanently discontinued he shall, subject to subsections (2) and (4) below, be entitled to surrender his licence and obtain relief from excise licence duty in respect of the period of the licence unexpired at the date when the trade was discontinued.

In this subsection " beer-primer " means a person who holds a licence under section 48 above.

(2) No relief shall be granted under subsection (1) above where the trade has been discontinued owing to the disqualification either of the premises or of the trader by reason of the conviction of the trader of some offence.

(3) Where a wholesaler satisfies the Commissioners that his trade has been temporarily discontinued—

> (a) by reason of the premises in respect of which his licence was granted having been destroyed or seriously damaged or closed with a view to their demolition or alteration ; or

    (*b*) by reason of any circumstances directly or indirectly attributable to any war in which Her Majesty may be or have been engaged ; or

    (*c*) in Great Britain, by reason of the compulsory acquisition or the proposed compulsory acquisition of the said premises ;

he shall, subject to subsection (4) below, on making application as provided in subsection (5) below and surrendering his licence, be entitled to relief from excise licence duty in respect of the period of the licence unexpired at the date when the trade was discontinued.

In this subsection, " compulsory acquisition " includes acquisition by agreement by any authority or persons for a purpose for which the authority or persons could be authorised to acquire the premises compulsorily.

(4) A wholesaler shall not be entitled to relief from duty under subsection (1) or (3) above unless his trade is discontinued within 9 months after the commencement of the licence year.

(5) An application for relief from duty under subsection (3) above shall be made to the Commissioners within one month after the discontinuance of the trade or within such longer period as the Commissioners may in any special case allow, and before making the application the licence holder shall give notice to the registered owner of the licensed premises of his intention to make it.

(6) Relief from excise licence duty under this section shall be granted by the Commissioners by repayment or, in so far as the duty has not been paid, by remission of the appropriate amount of duty.

(7) The appropriate amount of duty is, except where the relief is due to a wholesaler, such part of the full amount of duty for a year as bears to that amount the same proportion as the period in respect of which the licence holder is entitled to relief bears to a year.

(8) Where the relief is due to a wholesaler, the appropriate amount of duty is such proportion of the full amount of duty for the year as is specified in the following table in relation to the month during which the trade is discontinued, that is to say—

Month from the commencement of the licence year	*Proportion of full duty*
1st to 3rd	$\frac{3}{4}$
4th to 6th	$\frac{1}{2}$
7th to 9th	$\frac{1}{4}$

PART VI
Payment
of licence
duty in two
instalments.

88.—(1) Where the excise licence duty payable by any person on the grant to him of a licence as a distiller, rectifier, compounder, brewer, producer of wine or of made-wine or as a wholesaler, or the aggregate amount of the duties payable on two or more such licences granted to him in respect of the same premises, amounts to not less than £20, the licence or licences may, at the option of that person, be granted upon payment of half only of the duty or aggregate amount so payable.

(2) Where a licence is granted in pursuance of subsection (1) above upon payment of half only of the duty or aggregate amount of the duty, the second half of that duty or amount shall be paid immediately after the expiration of 6 months from the commencement of the appropriate licence year, or on 1st February next following the grant of the licence or licences, whichever is the earlier.

(3) If default is made in payment of the second half of the duty or amount payable under subsection (2) above the licence or licences shall be of no effect so long as the default continues.

(4) Any sum remaining unpaid in any case in respect of the said second half may be recovered either as a debt due to the Crown or by distress on the licensed premises, and the proper officer may, subject to subsection (5) below, for the purpose of such distress by warrant signed by him authorise any person to distrain upon the premises and to sell any thing so distrained by public auction after giving 6 days' notice of the sale.

(5) A distress shall not be levied under subsection (4) above unless notice in writing requiring the payment of the sum unpaid has been served on the holder of the licence or licences by leaving the notice at the premises or by sending it by post addressed to him at those premises.

(6) The proceeds of any such sale shall be applied in or towards payment of the costs and expenses of the distress and sale and the payment of the sum due, and the surplus, if any, shall be paid to the holder of the licence or licences.

(7) In the application of this section to Scotland, any reference to distress, or to levying distress, shall be construed as a reference to poinding.

PART VII

MISCELLANEOUS

Saving for certain privileges relating to sale of wine

Saving for
Cambridge
University
and Vintners
company.

89. Nothing in this Act shall affect—

    (a) any privilege in relation to the sale of wine enjoyed at 1st January 1953 by the University of Cambridge, or the chancellor, masters or scholars thereof, or by any person to whom that privilege has been transferred in pursuance of any Act ;

(b) the exemption from the obligation to take out an excise licence for the sale of wine enjoyed at that date by the Company of the master, wardens and commonalty of Vintners of the City of London.

But—

(i) the exemption in paragraph (b) above shall not extend to freemen of the said company who have obtained the freedom by redemption only ;

(ii) no freeman of the said company shall be entitled to that exemption in respect of more than one set of premises at any one time ; and

(iii) no person shall be entitled to that exemption unless he previously makes entry of the premises on which he intends to sell wine.

General

90.—(1) Any power to make regulations conferred by this Act shall be exercisable by statutory instrument. *Regulations.*

(2) A statutory instrument containing regulations under this Act shall be subject to annulment in pursuance of a resolution of either House of Parliament.

91. Directions given under any provision of this Act may make different provision for different circumstances and may be varied or revoked by subsequent directions thereunder. *Directions.*

92.—(1) The enactments specified in Schedule 3 to this Act shall be amended in accordance with the provisions of that Schedule. *Consequential amendments, repeals and saving and transitional provisions.*

(2) The enactments specified in Parts I and II of Schedule 4 to this Act are hereby repealed to the extent specified in the third column of that Schedule and the instrument specified in Part III of that Schedule is hereby revoked to the extent so specified.

(3) Any provision of this Act relating to anything done or required or authorised to be done under or by reference to that provision or any other provision of this Act shall have effect as if any reference to that provision, or that other provision, as the case may be, included a reference to the corresponding provision of the enactments repealed by this Act.

(4) Where an offence has been committed under section 129 of the Customs and Excise Act 1952 proceedings may be taken under section 51 of this Act in respect of the continuance of the *1952 c. 44.*

PART VII offence under section 129 after the commencement of this Act in the same manner as if the offence had been committed under section 51 of this Act.

1952 c. 44.

(5) Where an offence has been committed under section 102 of the Customs and Excise Act 1952 before the commencement of this Act subsection (4) of section 21 of this Act shall apply on a conviction of an offence under that section as it would apply had the earlier offence been committed under section 21.

(6) The repeal by this Act of sections 103 and 112 of the Customs and Excise Act 1952 shall not affect the right to draw-back under section 103 in respect of medicinal spirits in respect of which a repayment of duty had been made before 8th August 1972 or the right to a repayment of duty under section 112 in respect of spirits used for medical purposes before that date (being the date on which the amendments made in those provisions by section 57 of the Finance Act 1972 came into operation).

1972 c. 41.

(7) The repeal by this Act of section 243 of the Customs and Excise Act 1952 and section 3(4) of the Finance Act 1960 shall not affect the operation of the saving in relation to spirits dis-tilled before 1st August 1969 contained in paragraph 1 of Schedule 7 to the Finance Act 1969 (which repealed subsection (1)(*b*) of that section except in relation to spirits distilled before that date).

1960 c. 44.

1969 c. 32.

(8) Nothing in this section shall be taken as prejudicing the operation of sections 15 to 17 of the Interpretation Act 1978 (which relate to the effect of repeals).

1978 c. 30.

Citation and commence-ment.

93.—(1) This Act may be cited as the Alcoholic Liquor Duties Act 1979 and is included in the Acts which may be cited as the Customs and Excise Acts 1979.

(2) This Act shall come into operation on 1st April 1979.

SCHEDULES
SCHEDULE 1
WINE: RATES OF DUTY

Section 54.

Description of wine (in strengths measured by reference to the following percentages of alcohol by volume at a temperature of 20° C.)	Rates of duty (per gallon)
	£
Wine of an alcoholic strength—	
not exceeding 15 per cent. ...	3·2500
exceeding 15 but not exceeding 18 per cent.	3·7500
exceeding 18 but not exceeding 22 per cent.	4·4150
exceeding 22 per cent.	4·4150 plus £0·4700 for every 1 per cent. or part of 1 per cent. in excess of 22 per cent.; each of the above rates of duty being, in the case of sparkling wine, increased by £0·7150 per gallon.

SCHEDULE 2
MADE-WINE: RATES OF DUTY

Section 55.

Description of made-wine (in strengths measured by reference to the following percentages of alcohol by volume at a temperature of 20° C.)	Rates of duty (per gallon)
	£
Made-wine of an alcoholic strength—	
not exceeding 10 per cent. ...	2·1100
exceeding 10 but not exceeding 15 per cent.	3·1600
exceeding 15 but not exceeding 18 per cent.	3·4750
exceeding 18 per cent.	3·4750 plus £0·4700 for every 1 per cent. or part of 1 per cent. in excess of 18 per cent.; each of the above rates of duty being, in the case of sparkling made-wine, increased by £0·3300 per gallon.

SCHEDULE 3

CONSEQUENTIAL AMENDMENTS

1955 c. 16.   *Food and Drugs Act* 1955

1. In section 3(4) of the Food and Drugs Act 1955, for the words " section one hundred and sixty-one of the Customs and Excise Act 1952 " there shall be substituted the words " section 70 of the Alcoholic Liquor Duties Act 1979 ".

1956 c. 30.   *Food and Drugs (Scotland) Act* 1956

2. In section 3(4) of the Food and Drugs (Scotland) Act 1956, for the words " section one hundred and sixty-one of the Customs and Excise Act 1952 " there shall be substituted the words " section 70 of the Alcoholic Liquor Duties Act 1979 ".

1963 c. 31.   *Weights and Measures Act* 1963

3. In section 58 of the Weights and Measures Act 1963, in the definition of " intoxicating liquor ", for the words " has the same meaning as for the purposes of the Customs and Excise Act 1952 " there shall be substituted the words " means spirits, beer, wine, made-wine or cider as defined in section 1 of the Alcoholic Liquor Duties Act 1979 ; ".

4. In Part VI of Schedule 4 to the Weights and Measures Act 1963, for paragraph 1 there shall be substituted the following paragraph—

" 1. In this Part of this Schedule—

(*a*) the expressions " beer " and " cider " have the same meanings respectively as in the Alcoholic Liquor Duties Act 1979 ;

(*b*) the expression " wine " means imported wine ; and

(*c*) the expression " British wine " means any liquor which is made from fruit and sugar or from fruit or sugar mixed with any other material and which has undergone a process of fermentation in the manufacture thereof, and includes British wines, made wines, mead and metheglin."

1964 c. 26.   *Licensing Act* 1964

5.—(1) The Licensing Act 1964 shall be amended as provided in this paragraph.

(2) In section 181, for the words " dealer's licence under section 146 of the Customs and Excise Act 1952 " there shall be substituted the words " wholesaler's licence under section 65 of the Alcoholic Liquor Duties Act 1979 " and for the words " dealer's licence " in the other two places where they occur there shall be substituted the words " wholesaler's licence ".

(3) In section 201(1)—

(*a*) in the definition of " sale by retail ", for the words following " section " there shall be substituted the words " 4(4) of the Alcoholic Liquor Duties Act 1979 " ; and (*b*) in the appropriate place in alphabetical order there shall be inserted the following definition (in place of the definition repealed by this Act)—

"wine" means wine or made-wine as defined in section 1 of the Alcoholic Liquor Duties Act 1979.

(4) In Part II of Schedule 9, in paragraph 4, for the words "section 307 of the Customs and Excise Act 1952)" there shall be substituted the words "section 1 of the Alcoholic Liquor Duties Act 1979)".

Weights and Measures Act (Northern Ireland) 1967

6. In section 41 of the Weights and Measures Act (Northern Ireland) 1967, in the definition of "intoxicating liquor", for the words "has the same meaning as for the purposes of the Customs and Excise Act 1952" there shall be substituted the words "means spirits, beer, wine, made-wine or cider as defined in section 1 of the Alcoholic Liquor Duties Act 1979;".

7. In Part VI of Schedule 2 to the Weights and Measures Act (Northern Ireland) 1967, for paragraph 1 there shall be substituted the following paragraph—

"1. In this Part of this Schedule—

(*a*) the expressions "beer" and "cider" have the same meanings respectively as in the Alcoholic Liquor Duties Act 1979;

(*b*) the expression "wine" means imported wine; and

(*c*) the expression "British wine" means any liquor which is made from fruit and sugar or from fruit or sugar mixed with any other material and which has undergone a process of fermentation in the manufacture thereof, and includes British wines, made wines, mead and metheglin."

Licensing Act (Northern Ireland) 1971

8.—(1) The Licensing Act (Northern Ireland) 1971 shall be amended as provided in this paragraph.

(2) In section 76(1), for the words "section 146 of the Customs and Excise Act 1952" there shall be substituted the words "section 65 of the Alcoholic Liquor Duties Act 1979".

(3) In section 76(2)(*b*), for the words "section 146 or 167" there shall be substituted the words "section 65 or 84" and for the words "Act of 1952" there shall be substituted the words "Act of 1979".

(4) In section 84(5), for the words "section 148(4) of the Customs and Excise Act 1952" there shall be substituted the words "section 4(4) of the Alcoholic Liquor Duties Act 1979".

(5) In section 85(*c*), for the words "section 167 of the Customs and Excise Act 1952" there shall be substituted the words "section 84 of the Alcoholic Liquor Duties Act 1979".

Licensing (Scotland) Act 1976

9. In section 139(1) of the Licensing (Scotland) Act 1976 the following amendments shall be made, that is to say—

(a) in the definitions of "made-wine" and "wine", for the words "Customs and Excise Act 1952" there shall be substituted the words "section 1 of the Alcoholic Liquor Duties Act 1979";

(b) in the definition of "wholesaler's excise licence", for the words from "section 146" to the end, there shall be substituted the words "section 65 of the Alcoholic Liquor Duties Act 1979".

Section 92(2).

SCHEDULE 4

REPEALS

PART I

ENACTMENTS OF THE PARLIAMENT OF THE UNITED KINGDOM

Chapter	Short title	Extent of repeal
53 & 54 Vict. c. 8.	The Customs and Inland Revenue Act 1890.	Section 31(2).
15 & 16 Geo. 6 & 1 Eliz. 2. c. 44.	The Customs and Excise Act 1952.	Part IV. Sections 226 to 228. Section 237. Sections 241 to 243. Section 263(3) to (5). In section 307(1), the definitions of "authorised methylator", "beer", "beer-primer", "brewer" and "brewer for sale", "British compounded spirits", "British spirits", "case", "cider", "compounder", "dealer", "distiller" and "distillery", "distiller's warehouse", "gravity" and "original gravity", "intoxicating liquor", "justices' licence" and "justices' on-licence", "licensed methylator", "limited licence to brew beer", "made-wine", "methylated spirits", "producer of wine", "producer of made-wine", "proof", "rectifier", "registered club", "retail", "retailer", "spirits", "spirits of wine", "wholesale" and "wine". In section 315, paragraphs (c) and (d). In Schedule 10, paragraph 15.
1 & 2 Eliz. 2. c. 34.	The Finance Act 1953.	Section 2.

Chapter	Short title	Extent of repeal
6 & 7 Eliz. 2. c. 56.	The Finance Act 1958.	Section 6.
7 & 8 Eliz. 2. c. 58.	The Finance Act 1959.	Section 2(1) and (5). Section 3(2), (3), (4) and (5).
8 & 9 Eliz. 2. c. 44.	The Finance Act 1960.	Section 3. Schedule 1.
1963 c. 25.	The Finance Act 1963.	Section 6. Schedule 2.
1963 c. 31.	The Weights and Measures Act 1963.	Section 59. In Schedule 10, paragraph 1(*d*).
1964 c. 49.	The Finance Act 1964.	Section 1(5). Section 2(5) and (6).
1966 c. 18.	The Finance Act 1966.	In Schedule 2, in paragraph 1, the words from "section 107(1)" to "spirits)" and paragraph 2.
1967 c. 54.	The Finance Act 1967.	Section 1(5). Section 4 except, in subsection (5), paragraphs (*a*)(i) and (v). Section 6. In Schedule 5, paragraphs 2, 3 and 4. In Schedule 6, paragraphs 1, 3, 4, 7, 8, 9, 10 and 11. In Schedule 9, paragraphs 1 to 6.
1968 c. 44.	The Finance Act 1968.	Section 1(3).
1968 c. 54.	The Theatres Act 1968.	In Schedule 2 the amendment in section 162 of the Customs and Excise Act 1952.
1969 c. 32.	The Finance Act 1969.	Section 1(5)(*b*). In Schedule 7, paragraph 2.
1970 c. 24.	The Finance Act 1970.	Section 6(1) and (2)(*a*). Section 7, except subsections (5) and (8).
1972 c. 41.	The Finance Act 1972.	Section 57(3) and (4).
1974 c. 30.	The Finance Act 1974.	Section 4.
1975 c. 45.	The Finance (No. 2) Act 1975.	Sections 9 and 10. Sections 14 and 15. In Schedule 3, paragraphs 3 to 7, 9, 15, 24 to 37, 42, in paragraph 44, subparagraphs (*a*), (*b*) and (*d*) and paragraphs 45 to 47. Schedules 4 and 5. In Schedule 6, paragraphs 5, 6, 7 and 8.
1976 c. 40.	The Finance Act 1976.	Sections 2 and 3. In Schedule 3, paragraphs 1, 5, 7 and 9.
1976 c. 66.	The Licensing (Scotland) Act 1976.	In Schedule 7, paragraphs 3 and 4.
1977 c. 36.	The Finance Act 1977.	Section 1(1) to (5), (8) and (9). Schedules 1 and 2.
1978 c. 42.	The Finance Act 1978.	Section 2. In Schedule 12, paragraphs 1 to 5.

PART II

ENACTMENTS OF THE PARLIAMENT OF NORTHERN IRELAND

Chapter	Short title	Extent of repeal
1959 c. 9 (N.I.).	The Finance Act (Northern Ireland) 1959.	Section 12(1) and (5). Section 13(2) to (5). Section 18(5).
1963 c. 22 (N.I.).	The Finance Act (Northern Ireland) 1963.	Section 19. Section 22(6). Schedule 2.
1967 c. 20 (N.I.).	The Finance Act (Northern Ireland) 1967.	Section 15(1)(*b*) and (6). Section 17. Section 21(6). In Schedule 2, the amendment in the Finance Act (Northern Ireland) 1959.

PART III

NORTHERN IRELAND INSTRUMENT

Year and Number	Title	Extent of revocation
1976/1214 (N.I. 23).	The Poisons (Northern Ireland) Order 1976.	In Schedule 2, paragraph 1.

Hydrocarbon Oil Duties Act 1979

1979 CHAPTER 5

An Act to consolidate the enactments relating to the excise duties on hydrocarbon oil, petrol substitutes, power methylated spirits and road fuel gas.

[22nd February 1979]

BE IT ENACTED by the Queen's most Excellent Majesty, by and with the advice and consent of the Lords Spiritual and Temporal, and Commons, in this present Parliament assembled, and by the authority of the same, as follows:—

The dutiable commodities

1.—(1) Subsections (2) to (4) below define the various descriptions of oil referred to in this Act.

Hydrocarbon oil.

(2) "Hydrocarbon oil" means petroleum oil, coal tar, and oil produced from coal, shale, peat or any other bituminous substance, and all liquid hydrocarbons, but does not include such hydrocarbons or bituminous or asphaltic substances as are—

(a) solid or semi-solid at a temperature of 15° C, or

(b) gaseous at a temperature of 15°C and under a pressure of 1013·25 millibars.

(3) "Light oil" means hydrocarbon oil—

(a) of which not less than 90 per cent. by volume distils at a temperature not exceeding 210°C, or

(b) which gives off an inflammable vapour at a temperature of less than 23°C when tested in the manner prescribed by the Acts relating to petroleum.

(4) "Heavy oil" means hydrocarbon oil other than light oil.

H3

Provisions supplementing s. 1.

2.—(1) The method of testing oil for the purpose of ascertaining its classification in accordance with section 1 above shall, subject to subsection (3)(*b*) of that section, be such as the Commissioners may direct.

(2) Subject to subsection (3) below, the Treasury may from time to time direct that, for the purposes of any duty of excise for the time being chargeable on hydrocarbon oil, any specified description of light oil shall be treated as being heavy oil.

(3) The Treasury shall not give a direction under subsection (2) above in relation to any description of oil unless they are satisfied that the description is one which should, according to its use, be classed with heavy oil.

(4) For the purposes of the Customs and Excise Acts 1979, the production of hydrocarbon oil includes—

(*a*) the obtaining of one description of hydrocarbon oil from another description of hydrocarbon oil ; and

(*b*) the subjecting of hydrocarbon oil to any process of purification or blending,

as well as the obtaining of hydrocarbon oil from other substances or from any natural source.

(5) Where heavy oil having a temperature exceeding 15°C is measured for the purpose of ascertaining the amount of any duty of excise chargeable, or of any rebate or drawback allowable, on the oil and the Commissioners are satisfied that the oil is artificially heated, the duty shall be charged or the rebate or drawback shall be allowed on the number of litres which, in the opinion of the Commissioners, the oil would have measured if its temperature had been 15°C.

Hydrocarbon oil as ingredient of imported goods.

3. Where imported goods contain hydrocarbon oil as a part or ingredient thereof, the oil shall be disregarded in the application to the goods of section 126 of the Management Act (charge of duty on manufactured or composite imported articles) unless in the opinion of the Commissioners the goods should, according to their use, be classed with hydrocarbon oil.

Petrol substitutes and power methylated spirits.

4.—(1) In this Act " petrol substitute " means any liquid intended to take the place of petrol as fuel for internal combustion piston engines, being neither hydrocarbon oil nor power methylated spirits.

(2) In subsection (1) above, " liquid " does not include a substance which is gaseous at a temperature of 15°C and under a pressure of 1013·25 millibars.

(3) In this Act " power methylated spirits " means spirits methylated in such manner as may be prescribed by regulations made under section 77 of the Alcoholic Liquor Duties Act 1979 1979 c. 4. for methylated spirits of that class.

5. In this Act " road fuel gas " means any substance which is Road fuel gaseous at a temperature of 15°C and under a pressure of 1013·25 gas. millibars, and which is for use as fuel in road vehicles.

Charging provisions

6.—(1) Subject to subsection (2) below, there shall be charged Excise duty on on hydrocarbon oil— hydrocarbon oil.
  (a) imported into the United Kingdom ; or
  (b) produced in the United Kingdom and delivered for home use from a refinery or from other premises used for the production of hydrocarbon oil or from any bonded storage for hydrocarbon oil, not being hydro-carbon oil chargeable with duty under paragraph (a) above,

a duty of excise at the rate of £0·0660 a litre in the case of light oil and £0·0770 a litre in the case of heavy oil.

(2) Where imported hydrocarbon oil is removed to a refinery, the duty chargeable under subsection (1) above shall, instead of being charged at the time of the importation of that oil, be charged on the delivery of any goods from the refinery for home use and shall be the same as that which would be payable on the importation of like goods.

7. A duty of excise at the same rate as the duty of excise on Excise duty on light oil shall be charged— petrol
  (a) on any petrol substitute which is sent out from the substitutes premises of a person producing or dealing in petrol and power substitutes and which was not acquired by him duty methylated paid under this paragraph ; and spirits.
  (b) on spirits used for making power methylated spirits (payable by the methylator immediately after the spirits have been so used).

8.—(1) A duty of excise shall be charged on road fuel gas Excise duty on which is sent out from the premises of a person producing or road fuel gas. dealing in road fuel gas and on which the duty charged by this section has not been paid.

(2) The like duty of excise shall be charged on the setting aside for use, or on the use, by any person, as fuel in a road vehicle, of road fuel gas on which the duty charged by this section has not been paid.

(3) The rate of the duty under this section shall be prescribed by order made by the Treasury, and in exercising their power under this subsection the Treasury shall select the rate (whether for all road fuel gas or for a particular kind of road fuel gas) which in their opinion is for the time being the nearest convenient and suitable rate corresponding with the rate of excise duty on light oil.

In comparing the excise duty chargeable under this section with that on light oil account shall be taken of relative average calorific values and of other relevant factors.

(4) An order made under subsection (3) above—

(a) may express the rate of duty by reference to any method of measuring the road fuel gas ;

(b) may prescribe different rates for different kinds of road fuel gas ; and

(c) may prescribe a rate which depends in whole or in part on the rate for the time being of excise duty charged on light oil.

(5) The power to make orders under subsection (3) above shall be exercisable by statutory instrument, and any statutory instrument by which the power is exercised shall be subject to annulment in pursuance of a resolution of the House of Commons.

(6) For the purposes of this Act, so far as it relates to the excise duty chargeable under this section, road fuel gas shall be deemed to be used as fuel in a road vehicle if, but only if, it is used as fuel for the engine provided for propelling the vehicle, or for an engine which draws its fuel from the same supply as that engine.

(7) Subsection (2) above shall not apply to road fuel gas delivered to, or in the stock of, the person otherwise chargeable if it was delivered to, or stocked by, him before 3rd July 1972.

Delivery of oil without payment of duty

Oil delivered for home use for certain industrial purposes.

9.—(1) The Commissioners may permit hydrocarbon oil to be delivered for home use to an approved person, without payment of excise duty on the oil, where—

(a) it is to be put by him to a use qualifying for relief under this section ; or

(b) it is to be supplied by him in the course of a trade of supplying oil for any such use.

(2) The uses of hydrocarbon oil qualifying for relief under this section are—

(a) use in the manufacture or preparation of any article, not being hydrocarbon oil or an article which in the opinion of the Commissioners should, according to its use, be classed with hydrocarbon oil; and

(b) use for cleaning plant, in connection with the use of the plant in the manufacture or preparation of such an article,

but do not include the use of oil as fuel or, except as provided by subsection (3) below, as a lubricant.

(3) Where, in the manufacture or preparation of an article described in subsection (2)(a) above, hydrocarbon oil is used for preventing or reducing friction, adhesion or contact—

(a) between parts or components of the article; or

(b) between the article or a part or component of the article and any plant used in the manufacture or preparation, or any part or component of plant so used,

that use of the oil is to be included among the uses qualifying for relief under this section.

(4) Where the Commissioners are authorised to give permission under subsection (1) above in the case of any oil, but the permission is for any reason not given, they shall, if satisfied that the oil has been put by an approved person to a use qualifying for relief under this section, repay to him the amount of the excise duty paid on the oil, less any rebate allowed in respect of the duty.

(5) In this section—

(a) " an approved person " means a person for the time being approved in accordance with regulations made for any of the purposes of subsection (1) or (4) above under section 24(1) below; and

(b) " plant " means any machinery, apparatus, equipment or vessel.

10.—(1) Except with the consent of the Commissioners, no oil in whose case delivery without payment of duty has been permitted under section 9 above shall— Restrictions on the use of duty-free oil.

(a) be put to a use not qualifying for relief under that section; or

(b) be acquired or taken into any vehicle, appliance or storage tank in order to be put to such a use.

(2) In giving their consent for the purposes of subsection (1) above, the Commissioners may impose such conditions as they think fit.

(3) A person who—

(a) uses or acquires oil in contravention of subsection (1) above ; or

(b) is liable for oil being taken into a vehicle, appliance or storage tank in contravention of that subsection,

shall be liable on summary conviction to a penalty of three times the value of the oil or £100, whichever is the greater ; and the Commissioners may recover from him an amount equal to the excise duty on like oil at the rate in force at the time of the contravention.

(4) A person who supplies oil having reason to believe that it will be put to a use not qualifying for relief under section 9 above shall be liable on summary conviction to a penalty of three times the value of the oil or £100, whichever is the greater, if that use without the consent of the Commissioners would contravene subsection (1) above.

(5) A person who, with the intent that the restrictions imposed by subsection (1) above should be contravened,—

(a) uses or acquires oil in contravention of that subsection ; or

(b) supplies oil having reason to believe that it will be put to a use not qualifying for relief under section 9 above, being a use which, without the consent of the Commissioners, would contravene that subsection,

shall be guilty of an offence under this subsection.

(6) A person who is liable for oil being taken into a vehicle, appliance or storage tank in contravention of subsection (1) above shall be guilty of an offence under this subsection where the oil was taken in with the intent by him that the restrictions imposed by that subsection should be contravened.

(7) A person guilty of an offence under subsection (5) or (6) above shall be liable—

(a) on summary conviction, to a penalty of the prescribed sum or of three times the value of the oil in question, whichever is the greater, or to imprisonment for a term not exceeding 6 months, or to both ; or

(b) on conviction on indictment, to a penalty of any amount or to imprisonment for a term not exceeding 2 years, or to both.

(8) For the purposes of this section, a person is liable for oil being taken into a vehicle, appliance or storage tank in contravention of subsection (1) above if he is at the time the person having the charge of the vehicle, appliance or tank, or is its owner, except that if a person other than the owner is, or is for the time being, entitled to possession of it, that person and not the owner is liable.

(9) Any oil acquired, or taken into a vehicle, appliance or storage tank as mentioned in subsection (1) above, or supplied as mentioned in subsection (4) or (5) above, shall be liable to forfeiture.

Rebate of duty

11.—(1) Subject to sections 12 and 13 below, where heavy oil Rebate on charged with the excise duty on hydrocarbon oil is delivered heavy oil. for home use, there shall be allowed on the oil at the time of delivery a rebate of duty at a rate—

  (a) in the case of kerosene other than aviation turbine fuel, of £0·0022 a litre less than the rate at which the duty is for the time being chargeable ;

  (b) in the case of aviation turbine fuel, and heavy oil other than kerosene, of £0·0055 a litre less than the rate at which the duty is for the time being chargeable.

(2) In this section—

  (a) " aviation turbine fuel " means kerosene which is intended to be used as fuel for aircraft engines and is allowed to be delivered for that purpose without being marked in accordance with the regulations made for the purposes of this section ;

  (b) " kerosene " means heavy oil of which more than 50 per cent. by volume distils at a temperature not exceeding 240°C.

12.—(1) If, on the delivery of heavy oil for home use, it is Rebate not intended to use the oil as fuel for a road vehicle, a declaration allowed on shall be made to that effect in the entry for home use and fuel for road thereupon no rebate shall be allowed in respect of that oil. vehicles.

(2) No heavy oil on whose delivery for home use rebate has been allowed shall—

  (a) be used as fuel for a road vehicle ; or

  (b) be taken into a road vehicle as fuel,

unless an amount equal to the amount for the time being allowable in respect of rebate on like oil has been paid to the Commissioners in accordance with regulations made under section 24(1) below for the purposes of this section.

(3) For the purposes of this section and section 13 below—

(a) heavy oil shall be deemed to be used as fuel for a road vehicle if, but only if, it is used as fuel for the engine provided for propelling the vehicle or for an engine which draws its fuel from the same supply as that engine ; and

(b) heavy oil shall be deemed to be taken into a road vehicle as fuel if, but only if, it is taken into it as part of that supply.

Penalties for misuse of rebated heavy oil.

13.—(1) A person who—

(a) uses heavy oil in contravention of section 12(2) above ; or

(b) is liable for heavy oil being taken into a road vehicle in contravention of that subsection,

shall be liable on summary conviction to a penalty of three times the value of the oil or £100, whichever is the greater ; and the Commissioners may recover from him an amount equal to the rebate on like oil at the rate in force at the time of the contravention.

(2) A person who supplies heavy oil having reason to believe that it will be put to a particular use shall be liable on summary conviction to a penalty of three times the value of the oil or £100, whichever is the greater, where that use would, if a payment under subsection (2) of section 12 above were not made in respect of the oil, contravene that subsection.

(3) A person who, with the intent that the restrictions imposed by section 12 above should be contravened,—

(a) uses heavy oil in contravention of subsection (2) of that section ; or

(b) supplies heavy oil having reason to believe that it will be put to a particular use, being a use which would, if a payment under that subsection were not made in respect of the oil, contravene that subsection,

shall be guilty of an offence under this subsection.

(4) A person who is liable for heavy oil being taken into a road vehicle in contravention of subsection (2) of section 12 above shall be guilty of an offence under this subsection where the oil was taken in with the intent by him that the restrictions imposed by that section should be contravened.

(5) A person guilty of an offence under subsection (3) or (4) above shall be liable—

    (*a*) on summary conviction, to a penalty of the prescribed sum or of three times the value of the oil in question, whichever is the greater, or to imprisonment for a term not exceeding 6 months, or to both ; or

    (*b*) on conviction on indictment, to a penalty of any amount, or to imprisonment for a term not exceeding 2 years, or to both.

(6) Any heavy oil—

    (*a*) taken into a road vehicle as mentioned in section 12(2) above or supplied as mentioned in subsection (2) or (3) above ; or

    (*b*) taken as fuel into a vehicle at a time when it is not a road vehicle and remaining in the vehicle as part of its fuel supply at a later time when it becomes a road vehicle,

shall be liable to forfeiture.

(7) For the purposes of this section, a person is liable for heavy oil being taken into a road vehicle in contravention of section 12(2) above if he is at the time the person having the charge of the vehicle or is its owner, except that if a person other than the owner is, or is for the time being, entitled to possession of it, that person and not the owner is liable.

14.—(1) On light oil charged with the excise duty on hydro- Rebate on carbon oil, and delivered for home use as furnace fuel for burn- light oil for ing in vaporised or atomised form by a person for the time use as furnace being approved in accordance with regulations made for the fuel. purposes of this subsection under section 24(1) below, there shall be allowed at the time of delivery a rebate of duty at a rate of £0·0055 a litre less than the rate at which the duty is charged.

(2) Except with the consent of the Commissioners, no oil in whose case rebate has been allowed under this section shall—

    (*a*) be put to a use otherwise than as mentioned in subsection (1) above ; or

    (*b*) be acquired or taken into any vehicle, appliance or storage tank in order to be put to such a use.

(3) In giving their consent for the purposes of subsection (2) above, the Commissioners may impose such conditions as they think fit.

(4) A person who—

    (*a*) uses or acquires oil in contravention of subsection (2) above ; or (*b*) is liable for oil being taken into a vehicle, appliance or storage tank in contravention of that subsection,

shall be liable on summary conviction to a penalty of three times the value of the oil or £100, whichever is the greater; and the Commissioners may recover from him the amount of the rebate allowed on the oil.

  (5) A person who supplies oil having reason to believe that it will be used otherwise than as mentioned in subsection (1) above shall be liable on summary conviction to a penalty of three times the value of the oil or £100, whichever is the greater, if that use without the consent of the Commissioners would contravene subsection (2) above.

  (6) A person who, with the intent that the restrictions imposed by subsection (2) above should be contravened,—

  (*a*) uses or acquires oil in contravention of that subsection; or

  (*b*) supplies oil having reason to believe that it will be put to a use otherwise than as mentioned in subsection (1) above, being a use which, without the consent of the Commissioners, would contravene subsection (2) above,

shall be guilty of an offence under this subsection.

  (7) A person who is liable for oil being taken into a vehicle, appliance or storage tank in contravention of subsection (2) above shall be guilty of an offence under this subsection where the oil was taken in with the intent by him that the restrictions imposed by that subsection should be contravened.

  (8) A person guilty of an offence under subsection (6) or (7) above shall be liable—

  (*a*) on summary conviction, to a penalty of the prescribed sum or of three times the value of the oil in question, whichever is the greater, or to imprisonment for a term not exceeding 6 months, or to both; or

  (*b*) on conviction on indictment, to a penalty of any amount, or to imprisonment for a term not exceeding 2 years, or to both.

  (9) For the purposes of this section, a person is liable for oil being taken into a vehicle, appliance or storage tank in contravention of subsection (2) above if he is at the time the person having the charge of the vehicle, appliance or tank, or is its owner, except that if a person other than the owner is, or is for the time being, entitled to possession of it, that person and not the owner is liable.

(10) Any oil acquired, or taken into a vehicle, appliance or storage tank, as mentioned in subsection (2) above, or supplied as mentioned in subsection (5) or (6) above, shall be liable to forfeiture.

Drawback

15.—(1) A drawback equal to any amount shown to the satisfaction of the Commissioners to have been paid in respect of the goods in question by way of the excise duty on hydrocarbon oil shall be allowed on the exportation, shipment as stores or warehousing in an excise warehouse for use as stores of— Drawback of duty on exportation etc. of certain goods.

    (*a*) any hydrocarbon oil ; or

    (*b*) any article in which there is contained any hydrocarbon oil which was used, or which formed a component of any article used, as an ingredient in the manufacture or preparation of the article.

(2) The Treasury may by order direct as respects articles of any class or description specified in the order that, subject to the provisions of the order, drawback shall be allowed under subsection (1) above in respect of hydrocarbon oil (or goods containing it) used as a material, solvent, extractant, preservative or finish in the manufacture or preparation of the articles.

(3) On the making of an order under subsection (2) above this Act shall have effect, subject to the provisions of the order and of this section, as if the reference in subsection (1)(*b*) above to an article in which there is contained any hydrocarbon oil used as an ingredient in the manufacture or preparation of the article included a reference to an article of the class or description specified in the order.

(4) An order made under subsection (2) above as respects articles of any class or description—

    (*a*) may provide for drawback to be allowed in respect of hydrocarbon oil (or goods containing it) used as a material, solvent, extractant, preservative or finish in the manufacture or preparation not directly of articles of that class or description but of articles incorporated in them ; and

    (*b*) may provide that the quantity of hydrocarbon oil as respects duty on which drawback is to be allowed shall be determined by reference to average quantities or otherwise.

(5) The power to make orders under subsection (2) above shall be exercisable by statutory instrument, and any statutory instrument by which the power is exercised shall be subject to annulment in pursuance of a resolution of the House of Commons.

Drawback of
duty on
exportation
etc. of power
methylated
spirits.

16. On power methylated spirits which are exported, shipped as stores or warehoused in an excise warehouse for use as stores there shall be allowed a drawback equal to the amount of excise duty shown to the satisfaction of the Commissioners to have been paid in respect of those spirits.

Miscellaneous reliefs

Heavy oil
used by
horticultural
producers.

17.—(1) If, on an application made for the purposes of this section by a horticultural producer, it is shown to the satisfaction of the Commissioners that within the period for which the application is made any quantity of heavy oil has been used by the applicant as mentioned in subsection (2) below, then, subject as provided below, the applicant shall be entitled to obtain from the Commissioners repayment of the amount of any excise duty which has been paid in respect of the quantity so used, unless that amount is less than £2·50.

(2) A horticultural producer shall be entitled to repayment under this section in respect of oil used by him—

> (a) in the heating, for the growth of horticultural produce primarily with a view to the production of horticultural produce for sale, of any building or structure, or of the earth or other growing medium in it; or

> (b) in the sterilisation of the earth or other growing medium to be used for the growth of horticultural produce as mentioned in paragraph (a) above in any building or structure.

(3) Where any quantity of oil is used partly for any such purpose as is mentioned in subsection (2) above and partly for another purpose, such part of that quantity shall be treated as used for each purpose as may be determined by the Commissioners.

(4) An application under this section shall be made for a period of 6 months ending with June or December and within 3 months following that period, unless the Commissioners otherwise allow, and shall be made in such manner as the Commissioners may direct.

(5) The Commissioners may require an applicant for repayment under this section—

> (a) to state such facts concerning the hydrocarbon oil delivered to or used by him, or concerning the production of horticultural produce by him, as they may think necessary to deal with the application;

> (b) to furnish them in such form as they may require with proof of any statement so made; and

(c) to permit an officer to inspect any premises or plant used by him for the production of horticultural produce or in or for which any such oil was used.

(6) If—

(a) the facts required by the Commissioners under subsection (5)(a) above are not stated ; or

(b) proof of the matters referred to in subsection (5)(b) above is not furnished to the satisfaction of the Commissioners ; or

(c) an applicant fails to permit inspection of premises or plant as required under the subsection (5)(c) above,

the facts shall be deemed for the purposes of this section to be such as the Commissioners may determine.

(7) In this section—

(a) " horticultural produce " has the meaning assigned to it by Schedule 2 to this Act ; and

(b) " horticultural producer " means a person growing horticultural produce primarily for sale.

18.—(1) If, on an application made for the purposes of this subsection in such manner as the Commissioners may direct by the owner of a ship specified in the application, not being a pleasure yacht, it is shown to the satisfaction of the Commissioners— Fuel for ships in home waters.

(a) that at any time within the period of 6 months preceding the date of the application (or within such longer period preceding that date as the Commissioners may in any special case allow) any quantity of heavy oil has been used as fuel for the machinery of the ship while engaged on a voyage in home waters ; and

(b) that no drawback was allowable on the shipment of the oil,

the applicant shall be entitled to obtain from the Commissioners repayment of the amount of any excise duty which has been paid in respect of the quantity so used, unless that amount is less than £5.

(2) Subject to subsections (3) and (4) below, heavy oil in a warehouse or refinery may, on an application made for the purposes of this subsection in such manner as the Commissioners may direct by the owner of a ship specified in the application, not being a pleasure yacht, and on the prescribed security being given, be delivered without payment of excise duty to the applicant for use as fuel for the machinery of the ship while engaged on a voyage in home waters.

(3) At any time not later than 12 months after any oil has been delivered as mentioned in subsection (2) above the Commissioners may require the applicant to prove in the prescribed manner that the whole of the oil, or such part of it as is not on board the ship or has not been relanded with the sanction of the proper officer, has been used as so mentioned.

(4) If proof of any matter relating to the use of any oil, required by the Commissioners under subsection (3) above is not furnished to their satisfaction, any duty which but for the provisions of subsection (2) above would have been payable on the delivery of the oil shall become payable by the applicant on demand made by the Commissioners in the prescribed manner.

(5) If, where oil has been delivered from a warehouse or refinery without payment of duty on an application under subsection (2) above, a person—

> (a) uses the oil or any part of it otherwise than as fuel for the machinery of the ship specified in the application while engaged on a voyage in home waters ; or
>
> (b) relands the whole or any part of the oil at any place in the United Kingdom without the sanction of the proper officer,

he shall be liable on summary conviction to a penalty of three times the value of the whole of the oil so delivered or £100, whichever is the greater ; and in the case of an offence under paragraph (b) of this subsection the oil relanded shall be liable to forfeiture.

(6) In this section—

> (a) " owner ", in relation to an application, includes a charterer to whom the specified ship is demised, or, in a case where the application relates to oil used, or for use, on a ship while undergoing trials for the purpose of testing her hull or machinery, the builder or other person conducting the trials ;
>
> (b) " prescribed " means prescribed by regulations made by the Commissioners ; and
>
> (c) " voyage in home waters ", in relation to a ship, means a voyage in which the ship is at all times either at sea or within the limits of a port.

(7) This section shall apply as if references to ships included references to hovercraft (and " pleasure yacht ", " voyage ", " reland " and other expressions shall be construed accordingly).

Fuel used in fishing boats, etc.

1894 c. 60.

19.—(1) Subsection (3) below shall have effect in the case of—

> (a) any fishing boat entered in the fishing boat register under the Merchant Shipping Act 1894 and used for

the purposes of fishing by a person gaining a substantial part of his livelihood by fishing, whether he is the owner of the boat or not ; or

(b) any lifeboat owned by the Royal National Lifeboat Institution (in this subsection called " the Institution ") ; or

(c) any tractor or gear owned by the Institution and used for the purpose of launching or hauling in any lifeboat owned by it,

in respect of which an application is made to the Commissioners for the purposes of this section by the owner or master of the fishing boat or, as the case may be, by the Institution.

(2) Paragraphs (b) and (c) of subsection (1) above shall apply to hovercraft as if hovercraft were boats or vessels.

(3) Subject to the provisions of this section, if it appears to the satisfaction of the Commissioners that the applicant has at any time within the period of 6 months preceding the date of the application or within such longer period preceding that date as the Commissioners may in any special case allow, used any quantity of hydrocarbon oil on board that boat or for the purposes of that tractor or gear, the applicant shall be entitled to obtain from the Commissioners repayment of any excise duty which has been paid in respect of the oil so used.

(4) An application for the purposes of this section shall be made in such manner as the Commissioners may direct.

(5) No person who has previously made application under this section for repayment of duty shall be entitled to make a further application until the expiration of at least 3 months from the date on which the last preceding application was made.

(6) This section shall have effect in relation to excise duty paid in respect of power methylated spirits as it has effect in relation to excise duty paid in respect of hydrocarbon oil.

20.—(1) Where in the case of hydrocarbon oil which has been Oil delivered for home use it is shown to the satisfaction of the contaminated Commissioners— or accidentally

(a) that since it was so delivered the oil has been deposited mixed in unused in an oil warehouse ; and warehouse.

(b) that it has been so deposited by reason of having become contaminated or by reason of its consisting of different descriptions of hydrocarbon oil which have accidentally become mixed ; and

(c) that at the time when it was so deposited it was oil or, as the case may be, was a mixture of oils, on which the appropriate duty of excise had been paid and not repaid and on which drawback had not been allowed,

then, subject to any conditions which the Commissioners see fit to impose for the protection of the revenue, the Commissioners may make to the occupier of that warehouse a payment in accordance with subsection (2) below.

(2) The payment referred to in subsection (1) above shall be a payment of an amount appearing to the Commissioners to be equal to the excise duty which would have been payable if—

(a) the oil had not become contaminated or mixed ; and

(b) it had first been delivered for home use at the time when it was deposited in the warehouse and the duty had first become chargeable on that delivery.

(3) In this section " oil warehouse " means a place of security approved by the Commissioners under section 92 of the Management Act for the depositing, keeping and securing of hydrocarbon oil, and includes a refinery.

Administration and enforcement

Regulations with respect to hydrocarbon oil, petrol substitutes and road fuel gas.

21.—(1) The Commissioners may, with a view to the protection of the revenue, make regulations—

(a) for any of the purposes specified in Part I of Schedule 3 to this Act (which relates to hydrocarbon oil) ;

(b) for any of the purposes specified in Part II of that Schedule (which relates to petrol substitutes) ;

(c) for any of the purposes specified in Part III of that Schedule (which relates to road fuel gas).

(2) In the case of regulations made for the purposes mentioned in subsection (1)(a) above, different regulations may be made for different classes of hydrocarbon oil ; and the power to make such regulations shall include power to make regulations—

(a) regulating the allowance and payment of drawback under or by virtue of section 15 above ; and

(b) for making the allowance and payment of drawback by virtue of an order under subsection (2) of that section subject to such conditions as the Commissioners see fit to impose for the protection of the revenue.

(3) A person who contravenes or fails to comply with any regulation made under this section shall be liable on summary conviction to a penalty of three times the value of any goods in respect of which the offence was committed or £100, whichever is the greater ; and the goods shall be liable to forfeiture.

22.—(1) A person who uses as fuel for an internal combustion piston engine any liquid which is neither hydrocarbon oil nor power methylated spirits and on which he knows or has reasonable cause to believe that the excise duty on petrol substitutes has not been paid shall be liable on summary conviction to a penalty of three times the value of the goods in respect of which the offence was committed or £100, whichever is the greater; and the goods shall be liable to forfeiture.

Prohibition on use of petrol substitutes on which duty has not been paid.

(2) In subsection (1) above, "liquid" does not include any substance which is gaseous at a temperature of 15°C and under a pressure of 1013·25 millibars.

23.—(1) A person who—

    (*a*) uses as fuel in; or

    (*b*) takes as fuel into,

a road vehicle any road fuel gas on which he knows or has reasonable cause to believe that the excise duty chargeable under section 8 above has not been paid shall be liable on summary conviction to a penalty of three times the value of the goods in respect of which the offence was committed or £100, whichever is the greater; and the goods shall be liable to forfeiture.

Prohibition on use etc. of road fuel gas on which duty has not been paid.

(2) For the purposes of subsection (1)(*b*) above, road fuel gas shall be deemed to be taken into a road vehicle as fuel if, but only if, it is taken into it as part of the supply of fuel for the engine provided for propelling the vehicle or for an engine which draws its fuel from the same supply as that engine.

24.—(1) The Commissioners may make regulations for any of the purposes of section 9(1) or (4), section 12 or section 14(1) above, and in particular for the purposes specified in Schedule 4 to this Act.

Control of use of duty-free and rebated oil.

(2) Regulations made for the purposes of section 12 above may provide for restricting (whether by reference to locality, the obtaining of a licence from the Commissioners or other matters) the cases in which payments to the Commissioners under subsection (2) of that section are to be effective for the purposes of that subsection.

(3) For the purposes of the Customs and Excise Acts 1979, the presence in any hydrocarbon oil of a marker which, in regulations made under this section, is prescribed in relation to—

    (*a*) oil delivered without payment of duty under section 9 above; or

    (*b*) rebated heavy oil or rebated light oil,

shall be conclusive evidence that that oil has been so delivered or, as the case may be, that the rebate in question has been allowed.

(4) A person who contravenes or fails to comply with any regulation made under this section shall be liable on summary conviction to a penalty of three times the value of any goods in respect of which the offence was committed or £100, whichever is the greater ; and the goods shall be liable to forfeiture.

(5) Schedule 5 to this Act shall have effect with respect to any sample of hydrocarbon oil taken in pursuance of regulations made under this section.

Supplementary

Regulations.   **25.** Any power to make regulations under this Act shall be exercisable by statutory instrument, and any statutory instrument by which the power is exercised shall be subject to annulment in pursuance of a resolution of either House of Parliament.

Directions.   **26.** Directions given under any provision of this Act may make different provision for different circumstances and may be varied or revoked by subsequent directions thereunder.

Interpretation.   **27.**—(1) In this Act—

" heavy oil " has the meaning given by section 1(4) above ;

" hydrocarbon oil " has the meaning given by section 1(2) above ;

" light oil " has the meaning given by section 1(3) above ;

1979 c. 2.   " the Management Act " means the Customs and Excise Management Act 1979 ;

" petrol substitute " shall be construed in accordance with section 4(1) and (2) above ;

" power methylated spirits " has the meaning given by section 4(3) above ;

" the prescribed sum ", in relation to the penalty provided for an offence, means—

(a) if the offence was committed in England, Wales or Northern Ireland, the prescribed sum within the meaning of section 28 of the Criminal Law Act 1977 (£1,000 or other sum substituted by order under section 61(1) of that Act) ;

1977 c. 45.

(b) if the offence was committed in Scotland, the prescribed sum within the meaning of section 289B of the Criminal Procedure (Scotland) Act 1975 (£1,000 or other sum substituted by order under section 289D(1) of that Act) ;

1975 c. 21.

" rebate " means rebate of duty under section 11 or 14 above, and " rebated " has a corresponding meaning ;

" refinery " means any premises approved by the Commissioners for the treatment of hydrocarbon oil ;

" road fuel gas " has the meaning given by section 5 above ; and

" road vehicle " means a vehicle constructed or adapted for use on roads, but does not include any vehicle of a kind specified in Schedule 1 to this Act.

(2) This Act and the other Acts included in the Customs and Excise Acts 1979 shall be construed as one Act but where a provision of this Act refers to this Act that reference is not to be construed as including a reference to any of the others.

(3) Any expression used in this Act or in any instrument made under this Act to which a meaning is given by any other Act included in the Customs and Excise Acts 1979 has, except where the context otherwise requires, the same meaning in this Act or in any such instrument as in that Act ; and for ease of reference the Table below indicates the expressions used in this Act to which a meaning is given by any other such Act—

Management Act

" the Commissioners "
" container "
" the Customs and Excise Acts 1979 "
" excise warehouse "
" goods "
" hovercraft "
" occupier "
" officer " and " proper " in relation to an officer
" port "
" ship "
" shipment "
" stores "
" warehouse "

Alcoholic Liquor Duties Act 1979

" methylated spirits "
" spirits ".

28.—(1) The enactments and order specified in Schedule 6 to this Act shall be amended in accordance with the provisions of that Schedule.

(2) The enactments specified in Schedule 7 to this Act are hereby repealed to the extent specified in the third column of that Schedule.

(3) Any provision of this Act relating to anything done or required or authorised to be done under or by reference to that provision or any other provision of this Act shall have effect as if any reference to that provision, or that other provision, as the case may be, included a reference to the corresponding provision of the enactments repealed by this Act.

(4) The repeal by subsection (2) above of the Hydrocarbon Oil (Customs & Excise) Act 1971 shall not affect the operation of the saving in paragraph 2 in Part I of Schedule 14 to the

[margin note] Consequential amendments, repeals, savings and transitional provisions.

[margin note] 1971 c. 12.

1975 c. 45.   Finance (No. 2) Act 1975 in relation to the provisions of the said Act of 1971 repealed by section 75(5) of the said Act of 1975 and specified in that Part.

S.I. 1977/1866.   (5) The Amendment of Units of Measurement (Hydrocarbon Oil, etc) Order 1977 is hereby revoked.

1978 c. 30.   (6) Nothing in this section shall be taken as prejudicing the operation of sections 15 to 17 of the Interpretation Act 1978 (which relate to the effect of repeals).

Citation and commencement.   **29.**—(1) This Act may be cited as the Hydrocarbon Oil Duties Act 1979 and is included in the Acts which may be cited as the Customs and Excise Acts 1979.

(2) This Act shall come into operation on 1st April 1979.

SCHEDULES

SCHEDULE 1

Section 27(1).

VEHICLES WHICH ARE NOT ROAD VEHICLES WITHIN THE MEANING OF THIS ACT

Vehicles excluded from definition of " road vehicle "

1. Any vehicle while it is not used on a public road and no vehicle excise licence is in force in respect of it.

2. The following—

(a) any vehicle exempted from vehicle excise duty by section 4(1)(h) of the Vehicles (Excise) Act 1971 (road construction 1971 c. 10. vehicles) or section 7(1) of that Act (vehicles used only for passing to and from land in the same occupation);

(b) a vehicle of any of the following descriptions which is not chargeable with duty as a goods vehicle, namely an agricultural machine, digging machine, mobile crane, works truck, mowing machine or fisherman's tractor mentioned in Schedule 3 to that Act;

(c) a road roller.

Interpretation

3. In paragraph 1 above " public road " means a road which is repairable at the public expense.

4. In this Schedule "vehicle excise licence", "vehicle excise duty" and "duty" means a licence and duty under the Vehicles (Excise) Act 1971; but a vehicle in respect of which there is current a certificate or document in the form of a licence issued in pursuance of regulations under section 23 of that Act shall be treated as a vehicle for which a road licence is in force.

5. In the application of this Schedule to Northern Ireland, for any reference to the Vehicles (Excise) Act 1971 there shall be substituted a reference to the Vehicles (Excise) Act (Northern 1972 c. 10 (N.I.). Ireland) 1972.

SCHEDULE 2

Section 17(7).

MEANING OF " HORTICULTURAL PRODUCE " FOR PURPOSES OF RELIEF UNDER SECTION 17

In section 17 of this Act " horticultural produce " means—

(a) fruit;

(b) vegetables of a kind grown for human consumption, including fungi, but not including maincrop potatoes or peas grown for seed, for harvesting dry or for vining;

(c) flowers, pot plants and decorative foliage;

(d) herbs;

(e) seeds other than pea seeds, and bulbs and other material, being seeds, bulbs or material for sowing or planting for the production of—

(i) fruit,

(ii) vegetables falling within paragraph (*b*) above,

(iii) flowers, plants or foliage falling within paragraph (*c*) above, or

(iv) herbs,

or for reproduction of the seeds, bulbs or other material planted ; or

(*f*) trees and shrubs, other than trees grown for the purpose of afforestation ;

but does not include hops.

Section 21(1).

SCHEDULE 3

SUBJECTS FOR REGULATIONS UNDER SECTION 21

PART I

HYDROCARBON OIL

1. Prohibiting the production of hydrocarbon oil or any description of hydrocarbon oil except by a person holding a licence.

2. Fixing the date of expiration of any such licence.

3. Regulating the production, storage and warehousing of hydrocarbon oil or any description of hydrocarbon oil and the removal of any such oil to or from premises used for the production of any such oil.

4. Prohibiting the refining of hydrocarbon oil elsewhere than in a refinery.

5. Prohibiting the incorporation of gas in hydrocarbon oil elsewhere than in a refinery.

6. Regulating the use and storage of hydrocarbon oil in a refinery.

7. Regulating or prohibiting the removal to a refinery of hydrocarbon oil in respect of which any rebate has been allowed.

8. Regulating the removal of imported hydrocarbon oil to a refinery without payment of the excise duty on such oil.

9. Making provision for securing payment of the excise duty on any imported hydrocarbon oil received into a refinery.

10. Relieving from the excise duty chargeable on hydrocarbon oil produced in the United Kingdom any such oil intended for exportation or shipment as stores.

11. Generally for securing and collecting the excise duty chargeable on hydrocarbon oil produced in the United Kingdom.

PART II

PETROL SUBSTITUTES

12. Prohibiting the production of petrol substitutes, and dealing in petrol substitutes on which the excise duty has not been paid, except by persons holding a licence.

13. Fixing the date of expiration of any such licence.

14. Regulating the production, dealing in, storage and warehousing of petrol substitutes and their removal to and from premises used therefor.

15. Relieving from the excise duty petrol substitutes intended for exportation or shipment as stores.

16. Generally for securing and collecting the excise duty.

In this Part of this Schedule " the excise duty " means the excise duty on petrol substitutes.

PART III

ROAD FUEL GAS

17. Prohibiting the production of gas, and dealing in gas on which the excise duty has not been paid, except by persons holding a licence.

18. Fixing the date of expiration of any such licence.

19. Regulating the production, dealing in, storage and warehousing of gas and the removal of gas to and from premises used therefor.

20. Requiring containers for gas to be marked in the manner prescribed by the regulations.

21. Conferring power to require information relating to the supply or use of gas and containers for gas to be given by producers of and dealers in gas, and by the person owning or possessing or for the time being in charge of any road vehicle which is constructed or adapted to use gas as fuel.

22. Requiring a person owning or possessing a road vehicle which is constructed or adapted to use gas as fuel to keep such accounts and records in such manner as may be prescribed by the regulations, and to preserve such books and documents relating to the supply of gas to or by him, or the use of gas by him, for such period as may be so prescribed.

23. Requiring the production of books or documents relating to the supply or use of gas or the use of any road vehicle.

24. Authorising the entry and inspection of premises (other than private dwelling-houses) and the examination of road vehicles, and authorising, or requiring the giving of facilities for, the inspection of gas found on any premises entered or on or in any road vehicle.

25. Generally for securing and collecting the excise duty.

In this Part of this Schedule " the excise duty " means the excise duty chargeable under section 8 of this Act on gas, and " gas " means road fuel gas.

SCHEDULE 4

Section 24(1).

SUBJECTS FOR REGULATIONS UNDER SECTION 24

As to grant of relief under sections 9 and 14

1. Regulating the approval of persons for purposes of section 9(1) or (4) or 14(1) of this Act, whether individually or by reference to

SCH. 4   a class, and whether in relation to particular descriptions of oil or generally ; enabling approval to be granted subject to conditions and providing for the conditions to be varied, or the approval revoked, for reasonable cause.

2. Enabling permission under section 9(1) of this Act to be granted subject to conditions as to the giving of security and otherwise.

3. Requiring claims for repayment under section 9(4) of this Act to be made at such times and in respect of such periods as are prescribed ; providing that no such claim shall lie where the amount to be paid is less than the prescribed minimum ; and preventing, where such a claim lies, the payment of drawback.

As to mixing of oil
4. Imposing restrictions on the mixing with other oil of any rebated oil or oil delivered without payment of duty.

As to marking of oil
5. Requiring as a condition of allowing rebate on, or delivery without payment of duty of, any oil (subject to any exceptions provided by or under the regulations) that there shall have been added to that oil, at such times, in such manner and in such proportions as may be prescribed, one or more prescribed markers, with or without a prescribed colouring substance (not being a prescribed marker), and that a declaration to that effect is furnished.

6. Prescribing the substances which are to be used as markers.

7. Providing that the presence of a marker shall be disregarded if the proportion in which it is present is less than that prescribed for the purposes of this paragraph.

8. Prohibiting the addition to any oil of any prescribed marker or prescribed colouring substance except in such circumstances as may be prescribed.

9. Prohibiting the removal from any oil of any prescribed marker or prescribed colouring substance.

10. Prohibiting the addition to oil of any substance, not being a prescribed marker, which is calculated to impede the identification of a prescribed marker.

11. Regulating the storage or movement of prescribed markers.

12. Requiring any person who adds a prescribed marker to any oil to keep in such manner and to preserve for such period as may be prescribed such accounts and records in connection with his use of that marker as may be prescribed, and requiring the production of the accounts and records.

13. Requiring, in such circumstances or subject to such exceptions as may be prescribed, that any drum, storage tank, delivery pump or other container or outlet which contains any oil in which a prescribed marker is present shall be marked in the prescribed manner to indicate that the oil is not to be used as road fuel or for any other prohibited purpose.

14. Requiring any person who supplies oil in which a prescribed marker is present to deliver to the recipient a document containing a statement in the prescribed form to the effect that the oil is not to be used as road fuel or for any other prohibited purpose.

15. Prohibiting the sale of any oil the colour of which would prevent any prescribed colouring substance from being readily visible if present in the oil.

16. Prohibiting the importation of oil in which any prescribed marker, or any other substance which is calculated to impede the identification of a prescribed marker, is present.

As to control of storage, supply etc. of oil, entry of premises etc.

17. Regulating the storage or movement of oil.

18. Restricting the supplying of oil in respect of which rebate has been allowed and not repaid or on which excise duty has not been paid.

19. Requiring a person owning or possessing a road vehicle which is constructed or adapted to use heavy oil as fuel to keep such accounts and records in such manner as may be prescribed, and to preserve such books and documents relating to the supply of heavy oil to or by him, or the use of heavy oil by him, for such period as may be prescribed.

20. Requiring the production of books or documents relating to the supply or use of oil or the use of any vehicle.

21. Authorising the entry and inspection of premises (other than private dwelling-houses) and the examination of vehicles, and authorising, or requiring the giving of facilities for, the inspection of oil found on any premises entered or on or in any vehicle and the taking of samples of any oil inspected.

Interpretation

22. In this Schedule—

" oil " means hydrocarbon oil ;

" prescribed " means prescribed by regulations made under
    section 24 of this Act ;

and section 12(3)(*a*) of this Act shall apply for the purposes of paragraph 19 above as it applies for the purposes of that section.

SCHEDULE 5

SAMPLING

1. The person taking a sample—

    (*a*) if he takes it from a motor vehicle, shall if practicable do so in the presence of a person appearing to him to be the owner or person for the time being in charge of the vehicle ;

    (*b*) if he takes the sample on any premises but not from a motor vehicle, shall if practicable take it in the presence of a person appearing to him to be the occupier of the premises

SCH. 5

or for the time being in charge of the part of the premises from which it is taken.

2.—(1) The result of an analysis of a sample shall not be admissible—

(a) in criminal proceedings under the Customs and Excise Acts 1979 ; or

(b) on behalf of the Commissioners in any civil proceedings under those Acts,

unless the analysis was made by an authorised analyst and the requirements of paragraph 1 above (where applicable) and of the following provisions of this paragraph have been complied with.

(2) The person taking a sample must at the time have divided it into three parts (including the part to be analysed), marked and sealed or fastened up each part, and—

(a) delivered one part to the person in whose presence the sample was taken in accordance with paragraph 1 above, if he requires it ; and

(b) retained one part for future comparison.

(3) Where it was not practicable to comply with the relevant requirements of paragraph 1 above, the person taking the sample must have served notice on the owner or person in charge of the vehicle or, as the case may be, the occupier of the premises informing him that the sample has been taken and that one part of it is available for delivery to him, if he requires it, at such time and place as may be specified in the notice.

3.—(1) Subject to sub-paragraph (2) below, in any such proceedings as are mentioned in paragraph 2(1) above a certificate purporting to be signed by an authorised analyst and certifying the presence of any substance in any such sample of oil as may be specified in the certificate shall be evidence, and in Scotland sufficient evidence, of the facts stated in it.

(2) Without prejudice to the admissibility of the evidence of the analyst (which shall be sufficient in Scotland as well as in England), such a certificate shall not be admissible as evidence—

(a) unless a copy of it has, not less than 7 days before the hearing, been served by the prosecutor or, in the case of civil proceedings, the Commissioners on all other parties to the proceedings ; or

(b) if any of those other parties, not less than 3 days before the hearing or within such further time as the court may in special circumstances allow, serves notice on the prosecutor or, as the case may be, the Commissioners requiring the attendance at the hearing of the person by whom the analysis was made.

4.—(1) Any notice required or authorised to be given under this Schedule shall be in writing.

(2) Any such notice shall be deemed, unless the contrary is shown, to have been received by a person if it is shown to have been left for him at his last-known residence or place of business in the United Kingdom. SCH. 5

(3) Any such notice may be given by post, and the letter containing the notice may be sent to the last-known residence or place of business in the United Kingdom of the person to whom it is directed.

(4) Any such notice given to the secretary or clerk of a company or body of persons (incorporated or unincorporated) on behalf of the company or body shall be deemed to have been given to the company or body ; and for the purpose of the foregoing provisions of this paragraph any such company or body of persons having an office in the United Kingdom shall be treated as resident at that office or, if it has more than one, at the registered or principal office.

(5) Where any such notice is to be given to any person as the occupier of any land, and it is not practicable after reasonable inquiry to ascertain—

(a) what is the name of any person being the occupier of the land ; or

(b) whether or not there is a person being the occupier of the land,

the notice may be addressed to the person concerned by any sufficient description of the capacity in which it is given to him.

(6) In any case to which sub-paragraph (5) above applies, and in any other case where it is not practicable after reasonable inquiry to ascertain an address in the United Kingdom for the service of a notice to be given to a person as being the occupier of any land, the notice shall be deemed to have been received by the person concerned on being left for him on the land, either in the hands of a responsible person or conspicuously affixed to some building or object on the land.

(7) Sub-paragraphs (2) to (6) above shall not affect the validity of any notice duly given otherwise than in accordance with those sub-paragraphs.

5. In this Schedule " authorised analyst " means—

(a) the Government Chemist or a person acting under his direction ;

(b) the Government Chemist for Northern Ireland or a person acting under his direction ;

(c) any chemist authorised by the Treasury to make analyses for the purposes of this Schedule ; or

(d) any other person appointed as a public analyst or deputy public analyst under—

section 89 of the Food and Drugs Act 1955, 1955 c. 16.

section 27 of the Food and Drugs (Scotland) Act 1956, (4 & 5 Eliz. 2.) 1956 c. 30. or

section 31 of the Food and Drugs Act (Northern Ireland) 1958. 1958 c. 27 (N.I.).

SCH. 5   6. References in this Schedule to the taking of a sample or to a sample shall be construed respectively as references to the taking of a sample in pursuance of regulations under section 24 of this Act and to a sample so taken.

7. This Schedule shall have effect in its application to a vehicle of which a person other than the owner is, or is for the time being, entitled to possession as if for references to the owner there were substituted references to the person entitled to possession.

Section 28(1).

SCHEDULE 6

CONSEQUENTIAL AMENDMENTS

Finance Act 1965 *and Finance Act* (*Northern Ireland*) 1965

1965 c. 25.   1. In section 92(2) of the Finance Act 1965 and section 14(2) of the
1966 c. 21 (N.I.). Finance Act (Northern Ireland) 1966 (grants towards duty on bus fuel) for the words " hydrocarbon oil " there shall be substituted the words " heavy oil ".

Transport Act 1968

1968 c. 73.   2. In section 69 of the Transport Act 1968 (revocation etc. of operators' licences), in subsection (4)(*e*), after the words " section 200 of the Customs and Excise Act 1952 " there shall be inserted the words " section 11 of the Hydrocarbon Oil (Customs & Excise) Act 1971 or section 13 of the Hydrocarbon Oil Duties Act 1979 ".

Finance Act 1972

1972 c. 41.   3. In Item 4 of Group 7 in Schedule 4 to the Finance Act 1972 for the words " the Hydrocarbon Oil (Customs & Excise) Act 1971 " there shall be substituted the words " the Hydrocarbon Oil Duties Act 1979 ".

4. In Note (3) to Group 7 in Schedule 4 to the Finance Act 1972 for the words from " gas " to " road vehicles and " there shall be substituted the words " road fuel gas (within the meaning of the Hydrocarbon Oil Duties Act 1979) ".

5. In Note (4) to Group 7 in Schedule 4 to the Finance Act 1972 the words " or is to be " shall be omitted and at the end of that Note there shall be added the words " or on which a duty of excise has been or is to be charged without relief from, or rebate of, such duty by virtue of the provisions of the Hydrocarbon Oil Duties Act 1979 ".

Excise Duties (*Gas as Road Fuel*) *Order* 1972

S.I. 1972/567.   6. In Article 3 of the Excise Duties (Gas as Road Fuel) Order 1972 for the words " hydrocarbon oil " there shall be substituted the words " light oil ".

Finance (*No. 2*) *Act* 1975

1975 c. 45.   7. In Note (1) to Group 8 in Schedule 7 to the Finance (No. 2) Act 1975 for the words " the Hydrocarbon Oil (Customs & Excise) Act 1971 " there shall be substituted the words " the Hydrocarbon Oil Duties Act 1979 ".

SCHEDULE 7

REPEALS

Chapter	Short title	Extent of repeal
1971 c. 12.	The Hydrocarbon Oil (Customs & Excise) Act 1971.	The whole Act, except section 22 and paragraphs 1 and 2 of Schedule 6.
1971 c. 68.	The Finance Act 1971.	Section 3, except subsection (5). Section 6(2).
1972 c. 41.	The Finance Act 1972.	In Schedule 4, in Note (4) to Group 7, the words " or is to be ".
1975 c. 45.	The Finance (No. 2) Act 1975.	Section 11. In Schedule 3, paragraphs 2 and 16 to 22.
1976 c. 40.	The Finance Act 1976.	Sections 9 and 10.
1977 c. 36.	The Finance Act 1977.	Section 4.
1978 c. 42.	The Finance Act 1978.	In Schedule 12, paragraph 8.

Matches and Mechanical Lighters Duties Act 1979

1979 CHAPTER 6

An Act to consolidate the enactments relating to the excise duties on matches and mechanical lighters.

[22nd February 1979]

B E IT ENACTED by the Queen's most Excellent Majesty, by and with the advice and consent of the Lords Spiritual and Temporal, and Commons, in this present Parliament assembled, and by the authority of the same, as follows:—

Matches

Excise duty on matches. **1.**—(1) There shall be charged on matches—

(*a*) imported into the United Kingdom ; or

(*b*) manufactured in the United Kingdom and sent out from the premises of a manufacturer of matches,

a duty of excise at the rate of £0·49 for every 7,200 matches (and so in proportion for any less number of matches).

(2) For the purposes of the duty chargeable under subsection (1) above, a match which has more than one point of ignition shall be reckoned as so many matches as there are points of ignition.

Licences to manufacture matches. **2.**—(1) No person shall manufacture matches unless he holds an excise licence for that purpose granted under this section.

(2) A licence granted under this section shall expire on the 31st March next after it is granted.

(3) On any licence granted under this section there shall be charged an excise licence duty of £1.

(4) If any person manufactures matches otherwise than under and in accordance with a licence granted under this section, he shall be liable on summary conviction to a penalty of £50 and the matches shall be liable to forfeiture.

3.—(1) The Commissioners may, with a view to the protec- Regulations
tion of the revenue, make regulations— about
matches.

   (*a*) regulating the manufacture of matches and the removal of matches from the premises of a licensed manufacturer ;

   (*b*) for securing and collecting the excise duty chargeable on matches manufactured in the United Kingdom ;

   (*c*) providing for the remission or repayment of excise duty on defective matches ;

   (*d*) for authorising the removal from the premises of a licensed manufacturer without payment of excise duty of matches removed for exportation or shipment as stores or for warehousing, or removed to other premises of that manufacturer or to premises of another licensed manufacturer ;

   (*e*) for securing that there is on every container of matches a notification of the contents, or the minimum or maximum contents, of the container.

(2) In subsection (1) above " licensed manufacturer " means a person who holds a licence granted under section 2 above.

(3) If any person contravenes or fails to comply with any regulation made under subsection (1) above, he shall be liable on summary conviction to a penalty of £50, and any article in respect of which the offence was committed shall be liable to forfeiture.

(4) The power to make regulations under subsection (1) above shall be exercisable by statutory instrument and any statutory instrument by which the power is exercised shall be subject to annulment in pursuance of a resolution of either House of Parliament.

Mechanical lighters

4.—(1) For the purposes of this Act " mechanical lighter " Mechanical
means any portable contrivance intended to provide a means of lighters.
ignition, whether by spark, flame or otherwise, being a mechanical, chemical, electrical or similar contrivance.

(2) For the purposes of this Act—

(*a*) any component which is, in accordance with section 5 below, the prescribed component of a mechanical lighter ; or

(*b*) any assembly which includes such a component,

shall be deemed to be a mechanical lighter ; and any reference in this Act to a manufacturer of mechanical lighters includes a reference to a person by whom any prescribed component of a mechanical lighter, or assembly which includes such a component, has been manufactured in the course of a business carried on by him, notwithstanding that he has not carried on the manufacture at a time when such a component or assembly is deemed to be a mechanical lighter.

The prescribed component.

5.—(1) Until otherwise provided by an order under subsection (2) below, for the purposes of section 4(2) above the prescribed component of an imported mechanical lighter shall be the body.

(2) Subject to subsection (1) above, in section 4(2) above the " prescribed component ", in relation to a mechanical lighter falling within any class or description of mechanical lighters, means such one of the component parts of a lighter of that class or description as the Treasury may by order designate for this purpose as being the component part or one of the component parts in such a lighter least likely to require replacement.

(3) The power to make orders under subsection (2) above shall be exercisable by statutory instrument and any statutory instrument by which the power is exercised shall be laid before the House of Commons after being made.

(4) A statutory instrument made under subsection (2) above which extends the incidence of duty shall cease to have effect on the expiration of a period of 28 days from the date on which it is made unless at some time before the expiration of that period it has been approved by a resolution of the House of Commons, but without prejudice to anything previously done under it or to the making of a new order.

In reckoning any such period no account shall be taken of any time during which Parliament is dissolved or prorogued or during which the House of Commons is adjourned for more than 4 days.

(5) A statutory instrument made under subsection (2) above which does not extend the incidence of duty shall be subject to annulment in pursuance of a resolution of the House of Commons.

6.—(1) There shall be charged on mechanical lighters—
(*a*) imported into the United Kingdom ; or
(*b*) manufactured in the United Kingdom and sent out from the premises of a manufacturer of mechanical lighters,
a duty of excise at the rate of £0·20 for each lighter.

(2) The duty chargeable under subsection (1) above shall be chargeable on mechanical lighters which when imported or sent out as mentioned in that subsection are incomplete as well as on lighters which at that time are complete.

(3) No duty shall be chargeable under this section on a mechanical lighter which is shown to the satisfaction of the Commissioners to be constructed solely for the purposes of igniting gas for domestic use.

(4) The Commissioners may, subject to such conditions as they see fit to impose, exempt from the duty chargeable under this section any mechanical lighters which are shown to their satisfaction to be intended to be used as parts of miners' lamps.

(5) If, save as permitted under subsection (4) above or regulations under section 7(1) below, a manufacturer of mechanical lighters sends out from his premises any mechanical lighter without payment of the duty chargeable on it under this section, he shall be liable on summary conviction to a penalty of £50, and any article in respect of which the offence was committed shall be liable to forfeiture.

Excise duty on mechanical lighters.

7.—(1) The Commissioners may make regulations—
(*a*) prohibiting the manufacture of mechanical lighters (including the assembling of parts of mechanical lighters, whether to form complete mechanical lighters or not) except by a person who holds a licence granted for that purpose under the regulations ;
(*b*) for fixing the date of the expiration of licences granted under the regulations ;
(*c*) for regulating the manufacture of mechanical lighters and the removal of them from the place of manufacture with a view to securing and collecting the excise duty chargeable on them ;
(*d*) for requiring every manufacturer of mechanical lighters to give security by bond or otherwise—
(i) for the keeping of such records as, in pursuance of regulations under this subsection, he may be required to produce to an officer ; and
(ii) for the payment of all excise duty payable by him ;

Regulations about mechanical lighters.

13

(e) providing for the delivery to and receipt by manufacturers licensed under the regulations of mechanical lighters imported into or manufactured in the United Kingdom without payment of the excise duty chargeable on them ;

(f) for authorising the removal from the premises of a manufacturer licensed under the regulations without payment of excise duty of mechanical lighters for exportation or shipment as stores or for warehousing for exportation or for use as stores ;

(g) for the remission or repayment, subject to such conditions as may be prescribed in the regulations, of any excise duty chargeable or paid on mechanical lighters—

(i) which have been destroyed or have become unfit for use by unavoidable accident before removal from a manufacturer's premises ; or

(ii) which have been sent back to the place of manufacture as being defective.

(2) Where an officer finds that the number of mechanical lighters in the stock or possession of a manufacturer of mechanical lighters is less than the manufacturer's recorded number, then, except in so far as the deficiency is explained by the manufacturer to the satisfaction of the Commissioners, mechanical lighters to the number of the deficiency shall be deemed to have been sent out from the premises of the manufacturer on the day on which the deficiency first came to the notice of the officer.

(3) In subsection (2) above the " recorded number ", in relation to a manufacturer of mechanical lighters, means the number of mechanical lighters which, according to records or other documents produced by him in pursuance of regulations under subsection (1) above to the officer concerned, ought to be in his stock or possession.

(4) If any person contravenes or fails to comply with any regulation made under subsection (1) above, he shall be liable on summary conviction to a penalty of £50, and any article in respect of which the offence was committed shall be liable to forfeiture.

(5) The power to make regulations under subsection (1) above shall be exercisable by statutory instrument and any statutory instrument by which the power is exercised shall be subject to annulment in pursuance of a resolution of either House of Parliament.

Supplementary

8.—(1) In this Act "mechanical lighter" has the meaning Interpretation. given by section 4(1) above.

(2) This Act and the other Acts included in the Customs and Excise Acts 1979 shall be construed as one Act but where a provision of this Act refers to this Act that reference is not to be construed as including a reference to any of the others.

(3) Any expression used in this Act or in any instrument made under this Act to which a meaning is given by any other Act included in the Customs and Excise Acts 1979 has, except where the context otherwise requires, the same meaning in this Act or in any such instrument as in that Act ; and for ease of reference the Table below indicates the expressions used in this Act to which a meaning is given by any other such Act—

         Customs and Excise Management Act 1979

" the Commissioners "
" the Customs and Excise Acts 1979 "
" container "
" officer "
" shipment "
" stores "
" warehousing ".

9.—(1) The enactments specified in the Schedule to this Act Repeals and are hereby repealed to the extent specified in the third column consequential of that Schedule. amendments.

(2) In section 17 of the Finance Act 1972, after the subsection 1972 c. 41. (2A) inserted by paragraph 2 of Schedule 2 to the Customs and 1979 c. 3. Excise Duties (General Reliefs) Act 1979, there shall be inserted the following subsection—

> " (2B) Section 6(4) of the Matches and Mechanical Lighters Duties Act 1979 (exemption of certain mechanical lighters) shall also be excepted from the enactments which are to have effect as mentioned in subsection (1) of this section.".

(3) In Note (2) to Group 1 in Schedule 7 to the Finance 1975 c. 45. (No. 2) Act 1975, and in Note (2) to Group 8 in that Schedule, for the words " section 221(4) of the Customs and Excise Act 1952 " there shall be substituted the words " section 4(1) of the Matches and Mechanical Lighters Duties Act 1979 ".

(4) Nothing in subsection (2) or (3) above shall prejudice the operation of sections 15 to 17 of the Interpretation Act 1978 1978 c. 30. (which relate to the effect of repeals).

10.—(1) This Act may be cited as the Matches and Mecha- Citation nical Lighters Duties Act 1979 and is included in the Acts which and com- may be cited as the Customs and Excise Acts 1979. mencement.

(2) This Act shall come into operation on 1st April 1979.

SCHEDULE

                              REPEALS

Chapter	Short title	Extent of repeal
15 & 16 Geo. 6 & 1 Eliz. 2 c. 44.	The Customs and Excise Act 1952.	Sections 219 to 222.
1 & 2 Eliz. 2 c. 34.	The Finance Act 1953.	Section 3(3) and (5).
8 & 9 Eliz. 2 c. 44.	The Finance Act 1960.	In section 7, in subsection (1), from the beginning to the words " or similar contrivance " ", and subsections (3) and (4).
1963 c. 25.	The Finance Act 1963.	Section 4(2).
1975 c. 45.	The Finance (No. 2) Act 1975.	Sections 12 and 13. In Schedule 3, paragraphs 8, 12 and 38.
1978 c. 42.	The Finance Act 1978.	In Schedule 12, paragraph 6.

Tobacco Products Duty Act 1979

1979 CHAPTER 7

An Act to consolidate the enactments relating to the excise duty on tobacco products.

[22nd February 1979]

BE IT ENACTED by the Queen's most Excellent Majesty, by and with the advice and consent of the Lords Spiritual and Temporal, and Commons, in this present Parliament assembled, and by the authority of the same, as follows:—

1.—(1) In this Act " tobacco products " means any of the following products, namely,—

(*a*) cigarettes ;

(*b*) cigars ;

(*c*) hand-rolling tobacco ;

(*d*) other smoking tobacco ; and

(*e*) chewing tobacco,

which are manufactured wholly or partly from tobacco or any substance used as a substitute for tobacco, but does not include herbal smoking products.

Tobacco products.

(2) Subject to subsection (3) below, in this Act " hand-rolling tobacco " means tobacco—

(*a*) which is sold or advertised by the importer or manufacturer as suitable for making into cigarettes ; or

(*b*) of which more than 25 per cent. by weight of the tobacco particles have a width of less than 0·6 mm.

(3) The Treasury may by order made by statutory instrument provide that in this Act references to cigarettes, cigars, hand-rolling tobacco, other smoking tobacco and chewing tobacco shall or shall not include references to any product of a description specified in the order, being a product manufactured as mentioned in subsection (1) above but not including herbal smoking products ; and any such order may amend or repeal subsection (2) above.

(4) Subject to subsection (5) below, a statutory instrument by which there is made an order under subsection (3) above shall be laid before the House of Commons after being made ; and unless the order is approved by that House before the expiration of 28 days beginning with the date on which it was made, it shall cease to have effect on the expiration of that period, but without prejudice to anything previously done under it or to the making of a new order.

In reckoning any such period no account shall be taken of any time during which Parliament is dissovled or prorogued or during which the House of Commons is adjourned for more than 4 days.

(5) Subsection (4) above shall not apply to any order containing a statement by the Treasury that the order does not extend the incidence of the duty or involve a greater charge to duty or a reduction of any relief ; and a statutory instrument by which any such order is made shall be subject to annulment in pursuance of a resolution of the House of Commons.

(6) In this section " herbal smoking products " means products commonly known as herbal cigarettes or herbal smoking mixtures.

Charge and remission or repayment of tobacco products duty.

2.—(1) There shall be charged on tobacco products imported into or manufactured in the United Kingdom a duty of excise at the rates shown, subject to section 3 below, in the Table in Schedule 1 to this Act.

(2) Subject to such conditions as they see fit to impose, the Commissioners shall remit or repay the duty charged by this section where it is shown to their satisfaction that the products in question have been—

(a) exported or shipped as stores ; or

(b) used solely for the purposes of research or experiment ;

and the Commissioners may by regulations provide for the remission or repayment of the duty in such other cases as may be specified in the regulations and subject to such conditions as they see fit to impose.

3.—(1) In the case of any cigarette having a tar yield of not Additional duty on higher tar cigarettes. less than 20 mg. the Table in Schedule 1 to this Act shall have effect as if the rate of duty in paragraph 1 were increased by £2·25 per thousand cigarettes.

(2) The Commissioners may make regulations—

    (*a*) prescribing how the tar yield of cigarettes is to be determined for the purposes of this section ;

    (*b*) without prejudice to section 2(2) above, enabling the whole or any part of the additional duty imposed by this section to be remitted or repaid in such cases as may be specified in the regulations or determined by the Commissioners and subject to such conditions as they see fit to impose.

4. For the purposes of the references to a thousand cigarettes Calculation of duty in case of cigarettes more than 9 cm. long. in paragraph 1 in the Table in Schedule 1 to this Act and in section 3(1) above any cigarette more than 9 cm. long (excluding any filter or mouthpiece) shall be treated as if each 9 cm. or part thereof were a separate cigarette.

5.—(1) For the purposes of the duty chargeable at any time Retail price of cigarettes. under section 2 above in respect of cigarettes of any description, the retail price of the cigarettes shall be taken to be—

    (*a*) in a case in which paragraph (*b*) below does not apply, the highest price at which cigarettes of that description are normally sold by retail at that time in the United Kingdom ;

    (*b*) in any case where—

        (i) there is a price recommended by the importer or manufacturer for the sale by retail at that time in the United Kingdom of cigarettes of that description ; and

        (ii) duty is tendered and accepted by reference to that price,

    the price so recommended.

(2) The duty in respect of any number of cigarettes shall be charged by reference to the price which, in accordance with subsection (1) above, is applicable to cigarettes sold in packets of 20 or of such other number as the Commissioners may determine in relation to cigarettes of the description in question ; and the whole of the price of a packet shall be regarded as referable to the cigarettes it contains notwithstanding that it also contains a coupon, token, card or other additional item.

(3) In any case in which duty is chargeable in accordance with paragraph (*a*) of subsection (1) above—

    (*a*) the question as to what price is applicable under that paragraph shall, subject to subsection (4) below, be determined by the Commissioners ; and

    (*b*) the Commissioners may require security (by deposit of money or otherwise to their satisfaction) for the payment of duty to be given pending their determination.

(4) Any person who has paid duty in accordance with a determination of the Commissioners under subsection (3)(*a*) above and is dissatisfied with their determination may require the question of what price was applicable under subsection (1)(*a*) above to be referred to the arbitration of a referee appointed by the Lord Chancellor, not being an official of any government department.

(5) If, on a reference to him under subsection (4) above, the referee determines that the price was lower than that determined by the Commissioners, they shall repay the duty overpaid together with interest on the overpaid duty from the date of the overpayment at such rate as the referee may determine.

(6) The procedure on any reference to a referee under subsection (4) above shall be such as may be determined by the referee ; and the referee's decision on any such reference shall be final and conclusive.

Alteration of rates of duty.

6.—(1) The Treasury may by order made by statutory instrument increase or decrease any of the rates of duty for the time being in force under the Table in Schedule 1 to this Act by such percentage of the rate, not exceeding 10 per cent., as may be specified in the order, but any such order shall cease to be in force at the expiration of a period of one year from the date on which it takes effect unless continued in force by a further order made under this subsection.

(2) In relation to any order made under subsection (1) above to continue, vary or replace a previous order so made, the reference in that subsection to the rate for the time being in force is a reference to the rate that would be in force if no order under that subsection had been made.

(3) A statutory instrument under subsection (1) above by which there is made an order increasing the rate in force at the time of making the order shall be laid before the House of Commons after being made ; and unless the order is approved by that House before the expiration of 28 days beginning with the date on which it was made, it shall cease to have effect on the expiration of that period, but without prejudice to anything previously done under it or to the making of a new order.

In reckoning any such period no account shall be taken of any time during which Parliament is dissolved or prorogued or during which the House of Commons is adjourned for more than 4 days.

(4) A statutory instrument made under subsection (1) above to which subsection (3) above does not apply shall be subject to annulment in pursuance of a resolution of the House of Commons.

(5) For the purposes of this section—

    (a) the percentage and the amount per thousand cigarettes in paragraph 1 in the Table in Schedule 1 to this Act shall be treated as separate rates of duty ; and

    (b) the increase specified in section 3(1) above shall be treated as a rate of duty separate from that applying apart from the increase.

7.—(1) The Commissioners may with a view to managing the duty charged by section 2 above make regulations— *Regulations for management of duty.*

    (a) prescribing the method of charging the duty and for securing and collecting the duty ;

    (b) for the registration of premises for the safe storage of tobacco products and for requiring the deposit of tobacco products in, and regulating their treatment in and removal from, premises so registered ;

    (c) for the registration of premises where—

        (i) tobacco products are manufactured ;

        (ii) materials for the manufacture of tobacco products are grown, produced, stored or treated ; or

        (iii) refuse from the manufacture of tobacco products is stored or treated,

    and for regulating the storage and treatment in, and removal from, premises so registered of such materials and refuse ;

    (d) for requiring the keeping and preservation of such records, and the making of such returns, as may be specified in the regulations ; and

    (e) for the inspection of goods, documents and premises.

(2) If any person fails to comply with any regulation made under subsection (1) above he shall be liable on summary conviction to a penalty of £200, and any article in respect of which, or found on premises in respect of which, the offence was committed shall be liable to forfeiture.

Charge in
cases of
default.

8.—(1) Where the records or returns kept or made by any person in pursuance of regulations under section 2 or 7 above show that any tobacco products or materials for their manufacture are or have been in his possession or under his control, the Commissioners may from time to time require him to account for those products or materials.

(2) Unless a person required under subsection (1) above to account for any products or materials proves—

(a) that duty has been paid or secured under section 7 above in respect of the products or, as the case may be, products manufactured from the materials ; or

(b) that the products or materials are being or have been otherwise dealt with in accordance with regulations under section 2 or 7 above,

the Commissioners may require him to pay duty under section 2 above in respect of those products or, as the case may be, in respect of such products as in their opinion might reasonably be expected to be manufactured from those materials.

(3) Where a person has failed to keep or make any records or returns required by regulations under section 2 or 7 above, or it appears to the Commissioners that any such records or returns are inaccurate or incomplete, they may require him to pay any duty under section 2 above which they consider would have been shown to be due if proper records or returns had been kept or made.

Regulations.

9. Any power to make regulations under this Act shall be exercisable by statutory instrument and any statutory instrument by which the power is exercised shall be subject to annulment in pursuance of a resolution of either House of Parliament.

Interpretation.

10.—(1) In this Act—

" hand-rolling tobacco " has the meaning given by section 1(2) above ; and

" tobacco products " has the meaning given by section 1(1) above.

(2) This Act and the other Acts included in the Customs and Excise Acts 1979 shall be construed as one Act but where a provision of this Act refers to this Act that reference is not to be construed as including a reference to any of the others.

(3) Any expression used in this Act or in any instrument made under this Act to which a meaning is given by any other Act included in the Customs and Excise Acts 1979 has, except where the context otherwise requires, the same meaning in this Act or in any such instrument as in that Act ; and for ease of

reference the Table below indicates the expressions used in this Act to which a meaning is given by any other such Act—

Customs and Excise Management Act 1979
" the Commissioners "
" the Customs and Excise Acts 1979 "
" goods "
" importer "
" shipped "
" stores ".

11.—(1) The enactments specified in Schedule 2 to this Act are Repeals, hereby repealed to the extent specified in the third column of savings and that Schedule, but subject to the provision at the end of that transitional Schedule. and consequential

(2) Any provision of this Act relating to anything done or provisions. required or authorised to be done under or by reference to that provision or any other provision of this Act shall have effect as if any reference to that provision, or that other provision, as the case may be, included a reference to the corresponding provision of the enactments repealed by this Act.

(3) In section 3(2) of the Finance Act 1977 (which makes 1977 c. 36. provision in consequence of the replacement from 1st January 1978 of duty under section 4 of the Finance Act 1964 with duty 1964 c. 49. under section 4 of the Finance Act 1976) for the words " the 1976 c. 40. said Act of 1964 " there shall be substituted the words " the Finance Act 1964 ", for the words " the said Act of 1976 " there shall be substituted the words " the Finance Act 1976 " and after the words " the said 1st January " there shall be inserted the words " or under section 2 of the Tobacco Products Duty Act 1979 on or after 1st April 1979 ".

(4) Nothing in this section shall be taken as prejudicing the operation of sections 15 to 17 of the Interpretation Act 1978 1978 c. 30. (which relate to the effect of repeals).

12.—(1) This Act may be cited as the Tobacco Products Duty Citation Act 1979 and is included in the Acts which may be cited as the and com- Customs and Excise Acts 1979. mencement.

(2) This Act shall come into operation on 1st April 1979.

SCHEDULES

Section 2(1).

SCHEDULE 1

TABLE OF RATES OF TOBACCO PRODUCTS DUTY

TABLE

1. Cigarettes ... ... An amount equal to 30 per cent. of the retail price plus £9·00 per thousand cigarettes.
2. Cigars ... ... £9·50 per pound.
3. Hand-rolling tobacco ... £9·20 per pound.
4. Other smoking tobacco and chewing tobacco ... £7·30 per pound.

Section 11(1).

SCHEDULE 2

REPEALS

Chapter	Short Title	Extent of Repeal
15 & 16 Geo. 6 & 1 Eliz. 2 c. 44.	The Customs and Excise Act 1952.	In the proviso to section 271(3), paragraph (i).
1976 c. 40.	The Finance Act 1976.	Sections 4, 5, 6(1) to (5) and 7.
1977 c. 36.	The Finance Act 1977.	Sections 2(2) and (4) to (8) and 3(1) and (5).
1978 c. 42.	The Finance Act 1978.	Section 1. In Schedule 12, paragraph 7(2).

The repeal in section 271(3) of the Customs and Excise Act 1952 does not affect drawback by virtue of events occurring on or before 30th June 1978.

Excise Duties
(Surcharges or Rebates) Act
1979

1979 CHAPTER 8

An Act to consolidate the provisions of section 9 of and
Schedules 3 and 4 to the Finance Act 1961 with the
provisions amending them.   [22nd February 1979]

BE IT ENACTED by the Queen's most Excellent Majesty, by and
with the advice and consent of the Lords Spiritual and
Temporal, and Commons, in this present Parliament
assembled, and by the authority of the same, as follows:—

1.—(1) This section applies to the following groups of excise
duties, namely—

Surcharges or rebates of amounts due for excise duties.

    (*a*) those chargeable in respect of spirits (other than power
         methylated spirits), beer, wine, made-wine and cider ;

    (*b*) those chargeable in respect of hydrocarbon oil, petrol
         substitutes, power methylated spirits and road fuel gas ;

    (*c*) all other duties of excise except—

         (i) that chargeable on tobacco products ;

         (ii) those payable on a licence ; and

         (iii) those with respect to which the Parliament of
         Northern Ireland would, if the Northern Ireland
         Constitution Act 1973 had not been passed, have had
         power to make laws.

1973 c. 36.

(2) If it appears to the Treasury that it is expedient, with a
view to regulating the balance between demand and resources
in the United Kingdom, that an order under this section should
be made with respect to one or more of the groups of duties to

which this section applies, the Treasury may by order provide for an adjustment—

    (a) of every liability to a duty within that group or any of those groups ; and

    (b) of every right to a drawback, rebate or allowance in connection with such a duty,

by the addition to or deduction from the amount payable or allowable of such percentage, not exceeding 10 per cent, as may be specified in the order.

(3) The adjustment under this section of a liability to duty shall be made where the duty becomes due while the order is in force with respect to it, except that if the duty is pool betting duty it shall instead be made where the bets (whenever made) are made by reference to an event taking place while the order is in force with respect to the duty.

(4) The adjustment under this section of a right to any drawback, rebate or allowance in respect of a duty or goods charged with a duty shall be made where the right arises while the order is in force with respect to the duty (whenever the duty became due) ; but in calculating the amount to be adjusted any adjustment under this section of the liability to the duty shall be disregarded.

(5) A repayment of any duty within a group to which this section applies or of drawback or allowance in respect of such a duty or goods chargeable with such a duty shall be calculated by reference to the amount actually paid or allowed (after effect was given to any adjustment falling to be made under this section) but save as aforesaid this section does not require the adjustment of any such repayment.

1979 c. 2.　(6) Subsection (5) above shall apply to any payment under section 94 or 95 of the Customs and Excise Management Act 1979 (deficiency in goods in or from warehouse) in the case of goods warehoused on drawback which could not lawfully be entered for home use (being a payment of an amount equal to the drawback and any allowance paid in respect of the goods) as if it were a repayment of drawback or allowance.

1979 c. 5.　(7) The preceding provisions of this section shall apply to repayments of duty under the following provisions of the Hydrocarbon Oil Duties Act 1979—

    (a) section 9(4) (repayment of duty on oil put to an industrial use which would have qualified it for duty-free delivery) ;

    (b) section 17 (relief for heavy oil used by horticultural producers) ;

   (c) section 18 (relief for heavy oil used as fuel in ships in home waters);

   (d) section 19 (relief for oil etc. used in fishing boats, lifeboats and lifeboat launching gear),

as if the repayments were drawbacks and not repayments.

2.—(1) The following provisions of this section shall have effect with respect to orders under section 1 above.   Orders under s. 1.

(2) No order shall be made or continue in force after the end of August 1979 or such later date as Parliament may hereafter determine.

(3) An order may specify different percentages for different groups of duties but must apply uniformly to all the duties within the same group.

(4) An order may not provide for additions in the case of one or more groups and deductions in the case of another or others.

(5) An order may be made so as to come into operation at different times of day for different duties, whether or not within the same group.

(6) The power to make an order shall be exercisable by statutory instrument.

(7) Any statutory instrument by which an order is made shall be laid before the House of Commons after being made, and the order shall cease to have effect at the end of 21 days after that on which it is made unless at some time before the end of those 21 days the order is approved by a resolution of that House.

(8) Except in the case of such an order as is mentioned in subsection (9) below, in reckoning the period of 21 days specified in subsection (7) above no account shall be taken of any time during which Parliament is dissolved or prorogued or during which the House of Commons is adjourned for more than 4 days.

(9) Subsection (8) above does not apply to an order which, with respect to all or any of the groups of duties,—

   (a) specifies a percentage by way of addition to duty, or increases a percentage so specified; or

   (b) withdraws, or reduces, a percentage specified by way of deduction from duty.

Application of certain enactments.

3.—(1) The enactments relating to the collection or recovery or otherwise to the management of any duty within a group to which section 1 above applies shall apply to the amount of any adjustment under that section as if it were duty, drawback, rebate or allowance, as the case may be.

1901 c. 7.

(2) For the purposes of subsections (1) and (2) of section 10 of the Finance Act 1901 (adjustment of contract prices and variation of duties) the beginning or ending of a period during which an order under section 1 above is in force with respect to any duty, or the variation of a percentage specified in such an order, shall be treated as an increase or decrease (as the case may require) of that duty ; and references in those subsections to an amount paid on account of an increase of duty, to having had the benefit of a decrease of duty, and to the amount of the decrease of duty shall be construed accordingly.

1958 c. 11.

(3) For the purposes of section 2 of the Isle of Man Act 1958 (Isle of Man share of equal duties) the amount of equal duties collected in the Isle of Man and the United Kingdom, or in the Isle of Man, shall be calculated by reference to the amount so collected in respect of such duties after giving effect to any addition or deduction provided for under section 1 above or any corresponding provisions of the law of the Isle of Man.

Interpretation, consequential amendments, repeals and saving.

4.—(1) Any expression used in this Act and in any Act included in the Customs and Excise Acts 1979 has the same meaning in this Act as in that Act.

(2) The enactments specified in Schedule 1 to this Act shall be amended in accordance with the provisions of that Schedule.

(3) The enactments specified in Schedule 2 to this Act are hereby repealed to the extent specified in the third column of that Schedule.

1961 c. 36.

(4) If at the commencement of this Act an order under section 9 of the Finance Act 1961 is in force, the order shall have effect as if made under this Act.

Citation and commencement.

5.—(1) This Act may be cited as the Excise Duties (Surcharges or Rebates) Act 1979.

(2) This Act shall come into operation on 1st April 1979.

SCHEDULES

SCHEDULE 1

CONSEQUENTIAL AMENDMENTS

Finance (No. 2) Act 1964

1. In section 9(8) of the Finance (No. 2) Act 1964, for the words 1964 c. 92. " section 9 of the Finance Act 1961 " there shall be substituted the words " section 1 of the Excise Duties (Surcharges or Rebates) Act 1979 ".

Finance Act 1965

2. In section 92(2) of the Finance Act 1965, for the words " section 1965 c. 25. 9 of the Finance Act 1961 " there shall be substituted the words " section 1 of the Excise Duties (Surcharges or Rebates) Act 1979 ".

Finance Act 1966

3. In section 2(12) of the Finance Act 1966, for the words 1966 c. 18. " section 9 of the Finance Act 1961 " there shall be substituted the words " section 1 of the Excise Duties (Surcharges or Rebates) Act 1979 ".

SCHEDULE 2

REPEALS

Chapter	Short Title	Extent of Repeal
9 & 10 Eliz. 2 c. 36.	The Finance Act 1961.	Section 9. Schedules 3 and 4.
1964 c. 49.	The Finance Act 1964.	Section 8.
1968 c. 44.	The Finance Act 1968.	Section 10(2).
1971 c. 12.	The Hydrocarbon Oil (Customs & Excise) Act 1971.	In Schedule 6, paragraph 2.
1971 c. 68.	The Finance Act 1971.	Section 3(5).
1976 c. 40.	The Finance Act 1976.	Section 6(6). In Schedule 3, paragraph 8.
1978 c. 42.	The Finance Act 1978.	In section 6(4) the words preceding " any duty " and the words " and any such duty ". Section 10.

Films Act 1979

1979 CHAPTER 9

An Act to amend section 6 of the Films Act 1960.

[22nd February 1979]

BE IT ENACTED by the Queen's most Excellent Majesty, by and with the advice and consent of the Lords Spiritual and Temporal, and Commons, in this present Parliament assembled, and by the authority of the same, as follows:—

Amendment of section 6 of Films Act 1960.

1960 c. 57.

1. For subsection (1) of section 6 of the Films Act 1960 there shall be substituted the following subsection:—

" (1) Where—

    (a) a film registered as a foreign film (other than a Community film) is to be or is being exhibited at a cinema; and

    (b) before or while it is exhibited there an application for a direction under this section is made to the Secretary of State by the exhibitor who exhibits films at that cinema,

the Secretary of State may, if he thinks fit, direct that, if the period during which the film is exhibited at that cinema is or includes such a continuous period exceeding eight weeks as is specified in the direction, the requirements imposed by section 1 of this Act shall be deemed to be complied with in relation to that cinema in the relevant year, if they are so complied with in that year and the succeeding year taken together.".

Citation.

1972 c. 68.

2. This Act may be cited as the Films Act 1979; and the Films Acts 1960 to 1970, section 8 of the European Communities Act 1972 and this Act may be cited together as the Films Acts 1960 to 1979.

Public Lending Right Act 1979

1979 CHAPTER 10

An Act to provide public lending right for authors, and for connected purposes.   [22nd March 1979]

BE IT ENACTED by the Queen's most Excellent Majesty, by and with the advice and consent of the Lords Spiritual and Temporal, and Commons, in this present Parliament assembled, and by the authority of the same, as follows:—

1.—(1) In accordance with a scheme to be prepared and brought into force by the Secretary of State, there shall be conferred on authors a right, known as " public lending right ", to receive from time to time out of a Central Fund payments in respect of such of their books as are lent out to the public by local library authorities in the United Kingdom. Establishment of public lending right.

(2) The classes, descriptions and categories of books in respect of which public lending right subsists, and the scales of payments to be made from the Central Fund in respect of it, shall be determined by or in accordance with the scheme; and in preparing the scheme the Secretary of State shall consult with representatives of authors and library authorities and of others who appear to be likely to be affected by it.

(3) The Secretary of State shall appoint an officer to be known as the Registrar of Public Lending Right; and the Schedule to this Act has effect with respect to the Registrar.

(4) The Registrar shall be charged with the duty of establishing and maintaining in accordance with the scheme a register showing the books in respect of which public lending right subsists and the persons entitled to the right in respect of any registered book.

(5) The Registrar shall, in the case of any registered book determine in accordance with the scheme the sums (if any) due by way of public lending right; and any sum so determined to be due shall be recoverable from the Registrar as a debt due to the person for the time being entitled to that right in respect of the book.

(6) Subject to any provision made by the scheme, the duration of public lending right in respect of a book shall be from the date of the book's first publication (or, if later, the beginning of the year in which application is made for it to be registered) until 50 years have elapsed since the end of the year in which the author died.

(7) Provision shall be made by the scheme for the right—

    (a) to be established by registration;

    (b) to be transmissible by assignment or assignation, by testamentary disposition or by operation of law, as personal or moveable property;

    (c) to be claimed by or on behalf of the person for the time being entitled;

    (d) to be renounced (either in whole or in part, and either temporarily or for all time) on notice being given to the Registrar to that effect.

The Central Fund.

2.—(1) The Central Fund shall be constituted by the Secretary of State and placed under the control and management of the Registrar.

(2) There shall be paid into the Fund from time to time such sums, out of money provided by Parliament, as the Secretary of State with Treasury approval determines to be required for the purpose of satisfying the liabilities of the Fund; but in respect of the liabilities of any one financial year of the Fund the total of those sums shall not exceed £2 million less the total of any sums paid in that year, out of money so provided, under paragraph 2 of the Schedule to this Act (pay, pension, etc. of Registrar).

(3) With the consent of the Treasury, the Secretary of State may from time to time by order in a statutory instrument

increase the limit on the sums to be paid under subsection (2) above in respect of financial years beginning after that in which the order is made ; but no such order shall be made unless a draft of it has been laid before the House of Commons and approved by a resolution of that House.

(4) There shall be paid out of the Central Fund—

    (*a*) such sums as may in accordance with the scheme be due from time to time in respect of public lending right ; and

    (*b*) the administrative expenses of the Registrar and any other expenses and outgoings mentioned in this Act which are expressed to be payable from the Fund.

(5) Money received by the Registrar in respect of property disposed of, or otherwise in the course of his functions, or under this Act, shall be paid into the Central Fund, except in such cases as the Secretary of State otherwise directs with the approval of the Treasury ; and in any such case the money shall be paid into the Consolidated Fund.

(6) The Registrar shall keep proper accounts and other records and shall prepare in respect of each financial year of the Fund statements of account in such form as the Secretary of State may direct with Treasury approval ; and those statements shall, on or before 31st August next following the end of that year, be transmitted to the Comptroller and Auditor General, who shall examine and certify the statements and lay copies thereof, together with his report thereon, before each House of Parliament.

3.—(1) As soon as may be after this Act comes into force, The scheme the Secretary of State shall prepare the draft of a scheme for and its its purposes and lay a copy of the draft before each House of administration. Parliament.

(2) If the draft scheme is approved by a resolution of each House, the Secretary of State shall bring the scheme into force (in the form of the draft) by means of an order in a statutory instrument, to be laid before Parliament after it is made ; and the order may provide for different provisions of the scheme to come into force on different dates.

(3) The scheme shall be so framed as to make entitlement to public lending right dependent on, and its extent ascertainable by reference to, the number of occasions on which books are lent out from particular libraries, to be specified by the scheme or identified in accordance with provision made by it.

(4) For this purpose, " library "—

    (*a*) means any one of a local library authority's collections of books held by them for the purpose of being borrowed by the public ; and (*b*) includes any such collection which is taken about from place to place.

(5) The scheme may provide for requiring local library authorities—

(*a*) to give information as and when, and in the form in which, the Registrar may call for it or the Secretary of State may direct, as to loans made by them to the public of books in respect of which public lending right subsists, or of other books ; and

(*b*) to arrange for books to be numbered, or otherwise marked or coded, with a view to facilitating the maintenance of the register and the ascertainment and administration of public lending right.

(6) The Registrar shall, by means of payments out of the Central Fund, reimburse to local library authorities any expenditure incurred by them in giving effect to the scheme, the amount of that expenditure being ascertained in accordance with such calculations as the scheme may prescribe.

(7) Subject to the provisions of this Act (and in particular to the foregoing provisions of this section), the scheme may be varied from time to time by the Secretary of State, after such consultation as is mentioned in section 1(2) above, and the variation brought into force by an order in a statutory instrument, subject to annulment in pursuance of a resolution of either House of Parliament ; and the variation may comprise such incidental and transitional provisions as the Secretary of State thinks appropriate for the purposes of continuing the scheme as varied.

(8) The Secretary of State shall in each year prepare and lay before each House of Parliament a report on the working of the scheme.

The register. **4.**—(1) The register shall be kept in such form, and contain such particulars of books and their authors, as may be prescribed.

(2) No application for an entry in the register is to be entertained in the case of any book unless it falls within a class, description or category of books prescribed as one in respect of which public lending right subsists.

(3) The scheme shall provide for the register to be conclusive both as to whether public lending right subsists in respect of a particular book and also as to the persons (if any) who are for the time being entitled to the right.

(4) Provision shall be included in the scheme for entries in the register to be made and amended, on application made in the prescribed manner and supported by prescribed particulars (verified as prescribed) so as to indicate, in the case of any

book who (if any one) is for the time being entitled to public lending right in respect of it.

(5) The Registrar may direct the removal from the register of every entry relating to a book in whose case no sum has become due by way of public lending right for a period of at least 10 years, but without prejudice to a subsequent application for the entries to be restored to the register.

(6) The Registrar may require the payment of fees, according to prescribed scales and rates, for supplying copies of entries in the register ; and a copy of an entry, certified under the hand of the Registrar or an officer of his with authority in that behalf (which authority it shall be unnecessary to prove) shall in all legal proceedings be admissible in evidence as of equal validity with the original.

(7) It shall be an offence for any person, in connection with the entry of any matter whatsoever in the register, to make any statement which he knows to be false in a material particular or recklessly to make any statement which is false in a material particular ; and a person who commits an offence under this section shall be liable on summary conviction to a fine of not more than £1,000.

(8) Where an offence under subsection (7) above which has been committed by a body corporate is proved to have been committed with the consent or connivance of, or to be attributable to any neglect on the part of, a director, manager, secretary or other similar officer of the body corporate, or any person who was purporting to act in any such capacity, he (as well as the body corporate) shall be guilty of that offence and be liable to be proceeded against accordingly.

Where the affairs of a body corporate are managed by its members, this subsection applies in relation to the acts and defaults of a member in connection with his functions of management as if he were a director of the body corporate.

5.—(1) This Act may be cited as the Public Lending Right Citation, etc. Act 1979.

(2) In this Act any reference to " the scheme " is to the scheme prepared and brought into force by the Secretary of State in accordance with sections 1 and 3 of this Act (including the scheme as varied from time to time under section 3(7) ; and—

" local library authority " means—

   (a) a library authority under the Public Libraries 1964 c. 75. and Museums Act 1964,

   (b) a statutory library authority within the Public 1955 c. 27. Libraries (Scotland) Act 1955, and

S.I. 1972/1263
(N.I. 12).

(c) an Education and Library Board within the Education and Libraries (Northern Ireland) Order 1972 ;

" prescribed " means prescribed by the scheme ;

" the register " means the register required by section 1(4) to be established and maintained by the Registrar ; and

" the Registrar " means the Registrar of Public Lending Right.

(3) This Act comes into force on a day to be appointed by an order made by the Secretary of State in a statutory instrument to be laid before Parliament after it has been made.

(4) This Act extends to Northern Ireland.

SCHEDULE

THE REGISTRAR OF PUBLIC LENDING RIGHT

1. The Registrar shall hold and vacate office as such in accordance with the terms of his appointment; but he may at any time resign his office by notice in writing addressed to the Secretary of State; and the Secretary of State may at any time remove a person from the office of Registrar on the ground of incapacity or misbehaviour.

2.—(1) There shall be paid to the Registrar out of money provided by Parliament such remuneration and allowances as the Secretary of State may determine with the approval of the Minister for the Civil Service.

(2) In the case of any such holder of the office of Registrar as may be determined by the Secretary of State with that approval, there shall be paid out of money so provided such pension, allowance or gratuity to or in respect of him, or such contributions or payments towards provision of such a pension, allowance or gratuity, as may be so determined.

3. If, when a person ceases to hold office as Registrar, it appears to the Secretary of State that there are special circumstances which make it right that he should receive compensation, there may (with the approval of the Minister for the Civil Service) be paid to him out of the Central Fund a sum by way of compensation of such amount as may be so determined.

4. In the House of Commons Disqualification Act 1975, in Part III of Schedule 1 (other disqualifying offices), the following shall be inserted at the appropriate place in alphabetical order— 1975 c. 24.

"Registrar of Public Lending Right";

and the like insertion shall be made in Part III of Schedule 1 to the Northern Ireland Assembly Disqualification Act 1975. 1975 c. 25.

5.—(1) The Registrar of Public Lending Right shall be by that name a corporation sole, with a corporate seal.

(2) He is not to be regarded as the servant or agent of the Crown.

6. The Documentary Evidence Act 1868 shall have effect as if the Registrar were included in the first column of the Schedule to that Act, as if the Registrar and any person authorised to act on his behalf were mentioned in the second column of that Schedule, and as if the regulations referred to in that Act included any documents issued by the Registrar or by any such person. 1868 c. 37.

7.—(1) The Registrar may appoint such assistant registrars and staff as he thinks fit, subject to the approval of the Secretary of State as to their numbers; and their terms and conditions of service, and the remuneration and allowances payable to them, shall be such as the Registrar may determine.

(2) The Registrar may direct, in the case of persons appointed by him under this paragraph—

> (a) that there be paid to and in respect of them such pensions, allowances and gratuities as he may determine ;
>
> (b) that payments be made towards the provision for them of such pensions, allowances and gratuities as he may determine ; and
>
> (c) that schemes be provided and maintained (whether contributory or not) for the payment to and in respect of them of such pensions, allowances and gratuities as he may determine.

(3) Any money required for the payment of remuneration and allowances under this paragraph, and of pensions, allowances and gratuities, and otherwise for the purposes of sub-paragraph (2) above, shall be paid from the Central Fund.

(4) The approval of the Secretary of State and the Minister for the Civil Service shall be required for any directions or determination by the Registrar under this paragraph.

8. Anything authorised or required under this Act (except paragraph 7 of this Schedule), or by or under the scheme, to be done by the Registrar may be done by any assistant registrar or member of the Registrar's staff who is authorised generally or specially in that behalf in writing by the Registrar.

Electricity (Scotland) Act 1979

1979 CHAPTER 11

An Act to consolidate certain enactments relating to the North of Scotland Hydro-Electric Board and the South of Scotland Electricity Board and to functions of the Secretary of State in relation to the generation and distribution of electricity in Scotland with amendments to give effect to recommendations of the Scottish Law Commission. [22nd March 1979]

BE IT ENACTED by the Queen's most Excellent Majesty, by and with the advice and consent of the Lords Spiritual and Temporal, and Commons, in this present Parliament assembled, and by the authority of the same, as follows:—

PART I

THE BOARDS

Constitution

1.—(1) The North of Scotland Hydro-Electric Board estab- Constitution lished by section 1 of the Act of 1943 (in this Act referred to as of Boards. " the North Board ") and the South of Scotland Electricity Board established by section 2 of the Act of 1954 (in this Act referred to as " the South Board ") shall continue in existence, and are referred to in this Act as " the Boards ".

(2) Schedule 1 shall have effect in relation to the constitution and proceedings of the Boards.

2.—(1) Subject to the provisions of this section, the districts Definition of the North and South Boards shall continue to be as defined in and variation Parts I and II of Schedule 2 respectively. of districts.

(2) Subject to subsection (3), the Secretary of State may, after giving to each Board an opportunity to make representations, by order vary the districts defined in Schedule 2 and any such

PART I

variation may include the formation of a new district from any part of an existing district or parts of existing districts, or the amalgamation with an existing district of the whole or part of any other existing district.

(3) Part III of Schedule 2 shall have effect in relation to any order made under subsection (2).

(4) In subsection (2), " existing " means existing immediately before the order in question is made.

Principal functions

Functions of the Boards.

3.—(1) Subject to the provisions of this Act, the Boards shall be responsible for initiating and undertaking the development of all means of generation of electricity within their respective districts.

(2) Subject to any directions of the Secretary of State and the provisions of this Act, it shall, so far as practicable, be the duty—

(a) of the South Board—

(i) to plan and carry out an efficient and economic distribution of supplies of electricity to persons in their district ;

(ii) to provide supplies of electricity to meet the requirements for haulage or traction of railway undertakers in their district ;

(b) of the North Board—

(i) to provide supplies of electricity required to meet the demands of ordinary consumers in their district ;

(ii) to provide supplies of electricity suitable for the needs of large power users in their district, including the requirements for haulage or traction of railway undertakers.

(3) Subject to any duty of the North Board to supply electricity to the South Board, the duties imposed on the North Board under head (i) of paragraph (b) of subsection (2) shall have priority over all other demands for the electricity generated by them.

(4) Schedule 3 shall have effect in relation to the supply of electricity by the Boards to railway undertakers under subsection (2).

General duties in exercising functions.

4.—In exercising and performing their functions the Boards shall, subject to and in accordance with any directions given by the Secretary of State under section 33—

(a) promote the use of all economical methods of generating, transmitting and distributing electricity ;

(*b*) secure so far as practicable, the development, extension to rural areas and cheapening of supplies of electricity ;

(*c*) avoid undue preference in the provision of such supplies ;

(*d*) promote the simplification and standardisation of methods of charge for such supplies ;

(*e*) promote the standardisation of systems of supply and types of electrical fittings ;

(*f*) promote the welfare, health and safety of persons in their employment and in consultation with any organisation appearing to them to be appropriate make provision for advancing the skill of persons employed by them and for improving the efficiency of their equipment and of the manner in which that equipment is to be used, including provision by them, and the assistance of the provision by others, of facilities for training and education ;

(*g*) conduct research into matters affecting the supply of electricity and assist other persons conducting such research.

5.—(1) In the exercise of their functions the Boards shall have regard in relation to their respective districts to the desirability of preserving the beauty of the scenery and any object of architectural or historical interest and of avoiding as far as possible injury to fisheries and to the stock of fish in any waters.

(2) For the purpose of giving advice and assistance to the Secretary of State and to each of the Boards, the Secretary of State shall appoint two Committees (in this Act referred to as the Amenity Committee and the Fisheries Committee respectively) ; and Schedule 4 shall have effect in relation to the constitution, proceedings and functions of those Committees.

6. The North Board shall, so far as their powers and duties permit, collaborate in the carrying out of any measures for the economic development and social improvement of the whole or any part of their district.

Powers and duties

7.—(1) Subject to subsection (2), each of the Boards shall have power

(*a*) to manufacture electrical plant and electrical fittings ;

(*b*) to sell, hire or otherwise supply electrical plant and electrical fittings and to instal, repair, maintain or remove any electrical plant and electrical fittings ;

(c) to carry on all such other activities as may appear to the Board concerned to be requisite, advantageous or convenient for them to carry on for or in connection with the performance of their duties under this Act, or with a view to making the best use of any assets vested in them.

(2) Subsection (1) shall not apply to the manufacture of electrical plant or electrical fittings for export.

(3) The Boards may do anything and enter into any transaction (whether or not involving the expenditure, the borrowing in accordance with the provisions of this Act or the lending of money, the acquisition of any property or rights or the disposal of any property or rights not in their opinion required for the proper exercise and performance of their functions) which in their opinion is calculated to facilitate the proper exercise or performance of any of their functions under this Act or is incidental or conducive thereto.

(4) The Boards may collect for the purposes of their powers and duties under this Act information as to the requirements of the whole or any part of their respective districts in respect of electricity.

Powers of Boards to enter into agreements with each other, and with other persons.

8.—(1) Subject to this section and section 9 either of the Boards may by agreement—

(a) with each other—

(i) give to or acquire from the other Board bulk supplies of electricity ;

(ii) supply electricity to consumers in the district of the other Board ;

(b) with the Generating Board or with any person or body of persons carrying on an electricity undertaking outside Great Britain, provide bulk supplies of electricity for the Generating Board or for that undertaking.

(2) If either of the Boards are unable to obtain the agreement of the other Board under head (ii) of paragraph (a) of subsection (1), they may apply to the Secretary of State for an authorisation to supply electricity to consumers in such part of the district of the other Board as may be specified in the application, and if the Secretary of State gives such authorisation the Board which has applied for it shall have power to supply electricity in accordance with it.

(3) Either of the Boards may by agreement with the other Board use for the purposes of any of their functions any works, plant or other property of the other Board.

(4) If it appears to the Secretary of State that such use cannot be obtained by agreement between the Boards and is required by one of them for the purpose of securing efficient and economical services he may by order authorise such use by that Board on such terms and conditions (including the payment of money) as he may determine.

9.—(1) Either of the Boards may purchase electricity from the Purchase and other Board on such terms and conditions as they may agree. supply of electricity.

(2) Either of the Boards may purchase electricity from any other person (other than an Area Board) on such terms and conditions as may be agreed with that person but—

(a) where any purchase of electricity is made by either of the Boards from a person in the district of the other Board any such purchase shall require the approval of that other Board ; or

(b) where any purchase of electricity is made by either of the Boards from a person in the area of an Area Board, any such purchase shall require the approval of the Generating Board.

(3) The South Board and the North Board may enter into and carry into effect agreements for the construction by either Board of such main transmission lines as are necessary for the delivery of electricity purchased under this section, and for that purpose the powers of either Board shall be exerciseable in the district of the other.

(4) Any question between the Boards under this section shall be determined by an arbiter appointed by the Secretary of State.

10.—(1) Each of the Boards shall in respect of their respective Constructional districts prepare schemes (in this Act referred to as " construc- schemes. tional schemes ") with a view to the execution of works necessary for the generation of electricity by water power, other than works required for the replacement or renewal of works already authorised.

(2) Schedule 5 shall have effect in relation to constructional schemes.

PART I   (3) If the Secretary of State is satisfied that a proposed extension of existing works involves only works of a minor character he may, subject to such conditions as he may think fit to impose, authorise the Board concerned to execute those works without the preparation of a constructional scheme.

Acquisition   **11.**—(1) For the purpose of carrying out any scheme con-
of land etc. for firmed under section 10, the Board authorised to carry out the
purposes of   scheme so confirmed may, subject to the provisions of this Act,
constructional
schemes.   (*a*) acquire such land,

                     (*b*) abstract, divert and use such water,

                     (*c*) divert such roads, and

                     (*d*) construct, operate and maintain such works and plant,

as may be necessary for that purpose, and do any other thing necessary for the effective exercise and discharge of their powers and duties.

1963 c. 51.   (2) Subject to the provisions of the Land Compensation
1973 c. 56.   (Scotland) Acts 1963 and 1973, and of this section, the Lands
1845 c. 19.   Clauses Acts and section 6 and sections 70 to 78 of the Railways
1845 c. 33.   Clauses Consolidation (Scotland) Act 1845 shall apply in accordance with the provisions of Schedule 6 for the purposes of the acquisition of land which either of the Boards are authorised by a constructional scheme to acquire.

        (3) If it appears to the Board concerned necessary or expedient for the purpose of carrying out a constructional scheme to enter upon and take possession of any land which they are authorised by the scheme to acquire, they may, after giving not less than 28 days notice by registered post to the persons appearing from the valuation roll to be the owners and occupiers of that land, enter upon and take possession of that land, and may give such directions as appear to them to be necessary or expedient in connection with the taking of possession of that land.

        (4) A certified copy of any direction to give up possession of and remove from any land given under subsection (3) shall be sufficient warrant for ejection against any occupier or any party in his right in the event of non-compliance with any such direction.

        (5) Land of which either of the Boards are in possession in pursuance of subsection (3) may, notwithstanding any restriction imposed on the use of that land under any enactment or otherwise, be used, subject to the provisions of the scheme, by

the Board in such manner as they think expedient for the purpose of carrying out the scheme.

(6) Where in the exercise of the powers conferred on them by subsection (3) either of the Boards have taken possession of any land, they shall as soon as may be proceed with the acquisition of the land and shall, if they are unable to acquire the land by agreement, serve notice to treat.

12.—(1) This section applies to land required by either of the Boards for any purpose connected with the discharge of their functions, not being land required by them for the purposes of a constructional scheme under section 10.

(2) The Secretary of State may authorise either of the Boards to purchase compulsorily any land to which this section applies and the Acquisition of Land (Authorisation Procedure) (Scotland) Act 1947 shall apply in relation to any such compulsory purchase as if the Board making the purchase were a local authority within the meaning of that Act and as if this Act had been in force immediately before the commencement of that Act.

(3) Either of the Boards may be authorised under this section to purchase compulsorily a right to place an electric line across land, whether above or below ground, and a right to repair and maintain the line, without purchasing any other interest in the land.

(4) The said Act of 1947 shall have effect in relation to compulsory purchase under subsection (3) as if references to the land comprised in the compulsory purchase order were construed as references to the land across which the line is to be placed and as if references to the obtaining or taking possession of the land comprised in the order were construed as references to the exercise of the right to place the line across land.

(5) In this section " land " includes servitudes and other rights over land.

(6) Section 14 of the Schedule to the Electric Lighting (Clauses) Act 1899 shall, so far as it relates to the Post Office, apply to the placing of an electric line in pursuance of any right purchased under subsection (3) as it applies to the execution of works involving the placing of lines in, under, along or across any street or public bridge.

13.—(1) Without prejudice to any other rights of entry exercisable by the Boards, any person duly authorised in writing by either of the Boards may, subject to the provisions of this section, at any reasonable time enter upon and survey any land, not being land covered by buildings or used as a garden or pleasure ground, for the purpose of ascertaining whether the land would be suitable for use for the purposes of any functions of the Board.

(2) In subsection (1) the power conferred to survey land includes power, subject to subsection (4), to search and bore for the purpose of ascertaining the nature of the subsoil.

(3) Any person duly authorised by either of the Boards under subsection (1) to enter on any land shall, if so required, produce evidence of his authority before so entering and shall not demand admission as of right to any land which is occupied unless 28 days notice of the intended entry has been given to the occupier.

(4) Where a person proposes to carry out works authorised by virtue of subsection (2)—

    (*a*) he shall not carry out those works unless notice of his intention to do so was included in the notice given under subsection (3) ; and

    (*b*) if the land in question is held by statutory undertakers, and those undertakers object to the proposed works on the grounds that the carrying out of the works would be seriously detrimental to the carrying on of their undertaking, the works shall not be carried out except with the authority of the Secretary of State.

1972 c. 52.

In this subsection " statutory undertakers " has the meaning given by the Town and Country Planning (Scotland) Act 1972 and includes the Post Office.

(5) Any person who wilfully obstructs a person acting in the exercise of his powers under subsection (1) shall be guilty of an offence and liable on summary conviction to a fine not exceeding £20.

(6) Where in the exercise of any power conferred by subsection (1) any damage is caused to land or to corporeal moveables, any person interested in the land or moveables may recover compensation in respect of that damage from the Board by whom or on whose behalf the power is exercised ; and where in consequence of the exercise of any such power any person is disturbed in his enjoyment of any land or moveables he may recover from that Board compensation in respect of the disturbance.

1963 c. 51.

(7) Any question of disputed compensation under subsection (6) shall be referred to and determined by the Lands Tribunal for Scotland, and in relation to the determination of any such question sections 9 and 11 of the Land Compensation (Scotland) Act 1963 shall apply.

(8) Where either of the Boards—

(a) acquire a bulk supply of electricity which is received by them outside their district, or

(b) provide a supply of electricity outside their district,

that Board may, in accordance with proposals submitted by them to the Secretary of State and approved by him, exercise outside their district for the purpose of such acquisition or the provision of such supply any powers exercisable within their district by that Board under this Act or the Electricity (Supply) Acts or any local enactment, being powers relating to the breaking up of streets, railways and tramways which would not be so exercisable apart from this subsection.

(9) The powers conferred by subsection (8) shall be exercisable in like manner and subject to the like provisions and restrictions as they are exercisable by the Board concerned for the purpose of the supply of electricity in the district of that Board.

14. Either of the Boards may conduct experiments or trials for the improvement of methods of generation, distribution or use of electricity in the special conditions and circumstances in their respective districts and may for that purpose incur such expenditure as they may think fit.

Power to conduct experiments.

15.—(1) It shall be the duty of the Boards to investigate methods by which heat obtained from or in connection with the generation of electricity may be used for the heating of buildings in neighbouring localities or for any other useful purpose, and the Boards may accordingly conduct or assist others in conducting research into any matters relating to such methods of using heat.

Research into heating from electricity.

(2) Either of the Boards may provide or assist other persons to provide for the heating of buildings by any such methods or otherwise for the use of heat so obtained, and may, in accordance with a scheme submitted by the Board concerned to the Secretary of State and approved by order made with or without modification by him, exercise for those purposes the powers conferred by section 13(8) for the purposes of that section, and section 13(9) shall apply in relation to the manner in which those powers are exercisable.

16.—(1) The Boards may, with the consent of the Secretary of State, enter into and carry out agreements with the relevant Minister in pursuance of which the Boards, or one or other of

Agreements for technical assistance overseas.

K4

PART I

1966 c. 21.

them, may act at the expense of the Minister as the instrument by means of which technical assistance is furnished by him in exercise of the power conferred on him by section 1(1) of the Overseas Aid Act 1966.

(2) In this section " the relevant Minister " means the Minister of the Crown by whom is exercisable the powers conferred on the Minister of Overseas Development by that section 1(1) as originally enacted.

Consultation

Consultative
Councils.

17.—(1) The Consultative Councils established for the districts of each of the Boards under section 7A of the Act of 1947 shall continue in existence.

(2) Schedule 7 shall have effect in relation to the constitution, proceedings and functions of those Councils.

Finance

General fund.

18.—(1) It shall be the duty of each of the Boards so to exercise and perform their functions under this Act as to secure that their respective revenues are not less than sufficient to meet their outgoings properly chargeable to revenue account, taking one year with another.

(2) All sums received by the Boards on revenue account from whatever source, including any interest on money invested, shall in the case of each Board be credited to and form part of a fund to be called the " general fund "

General
reserve fund
of the South
Board.

19.—(1) The South Board shall continue to maintain the general reserve fund established in pursuance of section 11A of the Act of 1943.

(2) The South Board shall contribute to the general reserve fund such sums at such times as the Board may determine, and the management of the fund and the application of the monies contained in the fund shall, subject to the provisions of this section, be as the Board may determine.

(3) No part of the general reserve fund shall be applied otherwise than for the purposes of the South Board.

(4) The Secretary of State may, with the approval of the Treasury, give directions of a general or specific character to the South Board as to any matter relating to the management of the general reserve fund, the carrying of sums to the credit thereof, or the application thereof.

(5) One of the purposes of the general reserve fund is the prevention of frequent fluctuations in the charges made by the South Board, and the powers of the Board in relation to the said fund shall be exercised accordingly.

(6) The provisions of this section shall be without prejudice to the power of the South Board to establish appropriate reserves for replacements or other purposes.

20. The South Board shall charge to the general fund in every year all charges which are proper to be made to revenue account including in particular— Sums which are to be chargeable by the South Board to revenue account.

(a) proper allocations to the general reserve fund ;

(b) proper provision for the redemption of capital ;

(c) proper provision for depreciation of assets or for renewal of assets ; and

(d) all payments (including the payments which are by the relevant provision of this Act or by any other relevant enactment to be deemed to be capital payments) which fall to be made in that year to any local authority under this Act or the Act of 1947 in respect of any loan by that local authority ;

and references in this Act to outgoings properly chargeable to revenue account shall be construed accordingly.

21.—(1) Subject to the provisions of this section any excess of the revenues of the South Board for any financial year over their outgoings for that year properly chargeable to revenue account shall be applied for such purposes as that Board may determine. Application of surplus revenues of the South Board.

(2) No part of any such excess shall be applied otherwise than for the purposes of the South Board.

(3) The Secretary of State may, with the approval of the Treasury, give directions of a general or specific character to the South Board as to the application of any such excess.

22.—(1) The prices to be charged by each Board for the supply of electricity shall be in accordance with such tariffs as may be fixed by that Board from time to time.

(2) The tariffs fixed under subsection (1) shall be so framed as to show the methods by which, and the principles on which, the charges are to be made as well as the prices which are to be charged, and shall be published in such manner as in the opinion of each Board will secure adequate publicity for them.

(3) A tariff fixed by either of the Boards in respect of a supply of electricity by virtue of the provisions of this Act may include a rent or other charge in respect of electrical fittings provided by the Board on the premises of the consumer.

(4) Notwithstanding anything in the foregoing provisions of this section, in cases where the tariffs in force are not appropriate owing to special circumstances a Board may enter into an agreement with any consumer for the supply of electricity to him on such terms as may be specified in the agreement.

(5) The Boards in fixing tariffs and making agreements under this section shall not show undue preference to any person or class of persons and shall not exercise any undue discrimination against any person or class of persons.

Maximum
charges for
reselling
electricity
supplied by
the Boards.

23.—(1) Either of the Boards may publish a notice fixing maximum charges in consideration of which electricity supplied by the Board may be resold by persons to whom it is so supplied or by any class of such persons specified in the notice.

(2) Any notice under this section shall be published in such manner as in the opinion of the Board concerned will secure adequate publicity for it, and the maximum charges fixed by any such notice may be varied by a subsequent notice published by that Board in accordance with this subsection.

(3) Different maximum charges may be fixed by either Board under this section for different classes of cases, whether by reference to different parts of the district of the Board concerned or by reference to different tariffs under which electricity is supplied by that Board or by reference to any other relevant circumstances.

(4) If, in consideration of the resale of any electricity supplied by either of the Boards in circumstances to which a notice published by that Board under this section applies, any person requires the payment of charges exceeding the maximum charges applicable thereto in accordance with the notice, the amount

of the excess shall be recoverable by the person to whom the electricity is resold.

24.—(1) The Secretary of State may, with the approval of the Treasury, advance to the Boards or either of them any sums which the Boards have power to borrow.

(2) Any advances made by the Secretary of State under subsection (1) shall be repaid to him at such times and by such methods, and interest thereon shall be paid to him at such rates and at such times, as he may with the approval of the Treasury from time to time direct.

(3) The Treasury may issue out of the National Loans Fund to the Secretary of State such sums as are necessary to enable him to make advances under this section.

(4) Any sums received by the Secretary of State under subsection (2) shall be paid into the National Loans Fund.

(5) In respect of each financial year the Secretary of State shall prepare, in such form and manner as the Treasury may direct, an account of sums issued to him under this section and of the sums to be paid into the National Loans Fund under subsection (4) and of the disposal by him of those sums respectively, and shall send it to the Comptroller and Auditor General not later than the end of November following that financial year ; and the Comptroller and Auditor General shall examine, certify and report on the account and lay copies of it, together with his report, before each House of Parliament.

25.—(1) Subject to the provisions of this section, the Treasury may guarantee, in such manner and on such conditions as they think fit the payment of the interest and principal of any loan proposed to be raised by either Board, or of either the interest or the principal.

(2) Such sums as may from time to time be required by the Treasury for fulfilling any guarantees given under this section shall be charged on and issued out of the Consolidated Fund.

(3) The repayment to the Treasury of any sums so issued out of the Consolidated Fund, together with interest thereon at such rate as the Treasury may fix, shall be a charge on the undertaking and all the revenues of the Board next after the principal and interest of the guaranteed loan and any sinking fund payments for the repayment of the principal thereof, and in priority to any other charges not existing at the date on which the loan is raised.

PART I

Exchequer advances to the Boards.

Power to Treasury to guarantee loans to the Boards.

(4) All sums paid from time to time in or towards the repayment of any sum issued out of the Consolidated Fund under this section shall be paid into the Exchequer.

(5) Immediately after a guarantee is given under this section, the Treasury shall lay a statement of the guarantee before each House of Parliament.

(6) Where any sum is issued out of the Consolidated Fund under this section the Treasury shall forthwith lay before each House of Parliament a statement that that sum has been issued.

Power to
issue stock.

26.—(1) The Boards may for the purpose of raising money which they are authorised to borrow under this Act, create and issue stock.

(2) Any stock issued by either of the Boards and the interest thereon shall be charged on the undertaking and all the revenues of that Board.

(3) Subject to the provisions of this Act, any stock created by the Boards under this section shall be issued, transferred, dealt with, and redeemed according to regulations to be made by the Secretary of State with the approval of the Treasury.

(4) Regulations made under subsection (3) may apply for the purposes of this section, with or without modifications, any provisions of any Act relating to stock issued by a local authority.

Power of the
Boards to
borrow.

27.—(1) Subject to the provisions of this section, either of the Boards may for the purposes to which this section applies, with the consent of the Secretary of State (which shall require the approval of the Treasury) and subject to regulations to be made by the Secretary of State with the approval of the Treasury, borrow money in sterling or foreign currency from any source, whether within or outwith the United Kingdom, in such manner and subject to such provisions as to repayments as may be prescribed.

(2) Each Board shall have such powers as may be prescribed with respect to reborrowing for the purpose of paying off a loan previously raised under this section.

(3) Regulations under subsection (1) may provide—
    (a) for either of the Boards to borrow temporarily ; and
    (b) for the application, with or without modifications, of any enactments relating to borrowing by local authorities.

(4) The purposes to which this section applies are—
    (a) the acquisition of such land and the acquisition or construction of such works as the Boards are authorised to acquire or construct ;

(*b*) the provision of working capital ;

(*c*) providing temporarily for any current expenses properly chargeable to revenue ;

(*d*) the making of any other payment which the Boards are authorised to make and which ought in the opinion of the Secretary of State to be spread over a term of years, including the payment of interest on money borrowed for capital expenditure for such period as may be determined by the Secretary of State with the approval of the Treasury, not exceeding the period during which the expenditure remains unremunerative.

(5) Any money borrowed for any of the purposes to which this section applies, and the interest on any such money, shall be charged on the undertaking and all the revenues of the Board concerned.

(6) It shall be lawful for any annual provision required to be made by the North Board for the repayment of money borrowed under this section to be suspended subject to such conditions and for such period, not exceeding the period during which the relative expenditure remains unremunerative, as the Secretary of State, with the approval of the Treasury, may determine.

(7) Where any annual provision is suspended under subsection (6) that suspension shall not be for a period exceeding 5 years from the commencement of the financial year following that in which such expenditure is incurred.

(8) The amount outstanding in respect of the principal of any sums of foreign currency borrowed under this section or section 3 of the Gas and Electricity Act 1968, and of any sums of sterling borrowed from outwith the United Kingdom under this section, shall be included in the aggregate of the amounts outstanding in respect of loans raised by the Boards which is subject to the limit imposed by section 29.

1968 c. 39.

(9) Nothing in subsection (8) shall

(*a*) prevent the Boards from borrowing in excess of the limit mentioned in that subsection for the purpose of repaying the principal of any such sums borrowed by them under this section or the said section 3, or for the purpose of redeeming any securities issued under either of those sections which they are required or entitled to redeem ;

(*b*) be taken as exempting the Boards from the provisions of any order under section 1 of the Borrowing (Control and Guarantees) Act 1946 or from the provisions of the Exchange Control Act 1947.

1946 c. 58.

1947 c. 14.

28.—(1) All money borrowed by either of the Boards shall be applied to the purpose for which it is authorised to be borrowed up to the amount required for that purpose, and any excess over that amount and all other capital money received by the Board in respect of their undertaking, including money arising from the disposal of lands acquired by the Board for the purposes of any scheme, shall be applied towards the discharge of any loan, or, with the approval of the Secretary of State, to any other purpose to which capital may properly be applied.

(2) In the case of the North Board there shall be paid out of the general fund all the expenses of the Board which are properly chargeable to revenue including, without prejudice to the generality of this provision—

    (a) interest on money borrowed and the sums required to be set aside for the repayment thereof ;

    (b) payments to the reserve fund ;

    (c) the salaries, fees and allowances to members of the Board ;

    (d) the salaries, remuneration, allowances of, and payments made for the purpose of providing superannuation allowances and gratuities for, the members and the secretary, officers and servants of the Board or their representatives ; and

    (e) expenditure on the operation, maintenance and repair of the works, machinery and plant forming part of the undertaking of the Board.

(3) The North Board may provide out of revenue a reserve fund by setting aside such sums as they think reasonable and investing such sums, and the resulting income thereof, in securities of Her Majesty's Government in the United Kingdom or securities guaranteed as to principal and interest by the Government, not being securities of that Board.

(4) The reserve fund shall be applicable to meet any deficiency at any time existing in the income of the North Board from their undertaking or to meet any extraordinary claim or demand at any time arising against the Board in respect of their undertaking.

(5) The North Board may make provision for the carrying forward of such working balance as they may consider reasonably necessary and may, with the approval of the Secretary of State, apply any surplus revenues in payment of expenses chargeable to capital.

29.—(1) The aggregate of the amounts outstanding in respect of—

    (*a*) the principal of any stock issued (other than stock issued to the Central Authority under section 47 of the Act of 1947 and transferred to the South Board by virtue of section 5(1) of the Act of 1954) ; and

    (*b*) any loans raised by the Boards ; and

    (*c*) any advances, whether temporary or otherwise, made to either of those Boards under section 42 of the Finance Act 1956 or under section 2 of the Electricity and Gas Act 1963, or under section 24,

shall not at any time exceed the sum of £1,500 million, or such greater sum not exceeding £1,950 million as the Secretary of State may by order specify.

(2) Nothing in this section shall prevent the Boards from borrowing in excess of the said sum for the purposes of redeeming any stock which they are required or entitled to redeem or of repaying any such loans or any such advances.

30.—(1) The Boards shall each cause proper books of account and other books in relation thereto to be kept and shall prepare an annual statement of accounts in such form as the Secretary of State with the approval of the Treasury may direct, being a form which shall conform with the best commercial standards and which shall be such as to secure the provision of separate information as respects the generation of electricity, the distribution of electricity and each of the main other activities of the Board concerned and to show as far as may be the financial and operating results of each such activity.

(2) The accounts of each Board and their officers shall be audited by an auditor appointed by the Secretary of State and the audit shall be conducted in such manner as may be prescribed.

(3) As soon as the accounts of either of the Boards have been audited that Board shall send copies to the Secretary of State, together with copies of any report of the auditor, and shall publish the accounts in such manner as the Secretary of State may direct, and shall place copies of the accounts on sale at a reasonable price.

(4) The Secretary of State shall lay before each House of Parliament a copy of the accounts of each of the Boards and of any reports thereon sent to him under subsection (3).

31.—(1) Subject to the provisions of this section, nothing in this Act shall exempt either of the Boards from any liability for tax, duty, rate, levy or other charge whatsoever, whether general or local.

PART I
1946 c. 64.

(2) For the purposes of section 52 of the Finance Act 1946 (which exempts from stamp duty certain documents connected with nationalisation schemes) any transfer of property from one of the Boards to the other effected by an order made under this Act shall be deemed to be part of the initial putting into force of such a scheme.

PART II

POWERS OF SECRETARY OF STATE

Powers of the Secretary of State.

32. The Secretary of State shall continue to exercise the functions transferred to him by subsections (1) and (2) of section 1 of the Act of 1954 (functions relating to the generation and supply of electricity in Scotland and matters connected therewith).

Power to give directions.

33.—(1) The Secretary of State may after consultation with either of the Boards give to that Board such directions of a general character as to the exercise and performance by the Board of their functions under this Act as appear to the Secretary of State to be requisite in the national interest, and the Board shall give effect to any such directions.

(2) In carrying out such measures of reorganisation, or such works of development, as involve substantial outlay on capital account, the Boards shall act in accordance with a general programme settled from time to time in consultation with the Secretary of State.

(3) In the exercise and performance of their functions as to training, education and research the Boards shall act in accordance with a general programme settled from time to time in consultation with the Secretary of State.

(4) The Secretary of State may, after consultation with either of the Boards, give to that Board directions as to the use or disposal of any assets vested in them, being assets which are not connected with the generation, transmission or distribution of electricity; and the Board shall give effect to any such directions.

Transfer orders.

34. The Secretary of State may, after consulting the Boards, provide by order—

(*a*) for the transfer to either of the Boards of any property, rights, liabilities and obligations vested in the other Board ;

(*b*) for the modification of agreements so far as necessary for giving effect to the transfer of rights, liabilities and obligations thereunder from one of the Boards to the other, and, in a case where part only of the rights, liabilities and obligations under any agreement are transferred, for substituting for the agreement separate agreements in the requisite terms, and for any apportionments and indemnities consequent thereon ;

(c) in connection with the transfer to one of the Boards of part of the land comprised in any lease vested in the other Board, for the severance of that lease and for apportionments and indemnities consequent thereon ;

(d) for such other financial adjustments between the Boards as may be required in consequence of any such order, and for any other matters supplementary to or consequential on the matters aforesaid for which provision appears to the Secretary of State to be necessary or expedient, including the application to the Board to whom the transfer is made of the provisions of any local enactment applicable to the Board from whom the transfer is made.

35.—(1) It shall not be lawful, except with the consent of the Secretary of State given after consultation with the North Board or the South Board, as the case may be, for any body or person to establish in the district of either Board a new private generating station operated by water power and having plant with a rating exceeding 50 kilowatts, or to extend any existing private generating station so operated in that district by the installation of plant with a rating exceeding 50 kilowatts.

Control of new private hydro-electric generating stations.

(2) The Secretary of State shall not refuse his consent to the establishment or extension of any such station if he is satisfied that such establishment or extension would not prejudice the exercise or performance by the Board concerned of their powers or duties regarding the development of further means of generation of electricity by water power.

(3) Where consent is given by the Secretary of State under subsection (1) to any body or person, nothing in this Act shall prevent that body or person from exercising any powers otherwise competent to them in relation to the construction or extension of the station and the carrying out of any other works necessary for the operation of the station.

36.—(1) Where a person ceases otherwise than on the expiry of his term of office to be a member of either of the Boards and it appears to the Secretary of State that there are special circumstances which make it right that that person should receive compensation, the Secretary of State may, with the approval of

Compensation for members and officers of the Boards.

PART II   the Minister for the Civil Service, require the Board concerned to make to that person a payment of such amount as may be determined by the Secretary of State with the approval of the Minister for the Civil Service.

(2) The Secretary of State shall by regulations require the Boards and any Board established by order made under section 2 to pay, in such cases and to such extent as may be specified in the regulations, compensation to officers of those Boards who suffer loss of employment or loss or diminution of emoluments or pension rights or whose position is worsened in consequence of—

>   (a) the transfer of any property, rights, liabilities and obligations vested in one of those Boards to another of those Boards under section 34(a) or paragraph 6(a) of Schedule 2, or
>
>   (b) the disposal in any other manner of any such property, rights, liabilities or obligations.

(3) Different regulations may be made under subsection (2) in relation to different classes of persons, and any such regulations may be made so as to have effect from a date prior to the date of making, provided that any such regulation so made shall not place any person other than any of those Boards in a worse position than he would have been if the regulations had not been so made.

(4) Regulations made under subsection (2)—

>   (a) shall prescribe the procedure to be followed in making claims for compensation, and the manner in which, and the person by whom, the question whether any or all the compensation is payable is to be determined ; and
>
>   (b) may in particular contain provisions enabling appeals from any determination under paragraph (a) to be brought, in such cases and subject to such conditions as may be prescribed before a tribunal established 1964 c. 16.   under section 12 of the Industrial Training Act 1964 ; and
>
>   (c) shall, in such cases and to such extent as may be specified in the regulations, extend to persons to whom the said subsection would have applied, but for any service in Her Majesty's Forces and in such other employment as may be specified in the regulations.

Pension rights.   **37.**—(1) The Secretary of State may make regulations—

>   (a) for providing pensions to or in respect of persons who are or have been in the employment of either of the Boards or of a Consultative Council established for the district of either of the Boards ;

(b) for the establishment and administration of pension schemes and pension funds for the purpose of providing the pensions mentioned in paragraph (a) ;

(c) for the continuance, amendment, repeal or revocation of existing pension schemes, whenever constituted, relating in whole or in part to that purpose and of enactments relating thereto, and of trust deeds, rules or other instruments made for that purpose ;

(d) for the transfer in whole or in part, or for the extinguishing, of liabilities under any such existing pension schemes, and for the transfer in whole or in part, or winding up, of pension funds held for the purposes of any such existing pension scheme, not being, in the case of a transfer, a diversion of any such funds to purposes other than those mentioned in paragraph (a) ; and

(e) for making any consequential provision, including—

    (i) provision for the dissolution or winding up of any body whose continued existence has by reason of regulations made under this section become unnecessary ;

    (ii) provision as to the manner in which questions arising under the regulations are to be determined ; and

    (iii) provision for adapting, modifying or repealing enactments, whether of general or special application.

(2) Regulations made under subsection (1) may contain provisions authorising any person who, being a participant in any pension scheme to which the regulations relate, becomes a member of one of the Boards being treated as if his service as a member of the Board were service in the employment of the Board ; and the pension rights of any such person resulting from the operation of any such provision shall not be affected by any provision of this Act which requires that the pensions if any, which are to be paid in the case of members of the Board are to be determined by the Secretary of State with the approval of the Minister for the Civil Service.

(3) Subject to subsection (4), regulations made under subsection (1) shall be so framed as to ensure that persons having existing pension rights are not by reason of any provision of the regulations made under this section placed in any worse position than their position under the existing scheme.

PART II

(4) Regulations shall not be invalid by reason only that they do not comply with subsection (3), but if the Secretary of State is satisfied, or it is determined under subsection (5), that they do not so comply, the Secretary of State shall as soon as possible after being so satisfied, or, as the case may be, after it is so determined, make amending regulations to comply with subsection (3).

(5) Any dispute as to whether regulations made under subsection (1) comply with subsection (3) shall be referred to a tribunal established under section 12 of the Industrial Training Act 1964.

1964 c. 16.

(6) Regulations made under subsection (1) may be made so as to have effect from a date prior to the date of making, provided that any such regulation so made shall not place any person other than either of the Boards in a worse position than he would have been if the regulations had not been so made.

Inquiries.

38.—(1) The Secretary of State may in any case where he deems it advisable to do so cause an inquiry to be held in connection with any matter arising under this Act, the Act of 1957 or the Electricity (Supply) Acts.

(2) Schedule 8 shall have effect in relation to any inquiry caused to be held by the Secretary of State under this section.

PART III

GENERAL AND MISCELLANEOUS

Disputes between the Boards.

39.—(1) Subject to the provisions of this Act, any question or dispute arising between the Boards shall, failing agreement between them, be determined by the Secretary of State or by an arbiter appointed by the Secretary of State.

(2) Any arbiter so appointed shall have the like powers for securing the attendance of witnesses and the production of documents and with regard to the examination of witnesses on oath and the awarding of expenses as if the arbitration were under a submission.

(3) The arbiter may, and if so directed by the Court of Session shall, state a case for the opinion of that Court on any question of law arising in the proceedings.

(4) Any award of the Secretary of State or as the case may be of an arbiter under this section may be recorded in the Books of Council and Session for execution and may be enforced accordingly.

40.—(1) Any power of the Secretary of State to make regulations or orders under this Act shall be exercisable by statutory
instrument.

(2) A statutory instrument made under the powers conferred
by sections 8(4), 34, 37(1), paragraph 3 of Schedule 7, or,
subject to subsection (4), by section 2(2), shall be subject to
annulment in pursuance of a resolution of either House of
Parliament.

(3) A statutory instrument made under the powers conferred
by section 15(2) shall be subject to special parliamentary procedure.

(4) No order shall be made in the exercise of the power conferred by section 2(2) the effect of which is to increase or reduce
the total number of districts or to constitute a new district for
which a new Board is required to be established and no regulations shall be made under section 36(2) relating to compensation
to officers unless a draft of the order or regulations has been
laid before Parliament and has been approved by a resolution
of each House of Parliament.

(5) No order shall be made in the exercise of the power conferred by section 29 unless a draft of the order has been laid
before the Commons House of Parliament and has been approved
by resolution of that House.

(6) Where a power to make regulations or orders is exercisable by the Secretary of State by virtue of sections 2(2), 8(4),
15(2), 34, 36(2), 37(1) or paragraph 3 of Schedule 7, any regulations or order, as the case may be, made in the exercise of that
power may—

(a) provide for the determination of questions of fact or of
law which may arise in giving effect to the regulations
or order ;

(b) regulate (otherwise than in relation to any court proceedings) any matters relating to the practice and procedure to be followed in connection with the determination of such questions, including—

(i) provision as to the mode of proof of any
matters ;

(ii) provision as to parties and their representation ;

(iii) provision for the right of the Secretary of
State or other authorities to appear and be heard
in court proceedings or otherwise, and

     (iv) provision as to awarding expenses of proceedings for the determination of such questions, determining the amount of such expenses, and the enforcement of awards of expenses ;

(c) provide for extending any period prescribed by any such regulations or order as a period within which anything is required to be done ;

(d) in the case of regulations, provide that any person offending against them shall be liable on summary conviction to a fine not exceeding £100 and that, if the offence in respect of which he is so convicted is continued after the conviction, he shall be guilty of a further offence and shall be liable on summary conviction to a fine not exceeding £5 for each day on which the offence is so continued.

(7) Any power conferred on the Secretary of State by this Act to make orders includes power to vary or revoke any orders so made.

Offences and penalties.

41.—(1) If any person, in giving any information, making any claim or giving any notice for the purposes of sections 4(g), 12, 15, 36(2) to (4) and 37 or of any regulation made thereunder, knowingly or recklessly makes any statement which is false in a material particular, he shall be liable—

(a) on summary conviction, to imprisonment for a term not exceeding 3 months, or to a fine not exceeding £100, or to both ;

(b) on conviction on indictment, to imprisonment for a term not exceeding 2 years, or to a fine not exceeding £500, or to both.

(2) Where an offence under subsection (1) has been committed by a body corporate, every person who at the time of the commission of the offence was a director, general manager, or secretary or other similar officer of the body corporate, or was purporting to act in any such capacity, shall be deemed to be guilty of that offence unless he proves that the offence was committed without his consent or connivance and that he exercised all such diligence to prevent the commission of the offence as he ought to have exercised having regard to the nature of his functions in that capacity and to all the circumstances.

Annual reports, statistics and returns.

42.—(1) The Boards shall each annually, at such date and in such form as the Secretary of State may require, make to him a report dealing generally with the operations of the Board during the preceding year, and such report shall set out any direction given by the Secretary of State to the Board during that year unless the Secretary of State has notified the Board that

in his opinion it is against the interests of national security to do
so ; and any such report shall be laid before Parliament and shall
be on sale at a reasonable charge to the public at the offices of
the Board.

(2) Each of the Boards shall furnish to the Secretary of State
such returns, accounts and information regarding the property
and activities of the Board as he may require, and shall, in such
manner and at such times as he may require, afford to him
facilities for the verification of the information furnished.

43. The Boards may with the consent of the Secretary of Power of
State promote an order under the Private Legislation Procedure Boards to
(Scotland) Act 1936 and may oppose any such order. promote and
oppose
private
legislation.

44. Schedule 9 shall have effect in relation to the service of Service of
notices or other documents under this Act. notices etc.

45.—(1) In this Act, unless the context otherwise requires— Interpretation.
  " Act of 1943 " means the Hydro-Electric Development 1943 c. 32.
      (Scotland) Act 1943 ;
  " Act of 1947 " means the Electricity Act 1947 ; 1947 c. 54.
  " Act of 1954 " means the Electricity Reorganisation (Scot- 1954 c. 60.
      land) Act 1954 ;
  " Act of 1957 " means the Electricity Act 1957 ; 1957 c. 48.
  " Area Board " means an Area Board within the meaning of
      section 1 of the Act of 1947, being an Area Board
      whose area is within England and Wales ;
  " the Boards " has the meaning given by section 1, and any
      reference to a Board shall be construed as a reference to
      one or other of the Boards ;
  " bulk supply " means a supply of electricity to be used for
      the purposes of distribution ;
  " Central Authority " means the Central Electricity Auth-
      ority established by section 1 of the Act of 1947 and
      dissolved by section 1 of the Act of 1957 ;
  " constructional scheme " has the meaning given by section
      10 ;
  " Consultative Councils " shall be construed in accordance
      with section 17 ;
  " electric line " means a wire or wires, conductor, or other
      means used for the purpose of conveying, transmitting,
      or distributing electricity with any casing, coating, cover-
      ing, tube, pipe, or insulator enclosing, surrounding, or
      supporting the same, or any part thereof, or any appara-
      tus connected therewith for the purpose of conveying,
      transmitting, or distributing electricity or electric
      currents ;

" electrical fittings " means electric lines, fittings, apparatus and appliances designed for use by consumers of electricity for lighting, heating, motive power and other purposes for which electricity can be used ;

" electrical plant " means any plant, equipment, apparatus and appliances used for the purposes of generating, transmitting and distributing electricity, but not including any electrical fittings ;

" Electricity Council " means the Electricity Council established by section 3 of the Act of 1957 ;

" Electricity (Supply) Acts " means the Electricity (Supply) Acts 1882 to 1936 ;

" financial year " in relation to either of the Boards means the financial year prescribed for that Board by the Secretary of State under section 30 ;

" general fund " has the meaning given by section 18 ;

" general reserve fund " shall be construed in accordance with section 19 ;

" the Generating Board " means the Central Electricity Generating Board established by section 2 of the Act of 1957 ;

" generating station " has the meaning given by section 36 of the Electricity (Supply) Act 1919 ;

1919 c. 100.

" land " includes an interest in land and references to entering upon or taking possession of land shall be construed accordingly ; and any reference to land shall include a reference to salmon fishings ;

" large power user " means a consumer (other than either of the Boards) with a demand for a supply of not less than 5,000 kilowatts ;

" lease " includes an agreement for a lease and any tenancy agreement ;

" local authority " means a regional, islands or district council ;

" local enactment " means any enactment other than a public general act ;

" main transmission lines " has the meaning given by the Electricity (Supply) Act 1919 ;

" North Board " has the meaning given by section 1 ;

" ordinary consumer " means any consumer other than a large power user or the South Board ;

" pension ", in relation to any person, means a pension, whether contributory or not, of any kind whatsoever payable to or in respect of him, and includes a gratuity so payable and a return of contributions to a pension fund, with or without interest thereon or any other addition thereto ;

" pension fund " means a fund established for the purposes of paying pensions ;

" pension rights " includes, in relation to any person, all forms of right to or eligibility for the present or future payment of a pension to or in respect of that person, and any expectation of the accruer of a pension to or in respect of that person under any customary practice and includes a right of allocation in respect of the present or future payment of a pension ;

" pension scheme " includes any form of arrangements for the payment of pensions, whether subsisting by virtue of an Act, trust, contract or otherwise ;

" prescribed " means prescribed by regulations made by the Secretary of State ;

" railway undertakers " means any body authorised by any enactment to carry goods and passengers by railway ;

" South Board " has the meaning given by section 1 ;

" telegraphic line " has the meaning given by the Telegraph Act 1878. 1878 c. 76.

(2) Except insofar as the context otherwise requires, any reference in this Act to an enactment shall be construed as a reference to that enactment as amended by or under any other enactment including this Act.

(3) In this Act, except where otherwise indicated—

  (*a*) the reference to a numbered Part, section or schedule is a reference to the Part or section of, or the schedule to, this Act so numbered, and

  (*b*) the reference in a section to a numbered subsection is a reference to the subsection of that section so numbered, and

  (*c*) a reference in a section, subsection or schedule to a numbered or lettered paragraph is a reference to the paragraph of that section, subsection or schedule so numbered or lettered.

46.—(1) Schedule 10 (transitional and saving provisions) and Schedule 11 (consequential amendment) shall have effect, but the provisions of those Schedules shall not be taken as prejudicing the operation of section 38 of the Interpretation Act 1889 (which relates to the effect of repeals).

PART III   (2) The enactments specified in Schedule 12 are hereby repealed to the extent shown in column 3 of that Schedule.

Short title,
extent and
commence-
ment.

47.—(1) This Act may be cited as the Electricity (Scotland) Act 1979.

(2) Subject to subsection (3), this Act extends to Scotland only.

(3) Paragraph 1(*b*) of Schedule 3 shall extend also to England and Wales.

(4) This Act shall come into force on the expiry of the period of one month beginning on the date of its passing.

SCHEDULES

SCHEDULE 1

CONSTITUTION AND PROCEEDINGS OF THE BOARDS

1. The Boards shall each be appointed by the Secretary of State and shall consist of a Chairman, and not less than 4 nor more than 8 other members of whom one or more may be appointed Deputy Chairman or Chairmen.

2. A person shall be disqualified from being appointed or being a member of either of the Boards if he is an undischarged bankrupt or if he has granted a trust deed for behoof of creditors, or entered into a composition contract.

3. A member of either of the Boards shall hold office for such term and on such conditions as the Secretary of State may determine at the time of his appointment, but may at any time resign his office by notice in writing given to the Secretary of State.

4. Any member of either of the Boards shall, if he is interested in any company with which the Board has made or proposes to make any contract, disclose to the Board the fact and nature of his interest, and shall take no part in any deliberation or decision of the Board relating to that contract ; and the disclosure shall be forthwith recorded in the minutes of the Board.

5. Where any member of either of the Boards is absent from the meetings of the Board for more than 6 months consecutively, except for some reason approved by the Secretary of State, the Secretary of State shall forthwith declare the office of that member to be vacant and thereupon the office shall become vacant.

6. Each of the Boards shall be a body corporate and subject to the quorum of the Board not being less than 3, shall have power to regulate their own procedure.

7. Either of the Boards may act notwithstanding a vacancy in their number.

8. The Boards shall have their offices in Scotland.

9. Each Board shall have a common seal and the seal of each Board shall be authenticated by the signature of the secretary to the Board or some person authorised by the Board to act in that behalf.

10. Every document purporting to be an instrument issued by either of the Boards and
   (a) to be sealed with the seal of the Board authenticated in the manner provided by paragraph 9, or
   (b) to be signed by the secretary to the Board or by a person authorised by the Board to act in that behalf.

shall be received in evidence and be deemed to be such an instrument or document without further proof unless the contrary is shown.

11. Each Board shall appoint a secretary and such other officers and servants as the Board may determine.

12. There shall be paid to the members of each Board such salaries or fees and allowances for expenses as the Secretary of State with the approval of the Minister for the Civil Service may determine, and there shall be paid to the secretary, officers and servants of each Board such salaries, remuneration and allowances as the Board may determine ; and on the retirement or death of any member in whose case it may be so determined to make such provision there shall be paid such a pension to or in respect of that member as may be so determined.

Section 2.

SCHEDULE 2

DISTRICTS

PART I

NORTH DISTRICT

1. The district of the North Board (in this Act referred to as the North District) shall consist of—

    (*a*) the following Regions:—Highland, Grampian and Tayside, and

        (i) in the Central Region—In Stirling District, the former parishes of Balfron, Buchanan, Drymen, Fintry, Gargunnock, Killearn and Kippen ;

        (ii) in Strathclyde Region—Argyll and Bute District, that part of Cunninghame District, formerly in the County of Bute, and that part of Dunbarton District formerly comprising the parishes of Arrochar, Kilmaronock and Luss ;

    (*b*) the Islands Areas.

PART II

SOUTH DISTRICT

2. The district of the South Board (in this Act referred to as the South District) shall consist of all of Scotland other than the North District.

PART III

ORDERS VARYING DISTRICTS

3. If any question arises as to the exact boundary between the North District and the South District as defined by any order made under section 2 it shall be determined by the Secretary of State after giving to the Boards an opportunity to make representations in relation to that question.

4. An order so made shall state whether the districts affected by the order are to be regarded as the districts of the Boards or whether any such district is to be regarded as a new district.

5. An order so made which includes the formation of a new district shall establish for that district a new Board which shall

be known by such name as may be specified in the order and Schedule 1 shall have effect in relation to any such new Board as it has effect in relation to the Boards, and any such new Board shall have the like functions as the South Board.

6. An order made under section 2 shall, so far as it appears to the Secretary of State to be necessary or expedient in consequence of the variation of districts or the establishment of a new Board provide—

   (*a*) for the transfer of property, rights, liabilities and obligations from one Board to another ;

   (*b*) for the modification of agreements for the purposes of giving effect to the transfer of rights, liabilities and obligations under any such agreement from one Board to another and, in a case where part only of the rights, liabilities and obligations under any agreement are transferred, for substituting for that agreement separate agreements in the requisite terms and for any consequent apportionments and indemnities ;

   (*c*) for the purpose of transferring part of the land comprised in any lease vested in any such Board to another such Board, for the severance of that lease and for consequent apportionments and indemnities ;

   (*d*) for dissolving any Board the whole of whose functions are to be exercised by another Board or Boards and for winding up the affairs of the Board to be dissolved ; and

   (*e*) for such other financial adjustments between the Boards concerned as may be required in consequence of any such transfer,

and for any other matter supplementary to or consequential on the matters aforesaid, including the continuation of legal proceedings.

7. An order made under section 2 shall define by reference to a map the new districts or new boundaries constituted by the order, and copies of the map shall be made available for inspection at such places and such times as may be published by the Secretary of State in the Edinburgh Gazette and in such other newspapers circulating in the districts concerned as the Secretary of State thinks fit, and shall also be made available for inspection to Members of each House of Parliament when the order is laid before Parliament.

SCHEDULE 3

SUPPLY OF ELECTRICITY TO RAILWAYS

1. A supply of electricity to railway undertakers under section 3 may be provided—

   (*a*) by either of the Boards in their own district ;

   (*b*) in England or Wales by the South Board with the approval of the Generating Board ;

   (*c*) in the South District by the Generating Board with the approval of the South Board ;

SCH. 3   (d) in the district of either of the Boards by the other of them with the approval of the Board in whose district the supply is provided.

2. The terms and conditions on which electricity is supplied by either of the Boards to railway undertakers under section 3 shall be such as may be agreed between the Board concerned and the undertakers or in default of such agreement, as may be determined by the Secretary of State, being such terms and conditions as in the opinion of that Board or, as the case may be, of the Secretary of State, will not cause a financial loss to result to that Board from the provision of the supply.

3. Where the terms and conditions mentioned in paragraph 2 are determined by the Secretary of Sate that determination—

    (a) shall not extend to the terms and conditions on which any electricity so supplied may be used by the undertakers for other purposes, and

    (b) shall not be taken to preclude the Board concerned and the undertakers from subsequently varying the terms and conditions so determined by agreement between them.

4. Either of the Boards may enter into an agreement with any railway undertakers to whom the Board are to supply electricity under section 3 for purposes of haulage and traction whereby any of that electricity may be used by the undertakers for other purposes on such terms and conditions as may be specified in the agreement.

5. Without prejudice to any other enactment providing for protection of telegraphic lines belonging to or used by the Post Office, any electricity supplied to railway undertakers under section 3 shall be used in such manner as not to cause or to be likely to cause any interference (whether by induction or otherwise) with any such telegraphic line or with telegraphic communication by means of any such line.

Section 5(2).   **SCHEDULE 4**

CONSTITUTION AND FUNCTIONS OF AMENITY COMMITTEE
AND FISHERIES COMMITTEE

1. The Amenity Committee and the Fisheries Committee shall consist of such number of persons as the Secretary of State may think proper for them respectively, and shall have the function of giving advice and assistance to the Secretary of State and to each of the Boards on questions of amenity and fisheries respectively.

2. The Boards shall furnish to each of those Committees any maps, plans, drawings or information which the Committee may reasonably require, and shall give to each Committee reasonable facilities for inspection.

3. The Boards shall before and during the preparation of a constructional scheme under section 10, and may at any other time, consult the Amenity Committee and the Fisheries Committee; and upon being so consulted or at any other time each of those Committees may make recommendations to the Board concerned; and

that Board shall transmit a copy of every such recommendation to the Secretary of State, together with an intimation as to whether or not they are prepared to accept it.

4. If either of the Boards is not prepared to accept any recommendation made to them under paragraph 3, the Secretary of State after considering any representations made to him may—

(a) if the recommendation relates to a scheme which has been submitted to him for confirmation but has not yet been confirmed, refuse to confirm the scheme, and

(b) in the case of any other recommendation (not being a recommendation involving the execution by either of the Boards of any works authorised by a confirmed scheme otherwise than in the manner set out in that scheme), require that Board to give effect to it ;

and where a requirement is imposed on a Board under sub-paragraph (b) that Board shall thereupon be bound to carry out the requirement.

5. The Boards shall not, without giving prior notice to the Amenity Committee of their intention to do so, use or permit to be used for the exhibition of advertisements any part of any land or building owned or leased by them in connection with a constructional scheme under section 10.

6. Each of the Boards shall defray any expenses reasonably incurred by the Amenity Committee and the Fisheries Committee up to such amounts and in such proportions as the Secretary of State may from time to time approve.

SCHEDULE 5

CONSTRUCTIONAL SCHEMES

1. A constructional scheme shall contain particulars with regard to such matters, and shall be accompanied by such maps, drawings and plans, as the Secretary of State may require.

2. When either of the Boards have prepared a constructional scheme they shall submit it to the Secretary of State for confirmation and shall publish, in such form and in such newspapers as the Secretary of State may require, a notice stating that the scheme has been prepared and submitted for confirmation and specifying the situation of any works proposed to be undertaken and of any land proposed to be acquired.

3. The Board concerned shall send copies of that notice to the persons appearing from the valuation roll to be the owners and the occupiers of any land proposed to be acquired, and shall also deposit a copy of the scheme and keep copies available for inspection and sale at the offices of the Board and at one or more other convenient places ; and the notice so published shall state where the copies of

SCH. 5

the scheme are deposited and shall also specify a period of 40 days within which, and the manner in which objection thereto may be made to the Secretary of State.

4. Subject to paragraph 5, if on the expiry of the time within which objection may be made to a constructional scheme the Secretary of State on considering the scheme together with any objections made thereto, and after holding such inquiry (if any) as he thinks fit, is of the opinion that it is in the public interest that the Board should be authorised to carry out the scheme, he may make an order confirming the scheme without amendment or with such amendments as the Board may submit.

5. Where any person who has lodged an objection to the scheme requests that an inquiry shall be held, the Secretary of State shall, unless he is of the opinion that the objection is frivolous, cause an inquiry to be held before confirming the scheme.

6. Every order made by the Secretary of State confirming a constructional scheme shall be laid before Parliament as soon as may be after it is made, together with a copy of the scheme as confirmed, and shall be subject to annulment by a resolution of either House of Parliament.

7. A constructional scheme shall become operative on the expiry of the period within which the order confirming the scheme might be annulled without its being so annulled.

8. The Board shall thereon deposit copies of the scheme as confirmed and give notice of the places where such copies are available for inspection and sale in like manner as under paragraph 3.

9. As soon as may be after notice has been given in accordance with paragraph 8 the Board shall proceed with the construction of the works specified in the scheme and may do all things necessary for giving effect to the scheme.

10. A scheme confirmed under this Schedule may be amended or revoked by a subsequent scheme prepared and confirmed in the like manner and subject to the like conditions as the original scheme.

Section 11(2).

SCHEDULE 6

ADAPTATIONS AND MODIFICATIONS OF LANDS CLAUSES ACTS AND OF THE RAILWAYS CLAUSES CONSOLIDATION (SCOTLAND) ACT, 1845.

1. The scheme shall be deemed to be the special Act, and—

(a) in the Lands Clauses Acts references to the promoters of the undertaking shall be construed as references to the Board concerned, and

(b) in the Railways Clauses Consolidation (Scotland) Act, 1845—

> (i) references to the railway company shall be construed
> as references to that Board, and

> (ii) references to the railway shall be construed as
> references to the land acquired or to any works which have
> been or may be constructed thereon, or to any use to
> which the land is or may be put, according to the
> context.

2. Sections 83 to 88 and section 90 of the Lands Clauses
Consolidation (Scotland) Act, 1845, and the provisions of that Act
relating to access to the special Act, shall not apply.

3. No person shall be required to sell a part only of any house,
building or manufactory or of any land which forms part of a park
or garden belonging to a house, if he is willing and able to sell the
whole of the house, building, manufactory, park or garden, unless
the arbiter by whom compensation is to be assessed determines—

(a) in the case of a house, building or manufactory that the
part proposed to be taken can be taken without material
detriment to the house, building or manufactory ; or

(b) in the case of a park or garden, that such part can be taken
without seriously affecting the amenity or convenience of
the house ;

and if the arbiter so determines, compensation shall be awarded
in respect of the severance of the part so proposed to be taken, in
addition to the value of that part, and thereupon the person interested
shall be required to sell to the Board that part of the house,
building, manufactory, park or garden.

4.—(1) In assessing the sums to be included in the compensation
payable to any person by way of compensation in respect of the
injurious affection of, or the severance of the land acquired from, any
land in which that person has an interest, account shall be taken of
any increase, ascribable to any use to which the land acquired is
intended to be put, in the value of his interest in any land which
at the relevant time was held with the land acquired.

(2) In this paragraph the expression " the relevant time " means,
in connection with the acquisition of any land, immediately before
the date of the service of the notice to treat relating to the land, or,
if possession of the land had then already been taken by the Board
in exercise of the power conferred on them by section 11(3),
immediately before the taking of possession.

5. In assessing the compensation payable in respect of the
acquisition of any land, no account shall be taken of any change
in the value of the land attributable to anything done by the Board
in the exercise of their powers under section 11(5), but the value of
the land shall be computed by reference to the circumstances existing
at the date of the notice given in pursuance of section 11(3).

6. The compensation payable in respect of the acquisition of a
servitude over any land shall be the difference between the value
of the land free from that servitude and the value of that land subject
to that servitude.

7. Any person empowered to sell or convey any land to the Board shall have power to grant to them a servitude over that land.

8.—(1) The Board concerned may sell, feu, or lease for such periods and for such consideration as they may think fit any land and property for the time being belonging to them which they do not require for the purposes of any scheme.

(2) On so disposing of any land, the Board concerned may reserve to themselves all or any part of the water rights or any servitude belonging thereto, and may so dispose of any land subject to such other reservations, conditions, and restrictions as they may think fit.

SCHEDULE 7

CONSULTATIVE COUNCILS

Constitution, Proceedings and Functions

1. Each of the Consultative Councils established for the respective districts of the Boards shall consist of a chairman appointed by the Secretary of State and of not less than 20 or more than 30 other persons so appointed of whom—

(a) not less than two-fifths or more than three-fifths shall be appointed from a panel of persons nominated by such associations as appear to the Secretary of State to represent local authorities in the district ;

(b) the remainder shall be appointed after consultation with such bodies as the Secretary of State thinks fit to represent agriculture, commerce, industry, labour and the general interests of consumers of electricity and other persons or organisations interested in the development of electricity in the district.

2. In the appointment of any person under subparagraph (a) of paragraph 1, the Secretary of State shall have particular regard to that person's ability to exercise a wide and impartial judgment on the matters to be dealt with by the Council generally ; and in making appointments under subparagraph (b) of that paragraph the Secretary of State shall have particular regard to any nominations made to him by the bodies mentioned in that subparagraph of persons who are recommended by them as having both adequate knowledge of the requirements of the interests to be represented and also the ability to exercise a wide and impartial judgment on the matters to be dealt with by the Council generally.

3. The Secretary of State may make regulations with respect to—

(a) the appointment of, and the tenure and the vacation of office by, the members of a Consultative Council and the appointment of a person to act in the place of the Chairman of such a Council ;

(b) the quorum, proceedings, meetings and determinations of a Consultative Council ;

(c) any other matters supplementary or incidental to the matters aforesaid for which provision appears to the Secretary of State to be necessary or expedient.

4. Subject to the provisions of any regulations made under paragraph 3, a Consultative Council may regulate their own procedure.

5. Each of the Councils—

   (a) shall consider any matter affecting the distribution of electricity in their district, including the variation of tariffs and the provision of new or improved services and facilities within the district, being a matter which is the subject of a representation made to them by consumers or other persons requiring supplies of electricity in that district, or which appears to them to be a matter to which consideration ought to be given apart from any such representation, and where action appears to them to be requisite as to any such matter, shall notify their conclusions to the Board; and

   (b) shall consider and report to the Board on any such matter which may be referred to them by that Board.

6. Each of the Councils shall be informed by the Board of that Board's general plans and arrangements for exercising and performing their functions under this Act and may make representations thereon to that Board.

7. The Board shall consider any conclusion, reports and representations notified or made to them by the Council for their district under paragraphs 5 and 6, and the Council may after consultation with the Board make representations to the Secretary of State on matters arising therefrom.

8. Where representations have been so made to the Secretary of State and it appears to him after consultation with the Board and with the Council that a defect is disclosed in that Board's general plans and arrangements for the exercise and performance of their functions under this Act, the Secretary of State may give to the Board such directions as he thinks fit for remedying the defect.

9. Each of the Councils shall prepare and submit to the Secretary of State a scheme for the appointment by them of committees or individuals to be local representatives of the Council in such localities as may be specified in the scheme; and it shall be the duty of such committees and individuals to consider the particular circumstances and requirements of those localities with respect to the distribution of electricity and to make representations to the Council thereon, and to be available for receiving on behalf of the Council representations from consumers in those localities; and if the scheme is approved by the Secretary of State the Consultative Council shall put it into effect.

10. Under a scheme prepared and submitted under paragraph 8 a member of a Council shall be eligible for appointment either as a member of a Committee or as an individual, but membership of the Council shall not be a necessary qualification for such an appointment.

11. A Council may make to the Board concerned a report on the exercise and performance by the Council of their functions during any financial year of the Board and any such report shall be made to the Board as soon as possible after the end of that financial year and the Board shall include that report in the report made by them under section 42.

Council Chairmen

12. There shall be paid to the chairman of a Council such remuneration as the Secretary of State may determine ; and in the case of a person remunerated under this paragraph there shall be no obligation to remunerate him also under paragraph 12 of Schedule 1.

13. If the Secretary of State so determines in the case of a person who has been remunerated under paragraph 12, he shall pay such pension to or in respect of that person, or make such payments towards the provision of such a pension, as the Secretary of State may determine.

14. If a person in receipt of remuneration under paragraph 12 ceases to hold the office by virtue of which he receives it, and it appears to the Secretary of State that there are special circumstances which make it right that that person should receive compensation, that person shall be paid a sum of such amount as the Secretary of State may determine.

Council's Administration, Personnel etc.

15. A Council may, subject to the approval of the Secretary of State as to numbers, appoint such officers as appear to the Council to be requisite for the performance of their functions, including those of any committee or individual appointed under paragraph 9.

16. The Secretary of State shall provide the Council with funds wherewith to pay—

    (*a*) to their members, and to members of any such committee, or to any such individual, as is mentioned above such travelling and other allowances ; and

    (*b*) to the officers of a Council, such remuneration, and such travelling and other allowances,

as the Secretary of State may determine, and wherewith also to defray such other expenses in connection with their functions as he may determine to be appropriate ; and he may make arrangements for Councils to be provided with office accommodation.

17.—(1) There shall be paid, to or in respect of persons who are or have been officers of Consultative Councils such pensions as the Secretary of State may determine or arrangements shall be made for the payment of such pensions.

(2) A Consultative Council may, if the Secretary of State determines that they should do so, assume in respect of such persons as are referred to in sub-paragraph (1) any liabilities incurred by either of the Boards under or in pursuance of section 37.

(3) The Secretary of State shall provide Consultative Councils with funds wherewith to pay pensions under sub-paragraph (1) or to finance any arrangements under that sub-paragraph, and to discharge any liabilities assumed by Councils under sub-paragraph (2).

SCH. 7

Supplementary

18.—(1) The consent of the Minister for the Civil Service shall be required for any determination or approval by the Secretary of State under paragraphs 12 to 17.

(2) In this Schedule " pension " includes allowance and gratuity payable on retirement or otherwise.

SCHEDULE 8

PROVISIONS AS TO INQUIRIES

Section 38.

1. The Secretary of State shall appoint a person to hold the inquiry and to report thereon to him.

2. The person appointed to hold the inquiry shall notify the Board concerned and any person who has lodged objections to the matter which is the subject of the inquiry, and shall publish in such newspaper or newspapers as the Secretary of State may direct a notice of the time when and the place where the inquiry is to be held.

3. Except with the sanction of the person appointed to hold the inquiry, no person other than the Board or a person who has lodged objections to the matter which is the subject of the inquiry shall be entitled to appear or to be represented at the inquiry.

4. The person appointed to hold the inquiry may, on the motion of any party thereto, or of his own motion, require any person by notice in writing—

   (a) to attend at the time and place set forth in the notice to give evidence or to produce any books or documents in his custody or under his control which relate to any matter in question at the inquiry ; or

   (b) to furnish within such reasonable period as is specified in the notice such information relating to any matter in question at the inquiry as the person appointed to hold the inquiry may think fit and as the person so required is able to furnish:

Provided that no person shall be required in obedience to such a notice to attend at any place which is more than 10 miles from the place where he resides unless the necessary expenses are paid or tendered to him.

5. The person appointed to hold the inquiry may administer oaths and examine witnesses on oath and may accept, in lieu of evidence on oath by any person, a statement in writing by that person.

6. The inquiry shall be held in public.

L 3

7. Any person who refuses or wilfully neglects to attend in obedience to a notice issued under paragraph 4, or who wilfully alters, suppresses, conceals, destroys, or refuses to produce, any book or document which he may be required by any such notice to produce, or who refuses or wilfully neglects to comply with any requirement under paragraph 4 of the person appointed to hold the inquiry, shall be liable on summary conviction to a fine not exceeding £20 or to imprisonment for a period not exceeding 3 months.

8. The Secretary of State shall communicate to each party to the inquiry the recommendations made by the person appointed to hold it.

9. The expenses incurred by the Secretary of State in relation to the inquiry (including such reasonable sum as the Secretary of State may determine for the services of the person appointed to hold the inquiry) shall be paid by such of the parties to the inquiry as the Secretary of State may direct.

10. The Secretary of State may make directions as to the expenses incurred by the parties to the inquiry and as to the parties by whom such expenses shall be paid.

11. Any direction by the Secretary of State under paragraph 9 or paragraph 10 requiring any party to pay expenses may be recorded in the Books of Council and Session for execution and may be enforced accordingly.

Section 44.

SCHEDULE 9

SERVICE OF NOTICES

Any notice or other document required or authorised to be given, delivered or served by or under this Act, or under any enactment applied by this Act, may be given, delivered or served either—

(a) by delivering it to the person to whom it is to be given or delivered or on whom it is to be served ; or

(b) by leaving it at the usual or last known place of abode of that person ; or

(c) by sending it by registered post or recorded delivery service addressed to that person at his usual or last known place of abode ; or

(d) in the case of an incorporated company or body, by delivering it to the secretary or clerk of the company or body at their registered or principal office or sending it by registered post or recorded delivery service addressed to the secretary or clerk of the company or body at that office ; or

(e) if it is not practicable after reasonable enquiry to ascertain the name or address of a person to whom it should be given or delivered, or on whom it should be served, as being a person having any interest in land, by addressing it to him by the description of the person having that interest in the premises (naming them) to which it relates, and delivering it to some person on the premises or, if there is no person on the premises to whom it can be delivered, affixing it, or a copy of it, to some conspicuous part of the premises.

SCHEDULE 10
TRANSITIONAL AND SAVING PROVISIONS

1. In so far as any regulation, order, licence, permit, notice, entry, directive, warrant or other instrument made, issued or given, under any enactment repealed by this Act, or any such other thing done or having effect as if done under any such enactment, could have been made, issued, given or done under a corresponding provision of this Act, it shall not be invalidated by the repeal but shall have effect as if made, issued, given or done under that corresponding provision.

2. Without prejudice to paragraph 1, any provision of this Act relating to anything done or required or authorised to be done under or by reference to that provision or any other provision of this Act shall have effect as if any reference to that provision, or that other provision, as the case may be, included a reference to the corresponding provision of the enactments repealed by this Act.

3. Without prejudice to the generality of paragraphs 1 and 2, any scheme or agreement made, or any charge or tariff imposed, under any enactment repealed by this Act, shall continue to have effect as if made or imposed under the corresponding provision of this Act.

4.—(1) Nothing in this Act shall affect the enactments repealed by this Act in their operation in relation to offences committed before the commencement of this Act.

(2) Where an offence, for the continuance of which a penalty may be provided, has been committed under an enactment repealed by this Act, proceedings may be taken under this Act in respect of the continuance of the offence after the commencement of this Act in the same manner as if the offence had been committed under the corresponding provision of this Act.

5. Where any enactment or document refers, either expressly or by implication, to an enactment repealed by this Act, the reference shall, except where the context otherwise requires, be construed as, or as including, a reference to the corresponding provision of this Act.

6. Nothing in this Act shall affect the operation of the provisions of section 57(1) of or of Schedule 4 Part I to the Act of 1947 (adaptation and modification of Electricity (Supply) Acts) and references in any of the provisions of the Electricity (Supply) Acts, to those Acts, and any reference therein to one or more of those Acts, being a reference which, by virtue of the construction of those Acts as one, is to be construed as a reference to all the said Acts shall in their application to Scotland be construed as containing a reference to this Act.

7. Nothing in this Act shall affect the operation of the provisions of section 57(2) of or of Schedule 4 Part III to the Act of 1947 (incorporation of the Schedule to the Electric Lighting (Clauses) Act 1899) and those provisions shall have effect in relation to the provisions of this Act as they had effect immediately before the coming into operation of this Act in relation to the provisions of

SCH. 10   the Act of 1947, with the adaptations and modifications subject to which they so had effect.

8. Notwithstanding the repeal by this Act of section 2(9) of the Act of 1947 (capacity of Boards as statutory corporations), the provisions of that subsection shall continue to have effect in relation to the provisions of this Act as they had effect in relation to the provisions of the Act of 1947 immediately before the coming into operation of this Act.

1975 c. 55.
1968 c. 39.

9. The repeal by the Statutory Corporations (Financial Provisions) Act 1975 of section 3 of the Gas and Electricity Act 1968 shall not affect anything done or any right established under that section before the passing of the said Act of 1975.

1899 c. 19.

1936 c. 20.

10. Nothing in section 32 shall affect the functions of the Secretary of State under the Schedule to the Electric Lighting (Clauses) Act 1899 as incorporated with the Act of 1947, so far as that Schedule relates to the certification of meters and the measurement of electricity, or under the Electricity Supply (Meters) Act 1936, being the functions formerly exercised by the Minister of Fuel and Power and referred to in section 1(4) of the Act of 1954, as originally enacted.

11. Notwithstanding the repeal by this Act of Section 51 of the Act of 1947 (power to break up streets), any powers exerciseable by an Area Board in Scotland by virtue of that section immediately before the coming into force of this Act, shall continue to be so exerciseable thereafter.

12.—(1) Section 24 shall have effect without prejudice to the operation of any provisions of section 42 of the Finance Act 1956 in relation to advances made to the Boards before 18th December 1963, and the provisions of the said section 42 shall, notwithstanding its repeal by section 4(2) of the Electricity and Gas Act 1963, continue to operate in relation to any such advances.

(2) Notwithstanding the repeal by this Act of section 2(8) of the said Act of 1963, any account prepared under section 24(5) shall include any sums received by the Secretary of State under section 42(4) of the Finance Act 1956 in respect of the financial year to which the account relates ; and the Secretary of State shall not be required to prepare an account under the said section 42.

13. Notwithstanding the repeal by this Act—

    (a) of section 38(4) of the Act of 1947 (amendments to Schedule 4 of the Act of 1943) ;

    (b) of Schedule 4 Part II to the Act of 1947 (amendments to the Act of 1943) ;

    (c) of Schedule 1 Part 1 to the Act of 1954 (amendments to the Act of 1943) ;

    (d) of Schedule 1 Part II to the Act of 1954 (amendments to Act of 1947),

the amendments made by the said section 38(4) to Schedule 4 of the Act of 1943 and by the said Schedule 4 Part II to the Act of 1947 to sections 2(1)(d), 16(1), 17, 27 and Schedule 4 of the Act of 1943 and by the said Schedule 1 Part I to the Act of 1954 to sections

2(1)(*d*), 16(1), 17 and Schedule 4 and by the said Schedule 1 Part II to the Act of 1954 to sections 1(4) and (5), 2(8A), 4, 19, 60 and 67 of the Act of 1947 shall continue to have the same effect in relation to that Schedule and to those sections and Schedules as they had immediately before the coming into force of this Act.

14. Notwithstanding the repeal by this Act of section 55(6) of the Act of 1947 (saving of rights in respect of compensation), regulations made under section 36(2) shall not prejudice the rights of any person arising in consequence of events which occurred before 1st April 1948 under—

(*a*) section 16 of the Electricity (Supply) Act 1919 ;

(*b*) section 15 of and the Fourth Schedule to the Electricity (Supply) Act 1926 ;

(*c*) the Compensation of Displaced Officers (War Service) (Electricity Undertakings) Order 1946,

including those sections and that Schedule as applied by any other enactment, with or without modifications and adaptations.

SCHEDULE 11

Consequential Amendment

The Salmon Fisheries (Scotland) Act 1868

In Schedule G to the Salmon Fisheries (Scotland) Act 1868, at the end, add the following paragraph: —

" 8. Nothing in this Schedule shall apply to any dam, aqueduct, pipe or other work constructed under the Electricity (Scotland) Act 1979 or under any enactment repealed by that Act."

SCHEDULE 12

Repeals

Chapter	Short Title	Extent of Repeal
6 & 7 Geo. 6. c. 32.	The Hydro-Electric Development (Scotland) Act 1943.	The whole Act, except sections 2(1)(*d*), 16(1), 17, 27 in so far as it defines " maximum number of kilowatts " and other expressions, 28 and Schedule 4.
10 & 11 Geo. 6. c. 54.	The Electricity Act 1947.	The whole Act except sections 1(3), 2(8A), 4(8), 13, 22, 54(5), 57(1) and (2), 60, 67, 68(1) to (3) and 69, Schedule 2 and Schedule 4 Parts I and III, and in so far as they relate to any matter affecting one of the Boards and the Generating Board or an Area Board, sections 1(4) and (5), 2(7), 4(2) to (7), 11(2) and 19.
2 & 3 Eliz. 2. c. 60.	The Electricity Reorganisation (Scotland) Act 1954.	The whole Act, except sections 1(3), 10(2), 15(1), 16, 17 and, in Schedule 1, Part III.

Chapter	Short Title	Extent of Repeal
5 & 6 Eliz. 2. c. 48.	The Electricity Act 1957.	Sections 28 and 35. In section 29— in subsection (1), the words " or either of the Scottish Electricity Boards "; in subsection (3), the words " or District "; in subsection (4), the words " or Scottish Electricity Board "; In Schedule 4 Part II, the entries relating to section 2 and section 10A of the Act of 1943.
1963 c. 59.	The Electricity and Gas Act 1963.	In section 2— in subsection (1), the words from " and the Secretary of State " to the words " South of Scotland Electricity Board "; and the words " or Board in question "; in subsections (3) and (6), the words " or the Secretary of State "; in subsections (4) and (7), the words " and the Secretary of State "; subsection (8); in subsection (9), the words " and Boards ". In section 3— in subsection (2), paragraphs (*d*) and (*e*); subsection (3). In section 4, subsection (3); In Schedule 1, the entry relating to the Act of 1947; Schedule 3.
1968 c. 39.	The Gas and Electricity Act 1968.	The whole Act.
1969 c. 1.	The Electricity (Scotland) Act 1969.	The whole Act.
1972 c. 17.	The Electricity Act 1972.	The whole Act except sections 2 and 4.
1975 c. 55.	The Statutory Corporations (Financial Provisions) Act 1975.	In Schedule 2, the references to the North Board and the South Board. In Schedule 3, Part I, except paragraph 5. In Schedule 4, paragraphs 1 and 4.
1976 c. 61.	The Electricity (Financial Provisions) (Scotland) Act 1976.	Section 1.

Wages Councils Act 1979

1979 CHAPTER 12

An Act to consolidate the enactments relating to wages councils and statutory joint industrial councils.

[22nd March 1979]

BE IT ENACTED by the Queen's most Excellent Majesty, by and with the advice and consent of the Lords Spiritual and Temporal, and Commons, in this present Parliament assembled, and by the authority of the same, as follows:—

PART I

WAGES COUNCILS

1.—(1) Subject to the provisions of this Part of this Act, the Secretary of State may by order establish a wages council to perform, in relation to the workers described in the order and their employers, the functions specified in relation to wages councils in the subsequent provisions of this Part of this Act.

Establishment of wages councils.

(2) An order establishing a wages council may be made by the Secretary of State either—

(*a*) if he is of opinion that no adequate machinery exists for the effective regulation of the remuneration of the workers described in the order and that, having regard to the remuneration existing among those workers, or any of them, it is expedient that such a council should be established ; or

(*b*) if he thinks fit, to give effect to a recommendation of the Advisory, Conciliation and Arbitration Service (" the Service ") made on the reference to it, in accordance with section 2 below, of an application made in accordance therewith for the establishment of a wages council ; or

(c) if he thinks fit, to give effect to the recommendation of the Service made in a case where the Secretary of State, being of opinion that no adequate machinery exists for the effective regulation of the remuneration of any workers or the existing machinery is likely to cease to exist or be adequate for that purpose and a reasonable standard of remuneration among those workers will not be maintained, refers to the Service the question whether a wages council should be established with respect to any of those workers and their employers.

(3) Schedule 1 to this Act shall have effect with respect to the making of orders establishing wages councils.

(4) Schedule 2 to this Act shall have effect with respect to the constitution, officers and proceedings of wages councils.

Applications for wages council orders.   **2.**—(1) An application for the establishment of a wages council with respect to any workers and their employers may be made to the Secretary of State either—

(a) by a joint industrial council, conciliation board or other similar body constituted by organisations representative respectively of those workers and their employers; or

(b) jointly by any organisation of workers and any organisation of employers which claim to be organisations that habitually take part in the settlement of remuneration and conditions of employment for those workers;

on the ground, in either case, that the existing machinery for the settlement of remuneration and conditions of employment for those workers is likely to cease to exist or be adequate for that purpose.

(2) Where such an application as aforesaid is made to him, the Secretary of State—

(a) subject to subsection (3) below, if he is satisfied that there are sufficient grounds to justify the reference of the application to the Service, and, in the case of an application under paragraph (b) of subsection (1) above, that the claim of the organisations habitually to take part in the settlement of remuneration and conditions of employment for those workers is well-founded, shall refer the application to the Service to inquire into and report on the application;

(b) if he is not so satisfied shall notify the applicants to that effect, in which case no further steps shall be taken on the application unless and until he is so satisfied by fresh facts brought to his notice:

Provided that before taking either of the said courses, the Secretary of State may require the applicants to furnish such

information, if any, in relation to the application as he considers PART I
necessary.

(3) If, on considering an application under subsection (1) above, it appears to the Secretary of State either—

(a) that there is a joint industrial council, conciliation board or other similar body constituted by organisations of workers and organisations of employers, being a council, board or body which would or might be affected by the establishment of a wages council in pursuance of the application ; or

(b) that there are organisations of workers and organisa- tions of employers representative respectively of workers other than workers to whom the application relates and their employers, who would or might be affected by the establishment of a wages council as aforesaid ;

being a council, board or body, or, as the case may be, organisations, which are parties to joint voluntary machinery for the settlement of remuneration and conditions of employment but are not parties to the application for a wages council, the Secretary of State shall, before deciding to refer the application to the Service give notice of the application to that council, board or body or, as the case may be, to those organisations, shall consider any observations in writing which may be submitted to him by them within such period as he may direct, not being less than one month from the date of the notice, and, if he decides to refer the application to the Service, shall transmit a copy of the observations to the Service.

(4) If, before an application is referred to the Service, it is withdrawn by the applicants, no further proceedings shall be had thereon.

3.—(1) Where the Secretary of State makes any such refer- Proceedings on ence as is mentioned in paragraph (b) or (c) of subsection (2) references as to of section 1 above, it shall be the duty of the Service to establishment of wages consider not only the subject matter of the reference but also councils. any other question or matter which, in the opinion of the Service, is relevant thereto, and in particular to consider whether there are any other workers (being workers who, in the opinion of the Service, are engaged in work which is complementary, subsidiary or closely allied to the work performed by the workers specified in the reference or any of them) whose position should be dealt with together with that of the workers, or some of the workers, specified as aforesaid ; and in relation to any such reference, any reference in this Part of this Act to the workers with whom the Service is concerned shall be construed as a reference to the workers specified as aforesaid and any such other workers as aforesaid.

(2) If the Service is of opinion with respect to the workers with whom it is concerned or any of those workers whose position should, in the opinion of the Service be separately dealt with—

    (*a*) that there exists machinery set up by agreement between organisations representing workers and employers respectively which is, or can be made by improvements which it is practicable to secure, adequate for regulating the remuneration and conditions of employment of those workers ; and

    (*b*) that there is no reason to believe that that machinery is likely to cease to exist or be adequate for that purpose,

the Service shall report to the Secretary of State accordingly and may include in its report any suggestions which it may think fit to make as to the improvement of that machinery.

(3) Where any such suggestions are so included, the Secretary of State shall take such steps as appear to him to be expedient and practicable to secure the improvements in question.

(4) If the Service is of opinion with respect to the workers with whom it is concerned or any of those workers whose position should, in the opinion of the Service, be separately dealt with—

    (*a*) that machinery for regulating the remuneration and conditions of employment of those workers is not, and cannot be made by any improvements which it is practicable to secure, adequate for that purpose, or does not exist ; or

    (*b*) that the existing machinery is likely to cease to exist or be adequate for that purpose,

and that as a result a reasonable standard of remuneration among those workers is not being or will not be maintained, the Service may make a report to the Secretary of State embodying a recommendation for the establishment of a wages council in respect of those workers and their employers.

(5) In considering for the purposes of section 1 above whether any machinery is, or is likely to remain, adequate for regulating the remuneration and conditions of employment of any workers, the Service shall consider not only what matters are capable of being dealt with by that machinery, but also to what extent those matters are covered by the agreements or awards arrived at or given thereunder, and to what extent the practice is, or is likely to be, in accordance with those agreements or awards.

Abolition of, or variation of field of operation of, wages councils.

4.—(1) The Secretary of State may at any time abolish a wages council by order made—

    (*a*) to give effect to an application in that behalf made to him in accordance with section 5 below, or (*b*) without any such application, subject however to the provisions of section 6 below.

(2) The Secretary of State may at any time by order vary the field of operation of a wages council.

(3) The power of the Secretary of State to make an order under this section varying the field of operation of a wages council shall include power to vary that field by excluding from it any employers to whom there for the time being applies, as members of an organisation named in the order, an agreement, to which the organisation or any other organisation of which it is a member or on which it is represented, is a party, regulating remuneration or other terms or conditions of employment of their employees.

(4) Any organisation so named shall if it has not already done so furnish the Secretary of State with a list of its members and shall from time to time, and also if so required by the Secretary of State, furnish him with particulars of any changes in their membership which have occurred since the list was furnished or, as the case may be, when particulars were last furnished to him.

(5) An order under this section abolishing or varying the field of operation of one or more wages councils may include provision for the establishment of one or more wages councils operating in relation to all or any of the workers in relation to whom the first mentioned council or councils would have operated but for the order, and such other workers, if any, as may be specified in the order.

(6) Where an order of the Secretary of State under this section directs that any workers shall be excluded from the field of operation of one wages council and brought within the field of operation of another, the order may provide that anything done by, or to give effect to proposals made by, the first-mentioned council shall have effect in relation to those workers as if it had been done by, or to give effect to proposals made by, the second-mentioned council and may make such further provision as appears to the Secretary of State to be expedient in connection with the transition.

(7) Where an order of the Secretary of State under this section directs that a wages council shall be abolished or shall cease to operate in relation to any workers, then, save as is otherwise provided by the order, anything done by, or to give effect to proposals made by the wages council shall, except as respects things previously done or omitted to be done, cease to have effect or, as the case may be, cease to have effect in relation to the workers in relation to whom the council ceases to operate.

(8) Schedule 1 to this Act shall have effect with respect to the making of orders under this section.

5.—(1) An application such as is mentioned in paragraph (*a*) of subsection (1) of section 4 above may be made to the Secretary of State either—

> (*a*) by a joint industrial council, conciliation board or other similar body constituted by organisations of workers and organisations of employers which represent respectively substantial proportions of the workers and employers with respect to whom that wages council operates ; or
>
> (*b*) jointly by organisations of workers and organisations of employers which represent respectively substantial proportions of the workers and employers aforesaid ; or
>
> (*c*) by any organisation of workers which represents a substantial proportion of the workers with respect to whom that wages council operates.

(2) The grounds on which any such application may be made are that the existence of a wages council is no longer necessary for the purpose of maintaining a reasonable standard of remuneration for the workers with respect to whom that wages council operates.

References to
the Service as
to variation or
revocation of
wages council
orders.

6.—(1) The Secretary of State—

> (*a*) shall in any case where an application for the abolition of a wages council has been made to him under section 5 above and he does not thereupon proceed to the making of an order giving effect to the application,
>
> (*b*) may in any other case where he is considering whether to exercise his power under section 4 above to abolish or vary the field of operation of a wages council ;

refer to the Service the question whether the council should be abolished or, as the case may be, its field of operation varied.

(2) On a reference under this section of a question as to the abolition of a wages council the Service, if of the opinion that it is expedient to do so, may make a report to the Secretary of State recommending—

> (i) the abolition of the wages council to which the reference relates, or
>
> (ii) the narrowing of the field of operation of the council,

and (in either case), if the Service of the opinion that it is expedient as aforesaid, also recommending the transfer of workers to the field of operation of another wages council, whether already existing or to be established.

(3) On a reference under this section as to the variation of the field of operation of a wages council the Service may make a report to the Secretary of State recommending any such variation (including the transfer of workers to the field of operation of any other wages council, whether already existing or to be established) which appears to the Service desirable in all the circumstances.

7.—(1) On any references under this Part of this Act to the Service, the Service shall make all such investigations as appear to it to be necessary and shall publish in the prescribed manner a notice stating the questions which it is its duty to consider by virtue of the reference and further stating that it will consider representations with respect thereto made to it in writing within such period as may be specified in the notice, not being less than forty days from the date of the publication thereof ; and it shall consider any representations made to it within that period and then make such further inquiries as it considers necessary including, so far as it considers necessary, the hearing of oral evidence.

PART I
Supplemental provisions.

(2) Any power conferred by this Part of this Act on the Secretary of State to make an order giving effect to a recommendation of the Service shall be construed as including power to make an order giving effect to that recommendation with such modifications as he thinks fit, being modifications which, in his opinion, do not effect important alterations in the character of the recommendation.

(3) Where the Secretary of State receives any report from the Service he may, if he thinks fit, refer the report back to the Service and the Service shall thereupon reconsider it having regard to any observations made by him and shall make a further report, and the like proceedings shall be had on any such further report as in the case of an original report.

(4) The Secretary of State shall publish every report made to him by the Service under this Part of this Act:

Provided that where he refers a report back to the Service, he shall not be bound to publish it until he publishes the further report of the Service.

8.—(1) A wages council may request the Secretary of State to appoint a committee for any of the workers within the field of operation of the council and the Secretary of State shall appoint a committee accordingly, and the council may refer to it for a report and recommendations any matter relating to those workers which the council thinks it expedient so to refer.

Advisory committees.

(2) Schedule 3 to this Act shall have effect with respect to committees appointed under this section.

9.—(1) A wages council shall consider, as occasion requires, any matter referred to it by the Secretary of State or any government department with reference to the industrial conditions prevailing as respects the workers and employers in relation to whom it operates, and shall make a report upon the matter to the Secretary of State or, as the case may be, to that department.

General duty of wages councils to consider references by government departments.

(2) A wages council may, if it thinks it expedient so to do, make of its own motion a recommendation to the Secretary of State or any government department with reference to the said conditions and, where such a recommendation is so made, the Secretary of State or, as the case may be, that department, shall forthwith take it into consideration.

PART II

STATUTORY JOINT INDUSTRIAL COUNCILS

Conversion of wages councils to statutory joint industrial councils.

10.—(1) The Secretary of State may by order made in accordance with the following provisions of this section provide that a wages council shall become a statutory joint industrial council having the functions conferred on statutory joint industrial councils by the provisions of Part III of this Act.

(2) The Secretary of State may make an order under this section with respect to a wages council—

(a) on an application made to him by the employers' association or trade union nominated in relation to the council or by that association and union jointly ; or

(b) without an application under paragraph (a) above, but after consultation with the employers' association and trade union so nominated.

(3) An order under this section shall not be made on an application by an employers' association or trade union alone unless the Secretary of State has consulted every employers' association and trade union nominated in relation to the wages council in question and (whether so nominated or not) all organisations of employers and workers which in his opinion represent a substantial proportion of employers and workers respectively in relation to whom that council operates.

(4) The Secretary of State shall before making an order under this section refer the question whether he should do so to the Service, and the Service shall inquire into it and report on that question.

(5) Part I of Schedule 4 to this Act shall have effect with respect to the constitution, officers and proceedings of statutory joint industrial councils and Part II of that Schedule shall have effect with respect to the transition of a wages council to a statutory joint industrial council.

Disputes between employers' and workers' representatives.

11.—(1) If in the opinion of either the persons appointed to represent employers or the persons appointed to represent workers on a statutory joint industrial council, a dispute has arisen on any question and cannot be settled by the members of the council, those persons may request the Service to attempt to bring about a settlement of the dispute and the Service shall attempt to do so accordingly.

(2) If the Service is unable to bring about a settlement of any such dispute, the Service shall refer the dispute for settlement to the arbitration of—

> (a) one or more persons appointed by the Service for that purpose (not being an officer or servant of the Service) ; or

> (b) the Central Arbitration Committee.

(3) Where more than one arbitrator is appointed under subsection (2)(a) above, the Service shall appoint one of the arbitrators to act as chairman.

(4) Any determination of the arbitrator, arbitrators or Committee on a dispute referred to him, them or it under this section shall be final and binding on the statutory joint industrial council and its members, and the council shall make an order under section 14 below or take any other steps which may be necessary to give effect to the determination.

(5) Part I of the Arbitration Act 1950 shall not apply to 1950 c. 27. an arbitration under this section.

(6) In the application of this section to Scotland, references to an arbitrator shall be construed as references to an arbiter.

12.—(1) If the Secretary of State is of the opinion that, in Abolition of the event of the abolition of a statutory joint industrial council, statutory joint adequate machinery would be established for the effective regu- industrial lation of the remuneration and other terms and conditions of councils. employment of the workers within the council's field of operation and is likely thereafter to be maintained, he may by order abolish the council.

(2) An order under this section may be made on the application of the statutory joint industrial council concerned or without such an application, but shall not be made without such an application unless the Secretary of State has consulted the council.

(3) The Secretary of State shall before making an order under this section refer the question whether he should do so to the Service, and the Service shall inquire into it and report on that question.

(4) Where an order under this section abolishes a statutory joint industrial council, then, save as is otherwise provided by the order, anything done by the council shall, except as respects

things previously done or omitted to be done, cease to have effect.

Supplemental provisions.

13.—(1) In sections 10 to 12 above " nominated ", in relation to an employers' association or trade union, means, an association or union for the time being nominated under paragraph 1(2) of Schedule 2 to this Act to appoint persons to represent employers or workers on the wages council in question.

(2) Schedule 1 to this Act shall apply in relation to an order under section 10 above providing that a wages council shall become a statutory joint industrial council and in relation to an order under section 12 above abolishing a statutory joint industrial council.

PART III

ORDERS REGULATING TERMS AND CONDITIONS OF EMPLOYMENT

Power to fix terms and conditions of employment.

14.—(1) A wages council or a statutory joint industrial council may make an order, subject to and in accordance with the provisions of this section,—

   (a) fixing the remuneration,

   (b) requiring holidays to be allowed,

   (c) fixing any other terms and conditions,

for all or any of the workers in relation to whom the council operates.

(2) An order under this section requiring a holiday to be allowed for a worker—

   (a) shall not be made unless both holiday remuneration in respect of the period of the holiday and remuneration other than holiday remuneration have been or are being fixed under this Part of this Act for that worker ;

   (b) shall provide for the duration of the holiday being related to the duration of the period for which the worker has been employed or engaged to be employed by the employer who is to allow the holiday ; and

   (c) subject as aforesaid, may make provision as to the times at which or the periods within which, and the circumstances in which, the holiday shall be allowed.

(3) Any order under this section fixing holiday remuneration may contain provisions—

   (a) as to the times at which, and the conditions subject to which, that remuneration shall accrue and shall become payable, and (*b*) for securing that any such remuneration which has accrued due to a worker during his employment by any employer shall, in the event of his ceasing to be employed by that employer before he becomes entitled to be allowed a holiday by him, nevertheless become payable by the employer to the worker.

(4) Before making an order under this section the council shall make such investigations as it thinks fit and shall—

(*a*) publish in the prescribed manner notice of the council's proposals with respect to any new terms and conditions of employment (that is to say, any terms and conditions of employment differing from any then in force by virtue of an order made under this section) ; and

(*b*) give the prescribed notice for the purpose of informing, so far as practicable, all persons affected by the proposals, stating the place where copies of the proposals may be obtained and the period (which shall not be less than fourteen days from the date of publication of the notice) within which written representations with respect to the proposals may be sent to the council.

(5) After considering any written representations made with respect to any such proposals within the said period and making such further inquiries as the council considers necessary, or if no such representations are made within that period, after the expiration of that period, the council may make an order—

(*a*) giving effect to the proposals ; or

(*b*) giving effect to them with such modifications as the council thinks fit having regard to any such representations ;

but if it appears to the council that, having regard to the nature of any proposed modifications, an opportunity should be given to persons concerned to consider the modifications, the council shall again publish the proposals and give notice under subsection (4) above, and that subsection and this subsection shall apply accordingly.

(6) Subsections (4) and (5) above have effect subject to the provisions of subsection (1A) of section 4 of the Equal Pay Act 1970.   1970 c. 41.

(7) An order under this section shall have effect as regards any terms as to remuneration as from a date specified in the order, which may be a date earlier than the date of the order but not earlier than the date on which the council agreed on those terms prior to publishing the original proposals to which effect is given, with or without modifications, by the order ; but where any such order fixing workers' remuneration applies to any worker who is paid wages at intervals not exceeding seven days and the date so specified does not correspond with the beginning of the period for which the wages are paid (hereafter in this section referred

to as a wages period), the order shall, as respects that worker, have effect as from the beginning of the next wages period following the date specified in the order.

(8) Any increase in remuneration payable by virtue of an order under this section in respect of any time before the date of the order shall be paid by the employer within a period specified in the order, being—

(a) in the case of a worker who is in the employment of the employer on the date of the order, a period beginning with that date ;

(b) in the case of a worker who is no longer in the employment of the employer on that date, a period beginning with the date on which the employer receives from the worker or a person acting on his behalf a request in writing for the remuneration ;

but if, in the case of a worker falling within paragraph (a) of this subsection who is paid wages at intervals not exceeding seven days, pay day (the day on which wages are normally paid to him) for any wages period falling wholly or partly within the period so specified occurs within seven days from the end of that specified period, any such remuneration shall be paid not later than pay day.

(9) As soon as a council has made an order under this section it shall give the prescribed notice of the making and contents of the order and shall then and subsequently give such notice of other prescribed matters affecting its operation for the purpose of informing, so far as practicable, all persons who will be affected by it.

(10) An order under this section may make different provision for different cases and may amend or revoke previous orders under this section.

(11) A document purporting to be a copy of an order made by a council under this section and to be signed by the secretary of the council shall be taken to be a true copy of the order unless the contrary is proved.

(12) An order under this section shall not prejudice any rights conferred on any worker by or under any other enactment.

Effect and enforcement of orders under s. 14. **15.**—(1) If a contract between a worker to whom an order under section 14 above applies and his employer provides for the payment of less remuneration than the statutory minimum remuneration, it shall have effect as if the statutory minimum remuneration were substituted for the remuneration provided for in the contract, and if any such contract provides for the payment of any holiday remuneration at times or subject to conditions other than those specified in the order, it shall have effect as if the times or conditions specified in the order were substituted for those provided for in the contract.

(2) If any such contract fixes terms and conditions other than those relating to remuneration or wages which are less favourable than the corresponding terms and conditions specified in an order under section 14 above it shall have effect as if the corresponding terms and conditions were substituted for those fixed by the contract.

(3) If an employer fails—

   (*a*) to pay a worker to whom an order under section 14 above applies remuneration not less than the statutory minimum remuneration ; or

   (*b*) to pay him arrears of remuneration before the expiration of the period specified in the order ; or

   (*c*) to pay him holiday remuneration at the times and subject to the conditions specified in the order ; or

   (*d*) to allow to any such worker the holidays fixed by the order ;

he shall for each offence be liable on summary conviction to a fine not exceeding £100.

(4) Where proceedings are brought under subsection (3) above in respect of an offence consisting of a failure to pay remuneration not less than the statutory minimum remuneration, or to pay arrears of remuneration, and the employer or any other person charged as a person to whose act or default the offence was due is found guilty of the offence, then, subject to subsection (5) below,—

   (*a*) evidence may be given of any failure on the part of the employer to pay any such remuneration or arrears during the two years ending with the date of the offence to any worker employed by him ; and

   (*b*) on proof of the failure, the court may order the employer to pay such sum as is found by the court to represent the difference between the amount of any such remuneration or arrears which ought to have been paid during that period to any such worker, if the provisions of this Part of this Act had been complied with, and the amount actually so paid.

(5) Evidence of any failure to pay any such remuneration or arrears may be given under subsection (4) above only if—

> (a) the employer or any other person charged as aforesaid has been convicted of the offence consisting of the failure ; and
>
> (b) notice of intention to adduce such evidence has been served with the summons or warrant.

(6) The powers given by this section for the recovery of sums due from an employer to a worker shall not be in derogation of any right to recover such sums by civil proceedings.

(7) In the application of this section to Scotland—

> (a) in subsection (4), the words " or any other person charged as a person to whose act or default the offence was due " shall be omitted ; and
>
> (b) in subsection (5), in paragraph (a) the words " or any other person charged as aforesaid " shall be omitted, and in paragraph (b) for the words " summons or warrant " there shall be substituted the word " complaint ".

Permits to infirm and incapacitated persons.

16.—(1) If, as respects any worker employed or desiring to be employed in such circumstances that an order under section 14 above applies or will apply to him, the council which made the order is satisfied, on application being made to it for a permit under this section either by the worker or the employer or a prospective employer, that the worker is affected by infirmity or physical incapacity which renders him incapable of earning the statutory minimum remuneration or makes it inappropriate for other terms and conditions fixed by the order to apply to him, it may, if it thinks fit, grant, subject to any conditions it may determine, a permit authorising his employment at less than the statutory minimum remuneration or dispensing with a term or condition specified in the permit ; and while the permit is in force the remuneration authorised by the permit shall, if the conditions specified in the permit are complied with, be deemed to be the statutory minimum remuneration or, as the case may be, the terms and conditions fixed by the order shall be deemed to be observed.

(2) Where an employer employs any worker in reliance on any document purporting to be a permit granted under subsection (1) above authorising the employment of that worker at less than the statutory minimum remuneration, or dispensing with a term or condition specified in the permit, then, if the employer has notified the council in question that, relying on that document, he is employing or proposing to employ that worker at a specified remuneration or without compliance with

any such term or condition, the document shall, notwithstanding
that it is not or is no longer a valid permit relating to that
worker, be deemed, subject to the terms thereof and as respects
only any period after the notification, to be such a permit until
notice to the contrary is received by the employer from the
council.

17.—(1) Subject to the provisions of this Part of this Act, Computation
any reference therein to remuneration shall be construed as a of
reference to the amount obtained or to be obtained in cash by remuneration.
the worker from his employer after allowing for the worker's
necessary expenditure, if any, in connection with his employment, and clear of all deductions in respect of any matter whatsoever, except any reduction lawfully made—

(a) under the Income Tax Acts, the enactments relating
to social security or any enactment requiring or authorising deductions to be made for the purposes of a
superannuation scheme ;

(b) at the request in writing of the worker, either for the
purposes of a superannuation scheme or a thrift scheme
or for any purpose in the carrying out of which the
employer has no beneficial financial interest, whether
directly or indirectly ; or

(c) in pursuance of, or in accordance with, such a contract
in that behalf as is mentioned in section 1, 2 or 3 of
the Truck Act 1896 and in accordance with the pro- 1896 c. 44.
visions of that section.

(2) Notwithstanding subsection (1) above, orders under section
14 above may contain provisions authorising specified benefits
or advantages, being benefits or advantages provided, in pursuance of the terms and conditions of the employment of
workers, by the employer or by some other person under arrangements with the employer and not being benefits or advantages
the provision of which is illegal by virtue of the Truck Acts
1831 to 1940, or of any other enactment, to be reckoned as
payment of wages by the employer in lieu of payment in cash,
and defining the value at which any such benefits or advantages
are to be reckoned.

(3) If any payment is made by a worker in respect of any
benefit or advantage provided as mentioned in the foregoing
subsection, then,—

(a) if the benefit or advantage is authorised by virtue of
that subsection to be reckoned as therein mentioned,
the amount of the payment shall be deducted from the
defined value for the purposes of the reckoning ;

    (*b*) if the benefit or advantage is authorised by virtue of that subsection to be reckoned as therein mentioned, any excess of the amount of the payment over the defined value shall be treated for the purposes of subsection (1) above as if it had been a deduction not being one of the excepted deductions therein mentioned ;

    (*c*) if the benefit or advantage is specified in an order under section 14 above as one which has been taken into account in fixing the statutory minimum remuneration, the whole of the payment shall be treated for the purposes of subsection (1) above as if it had been a deduction not being one of the excepted deductions therein mentioned.

(4) Nothing in this section shall be construed as authorising the making of any deduction, or the giving of remuneration in any manner, which is illegal by virtue of the Truck Acts 1831 to 1940, or of any other enactment.

Apportionment of remuneration.

18. Where for any period a worker receives remuneration for work for part of which he is entitled to statutory minimum remuneration at one or more time rates and for the remainder of which no statutory minimum remuneration is fixed, the amount of the remuneration which is to be attributed to the work for which he is entitled to statutory minimum remuneration shall, if not apparent from the terms of the contract between the employer and the worker, be deemed for the purposes of this Part of this Act to be the amount which bears to the total amount of the remuneration the same proportion as the time spent on the part of the work for which he is entitled to statutory minimum remuneration bears to the time spent on the whole of the work.

Employers not to receive premiums.

19.—(1) Where a worker to whom an order under section 14 above applies is an apprentice or learner, it shall not be lawful for his employer to receive directly or indirectly from him, or on his behalf or on his account, any payment by way of premium :

Provided that nothing in this section shall apply to any such payment duly made in pursuance of any instrument of apprenticeship not later than four weeks after the commencement of the apprenticeship or to any such payment made at any time if duly made in pursuance of any instrument of apprenticeship approved for the purposes of this proviso by a wages council or by a statutory joint industrial council.

(2) If any employer acts in contravention of this section, he shall be liable on summary conviction in respect of each offence to a fine not exceeding £100, and the court may, in addition to imposing a fine, order him to repay to the worker or other person by whom the payment was made the sum improperly received by way of premium.

20.—(1) The employer of any workers to whom an order under section 14 above applies shall keep such records as are necessary to show whether or not the provisions of this Part and Part IV of this Act are being complied with as respects them, and the records shall be retained by the employer for three years.

(2) The employer of any workers shall post in the prescribed manner such notices as may be prescribed for the purpose of informing them of any proposal or order under section 14 above affecting them, and, if it is so prescribed, shall give notice in any other prescribed manner to the said workers of the said matters and of such other matters, if any, as may be prescribed.

(3) If an employer fails to comply with any of the requirements of this section he shall be liable on summary conviction to a fine not exceeding £100.

PART IV

MISCELLANEOUS

Offences and enforcement

21.—(1) Where the immediate employer of any worker is himself in the employment of some other person and that worker is employed on the premises of that other person, that other person shall for the purposes of Part III and this Part of this Act be deemed to be the employer of that worker jointly with the immediate employer.

(2) Where an employer is charged with an offence under Part III or this Part of this Act, he shall be entitled, upon information duly laid by him and on giving to the prosecution not less than three days' notice in writing of his intention, to have any other person to whose act or default he alleges that the offence in question was due brought before the court at the time appointed for the hearing of the charge; and if, after the commission of the offence has been proved, the employer proves that the offence was due to the act or the default of that other person, that other person may be convicted of the offence, and, if the employer further proves that he has used all due diligence to secure that the provisions of Part III and this Part of this Act and any relevant regulation or order made thereunder are complied with, he shall be acquitted of the offence.

(3) Where a defendant seeks to avail himself of the provisions of subsection (2) above—

    (a) the prosecution, as well as the person whom the defendant charges with the offence, shall have the right to cross-examine him if he gives evidence and any witnesses called by him in support of his pleas and to call rebutting evidence ;

(b) the court may make such order as it thinks fit for the payment of costs by any party to the proceedings to any other party thereto.

(4) Where it appears to an officer acting for the purposes of Part III and this Part of this Act that an offence has been committed in respect of which proceedings might be taken under this Act against an employer, and the officer is reasonably satisfied that the offence of which complaint is made was due to an act or default of some other person and that the employer could establish a defence under subsection (2) above, the officer may cause proceedings to be taken against that other person without first causing proceedings to be taken against the employer.

In any such proceedings the defendant may be charged with and, on proof that the offence was due to his act or default, be convicted of, the offence with which the employer might have been charged.

(5) Subsections (2) to (4) above shall not apply to Scotland, but—

(a) where an offence for which an employer is, under this Act, liable to a fine was due to an act or default of an agent of the employer or other person, then, whether proceedings are or are not taken against the employer, that agent or other person may be charged with and convicted of the offence, and shall be liable on conviction to the same punishment as might have been inflicted on the employer if he had been convicted of the offence ;

(b) where an employer who is charged with an offence under this Act proves to the satisfaction of the court that he has used due diligence to secure compliance with the provisions of Part III and this Part of this Act and any relevant regulation or order made thereunder and that the offence was due to the act or default of some other person, he shall be acquitted of the offence.

Officers.

22.—(1) The Secretary of State, with the approval of the Minister for the Civil Service as to numbers and salaries, may appoint officers to act for the purposes of Part III and this Part of this Act, and may, in lieu of or in addition to appointing any officers under this section, arrange with any government department that officers of that department shall act for the said purposes.

(2) Every officer acting for the purposes of Part III and this Part of this Act shall be furnished by the Secretary of State with a certificate of his appointment or authority so to act, and, when

so acting, shall, if so required by any person affected, produce
the certificate to him.

(3) An officer acting for the purposes of Part III and this
Part of this Act shall have power for the performance of his
duties—

(a) to require the production of wages sheets or other records
of wages kept by an employer, and records of payments
made to homeworkers by persons giving out work, and
any other such records as are required by this Act
to be kept by employers, and to inspect and examine
those sheets or records and copy any material part
thereof;

(b) to require the production of any licence or certificate
granted under the Transport Act 1968, and of any 1968 c. 73.
records kept in pursuance of Part VI of the Transport
Act 1968 or of the applicable Community rules within
the meaning of the said Part VI, and to examine any
such licence, certificate or records and copy it or them
or any material part thereof;

(c) to require any person giving out work and any homeworker to give any information which it is in his
power to give with respect to the names and addresses
of the persons to whom the work is given out or from
whom the work is received, as the case may be, and
with respect to the payments to be made for the work;

(d) at all reasonable times to enter any premises at which
any employer to whom an order under section 14
above applies carries on his business (including any
place used, in connection with that business, for giving
out work to homeworkers and any premises which the
officer has reasonable cause to believe to be used by or
by arrangement with the employer to provide living
accommodation for workers);

(e) to inspect and copy any material part of any list of homeworkers kept by an employer or person giving out
work to homeworkers;

(f) to examine, either alone or in the presence of any other
person, as he thinks fit, with respect to any matters
under Part III or this Part of this Act, any person
whom he has reasonable cause to believe to be or to
have been a worker to whom an order under section
14 above applies or applied or the employer of any
such person or a servant or agent of the employer
employed in the employer's business, and to require
every such person to be so examined, and to sign a
declaration of the truth of the matters in respect of
which he is so examined:

Provided that no person shall be required under paragraph (*f*) above to give any information tending to criminate himself or, in the case of a person who is married, his or her wife or husband.

(4) In England or Wales, an officer acting for the purposes of Part III and this Part of this Act may institute proceedings for any offence under this Act and may, although not of counsel or a solicitor, conduct any such proceedings:

Provided that an officer may not conduct proceedings for an offence under section 24 below unless he instituted those proceedings.

(5) An officer acting for the purposes of Part III and this Part of this Act who is authorised in that behalf by general or special directions of the Secretary of State may, if it appears to him that a sum is due from an employer to a worker on account of the payment to him of remuneration less than the statutory minimum remuneration, institute on behalf of and in the name of that worker civil proceedings for the recovery of that sum and in any such proceedings the court may make an order for the payment of costs by the officer as if he were a party to the proceedings.

The power given by this subsection for the recovery of sums due from an employer to a worker shall not be in derogation of any right of the worker to recover such sums by civil proceedings.

(6) Any person who obstructs an officer acting for the purposes of Part III and this Part of this Act in the exercise of any power conferred by this section, or fails to comply with any requirement of such an officer made in the exercise of any such power, shall be liable on summary conviction to a fine not exceeding £100:

Provided that it shall be a defence for a person charged under this subsection with failing to comply with a requirement to prove that it was not reasonably practicable to comply therewith.

Penalties for false entries in records, producing false records or giving false information.

23. If any person makes or causes to be made or knowingly allows to be made any entry in a record required by this Act to be kept by employers, which he knows to be false in a material particular, or for purposes connected with Part III or the preceding provisions of this Part of this Act produces or furnishes, or causes or knowingly allows to be produced or furnished, any wages sheet, record, list or information which he knows to be false in a material particular, he shall be liable on summary conviction to a fine not exceeding £400 or to imprisonment for a term not exceeding three months, or to both such fine and such imprisonment.

24.—(1) The Secretary of State may, for the purpose of, or in connection with the enforcement of, an order under section 14 above, by notice in writing require an employer within the field of operation of a council making such an order to furnish such information as may be specified or described in the notice.

(2) A notice under this section may specify the way in which, and the time within which, it is to be complied with, and may be varied or revoked by a subsequent notice so given.

(3) If a person refuses or wilfully neglects to furnish any information which he has been required to furnish by a notice under subsection (1) above, he shall be liable on summary conviction to a fine not exceeding £100.

(4) If a person, in purporting to comply with a requirement of a notice under subsection (1) above, knowingly or recklessly makes any false statement he shall be liable on summary conviction to a fine not exceeding £400.

(5) Section 21 above shall not apply in relation to an offence under this section.

(6) Where an offence under this section committed by a body corporate is proved to have been committed with the consent or connivance of, or to be attributable to any neglect on the part of, any director, manager, secretary or other similar officer of the body corporate, or any person who was purporting to act in any such capacity, he as well as the body corporate shall be guilty of that offence and shall be liable to be proceeded against and punished accordingly.

(7) Where the affairs of the body corporate are managed by its members, subsection (6) above shall apply in relation to the acts and defaults of a member in connection with his functions of management as if he were a director of the body corporate.

Central co-ordinating committees

25.—(1) The Secretary of State may, if he thinks fit to do so, by order establish a central co-ordinating committee in relation to any two or more wages councils or statutory joint industrial councils, or wages councils and statutory joint industrial councils, or abolish, or vary the field of operation of, any central co-ordinating committee so established:

Provided that, except where subsection (2) or (3) below applies, the Secretary of State shall, before making any such order, consult the wages councils or statutory joint industrial councils, or, as the case may be, the wages councils and the statutory joint industrial councils, concerned.

(2) Where the Service makes a recommendation for the establishment of a wages council or statutory joint industrial council

it may include in its report a recommendation for the establishment, in relation to any council established in accordance with the recommendation and any other council (including a council proposed to be established by another recommendation embodied in the same report), of a central co-ordinating committee, or for the variation of the field of operation of an existing central co-ordinating committee so that it operates also in connection with any council established in accordance with the recommendation.

(3) Where the Service makes a recommendation for the abolition of a wages council or statutory joint industrial council, it may include in its report a recommendation for the variation of the field of operation of an existing central co-ordinating committee so that it no longer operates in relation to the council to be abolished, or a recommendation for the abolition of any central co-ordinating committee theretofore operating in relation to the council to be abolished.

(4) The Secretary of State may by order give effect to a recommendation made under subsection (2) or (3) above.

(5) It shall be the duty of any central co-ordinating committee from time to time—

    (*a*) to consider whether the field of operation of the councils in relation to which it is established is properly divided as between the councils and to report thereon to the Secretary of State ;

    (*b*) to make recommendations to the councils with respect to the principles to be followed by them in the exercise of their powers under this Act ;

    (*c*) to consider any question referred to it by the Secretary of State or by the councils or any two or more of them, and to report thereon to the Secretary of State, or to the councils which referred the question, as the case may be.

(6) Schedule 2 to this Act shall have effect with respect to the constitution, officers and proceedings of central co-ordinating committees.

Reports on regulation of terms and conditions of employment

Reports by Service on regulation of terms and conditions of employment.

26. The Service shall, if requested to do so by the Secretary of State—

    (*a*) inquire into and report on the development by agreement of machinery for the regulation of the remuneration and terms and conditions of employment of workers within the field of operation of a wages council or statutory joint industrial council and the question whether, in order to maintain a reasonable standard of remuneration and terms and conditions of employment of those workers, it is necessary to regulate their remuneration and other terms and conditions of employment by means of orders under section 14 above ;

(*b*) inquire into and report on the operation generally of this Act ;

(*c*) publish a report made under paragraph (*a*) or (*b*) above.

Power to extend wages councils legislation

27.—(1) Her Majesty may by Order in Council provide that—

(*a*) the provisions of this Act, and

(*b*) the provisions of any legislation (that is to say any enactment of the Parliament of Northern Ireland and any provision made by or under a Measure of the Northern Ireland Assembly) for the time being in force in Northern Ireland which makes provision for purposes corresponding to any of the purposes of the provisions of this Act,

shall, to such extent and for such purposes as may be specified in the Order, apply (with or without modification) to or in relation to any person in employment to which this section applies.

Extension of this Act and N.I. legislation.

(2) This section applies to employment for the purposes of any activities—

(*a*) in the territorial waters of the United Kingdom ; or

(*b*) connected with the exploration of the sea bed or subsoil or the exploitation of their natural resources in any designated area ; or

(*c*) connected with the exploration or exploitation, in a foreign sector of the continental shelf, of a cross-boundary petroleum field.

(3) An Order in Council under subsection (1) above—

(*a*) may make different provision for different cases ;

(*b*) may provide that all or any of the provisions of any Act mentioned in that subsection, as applied by such an Order, shall apply to individuals whether or not they are British subjects and to bodies corporate whether or not they are incorporated under the law of any part of the United Kingdom (notwithstanding that the application may affect their activities outside the United Kingdom) ;

(*c*) may make provision for conferring jurisdiction on any court or class of court specified in the Order, or on industrial tribunals, in respect of offences, causes of action or other matters arising in connection with employment to which this section applies;

(d) without prejudice to the generality of subsection (1) above or of paragraph (a) above, may provide that the enactments referred to in that subsection shall apply in relation to any person in employment for the purposes of such activities as are referred to in subsection (2) above in any part of the areas specified in paragraphs (a) and (b) of that subsection;

(e) may exclude from the operation of section 3 of the Territorial Waters Jurisdiction Act 1878 (consents required for prosecutions) proceedings for offences under the enactments referred to in subsection (1) above in connection with employment to which this section applies;

(f) may provide that such proceedings shall not be brought without such consent as may be required by the Order.

(4) Any jurisdiction conferred on any court or tribunal under this section shall be without prejudice to jurisdiction exercisable apart from this section by that or any other court or tribunal.

(5) In this section—

" cross-boundary petroleum field " means a petroleum field that extends across the boundary between a designated area and a foreign sector of the continental shelf;

" designated area " means an area designated under section 1(7) of the Continental Shelf Act 1964;

" foreign sector of the continental shelf " means an area which is outside the territorial waters of any State and within which rights are exercisable by a State other than the United Kingdom with respect to the sea bed and subsoil and their natural resources;

" petroleum field " means a geological structure identified as an oil or gas field by the Order in Council concerned.

Supplemental

28. In this Act—

" employers' association " means any organisation representing employers and any association of such organisations or of employers and such organisations;

" homeworker " means a person who contracts with a person, for the purposes of that person's business, for the execution of work to be done in a place not under the control or management of the person with whom he contracts, and who does not normally make use of the services of more than two persons in the carrying

out of contracts for the execution of work with statutory
minimum remuneration ;

" organisation ", in relation to workers, means a trade union
and, in relation to employers, means an employers'
association ;

" prescribed " means prescribed by regulations made by the
Secretary of State ;

" the Service " means the Advisory, Conciliation and
Arbitration Service ;

" statutory joint industrial council " means a council established by an order made under section 10 above ;

" statutory minimum remuneration " means remuneration
(including holiday remuneration) fixed by an order
made under section 14 above ;

" statutory provision " means a provision contained in or
having effect under any enactment ;

" superannuation scheme " means any enactment, rules,
deed or other instrument, providing for the payment
of annuities or lump sums to the persons with respect
to whom the instrument has effect on their retirement
at a specified age or on becoming incapacitated at some
earlier age, or to the personal representatives or the
widows, relatives or dependants of such persons on
their death or otherwise, whether with or without any
further or other benefits ;

" thrift scheme " means any arrangement for savings, for
providing money for holidays or for other purposes,
under which a worker is entitled to receive in cash
sums equal to or greater than the aggregate of any sums
deducted from his remuneration or paid by him for
the purposes of the scheme ;

" time rate " means a rate where the amount of the
remuneration is to be calculated by reference to the
actual number of hours worked ;

" trade union " has the meaning given by section 28 of the
Trade Union and Labour Relations Act 1974 ;   1974 c. 52.

" wages council " means a wages council established by an
order under section 1 above ;

" worker " means any person—

> (a) who has entered into or works under a contract
with an employer (whether express or implied, and, if
express, whether oral or in writing) whether it be a

M 2

contract of service or of apprenticeship or any other contract whereby he undertakes to do or perform personally any work or services for another party to the contract who is not a professional client of his; or

(b) whether or not he falls within the foregoing provision, who is a homeworker;

but does not include any person who is employed casually and otherwise than for the purposes of the business of the employer or other party to the contract;

" work with statutory minimum remuneration " means work of a description for which, when executed by a worker, statutory minimum remuneration is provided under Part III of this Act.

Orders and regulations.

29.—(1) The Secretary of State may make regulations for prescribing anything which by this Act is authorised or required to be prescribed.

(2) Any power to make orders or regulations conferred on the Secretary of State by this Act shall be exercisable by statutory instrument.

(3) Any statutory instrument containing any order of the Secretary of State made under Part I or II of this Act or regulations made under any of the provisions of this Act shall (together, in the case of an order, with any report of the Service relating thereto) be laid before Parliament after being made, and shall be subject to annulment in pursuance of a resolution of either House of Parliament.

(4) Any power conferred by this Act to prescribe the manner in which anything is to be published shall include power to prescribe the date which is to be taken for the purposes of this Act as the date of publication.

Expenses.

30. The expenses of the Secretary of State in carrying this Act into effect, and any expenses authorised by the Secretary of State with the consent of the Treasury to be incurred by a wages council, the Service, or a central co-ordinating committee established under this Act by order of the Secretary of State, shall be defrayed out of moneys provided by Parliament.

Transitional provisions, amendments and repeals.
1978 c. 30.

31.—(1) The transitional provisions and savings in Schedule 5 to this Act shall have effect, but nothing in that Schedule shall be construed as prejudicing section 16 of the Interpretation Act 1978 (effect of repeals).

(2) The enactments specified in Schedule 6 to this Act shall have effect subject to the amendments specified in that Schedule.

(3) The enactments specified in the first column of Schedule PART IV 7 to this Act are hereby repealed to the extent specified in the third column of that Schedule.

32.—(1) This Act may be cited as the Wages Councils Act Citation, 1979. commencement and
(2) This Act shall come into force on the expiry of the period extent. of one month beginning with the date on which it is passed.

(3) This Act, except section 27, paragraphs 4 and 5 of Schedule 6 and the repeal of section 127(1)(*a*) of the Employment Protection Act 1975 provided for in Schedule 7, shall not extend to 1975 c. 71. Northern Ireland.

SCHEDULES

SCHEDULE 1

ORDERS RELATING TO WAGES COUNCILS AND STATUTORY JOINT
INDUSTRIAL COUNCILS

1. In this Schedule, except in so far as the context otherwise
requires, " order " means an order, whether made in pursuance of
the recommendation of the Service or not, under section 1, 4, 10 or
12 of this Act.

2. Before making an order, the Secretary of State shall publish, in
the prescribed manner, notice of his intention to make the order,
specifying a place where copies of a draft thereof may be obtained
and the time (which shall not be less than forty days from the date
of the publication) within which any objection made with respect to
the draft order must be sent to him.

3. In relation to the making of an order under section 4 of this
Act in pursuance of an application made in accordance with section
5(1)(c) of this Act, paragraph 2 above shall have effect as if, before
the words " shall publish ", there were inserted the words " after
consultation with the wages council concerned and with all such
organisations of employers as in his opinion represent a substantial
proportion of employers with respect to whom the wages council
operates ".

4. Every objection made with respect to the draft order must be
in writing, and must state—

    (*a*) the specific grounds of objection, and

    (*b*) the omissions, additions or modifications asked for,

and the Secretary of State shall consider any such objection made
by or on behalf of any person appearing to him to be affected,
being an objection sent to him within the time specified in the notice,
but shall not be bound to consider any other objection.

5.—(1) If there is no objection which the Secretary of State is
required by paragraph 4 above to consider or if, after considering
any such objection, he is of the opinion that it satisfies one of the
following conditions, that is to say—

    (*a*) in the case of an order to be made in pursuance of a recom-
mendation of the Service, the objection was made to the
Service and was expressly dealt with in the report embodying the recommendations ; or

    (*b*) in the case of such an order as is referred to in paragraph
(*a*) above, the objection is one the subject-matter of which
was considered by the Service and was expressly dealt with
in that report or is such that a further inquiry into that
subject-matter would serve no useful purpose ; or

(*c*) in any case, the objection will be met by a modification which he proposes to make under this paragraph, or is frivolous,

he may make the order either in the terms of the draft or subject to such modifications, if any, as he thinks fit, being modifications which, in his opinion, do not effect important alterations in the character of the draft order as published.

(2) The Secretary of State shall not form an opinion as to any matter mentioned in paragraph (*b*) of sub-paragraph (1) above without consulting the Service.

6. Where the Secretary of State does not proceed under paragraph 5 above, he may, if he thinks fit, either—

(*a*) amend the draft order, in which case all the provisions of this Schedule shall have effect in relation to the amended draft order as they have effect in relation to an original draft order ; or

(*b*) refer the draft order to the Service for inquiry and report, in which case he shall consider the report of the Service and may then, if he thinks fit, make an order either in the terms of the draft or with such modifications as he thinks fit.

7.—(1) Where any objection is made to the Secretary of State and, under sub-paragraph (*b*) of paragraph 6 above, he refers the draft order to the Service, the Secretary of State shall notify to the Service the objections which he wishes the Service to take into account, and the questions which it is the duty of the Service to consider and report on by virtue of the reference shall be all questions affecting the draft order which arise on or in connection with the objections so notified.

(2) The Secretary of State shall include in the objections which he notifies to the Service all the objections which, under paragraph 4 above, he is himself required to consider, other than any objections which he thinks fit to exclude, in the case of an order in pursuance of a recommendation of the Service, on the ground that, in his opinion, they were made to the Service and were expressly dealt with in the report embodying the recommendation or, in any case, on the ground that they are in the Secretary of State's opinion frivolous.

8.—(1) Where any of the councils affected by an order under section 4 or 12 of this Act is one of the councils in relation to which a central co-ordinating committee has been established under section 25 of this Act, the Secretary of State, before making the order, shall consult that committee and take into consideration any observations which it may make to him within fourteen days from the date on which he consults it.

(2) Where an order under section 4 of this Act directs that a wages council shall cease to operate in relation to any workers, and that another existing wages council shall operate in relation

M 4

to them, but, save as aforesaid, does not affect the field of operation of any wages council, paragraphs 2 to 7 above shall not apply but before making the order the Secretary of State shall consult the councils concerned.

(3) On the reference under sub-paragraph (*b*) of paragraph 6 above of a draft order for the abolition, or variation of the field of operation, of a wages council, subsection (2), or, as the case may be, (3) of section 6 of this Act shall apply as it would apply to the like reference under that section ; and the power of the Secretary of State under the said sub-paragraph (*b*) to modify the draft in making an order shall include power to make any alterations necessary to give effect to a recommendation of the Service, with or without modifications.

9. An order shall come into operation on the date on which it is first issued by Her Majesty's Stationery Office or on such later date as is specified in the order.

SCHEDULE 2

Constitution, Officers and Proceedings of Wages Councils and Co-ordinating Committees

1.—(1) A wages council or, subject to paragraph 2 below, a central co-ordinating committee shall consist of—

  (*a*) not more than three persons appointed by the Secretary of State as being independent persons ;

  (*b*) such number of persons appointed to represent employers and workers on the council or committee as falls within the limits for the time being specified for the purposes of this paragraph by the Secretary of State.

(2) Subject to sub-paragraphs (4) and (5) below, the persons appointed under sub-paragraph (1) above to represent employers shall be appointed by one or more employers' associations for the time being nominated for that purpose by the Secretary of State and those so appointed to represent workers shall be appointed by one or more trade unions so nominated.

(3) A nominated employers' association or trade union shall on making such an appointment inform the secretary of the wages council or central co-ordinating committee, in writing, of that appointment.

(4) If the nominated employers' association or the nominated trade union are unable to agree on such an appointment, they shall consult the Secretary of State who may make the appointment on their behalf.

(5) If it appears to the Secretary of State that an insufficient number of persons has been appointed to represent either employers or workers on a wages council or central co-ordinating committee

he may, after consultation with such persons or organisations as as he thinks fit, himself appoint such number of persons for the purpose as will secure a sufficiency of representatives of employers or workers, as the case may be, on the council or committeee.

(6) Of the independent persons appointed under sub-paragraph (1)(*a*) above, one shall be appointed by the Secretary of State to act as chairman, and another may be appointed by the Secretary of State to act as chairman in the absence of the chairman.

2.—(1) A central co-ordinating committee operating in relation only to two or more statutory joint industrial councils shall consist of equal numbers of persons appointed by one or more employers' associations to represent employers on the committee and of persons appointed by one or more trade unions to represent workers on the committee.

(2) Any such committee shall elect a chairman and deputy chairman from among its members.

3. The Secretary of State may on the application of a wages council or central co-ordinating committee make such changes in the number of members or the machinery for appointing them as is necessary or expedient in the circumstances.

4. The Secretary of State may appoint a secretary and such other officers as he thinks fit of a wages council or central co-ordinating committee.

5. The proceedings of a wages council or central co-ordinating committee shall not be invalidated by reason of any vacancy therein or by any defect in the appointment of a member.

6.—(1) A wages council or central co-ordinating committee may delegate any of its functions, other than the power to make orders under section 14 of this Act, to a committee or sub-committee consisting of such number of members of the council as the council or committee thinks fit.

(2) The number of members representing employers and the number of members representing workers on a committee of a council or any such sub-committee shall be equal.

7. The Secretary of State may make regulations as to the meetings and procedure of a wages council or central co-ordinating committee and of any committee or, as the case may be, sub-committee thereof, including regulations as to the quorum and the method of voting, but, subject to the provisions of this Act and to any regulations so made, a wages council or central co-ordinating committee and any committee or, as the case may be, sub-committee thereof may regulate its procedure in such manner as it thinks fit.

8.—(1) A member of a wages council or central co-ordinating committee shall hold and vacate office in accordance with the terms of his appointment, but the period for which he is to hold office, shall, without prejudice to his re-appointment, not exceed five years.

(2) Where the term for which the members of a wages council or central co-ordinating committee were appointed comes to an end before their successors are appointed, those members shall, except so far as the Secretary of State or, as the case may be, the appointing body otherwise directs, continue in office until the new appointments take effect.

9. There may be paid to the members of a wages council or central co-ordinating committee appointed under paragraph 1(*a*) above such remuneration, and to any member of any such council or committee such travelling and other allowances, as the Secretary of State may, with the consent of the Minister for the Civil Service, determine, and all such remuneration and allowances shall be defrayed as part of the expenses of the Secretary of State in carrying this Act into effect.

SCHEDULE 3

PROVISIONS AS TO ADVISORY COMMITTEES

1.—(1) Any committee appointed by the Secretary of State at the request of a wages council shall consist of—

    (*a*) a chairman chosen as being an independent person ;

    (*b*) persons who appear to the Secretary of State to represent the employers in relation to whom the committee will operate ; and

    (*c*) persons who appear to the Secretary of State to represent the workers in relation to whom the committee will operate.

(2) On any such committee the persons appointed under head (*b*), and the persons appointed under head (*c*), of sub-paragraph (1) above shall be equal in number.

2.—(1) The appointment of a member of any such committee as aforesaid shall be for such term as may be determined by the Secretary of State before his appointment and shall be subject to such conditions as may be so determined.

(2) Where the term for which the members of an advisory committee were appointed comes to an end before the Secretary of State has appointed the persons who are to serve as members of the committee after the expiration of that term, they shall, except so far as the Secretary of State otherwise directs, continue in office until the new appointments take effect.

3. There may be paid to the chairman of any such committee as aforesaid such fees, and to any member of any such committee such travelling and other allowances, as the Secretary of State may, with the consent of the Minister for the Civil Service, determine, and all such fees and allowances shall be defrayed out of moneys provided by Parliament.

SCHEDULE 4

STATUTORY JOINT INDUSTRIAL COUNCILS

PART I

CONSTITUTION, ETC.

1.—(1) A statutory joint industrial council (hereafter in this Part of this Schedule referred to as a council) shall consist of equal numbers (being numbers within the limits specified by the Secretary of State) of persons appointed by a nominated employers' association to represent employers on the council and of persons appointed by a nominated trade union to represent workers on the council.

(2) A nominated employers' association or trade union shall on making such an appointment inform the secretary of the council, in writing, of that appointment.

2.—(1) On the conversion of a wages council to a statutory joint industrial council—

(a) the limits as to the number of persons to be appointed to represent employers and workers on that wages council which are immediately before the date on which that council becomes a statutory joint industrial council for the time being specified by the Secretary of State, shall continue, subject to sub-paragraph (2) below, to be the limits in relation to that statutory joint industrial council; and

(b) an employers' association or trade union which immediately before the date on which that wages council becomes a statutory joint industrial council is for the time being nominated by the Secretary of State for the purpose of appointing persons to represent employers or workers on that wages council, shall continue, subject to sub-paragraph (2) below, to be so nominated in relation to that statutory joint industrial council.

(2) The Secretary of State may, on the application of a statutory joint industrial council, make such changes in the number of members of the council or in the machinery for appointing them as are necessary or expedient in the circumstances.

3. A council shall elect a chairman and deputy chairman from among its members.

4. The proceedings of a council shall not be invalidated by reason of any vacancy among its members or by any defect in the appointment of a member.

Sch. 4   5.—(1) A council may delegate any of its functions, other than the power to make orders under section 14 of this Act, to a committee consisting of such number of members of the council as the council thinks fit.

(2) The number of members representing employers and the number of members representing workers on a committee of a council shall be equal.

6. A council may regulate its own procedure.

7.—(1) A member of a council shall hold and vacate office in accordance with the terms of his appointment, but the period for which he is to hold office shall, without prejudice to his re-appointment, not exceed five years.

(2) Where the term for which the members of a council were appointed comes to an end before their successors are appointed, those members shall, except so far as the appointing body otherwise directs, continue in office until the new appointments take effect.

8. The Secretary of State may pay to the members of a council such travelling and other allowances, including allowances for loss of remunerative time, as the Secretary of State may, with the consent of the Minister for the Civil Service, determine.

9. The expenses of a statutory joint industrial council, to such an extent as may be approved by the Secretary of State with the consent of the Treasury, shall be paid by the Secretary of State.

10. The Secretary of State may appoint a secretary and such other officers of a council as he thinks fit.

Part II

Transitional Provisions

11. Any of the following things done by, to or in relation to a wages council, that is to say—

any order made under section 14 of this Act ;

any proposals published in relation to making of such an order, any notice published and representations made with respect thereto ;

any permit issued under section 16 of this Act ;

any approval given under the proviso to section 19(1) of this Act ;

shall as from the date when that council becomes a statutory joint industrial council be treated as having been done by, to or in relation to the latter council.

12. The persons who immediately before the date on which a wages council becomes a statutory joint industrial council are the

members of the wages council appointed by an employers' associa- SCH. 4
tion or trade union shall, subject to paragraph 2(2) above, become
and continue to be members of the statutory joint industrial council
as if they had been appointed under paragraph 1 above.

13. The persons who immediately before the date on which a
wages council becomes a statutory joint industrial council are the
secretary and officers of the wages council shall on that date become
the secretary and officers of the statutory joint industrial council.

SCHEDULE 5

TRANSITIONAL PROVISIONS

Section 31.

1. The repeals effected by this Act shall not affect any right of a
worker to recover sums from his employer on account of the payment to the worker of remuneration less than the statutory minimum
remuneration, or the power of an officer of the Secretary of State to
institute on behalf of and in the name of the worker civil proceedings
for the enforcement of that right or the power of the court in such
proceedings to make an order for the payment of costs by the officer.

2. A member of a wages council or central co-ordinating committee who, immediately before the commencement of this Act, is
by virtue of paragraph 11(3) of Schedule 17 to the Employment Pro- 1975 c. 71.
tection Act 1975 treated as having been appointed by a nominated
employers' association or trade union shall continue to be so treated.

3. Any reference in any enactment or document made before the
passing of the Wages Councils Act 1945 (28th March 1945), other 8 & 9 Geo. 6
than an enactment repealed by that Act, to a trade board shall be c. 17.
construed as including a reference to a wages council.

SCHEDULE 6

CONSEQUENTIAL AMENDMENTS

Post Office Act 1969 (c. 48)

Section 31.

1. In section 81(1) of the Post Office Act 1969, for the words " the
Wages Councils Act 1959 " there are substituted the words " Wages
Councils Act 1979 ".

Equal Pay Act 1970 (c. 41)

2. In section 4 of the Equal Pay Act 1970—

    (*a*) in subsections (1), (1A), and (2), for the words " section 11
    of the Wages Councils Act 1959 ", in each place where they
    occur, there are substituted the words " section 14 of the
    Wages Councils Act 1979 " ; and

(*b*) in subsection (1A), for the words " subsections (3) and (3A) of the said section 11 " there are substituted the words " subsections (4) and (5) of the said section 14 " ; and

(*c*) in subsection (3), for the words " section 12(1) or (1A) of the Wages Councils Act 1959 ", " in section 12(1) or (1A) " and " section 11(8) " there are substituted the words " section 15(1) or (2) of the Wages Councils Act 1979 ", " in section 15(1) or (2) " and " section 14(12) " respectively.

Attachment of Earnings Act 1971 (c. 32)

3. In Schedule 3 to the Attachment of Earnings Act 1971, in paragraph 3(*c*), for the words " Wages Councils Act 1959 " there are substituted the words " Wages Councils Act 1979 ".

House of Commons Disqualification Act 1975 (c. 24)

4. In Part III of Schedule 1 to the House of Commons Disqualification Act 1975, in the first entry relating to wages councils, for the words " paragraph 1(*a*) of Schedule 2 to the Wages Councils Act 1959 or Chairman of a Committee appointed under paragraph 1(1)(*a*) of Schedule 3 to that Act " there are substituted the words " paragraph 1(1)(*a*) of Schedule 2 to the Wages Councils Act 1979 or chairman of a committee appointed under paragraph 1(1)(*a*) of Schedule 3 to that Act ".

Northern Ireland Assembly Disqualification Act 1975 (c. 25)

5. In Part III of Schedule 1 to the Northern Ireland Assembly Disqualification Act 1975, in the first entry relating to wages councils, for the words " paragraph 1(*a*) of Schedule 2 to the Wages Councils Act 1959 or Chairman of a Committee appointed under paragraph 1(1)(*a*) of Schedule 3 to that Act " there are substituted the words " paragraph 1(1)(*a*) of Schedule 2 to the Wages Councils Act 1979 or chairman of a committee appointed under paragraph 1(1)(*a*) of Schedule 3 to that Act ".

Employment Protection (Consolidation) Act 1978 (c. 44)

6. In section 18(2) of the Employment Protection (Consolidation) Act 1978 for paragraph (*a*) there is substituted the following paragraph—

" (*a*) section 14 of the Wages Councils Act 1979 ; ".

SCHEDULE 7

REPEALS

Section 31.

Chapter	Short title	Extent of repeal
7 & 8 Eliz. 2 c. 69.	Wages Councils Act 1959.	The whole Act.
1968 c. 64.	Civil Evidence Act 1968.	In the Schedule, the paragraph relating to the Wages Councils Act 1959.
1968 c. 73.	Transport Act 1968.	In Schedule 11, the paragraph relating to the Wages Councils Act 1959.
1972 c. 68.	European Communities Act 1972.	In Schedule 4, in paragraph 9(4), the words " and in section 19(3)(*b*) of the Wages Councils Act 1959 ".
1973 c. 38.	Social Security Act 1973.	In Schedule 27, paragraph 21.
1974 c. 52.	Trade Union and Labour Relations Act 1974.	In Schedule 3, paragraph 9.
1975 c. 71.	Employment Protection Act 1975.	Sections 89 to 96. In section 127(1), paragraph (*a*). Schedules 7 and 8. In Schedule 17, paragraph 11 and, in paragraph 12, the words " section 11 of the Wages Councils Act 1959 ".
1976 c. 3.	Road Traffic (Drivers' Ages and Hours of Work) Act 1976.	In section 2(3), the words " section 19(3)(*b*) of the Wages Councils Act 1959 ".

Agricultural Statistics Act 1979

1979 CHAPTER 13

An Act to consolidate certain enactments relating to agricultural statistics. [22nd March 1979]

BE IT ENACTED by the Queen's most Excellent Majesty, by and with the advice and consent of the Lords Spiritual and Temporal, and Commons, in this present Parliament assembled, and by the authority of the same, as follows:—

Power to obtain agricultural statistics.

1.—(1) Where it appears to the appropriate Minister expedient so to do for the purpose of obtaining statistical information relating to agriculture, he may serve on any owners or occupiers of land used for agriculture, or of land which he has reason to believe may be so used, notices requiring them to furnish in writing, in such form and manner and to such person as may be specified in the notice, and within such time and with respect to such date or dates or such period or periods as may be so specified, the information referred to in the notice (including, as respects paragraphs (*d*) to (*f*) of this subsection, the information referred to in the notice as to quantities, values, expenditure and receipts) relating to—

(*a*) the situation, area and description of relevant land owned or occupied by them, the date of acquisition of the land, and the date at which so much of it as is comprised in any agricultural unit became comprised in that unit, and the rates payable in respect of the land,

(*b*) the names and addresses of the owners and occupiers of the land,

(*c*) whether the land or any, and if so what, part of it is let and at what rent,

(d) the character and use of different parts of the land, the time at which any use of such parts was begun or will become fully effective, and their produce at any time during the period beginning one year before, and ending one year after, the time at which the information is required to be furnished,

(e) fixed and other equipment, livestock, and the stocks of agricultural produce and requisites held in respect of the land, and the provision and maintenance of such equipment, livestock and requisites and the provision of agricultural services for the benefit of the land,

(f) the methods and operations used on the land, the marketing or other disposal of its produce, any payments received under any enactment in respect of such produce, and the provision of agricultural services otherwise than for the benefit of the land,

(g) the number and description of persons employed on the land, or employed by the occupier in disposing of its produce, and the remuneration paid to, and hours worked by, persons so employed or such persons of different descriptions.

(2) For the purpose of obtaining statistical information relating to agriculture, any person authorised by the appropriate Minister in that behalf may, after giving not less than 24 hours notice and on producing if so required evidence of his authority to act for the purposes of this subsection, orally require the owner or occupier of land to furnish to him within a reasonable time, and either orally or in writing as the said owner or occupier may elect, such information, whether or not specified in the notice, as the said person authorised by the appropriate Minister may require, being information which the owner or occupier, as the case may be, could have been required to furnish under subsection (1) above.

(3) References in subsections (1) and (2) above to the owner of land include references to a person exercising, as servant or agent of the owner, functions of estate management in relation to the land, and references in those subsections to the occupier of land include references to a person responsible for the control of the farming of the land as servant or agent of the occupier of the land.

(4) No person shall be required under this section to furnish any balance sheet or profit and loss account, but this subsection shall not prevent the requiring of information by reason only that it is or might be contained as an item in such a balance sheet or account.

(5) Section 106 of the Agriculture Act 1947 (provisions as to entry and inspection) shall have effect for the purposes of this section as it has effect for the purposes of that Act.

Information as to dealings in land used for agriculture.

2.—(1) The appropriate Minister may by regulation require that parties to any sale of land which immediately before the completion of the transaction was being used for agriculture, or to any grant, assignment or surrender of a tenancy of such land for an interest not less than that of a tenant for a year, shall within the period from the completion of the transaction prescribed by the regulations furnish to him, in such manner as may be so prescribed, information as to the names and addresses of the parties to the transaction and the situation and extent of the land affected by it.

(2) Regulations under subsection (1) above shall be made by statutory instrument and shall be laid before Parliament forthwith after being made, and if either House of Parliament, within the period of 40 days beginning with the day on which the regulations are laid before it, resolves that an Address be presented to Her Majesty praying that the regulations be annulled, no further proceedings shall be taken under the regulations after the date of the resolution, and Her Majesty may by Order in Council revoke the regulations, so, however, that any such resolution and revocation shall be without prejudice to the validity of anything previously done under the regulations or to the making of new regulations.

Restriction on disclosure of information.

3.—(1) Subject to subsection (2) below, no information relating to any particular land or business which has been obtained under section 1 or 2 above shall be published or otherwise disclosed without the previous consent in writing of the person by whom the information was furnished and every other person who is an owner or the occupier of the land and whose interests may in the opinion of the appropriate Minister be affected by the disclosure.

(2) Nothing in subsection (1) above shall restrict the disclosure of information—

(a) to the Minister in charge of any Government department, to any authority acting under an enactment for regulating the marketing of any agricultural produce, or to any person exercising functions on behalf of any such Minister or authority for the purpose of the exercise of those functions ;

(b) to an authority having power under any enactment to give permission for the development of land, for the purpose of assisting that authority in the preparation of proposals relating to such development or in considering whether or not to give such permission ;

(c) if the disclosure is confined to situation, extent, number and kind of livestock, character of land, and name and address of owner and occupier, to any person to whom the appropriate Minister considers that the disclosure is required in the public interest;

(d) to any person for the purposes of any criminal proceedings under section 4 below or for the purposes of any report of such proceedings;

(e) to the Agricultural Training Board under section 2B of the Industrial Training Act 1964; or   1964 c. 16.

(f) to an institution of the European Communities under section 12 of the European Communities Act 1972,   1972 c. 68.

or the use of information in any manner which the appropriate Minister thinks necessary or expedient in connection with the maintenance of the supply of food in the United Kingdom.

4.—(1) Any person who without reasonable excuse fails to Penalties. furnish information in compliance with a requirement under section 1 or 2 above shall be liable on summary conviction to a fine not exceeding £50.

(2) If any person—

(a) in purported compliance with a requirement imposed under section 1 or 2 above knowingly or recklessly furnishes any information which is false in any material particular, or

(b) publishes or otherwise discloses any information in contravention of section 3 above,

he shall be liable on summary conviction to imprisonment for a term not exceeding 3 months or to a fine not exceeding the prescribed sum or to both, or on conviction on indictment to imprisonment for a term not exceeding 2 years or to a fine or to both.

5.—(1) Any notice authorised by this Act to be served on any Service of person shall be duly served if it is delivered to him, or left at notices. his proper address or sent to him by post in a registered letter.

(2) Any such notice authorised to be served on an incorporated company or body shall be duly served if served on the secretary or clerk of the company or body.

(3) For the purposes of this section and of section 7 of the Interpretation Act 1978, the proper address of any person on 1978 c. 30. whom any such notice is to be served shall, in the case of the

secretary or clerk of any incorporated company or body be that of the registered or principal office of the company or body, and in any other case be the last known address of the person in question.

(4) Where any such notice is to be served on a person as being the person having any interest in land, and it is not practicable after reasonable inquiry to ascertain his name or address, the notice may be served by addressing it to him by the description of the person having that interest in the land (naming it), and delivering the notice to some responsible person on the land or by affixing it, or a copy of it, to some conspicuous object on the land.

(5) Where any such notice is to be served on any person as being the owner of the land and the land belongs to an ecclesiastical benefice a copy shall be served on the Church Commissioners.

(6) Without prejudice to subsections (1) to (5) above, any notice under this Act to be served on an occupier shall be deemed to be duly served if it is addressed to him by the description of " the occupier " of the land in question and sent by post to, or delivered to some person on, the land.

Interpretation. **6.**—(1) In this Act—

" the appropriate Minister " means, in relation to England, the Minister of Agriculture, Fisheries and Food and, in relation to Wales, the Secretary of State ;

" land " includes messuages, tenements and hereditaments, houses and buildings of any tenure ;

" livestock " includes creatures kept for any purpose ;

" owner " means, in relation to land, a person, other than a mortgagee not in possession, who is for the time being entitled to dispose of the fee simple of the land, and includes also a person holding, or entitled to the rents and profits of, the land under a lease or agreement ;

1977 c. 45.
" the prescribed sum " means the prescribed sum within the meaning of section 28 of the Criminal Law Act 1977 (£1,000 or other sum substituted by order under section 61(1) of that Act) ; and

" relevant land " in the case of any owner or occupier of land used for agriculture, means the aggregate of—

(a) the land owned or occupied by him which is comprised in any agricultural unit ; and

(b) any other land owned or occupied by him which is either—

(i) used for forestry ; or

(ii) not used for any purpose, but capable of use for agriculture or forestry,

but which, if used as agricultural land by the occupier of that agricultural unit, would be comprised in that unit.

(2) Section 109 of the Agriculture Act 1947 (interpretation) 1947 c. 48. shall have effect for the purposes of this Act as it has effect for the purposes of that Act except that the definition of " livestock " shall be omitted from subsection (3).

7.—(1) The enactments specified in Schedule 1 to this Act Amendments shall have effect subject to the amendments set out in that and repeals. Schedule, being amendments consequential on the foregoing provisions of this Act.

(2) The enactments specified in Schedule 2 to this Act are hereby repealed to the extent specified in column 3 of that Schedule.

8.—(1) This Act may be cited as the Agricultural Statistics Citation, etc. Act 1979.

(2) This Act shall come into force at the expiry of the period of one month beginning on the date on which it is passed.

(3) This Act does not extend to Scotland or Northern Ireland.

Section 7.

SCHEDULES

SCHEDULE 1

CONSEQUENTIAL AMENDMENTS

1958 c. 47.

Agricultural Marketing Act 1958

1. In section 5(4) of the Agricultural Marketing Act 1958 (list of producers) for the words "eighty of the Agriculture Act 1947" there shall be substituted the words "three of the Agricultural Statistics Act 1979".

1958 c. 51.

Public Records Act 1958

2. At the end of Schedule 2 to the Public Records Act 1958 (enactments prohibiting disclosure of information obtained from the public) there shall be added—

"The Agricultural Statistics Act 1979   Section 3."

1964 c. 16.

Industrial Training Act 1964

3. At the end of section 2B of the Industrial Training Act 1964 (disclosure of information to Agricultural Training Board) there shall be added the words "or section 1 of the Agricultural Statistics Act 1979".

1972 c. 68

European Communities Act 1972

4. In section 12 of the European Communities Act 1972 (furnishing of information to Communities) for the words "80 of the Agriculture Act 1947" there shall be substituted the words "3 of the Agricultural Statistics Act 1979".

Section 7.

SCHEDULE 2

ENACTMENTS REPEALED

Chapter	Short Title	Extent of Repeals
10 & 11 Geo. 6. c. 48.	Agriculture Act 1947.	Sections 78 to 81.
6 & 7 Eliz. 2. c. 51.	Public Records Act 1958.	In Schedule 2, the entry relating to section 80 of the Agriculture Act 1947.
1972 c. 62.	Agriculture (Miscellaneous Provisions) Act 1972.	Section 18.
1976 c. 55.	Agriculture (Miscellaneous Provisions) Act 1976.	Section 6. Schedule 2.

Capital Gains Tax Act 1979

1979 CHAPTER 14

An Act to consolidate Part III of the Finance Act 1965 with related provisions in that Act and subsequent Acts. [22nd March 1979]

BE IT ENACTED by the Queen's most Excellent Majesty, by and with the advice and consent of the Lords Spiritual and Temporal, and Commons, in this present Parliament assembled, and by the authority of the same, as follows:—

PART I

GENERAL

Capital gains tax and corporation tax

1.—(1) Tax shall be charged in accordance with this Act in respect of capital gains, that is to say chargeable gains computed in accordance with this Act and accruing to a person on the disposal of assets.

Taxation of capital gains.

(2) In the circumstances prescribed by the provisions of Part XI of the Taxes Act (taxation of companies and certain other bodies and associations) the tax shall be chargeable in accordance with those provisions, and all the provisions of this Act have effect subject to those provisions.

(3) Subject to the said provisions, capital gains tax shall be charged for all years of assessment in accordance with the following provisions of this Act.

Persons
chargeable.

Capital gains tax

2.—(1) Subject to any exceptions provided by this Act, a person shall be chargeable to capital gains tax in respect of chargeable gains accruing to him in a year of assessment during any part of which he is resident in the United Kingdom, or during which he is ordinarily resident in the United Kingdom.

(2) This section is without prejudice to the provisions of section 12 below (non-resident with UK branch or agency), and of section 38 of the Finance Act 1973 (territorial sea of the United Kingdom).

1973 c. 51.

Rate of tax.

3. The rate of capital gains tax shall be 30 per cent.

Gains
chargeable
to tax.

4.—(1) Capital gains tax shall be charged on the total amount of chargeable gains accruing to the person chargeable in the year of assessment, after deducting—

(a) any allowable losses accruing to that person in that year of assessment, and

(b) so far as they have not been allowed as a deduction from chargeable gains accruing in any previous year of assessment, any allowable losses accruing to that person in any previous year of assessment (not earlier than the year 1965-66).

(2) In the case of a woman who in a year of assessment is a married woman living with her husband any allowable loss which, under subsection (1) above, would be deductible from the chargeable gains accruing in that year of assessment to the one but for an insufficiency of chargeable gains shall, for the purposes of that subsection, be deductible from chargeable gains accruing in that year of assessment to the other:

Provided that this subsection shall not apply in relation to losses accruing in a year of assessment to either if, before 6th July in the year next following that year of assessment, an application is made by the man or the wife to the inspector in such form and manner as the Board may prescribe.

Relief for
gains less
than £9,500.

5.—(1) An individual shall not be chargeable to capital gains tax for a year of assessment if his taxable amount for that year does not exceed £1,000.

(2) If an individual's taxable amount for a year of assessment exceeds £1,000 but does not exceed £5,000, the amount of capital gains tax to which he is chargeable for that year shall be 15 per cent. of the excess over £1,000.

(3) If an individual's taxable amount for a year of assessment exceeds £5,000, the amount of capital gains tax to which he is

chargeable for that year shall not exceed £600 plus one-half of
the excess over £5,000.

(4) For the purposes of this section an individual's taxable
amount for a year of assessment is the amount on which he is
chargeable under section 4(1) above for that year but—

  (a) where the amount of chargeable gains less allowable
      losses accruing to an individual in any year of assess-
      ment does not exceed £1,000, no deduction from that
      amount shall be made for that year in respect of allow-
      able losses carried forward from a previous year or
      carried back from a subsequent year in which the
      individual dies, and

  (b) where the amount of chargeable gains less allowable
      losses accruing to an individual in any year of assess-
      ment exceeds £1,000, the deduction from that amount
      for that year in respect of allowable losses carried for-
      ward from a previous year or carried back from a
      subsequent year in which the individual dies shall not
      be greater than the excess.

(5) Where in a year of assessment—

  (a) the amount of chargeable gains accruing to an indi-
      vidual does not exceed £1,000, and

  (b) the aggregate amount or value of the consideration for
      all the disposals of assets made by him (other than
      disposals gains accruing on which are not chargeable
      gains) does not exceed £5,000,

a statement to the effect of paragraphs (a) and (b) above shall,
unless the inspector otherwise requires, be sufficient compliance
with any notice under section 8 of the Taxes Management Act 1970 c. 9.
1970 requiring the individual to make a return of the chargeable
gains accruing to him in that year.

(6) Schedule 1 to this Act shall have effect as respects the
application of this section to husbands and wives, personal
representatives and trustees.

6. A gain accruing to an individual on a disposal by way of Small gifts.
gift of an asset the market value of which does not exceed £100
shall not be a chargeable gain, but this section shall not apply
to gifts made by the same individual in the same year of assessment the total value of which exceeds £100.

7. Capital gains tax assessed on any person in respect of gains Time for
accruing in any year shall be payable by that person at or before payment
the expiration of the three months following that year, or at the tax.
expiration of a period of thirty days beginning with the date
of the issue of the notice of assessment, whichever is the later.

PART I
Postponement
of payment
of tax.

8.—(1) Where the whole or part of any assets falling within subsection (3) below—

    (*a*) is disposed of by way of gift, or

    (*b*) is under section 54(1) or 55(1) below (settled property) deemed to be disposed of,

the capital gains tax chargeable on a gain accruing on the disposal may, at the option of the person liable to pay it, be paid by eight equal yearly instalments or sixteen half-yearly instalments.

(2) Payment of capital gains tax in accordance with subsection (1) above shall be subject to the payment of interest under Part IX (except sections 87 and 88) of the Taxes Management Act 1970 except as provided by section 9 below.

1970 c. 9.

(3) The assets referred to in subsection (1) above are—

    (*a*) land or an estate or interest in land,

    (*b*) any shares or securities of a company which, immediately before the disposal, gave control of the company to the person by whom the disposal was made or deemed to be made,

    (*c*) any shares or securities of a company not falling under paragraph (*b*) above and not quoted on a recognised stock exchange in the United Kingdom or elsewhere, and

    (*d*) any assets used exclusively for the purposes of a trade, profession or vocation which, immediately before the disposal, was carried on (whether alone or in partnership) by the person by whom the disposal was made or deemed to be made.

(4) Where tax is payable by instalments by virtue of this section the first instalment shall be due at the expiration of twelve months from the time of the disposal, and subject to section 9 below, the interest on the unpaid portion of the tax shall be added to each instalment and paid accordingly; but the tax for the time being unpaid, with interest to the date of payment, may be paid at any time, and shall become due and payable forthwith if—

    (*a*) the disposal was by way of gift to a person connected with the donor, or was deemed to be made under section 54(1) or 55(1) below, and

    (*b*) the assets are disposed of for valuable consideration under a subsequent disposal (whether or not the subsequent disposal is made by the person who acquired them under the first disposal).

9.—(1) Subject to the following provisions of this section, where capital gains tax is payable—

(a) by instalments under section 8 above, and

(b) in respect of the disposal of assets falling within paragraph (b), (c) or (d) of subsection (3) of that section,

the tax shall, for the purpose of any interest to be added to each instalment, be treated as carrying interest from the date at which the instalment is payable.

(2) Subsection (1) above does not apply to tax payable in respect of the disposal of shares or securities of a company falling within paragraph (a) of subsection (3) below unless it also falls within paragraph (b) or (c) of that subsection.

(3) The companies referred to in subsection (2) above are—

(a) any company whose business consists wholly or mainly of one or more of the following, that is to say, dealing in shares or securities, land or buildings, or making or holding investments,

(b) any company whose business consists wholly or mainly in being a holding company (within the meaning of section 154 of the Companies Act 1948) of one or more companies not falling within paragraph (a) above and

(c) any company whose business is that of a jobber (as defined in section 477 of the Taxes Act) or discount house and is carried on in the United Kingdom.

(4) Subsection (1) above applies only to the extent to which—

(a) the market value of the assets in respect of the disposal of which the tax concerned is payable, plus

(b) the market value of any assets which the same person has or is deemed to have previously disposed of and in respect of the disposal of which the tax also fell within that subsection,

does not exceed £250,000.

The foreign element

10.—(1) For the purpose of giving relief from double taxation in relation to capital gains tax and tax on chargeable gains charged under the law of any country outside the United Kingdom, in Chapters I and II of Part XVIII of the Taxes Act, as they apply for the purposes of income tax, for references to income there shall be substituted references to capital gains and for references to income tax there shall be substituted references to capital gains tax meaning, as the context may require, tax charged under the law of the United Kingdom or tax charged under the law of a country outside the United Kingdom.

(2) Any arrangements set out in an order made under section 347 of the Income Tax Act 1952 before 5th August 1965 (the date of the passing of the Finance Act 1965) shall so far as they provide (in whatever terms) for relief from tax chargeable in the United Kingdom on capital gains have effect in relation to capital gains tax.

(3) So far as by virtue of this section capital gains tax charged under the law of a country outside the United Kingdom may be brought into account under the said Chapters I and II as applied by this section, that tax, whether relief is given by virtue of this section in respect of it or not, shall not be taken into account for the purposes of those Chapters as they apply apart from this section.

(4) Section 518 of the Taxes Act (disclosure of information for purposes of double taxation) shall apply in relation to capital gains tax as it applies in relation to income tax.

Allowance for foreign tax.
11. Subject to section 10 above, the tax chargeable under the law of any country outside the United Kingdom on the disposal of an asset which is borne by the person making the disposal shall be allowable as a deduction in the computation under Chapter II of Part II of this Act.

Non-resident with United Kingdom branch or agency.
12.—(1) Subject to any exceptions provided by this Act, a person shall be chargeable to capital gains tax in respect of chargeable gains accruing to him in a year of assessment in which he is not resident and not ordinarily resident in the United Kingdom but is carrying on a trade in the United Kingdom through a branch or agency, and shall be so chargeable on chargeable gains accruing on the disposal—

    (a) of assets situated in the United Kingdom and used in or for the purposes of the trade at or before the time when the capital gain accrued, or

    (b) of assets situated in the United Kingdom and used or held for the purposes of the branch or agency at or before that time, or assets acquired for use by or for the purposes of the branch or agency.

(2) This section shall not apply to a person who, by virtue of Part XVIII of the Taxes Act (double taxation agreements), is exempt from income tax chargeable for the year of assessment in respect of the profits or gains of the branch or agency.

(3) In this Act, unless the context otherwise requires, " branch or agency " means any factorship, agency, receivership, branch or management, but does not include any person within the

exemptions in section 82 of the Taxes Management Act 1970 (general agents and brokers). PART 1
1970 c. 9.

13.—(1) Subsection (2) below applies where—

(a) chargeable gains accrue from the disposal of assets situated outside the United Kingdom, and

(b) the person charged or chargeable makes a claim and shows that the conditions set out in subsection (3) below are, so far as applicable, satisfied as respects those gains (" the qualifying gains ").

Foreign assets: delayed remittances.

(2) For the purposes of capital gains tax—

(a) the amount of the qualifying gains shall be deducted from the amounts on which the claimant is assessed to capital gains tax for the year in which the qualifying gains accrued to the claimant, but

(b) the amount so deducted shall be assessed to capital gains tax on the claimant (or his personal representatives) as if it were an amount of chargeable gains accruing in the year of assessment in which the conditions set out in subsection (3) below cease to be satisfied.

(3) The said conditions are—

(a) that the claimant was unable to transfer the qualifying gains to the United Kingdom, and

(b) that that inability was due to the laws of the territory where the income arose, or to the executive action of its government, or to the impossibility of obtaining foreign currency in that territory, and

(c) that the inability was not due to any want of reasonable endeavours on the part of the claimant.

(4) Where under an agreement entered into under arrangements made by the Secretary of State in pursuance of section 1 of the Overseas Investment and Export Guarantees Act 1972 or section 11 of the Export Guarantees and Overseas Investment Act 1978 any payment is made by the Exports Credits Guarantee Department in respect of any gains which cannot be transferred to the United Kingdom, then, to the extent of the payment, the gains shall be treated as gains with respect to which the conditions mentioned in subsection (3) above are not satisfied (and accordingly cannot cease to be satisfied). 1972 c. 40.
1978 c. 18.

(5) No claim under this section shall be made in respect of any chargeable gain more than six years after the end of the year of assessment in which that gain accrues.

(6) The personal representatives of a deceased person may make any claim which he might have made under this section if he had not died.

PART I
Foreign
assets of
person with
foreign
domicile.

14.—(1) In the case of individuals resident or ordinarily resident but not domiciled in the United Kingdom, capital gains tax shall not be charged in respect of gains accruing to them from the disposal of assets situated outside the United Kingdom (that is chargeable gains accruing in the year 1965-66 or a later year of assessment) except that the tax shall be charged on the amounts (if any) received in the United Kingdom in respect of those chargeable gains, any such amounts being treated as gains accruing when they are received in the United Kingdom.

(2) For the purposes of this section there shall be treated as received in the United Kingdom in respect of any gain all amounts paid, used or enjoyed in or in any manner or form transmitted or brought to the United Kingdom, and subsections (4) to (7) of section 122 of the Taxes Act (under which income applied outside the United Kingdom in payment of debts is, in certain cases, treated as received in the United Kingdom) shall apply as they would apply for the purposes of subsection (3) of the said section 122 if the gain were income arising from possessions out of the United Kingdom.

15.—(1) This section applies as respects chargeable gains accruing to a company—

(a) which is not resident in the United Kingdom, and

(b) which would be a close company if it were resident in the United Kingdom.

(2) Subject to this section, every person who at the time when the chargeable gain accrues to the company is resident or ordinarily resident in the United Kingdom, who, if an individual, is domiciled in the United Kingdom, and who holds shares in the company, shall be treated for the purposes of this Act as if a part of the chargeable gain had accrued to him.

(3) That part shall be equal to the proportion of the assets of the company to which that person would be entitled on a liquidation of the company at the time when the chargeable gain accrues to the company.

(4) If the part of a chargeable gain attributable to a person under subsection (2) above is less than one-twentieth, the said subsection (2) shall not apply to that person.

(5) This section shall not apply in relation to—

(a) any amount in respect of the chargeable gain which is distributed, whether by way of dividend or distribution of capital or on the dissolution of the company, to persons holding shares in the company, or creditors of the company, within two years from the time when the chargeable gain accrued to the company, or (*b*) a chargeable gain accruing on the disposal of assets, being tangible property, whether movable or immovable, or a lease of such property, where the property was used, and used only, for the purposes of a trade carried on by the company wholly outside the United Kingdom, or

(*c*) a chargeable gain accruing on the disposal of currency or of a debt within section 135(1) below (foreign currency bank accounts), where the currency or debt is or represents money in use for the purposes of a trade carried on by the company wholly outside the United Kingdom, or

(*d*) to a chargeable gain in respect of which the company is chargeable to tax by virtue of section 246(2)(*b*) of the Taxes Act (gains corresponding to those charged under section 12 above).

(6) Subsection (5)(*a*) above shall not prevent the making of an assessment in pursuance of this section but if, by virtue of that paragraph, this section is excluded all such adjustments, whether by way of repayment or discharge of tax or otherwise, shall be made as will give effect to the provisions of that paragraph.

(7) The amount of capital gains tax paid by a person in pursuance of subsection (2) above (so far as not reimbursed by the company) shall be allowable as a deduction in the computation under this Act of a gain accruing on the disposal by him of the shares by reference to which the tax was paid.

(8) So far as it would go to reduce or extinguish chargeable gains accruing by virtue of this section to a person in a year of assessment this section shall apply in relation to a loss accruing to the company on the disposal of an asset in that year of assessment as it would apply if a gain instead of a loss had accrued to the company on the disposal, but shall only so apply in relation to that person ; and subject to the preceding provisions of this subsection this section shall not apply in relation to a loss accruing to the company.

(9) If the person owning any of the shares in the company at the time when the chargeable gain accrues to the company is itself a company which is not resident in the United Kingdom but which would be a close company if it were resident in the United Kingdom, an amount equal to the amount apportioned under subsection (3) above out of the chargeable gain to the shares so owned shall be apportioned among the issued shares of the second-mentioned company, and the holders of those shares shall be treated in accordance with subsection (2) above, and so on through any number of companies.

PART I

(10) If any tax payable by any person by virtue of subsection (2) above is paid by the company to which the chargeable gain accrues, or in a case under subsection (9) above is paid by any such other company, the amount so paid shall not for the purposes of income tax, capital gains tax or corporation tax be regarded as a payment to the person by whom the tax was originally payable.

Non-resident
group of
companies.

16.—(1) This section has effect for the purposes of section 15 above.

(2) Sections 273 to 275 and 276 (1) of the Taxes Act shall apply in relation to non-resident companies which are members of a non-resident group of companies, as they apply in relation to companies resident in the United Kingdom which are members of a group of companies.

(3) Sections 278 and 279 of the Taxes Act shall apply for the said purposes as if for any reference therein to a group of companies there were substituted a reference to a non-resident group of companies, and as if references to companies were references to companies not resident in the United Kingdom.

(4) For the purposes of this section—

(*a*) a " non-resident group " of companies—

(i) in the case of a group, none of the members of which are resident in the United Kingdom, means that group, and

(ii) in the case of a group, two or more members of which are not resident in the United Kingdom means the members which are not resident in the United Kingdom ;

(*b*) " group " shall be construed in accordance with subsections (1) (without paragraph (*a*)), (3) and (4) of section 272 of the Taxes Act.

Non-resident
trust.

17.—(1) This section applies as respects chargeable gains accruing to the trustees of a settlement if the trustees are not resident and not ordinarily resident in the United Kingdom, and if the settlor, or one of the settlors, is domiciled and either resident or ordinarily resident in the United Kingdom, or was domiciled and either resident or ordinarily resident in the United Kingdom when he made his settlement.

(2) Any beneficiary under the settlement who is domiciled and either resident or ordinarily resident in the United Kingdom during any year of assesment shall be treated for the purposes of this Act as if an apportioned part of the amount, if any, on which the trustees would have been chargeable to capital gains tax under section 4(1) above, if domiciled and either resident or

ordinarily resident in the United Kingdom in that year of assessment, had been chargeable gains accruing to the beneficiary in that year of assessment; and for the purposes of this section any such amount shall be apportioned in such manner as is just and reasonable between persons having interests in the settled property, whether the interest be a life interest or an interest in reversion, and so that the chargeable gain is apportioned, as near as may be, according to the respective values of those interests, disregarding in the case of a defeasible interest the possibility of defeasance.

(3) For the purposes of this section—

> (*a*) if in any of the three years ending with that in which the chargeable gain accrues a person has received a payment or payments out of the income of the settled property made in exercise of a discretion he shall be regarded, in relation to that chargeable gain, as having an interest in the settled property of a value equal to that of an annuity of a yearly amount equal to one-third of the total of the payments so received by him in the said three years, and

> (*b*) if a person receives at any time after the chargeable gain accrues a capital payment made out of the settled property in exercise of a discretion, being a payment which represents the chargeable gain in whole or part then, except so far as any part of the gain has been attributed under this section to some other person who is domiciled and resident or ordinarily resident in the United Kingdom, that person shall, if domiciled and resident or ordinarily resident in the United Kingdom, be treated as if the chargeable gain, or as the case may be the part of the chargeable gain represented by the capital payment, had accrued to him at the time when he received the capital payment.

(4) In the case of a settlement made before 6th April 1965—

> (*a*) subsection (2) above shall not apply to a beneficiary whose interest is solely in the income of the settled property, and who cannot, by means of the exercise of any power of appointment or power of revocation or otherwise, obtain for himself, whether with or without the consent of any other person, any part of the capital represented by the settled property, and

> (*b*) payment of capital gains tax chargeable on a gain apportioned to a beneficiary in respect of an interest in reversion in any part of the capital represented by the settled property may be postponed until that person becomes absolutely entitled to that part of the settled

property, or disposes of the whole or any part of his interest, unless he can, by any means described in paragraph (*a*) above, obtain for himself any of it at any earlier time,

and for the purposes of this subsection, property added to a settlement after the settlement is made shall be regarded as property under a separate settlement made at the time when the property is so added.

(5) In any case in which the amount of any capital gains tax payable by a beneficiary under a settlement in accordance with the provisions of this section is paid by the trustees of the settlement that amount shall not for the purposes of taxation be regarded as a payment to the beneficiary.

(6) This section shall not apply in relation to a loss accruing to the trustees of the settlement.

(7) In this section " settlement " and " settlor " have the meanings given by section 454(3) of the Taxes Act and " settled property " shall be construed accordingly.

18.—(1) In this Act " resident " and " ordinarily resident " have the same meanings as in the Income Tax Acts.

(2) Section 207 of the Taxes Act (disputes as to domicile or ordinary residence) shall apply in relation to capital gains tax as it applies for the purposes mentioned in that section.

(3) Subject to section 12(1) above, an individual who is in the United Kingdom for some temporary purpose only and not with any view or intent to establish his residence in the United Kingdom shall be charged to capital gains tax on chargeable gains accruing in any year of assessment if and only if the period (or the sum of the periods) for which he is resident in the United Kingdom in that year of assessment exceeds six months.

(4) For the purposes of this Act—

    (*a*) the situation of rights or interests (otherwise than by way of security) in or over immovable property is that of the immovable property,

    (*b*) subject to the following provisions of this subsection, the situation of rights or interests (otherwise than by way of security) in or over tangible movable property is that of the tangible movable property,

    (*c*) subject to the following provisions of this subsection, a debt, secured or unsecured, is situated in the United Kingdom if and only if the creditor is resident in the United Kingdom,

(d) shares or securities issued by any muncipal or govern-
mental authority, or by any body created by such an
authority, are situated in the country of that authority,

(e) subject to paragraph (d) above, registered shares or
securities are situated where they are registered and,
if registered in more than one register, where the
principal register is situated,

(f) a ship or aircraft is situated in the United Kingdom if
and only if the owner is then resident in the United
Kingdom, and an interest or right in or over a ship or
aircraft is situated in the United Kingdom if and only
if the person entitled to the interest or right is resident
in the United Kingdom,

(g) the situation of good-will as a trade, business or professional asset is at the place where the trade, business
or profession is carried on,

(h) patents, trade-marks and designs are situated where they
are registered, and if registered in more than one
register, where each register is situated, and copyright,
franchises, rights and licences to use any copyright
material, patent, trade-mark or design are situated in
the United Kingdom if they, or any rights derived from
them, are exercisable in the United Kingdom,

(i) a judgment debt is situated where the judgment is
recorded.

PART II

GAINS AND LOSSES

CHAPTER I

DISPOSALS

19.—(1) All forms of property shall be assets for the purposes Disposal of
of this Act, whether situated in the United Kingdom or not, assets.
including—

(a) options, debts and incorporeal property generally, and

(b) any currency other than sterling, and

(c) any form of property created by the person disposing
of it, or otherwise coming to be owned without being
acquired.

(2) For the purposes of this Act—

(a) references to a disposal of an asset include, except where
the context otherwise requires, references to a part
disposal of an asset, and

     (*b*) there is a part disposal of an asset where an interest or right in or over the asset is created by the disposal, as well as where it subsists before the disposal, and generally, there is a part disposal of an asset where, on a person making a disposal, any description of property derived from the asset remains undisposed of.

(3) Subject to the provisions of this Act, a person's acquisition of an asset and the disposal of it to him shall for the purposes of this Act be deemed to be for a consideration equal to the market value of the asset—

     (*a*) where he acquires the asset otherwise than by way of a bargain made at arm's length and in particular where he acquires it by way of gift or by way of distribution from a company in respect of shares in the company, or

     (*b*) where he acquires the asset wholly or partly for a consideration that cannot be valued, or in connection with his own or another's loss of office or employment or diminution of emoluments, or otherwise in consideration for or recognition of his or another's services or past services in any office or employment or of any other service rendered or to be rendered by him or another.

(4) It is hereby declared that winnings from betting, including pool betting, or lotteries or games with prizes are not chargeable gains, and no chargeable gain or allowable loss shall accrue on the disposal of rights to winnings obtained by participating in any pool betting or lottery or game with prizes.

(5) It is hereby declared that sums obtained by way of compensation or damages for any wrong or injury suffered by an individual in his person or in his profession or vocation are not chargeable gains.

Capital sums derived from assets.

     20.—(1) Subject to sections 21 and 23(1) below, and to any other exceptions in this Act, there is for the purposes of this Act a disposal of assets by their owner where any capital sum is derived from assets notwithstanding that no asset is acquired by the person paying the capital sum, and this subsection applies in particular to—

     (*a*) capital sums received by way of compensation for any kind of damage or injury to assets or for the loss, destruction or dissipation of assets or for any depreciation or risk of depreciation of an asset,

     (*b*) capital sums received under a policy of insurance of the risk of any kind of damage or injury to, or the loss or depreciation of, assets,

    (c) capital sums received in return for forfeiture or surrender of rights, or for refraining from exercising rights, and

    (d) capital sums received as consideration for use or exploitation of assets.

(2) In the case of a disposal within paragraph (a), (b), (c) or (d) of subsection (1) above the time of the disposal shall be the time when the capital sum is received as described in that subsection.

(3) In this section " capital sum " means any money or money's worth which is not excluded from the consideration taken into account in the computation under Chapter II below.

21.—(1) If the recipient so claims, receipt of a capital sum within paragraph (a), (b), (c) or (d) of section 20(1) above derived from an asset which is not lost or destroyed shall not be treated for the purposes of this Act as a disposal of the asset if— *Capital sums: compensation and insurance money.*

    (a) the capital sum is wholly applied in restoring the asset, or

    (b) (subject to subsection (2) below), the capital sum is applied in restoring the asset except for a part of the capital sum which is not reasonably required for the purpose and which is small as compared with the whole capital sum, or

    (c) (subject to subsection (2) below), the amount of the capital sum is small, as compared with the value of the asset,

but, if the receipt is not treated as a disposal, all sums which would, if the receipt had been so treated, have been brought into account as consideration for that disposal in the computation under Chapter II below of a gain accruing on the disposal shall be deducted from any expenditure allowable under Chapter II below as a deduction in computing a gain on the subsequent disposal of the asset.

(2) If the allowable expenditure is less than the consideration for the disposal constituted by the receipt of the capital sum (or is nil)—

    (a) paragraphs (b) and (c) of subsection (1) above shall not apply, and

    (b) if the recipient so elects (and there is any allowable expenditure)—

        (i) the amount of the consideration for the disposal shall be reduced by the amount of the allowable expenditure, and

N 3

(ii) none of that expenditure shall be allowable as a deduction in computing a gain accruing on the occasion of the disposal or any subsequent occasion.

In this subsection " allowable expenditure " means expenditure which, immediately before the disposal, was attributable to the asset under paragraphs (*a*) and (*b*) of section 32(1) below.

(3) If, in a case not falling within subsection (1)(*b*) above, a part of a capital sum within paragraph (*a*) or paragraph (*b*) of section 20(1) above derived from an asset which is not lost or destroyed is applied in restoring the asset, then if the recipient so claims, that part of the capital sum shall not be treated as consideration for the disposal deemed to be effected on receipt of the capital sum but shall be deducted from any expenditure allowable under Chapter II below as a deduction in computing a gain on the subsequent disposal of the asset.

(4) If an asset is lost or destroyed and a capital sum received by way of compensation for the loss or destruction, or under a policy of insurance of the risk of the loss or destruction, is within one year of receipt, or such longer period as the inspector may allow, applied in acquiring an asset in replacement of the asset lost or destroyed the owner shall if he so claims be treated for the purposes of this Act—

(*a*) as if the consideration for the disposal of the old asset were (if otherwise of a greater amount) of such amount as would secure that on the disposal neither a gain nor a loss accrues to him, and

(*b*) as if the amount of the consideration for the acquisition of the new asset were reduced by the excess of the amount of the capital sum received by way of compensation or under the policy of insurance, together with any residual or scrap value, over the amount of the consideration which he is treated as receiving under paragraph (*a*) above.

(5) A claim shall not be made under subsection (4) above if part only of the capital sum is applied in acquiring the new asset but if all of that capital sum except for a part which is less than the amount of the gain (whether all chargeable gain or not) accruing on the disposal of the old asset is so applied, then the owner shall if he so claims be treated for the purposes of this Act—

(*a*) as if the amount of the gain so accruing were reduced to the amount of the said part (and, if not all chargeable gain, with a proportionate reduction in the amount of the chargeable gain), and

(b) as if the amount of the consideration for the acquisition of the new asset were reduced by the amount by which the gain is reduced under paragraph (a) of this subsection.

(6) Subsections (4) and (5) above have effect subject to paragraph 18 of Schedule 5 to this Act (application to gain which in consequence of that Schedule is not all chargeable gain).

(7) This section shall not apply in relation to a wasting asset.

22.—(1) Subject to the provisions of this Act and, in particular to section 137 below (options), the occasion of the entire loss, destruction, dissipation or extinction of an asset shall, for the purposes of this Act, constitute a disposal of the asset whether or not any capital sum by way of compensation or otherwise is received in respect of the destruction, dissipation or extinction of the asset.

Assets lost or destroyed, or whose value becomes negligible.

(2) If, on a claim by the owner of an asset, the inspector is satisfied that the value of an asset has become negligible, he may allow the claim and thereupon this Act shall have effect as if the claimant had sold, and immediately re-acquired, the asset for a consideration of an amount equal to the value specified in the claim.

(3) For the purposes of subsections (1) and (2) above, a building and any permanent or semi-permanent structure in the nature of a building, may be regarded as an asset separate from the land on which it is situated, but where either of those subsections applies in accordance with this subsection, the person deemed to make the disposal of the building or structure shall be treated as if he had also sold, and immediately re-acquired, the site of the building or structure (including in the site any land occupied for purposes ancillary to the use of the building or structure) for a consideration equal to its market value at that time.

23.—(1) The conveyance or transfer by way of security of an asset or of an interest or right in or over it, or transfer of a subsisting interest or right by way of security in or over an asset (including a retransfer on redemption of the security), shall not be treated for the purposes of this Act as involving any acquisition or disposal of the asset.

Mortgages and charges.

(2) Where a person entitled to an asset by way of security or to the benefit of a charge or incumbrance on an asset deals with the asset for the purpose of enforcing or giving effect to the security, charge or incumbrance his dealings with it shall be treated for the purposes of this Act as if they were done through him as nominee by the person entitled to it subject to

PART II   the security, charge or incumbrance ; and this subsection shall apply to the dealings of any person appointed to enforce or give effect to the security, charge or incumbrance as receiver and manager or judicial factor as it applies to the dealings of the person entitled as aforesaid.

(3) An asset shall be treated as having been acquired free of any interest or right by way of security subsisting at the time of any acquisition of it, and as being disposed of free of any such interest or right subsisting at the time of the disposal ; and where an asset is acquired subject to any such interest or right the full amount of the liability thereby assumed by the person acquiring the asset shall form part of the consideration for the acquisition and disposal in addition to any other consideration.

Hire-purchase.   **24.** A hire-purchase or other transaction under which the use and enjoyment of an asset is obtained by a person for a period at the end of which the property in the asset will or may pass to that person shall be treated for the purposes of this Act, both in relation to that person and in relation to the person from whom he obtains the use and enjoyment of the asset, as if it amounted to an entire disposal of the asset to that person at the beginning of the period for which he obtains the use and enjoyment of the asset, but subject to such adjustments of tax, whether by way of repayment or discharge of tax or otherwise, as may be required where the period for which that person has the use and enjoyment of the asset terminates without the property in the asset passing to him.

Value shifting.   **25.**—(1) Without prejudice to the generality of the provisions of this Act as to the transactions which are disposals of assets, any transaction which under the following subsections is to be treated as a disposal of an asset shall be so treated (with a corresponding acquisition of an interest in the asset) notwithstanding that there is no consideration and so far as, on the assumption that the parties to the transaction were at arm's length, the party making the disposal could have obtained consideration, or additional consideration, for the disposal the transaction shall be treated as not being at arm's length and the consideration so obtainable, or the additional consideration so obtainable added to the consideration actually passing, shall be treated as the market value of what is acquired.

(2) If a person having control of a company exercises his control so that value passes out of shares in the company owned by him or a person with whom he is connected, or out of rights over the company exercisable by him or by a person with whom he is connected, and passes into other shares in or rights over the company, that shall be a disposal of the shares or rights out

of which the value passes by the person by whom they were owned or exercisable.

(3) A loss on the disposal of an asset shall not be an allowable loss to the extent to which it is attributable to value having passed out of other assets, being shares in or rights over a company which by virtue of the passing of value are treated as disposed of under subsection (2) above.

(4) If, after a transaction which results in the owner of land or of any other description of property becoming the lessee of the property there is any adjustment of the rights and liabilities under the lease, whether or not involving the grant of a new lease, which is as a whole favourable to the lessor, that shall be a disposal by the lessee of an interest in the property.

(5) If an asset is subject to any description of right or restriction the extinction or abrogation, in whole or in part, of the right or restriction by the person entitled to enforce it shall be a disposal by him of the right or restriction.

26.—(1) This section has effect as respects the disposal of an asset if a scheme has been effected or arrangements have been made (whether before or after the disposal) whereby—

> Value shifting: further provisions.

    (*a*) the value of the asset has been materially reduced, and

    (*b*) a tax-free benefit has been or will be conferred—

        (i) on the person making the disposal or a person with whom he is connected, or

        (ii) subject to subsection (3) below, on any other person.

(2) For the purposes of subsection (1)(*b*) above a benefit is conferred on a person if he becomes entitled to any money or money's worth or the value of any asset in which he has an interest is increased or he is wholly or partly relieved from any liability to which he is subject; and a benefit is tax-free unless it is required, on the occasion on which it is conferred on the person in question, to be brought into account in computing his income, profits or gains for the purposes of income tax, capital gains tax or corporation tax.

(3) This section shall not apply by virtue of subsection (1)(*b*)(ii) above if it is shown that avoidance of tax was not the main purpose or one of the main purposes of the scheme or arrangements in question.

(4) Where this section has effect in relation to any disposal, any allowable loss or chargeable gain accruing on the disposal shall be calculated as if the consideration for the disposal were increased by such amount as appears to the inspector, or on appeal the Commissioners concerned, to be just and reasonable having regard to the scheme or arrangements and the tax-free benefit in question.

(5) Where—

    (*a*) by virtue of subsection (4) above the consideration for the disposal of an asset has been treated as increased, and

    (*b*) the benefit taken into account under subsection (1)(*b*) above was an increase in the value of another asset,

any allowable loss or chargeable gain accruing on the first disposal of the other asset after the increase in its value shall be calculated as if the consideration for that disposal were reduced by such amount as appears to the inspector, or on appeal the Commissioners concerned, to be just and reasonable having regard to the scheme or arrangements in question and the increase made in relation to the disposal mentioned in paragraph (*a*) above.

(6) References in this section to a disposal do not include references to any disposal falling within—

    (*a*) section 44(1) below (disposals between husband and wife), or

    (*b*) section 49(4) below (disposals by personal representatives to legatees), or

    (*c*) section 273(1) of the Taxes Act (disposals within a group of companies).

(7) In relation to the disposal by a company of an asset consisting of shares in another company the reference in subsection (1)(*a*) above to a reduction in the value of the asset does not include a reference to any reduction attributable to—

    (*a*) the payment of a dividend by the second company at a time when it and the first company are members of the same group of companies within the meaning of section 272 of the Taxes Act, or

    (*b*) the disposal of any asset by the second company at such a time, being a disposal falling within section 273(1) of that Act.

(8) In relation to a case in which the disposal of an asset precedes its acquisition the reference in subsection (1)(*a*) above to a reduction shall be read as including a reference to an increase.

Time of disposal and acquisition where asset disposed of under contract.

    27.—(1) Where an asset is disposed of and acquired under a contract the time at which the disposal and acquisition is made is the time the contract is made (and not, if different, the time at which the asset is conveyed or transferred).

    This subsection has effect subject to section 20(2) above, and subsection (2) below.

(2) If the contract is conditional (and in particular if it is
conditional on the exercise of an option) the time at which the
disposal and acquisition is made is the time when the condition
is satisfied.

CHAPTER II

COMPUTATION

28.—(1) The amount of the gains accruing on the disposal of Chargeable
assets shall be computed in accordance with this Chapter, gains.
and subject to the other provisions of this Act.

(2) Every gain shall, except as otherwise expressly provided,
be a chargeable gain.

(3) Schedule 5 to this Act (which restricts the amount of
chargeable gains accruing on the disposal of assets owned on
6th April 1965) shall have effect.

29.—(1) Except as otherwise expressly provided, the amount Losses.
of a loss accruing on a disposal of an asset shall be computed
in the same way as the amount of a gain accruing on a disposal
is computed.

(2) Except as otherwise expressly provided, all the provisions
of this Act which distinguish gains which are chargeable gains
from those which are not, or which make part of a gain a
chargeable gain, and part not, shall apply also to distinguish
losses which are allowable losses from those which are not,
and to make part of a loss an allowable loss, and part not ; and
references in this Act to an allowable loss shall be construed
accordingly.

(3) A loss accruing to a person in a year of assessment during
no part of which he is resident or ordinarily resident in the United
Kingdom shall not be an allowable loss for the purposes of this
Act unless, under section 12 above (non-resident with U.K.
branch or agency), he would be chargeable to capital gains tax
in respect of a chargeable gain if there had been a gain instead
of a loss on that occasion.

(4) In accordance with section 14(1) above (foreign assets of
person with foreign domicile), losses accruing on the disposal of
assets situated outside the United Kingdom to an individual
resident or ordinarily resident but not domiciled in the United
Kingdom shall not be allowable losses.

(5) Except as provided by section 49 below (death), an allowable loss accruing in a year of assessment shall not be allowable
as a deduction from chargeable gains accruing in any earlier

PART II   year of assessment, and relief shall not be given under this Act more than once in respect of any loss or part of a loss, and shall not be given under this Act if and so far as relief has been or may be given in respect of it under the Income Tax Acts.

Computation of gains

Introductory.   **30.** The following provisions of this Chapter, and Schedule 5 to this Act, shall have effect for computing for the purposes of this Act the amount of a gain accruing on the disposal of an asset.

Consideration chargeable to tax on income.   **31.**—(1) There shall be excluded from the consideration for a disposal of assets taken into account in the computation under this Chapter of the gain accruing on that disposal any money or money's worth charged to income tax as income of, or taken into account as a receipt in computing income or profits or gains or losses of, the person making the disposal for the purposes of the Income Tax Acts.

(2) Subsection (1) above shall not be taken as excluding from the consideration so taken into acount any money or money's worth which is taken into account in the making of a balancing

1968 c. 3.   charge under the Capital Allowances Act 1968 (including the provisions of the Taxes Act which under that Act are to be treated as contained in the said Act of 1968).

(3) This section shall not preclude the taking into account in a computation under this Chapter, as consideration for the disposal of an asset, of the capitalised value of a rentcharge (as in a case where a rentcharge is exchanged for some other asset) or of the capitalised value of a ground annual or feu duty, or of a right of any other description to income or to payments in the nature of income over a period, or to a series of payments in the nature of income.

Expenditure: general.   **32.**—(1) Except as otherwise expressly provided, the sums allowable as a deduction from the consideration in the computation under this Chapter of the gain accruing to a person on the disposal of an asset shall be restricted to—

    (*a*) the amount or value of the consideration, in money or money's worth, given by him or on his behalf wholly and exclusively for the acquisition of the asset, together with the incidental costs to him of the acquisition or, if the asset was not acquired by him, any expenditure wholly and exclusively incurred by him in providing the asset,

    (*b*) the amount of any expenditure wholly and exclusively incured on the asset by him or on his behalf for the purpose of enhancing the value of the asset, being expenditure reflected in the state or nature of the asset at the time of the disposal, and any expenditure wholly and exclusively incurred by him in establishing, preserving or defending his title to, or to a right over, the asset,

(c) the incidental costs to him of making the disposal.

(2) For the purposes of this section and for the purposes of all other provisions of this Act the incidental costs to the person making the disposal of the acquisition of the asset or of its disposal shall consist of expenditure wholly and exclusively incurred by him for the purposes of the acquisition or, as the case may be, the disposal, being fees, commission or remuneration paid for the professional services of any surveyor or valuer, or auctioneer, or accountant, or agent or legal adviser and costs of transfer or conveyance (including stamp duty) together—

(a) in the case of the acquisition of an asset, with costs of advertising to find a seller, and

(b) in the case of a disposal, with costs of advertising to find a buyer and costs reasonably incurred in making any valuation or apportionment required for the purposes of the computation under this Chapter, including in particular expenses reasonably incurred in ascertaining market value where required by this Act.

(3) Except as provided by section 269 of the Taxes Act (companies: interest charged to capital), no payment of interest shall be allowable under this section.

(4) Any provision in this Act introducing the assumption that assets are sold and immediately re-acquired shall not imply that any expenditure is incurred as incidental to the sale or re-acquisition.

33.—(1) There shall be excluded from the sums allowable under section 32 above as a deduction in the computation under this Chapter any expenditure allowable as a deduction in computing the profits or gains or losses of a trade, profession or vocation for the purposes of income tax or allowable as a deduction in computing any other income or profits or gains or losses for the purposes of the Income Tax Acts and any expenditure which, although not so allowable as a deduction in computing any losses, would be so allowable but for an insufficiency of income or profits or gains ; and this subsection applies irrespective of whether effect is or would be given to the deduction in computing the amount of tax chargeable or by discharge or repayment of tax or in any other way.

Exclusion of expenditure by reference to tax on income.

(2) Without prejudice to the provisions of subsection (1) above there shall be excluded from the sums allowable under section 32 above as a deduction in the computation under this Chapter any expenditure which, if the assets, or all the assets to which the computation relates, were, and had at all times been, held or used as part of the fixed capital of a trade the profits or gains of which were (irrespective of whether the person making the disposal is a company or not) chargeable to income tax would be allowable as a deduction in computing the profits or gains or losses of the trade for the purposes of income tax.

Restriction of losses by reference to capital allowances and renewals allowances.

34.—(1) Section 33 above shall not require the exclusion from the sums allowable as a deduction in the computation under this Chapter of any expenditure as being expenditure in respect of which a capital allowance or renewals allowance is made, but the amount of any losses accruing on the disposal of an asset shall be restricted by reference to capital allowances and renewals allowances as follows.

(2) In the computation under this Chapter of the amount of a loss accruing to the person making the disposal, there shall be excluded from the sums allowable as a deduction any expenditure to the extent to which any capital allowance or renewals allowance has been or may be made in respect of it.

(3) If the person making the disposal acquired the asset—

1968 c. 3.

(a) by a transfer by way of sale in relation to which an election under paragraph 4 of Schedule 7 to the Capital Allowances Act 1968 was made, or

(b) by a transfer to which section 35(2) to (4) or section 48(2) of that Act applies,

(being enactments under which a transfer is treated for the purposes of capital allowances as being made at written down value), the preceding provisions of this section shall apply as if any capital allowance made to the transferor in respect of the asset had (except so far as any loss to the transferor was restricted under those provisions) been made to the person making the disposal (that is the transferee) ; and where the transferor acquired the asset by such a transfer, capital allowances which by virtue of this subsection can be taken into account in relation to the transferor shall also be taken into account in relation to the transferee (that is the person making the disposal), and so on for any series of transfers before the disposal.

(4) In this section " capital allowance " means—

1971 c. 68.

(a) any allowance under the Capital Allowances Act 1968 (including the provisions of the Taxes Act which under that Act are to be treated as contained in the said Act of 1968) or under Chapter I of Part III of the Finance

Act 1971, other than an allowance under section 79(1) of the Taxes Act (relief for cost of maintenance of agricultural land),

(b) any relief given under section 76 of the Taxes Act (expenditure on sea walls), and

(c) any deduction in computing profits or gains allowable under section 141 of the Taxes Act (cemeteries).

(5) In this section " renewals allowance " means a deduction allowable in computing the profits or gains of a trade, profession or vocation for the purpose of income tax by reference to the cost of acquiring an asset for the purposes of the trade, profession or vocation in replacement of another asset, and for the purposes of this Chapter a renewals allowance shall be regarded as a deduction allowable in respect of the expenditure incurred on the asset which is being replaced.

(6) The amount of capital allowances to be taken into account under this section in relation to a disposal include any allowances falling to be made by reference to the event which is the disposal, and there shall be deducted from the amount of the allowances the amount of any balancing charge to which effect has been or is to be given by reference to the event which is the disposal, or any earlier event, and of any balancing charge to which effect might have been so given but for the making of an election under section 40 of the Capital Allowances Act 1968 (option in case of replacement of machinery or plant).

(7) Where the disposal is of machinery or plant in relation to expenditure on which allowances or charges have been made under Chapter I of Part III of the Finance Act 1971, and neither 1971 c. 68. paragraph 5 (assets used partly for trade purposes and partly for other purposes) nor paragraph 6 (wear and tear subsidies) of Schedule 8 to that Act applies, the capital allowances to be taken into account under this section are to be regarded as equal to the difference between the capital expenditure incurred, or treated as incurred, under that Chapter on the provision of the machinery or plant by the person making the disposal and the disposal value required to be brought into account in respect of the machinery or plant.

35.—(1) Where a person disposes of an interest or right in or Part disposals. over an asset, and generally wherever on the disposal of an asset any description of property derived from that asset remains undisposed of, the sums which under paragraphs (a) and (b) of section 32(1) above are attributable to the asset shall, both for the purposes of the computation under this Chapter of the gain accruing on the disposal and for the purpose of applying this Chapter in relation to the property which remains undisposed of, be apportioned.

(2) The apportionment shall be made by reference—

> (*a*) to the amount or value of the consideration for the disposal on the one hand (call that amount or value A), and
>
> (*b*) to the market value of the property which remains undisposed of on the other hand (call that market value B),

and accordingly the fraction of the said sums allowable as a deduction in computing under this Chapter the amount of the gain accruing on the disposal shall be $\dfrac{A}{A+B}$, and the remainder shall be attributed to the property which remains undisposed of.

(3) Any apportionment to be made in pursuance of this section shall be made before operating the provisions of section 34 above and if, after a part disposal, there is a subsequent disposal of an asset the capital allowances or renewals allowances to be taken into account in pursuance of that section in relation to the subsequent disposal shall, subject to subsection (4) below, be those referable to the sums which under paragraphs (*a*) and (*b*) of section 32(1) above are attributable to the asset whether before or after the part disposal, but those allowances shall be reduced by the amount (if any) by which the loss on the earlier disposal was restricted under the provisions of section 34 above.

(4) This section shall not be taken as requiring the apportionment of any expenditure which, on the facts, is wholly attributable to what is disposed of, or wholly attributable to what remains undisposed of.

(5) It is hereby declared that this section, and all other provisions for apportioning on a part disposal expenditure which is deductible in computing a gain, are to be operated before the operation of, and without regard to—

> (*a*) section 44(1) below (disposals between husband and wife),
>
> (*b*) sections 115 to 121 below (replacement of business assets), but without prejudice to the provisions of subsection (8) of the said section 115,
>
> (*c*) section 273(1) of the Taxes Act (transfers within a group of companies), or
>
> (*d*) any other enactment making an adjustment to secure that neither a gain nor a loss occurs on a disposal.

Assets
derived from
other assets.

36. If and so far as, in a case where assets have been merged or divided or have changed their nature or rights or interests in or over assets have been created or extinguished, the value

of an asset is derived from any other asset in the same owner- PART II
ship, an appropriate proportion of the sums allowable as a
deduction in a computation under this Chapter in respect of the
other asset under paragraphs (*a*) and (*b*) of section 32(1) above
shall, both for the purpose of the computation of a gain accruing on the disposal of the first-mentioned asset and, if the other
asset remains in existence, on a disposal of that other asset, be
attributed to the first-mentioned asset.

37.—(1) In this Chapter " wasting asset " means an asset with Wasting assets.
a predictable life not exceeding fifty years but so that—

(*a*) freehold land shall not be a wasting asset whatever its
nature, and whatever the nature of the buildings or
works on it,

(*b*) " life ", in relation to any tangible movable property,
means useful life, having regard to the purpose for
which the tangible assets were acquired or provided
by the person making the disposal,

(*c*) plant and machinery shall in every case be regarded as
having a predictable life of less than fifty years, and in
estimating that life it shall be assumed that its life
will end when it is finally put out of use as being unfit
for further use, and that it is going to be used in the
normal manner and to the normal extent and is going
to be so used throughout its life as so estimated,

(*d*) a life interest in settled property shall not be a wasting
asset until the predictable expectation of life of the
life tenant is fifty years or less, and the predictable
life of life interests in settled property and of annuities shall be ascertained from actuarial tables approved
by the Board.

(2) In this Chapter " the residual or scrap value ", in relation to a wasting asset, means the predictable value, if any,
which the wasting asset will have at the end of its predictable
life as estimated in accordance with this section.

(3) The question what is the predictable life of an asset, and
the question what is its predictable residual or scrap value at
the end of that life, if any, shall, so far as those questions are not
immediately answered by the nature of the asset, be taken, in
relation to any disposal of the asset, as they were known or
ascertainable at the time when the asset was acquired or provided by the person making the disposal.

PART II
Wasting
assets:
straightline
restriction of
allowable
expenditure.

38.—(1) In the computation under this Chapter of the gain accruing on the disposal of a wasting asset it shall be assumed—

    (*a*) that any expenditure attributable to the asset under section 32(1)(*a*) above after deducting the residual or scrap value, if any, of the asset, is written off at a uniform rate from its full amount at the time when the asset is acquired or provided to nothing at the end of its life, and

    (*b*) that any expenditure attributable to the asset under section 32(1)(*b*) above is written off from the full amount of that expenditure at the time when that expenditure is first reflected in the state or nature of the asset to nothing at the end of its life,

so that an equal daily amount is written off day by day.

(2) Thus, calling the predictable life of a wasting asset at the time when it was acquired or provided by the person making the disposal L, the period from that time to the time of disposal T(1), and, in relation to any expenditure attributable to the asset under section 32(1)(b) above, the period from the time when that expenditure is first reflected in the state or nature of the asset to the said time of disposal T(2), there shall be excluded from the computation under this Chapter—

    (*a*) out of the expenditure attributable to the asset under section 32(1)(*a*) above a fraction $\dfrac{T(1)}{L}$ of an amount equal to the amount of that expenditure minus the residual or scrap value, if any, of the asset, and

    (*b*) out of the expenditure attributable to the asset under section 32(1)(*b*) above a fraction $\dfrac{T(2)}{L-(T(1)-T(2))}$ of the amount of the expenditure.

(3) If any expenditure attributable to the asset under section 32(1)(*b*) above creates or increases a residual or scrap value of the asset, the provisions of subsection (1)(*a*) above shall be applied so as to take that into account.

39.—(1) Section 38 above shall not apply in relation to a disposal of an asset—

    (*a*) which, from the beginning of the period of ownership of the person making the disposal to the time when the disposal is made, is used and used solely for the purposes of a trade, profession or vocation and in respect of which that person has claimed or could have claimed any capital allowance in respect of any expenditure attributable to the asset under paragraph (a) or paragraph (b) of section 32(1) above, or

(b) on which the person making the disposal has incurred any expenditure which has otherwise qualified in full for any capital allowance.

(2) In the case of the disposal of an asset which, in the period of ownership of the person making the disposal, has been used partly for the purposes of a trade, profession or vocation and partly for other purposes, or has been used for the purposes of a trade, profession or vocation for part of that period, or which has otherwise qualified in part only for capital allowances—

(a) the consideration for the disposal, and any expenditure attributable to the asset by paragraph (a) or paragraph (b) of section 32(1) above shall be apportioned by reference to the extent to which that expenditure qualified for capital allowances, and

(b) the computation under this Chapter shall be made separately in relation to the apportioned parts of the expenditure and consideration, and

(c) section 38 above shall not apply for the purposes of the computation in relation to the part of the consideration apportioned to use for the purposes of the trade, profession or vocation, or to the expenditure qualifying for capital allowances, and

(d) if an apportionment of the consideration for the disposal has been made for the purposes of making any capital allowance to the person making the disposal or for the purpose of making any balancing charge on him, that apportionment shall be employed for the purposes of this section, and

(e) subject to paragraph (d) above, the consideration for the disposal shall be apportioned for the purposes of this section in the same proportions as the expenditure attributable to the asset is apportioned under paragraph (a) above.

40.—(1) If the consideration, or part of the consideration, taken into account in the computation under this Chapter is payable by instalments over a period beginning not earlier than the time when the disposal is made, being a period exceeding eighteen months, then, if the person making the disposal satisfies the Board that he would otherwise suffer undue hardship, the tax on a chargeable gain accruing on the disposal may, at his option, be paid by such instalments as the Board may allow over a period not exceeding eight years and ending not later than the time at which the last of the first-mentioned instalments is payable.

PART II

(2) In the computation under this Chapter consideration for the disposal shall be brought into account without any discount for postponement of the right to receive any part of it and, in the first instance, without regard to a risk of any part of the consideration being irrecoverable or to the right to receive any part of the consideration being contingent; and if any part of the consideration so brought into account is subsequently shown to the satisfaction of the inspector to be irrecoverable, such adjustment, whether by way of discharge or repayment of tax or otherwise, shall be made as is required in consequence.

Contingent liabilities.

41.—(1) In the first instance no allowance shall be made in the computation under this Chapter—

(a) in the case of a disposal by way of assigning a lease of land or other property, for any liability remaining with, or assumed by, the person making the disposal by way of assigning the lease which is contingent on a default in respect of liabilities thereby or subsequently assumed by the assignee under the terms and conditions of the lease,

(b) for any contingent liability of the person making the disposal in respect of any covenant for quiet enjoyment or other obligation assumed as vendor of land, or of any estate or interest in land, or as a lessor,

(c) for any contingent liability in respect of a warranty or representation made on a disposal by way of sale or lease of any property other than land.

(2) If it is subsequently shown to the satisfaction of the inspector that any such contingent liability has become enforceable, and is being or has been enforced, such adjustment, whether by way of discharge or repayment of tax or otherwise, shall be made as is required in consequence.

Expenditure reimbursed out of public money.

42. There shall be excluded from the computation under this Chapter any expenditure which has been or is to be met directly or indirectly by the Crown or by any Government, public or local authority whether in the United Kingdom or elsewhere.

Supplemental.

43.—(1) No deduction shall be allowable in a computation under this Chapter more than once from any sum or from more than one sum.

(2) References in this Chapter to sums taken into account as receipts or as expenditure in computing profits or gains or losses for the purposes of income tax shall include references to sums which would be so taken into account but for the fact that any profits or gains of a trade, profession, employment or

vocation are not chargeable to income tax or that losses are not allowable for those purposes.

(3) In this Chapter references to income or profits charged or chargeable to tax include references to income or profits taxed or as the case may be taxable by deduction at source.

(4) For the purposes of any computation under this Chapter any necessary apportionments shall be made of any consideration or of any expenditure and the method of apportionment adopted shall, subject to the express provisions of this Chapter, be such method as appears to the inspector or on appeal the Commissioners concerned to be just and reasonable.

(5) In this Chapter " capital allowance " and " renewals allowance " have the meanings given by subsections (4) and (5) of section 34 above.

PART III

PERSONS AND TRUSTS

Married persons

44.—(1) If, in any year of assessment, and in the case of a Husband and woman who in that year of assessment is a married woman wife. living with her husband, the man disposes of an asset to the wife, or the wife disposes of an asset to the man, both shall be treated as if the asset was acquired from the one making the disposal for a consideration of such amount as would secure that on the disposal neither a gain nor a loss would accrue to the one making the disposal.

(2) This section shall not apply—

(a) if until the disposal the asset formed part of trading stock of a trade carried on by the one making the disposal, or if the asset is acquired as trading stock for the purposes of a trade carried on by the one acquiring the asset, or

(b) if the disposal is by way of donatio mortis causa,

but this section shall have effect notwithstanding the provisions of section 62 (transactions between connected persons) or section 122 (appropriations to and from stock in trade) below, or of any other provisions of this Act fixing the amount of the consideration deemed to be given on a disposal or acquisition.

Part III
Tax on married
woman's
gains.
45.—(1) Subject to this section, the amount of capital gains tax on chargeable gains accruing to a married woman in—

    (*a*) a year of assessment, or

    (*b*) any part of a year of assessment, being a part beginning with 6th April,

during which she is a married woman living with her husband shall be assessed and charged on the husband and not otherwise but this subsection shall not affect the amount of capital gains tax chargeable on a man apart from this subsection nor result in the additional amount of capital gains tax charged on a man by virtue of this subsection being different from the amount which would otherwise have remained chargeable on the married woman.

(2) Subsection (1) above shall not apply in relation to a husband and wife in any year of assessment if, before 6th July in the year next following that year of assessment, an application is made by either the husband or wife, and such an application duly made shall have effect not only as respects the year of assessment for which it is made but also for any subsequent year of assessment:

Provided that the applicant may give, for any subsequent year of assessment, a notice to withdraw that application and where such a notice is given the application shall not have effect with respect to the year for which the notice is given or any subsequent year.

A notice of withdrawal under this proviso shall not be valid unless it is given within the period for making, for the year for which the notice is given, an application similar to that to which the notice relates.

1970 c. 9.
(3) Returns under section 8 or 42(5) of the Taxes Management Act 1970 as respects chargeable gains accruing to a married woman may be required either from her or, if her husband is liable under subsection (1) above, from him.

(4) Section 40 (collection from wife of tax assessed on husband attributable to her income) and section 41 (right of husband to disclaim liability for tax on deceased wife's income) of the Taxes Act shall apply with any necessary modifications in relation to capital gains tax as they apply in relation to income tax.

(5) An application or notice of withdrawal under this section shall be in such form and made in such manner as may be prescribed by the Board.

Trustees, nominees and personal representatives

46.—(1) In relation to assets held by a person as nominee Nominees and for another person, or as trustee for another person absolutely bare trustees. entitled as against the trustee, or for any person who would be so entitled but for being an infant or other person under disability (or for two or more persons who are or would be jointly so entitled), this Act shall apply as if the property were vested in, and the acts of the nominee or trustee in relation to the assets were the acts of, the person or persons for whom he is the nominee or trustee (acquisitions from or disposals to him by that person or persons being disregarded accordingly).

(2) It is hereby declared that references in this Act to any asset held by a person as trustee for another person absolutely entitled as against the trustee are references to a case where that other person has the exclusive right, subject only to satisfying any outstanding charge, lien or other right of the trustees to resort to the asset for payment of duty, taxes, costs or other outgoings, to direct how that asset shall be dealt with.

47.—(1) In the case of a gain accruing to a person on the Expenses in disposal of, or of a right or interest in or over, an asset to which adminis- he became absolutely entitled as legatee or as against the trustees tration of of settled property— estates and trusts.

> (*a*) any expenditure within section 32(2) above incurred by him in relation to the transfer of the asset to him by the personal representatives or trustees, and
>
> (*b*) any such expenditure incurred in relation to the transfer of the asset by the personal representatives or trustees,

shall be allowable as a deduction in the computation under Chapter II of Part II above of the gain accruing to that person on the disposal.

(2) In this Act, unless the context otherwise requires, " legatee " includes any person taking under a testamentary disposition or on an intestacy or partial intestacy, whether he takes beneficially or as trustee, and a person taking under a donatio mortis causa shall be treated (except for the purposes of section 49 below (death)) as a legatee and his acquisition as made at the time of the donor's death.

(3) For the purposes of the definition of " legatee " above, and of any reference in this Act to a person acquiring an asset " as legatee ", property taken under a testamentary disposition or on an intestacy or partial intestacy includes any asset appropriated by the personal representatives in or towards satisfaction of a pecuniary legacy or any other interest or share in the property devolving under the disposition or intestacy.

48.—(1) Capital gains tax chargeable in respect of chargeable gains accruing to the trustees of a settlement or capital gains tax due from the personal representatives of a deceased person may be assessed and charged on and in the name of any one or more of those trustees or personal representatives, but where an assessment is made in pursuance of this subsection otherwise than on all the trustees or all the personal representatives the persons assessed shall not include a person who is not resident or ordinarily resident in the United Kingdom.

(2) Subject to section 46 above, chargeable gains accruing to the trustees of a settlement or to the personal representatives of a deceased person, and capital gains tax chargeable on or in the name of such trustees or personal representatives, shall not be regarded for the purposes of this Act as accruing to, or chargeable on, any other person, nor shall any trustee or personal representative be regarded for the purposes of this Act as an individual.

Death

49.—(1) For the purposes of this Act the assets of which a deceased person was competent to dispose—

(a) shall be deemed to be acquired on his death by the personal representatives or other person on whom they devolve for a consideration equal to their market value at the date of the death, but

(b) shall not be deemed to be disposed of by him on his death (whether or not they were the subject of a testamentary disposition).

(2) Allowable losses sustained by an individual in the year of assessment in which he dies may, so far as they cannot be deducted from chargeable gains accruing in that year, be deducted from chargeable gains accruing to the deceased in the three years of assessment preceding the year of assessment in which the death occurs, taking chargeable gains accruing in a later year before those accruing in an earlier year.

(3) In relation to property forming part of the estate of a deceased person the personal representatives shall for the purposes of this Act be treated as being a single and continuing body of persons (distinct from the persons who may from time to time be the personal representatives), and that body shall be treated as having the deceased's residence, ordinary residence, and domicile at the date of death.

(4) On a person acquiring any asset as legatee (as defined in section 47 above)—

(*a*) no chargeable gain shall accrue to the personal representatives, and

(*b*) the legatee shall be treated as if the personal representatives' acquisition of the asset had been his acquisition of it.

(5) Notwithstanding section 19(3) above (gifts) no chargeable gain shall accrue to any person on his making a disposal by way of donatio mortis causa.

(6) Subject to subsections (7) and (8) below, where within the period of two years after a person's death any of the dispositions (whether effected by will, under the law relating to intestacy or otherwise) of the property of which he was competent to dispose are varied, or the benefit conferred by any of those dispositions is disclaimed, by an instrument in writing made by the persons or any of the persons who benefit or would benefit under the dispositions—

(*a*) the variation or disclaimer shall not constitute a disposal for the purposes of this Act, and

(*b*) this section shall apply as if the variation had been effected by the deceased or, as the case may be, the disclaimed benefit had never been conferred.

(7) Subsection (6) above does not apply to a variation unless the person or persons making the instrument so elect by written notice given to the Board within six months after the date of the instrument or such longer time as the Board may allow.

(8) Subsection (6) above does not apply to a variation or disclaimer made for any consideration in money or money's worth other than consideration consisting of the making of a variation or disclaimer in respect of another of the dispositions.

(9) Subsection (6) above applies whether or not the administration of the estate is complete or the property has been distributed in accordance with the original dispositions.

(10) In this section references to assets of which a deceased person was competent to dispose are references to assets of the deceased which (otherwise than in right of a power of appointment or of the testamentary power conferred by statute to dispose of entailed interests) he could, if of full age and capacity, have disposed of by his will, assuming that all the assets were situated in England and, if he was not domiciled in the United Kingdom, that he was domiciled in England, and include references to his severable share in any assets to which, immediately before his death, he was beneficially entitled as a joint tenant.

50.—(1) The provisions of this Act, so far as relating to the consequences of the death of an heir of entail in possession of any property in Scotland subject to an entail, whether sui juris or not, or of a proper liferenter of any property, shall have effect subject to the provisions of this section.

(2) For the purposes of this Act, on the death of any such heir or liferenter the heir of entail next entitled to the entailed property under the entail or, as the case may be, the person (if any) who, on the death of the liferenter, becomes entitled to possession of the property as fiar shall be deemed to have acquired all the assets forming part of the property at the date of the deceased's death for a consideration equal to their market value at that date.

Settlements

51. In this Act, unless the context otherwise requires, " settled property " means any property held in trust other than property to which section 46 above (nominees and bare trustees) applies.

This definition has effect subject to section 61(4) (insolvents' assets) and 93 (unit trusts) below.

52.—(1) In relation to settled property, the trustees of the settlement shall for the purposes of this Act be treated as being a single and continuing body of persons (distinct from the persons who may from time to time be the trustees), and that body shall be treated as being resident and ordinarily resident in the United Kingdom unless the general administration of the trusts is ordinarily carried on outside the United Kingdom and the trustees or a majority of them for the time being are not resident or not ordinarily resident in the United Kingdom.

(2) Notwithstanding subsection (1) above, a person carrying on a business which consists of or includes the management of trusts, and acting as trustee of a trust in the course of that business, shall be treated in relation to that trust as not resident in the United Kingdom if the whole of the settled property consists of or derives from property provided by a person not at the time (or, in the case of a trust arising under a testamentary disposition or on an intestacy or partial intestacy, at his death) domiciled, resident or ordinarily resident in the United Kingdom, and if in such a case the trustees or a majority of them are or are treated in relation to that trust as not resident in the United Kingdom, the general administration of the trust shall be treated as ordinarily carried on outside the United Kingdom.

(3) For the purposes of this section, and of sections 54(1) and 55(1) below, where part of the property comprised in a settle-

ment is vested in one trustee or set of trustees and part in another (and in particular where settled land within the meaning of the Settled Land Act 1925 is vested in the tenant for life and investments representing capital money are vested in the trustees of the settlement), they shall be treated as together constituting and, in so far as they act separately, as acting on behalf of a single body of trustees.

(4) If tax assessed on the trustees, or any one trustee, of a settlement in respect of a chargeable gain accruing to the trustees is not paid within six months from the date when it becomes payable by the trustees or trustee, and before or after the expiration of that period of six months the asset in respect of which the chargeable gain accrued, or any part of the proceeds of sale of that asset, is transferred by the trustees to a person who as against the trustees is absolutely entitled to it, that person may at any time within two years from the time when the tax became payable be assessed and charged (in the name of the trustees) to an amount of capital gains tax not exceeding tax chargeable on an amount equal to the amount of the chargeable gain and, where part only of the asset or of the proceeds was transferred, not exceeding a proportionate part of that amount.

53. A gift in settlement, whether revocable or irrevocable, is Gifts in a disposal of the entire property thereby becoming settled settlement. property notwithstanding that the donor has some interest as a beneficiary under the settlement and notwithstanding that he is a trustee, or the sole trustee, of the settlement.

54.—(1) On the occasion when a person becomes absolutely Person entitled to any settled property as against the trustee all the becoming assets forming part of the settled property to which he becomes absolutely so entitled shall be deemed to have been disposed of by the settled trustee, and immediately reacquired by him in his capacity as property. a trustee within section 46(1) above, for a consideration equal to their market value.

(2) On the occasion when a person becomes absolutely entitled to any settled property as against the trustee, any allowable loss which has accrued to the trustee in respect of property which is, or is represented by, the property to which that person so becomes entitled (including any allowable loss carried forward to the year of assessment in which that occasion falls), being a loss which cannot be deducted from chargeable gains accruing to the trustee in that year, but before that occasion, shall be treated as if it were an allowable loss accruing at that time to the person becoming so entitled, instead of to the trustee.

55.—(1) On the termination at any time after 6th April 1965 of a life interest in possession in all or any part of settled property, the whole or a corresponding part of each of the assets forming part of the settled property and not ceasing at that time to be settled property shall be deemed for the purposes of this Act at that time to be disposed of and immediately reacquired by the trustee for a consideration equal to the whole or a corresponding part of the market value of the asset.

For the purposes of this subsection a life interest which is a right to part of the income of settled property shall be treated as a life interest in a corresponding part of the settled property.

(2) Subsection (1) above shall not apply on the occasion of the termination of the trusts of the settlement as respects any part of the settled property by the exercise of a power for that purpose contained in the settlement or of a statutory power of advancement or by the surrender of a life interest in such a part for the purpose of advancement, if all the property as respects which the life interest terminates thereby ceases to be settled property under the settlement.

(3) Subsection (1) above shall apply where the person entitled to a life interest in possession in all or any part of settled property dies (although the interest does not then terminate) as it applies on the termination of such a life interest.

(4) In this section " life interest " in relation to a settlement—

    (*a*) includes a right under the settlement to the income of, or the use or occupation of, settled property for the life of a person other than the person entitled to the right, or for lives,

    (*b*) does not include any right which is contingent on the exercise of the discretion of the trustee or the discretion of some other person, and

    (*c*) subject to subsection (5) below, does not include an annuity, notwithstanding that the annuity is payable out of or charged on settled property or the income of settled property.

(5) In this section the expression " life interest " shall include entitlement to an annuity created by the settlement if—

    (*a*) some or all of the settled property is appropriated by the trustees as a fund out of which the annuity is payable, and

    (*b*) there is no right of recourse to settled property not so appropriated, or to the income of settled property not so appropriated, and, without prejudice to subsection (6) below, the settled property so appropriated shall, while the annuity is payable, and on the occasion of the death of the annuitant, be treated for the purposes of this section as being settled property under a separate settlement.

(6) If there is a life interest in a part of the settled property and, where that is a life interest in income, there is no right of recourse to, or to the income of, the remainder of the settled property, the part of the settled property in which the life interest subsists shall while it subsists be treated for the purposes of this section as being settled property under a separate settlement.

56.—(1) Where, by virtue of section 54(1) above, the assets Death of life forming part of any settled property are deemed to be disposed tenant: of and re-acquired by the trustee on the occasion when a person exclusion of becomes absolutely entitled thereto as against the trustee, then, chargeable gain. if that occasion is the termination of a life interest (within the meaning of section 55 above) by the death of the person entitled to that interest—

    (*a*) no chargeable gain shall accrue on the disposal, and

    (*b*) if on the death the property reverts to the disponer the disposal and re-acquisition under that subsection shall be deemed to be for such consideration as to secure that neither a gain nor a loss accrues to the trustee, and shall, if the trustee had first acquired the property at a date earlier than 6th April 1965, be deemed to be at that earlier date.

(2) Where section 55(1) above applies on the death of the person entitled to the life interest referred to therein, no chargeable gain shall accrue on the disposal deemed to be made under that section.

57. Sections 54(1) and 55(1) above shall apply, where an Death of annuity which is not a life interest is terminated by the death of annuitant. the annuitant, as they apply on the termination of a life interest by the death of the person entitled thereto.

In this section " life interest " has the same meaning as in section 55 above.

58.—(1) No chargeable gain shall accrue on the disposal of Disposal of an interest created by or arising under a settlement (including, interests in in particular, an annuity or life interest, and the reversion to settled an annuity or life interest) by the person for whose benefit property. the interest was created by the terms of the settlement or by any other person except one who acquired, or derives his title from one who acquired, the interest for a consideration in money or money's worth, other than consideration consisting of another interest under the settlement.

(2) Subject to subsection (1) above, where a person who has acquired an interest in settled property (including in particular the reversion to an annuity or life interest) becomes, as the holder of that interest, absolutely entitled as against the trustee to any settled property, he shall be treated as disposing of the interest in consideration of obtaining that settled property (but without prejudice to any gain accruing to the trustee on the disposal of that property deemed to be effected by him under section 54(1) above).

Other cases

Gifts: recovery from donee.

59.—(1) If in any year of assessment a chargeable gain accrues to any person on the disposal of an asset by way of gift and any amount of capital gains tax assessed on that person for that year of assessment is not paid within twelve months from the date when the tax becomes payable the donee may, by an assessment made not later than two years from the date when the tax became payable, be assessed and charged (in the name of the donor) to capital gains tax on an amount not exceeding the amount of the chargeable gain so accruing, and not exceeding the grossed up amount of that capital gains tax unpaid at the time when he is so assessed, grossing up at the marginal rate of tax, that is to say taking capital gains tax on a chargeable gain at the amount which would not have been chargeable but for that chargeable gain.

(2) A person paying any amount of tax in pursuance of this section shall be entitled to recover a sum of that amount from the donor.

(3) References in this section to a donor include, in the case of an individual who has died, references to his personal representatives.

(4) In this section references to a gift include references to any transaction otherwise than by way of a bargain made at arm's length so far as money or money's worth passes under the transaction without full consideration in money or money's worth, and " donor " and " donee " shall be construed accordingly ; and this section shall apply in relation to a gift made by two or more donors with the necessary modifications and subject to any necessary apportionments.

Partnerships.

60. Where two or more persons carry on a trade or business in partnership—

    (a) tax in respect of chargeable gains accruing to them on the disposal of any partnership assets shall, in Scotland as well as elsewhere in the United Kingdom, be assessed and charged on them separately, and

(*b*) any partnership dealings shall be treated as dealings by the partners and not by the firm as such, and

(*c*) section 153(1)(2) of the Taxes Act (residence of partnerships) shall apply in relation to tax chargeable in pursuance of this Act as it applies in relation to income **tax.**

61.—(1) In relation to assets held by a person as trustee or assignee in bankruptcy or under a deed of arrangement this Act shall apply as if the assets were vested in, and the acts of the trustee or assignee in relation to the assets were the acts of, the bankrupt or debtor (acquisitions from or disposals to him by the bankrupt or debtor being disregarded accordingly), and tax in respect of any chargeable gains which accrue to any such trustee or assignee shall be assessable on and recoverable from him.

Insolvents' assets.

(2) Assets held by a trustee or assignee in bankruptcy or under a deed of arrangement at the death of the bankrupt or debtor shall for the purposes of this Act be regarded as held by a personal representative of the deceased and—

(*a*) subsection (1) above shall not apply after the death, and

(*b*) section 49(1) above (under which assets passing on a death are deemed to be acquired by the persons on whom they devolve) shall apply as if any assets held by a trustee or assignee in bankruptcy or under a deed of arrangement at the death of the bankrupt or debtor were assets of which the deceased was competent to dispose and which then devolved on the trustee or assignee as if he were a personal representative.

(3) Assets vesting in a trustee in bankruptcy after the death of the bankrupt or debtor shall for the purposes of this Act be regarded as held by a personal representative of the deceased, and subsection (1) above shall not apply.

(4) The definition of " settled property " in section 51 above shall not include any property as being property held by a trustee or assignee in bankruptcy or under a deed of arrangement.

(5) In this section " deed of arrangement " means a deed of arrangement to which the Deeds of Arrangement Act 1914 or any corresponding enactment forming part of the law of Scotland or Northern Ireland applies.

1914 c. 47.

62.—(1) This section shall apply where a person acquires an asset and the person making the disposal is connected with him.

(2) Without prejudice to the generality of section 19(3) above the person acquiring the asset and the person making the disposal shall be treated as parties to a transaction otherwise than by way of a bargain made at arm's length.

(3) If on the disposal a loss accrues to the person making the disposal, it shall not be deductible except from a chargeable gain accruing to him on some other disposal of an asset to the person acquiring the asset mentioned in subsection (1) above, being a disposal made at a time when they are connected persons:

Provided that this subsection shall not apply to a disposal by way of gift in settlement if the gift and the income from it is wholly or primarily applicable for educational, cultural or recreational purposes, and the persons benefiting from the application for those purposes are confined to members of an association of persons for whose benefit the gift was made, not being persons all or most of whom are connected persons.

(4) Where the asset mentioned in subsection (1) above is an option to enter into a sale or other transaction given by the person making the disposal a loss accruing to the person acquiring the asset shall not be an allowable loss unless it accrues on a disposal of the option at arm's length to a person who is not connected with him.

(5) In a case where the asset mentioned in subsection (1) above is subject to any right or restriction enforceable by the person making the disposal, or by a person connected with him, then (the amount of the consideration for the acquisition being, in accordance with subsection (2) above, deemed to be equal to the market value of the asset) that market value shall be—

(a) what its market value would be if not subject to the right or restriction, minus—

(b) the market value of the right or restriction or the amount by which its extinction would enhance the value of the asset to its owner, whichever is the less:

Provided that if the right or restriction is of such a nature that its enforcement would or might effectively destroy or substantially impair the value of the asset without bringing any countervailing advantage either to the person making the disposal or a person connected with him or is an option or other right to acquire the asset or, in the case of incorporeal property, is a right to extinguish the asset in the hands of the person giving the consideration by forfeiture or merger or otherwise, that market value of the asset shall be determined, and the amount of the gain accruing on the disposal shall be computed, as if the right or restriction did not exist.

(6) Subsection (5) above shall not apply to a right of forfeiture or other right exercisable on breach of a covenant contained in a lease of land or other property, and shall not apply to any right or restriction under a mortgage or other charge.

63.—(1) Any question whether a person is connected with another shall for the purposes of this Act be determined in accordance with the following subsections of this section (any provision that one person is connected with another being taken to mean that they are connected with one another).

(2) A person is connected with an individual if that person is the individual's husband or wife, or is a relative, or the husband or wife of a relative, of the individual or of the individual's husband or wife.

(3) A person, in his capacity as trustee of a settlement, is connected with any individual who in relation to the settlement is a settlor, with any person who is connected with such an individual and with a body corporate which, under section 454 of the Taxes Act, is deemed to be connected with that settlement ("settlement" and "settlor" having for the purposes of this subsection the meanings assigned to them by subsection (3) of the said section 454).

(4) Except in relation to acquisitions or disposals of partnership assets pursuant to bona fide commercial arrangements, a person is connected with any person with whom he is in partnership, and with the husband or wife or a relative of any individual with whom he is in partnership.

(5) A company is connected with another company—

    (*a*) if the same person has control of both, or a person has control of one and persons connected with him, or he and persons connected with him, have control of the other, or

    (*b*) if a group of two or more persons has control of each company, and the groups either consist of the same persons or could be regarded as consisting of the same persons by treating (in one or more cases) a member of either group as replaced by a person with whom he is connected.

(6) A company is connected with another person, if that person has control of it or if that person and persons connected with him together have control of it.

(7) Any two or more persons acting together to secure or exercise control of a company shall be treated in relation to that company as connected with one another and with any person

PART III   acting on the directions of any of them to secure or exercise control of the company.

(8) In this section " relative " means brother, sister, ancestor or lineal descendant.

PART IV

SHARES AND SECURITIES

CHAPTER I

GENERAL

Interpretation.   **64.**—(1) In this Act, unless the context otherwise requires—

" gilt-edged securities " has the meaning given by Schedule 2 to this Act,

" shares " includes stock,

" class ", in relation to shares or securities, means a class of shares or securities of any one company.

(2) For the purposes of this Act shares or debentures comprised in any letter of allotment or similar instrument shall be treated as issued unless the right to the shares or debentures thereby conferred remains provisional until accepted, and there has been no acceptance.

Rules of identification

Pooling.   **65.**—(1) This section has effect subject to—

(*a*) section 66 below, and

(*b*) paragraphs 3 and 13(2) of Schedule 5 to this Act,

and this section shall not apply to gilt-edged securities.

(2) Any number of securities of the same class held by one person in one capacity shall for the purposes of this Act be regarded as indistinguishable parts of a single asset (in this section referred to as a holding) growing or diminishing on the occasions on which additional securities of the class in question are acquired, or some of the securities of the class in question are disposed of.

(3) Without prejudice to the generality of subsection (2) above, a disposal of securities in a holding, other than the disposal outright of the entire holding, is a disposal of part of an asset and the provisions of this Act relating to the computation of a gain accruing on a disposal of part of an asset shall apply accordingly.

(4) Shares, or securities of a company, shall not be treated for the purposes of this section as being of the same class unless they are so treated by the practice of a recognised stock exchange in the United Kingdom or elsewhere or would be so treated if dealt with on such a stock exchange, but shall be treated in accordance with this section notwithstanding that they are identified in some other way by the disposal or by the transfer or delivery giving effect to it.

(5) This section shall apply separately in relation to any securities held by a person to whom they were issued as an employee of the company or of any other person on terms which restrict his rights to dispose of them, so long as those terms are in force, and, while applying separately to any such securities, shall have effect as if the owner held them in a capacity other than that in which he holds any other securities of the same class.

(6) Nothing in this section shall be taken as affecting the manner in which the market value of any asset is to be ascertained.

(7) In this section " securities " means—

    (*a*) shares, or securities of a company, and

    (*b*) subject to the exclusion of gilt-edged securities in sub-section (1) above, any other assets where they are of a nature to be dealt in without identifying the particular assets disposed of or acquired.

66.—(1) The following provisions shall apply where securities Disposal on of the same kind are acquired or disposed of by the same or before person on the same day and in the same capacity— day of acquisition.

    (*a*) all the securities so acquired shall be treated as acquired by a single transaction and all the securities so disposed of shall be treated as disposed of by a single transaction, and

    (*b*) all the securities so acquired shall, so far as their quantity does not exceed that of the securities so disposed of, be identified with those securities.

(2) Where the quantity of the securities so disposed of exceeds the quantity of the securities so acquired, then so far as the excess—

    (*a*) is not required by paragraph 2(2), 3(3) or 13(3) of Schedule 5 to this Act to be identified with securities held on or acquired before 6th April 1965, and

    (*b*) cannot be treated under section 65 above as diminishing a holding, it shall be treated as diminishing a quantity subsequently acquired, and a quantity so acquired at an earlier date, rather than one so acquired at a later date.

(3) Shares shall not be treated for the purposes of this section as being of the same kind unless they are treated as being of the same class by the practice of a recognised stock exchange in the United Kingdom or elsewhere or would be so treated if dealt with on such a stock exchange.

(4) In this section " securities " includes shares and any assets dealt with without identifying the particular assets disposed of or acquired, and in the case of gilt-edged securities subsection (2) above has effect subject to section 68 below.

Gilt-edged securities

Exemption for long-term gains.

67.—(1) A gain which accrues on the disposal by any person of gilt-edged securities shall not be a chargeable gain except where the disposal occurs within 12 months after the acquisition of the securities.

(2) So much of subsection (1) above as excepts a disposal occurring within 12 months after the acquisition of the securities shall not apply where the person disposing of the securities had acquired them—

    (*a*) by devolution on death or as legatee, or

    (*b*) if they were settled property, on becoming absolutely entitled thereto as against the trustee.

(3) Where, in the case of a man and his wife, section 44 above applies in relation to the acquisition of any securities by the one from the other, and the one making the acquisition subsequently disposes of the securities by a disposal to which that section does not apply, he shall be treated for the purposes of the exception in subsection (1) above as if he had acquired the securities when the other did.

Identification (general).

68.—(1) The following provisions shall apply, for the purpose of identifying gilt-edged securities disposed of by any person with securities of the same kind acquired by him in the same capacity.

(2) Securities disposed of at an earlier date shall be identified before securities disposed of at a later date, and their identification shall have effect also for determining what securities might be comprised in the later disposal.

(3) Securities disposed of shall be identified with securities acquired within the twelve months preceding the disposal rather than with securities not so acquired, and with securities so acquired at an earlier date rather than with securities so acquired at a later date.

(4) This section has effect subject to section 66(1) above, and PART IV
69 below.

69.—(1) Where, in the case of a man and his wife living with Identification:
him, one of them— disposal to
husband or
    (a) disposes of gilt-edged securities of any kind to the other, wife and
       and third person.

    (b) disposes of gilt-edged securities of the same kind to a
       third person,

then, if under the preceding provisions of this Chapter any of
the securities disposed of to the husband or wife would be
identified with securities acquired within the twelve months
preceding the disposal and any of the securities disposed of to
the third person with securities not so acquired, the securities
disposed of to the third person shall be identified with securities
so acquired before any securities disposed of to the husband or
wife are so identified.

(2) If there is more than one disposal to the wife or husband,
or to a third party, the provisions of this section shall be applied
to securities disposed of at an earlier date before they are applied
to securities disposed of at a later date, and the identification
of the securities disposed of at the earlier date shall have effect
also for determining what securities might be comprised in the
later disposal.

70.—(1) Where a loss accrues to a person on the disposal of Re-acquisition
gilt-edged securities and he re-acquires the same securities after sale at a
within the prescribed period after the disposal that loss shall not loss.
be deductible except from a chargeable gain accruing to him on
the disposal of the securities re-acquired.

(2) Where a person disposes of gilt-edged securities and
acquires gilt-edged securities of the same kind within the
prescribed period after the disposal he shall be treated for the
purposes of subsection (1) above as re-acquiring the securities
disposed of (or such quantity of them as does not exceed the
quantity acquired) but so that—

    (a) there cannot be in relation to the same disposal more
       than one re-acquisition of the same security, nor can
       there be by the same acquisition of a security a
       re-acquisition in relation to more than one disposal,
       and

    (b) if an acquisition could be treated as a re-acquisition of
       securities disposed of either at an earlier or at a later
       date it shall be treated as a re-acquisition of the
       securities disposed of at the earlier date, and

O 3

(c) if securities disposed of by the same disposal could be treated as re-acquired at an earlier or at a later date they shall be treated as re-acquired at the earlier date.

(3) Where a person who holds gilt-edged securities (the " original holding ") acquires securities of the same kind (an " additional holding ") and within the prescribed period after the acquisition disposes of securities of that kind, he shall be treated for the purposes of subsection (1) above as if he had within the prescribed period after the disposal re-acquired the securities disposed of or such quantity of them as does not exceed the original holding or the additional holding, whichever is the less.

Paragraphs (a), (b) and (c) of subsection (2) above shall have effect in relation to the acquisition of the additional holding as if it were a re-acquisition of the securities disposed of.

(4) In the case of a man and his wife living with him—

(a) the preceding provisions of this section shall, with the necessary modifications, apply also where a loss on the disposal accrues to one of them and the acquisition after the disposal is made by the other,

(b) paragraph (a) above shall have effect in relation to subsection (3) above as if the acquisition of the additional holding were an acquisition after the disposal.

(5) In the case of companies in the same group subsections (1), (2) and (3) above shall, with the necessary modifications, apply also where a loss on the disposal accrues to one of them and the acquisition is made by the other.

(6) In this section references to the acquisition of securities shall not include references—

(a) to acquisition as trading stock, or

(b) in the case of a company which is a member of a group, to acquisition from another company which is a member of that group throughout the prescribed period before and after the disposal.

(7) In this section—

" group " has the meaning given in section 272 of the Taxes Act ;

" the prescribed period " means—

(a) in the case of an acquisition through a stock exchange, one month ;

(b) in the case of an acquisition otherwise than as aforesaid, six months ;

" trading stock ", in relation to a company carrying on life assurance business as defined in section 323 of the Taxes Act, does not include investments held in connection with that business except in so far as they are referable to general annuity business or pension business as defined in that section ;

PART IV

and references to a person's holding, acquiring and disposing of securities are references to his doing so in the same capacity.

Savings certificates, etc.

71.—(1) Savings certificates and non-marketable securities issued under the National Loans Act 1968 or the National Loans Act 1939, or any corresponding enactment forming part of the law of Northern Ireland, shall not be chargeable assets, and accordingly no chargeable gain shall accrue on their disposal.

Exemption for government non-marketable securities.

1968 c. 13.

1939 c. 117.

(2) In this section—

(a) " savings certificates " means savings certificates issued under section 12 of the National Loans Act 1968, or section 7 of the National Debt Act 1958, or section 59 of the Finance Act 1920, and any war savings certificates as defined in section 9(3) of the National Debt Act 1972, together with any savings certificates issued under any enactment forming part of the law of Northern Ireland and corresponding to the said enactments, and

1958 (7 & 8 Eliz. 2) c. 6.

1920 c. 18.

1972 c. 65.

(b) " non-marketable securities " means securities which are not transferable, or which are transferable only with the consent of some Minister of the Crown, or the consent of a department of the Government of Northern Ireland, or only with the consent of the National Debt Commissioners.

Capital distribution in respect of shares, etc.

72.—(1) Where a person receives or becomes entitled to receive in respect of shares in a company any capital distribution from the company (other than a new holding as defined in section 77 below) he shall be treated as if he had in consideration of that capital distribution disposed of an interest in the shares.

Distribution which is not a new holding within Chapter II.

(2) If the inspector is satisfied that the amount distributed is small, as compared with the value of the shares in respect of which it is distributed, and so directs—

(a) the occasion of the capital distribution shall not be treated for the purposes of this Act as a disposal of the asset, and (*b*) the amount distributed shall be deducted from any expenditure allowable under this Act as a deduction in computing a gain or loss on the disposal of the shares by the person receiving or becoming entitled to receive the distribution of capital.

(3) A person who is dissatisfied with the refusal of the inspector to give a direction under this section may appeal to the Commissioners having jurisdiction on an appeal against an assessment to tax in respect of a gain accruing on the disposal.

(4) Where the allowable expenditure is less than the amount distributed (or is nil)—

    (*a*) subsections (2) and (3) above shall not apply, and

    (*b*) if the recipient so elects (and there is any allowable expenditure)—

        (i) the amount distributed shall be reduced by the amount of the allowable expenditure, and

        (ii) none of that expenditure shall be allowable as a deduction in computing a gain accruing on the occasion of the capital distribution, or on any subsequent occasion.

In this subsection " allowable expenditure " means the expenditure which immediately before the occasion of the capital distribution was attributable to the shares under paragraphs (*a*) and (*b*) of section 32(1) above.

(5) In this section—

    (*a*) the " amount distributed " means the amount or value of the capital distribution,

    (*b*) " capital distribution " means any distribution from a company, including a distribution in the course of dissolving or winding up the company, in money or money's worth except a distribution which in the hands of the recipient constitutes income for the purposes of income tax.

Disposal of right to acquire shares.

73.—(1) Where a person receives or becomes entitled to receive in respect of any shares in a company a provisional allotment of shares in or debentures of the company and he disposes of his rights section 72 above shall apply as if the amount of the consideration for the disposal were a capital distribution received by him from the company in respect of the first-mentioned shares, and as if that person had, instead of disposing of the rights, disposed of an interest in those shares.

(2) If under Schedule 5 to this Act it is to be assumed that, at a time after the creation of the rights and before their disposal, the said person sold and immediately re-acquired the

shares in respect of which the rights were created, the same assumption shall be made as respect the rights.

(3) This section shall apply in relation to rights obtained in respect of debentures of a company as it applies in relation to rights obtained in respect of shares in a company.

Close companies

74.—(1) If in pursuance of paragraph 5 of Schedule 16 to the Finance Act 1972 (consequences for income tax of apportionment of income etc. of close company) a person is assessed to income tax, then, in the computation under Chapter II of Part II of this Act of the gain accruing on a disposal by him of any shares forming part of his interest in the company to which the relevant apportionment relates, the amount of the income tax paid by him, so far as attributable to those shares, shall be allowable as a deduction.

Disposal of shares: relief in respect of income tax consequent on shortfall in distributions. 1972 c. 41.

(2) Subsection (1) above shall not apply in relation to tax charged in respect of undistributed income which has, before the disposal, been subsequently distributed and is then exempt from tax by virtue of sub-paragraph (6) of the said paragraph 5 or in relation to tax treated as having been paid by virtue of sub-paragraph (2)(b) of that paragraph.

(3) For the purposes of this section the income assessed to tax shall be the highest part of the individual's income for the year of assessment in question, but so that if the highest part of the said income is taken into account under this section in relation to an assessment to tax the next highest part shall be taken into account in relation to any other relevant assessment, and so on.

(4) For the purpose of identifying shares forming part of an interest in a company with shares subsequently disposed of which are of the same class, shares bought at an earlier time shall be deemed to have been disposed of before shares bought at a later time.

(5) The provisions of this section shall be construed as if this section formed part of the said paragraph 5.

75.—(1) If after 6th April 1965 a company which is a close company transfers an asset to any person otherwise than by way of a bargain made at arm's length and for a consideration of an amount or value less than the market value of the asset an amount equal to the difference shall be apportioned among the issued shares of the company, and the holders of those shares shall be treated in accordance with the following provisions of this section.

Shares in close company transferring assets at an undervalue.

(2) For the purposes of the computation under Chapter II of Part II of this Act of a gain accruing on the disposal of any of those shares by the person owning them on the date of transfer an amount equal to the amount so apportioned to that share shall be excluded from the expenditure allowable as a deduction under section 32(1)(a) above from the consideration for the disposal.

(3) If the person owning any of the said shares at the date of transfer is itself a close company an amount equal to the amount apportioned to the shares so owned under subsection (1) above to that close company shall be apportioned among the issued shares of that close company, and the holders of those shares shall be treated in accordance with subsection (2) above, and so on through any number of close companies.

(4) This section shall not apply where the transfer of the asset is a disposal to which section 273(1) of the Taxes Act (transfers within a group of companies) applies.

Share option schemes

76. Section 19(3) above (assets deemed acquired and disposed of at market value) shall not apply in calculating the consideration for the acquisition of shares in pursuance of a share option scheme as defined in Schedule 12 to the Finance Act 1972.

CHAPTER II

REORGANISATION OF SHARE CAPITAL, CONVERSION OF SECURITIES, ETC.

Reorganisation or reduction of share capital

77.—(1) For the purposes of this section and sections 78 to 81 below " reorganisation " means a reorganisation or reduction of a company's share capital, and in relation to the reorganisation—

(a) " original shares " means shares held before and concerned in the reorganisation,

(b) " new holding " means, in relation to any original shares, the shares in and debentures of the company which as a result of the reorganisation represent the original shares (including such, if any, of the original shares as remain).

(2) The reference in subsection (1) above to the reorganisation of a company's share capital includes—

(a) any case where persons are, whether for payment or not, allotted shares in or debentures of the company in respect of and in proportion to (or as nearly as may be in proportion to) their holdings of shares in the company or of any class of shares in the company, and

(*b*) any case where there are more than one class of share and the rights attached to shares of any class are altered.

(3) The reference in subsection (1) above to a reduction of share capital does not include the paying off of redeemable share capital, and where shares in a company are redeemed by the company otherwise than by the issue of shares or debentures (with or without other consideration) and otherwise than in a liquidation, the shareholder shall be treated as disposing of the shares at the time of the redemption.

78. Subject to sections 79 to 81 below, a reorganisation shall not be treated as involving any disposal of the original shares or any acquisition of the new holding or any part of it, but the original shares (taken as a single asset) and the new holding (taken as a single asset) shall be treated as the same asset acquired as the original shares were acquired.

Equation of original shares and new holding.

79.—(1) Where, on a reorganisation, a person gives or becomes liable to give any consideration for his new holding or any part of it, that consideration shall in relation to any disposal of the new holding or any part of it be treated as having been given for the original shares, and if the new holding or part of it is disposed of with a liability attaching to it in respect of that consideration, the consideration given for the disposal shall be adjusted accordingly:

Consideration given or received by holder.

Provided that there shall not be treated as consideration given for the new holding or any part of it any surrender, cancellation or other alteration of the original shares or of the rights attached thereto, or any consideration consisting of any application, in paying up the new holding or any part of it, of assets of the company or of any dividend or other distribution declared out of those assets but not made.

(2) Where on a reorganisation a person receives (or is deemed to receive), or becomes entitled to receive, any consideration, other than the new holding, for the disposal of an interest in the original shares, and in particular—

(*a*) where under section 72 above he is to be treated as if he had in consideration of a capital distribution disposed of an interest in the original shares, or

(*b*) where he receives (or is deemed to receive) consideration from other shareholders in respect of a surrender of rights derived from the original shares, he shall be treated as if the new holding resulted from his having for that consideration disposed of an interest in the original shares (but without prejudice to the original shares and the new holding being treated in accordance with section 78 above as the same asset).

(3) Where for the purpose of subsection (2) above it is necessary in computing the gain or loss accruing on the disposal of the interest in the original shares mentioned in subsection (2) above to apportion the cost of acquisition of the original shares between what is disposed of and what is retained, the apportionment shall be made in the like manner as under section 80(1) below.

Part disposal of new holding.

80.—(1) Where for the purpose of computing the gain or loss accruing to a person from the acquisition and disposal of any part of the new holding it is necessary to apportion the cost of acquisition of any of the original shares between what is disposed of and what is retained, the apportionment shall be made by reference to market value at the date of the disposal (with such adjustment of the market value of any part of the new holding as may be required to offset any liability attaching thereto but forming part of the cost to be apportioned).

(2) This section has effect subject to section 81(2) below.

Composite new holdings.

81.—(1) This section shall apply to a new holding—

(a) if it consists of more than one class of shares in or debentures of the company and one or more of those classes is of shares or debentures which, at any time not later than the end of the period of three months beginning with the date on which the reorganisation took effect, or of such longer period as the Board may by notice in writing allow, had quoted market values on a recognised stock exchange in the United Kingdom or elsewhere, or

(b) if it consists of more than one class of rights of unit holders and one or more of those classes is of rights the prices of which were published daily by the managers of the scheme at any time not later than the end of that period of three months (or longer if so allowed).

(2) Where for the purpose of computing the gain or loss accruing to a person from the acquisition and disposal of the whole or any part of any class of shares or debentures or rights of unit holders forming part of a new holding to which this section applies it is necessary to apportion costs of acquisition between what is disposed of and what is retained, the cost of

acquisition of the new holding shall first be apportioned between   PART IV
the entire classes of shares or debentures or rights of which
it consists by reference to market value on the first day (whether
that day fell before the reorganisation took effect or later) on
which market values or prices were quoted or published for the
shares, debentures or rights as mentioned in subsection (1)(*a*) or
(1)(*b*) above (with such adjustment of the market value of any
class as may be required to offset any liability attaching thereto
but forming part of the cost to be apportioned).

(3) For the purposes of this section the day on which a reorganisation involving the allotment of shares or debentures
or unit holders' rights takes effect is the day following the day
on which the right to renounce any allotment expires.

Conversion of securities

82.—(1) Sections 78 to 81 above shall apply with any neces- Equation of
sary adaptations in relation to the conversion of securities as converted
they apply in relation to a reorganisation (that is to say a re- securities and
organisation or reduction of a company's share capital). new holding.

(2) This section has effect subject to sections 83 and 84
below.

(3) For the purposes of this section and section 83 below—

    (*a*) " conversion of securities " includes—

        (i) a conversion of securities of a company into
shares in the company, and

        (ii) a conversion at the option of the holder of the
securities converted as an alternative to the redemp-
ion of those securities for cash, and

        (iii) any exchange of securities effected in
pursuance of any enactment (including an enactment
passed after this Act) which provides for the compulsory acquisition of any shares or securities and
the issue of securities or other securities instead,

    (*b*) " security " includes any loan stock or similar security
whether of the Government of the United Kingdom
or of any other government, or of any public or local
authority in the United Kingdom or elsewhere, or of
any company, and whether secured or unsecured.

83.—(1) This section applies where, on a conversion of securi- Premiums on
ties, a person receives, or becomes entitled to receive, any sum conversion of
of money (in this section called " the premium ") which is by securities.
way of consideration (in addition to his new holding) for the
disposal of the converted securities.

(2) If the inspector is satisfied that the premium is small, as compared with the value of the converted securities, and so directs—

(a) receipt of the premium shall not be treated for the purposes of this Act as a disposal of part of the converted securities, and

(b) the premium shall be deducted from any expenditure allowable under this Act as a deduction in computing a gain or loss on the disposal of the new holding by the person receiving or becoming entitled to receive the premium.

(3) A person who is dissatisfied with the refusal of the inspector to give a direction under subsection (2) above may appeal to the Commissioners having jurisdiction on an appeal against an assessment to tax in respect of a gain accruing to him on a disposal of the securities.

(4) Where the allowable expenditure is less than the premium (or is nil)—

(a) subsections (2) and (3) above shall not apply, and

(b) if the recipient so elects (and there is any allowable expenditure)—

(i) the amount of the premium shall be reduced by the amount of the allowable expenditure, and

(ii) none of that expenditure shall be allowable as a deduction in computing a gain accruing on the occasion of the conversion, or on any subsequent occasion.

(5) In subsection (4) above " allowable expenditure " means expenditure which immediately before the conversion was attributable to the converted securities under paragraphs (a) and (b) of section 32(1) above.

Compensation stock.

84.—(1) This section has effect where gilt-edged securities are exchanged for shares in pursuance of any enactment (including an enactment passed after this Act) which provides for the compulsory acquisition of any shares and the issue of gilt-edged securities instead.

(2) The exchange shall not constitute a conversion of securities within section 82 above and accordingly the gilt-edged securities shall not be treated as having been acquired on any date earlier than that on which they were issued or for any consideration other than the value of the shares as determined for the purposes of the exchange.

(3) The exchange shall be treated as not involving any disposal of the shares by the person from whom they were compulsorily acquired but—

> (a) there shall be calculated the gain or loss that would have accrued to him if he had then disposed of the shares for a consideration equal to the value mentioned in subsection (2) above, and

> (b) on a subsequent disposal of the whole or part of the gilt-edged securities by the person to whom they were issued—

>> (i) there shall be deemed to accrue to him (in addition to any gain or loss that actually accrues) the whole or a corresponding part of the gain or loss mentioned in paragraph (a) above, and

>> (ii) if the disposal is within section 67(1) above (exemption for gilt-edged securities) that section shall have effect only in relation to any gain or loss that actually accrues and not in relation to any gain or loss that is deemed to accrue as aforesaid.

(4) Where a person to whom gilt-edged securities of any kind were issued as mentioned in subsection (1) above disposes of securities of that kind, the securities of which he disposes—

> (a) shall, so far as possible, be identified with any securities of that kind which he has acquired otherwise than as mentioned in subsection (1) above within the twelve months preceding the disposal, and

> (b) so far as they cannot be identified as aforesaid, shall be identified (without regard to sections 66, 68(3) and 69 above) with securities which were issued to him as mentioned in subsection (1) above, taking those issued earlier before those issued later.

(5) Subsection (3)(b) above shall not apply to any disposal falling within the provisions of—

> (a) section 44(1) above (disposals between husband and wife),

> (b) section 49(4) above (disposals by personal representatives to legatees), or

> (c) section 273(1) of the Taxes Act (disposals within a group of companies);

but a person who has acquired the securities on a disposal falling within those provisions (and without there having been a previous disposal not falling within those provisions or a devolution on death) shall be treated for the purposes of subsections (3)(b) and (4) above as if the securities had been issued to him.

(6) Where the gilt-edged securities to be exchanged for any shares are not issued until after the date on which the shares are compulsorily acquired but on that date a right to the securities is granted, this section shall have effect as if the exchange had taken place on that date, as if references to the issue of the securities and the person to whom they were issued were references to the grant of the right and the person to whom it was granted and references to the disposal of the securities included references to disposals of the rights.

(7) In this section " shares " includes securities within the meaning of section 82 above.

(8) This section has effect subject to section 54 of the Finance Act 1976 (compulsory acquisition from certain companies of aircraft and shipbuilding shares).

Company reconstructions and amalgamations

85.—(1) Subsection (3) below has effect where a company (company A) issues shares or debentures to a person in exchange for shares in or debenture of another company (company B) and—

    (a) company A holds, or in consequence of the exchange will hold, more than one quarter of the ordinary share capital (as defined in section 526(5) of the Taxes Act) of company B, or

    (b) company A issues the shares or debentures in exchange for shares as the result of a general offer—

        (i) which is made to members of company B or any class of them (with or without exceptions for persons connected with company A), and

        (ii) which is made in the first instance on a condition such that if it were satisfied company A would have control of company B.

(2) Subsection (3) below also has effect where under section 86 below persons are to be treated as exchanging shares or debentures for shares or debentures held by them in consequence of the arrangement there mentioned.

(3) Subject to the provisions of sections 87 and 88 below, sections 78 to 81 above shall apply with any necessary adaptations as if the two companies mentioned in subsection (1) above, or as the case may be in section 86 below, were the same company and the exchange were a reorganisation of its share capital.

86.—(1) Where—

(*a*) an arrangement between a company and the persons holding shares in or debentures of the company, or any class of such shares or debentures, is entered into for the purposes of or in connection with a scheme of reconstruction or amalgamation, and

(*b*) under the arrangement another company issues shares or debentures to those persons in respect of and in proportion to (or as nearly as may be in proportion to) their holdings of shares in or debentures of the first-mentioned company, but the shares in or debentures of the first-mentioned company are either retained by those persons or cancelled,

then those persons shall be treated as exchanging the first-mentioned shares or debentures for those held by them in consequence of the arrangement (any shares or debentures retained being for this purpose regarded as if they had been cancelled and replaced by a new issue), and subsections (2) and (3) of section 85 above shall apply accordingly.

(2) In this section " scheme of reconstruction or amalgamation " means a scheme for the reconstruction of any company or companies or the amalgamation of any two or more companies, and references to shares or debentures being retained include their being retained with altered rights or in an altered form whether as the result of reduction, consolidation, division or otherwise.

(3) This section, and section 85(2) above, shall apply in relation to a company which has no share capital as if references to shares in or debentures of a company included references to any interests in the company possessed by members of the company.

87.—(1) Subject to subsection (2) below, and section 88 below, neither section 85 nor section 86 above shall apply to any issue by a company of shares in or debentures of that company in exchange for or in respect of shares in or debentures of another company unless the exchange, reconstruction or amalgamation in question is effected for bona fide commercial reasons and does not form part of a scheme or arrangements of which the main purpose, or one of the main purposes, is avoidance of liability to capital gains tax or corporation tax.

(2) Subsection (1) above shall not affect the operation of section 85 or 86 in any case where the person to whom the shares or debentures are issued does not hold more than 5 per cent. of, or of any class of, the shares in or debentures of the second company mentioned in subsection (1) above.

(3) For the purposes of subsection (2) above shares or debentures held by persons connected with the person there mentioned shall be treated as held by him.

(4) If any tax assessed on a person (the chargeable person) by virtue of subsection (1) above is not paid within six months from the date when it is payable, any other person who—

(a) holds all or any part of the shares or debentures that were issued to the chargeable person, and

(b) has acquired them without there having been, since their acquisition by the chargeable person, any disposal of them not falling within section 44(1) above or section 273 of the Taxes Act (disposals between spouses or members of a group of companies),

may, at any time within two years from the time when the tax became payable, be assessed and charged (in the name of the chargeable person) to all or, as the case may be, a corresponding part of the unpaid tax ; and a person paying any amount of tax under this subsection shall be entitled to recover a sum of that amount from the chargeable person.

(5) In this section references to shares or debentures include references to any interests or options to which this Chapter applies by virtue of section 86(3) above (interests in a company with no share capital) or section 139 below (quoted options).

Procedure for clearance in advance.

88.—(1) Section 87 above shall not affect the operation of section 85 or 86 above in any case where, before the issue is made, the Board have, on the application of either company mentioned in section 87(1) above, notified the company that the Board are satisfied that the exchange, reconstruction or amalgamation will be effected for bona fide commercial reasons and will not form part of any such scheme or arrangements as are mentioned in section 87(1) above.

(2) Any application under subsection (1) above shall be in writing and shall contain particulars of the operations that are to be effected and the Board may, within thirty days of the receipt of the application or of any further particulars previously required under this subsection, by notice require the applicant to furnish further particulars for the purpose of enabling the Board to make their decision ; and if any such notice is not complied with within thirty days or such longer period as the Board may allow, the Board need not proceed further on the application.

(3) The Board shall notify their decision to the applicant within thirty days of receiving the application or, if they give a notice under subsection (2) above, within thirty days of the notice being complied with.

(4) If the Board notify the applicant that they are not satisfied as mentioned in subsection (1) above or do not notify their decision to the applicant within the time required by subsection (3) above, the applicant may within thirty days of the notification or of that time require the Board to transmit the application, together with any notice given and further particulars furnished under subsection (2) above, to the Special Commissioners ; and in that event any notification by the Special Commissioners shall have effect for the purposes of subsection (1) above as if it were a notification by the Board.

(5) If any particulars furnished under this section do not fully and accurately disclose all facts and considerations material for the decision of the Board or the Special Commissioners, any resulting notification that the Board or Commissioners are satisfied as mentioned in subsection (1) above shall be void.

Stock dividends

89.—(1) In applying section 79(1) above in relation to the Stock issue of any share capital to which section 34 of the Finance dividends: (No. 2) Act 1975 (stock dividends) applies as involving a re- consideration organisation of the company's share capital, there shall be holding. allowed, as consideration given for so much of the new holding 1975 c. 45. as was issued as mentioned in—

    (*a*) subsection (4), (5) or (6) of the said section 34, or

    (*b*) paragraph 3(1) of Schedule 8 to that Act,

(read in each case with subsection (3) of the said section 34) an amount equal to what is, for that much of the new holding, the appropriate amount in cash within the meaning of paragraph 1 of the said Schedule 8.

(2) This section shall have effect notwithstanding the proviso to section 79(1) above.

90.—(1) This section applies where a company issues any Capital gains share capital to which section 34 of the Finance (No. 2) Act on certain 1975 applies in respect of shares in the company held by a stock person as trustee, and another person is at the time of the issue dividends. absolutely entitled thereto as against the trustee or would be so entitled but for being an infant or other person under disability (or two or more other persons are or would be jointly so entitled thereto).

(2) Notwithstanding paragraph (*a*) of section 77(2) above the case shall not constitute a reorganisation of the company's share capital for the purposes of sections 77 to 79 above.

(3) Notwithstanding section 19(3)(*a*) above (disposal at market value) the person who is or would be so entitled to the share

PART IV

1975 c. 45.

capital (or each of the persons who are or would be jointly so entitled thereto) shall be treated for the purposes of section 32(1) (*a*) above as having acquired that share capital, or his interest in it, for a consideration equal to the appropriate amount in cash within the meaning of paragraph 1 of Schedule 8 to the Finance (No. 2) Act 1975.

Quoted options

Application of Chapter II to quoted options.

91. The preceding provisions of this Chapter have effect subject to section 139 below (quoted option to be regarded for the purposes of this Chapter as the shares which could be acquired by exercising the option).

CHAPTER III

UNIT TRUSTS ETC.

Preliminary

Interpretation.

1958 c. 45.
1940 c. 9 (N.I.).

92. In this Act—

> (*a*) " unit trust scheme " has the meaning given by section 26(1) of the Prevention of Fraud (Investments) Act 1958 or section 22 of the Prevention of Fraud (Investments) Act (Northern Ireland) 1940,
>
> (*b*) " authorised unit trust " has the meaning given by section 358 of the Taxes Act,
>
> (*c*) " investment trust " has the meaning given by section 359 of the Taxes Act,
>
> (*d*) " court investment fund " means a common investment fund established under section 1 of the Administration of Justice Act 1965.

1965 c. 2.

Application of Act to unit trusts.

93. This Act shall apply in relation to any unit trust scheme as if—

> (*a*) the scheme were a company,
>
> (*b*) the rights of the unit holders were shares in the company, and
>
> (*c*) in the case of an authorised unit trust, the company were resident and ordinarily resident in the United Kingdom.

General

Reduction of tax liability on disposal of units or shares.

94.—(1) Subject to subsections (2) and (6) below, this section applies to disposals of shares in—

> (*a*) authorised unit trusts,
>
> (*b*) unit trust schemes to which section 97 below applies,
>
> (*c*) investment trusts, and
>
> (*d*) any court investment fund.

(2) Paragraphs (*a*), (*b*) and (*c*) of subsection (1) above do not apply to any share of a class to which there would not be attributable in a liquidation of the trust the whole or a substantial part—

> (*a*) of the assets of the trust representing gains on capital, or
>
> (*b*) if those assets would be so attributable to two or more classes of shares, of a proportion of those assets corresponding to the proportion of all the issued shares of those classes represented by the issued shares of the class in question.

Where there are shares on which different amounts have been paid up the proportion mentioned in paragraph (*b*) above shall be calculated by reference to the amount paid up on the issued share capital of each class of shares.

(3) Where gains accrue to a person in any year of assessment on any disposals to which this section applies, the capital gains tax to which he is chargeable for that year shall be reduced by a credit equal to whichever of the following amounts is the smallest—

> (*a*) the amount of that tax,
>
> (*b*) an amount equal to 10 per cent. of the total chargeable gains accruing to him in that year on disposals to which this section applies,
>
> (*c*) an amount equal to 10 per cent. of the total amount of chargeable gains accruing to him in that year on which capital gains tax is chargeable.

(4) Subsection (3) above shall have effect in relation to the corporation tax chargeable on a company for an accounting period in which gains accrue to it on any disposals to which this section applies as it has effect in relation to the capital gains tax chargeable on a person other than a company, and shall so have effect as if—

> (*a*) references to a year of assessment were references to an accounting period, and
>
> (*b*) for the total amount of chargeable gains mentioned in paragraph (*c*) of that subsection there were substituted the amount of gains charged to corporation tax for the accounting period in question increased, where subsection (5) below applies, in accordance with that subsection.

In this subsection " gains charged to corporation tax " means the profits on which corporation tax falls finally to be borne after deducting the income charged to corporation tax as defined in section 85(6) of the Finance Act 1972 (read with section 110(4) of that Act) except that, in relation to an accounting period for

1972 c. 41.

which the company claims a credit for foreign tax, those gains shall be determined in accordance with section 100(5) of that Act.

(5) In relation to an accounting period for which any reduction falls to be made under section 93 of the Finance Act 1972 in the amount to be included in respect of chargeable gains in the company's total profits, the gains mentioned in sub-section (4)(*b*) above shall be increased by multiplying by the inverse of the fraction of that amount remaining after the reduction ; and if under subsection (3) or (4) of the said section 93 the reduction falls to be made by reference to different portions of that amount, the increase under this subsection shall be made similarly, using the inverse of the fractions of those portions remaining after any reduction.

(6) Where a person disposes of a share—

    (*a*) which at the time of disposal is a qualifying share (that is to say, a share falling within subsection (1)(*a*), (*b*) or (*c*) above) but has not at all times while in the owner-ship of that person been a qualifying share, or

    (*b*) which at the time of disposal is not a qualifying share but has previously while in his ownership been such a share,

this section shall apply to the disposal, but for the purposes of subsection (3)(*b*) above the gain accruing on the disposal shall be treated as reduced in proportion to the time for which the share was in the ownership of that person without being a qualifying share.

(7) Where under Chapter II above the share of which a person disposes falls to be identified with another asset or other assets previously held by him, subsection (6) above shall have effect as if—

    (*a*) his period of ownership of the share disposed of included his period of ownership of the other asset or assets, and

    (*b*) the share disposed of had or had not been a qualifying share at any time during that additional period accord-ing to whether or not the other asset or any of those other assets was a qualifying share at that time.

(8) Where a person disposes of a share which at the time of disposal is a qualifying share and which he has received on a conversion of—

    (*a*) a share other than a qualifying share, or

    (*b*) loan stock,

previously held by him, being a conversion pursuant to rights in that behalf attached to the share or stock previously held, subsections (6) and (7) above shall have effect as if that share or stock had been a qualifying share throughout any time for which the company by which it was issued was a body of the kind mentioned in paragraph (*a*), (*b*) or (*c*) of subsection (1) above.

(9) Where the gain accruing on a disposal to which this section applies falls to be computed in accordance with paragraph 14(2)(*b*) of Schedule 5 to this Act (unquoted securities held before 6th April 1965 which are subsequently converted or exchanged)—

> (*a*) the period of ownership of the share disposed of shall not be treated under subsection (7)(*a*) above as having begun before the time mentioned in the said paragraph 14(2)(*b*) ; and

> (*b*) for the purposes of subsection (3)(*b*) above the gain shall be taken to be that mentioned in sub-paragraph (ii) of the said paragraph 14(2)(*b*) reduced, where applicable, in accordance with subsections (6) and (7) above.

(10) For the purposes of subsections (6) to (8) above no account shall be taken of any period of ownership before 6th April 1965 ; and nothing in Chapter II above shall be construed as enabling any asset to be treated as having been a qualifying share at any time when it was not such in fact.

(11) For the purposes of this section loan stock issued by an investment trust before 11th April 1972, being loan stock to which there would be attributable in a liquidation of the trust the whole of the assets of the trust representing gains on capital, shall be treated as shares in the trust falling within subsection (1) above.

Unit trusts

95. Nothing in any trust deed executed before 1st September 1972 and regulating any authorised unit trust, or any unit trust scheme to which section 97 below applies, shall preclude the managers of the trust or the trustee, in valuing the assets of the trust at any time during an accounting period, from making a deduction for any tax for which the trust may become liable in respect of its net gains in that period up to that time.

In this section " net gains " means the excess, if any, of chargeable gains over the allowable losses deductible from those gains as those gains and losses are computed for the charge to tax on the trust.

Valuation of assets and rights.

96. If throughout a year of assessment all the issued units in a unit trust scheme are assets such that any gain accruing if they were disposed of by the unit holder would be wholly exempt from capital gains tax or corporation tax (otherwise than by

Unit trusts for exempt unit holders.

reason of residence) gains accruing to the unit trust scheme in that year of assessment shall not be chargeable gains.

Unit trusts
for pension
schemes.
1970 c. 24.

97.—(1) This section applies to a unit trust scheme for any year of assessment if throughout that year all the issued units in the unit trust scheme constitute investments to which section 208(2) of the Taxes Act or section 21(7) of the Finance Act 1970 (pension schemes) applies, each being an investment such that any gain accruing if it were disposed of by the unit holder would either be wholly exempt from capital gains tax or corporation tax, or be so exempt as to not less than 85 per cent.

(2) Of all the gains accruing to the unit trust scheme in the year of assessment one-tenth (that is one-tenth of what would apart from this subsection be chargeable gains) shall be chargeable gains.

(3) The rate of capital gains tax payable on chargeable gains accruing to a unit trust scheme to which this section applies in the year of assessment shall be 10 per cent.

Transfer of
company's
assets to unit
trust which
later comes
within section
96 or 97.

98.—(1) Where section 267 of the Taxes Act (roll-over for assets transferred on company reconstruction or amalgamation) has applied on the transfer of a company's business (in whole or in part) to a unit trust scheme to which at the time of the transfer neither section 96 nor section 97 applied, then if—

(a) at any time after the transfer the unit trust scheme becomes in a year of assessment one to which either of those sections does apply, and

(b) at the beginning of that year of assessment the unit trust scheme still owns any of the assets of the business transferred,

the unit trust scheme shall be treated for all the purposes of this Act as if immediately after the transfer it had sold, and immediately re-acquired, the assets referred to in paragraph (b) above at their market value at that time.

(2) Notwithstanding any limitation on the time for making assessments, an assessment to corporation tax chargeable in consequence of subsection (1) above may be made at any time within six years after the end of the year of assessment referred to in subsection (1) above, and where under this section a unit trust scheme is to be treated as having disposed of, and re-acquired, an asset of a business, all such recomputations of liability in respect of other disposals and all such adjustments of tax, whether by way of assessment or by way of discharge or repayment of tax, as may be required in consequence of the provisions of this section shall be carried out.

Court investment funds etc.   PART IV

99.—(1) For the purposes of section 46 above (nominees and Funds in bare trustees) funds in court held by the Accountant General court. shall be regarded as held by him as nominee for the persons entitled to or interested in the funds, or as the case may be for their trustees.

(2) Where funds in court standing to an account are invested or, after investment, are realised the method by which the Accountant General effects the investment or the realisation of investments shall not affect the question whether there is for the purposes of this Act an acquisition, or as the case may be a disposal, of an asset representing funds in court standing to the account, and in particular there shall for those purposes be an acquisition or disposal of shares in a court investment fund notwithstanding that the investment in such shares of funds in court standing to an account, or the realisation of funds which have been so invested, is effected by setting off, in the Accountant General's accounts, investment in one account against realisation of investments in another.

(3) In this section " funds in court " means—

    (a) money in the Supreme Court, money in county courts and statutory deposits described in section 14 of the Administration of Justice Act 1965, and   1965 c. 2.

    (b) any such moneys as are mentioned in section 30 of the said Act of 1965 (which relates to Northern Ireland) and money in a county court in Northern Ireland,

and investments representing such money ; and references in this section to the Accountant General are references to the Accountant General of the Supreme Court of Judicature in England and, in relation to money within paragraph (b) above and investments representing such money, include references to the Accountant General of the Supreme Court of Judicature of Northern Ireland or any other person by whom such funds are held.

100. The rate of capital gains tax payable on chargeable Reduced rate gains accruing to a court investment fund shall be 10 per cent. of tax.

Part V

Land

Private residences

101.—(1) This section applies to a gain accruing to an individual so far as attributable to the disposal of, or of an interest in—

    (*a*) a dwelling-house or part of a dwelling-house which is, or has at any time in his period of ownership been, his only or main residence, or

    (*b*) land which he has for his own occupation and enjoyment with that residence as its garden or grounds up to the permitted area.

(2) In this section " the permitted area " means, subject to subsections (3) and (4) below, an area (inclusive of the site of the dwelling-house) of one acre.

(3) In any particular case the permitted area shall be such area, larger than one acre, as the Commissioners concerned may determine if satisfied that, regard being had to the size and character of the dwelling-house, that larger area is required for the reasonable enjoyment of it (or of the part in question) as a residence.

(4) Where part of the land occupied with a residence is and part is not within subsection (1) above, then (up to the permitted area) that part shall be taken to be within subsection (1) above which, if the remainder were separately occupied, would be the most suitable for occupation and enjoyment with the residence.

(5) So far as it is necessary for the purposes of this section to determine which of two or more residences is an individual's main residence for any period—

    (*a*) the individual may conclude that question by notice in writing to the inspector given within two years from the beginning of that period, or given by the end of the year 1966-67, if that is later, but subject to a right to vary that notice by a further notice in writing to the inspector as respects any period beginning not earlier than two years before the giving of the further notice,

    (*b*) subject to paragraph (*a*) above, the question shall be concluded by the determination of the inspector, which may be as respects either the whole or specified parts of the period of ownership in question,

and notice of any determination of the inspector under paragraph (*b*) above shall be given to the individual who may appeal to the General Commissioners or the Special Commissioners against that determination within thirty days of service of the notice.

(6) In the case of a man and his wife living with him—

    (*a*) there can only be one residence or main residence for both, so long as living together, and, where a notice under subsection (5)(*a*) above affects both the husband and the wife, it must be given by both, and

    (*b*) any notice under subsection (5)(*b*) above which affects a residence owned by the husband and a residence owned by the wife shall be given to each and either may appeal under that subsection.

(7) In this section, and sections 102 to 105 below, " the period of ownership " where the individual has had different interests at different times shall be taken to begin from the first acquisition taken into account in arriving at the expenditure which under Chapter II of Part II of this Act is allowable as a deduction in computing under that Chapter the amount of the gain to which this section applies, and in the case of a man and his wife living with him—

    (*a*) if the one disposes of, or of his or her interest in, the dwelling-house or part of a dwelling-house which is their only or main residence to the other, and in particular if it passes on death to the other as legatee, the other's period of ownership shall begin with the beginning of the period of ownership of the one making the disposal, and

    (*b*) if paragraph (*a*) above applies, but the dwelling-house or part of a dwelling-house was not the only or main residence of both throughout the period of ownership of the one making the disposal, account shall be taken of any part of that period during which it was his only or main residence as if it was also that of the other.

(8) If at any time (being a time after 30th July 1978) during an individual's period of ownership of a dwelling-house or part of a dwelling-house he—

    (*a*) resides in living accommodation which is for him job-related within the meaning of paragraph 4A of Schedule 1 to the Finance Act 1974, and

    (*b*) intends in due course to occupy the dwelling-house or part of a dwelling-house as his only or main residence,

this section, and sections 102 to 105 below, shall apply as if the dwelling-house or part of a dwelling-house were at that time occupied by him as a residence.

(9) Apportionments of consideration shall be made wherever required by this section or sections 102 to 105 below and, in

particular, where a person disposes of a dwelling-house only part of which is his only or main residence.

Amount of
relief.

102.—(1) No part of a gain to which section 101 above applies shall be a chargeable gain if the dwelling-house or part of a dwelling-house has been the individual's only or main residence throughout the period of ownership, or throughout the period of ownership except for all or any part of the last twelve months of that period.

(2) Where subsection (1) above does not apply, a fraction of the gain shall not be a chargeable gain, and that fraction shall be—

> (a) the length of the part or parts of the period of ownership during which the dwelling-house or the part of the dwelling-house was the individual's only or main residence, but inclusive of the last twelve months of the period of ownership in any event, divided by
>
> (b) the length of the period of ownership.

(3) For the purposes of subsections (1) and (2) above—

> (a) a period of absence not exceeding three years (or periods of absence which together did not exceed three years), and in addition
>
> (b) any period of absence throughout which the individual worked in an employment or office all the duties of which were performed outside the United Kingdom, and in addition
>
> (c) any period of absence not exceeding four years (or periods of absence which together did not exceed four years) throughout which the individual was prevented from residing in the dwelling-house or part of the dwelling-house in consequence of the situation of his place of work or in consequence of any condition imposed by his employer requiring him to reside elsewhere, being a condition reasonably imposed to secure the effective performance by the employee of his duties,

shall be treated as if in that period of absence the dwelling-house or the part of the dwelling-house was the individual's only or main residence if both before and after the period there was a time when the dwelling-house was the individual's only or main residence.

In this subsection " period of absence " means a period during which the dwelling-house or the part of the dwelling-house was not the individual's only or main residence and throughout which he had no residence or main residence eligible for relief under this section.

(4) In this section " period of ownership " does not include any period before 6th April 1965.

103.—(1) If the gain accrues from the disposal of a dwelling-house or part of a dwelling-house part of which is used exclusively for the purposes of a trade or business, or of a profession or vocation, the gain shall be apportioned and section 102 above shall apply in relation to the part of the gain apportioned to the part which is not exclusively used for those purposes.

PART V
Amount of relief: further provisions.

(2) If at any time in the period of ownership there is a change in what is occupied as the individual's residence, whether on account of a reconstruction or conversion of a building or for any other reason, or there have been changes as regards the use of part of the dwelling-house for the purpose of a trade or business, or of a profession or vocation, or for any other purpose, the relief given by section 102 above may be adjusted in such manner as the Commissioners concerned may consider to be just and reasonable.

(3) Section 102 above shall not apply in relation to a gain if the acquisition of, or of the interest in, the dwelling-house or the part of a dwelling-house was made wholly or partly for the purpose of realising a gain from the disposal of it, and shall not apply in relation to a gain so far as attributable to any expenditure which was incurred after the beginning of the period of ownership and was incurred wholly or partly for the purpose of realising a gain from the disposal.

104. Sections 101 to 103 above shall also apply in relation to a gain accruing to a trustee on a disposal of settled property being an asset within section 101(1) above where during the period of ownership of the trustee the dwelling-house or part of the dwelling-house mentioned in that subsection has been the only or main residence of a person entitled to occupy it under the terms of the settlement, and in those sections as so applied—

Private residence occupied under terms of settlement.

(a) references to the individual shall be taken as references to the trustee except in relation to the occupation of the dwelling-house or part of the dwelling-house, and

(b) the notice which may be given to the inspector under section 101(5)(a) above shall be a joint notice by the trustee and the person entitled to occupy the dwelling-house or part of the dwelling-house.

105.—(1) This section applies to a gain accruing to an individual so far as attributable to the disposal of, or of an interest in, a dwelling-house or part of a dwelling-house which is, or has at any time in his period of ownership been, the sole residence of a dependent relative of the individual, provided rent-free and without any other consideration.

Private residence occupied by dependent relative.

(2) If the individual so claims, such relief shall be given in respect of it and its garden or grounds as would be given under sections 101 to 103 above if the dwelling-house (or part of the dwelling-house) had been the individual's only or main residence in the period of residence by the dependent relative, and shall be so given in addition to any relief available under those sections apart from this section.

(3) Not more than one dwelling-house (or part of a dwelling-house) may qualify for relief as being the residence of a dependent relative of the claimant at any one time nor, in the case of a man and his wife living with him, as being the residence of a dependent relative of the claimant or of the claimant's husband or wife at any one time.

(4) The inspector, before allowing a claim, may require the claimant to show that the giving of the relief claimed will not under subsection (3) above preclude the giving of relief to the claimant's wife or husband or that a claim to any such relief has been relinquished.

(5) In this section " dependent relative " means, in relation to an individual—

> (*a*) any relative of his or of his wife who is incapacitated by old age or infirmity from maintaining himself, or
>
> (*b*) his or his wife's mother who, whether or not incapacitated, is either widowed, or living apart from her husband, or a single woman in consequence of dissolution or annulment of marriage.

(6) If the individual mentioned in subsection (5) above is a woman the references in that subsection to the individual's wife shall be construed as references to the individual's husband.

Leases

Leases of land and other assets.

106. Schedule 3 to this Act shall have effect as respects leases of land and of other assets.

Part disposals

Small part disposals.

107.—(1) This section applies to a transfer of land forming part only of a holding of land, where—

> (*a*) the amount or value of the consideration for the transfer is small, as compared with the market value of the holding as it subsisted immediately before the transfer, and
>
> (*b*) the transfer is not one which, by virtue of section 44 above (transfers between husband and wife) or section 273(1) of the Taxes Act (transfers within groups of

companies), is treated as giving rise to neither a gain nor
a loss.

(2) Subject to subsection (3) below, if the transferor so claims, the transfer shall not be treated for the purposes of this Act as a disposal, but all sums which, if it had been so treated, would have been brought into account as consideration for that disposal in the computation under Chapter II of Part II of this Act of a gain accruing on the disposal shall be deducted from any expenditure allowable under that Chapter as a deduction in computing a gain on any subsequent disposal of the holding.

(3) This section shall not apply—

    (*a*) if the amount or value of the consideration for the transfer exceeds £10,000, or

    (*b*) where in the year of assessment in which the transfer is made, the transferor made any other disposal of land, if the total amount or value of the consideration for all disposals of land made by the transferor in that year exceeds £10,000.

(4) No account shall be taken under subsection (3) above of any tranfer of land to which section 108 below applies.

(5) In relation to a transfer which is not for full consideration in money or money's worth " the amount or value of the consideration " in this section shall mean the market value of the land transferred.

(6) For the purposes of this section the holding of land shall comprise only the land in respect of which the expenditure allowable under paragraphs (*a*) and (*b*) of section 32(1) above would be apportioned under section 35 above if the transfer had been treated as a disposal (that is, as a part disposal of the holding).

(7) In this section references to a holding of land include references to any estate or interest in a holding of land, not being an estate or interest which is a wasting asset, and references to part of a holding shall be construed accordingly.

108.—(1) This section applies to a transfer of land forming Part disposal
part only of a holding of land to an authority exercising or to authority
having compulsory powers where— with
                                                                                                               compulsory
    (*a*) the amount or value of the consideration for the powers.
transfer, or if the transfer is not for full consideration in money or money's worth, the market value of the land transferred, is small, as compared with the market value of the holding as it subsisted immediately before the transfer, and

(*b*) the transferor had not taken any steps by advertising or otherwise to dispose of any part of the holding or to make his willingness to dispose of it known to the authority or others.

(2) If the transferor so claims, the transfer shall not be treated for the purposes of this Act as a disposal, but all sums which, if it had been so treated, would have been brought into account as consideration for that disposal in the computation under Chapter II of Part II of this Act of a gain accruing on the disposal shall be deducted from any expenditure allowable under that Chapter as a deduction in computing a gain on any subsequent disposal of the holding.

(3) For the purposes of this section the holding of land shall comprise only the land in respect of which the expenditure allowable under paragraphs (*a*) and (*b*) of section 32(1) above would be apportioned under section 35 above if the transfer had been treated as a disposal (that is, as a part disposal of the holding).

(4) In this section references to a holding of land include references to an estate or interest in a holding of land, not being an estate or interest which is a wasting asset, and references to part of a holding shall be construed accordingly.

(5) In this section " authority exercising or having compulsory powers " means, in relation to the land transferred, a person or body of persons acquiring it compulsorily or who has or have been, or could be, authorised to acquire it compulsorily for the purposes for which it is acquired, or for whom another person or body of persons has or have been, or could be, authorised so to acquire it.

Part disposal: consideration exceeding allowable expenditure.

109.—(1) The provisions of sections 107(2) and 108(2) above shall have effect subject to this section.

(2) Where the allowable expenditure is less than the consideration for the part disposal (or is nil)—

(*a*) the said provisions shall not apply, and

(*b*) if the recipient so elects (and there is any allowable expenditure)—

(i) the consideration for the part disposal shall be reduced by the amount of the allowable expenditure, and

(ii) none of that expenditure shall be allowable as a deduction in computing a gain accruing on the occasion of the part disposal or on any subsequent occasion.

In this subsection "allowable expenditure" means expenditure which, immediately before the part disposal, was attributable to the holding of land under paragraphs (*a*) and (*b*) of section 32(1) above.

Compulsory acquisition

110.—(1) Where land or an interest in or right over land is acquired and the acquisition is, or could have been, made under compulsory powers, then in considering whether, under section 43(4) above, the purchase price or compensation or other consideration for the acquisition should be apportioned and treated in part as a capital sum within section 20(1)(*a*) above (disposal arising on receipt of capital sum), whether as compensation for loss of goodwill or for disturbance or otherwise, or should be apportioned in any other way, the fact that the acquisition is or could have been made compulsorily, and any statutory provision treating the purchase price or compensation or other consideration as exclusively paid in respect of the land itself, shall be disregarded.

Compensation paid on compulsory acquisition.

(2) In any case where land or an interest in land is acquired as mentioned in subsection (1) above from any person and the compensation or purchase price includes an amount in respect of severance of the land comprised in the acquisition or sale from other land in which that person is entitled in the same capacity to an interest, or in respect of that other land as being injuriously affected, there shall be deemed for the purposes of this Act to be a part disposal of that other land.

111. Where an interest in land is acquired, otherwise than under a contract, by an authority possessing compulsory purchase powers the time at which the disposal and acquisition is made is the time at which the compensation for the acquisition is agreed or otherwise determined (variations on appeal being disregarded for this purpose) or, if earlier (but after 20th April 1971), the time when the authority enter on the land in pursuance of their powers.

Time of disposal and acquisition.

Agricultural land and woodlands

112. For the purposes of capital gains tax, a sum payable to an individual by virtue of a scheme under section 27 of the Agriculture Act 1967 (grants for relinquishing occupation of uncomercial agricultural units) shall not be treated as part of the consideration obtained by him for, or otherwise as accruing to him on, the disposal of any asset.

Grants for giving up agricultural land.
1967 c. 22.

113.—(1)(*a*) Consideration for the disposal of trees standing or felled or cut on land assessed to income tax or corporation tax under Schedule B, and

Woodlands.

> (*b*) capital sums received under a policy of insurance in respect of the destruction of or damage or injury to trees by fire or other hazard on such land,

shall be excluded from the computation under Chapter II of Part II of this Act of the gain accruing on the disposal if the person making the disposal is the person assessed to the tax under Schedule B.

(2) Subsection (1)(*b*) above has effect notwithstanding section 20(1) above (disposal arising on receipt of capital sum).

(3) In the computation under Chapter II of Part II above so much of the cost of woodland in the United Kingdom shall be disregarded as is attributable to trees growing on the land.

(4) In the computation under Chapter II of Part II above of the gain accruing on a disposal of woodland in the United Kingdom so much of the consideration for the disposal as is attributable to trees growing on the land shall be excluded.

(5) References in this section to trees include references to saleable underwood.

Development land tax etc.

114. The provisions of this Act have effect subject to—

Interaction with development land tax and other taxation.
1976 c. 24.
1974 c. 30.

> (*a*) the Development Land Tax Act 1976, and in particular Schedule 6 to that Act,
>
> (*b*) the taxation of development gains under Part III of the Finance Act 1974, which is to be terminated in accordance with the provisions of the Development Land Tax Act 1976,
>
> (*c*) the extension of the taxation of chargeable gains by Chapter II of the said Part III (the first letting charge), subject to termination in accordance with the said Act of 1976.

Part VI

Property: Further Provisions

Replacement of business assets

Roll-over relief.

115.—(1) If the consideration which a person carrying on a trade obtains for the disposal of, or of his interest in, assets (in this section referred to as " the old assets ") used, and used only, for the purposes of the trade throughout the period of ownership is applied by him in acquiring other assets, or an interest in other assets (in this section referred to as " the new assets ") which on the acquisition are taken into use, and used only, for the purposes of the trade, and the old assets and new

assets are within the classes of assets listed in section 118 below,
then the person carrying on the trade shall, on making a claim
as respects the consideration which has been so applied, be
treated for the purposes of this Act—

> (a) as if the consideration for the disposal of, or of the
> interest in, the old assets were (if otherwise of a greater
> amount or value) of such amount as would secure that
> on the disposal neither a gain nor a loss accrues to him,
> and
>
> (b) as if the amount or value of the consideration for the
> acquisition of, or of the interest in, the new assets were
> reduced by the excess of the amount or value of the
> actual consideration for the disposal of, or of the
> interest in, the old assets over the amount of the con-
> sideration which he is treated as receiving under
> paragraph (a) above,

but neither paragraph (a) nor paragraph (b) above shall affect
the treatment for the purposes of this Act of the other party to
the transaction involving the old assets, or of the other party
to the transaction involving the new assets.

(2) Where subsection (1)(a) above applies to exclude a gain
which, in consequence of Schedule 5 to this Act, is not all
chargeable gain, the amount of the reduction to be made under
subsection (1)(b) above shall be the amount of the chargeable
gain, and not the whole amount of the gain.

(3) This section shall only apply if the acquisition of, or of
the interest in, the new assets takes place, or an unconditional
contract for the acquisition is entered into, in the period beginning twelve months before and ending three years after the
disposal of, or of the interest in, the old assets, or at such earlier
or later time as the Board may by notice in writing allow:

Provided that, where an unconditional contract for the acquisition is so entered into, this section may be applied on a provisional basis without waiting to ascertain whether the new
assets, or the interest in the new assets, is acquired in pursuance
of the contract, and, when that fact is ascertained, all necessary
adjustments shall be made by making assessments or by repayment or discharge of tax, and shall be so made notwithstanding
any limitation on the time within which assessments may be
made.

(4) This section shall not apply unless the acquisition of, or
of the interest in, the new assets was made for the purpose of
their use in the trade, and not wholly or partly for the purpose
of realising a gain from the disposal of, or of the interest in,
the new assets.

(5) If, over the period of ownership or any substantial part of the period of ownership, part of a building or structure is, and part is not, used for the purposes of a trade, this section shall apply as if the part so used, with any land occupied for purposes ancillary to the occupation and use of that part of the building or structure, were a separate asset, and subject to any necessary apportionments of consideration for an acquisition or disposal of, or of an interest in, the building or structure and other land.

(6) If the old assets were not used for the purposes of the trade throughout the period of ownership this section shall apply as if a part of the asset representing its use for the purposes of the trade having regard to the time and extent to which it was, and was not, used for those purposes, were a separate asset which had been wholly used for the purposes of the trade, and this subsection shall apply in relation to that part subject to any necessary apportionment of consideration for an acquisition or disposal of, or of the interest in, the asset.

(7) This section shall apply in relation to a person who, either successively or at the same time, carries on two or more trades as if both or all of them were a single trade.

(8) The provisions of this Act fixing the amount of the consideration deemed to be given for the acquisition or disposal of assets shall be applied before this section is applied.

(9) Without prejudice to section 43(4) above (general provision for apportionments), where consideration is given for the acquisition or disposal of assets some or part of which are assets in relation to which a claim under this section applies, and some or part of which are not, the consideration shall be apportioned in such manner as is just and reasonable.

Assets only partly replaced.

116.—(1) Section 115(1) above shall not apply if part only of the amount or value of the consideration for the disposal of, or of the interest in, the old assets is applied as described in that subsection, but if all of the amount or value of the consideration except for a part which is less than the amount of the gain (whether all chargeable gain or not) accruing on the disposal of, or of the interest in, the old assets is so applied, then the person carrying on the trade, on making a claim as respects the consideration which has been so applied, shall be treated for the purposes of this Act—

(a) as if the amount of the gain so accruing were reduced to the amount of the said part (and, if not all chargeable gain, with a proportionate reduction in the amount of the chargeable gain), and

(b) as if the amount or value of the consideration for the acquisition of, or of the interest in, the new assets were reduced by the amount by which the gain is reduced (or as the case may be the amount by which the chargeable gain is proportionately reduced) under paragraph (a) of this subsection,

but neither paragraph (a) nor paragraph (b) above shall affect the treatment for the purposes of this Act of the other party to the transaction involving the old assets, or of the other party to the transaction involving the new assets.

(2) Subsections (3) to (9) of section 115 above shall apply as if this section formed part of that section.

117.—(1) Sections 115 and 116 above shall have effect subject to the provisions of this section in which—

> (a) the " held over gain " means the amount by which, under those sections, and apart from the provisions of this section, any chargeable gain on one asset (called " asset No. 1 ") is reduced, with a corresponding reduction of the expenditure allowable in respect of another asset (called " asset No. 2 "),

> (b) any reference to a gain of any amount being carried forward to any asset is a reference to a reduction of that amount in a chargeable gain coupled with a reduction of the same amount in expenditure allowable in respect of that asset.

(2) If asset No. 2 is a depreciating asset, the held over gain shall not be carried forward, but the claimant shall be treated as if so much of the chargeable gain on asset No. 1 as is equal to the held over gain did not accrue until—

> (a) the claimant disposes of asset No. 2, or

> (b) he ceases to use asset No. 2 for the purposes of a trade carried on by him, or

> (c) the expiration of a period of ten years beginning with the acquisition of asset No. 2,

whichever event comes first.

(3) If, in the circumstances specified in subsection (4) below, the claimant acquires an asset (called " asset No. 3 ") which is not a depreciating asset, and so claims under section 115 or 116 above—

> (a) the gain held over from asset No. 1 shall be carried forward to asset No. 3, and

> (b) the claim which applies to asset No. 2 shall be treated as withdrawn (so that subsection (2) above does not apply).

(4) The circumstances are that asset No. 3 is acquired not later than the time when the chargeable gain postponed under subsection (2) above would accrue and, assuming—

(a) that the consideration for asset No. 1 was applied in acquiring asset No. 3, and

(b) that the time between the disposal of asset No. 1 and the acquisition of asset No. 3 was within the time limited by section 115(3) above,

the whole amount of the postponed gain could be carried forward from asset No. 1 to asset No. 3 ; and the claim under subsection (3) above shall be accepted as if those assumptions were true.

(5) If part only of the postponed gain could be carried forward from asset No. 1 to asset No. 3, and the claimant so requires, that and the other part of the postponed gain shall be treated as derived from two separate assets, so that, on that claim—

(a) subsection (3) above applies to the first-mentioned part, and

(b) the other part remains subject to subsection (2) above.

(6) For the purposes of this section, an asset is a depreciating asset at any time if—

(a) at that time it is a wasting asset, as defined in section 37 above, or

(b) within the period of ten years beginning at that time it will become a wasting asset (so defined).

Relevant classes of assets.   **118.** The classes of assets for the purposes of section 115 (1) above are as follows.

Class 1.   Assets within heads A and B below.

Head A

1. Any building or part of a building and any permanent or semi-permanent structure in the nature of a building, occupied (as well as used) only for the purposes of the trade.

2. Any land occupied (as well as used) only for the purposes of the trade.

Head A has effect subject to section 119 below.

Head B

Fixed plant or machinery which does not form part of a building or of a permanent or semi-permanent structure in the nature of a building.

Class 2

Ships, aircraft and hovercraft ("hovercraft" having the same meaning as in the Hovercraft Act 1968).

Class 3

Goodwill.

119.—(1) This section has effect as respects head A of Class 1 in section 118 above.

(2) Head A shall not apply where the trade is a trade—

(a) of dealing in or developing land, or

(b) of providing services for the occupier of land in which the person carrying on the trade has an estate or interest.

(3) Where the trade is a trade of dealing in or developing land, but a profit on the sale of any land held for the purposes of the trade would not form part of the trading profits, then, as regards that land, the trade shall be treated for the purposes of subsection (2)(a) of this section as if it were not a trade of dealing in or developing land.

(4) A person who is a lessor of tied premises shall be treated as if he occupied (as well as used) those tied premises only for the purposes of the relevant trade.

This subsection shall be construed in accordance with section 140(2) of the Taxes Act (income tax and corporation tax on tied premises).

120. In relation to a case where—

(a) the person disposing of, or of his interest in, the old assets and acquiring the new assets, or an interest in them, is an individual, and

(b) the trade or trades in question are carried on not by that individual but by a company which, both at the time of the disposal and at the time of the acquisition referred to in paragraph (a) above, is his family company, within the meaning of section 124 below,

any reference in sections 115 to 119 above to the person carrying on the trade (or the two or more trades) includes a reference to that individual.

121.—(1) Sections 115 to 120 above shall apply with the necessary modifications—

(a) in relation to the discharge of the functions of a public authority, and

(b) in relation to the occupation of woodlands where the woodlands are managed by the occupier on a commercial basis and with a view to the realisation of profits, and

(c) in relation to a profession, vocation, office or employment, and

(d) in relation to such of the activities of a body of persons whose activities are carried on otherwise than for profit and are wholly or mainly directed to the protection or promotion of the interests of its members in the carrying on of their trade or profession as are so directed, and

(e) in relation to the activities of an unincorporated association or other body chargeable to corporation tax, being a body not established for profit whose activities are wholly or mainly carried on otherwise than for profit, but in the case of assets within head A of class 1 only if they are both occupied and used by the body, and in the case of other assets only if they are used by the body,

as they apply in relation to a trade.

(2) In sections 115 to 120 above and this section the expressions " trade ", " profession ", " vocation ", " office " and " employment " have the same meanings as in the Income Tax Acts, but not so as to apply the provisions of the Income Tax Acts as to the circumstances in which, on a change in the persons carrying on a trade, a trade is to be regarded as discontinued, or as set up and commenced.

(3) Sections 115 to 120 above, and this section, shall be construed as one.

Stock in trade

Appropriations to and from stock.   **122.**—(1) Subject to subsection (3) below, where an asset acquired by a person otherwise than as trading stock of a trade carried on by him is appropriated by him for the purposes of the trade as trading stock (whether on the commencement of the trade or otherwise) and, if he had then sold the asset for its market value, a chargeable gain or allowable loss would have accrued to him, he shall be treated as having thereby disposed of the asset by selling it for its then market value.

(2) If at any time an asset forming part of the trading stock of a person's trade is appropriated by him for any other purpose, or is retained by him on his ceasing to carry on the trade, he

shall be treated as having acquired it at that time for a consideration equal to the amount brought into the accounts of the trade
in respect of it for tax purposes on the appropriation or on
his ceasing to carry on the trade, as the case may be.

(3) Subsection (1) above shall not apply in relation to a
person's appropriation of an asset for the purposes of a trade
if he is chargeable to income tax in respect of the profits of
the trade under Case I of Schedule D, and elects that instead
the market value of the asset at the time of the appropriation
shall, in computing the profits of the trade for purposes of
tax, be treated as reduced by the amount of the chargeable
gain or increased by the amount of the allowable loss referred
to in that subsection, and where that subsection does not apply
by reason of such an election, the profits of the trade shall be
computed accordingly:

Provided that if a person making an election under this
subsection is at the time of the appropriation carrying on the
trade in partnership with others, the election shall not have
effect unless concurred in by the others.

Transfer of business to a company

123.—(1) This section shall apply for the purposes of this
Act where a person who is not a company transfers to a company a business as a going concern, together with the whole
assets of the business, or together with the whole of those
assets other than cash, and the business is so transferred wholly
or partly in exchange for shares issued by the company to the
person transferring the business.

Any shares so received by the transferor in exchange for the
business are referred to below as " the new assets ".

Roll-over relief on transfer of business.

(2) The amount determined under subsection (4) below shall
be deducted from the aggregate (referred to below as " the
amount of the gain on the old assets ") of the chargeable gains
less allowable losses.

(3) For the purpose of computing any chargeable gain accruing on the disposal of any new asset—

  (a) the amount determined under subsection (4) below
      shall be apportioned between the new assets as a
      whole, and

  (b) the sums allowable as a deduction under section 32
      (1)(a) above shall be reduced by the amount appor-
      tioned to the new asset under paragraph (a) above;

and if the shares which comprise the new assets are not all
of the same class, the apportionment between the shares under
paragraph (a) above shall be in accordance with their market
values at the time they were acquired by the transferor.

(4) The amount referred to in subsections (2) and (3)(*a*) above shall not exceed the cost of the new assets but, subject to that, the said amount shall be a fraction $\dfrac{A}{B}$ of the amount of the gain on the old assets where—

" A " is the cost of the new assets, and

" B " is the value of the whole of the consideration received by the transferor in exchange for the business ;

and for the purposes of this subsection " the cost of the new assets " means any sums which would be allowable as a deduction under section 32(1)(*a*) above if the new assets were disposed of as a whole in circumstances giving rise to a chargeable gain.

(5) References in this section to the business, in relation to shares or consideration received in exchange for the business, include references to such assets of the business as are referred to in subsection (1) above.

Transfer of business on retirement

124.—(1) If an individual who has attained the age of 60 years—

(*a*) disposes by way of sale or gift of the whole or part of a business, or

(*b*) disposes by way of sale or gift of shares or securities of a company,

and throughout a period of at least one year ending with the disposal the relevant conditions have been fulfilled, relief shall be given under this section in respect of gains accruing to him on the disposal.

(2) For the purposes of subsection (1) above the relevant conditions are fulfilled at any time if at that time,—

(*a*) in the case of a disposal falling within paragraph (*a*) of that subsection, the business in question is owned either by the individual or by a company with respect to which the following conditions are at that time fulfilled, namely,—

(i) it is a trading company,

(ii) it is the individual's family company, and

(iii) he is a full-time working director of it ;

and

(*b*) in the case of a disposal falling within paragraph (*b*) of that subsection, either the conditions in sub-paragraphs (i) to (iii) of paragraph (*a*) above are fulfilled with respect to the company in question or the individual owns the business which, at the time of the disposal, is owned by the company ;

and in relation to a particular disposal the period, up to a maximum of 10 years, which ends with the disposal and throughout which the relevant conditions are fulfilled is in this section referred to as " the qualifying period ".

(3) The amount available for relief under this section shall be—

(a) in the case of an individual who has attained the age of 65 years, the relevant percentage of £50,000, and

(b) in the case of an individual who has not attained that age, the relevant percentage of the aggregate of £10,000 for every year by which his age exceeds 60 and a corresponding part of £10,000 for any odd part of a year ;

and for the purpose of this subsection " the relevant percentage " means a percentage determined according to the length of the qualifying period on a scale rising arithmetically from 10 per cent. where that period is precisely one year to 100 per cent. where it is ten years.

(4) Where subsection (1)(a) above applies the gains accruing to the individual on the disposal of chargeable business assets comprised in the disposal by way of sale or gift shall be aggregated, and only so much of that aggregate as exceeds the amount available for relief under this section shall be chargeable gains (but not so as to affect liability in respect of gains accruing on the disposal of assets other than chargeable business assets).

(5) Where subsection (1)(b) above applies—

(a) the gains which accrue to the individual on the disposal of the shares or securities shall be aggregated, and

(b) of a proportion of that aggregate sum which is equal to the proportion which the part of the value of the company's chargeable assets at the time of the disposal which is attributable to the value of the company's chargeable business assets bears to the whole of that value, only so much as exceeds the amount available for relief under this section shall constitute chargeable gains (but not so as to affect liability in respect of gains representing the balance of the said aggregate sum),

and for the purposes of paragraph (b) above every asset is a chargeable asset except one, on the disposal of which by the company at the time of the disposal of the shares or securities, no chargeable gain would accrue.

(6) So far as the amount available for relief under this section is applied in giving relief to an individual as respects a disposal it shall not be applied in giving relief to that individual as respects any other disposal (and the relief shall be applied in the order in which any disposals take place).

(7) In arriving at the aggregate under subsection (4) or subsection (5) above—

(*a*) the respective amounts of the gains shall be computed in accordance with the provisions of this Act (other than this section) fixing the amount of chargeable gains, and

(*b*) any allowable loss which accrues on the disposal shall be deducted,

and the provisions of this section shall not affect the computation of the amount of any allowable loss.

(8) In this section—

"chargeable business asset" means an asset (including goodwill but not including shares or securities or other assets held as investments) which is, or is an interest in, an asset used for the purposes of a trade, profession, vocation, office or employment carried on by the individual, or as the case may be by the individual's family company, other than an asset on the disposal of which no chargeable gain accrues or (where the disposal is of shares or securities in the family company) on the disposal of which no chargeable gain would accrue if the family company disposed of the asset at the time of the disposal of the shares or securities,

"family company" means, in relation to an individual, a company the voting rights in which are—

(*a*) as to not less than 25 per cent., exercisable by the individual, or

(*b*) as to not less than 51 per cent., exercisable by the individual or a member of his family, and, as to not less than 5 per cent., exercisable by the individual himself,

"family" means, in relation to an individual, the husband or wife of the individual, and a relative of the individual or the individual's husband or wife, and "relative" means brother, sister, ancestor or lineal descendant,

"full time working director" means a director who is required to devote substantially the whole of his time to the service of the company in a managerial or technical capacity,

" trade ", " profession ", " vocation ", " office " and " employment " have the same meanings as in the Income Tax Acts,

" trading company " has the meaning given by paragraph 11 of Schedule 16 to the Finance Act 1972 ;

and in this section references to the disposal of the whole or part of a business include references to the disposal of the whole or part of the assets provided or held for the purposes of an office or employment by the person exercising that office or employment.

125.—(1) Subject to subsection (2) below, section 124(1)(*b*) above shall apply where under section 72 above (distribution which is not a new holding) the individual is treated as disposing of interests in shares or securities of a company in consideration of a capital distribution from the company in the course of dissolving or winding up the company as it applies where he disposes of shares or securities of a company by way of sale or gift.

(2) Subsection (1) above shall not apply if the capital distribution consists wholly of chargeable business assets of the company, and if it consists partly of chargeable business assets (and partly of money or money's worth), relief shall only be given under section 124 above in respect of that proportion of the gains accruing on the disposal which the part of the capital distribution not consisting of chargeable business assets bears to the entire capital distribution.

Gifts of business assets

126.—(1) If an individual (in this section referred to as " the transferor ") makes a disposal, otherwise than under a bargain at arm's length, to a person resident or ordinarily resident in the United Kingdom (in this section referred to as " the transferee ") of—

(*a*) an asset which is, or is an interest in, an asset used for the purposes of a trade, profession or vocation carried on by the transferor or by a company which is his family company, or

(*b*) shares or securities of a trading company which is the transferor's family company,

then, subject to subsection (2) below, the provisions of subsection (3) below shall apply in relation to the disposal if a claim for relief under this section is made by the transferor and the transferee.

(2) Subsection (3) below does not apply in relation to a disposal if—

> (a) in the case of a disposal of an asset, any gain accruing to the transferor on the disposal is (apart from this section) wholly relieved under section 124 above, or
>
> (b) in the case of a disposal of shares or securities, the proportion determined under subsection (5)(b) of section 124 above of any gain accruing to the transferor on the disposal is (apart from this section) wholly relieved under that section.

(3) Where a claim for relief is made under this section in respect of a disposal—

> (a) the amount of any chargeable gain which, apart from this section, would accrue to the transferor on the disposal, and
>
> (b) the amount of the consideration for which, apart from this section, the transferee would be regarded for the purposes of capital gains tax as having acquired the asset or, as the case may be, the shares or securities,

shall each be reduced by an amount equal to the held-over gain on the disposal.

(4) Part I of Schedule 4 to this Act shall have effect for extending the relief provided for by virtue of subsections (1) to (3) above in the case of agricultural property and for applying it in relation to settled property.

(5) Subject to Part II of Schedule 4 to this Act (which provides for reductions in the held-over gain in certain cases) and subsection (6) below, the reference in subsection (3) above to the held-over gain on a disposal is a reference to the chargeable gain which would have accrued on that disposal apart from subsection (3) above and (in appropriate cases) section 124 above, and in subsection (6) below that chargeable gain is referred to as the unrelieved gain on the disposal.

(6) In any case where—

> (a) there is actual consideration (as opposed to the consideration equal to the market value which is deemed to be given by virtue of section 19(3) above) for a disposal in respect of which a claim for relief is made under this section, and
>
> (b) that actual consideration exceeds the sums allowable as a deduction under section 32 above,

the held-over gain on the disposal shall be the amount by which the unrelieved gain on the disposal exceeds the excess referred to in paragraph (b) above.

(7) Subject to subsection (8) below, in this section and Schedule 4 to this Act—

   (a) " family company " has the meaning given by section 124(8) above,

   (b) " trading company " has the meaning given by paragraph 11 of Schedule 16 to the Finance Act 1972, and 1972 c. 41.

   (c) " trade ", " profession " and " vocation " have the same meaning as in the Income Tax Acts.

(8) In this section and Schedule 4 to this Act and in determining whether a company is a trading company for the purposes of this section and that Schedule, the expression " trade " shall be taken to include the occupation of woodlands where the woodlands are managed by the occupier on a commercial basis and with a view to the realisation of profits.

Movable property

127.—(1) Subject to the provisions of this section, no charge- Wasting able gain shall accrue on the disposal of, or of an interest in, an assets. asset which is tangible movable property and which is a wasting asset.

(2) Subsection (1) above shall not apply to a disposal of, or of an interest in, an asset—

   (a) if, from the beginning of the period of ownership of the person making the disposal to the time when the disposal is made, the asset has been used and used solely for the purposes of a trade, profession or vocation and if that person has claimed or could have claimed any capital allowance in respect of any expenditure attributable to the asset or interest under paragraph (a) or paragraph (b) of section 32(1) above (allowable expenditure), or

   (b) if the person making the disposal has incurred any expenditure on the asset or interest which has otherwise qualified in full for any capital allowance.

(3) In the case of the disposal of, or of an interest in, an asset which, in the period of ownership of the person making the disposal, has been used partly for the purposes of a trade, profession or vocation and partly for other purposes, or has been used for the purposes of a trade, profession or vocation for part of that period, or which has otherwise qualified in part only for capital allowances—

   (a) the consideration for the disposal, and any expenditure attributable to the asset or interest by virtue of section

32(1)(*a*) and (*b*) above, shall be apportioned by refer-ence to the extent to which that expenditure qualified for capital allowances, and

(*b*) the computation under Chapter II of Part II above shall be made separately in relation to the apportioned parts of the expenditure and consideration, and

(*c*) subsection (1) above shall not apply to any gain accru-ing by reference to the computation in relation to the part of the consideration apportioned to use for the purposes of the trade, profession or vocation, or to the expenditure qualifying for capital allowances.

(4) Subsection (1) above shall not apply to a disposal of com-modities of any description by a person dealing on a terminal market or dealing with or through a person ordinarily engaged in dealing on a terminal market.

(5) This section shall be construed as one with Chapter II of Part II above.

Chattel exemption.

128.—(1) Subject to this section a gain accruing on a dis-posal of an asset which is tangible movable property shall not be a chargeable gain if the amount or value of the consideration for the disposal does not exceed £2,000.

(2) Where the amount or value of the consideration for the disposal of an asset which is tangible movable property exceeds £2,000, there shall be excluded from any chargeable gain accru-ing on the disposal so much of it as exceeds five-thirds of the difference between—

(*a*) the amount or value of the consideration, and

(*b*) £2,000.

(3) Subsections (1) and (2) above shall not affect the amount of an allowable loss accruing on the disposal of an asset, but for the purposes of computing under this Act the amount of a loss accruing on the disposal of tangible movable property the consideration for the disposal shall, if less than £2,000, be deemed to be £2,000 and the losses which are allowable losses shall be restricted accordingly.

(4) If two or more assets which have formed part of a set of articles of any description all owned at one time by one person are disposed of by that person, and—

(*a*) to the same person, or

(*b*) to persons who are acting in concert or who are con-nected persons,

whether on the same or different occasions, the two or more
transactions shall be treated as a single transaction disposing of
a single asset, but with any necessary apportionments of the
reductions in chargeable gains, and in allowable losses, under
subsections (2) and (3) above.

(5) If the disposal is of a right or interest in or over tangible movable property—

    (*a*) in the first instance subsections (1), (2) and (3) above
        shall be applied in relation to the asset as a whole,
        taking the consideration as including the market value
        of what remains undisposed of, in addition to the actual
        consideration,

    (*b*) where the sum of the actual consideration and that
        market value exceeds £2,000, the part of any charge-
        able gain that is excluded from it under subsection (2)
        above shall be so much of the gain as exceeds five-
        thirds of the difference between that sum and £2,000
        multiplied by the fraction equal to the actual con-
        sideration divided by the said sum, and

    (*c*) where that sum is less than £2,000 any loss shall be
        restricted under subsection (3) above by deeming the
        consideration to be the actual consideration plus the
        said fraction of the difference between the said sum
        and £2,000.

(6) This section shall not apply—

    (*a*) in relation to a disposal of commodities of any des-
        cription by a person dealing on a terminal market or
        dealing with or through a person ordinarily engaged
        in dealing on a terminal market, or

    (*b*) in relation to a disposal of currency of any description.

129. Schedule 3 to this Act has effect, to the extent specified   Leases of
in paragraph 9 of that Schedule, as respects leases of property   property other
other than land.   than land.

130. A mechanically propelled road vehicle constructed or   Passenger
adapted for the carriage of passengers, except for a vehicle of   vehicles.
a type not commonly used as a private vehicle and unsuitable
to be so used, shall not be a chargeable asset ; and accordingly
no chargeable gain or allowable loss shall accrue on its disposal.

131. A gain shall not be a chargeable gain if accruing on   Decorations
the disposal by any person of a decoration awarded for valour   for valour or
or gallant conduct which he acquired otherwise than for con-   gallant
sideration in money or money's worth.   conduct.

Other property

Commodities
and other
assets without
earmark.

132. Sections 65 and 66 above (rules of identification), and
paragraph 13 of Schedule 5 to this Act (assets held on 6th
April 1965) have effect, to the extent there specified, as respects
assets dealt with without identifying the particular assets disposed of or acquired.

Foreign
currency for
personal
expenditure.

133. A gain shall not be a chargeable gain if accruing on the
disposal by an individual of currency of any description acquired
by him for the personal expenditure outside the United Kingdom
of himself or his family or dependants (including expenditure
on the provision or maintenance of any residence outside the
United Kingdom).

Debts.

134.—(1) Where a person incurs a debt to another, whether
in sterling or in some other currency, no chargeable gain shall
accrue to that (that is the original) creditor or his personal
representative or legatee on a disposal of the debt, except in the
case of the debt on a security (as defined in section 82 above).

(2) Subject to the provisions of sections 82 and 85 above
(conversion of securities and company amalgamations), and
subject to subsection (1) above, the satisfaction of a debt or
part of it (including a debt on a security as defined in section
82 above) shall be treated as a disposal of the debt or of
that part by the creditor made at the time when the debt or
that part is satisfied.

(3) Where property is acquired by a creditor in satisfaction
of his debt or part of it, then subject to the provisions of
sections 82 and 85 above the property shall not be treated as
disposed of by the debtor or acquired by the creditor for a
consideration greater than its market value at the time of the
creditor's acquisition of it; but if under subsection (1) above
(and in a case not falling within either of the said sections 82
and 85) no chargeable gain is to accrue on a disposal of the
debt by the creditor (that is the original creditor), and a chargeable gain accrues to him on a disposal by him of the property,
the amount of the chargeable gain shall (where necessary) be
reduced so as not to exceed the chargeable gain which would
have accrued if he had acquired the property for a consideration equal to the amount of the debt or that part of it.

(4) A loss accruing on the disposal of a debt acquired by
the person making the disposal from the original creditor or
his personal representative or legatee at a time when the creditor
or his personal representative or legatee is a person connected
with the person making the disposal, and so acquired either

directly or by one or more purchases through persons all of whom are connected with the person making the disposal, shall not be an allowable loss.

(5) Where the original creditor is a trustee and the debt, when created, is settled property, subsections (1) and (4) above shall apply as if for the references to the original creditor's personal representative or legatee there were substituted references to any person becoming absolutely entitled, as against the trustee, to the debt on its ceasing to be settled property, and to that person's personal representative or legatee.

135.—(1) Subject to subsection (2) below, section 134(1) above shall not apply to a debt owed by a bank which is not in sterling and which is represented by a sum standing to the credit of a person in an account in the bank.

(2) Subsection (1) above shall not apply to a sum in an individual's bank account representing currency acquired by the holder for the personal expenditure outside the United Kingdom of himself or his family or dependants (including expenditure on the provision or maintenance of any residence outside the United Kingdom).

136.—(1) In this section " a qualifying loan " means a loan in the case of which—

(a) the money lent is used by the borrower wholly for the purposes of a trade carried on by him, not being a trade which consists of or includes the lending of money, and

(b) the borrower is resident in the United Kingdom, and

(c) the borrower's debt is not a debt on a security as defined in section 82 above ;

and for the purposes of paragraph (a) above money used by the borrower for setting up a trade which is subsequently carried on by him shall be treated as used for the purposes of that trade.

(2) In subsection (1) above references to a trade include references to a profession or vocation ; and where money lent to a company is lent by it to another company in the same group, being a trading company, that subsection shall apply to the money lent to the first-mentioned company as if it had used it for any purpose for which it is used by the other company while a member of the group.

(3) If, on a claim by a person who has made a qualifying loan, the inspector is satisfied that—

(a) any outstanding amount of the principal of the loan has become irrecoverable, and

(b) the claimant has not assigned his right to recover that amount, and

(c) the claimant and the borrower were not each other's spouses, or companies in the same group, when the loan was made or at any subsequent time,

this Act shall have effect as if an allowable loss equal to that amount had accrued to the claimant when the claim was made.

(4) If, on a claim by a person who has guaranteed the repayment of a loan which is, or but for subsection (1)(c) above would be, a qualifying loan, the inspector is satisfied that—

(a) any outstanding amount of, or of interest in respect of, the principal of the loan has become irrecoverable from the borrower, and

(b) the claimant has made a payment under the guarantee (whether to the lender or a co-guarantor) in respect of that amount, and

(c) the claimant has not assigned any right to recover that amount which has accrued to him (whether by operation of law or otherwise) in consequence of his having made the payment, and

(d) the lender and the borrower were not each other's spouses, or companies in the same group, when the loan was made or at any subsequent time and the claimant and the borrower were not each other's spouses, and the claimant and the lender were not companies in the same group, when the guarantee was given or at any subsequent time,

this Act shall have effect as if an allowable loss had accrued to the claimant when the payment was made ; and the loss shall be equal to the payment made by him in respect of the amount mentioned in paragraph (a) above less any contribution payable to him by any co-guarantor in respect of the payment so made.

(5) Where an allowable loss has been treated under subsection (3) or (4) above as accruing to any person and the whole or any part of the outstanding amount mentioned in subsection (3)(a) or, as the case may be, subsection (4)(a) is at any time recovered by him, this Act shall have effect as if there had accrued to him at that time a chargeable gain equal to so much of the allowable loss as corresponds to the amount recovered.

(6) For the purposes of subsection (5) above, a person shall be treated as recovering an amount if he (or any other person by his direction) receives any money or money's worth in satisfaction of his right to recover that amount or in consideration of his assignment of the right to recover it ; and where a person assigns such a right otherwise than by way of a bargain made at

arm's length he shall be treated as receiving money or money's worth equal to the market value of the right at the time of the assignment.

(7) No amount shall be treated under this section as giving rise to an allowable loss or chargeable gain in the case of any person if it falls to be taken into account in computing his income for the purposes of income tax or corporation tax.

(8) Where an allowable loss has been treated as accruing to a person under subsection (4) above by virtue of a payment made by him at any time under a guarantee—

> (*a*) no chargeable gain shall accrue to him otherwise than under subsection (5) above, and

> (*b*) no allowable loss shall accrue to him under this Act,

on his disposal of any rights that have accrued to him (whether by operation of law or otherwise) in consequence of his having made any payment under the guarantee at or after that time.

(9) References in this section to an amount having become irre-coverable do not include references to cases where the amount has become irrecoverable in consequence of the terms of the loan, of any arrangements of which the loan forms part, or of any act or omission by the lender or, in a case within subsection (4) above, the guarantor.

(10) In this section—

> (*a*) " spouses " means spouses who are living together (con-strued in accordance with section 155(2) below),

> (*b*) " trading company " has the meaning given by para-graph 11 of Schedule 16 to the Finance Act 1972, and   1972 c. 41.

> (*c*) " group " shall be construed in accordance with section 272 of the Taxes Act.

(11) Subsection (3) above applies where the loan is made after 11th April 1978 and subsection (4) above applies where the guarantee is given after that date.

137.—(1) Without prejudice to section 19 above (general Options and provisions about the disposal of assets), the grant of an option, forfeited and in particular— deposits.

> (*a*) the grant of an option in a case where the grantor binds himself to sell what he does not own, and because the option is abandoned, never has occasion to own, and

> (*b*) the grant of an option in a case where the grantor binds himself to buy what, because the option is abandoned, he does not acquire,

is the disposal of an asset (namely of the option), but subject to the following provisions of this section as to treating the grant of an option as part of a larger transaction.

(2) If an option is exercised the grant of the option and the transaction entered into by the grantor in fulfilment of his obligations under the option shall be treated as a single transaction and accordingly—

(*a*) if the option binds the grantor to sell, the consideration for the option is part of the consideration for the sale, and

(*b*) if the option binds the grantor to buy, the consideration for the option shall be deducted from the cost of acquisition incurred by the grantor in buying in pursuance of his obligations under the option.

(3) The exercise of an option by the person for the time being entitled to exercise it shall not constitute the disposal of an asset by that person, but, if an option is exercised then the acquisition of the option (whether directly from the grantor or not) and the transaction entered into by the person exercising the option in exercise of his rights under the option shall be treated as a single transaction and accordingly—

(*a*) if the option binds the grantor to sell, the cost of acquiring the option shall be part of the cost of acquiring what is sold, and

(*b*) if the option binds the grantor to buy, the cost of the option shall be treated as a cost incidental to the disposal of what is bought by the grantor of the option.

(4) The abandonment of—

(*a*) a quoted option to subscribe for shares in a company, or

(*b*) an option to acquire assets exercisable by a person intending to use them, if acquired, for the purpose of a trade carried on by him,

shall constitute the disposal of an asset (namely of the option) ; but the abandonment of any other option by the person for the time being entitled to exercise it shall not constitute the disposal of an asset by that person.

(5) In the case of an option relating to shares or securities this section shall apply subject to the provisions of section 65 above (rules for identification: pooling) and, accordingly, the option may be regarded, in relation to the grantor or in relation to the person entitled to exercise the option, as relating to part of a holding (as defined in section 65 above) of shares or securities.

(6) This section shall apply in relation to an option binding the grantor both to sell and to buy as if it were two separate options with half the consideration attributed to each.

(7) In this section references to an option include references to an option binding the grantor to grant a lease for a premium

or enter into any other transaction which is not a sale, and references to buying and selling in pursuance of an option shall be construed accordingly.

(8) This section shall apply in relation to a forfeited deposit of purchase money or other consideration money for a prospective purchase or other transaction which is abandoned as it applies in relation to the consideration for an option which binds the grantor to sell and which is not exercised.

(9) In subsection (4)(*a*) above, and in sections 138 and 139 below, " quoted option " means an option of a kind which, at the time of the abandonment or other disposal, is quoted on a recognised stock exchange within the meaning of section 535 of the Taxes Act, and there dealt in in the same manner as shares.

138.—(1) Section 38 above (wasting assets: restriction of allowable expenditure) shall not apply—

  (*a*) to a quoted option to subscribe for shares in a company, or

  (*b*) to an option to acquire assets exercisable by a person intending to use them, if acquired, for the purpose of a trade carried on by him.

Options: application of rules as to wasting assets.

(2) In relation to the disposal by way of transfer of an option (other than a quoted option to subscribe for shares in a company) binding the grantor to sell or buy quoted shares or securities, the option shall be regarded as a wasting asset the life of which ends when the right to exercise the option ends, or when the option becomes valueless, whichever is the earlier.

Subsections (6) and (7) of section 137 above shall apply in relation to this subsection as they apply in relation to that section.

(3) The preceding provisions of this section are without prejudice to the application of sections 37 to 39 above (wasting assets) to options not within those provisions.

(4) In this section—

  (*a*) " quoted option " has the meaning given by section 137(9) above,

  (*b*) " quoted shares or securities " means shares or securities which have a quoted market value on a recognised stock exchange in the United Kingdom or elsewhere.

139.—(1) If a quoted option to subscribe for shares in a company is dealt in (on the stock exchange where it is quoted) within three months after the taking effect, with respect to the company granting the option, of any reorganisation, reduction, conversion or amalgamation to which Chapter II of Part

Quoted options treated as part of new holdings.

IV above applies, or within such longer period as the Board may by notice in writing allow—

> (*a*) the option shall, for the purposes of the said Chapter II (under which a holding prior to the reorganisation or reduction of capital, conversion or amalgamation is to be treated as the same as the resulting new holding) be regarded as the shares which could be acquired by exercising the option, and

> (*b*) section 150(3) below shall apply for determining its market value.

(2) In this section " quoted option " has the meaning given by section 137(9) above.

PART VII

OTHER PROVISIONS

Insurance

Policies of insurance.

140.—(1) The rights of the insurer under any policy of insurance shall not constitute an asset on the disposal of which a gain may accrue, whether the risks insured relate to property or not; and the rights of the insured under any policy of insurance of the risk of any kind of damage to, or the loss or depreciation of, assets shall constitute an asset on the disposal of which a gain may accrue only to the extent that those rights relate to assets on the disposal of which a gain may accrue or might have accrued.

(2) Notwithstanding subsection (1) above, sums received under a policy of insurance of the risk of any kind of damage to, or the loss or depreciation of, assets are for the purposes of this Act, and in particular for the purposes of section 20 above (disposal of assets by owner where any capital sum is derived from assets), sums derived from the assets.

(3) In this section " policy of insurance " does not include a policy of assurance on human life.

Disallowance of insurance premiums as expenses.

141. Without prejudice to the provisions of section 33 above (exclusion of expenditure by reference to tax on income), there shall be excluded from the sums allowable as a deduction in the computation under Part II of Chapter II above of the gain accruing to a person on the disposal of an asset any premiums or other payments made under a policy of insurance of the risk of any kind of damage or injury to, or loss or depreciation of, the asset.

142.—(1) An underwriting member of Lloyd's or of an approved association of underwriters shall, subject to the follow-ing provisions of this section, be treated for the purposes of this Act as absolutely entitled as against the trustees to the invest-ments of his premiums trust fund, his special reserve fund (if any) and any other trust fund required or authorised by the rules of Lloyd's or the association in question, or required by the underwriting agent through whom his business or any part of it is carried on, to be kept in connection with the business.

(2) The trustees of any premiums trust fund shall, subject to subsection (3) below, be assessed and charged to capital gains tax as if subsection (1) above had not been passed.

(3) The assessment to be made on the trustees of a fund by virtue of subsection (2) above for any year of assessment shall not take account of losses accruing in any previous year of assessment, and if for that or any other reason the tax paid on behalf of an underwriting member for any year of assessment by virtue of assessments so made exceeds the capital gains tax for which he is liable, the excess shall, on a claim by him, be repaid.

(4) For the purposes of subsections (2) and (3) above the under-writing agent may be treated as a trustee of the premiums trust fund.

143.—(1) This section has effect as respects any policy of assurance or contract for a deferred annuity on the life of any person.

(2) No chargeable gain shall accrue on the disposal of, or of an interest in, the rights under any such policy of assurance or contract except where the person making the disposal is not the original beneficial owner and acquired the rights or interest for a consideration in money or money's worth.

(3) Subject to subsection (2) above, the occasion of—

   (a) the payment of the sum or sums assured by a policy of assurance, or

   (b) the transfer of investments or other assets to the owner of a policy of assurance in accordance with the policy,

and the occasion of the surrender of a policy of assurance, shall be the occasion of a disposal of the rights under the policy of assurance.

(4) Subject to subsection (2) above, the occasion of the pay-ment of the first instalment of a deferred annuity, and the occasion of the surrender of the rights under a contract for a deferred annuity, shall be the occasion of a disposal of the rights

PART VII

under the contract for a deferred annuity and the amount of the consideration for the disposal of a contract for a deferred annuity shall be the market value at that time of the right to that and further instalments of the annuity.

Superannuation funds, annuities and annual payments

Superannua-
tion funds,
annuities and
annual
payments.

144. No chargeable gain shall accrue to any person on the disposal of a right to, or to any part of—

    (a) any allowance, annuity or capital sum payable out of any superannuation fund, or under any superannuation scheme, established solely or mainly for persons employed in a profession, trade, undertaking or employment, and their dependants,

    (b) an annuity granted otherwise than under a contract for a deferred annuity by a company as part of its business of granting annuities on human life, whether or not including instalments of capital, or an annuity

1929 c. 29.

         granted or deemed to be granted under the Government Annuities Act 1929, or

    (c) annual payments which are due under a covenant made by any person and which are not secured on any property.

Other exemptions and reliefs

Charities.

145.—(1) Subject to subsection (2) below a gain shall not be a chargeable gain if it accrues to a charity and is applicable and applied for charitable purposes.

(2) If property held on charitable trusts ceases to be subject to charitable trusts—

    (a) the trustees shall be treated as if they had disposed of, and immediately re-acquired, the property for a consideration equal to its market value, any gain on the disposal being treated as not accruing to a charity, and

    (b) if and so far as any of that property represents, directly or indirectly, the consideration for the disposal of assets by the trustees, any gain accruing on that disposal shall be treated as not having accrued to a charity,

and an assessment to capital gains tax chargeable by virtue of paragraph (b) above may be made at any time not more than three years after the end of the year of assessment in which the property ceases to be subject to charitable trusts.

146.—(1) Subsection (2) below shall apply where a disposal
of an asset is made otherwise than under a bargain at arm's
length—

   (*a*) to a charity, or

   (*b*) to any of the bodies mentioned in paragraph 12 of
       Schedule 6 to the Finance Act 1975 (gifts for national
       purposes, etc.).

(2) Section 19(3) above (consideration deemed to be equal
to market value) and section 147(3) below shall not apply ; but
if the disposal is by way of gift (including a gift in settlement)
or for a consideration not exceeding the sums allowable as a
deduction under section 32 above, then—

   (*a*) the disposal and acquisition shall be treated for the
       purposes of this Act as being made for such considera-
       tion as to secure that neither a gain nor a loss accrues
       on the disposal, and

   (*b*) where, after the disposal, the asset is disposed of by
       the person who acquired it under the disposal, its
       acquisition by the person making the earlier disposal
       shall be treated for the purposes of this Act as the
       acquisition of the person making the later disposal.

(3) Where, otherwise than on the termination of a life interest
(within the meaning of section 55 above) by the death of the
person entitled thereto, any assets or parts of any assets forming
part of settled property are, under section 54 or 55 above,
deemed to be disposed of and re-acquired by the trustee, and—

   (*a*) the person becoming entitled as mentioned in section
       54(1) above is a charity, or a body mentioned in para-
       graph 12 of Schedule 6 to the Finance Act 1975 (gifts
       for national purposes, etc.), or

   (*b*) any of the assets which, or parts of which, are deemed
       to be disposed of and re-acquired under section 55(1)
       above are held for the purposes of a charity, or a body
       mentioned in the said paragraph 12,

then, if no consideration is received by any person for or in
connection with any transaction by virtue of which the charity
or other body becomes so entitled or the assets are so held,
the disposal and re-acquisition of the assets to which the charity
or other body becomes so entitled or of the assets or parts of
the assets which are held as mentioned in paragraph (*b*) above
shall, notwithstanding sections 54 and 55 above, be treated for
the purposes of this Act as made for such consideration as to
secure that neither a gain nor a loss accrues on the disposal.

147.—(1) A gain accruing on the disposal of an asset by way of gift shall not be a chargeable gain if the asset is property falling within sub-paragraph (2) of paragraph 13 of Schedule 6 to the Finance Act 1975 (gifts for public benefit) and the Treasury give a direction in relation to it under sub-paragraph (1) of that paragraph.

(2) A gain shall not be a chargeable gain if it accrues on the disposal of an asset with respect to which a capital transfer tax undertaking or an undertaking under the following provisions of this section has been given and—

(a) the disposal is by way of sale by private treaty to a body mentioned in paragraph 12 of the said Schedule 6 (museums, etc), or is to such a body otherwise than by sale, or

(b) the disposal is to the Board in pursuance of paragraph 17 of Schedule 4 to the said Act of 1975 or in accordance with directions given by the Treasury under section 50 or 51 of the Finance Act 1946 (acceptance of property in satisfaction of tax).

(3) Subsection (4) below shall have effect in respect of the disposal of any asset which is property which has been or could be designated under section 77 of the Finance Act 1976, being—

(a) a disposal by way of gift, including a gift in settlement, or

(b) a disposal of settled property by the trustee on an occasion when, under section 54(1) or 55(1) above, the trustee is deemed to dispose of and immediately re-acquire settled property (other than any disposal on which by virtue of section 56 above no chargeable gain or allowable loss accrues to the trustee).

if the requisite undertaking described in the said section 77 (maintenance, preservation and access) is given by such person as the Treasury think appropriate in the circumstances of the case.

(4) The person making a disposal to which subsection (3) above applies and the person acquiring the asset on the disposal shall be treated for all the purposes of this Act as if the asset was acquired from the one making the disposal for a consideration of such an amount as would secure that on the disposal neither a gain nor a loss would accrue to the one making the disposal.

(5) If—

(a) there is a sale of the asset and capital transfer tax is chargeable under section 78 of the Finance Act 1976

(or would be chargeable if a capital transfer tax undertaking as well as an undertaking under this section
had been given), or

(b) the Treasury are satisfied that at any time during the
period for which any such undertaking was given it
has not been observed in a material respect,

the person selling that asset or, as the case may be, the owner
of the asset shall be treated for the purposes of this Act as
having sold the asset for a consideration equal to its market
value, and, in the case of a failure to comply with the undertaking, having immediately re-acquired it for a consideration
equal to its market value.

(6) The period for which an undertaking under this section is
given shall be until the person beneficially entitled to the asset
dies or it is disposed of, whether by sale or gift or otherwise ;
and if the asset subject to the undertaking is disposed of—

(a) otherwise than on sale, and

(b) without a further undertaking being given under this
section,

subsection (5) above shall apply as if the asset had been sold to
an individual.

References in this subsection to a disposal shall be construed
without regard to any provision of this Act under which an asset
is deemed to be disposed of.

(7) Where under subsection (5) above a person is treated as
having sold for a consideration equal to its market value any
asset within section 77(1)(c), (d) or (e) of the Finance Act 1976, 1976 c. 40.
he shall also be treated as having sold and immediately re-
acquired for a consideration equal to its market value any asset
associated with it ; but the Treasury may direct that the preceding
provisions of this subsection shall not have effect in any case in
which it appears to them that the entity consisting of the asset
and any assets associated with it has not been materially
affected.

For the purposes of this subsection two or more assets are
associated with each other if one of them is a building falling
within the said section 77(1)(c) and the other or others such land
or objects as, in relation to that building, fall within the said
section 77(1)(d) or (e).

(8) If in pursuance of subsection (5) above a person is treated
as having on any occasion sold an asset and capital transfer tax
becomes chargeable on the same occasion, then, in determining
the value of the asset for the purposes of that tax, an allowance
shall be made for the capital gains tax chargeable on any chargeable gain accruing on that occasion.

PART VII
1976 c. 40.
1975 c. 7.

(9) In this section " capital transfer tax undertaking " means an undertaking under sections 76 to 81 of the Finance Act 1976 or section 31 or 34 of the Finance Act 1975.

Maintenance funds for historic buildings.

148.—(1) This section applies where a person disposes of an asset to trustees in circumstances such that the disposal is a transfer of value which by virtue of section 84 of the Finance Act 1976 (capital transfer tax: maintenance funds for historic buildings) is an exempt transfer.

(2) The person making the disposal and the person acquiring the asset on the disposal shall be treated for all the purposes of this Act as if the asset was acquired from the one making the disposal for a consideration of such an amount as would secure that on the disposal neither a gain nor a loss would accrue to the one making the disposal.

Employee trusts.

149.—(1) Where—

(a) a close company disposes of an asset to trustees in circumstances such that the disposal is a disposition which by virtue of section 90 of the Finance Act 1976 (employee trusts) is not a transfer of value for the purposes of capital transfer tax, or

(b) an individual disposes of an asset to trustees in circumstances such that the disposal is an exempt transfer by virtue of section 67 of the Finance Act 1978 (employee trusts: capital transfer tax),

1978 c. 42.

this Act shall have effect in relation to the disposal in accordance with subsections (2) and (3) below.

(2) Section 19(3) above (consideration deemed to be equal to market value) shall not apply to the disposal ; and if the disposal is by way of gift or is for a consideration not exceeding the sums allowable as a deduction under section 32 above—

(a) the disposal, and the acquisition by the trustees, shall be treated for the purposes of this Act as being made for such consideration as to secure that neither a gain nor a loss accrues on the disposal, and

(b) where the trustees dispose of the asset, its acquisition by the company or individual shall be treated as its acquisition by the trustees.

(3) Where the disposal is by a close company, section 75(1) above (assets disposed of for less than market value) shall apply to the disposal as if for the reference to market value there were substituted a reference to market value or the sums allowable as a deduction under section 32 above, whichever is the less.

(4) Subject to subsection (5) below, this Act shall also have effect in accordance with subsection (2) above in relation to any disposal made by a company other than a close company if—

    (*a*) the disposal is made to trustees otherwise than under a bargain made at arm's length, and

    (*b*) the property disposed of is to be held by them on trusts of the description specified in paragraph 17(1) of Schedule 5 to the Finance Act 1975 (that is to say, those in relation to which the said section 90 of the Finance Act 1976 has effect) and the persons for whose benefit the trusts permit the property to be applied include all or most of either—

        (i) the persons employed by or holding office with the company, or

        (ii) the persons employed by or holding office with the company or any one or more subsidiaries of the company.

(5) Subsection (4) above does not apply if the trusts permit any of the property to be applied at any time (whether during any such period as is referred to in the said paragraph 17(1) or later) for the benefit of—

    (*a*) a person who is a participator in the company (" the donor company "), or

    (*b*) any other person who is a participator in any other company that has made a disposal of property to be held on the same trusts as the property disposed of by the donor company, being a disposal in relation to which this Act has had effect in accordance with subsection (2) above, or

    (*c*) any other person who has been a participator in the donor company or any such company as is mentioned in paragraph (*b*) above at any time after, or during the ten years before, the disposal made by that company, or

    (*d*) any person who is connected with a person within paragraph (*a*), (*b*) or (*c*) above.

(6) The participators in a company who are referred to in subsection (5) above do not include any participator who—

    (*a*) is not beneficially entitled to, or to rights entitling him to acquire, 5 per cent. or more of, or of any class of the shares comprised in, its issued share capital, and

    (*b*) on a winding-up of the company would not be entitled to 5 per cent. or more of its assets :

PART VII

and in determining whether the trusts permit property to be applied as mentioned in that subsection, no account shall be taken—

>   (i) of any power to make a payment which is the income of any person for any of the purposes of income tax, or would be the income for any of those purposes of a person not resident in the United Kingdom if he were so resident, or

1978 c. 42.

>   (ii) if the trusts are those of a profit sharing scheme approved under the Finance Act 1978, of any power to appropriate shares in pursuance of the scheme.

1948 c. 38.

(7) In subsection (4) above " subsidiary " has the same meaning as in the Companies Act 1948 and in subsections (5) and (6) above " participator " has the meaning given in section 303(1) of the Taxes Act, except that it does not include a loan creditor.

(8) In this section " close company " includes a company which, if resident in the United Kingdom, would be a close company as defined in section 155(1) below.

PART VIII

SUPPLEMENTAL

Valuation

Valuation: general.

150.—(1) In this Act " market value " in relation to any assets means the price which those assets might reasonably be expected to fetch on a sale in the open market.

(2) In estimating the market value of any assets no reduction shall be made in the estimate on account of the estimate being made on the assumption that the whole of the assets is to be placed on the market at one and the same time.

(3) The market value of shares or securities listed in The Stock Exchange Daily Official List shall, except where in consequence of special circumstances prices quoted in that List are by themselves not a proper measure of market value, be as follows—

>   (a) the lower of the two prices shown in the quotations for the shares or securities in The Stock Exchange Daily Official List on the relevant date plus one-quarter of the difference between those two figures, or

>   (b) halfway between the highest and lowest prices at which bargains, other than bargains done at special prices, were recorded in the shares or securities for the relevant date,

choosing the amount under paragraph (a) if less than that under paragraph (b), or if no such bargains were recorded for the rele-

vant date, and choosing the amount under paragraph (b) if less
than that under paragraph (a):

Provided that—

(i) this subsection shall not apply to shares or securities for which The Stock Exchange provides a more active market elswhere than on the London trading floor, and

(ii) if the London trading floor is closed on the relevant date the market value shall be ascertained by reference to the latest previous date or earliest subsequent date on which it is open, whichever affords the lower market value.

(4) In this Act " market value " in relation to any rights of unit holders in any unit trust scheme the buying and selling prices of which are published regularly by the managers of the scheme shall mean an amount equal to the buying price (that is the lower price) so published on the relevant date, or if none were published on that date, on the latest date before.

(5) In relation to an asset of a kind the sale of which is subject to restrictions imposed under the Exchange Control Act 1947 c. 14.
1947 such that part of what is paid by the purchaser is not retainable by the seller the market value, as arrived at under subsection (1), subsection (3) or subsection (4) above, shall be subject to such adjustment as is appropriate having regard to the difference between the amount payable by a purchaser and the amount receivable by a seller.

(6) The provisions of this section, with sections 151 to 153 below, have effect subject to Part I of Schedule 6 to this Act (market value at a time before the commencement of this Act).

151. If a person is given, or acquires from one or more per- Assets sons with whom he is connected, by way of two or more gifts disposed of or other transactions, assets of which the aggregate market in a series of value, when considered separately in relation to the separate transactions. gifts or other transactions, is less than their aggregate market value when considered together, then for the purposes of this Act their market value, where relevant, shall be taken to be the larger market value, to be apportioned rateably to the respective disposals.

152.—(1) The provisions of subsection (3) below shall have Unquoted effect in any case where, in relation to an asset to which this shares and section applies, there falls to be determined by virtue of section securities. 150(1) above the price which the asset might reasonably be expected to fetch on a sale in the open market.

(2) The assets to which this section applies are shares and securities which are not quoted on a recognised stock exchange, within the meaning of section 535 of the Taxes Act,

at the time as at which their market value for the purposes of tax on chargeable gains falls to be determined.

(3) For the purposes of a determination falling within subsection (1) above, it shall be assumed that, in the open market which is postulated for the purposes of that determination, there is available to any prospective purchaser of the asset in question all the information which a prudent prospective purchaser of the asset might reasonably require if he were proposing to purchase it from a willing vendor by private treaty and at arm's length.

Value determined for capital transfer tax.

153. Where on the death of any person capital transfer tax is chargeable on the value of his estate immediately before his death and the value of an asset forming part of that estate has been ascertained (whether in any proceedings or otherwise) for the purposes of that tax, the value so ascertained shall be taken for the purposes of this Act to be the market value of that asset at the date of the death.

Other provisions

Income tax decisions.

154. Any assessment to income tax or decision on a claim under the Income Tax Acts, and any decision on an appeal under the Income Tax Acts against such an assessment or decision, shall be conclusive so far as under Chapter II of Part II of this Act, or any other provision of this Act, liability to tax depends on the provisions of the Income Tax Acts.

Interpretation.

155.—(1) In this Act, unless the context otherwise requires—

" allowable loss " has the meaning given by section 29 above,

" the Board " means the Commissioners of Inland Revenue,

" chargeable gain " has the meaning given by section 28(2) above,

" chargeable period " means a year of assessment or an accounting period of a company for purposes of corporation tax,

" close company " has the meaning given by sections 282 and 283 of the Taxes Act,

" company " includes any body corporate or unincorporated association but does not include a partnership, and shall be construed in accordance with section 93 above (application of Act to unit trusts),

" control " shall be construed in accordance with section
302 of the Taxes Act,

" inspector " means any inspector of taxes,

" land " includes messuages, tenements, and hereditaments, houses and buildings of any tenure,

" married woman living with her husband ": see subsection (2) below,

" part disposal " has the meaning given by section 19(2) above,

" personal representatives " has the meaning given by section 432(4) of the Taxes Act,

" quoted " on a stock exchange, or recognised stock exchange, in the United Kingdom: see subsection (3) below,

" the Taxes Act " means the Income and Corporation 1970 c. 10. Taxes Act 1970,

" trade " has the same meaning as in the Income Tax Acts,

" trading stock " has the meaning given by section 137(4) of the Taxes Act,

" wasting asset " has the meaning given by section 37 above and paragraph 1 of Schedule 3 to this Act,

" year of assessment " means, in relation to capital gains tax, a year beginning on 6th April and ending on 5th April in the following calendar year, and " 1979-80 " and so on indicate years of assessment as in the Income Tax Acts.

(2) References in this Act to a married woman living with her husband shall be construed in accordance with section 42(1)(2) of the Taxes Act.

(3) References in this Act to quotation on a stock exchange in the United Kingdom or a recognised stock exchange in the United Kingdom shall be construed as references to listing in the Official List of The Stock Exchange.

(4) The Table below indexes other general definitions in this Act.

Q2

PART VIII

Expression defined	Reference
"Absolutely entitled as against the trustee " ...	S. 46(2).
"Authorised unit trust "	S. 92.
" Branch or agency "	S. 12(3).
" Class ", in relation to shares or securities	S. 64(1).
" Connected ", in references to persons being connected with one another.	S. 63.
" Court investment fund "	S. 92.
" Gilt-edged securities "	Schedule 2.
" Investment trust "	S. 92.
" Issued ", in relation to shares or debentures ...	S. 64(2).
" Lease " and cognate expressions	Paragraph 10(1) of Schedule 3.
" Legatee "	S. 47(2)(3).
" Market value "	Ss. 150 to 153; Part I of Schedule 6.
" Resident " and " ordinarily resident "	S. 18(1).
" Settled property "	S. 51.
" Shares "	S. 64(1).
" Unit trust scheme "	S. 92.

(5) References in the Income Tax Acts to profits or gains shall not include references to chargeable gains.

PART IX

GENERAL

Commencement.

156.—(1) Except as otherwise provided by this Part of this Act, this Act shall come into force in relation to tax for the year 1979-80 and subsequent years of assessment, and tax for other chargeable periods beginning after 5th April 1979.

(2) The following provisions of this Act, that is—

    (a) so much of any provision of this Act as authorises the making of any order or other instrument,

    (b) except where the tax concerned is all tax for chargeable periods to which this Act does not apply, so much of any provision of this Act as confers any power or imposes any duty the exercise or performance of which operates or may operate in relation to tax for more than one chargeable period,

shall come into force for all purposes on 6th April 1979 to the exclusion of the corresponding enactments repealed by this Act.

Savings, transitory provisions and consequential amendments.

157.—(1) Schedule 6 to this Act, which contains transitory provisions and savings, shall have effect, and the repeals made by section 158(1) below have effect subject to that Schedule.

(2) For the avoidance of doubt it is hereby declared that PART IX
this Act has effect subject to those provisions of the Taxes Act
and other enactments relating to chargeable gains which are
not repealed by this Act; and with a view to preserving the
existing effect of such enactments as are mentioned in Schedule
7 to this Act, they shall be amended in accordance with that
Schedule.

(3) The provisions of the said Schedule 7, and the other
provisions of this Part of this Act, are without prejudice to the
provisions of the Interpretation Act 1978 as respects the effect 1978 c. 30.
of repeals.

(4) This section and the said Schedules 6 and 7 shall come
into force on the passing of this Act.

158.—(1) The enactments and instruments mentioned in Repeals.
Schedule 8 to this Act are hereby repealed to the extent specified in the third column of that Schedule.

(2) The said repeals shall come into force in accordance with
section 156 above.

159.—(1) The continuity of the operation of the law relating Continuity and
to chargeable gains shall not be affected by the substitution of construction
this Act for the repealed enactments. of references
to old and
(2) Any reference, whether express or implied, in any enact- new law.
ment, instrument or document (including this Act and any enactment amended by Schedule 7 to this Act) to, or to things done
or falling to be done under or for the purposes of, any provision of this Act shall, if and so far as the nature of the reference
permits, be construed as including, in relation to the times,
years or periods, circumstances or purposes in relation to which
the corresponding provision in the repealed enactments has or
had effect, a reference to, or as the case may be to things done
or falling to be done under or for the purposes of, that corresponding provision.

(3) Any reference, whether express or implied, in any enactment, instrument or document (including the repealed enactments and enactments, instruments and documents passed or
made after the passing of this Act) to, or to things done or
falling to be done under or for the purposes of, any of the
repealed enactments shall, if and so far as the nature of the
reference permits, be construed as including, in relation to the
times, years or periods, circumstances or purposes in relation
to which the corresponding provision of this Act has effect, a
reference to, or as the case may be to things done or falling
to be done under or for the purposes of, that corresponding
provision.

Q3

PART IX   (4) In this section " the repealed enactments " means the enactments repealed by this Act.

Short title.   **160.** This Act may be cited as the Capital Gains Tax Act 1979.

SCHEDULES

SCHEDULE 1

Relief for Gains Less than £9,500

Preliminary

1. In this Schedule references to any subsections not otherwise identified are references to subsections of section 5 of this Act.

Husband and wife

2.—(1) For any year of assessment during which a married woman is living with her husband subsections (1) to (4) shall apply to them as if the amounts of £1,000, £5,000 and £600 were divided between them—

(a) in proportion to their respective taxable amounts for that year (disregarding for this purpose paragraphs (a) and (b) of subsection (4)), or

(b) where the aggregate of those amounts does not exceed £1,000 and allowable losses accruing to either of them in a previous year are carried forward from that year, in such other proportion as they may agree.

(2) Sub-paragraph (1) above shall also apply for any year of assessment during a part of which (being a part beginning with 6th April) a married woman is living with her husband but—

(a) her taxable amount for that year shall not include chargeable gains or allowable losses accruing to her in the remainder of the year, and

(b) subsections (1) to (4) shall apply to her (without the modification in sub-paragraph (1) above) for the remainder of the year as if it were a separate year of assessment.

3.—(1) For any year of assessment during which or during a part of which (being a part beginning with 6th April) the individual is a married man whose wife is living with him and in relation to whom section 45(1) of this Act applies subsection (5) shall apply as if—

(a) the chargeable gains accruing to him in the year included those accruing to her in the year or the part of the year, and

(b) all the disposals of assets made by her in the year or the part of the year were made by him.

(2) Subsection (5) shall not apply for any year of assessment during which or during a part of which (being a part beginning with 6th April)—

(a) the individual is a married man whose wife is living with him but in relation to whom the said section 45(1) does not apply, or

(b) the individual is a married woman living with her husband.

Q4

Personal representatives

4. For the year of assessment in which an individual dies and for the two next following years of assessment, subsections (1) to (5) shall apply to his personal representatives as they apply to an individual.

Trustees

5.—(1) For any year of assessment during the whole or part of which settled property is held on trusts which secure that, during the lifetime of a mentally disabled person or a person in receipt of attendance allowance, any of the property which is applied, and any income arising from the property, is applied only or mainly for the benefit of that person, subsections (1) to (5) shall apply to the trustees of the settlement as they apply to an individual.

(2) In this paragraph " mentally disabled person " means a person who by reason of mental disorder within the meaning of the Mental Health Act 1959 is incapable of administering his property or managing his affairs and " attendance allowance " means an allowance under section 35 of the Social Security Act 1975 or the Social Security (Northern Ireland) Act 1975.

1959 c. 72.

1975 c. 14.
1975 c. 15.

6.—(1) For any year of assessment during the whole or part of which any property is settled property, not being a year of assessment for which paragraph 5(1) above applies, subsections (1) to (5) shall apply to the trustees of a settlement as they apply to an individual but with the following modifications.

(2) In subsections (1), (4) and (5) for " £1,000 " there shall be substituted " £500 ".

(3) For subsections (2) and (3) there shall be substituted—

" (2) If an individual's taxable amount for a year of assessment exceeds £500 the amount of capital gains tax to which he is chargeable for that year shall not exceed one-half of the excess."

(4) In subsection (5) for " £5,000 " there shall be substituted " £2,500 ".

(5) This paragraph applies where the settlement was made before 7th June 1978.

Section 64(1).

SCHEDULE 2
GILT-EDGED SECURITIES

PART I

1. For the purposes of this Act " gilt-edged securities " means the securities specified in Part II of this Schedule, and such of the following securities, denominated in sterling and issued after 15th April 1969, as may be specified by order made by the Treasury by statutory instrument, namely—

1968 c. 13.

(a) stocks and bonds issued under section 12 of the National Loans Act 1968, and (*b*) stocks and bonds guaranteed by the Treasury and issued under the Electricity (Scotland) Acts 1943 to 1954, the Electricity Acts 1947 and 1957 and the Gas Act 1972. SCH. 2 1972 c. 60.

2. The Treasury shall cause particulars of any order made under paragraph 1 above to be published in the London and Edinburgh Gazettes as soon as may be after the order is made.

3. Section 14(*b*) of the Interpretation Act 1978 (implied power to amend orders made by statutory instrument) shall not apply to the power of making orders under paragraph 1 above. 1978 c. 30.

PART II

EXISTING GILT-EDGED SECURITIES

Stocks and bonds charged on the National Loans Fund

11½%	Treasury Stock 1979
3 %	Treasury Stock 1979
10½%	Treasury Stock 1979
9 %	Treasury Convertible Stock 1980
4 %	British Overseas Airways Stock 1974-80
9½%	Treasury Stock 1980
3½%	Treasury Stock 1977-80
5¼%	Funding Loan 1978-80
13 %	Exchequer Stock 1980
11½%	Treasury Stock 1981
3½%	Treasury Stock 1979-81
9¾%	Treasury Stock 1981
8¼%	Exchequer Stock 1981
9½%	Exchequer Stock 1981
3 %	Exchequer Stock 1981
	Variable Rate Treasury Stock 1981
12¾%	Exchequer Stock 1981
8½%	Treasury Loan 1980-82
3 %	Treasury Stock 1982
14 %	Treasury Stock 1982
2½%	British Overseas Airways Stock 1977-82
	Variable Rate Treasury Stock 1982
8¼%	Treasury Stock 1982
9¼%	Exchequer Stock 1982
8¾%	Exchequer Stock 1983
3 %	British Overseas Airways Stock 1980-83
3 %	Exchequer Stock 1983
12 %	Treasury Loan 1983
9¼%	Treasury Stock 1983
10 %	Exchequer Stock 1983
5½%	Funding Stock 1982-84
12¼%	Exchequer Stock 1985
8½%	Treasury Loan 1984-86
6½%	Funding Loan 1985-87
7¾%	Treasury Loan 1985-88
3 %	British Transport Stock 1978-88
5 %	Treasury Stock 1986-89

13 %	Treasury Stock 1990
8¼%	Treasury Loan 1987-90
11¾%	Treasury Stock 1991
5¾%	Funding Loan 1987-91
12¾%	Treasury Loan 1992
10 %	Treasury Stock 1992
12¼%	Exchequer Stock 1992
12½%	Treasury Loan 1993
6 %	Funding Loan 1993
13¾%	Treasury Loan 1993
14½%	Treasury Loan 1994
12½%	Exchequer Stock 1994
9 %	Treasury Loan 1994
12 %	Treasury Stock 1995
10¼%	Exchequer Stock 1995
12¾%	Treasury Loan 1995
9 %	Treasury Loan 1992-96
15¼%	Treasury Loan 1996
13¼%	Exchequer Loan 1996
13¼%	Treasury Loan 1997
10½%	Exchequer Stock 1997
8¾%	Treasury Loan 1997
6¾%	Treasury Loan 1995-98
15½%	Treasury Loan 1998
12 %	Exchequer Stock 1998
9½%	Treasury Loan 1999
10½%	Treasury Stock 1999
12 %	Exchequer Stock 1999-2002
3½%	Funding Stock 1999-2004
12½%	Treasury Stock 2003-2005
8 %	Treasury Loan 2002-2006
5½%	Treasury Stock 2008-2012
7¾%	Treasury Loan 2012-2015
2½%	Treasury Stock 1986-2016
12 %	Exchequer Stock 2013-2017
2½%	Annuities 1905 or after
2¾%	Annuities 1905 or after
2½%	Consolidated Stock 1923 or after
4 %	Consolidated Loan 1957 or after
3½%	Conversion Loan 1961 or after
2½%	Treasury Stock 1975 or after
3 %	Treasury Stock 1966 or after
3½%	War Loan 1952 or after

Securities issued by the Treasury under Part II of the Tithe Act 1936

3 %	Redemption Stock 1986-96

Securities issued by certain public corporations and guaranteed by the Treasury

4¼%	North of Scotland Electricity Stock 1974-79
4¼%	British Electricity Stock 1974-79
3½%	British Electricity Stock 1976-79
3½%	North of Scotland Electricity Stock 1977-80

3 % British European Airways Stock 1980-83 Sch. 2
3 % North of Scotland Electricity Stock 1989-92
3 % British Gas Stock 1990-95.

SCHEDULE 3 Section 106.

LEASES

*Leases of land as wasting assets: curved line restriction of allow-
able expenditure*

1.—(1) A lease of land shall not be a wasting asset until the time
when its duration does not exceed fifty years.

(2) If at the beginning of the period of ownership of a lease of
land it is subject to a sub-lease not at a rackrent and the value of
the lease at the end of the duration of the sub-lease, estimated as at
the beginning of the period of ownership, exceeds the expenditure
allowable under section 32(1)(*a*) of this Act in computing the gain
accruing on a disposal of the lease, the lease shall not be a wasting
asset until the end of the duration of the sub-lease.

(3) In the case of a wasting asset which is a lease of land the rate
at which expenditure is assumed to be written off shall, instead of
being a uniform rate as provided by section 38 of this Act, be a rate
fixed in accordance with the Table below.

(4) Accordingly, for the purposes of the computation under Chapter II of Part II of this Act of the gain accruing on a disposal of a
lease, and given that —

(*a*) the percentage derived from the Table for the duration of
the lease at the beginning of the period of ownership is $P(1)$,

(*b*) the percentage so derived for the duration of the lease at
the time when any item of expenditure attributable to the
lease under section 32(1)(*b*) of this Act is first reflected in
the nature of the lease is $P(2)$, and

(*c*) the percentage so derived for the duration of the lease at
the time of the disposal is $P(3)$,

then—

(i) there shall be excluded from the expenditure attributable to
the lease under section 32(1)(*a*) of this Act a fraction equal
to $\dfrac{P(1)-P(3)}{P(1)}$, and

(ii) there shall be excluded from any item of expenditure attributable to the lease under section 32(1)(*b*) of this Act a
fraction equal to $\dfrac{P(2)-P(3)}{P(2)}$.

(5) This paragraph applies notwithstanding that the period of
ownership of the lease is a period exceeding fifty years and, accordingly, no expenditure shall be written off under this paragraph in
respect of any period earlier than the time when the lease becomes
a wasting asset.

SCH. 3   (6) Section 39 of this Act (wasting assets qualifying for capital allowances) shall apply in relation to this paragraph as it applies in relation to section 38.

TABLE

Years			Percentage	Years			Percentage
50 (or more)	...	...	100	25	...	...	81·100
49	...	...	99·657	24	...	...	79·622
48	...	...	99·289	23	...	...	78·055
47	...	...	98·902	22	...	...	76·399
46	...	...	98·490	21	...	...	74·635
45	...	...	98·059	20	...	...	72·770
44	...	...	97·595	19	...	...	70·791
43	...	...	97·107	18	...	...	68·697
42	...	...	96·593	17	...	...	66·470
41	...	...	96·041	16	...	...	64·116
40	...	...	95·457	15	...	...	61·617
39	...	...	94·842	14	...	...	58·971
38	...	...	94·189	13	...	...	56·167
37	...	...	93·497	12	...	...	53·191
36	...	...	92·761	11	...	...	50·038
35	...	...	91·981	10	...	...	46·695
34	...	...	91·156	9	...	...	43·154
33	...	...	90·280	8	...	...	39·399
32	...	...	89·354	7	...	...	35·414
31	...	...	88·371	6	...	...	31·195
30	...	...	87·330	5	...	...	26·722
29	...	...	86·226	4	...	...	21·983
28	...	...	85·053	3	...	...	16·959
27	...	...	83·816	2	...	...	11·629
26	...	...	82·496	1	...	...	5·983
				0	...	...	0

If the duration of the lease is not an exact number of years the percentage to be derived from the Table above shall be the percentage for the whole number of years plus one twelfth of the difference between that and the percentage for the next higher number of years for each odd month counting an odd 14 days or more as one month.

Premiums for leases

2.—(1) Subject to this Schedule where the payment of a premium is required under a lease of land, or otherwise under the terms subject to which a lease of land is granted, there is a part disposal of the freehold or other asset out of which the lease is granted.

(2) In applying section 35 of this Act to such a part disposal, the property which remains undisposed of includes a right to any rent or other payments, other than a premium, payable under the lease, and that right shall be valued as at the time of the part disposal.

3.—(1) This paragraph applies in relation to a lease of land.

(2) Where, under the terms subject to which a lease is granted, a sum becomes payable by the tenant in lieu of the whole or part of the rent for any period, or as consideration for the surrender of the lease, the lease shall be deemed for the purposes of this Schedule

to have required the payment of a premium to the landlord (in
addition to any other premium) of the amount of that sum for the
period in relation to which the sum is payable.

(3) Where, as consideration for the variation or waiver of any of
the terms of a lease, a sum becomes payable by the tenant otherwise
than by way of rent, the lease shall be deemed for the purposes of
this Schedule to have required the payment of a premium to the
landlord (in addition to any other premium) of the amount of that
sum for the period from the time when the variation or waiver takes
effect to the time when it ceases to have effect.

(4) If under sub-paragraph (2) or (3) above a premium is deemed
to have been received by the landlord, otherwise than as consideration
for the surrender of the lease, then subject to sub-paragraph (5)
below, both the landlord and the tenant shall be treated as if that
premium were, or were part of, the consideration for the grant of
the lease due at the time when the lease was granted, and the gain
accruing to the landlord on the disposal by way of grant of the lease
shall be recomputed and any necessary adjustments of tax, whether
by way of assessment for the year in which the premium is deemed
to have been received, or by way of discharge or repayment of tax,
made accordingly.

(5) If under sub-paragraph (2) or (3) above a premium is deemed
to have been received by the landlord, otherwise than as consideration
for the surrender of the lease, and the landlord is a tenant under a
lease the duration of which does not exceed fifty years this Schedule
shall apply as if an amount equal to the amount of that premium
deemed to have been received had been given by way of consideration
for the grant of the part of the sub-lease covered by the period in
respect of which the premium is deemed to have been paid as if
that consideration were expenditure incurred by the sub-lessee and
attributable to that part of the sub-lease under section 32(1)(*b*) of
this Act.

(6) Where under sub-paragraph (2) above a premium is deemed to
have been received as consideration for the surrender of a lease the
surrender of the lease shall not be the occasion of any recomputation
of the gain accruing on the receipt of any other premium, and the
premium which is consideration for the surrender of the lease shall
be regarded as consideration for a separate transaction consisting of
the disposal by the landlord of his interest in the lease.

(7) Sub-paragraph (3) above shall apply in relation to a transaction
not at arm's length, and in particular in relation to a transaction
entered into gratuitously, as if such sum had become payable by the
tenant otherwise than by way of rent as might have been required of
him if the transaction had been at arm's length.

Sub-leases out of short leases

4.—(1) In the computation under Chapter II or Part II of this Act
of the gain accruing on the part disposal of a lease which is a wasting
asset by way of the grant of a sub-lease for a premium the expenditure
attributable to the lease under paragraphs (*a*) and (*b*) of section 32(1)

of this Act shall be apportioned in accordance with this paragraph, and section 35 of this Act shall not apply.

(2) Out of each item of the expenditure attributable to the lease under paragraphs (*a*) and (*b*) of section 32(1) of this Act there shall be apportioned to what is disposed of—

> (*a*) if the amount of the premium is not less than what would be obtainable by way of premium for the said sub-lease if the rent payable under that sub-lease were the same as the rent payable under the lease, the fraction which, under paragraph 1(3) of this Schedule, is to be written off over the period which is the duration of the sub-lease, and

> (*b*) if the amount of the premium is less than the said amount so obtainable, the said fraction multiplied by a fraction equal to the amount of the said premium divided by the said amount so obtainable.

(3) If the sub-lease is a sub-lease of part only of the land comprised in the lease this paragraph shall apply only in relation to a proportion of the expenditure attributable to the lease under paragraphs (*a*) and (*b*) of section 32(1) of this Act which is the same as the proportion which the value of the land comprised in the sub-lease bears to the value of that and the other land comprised in the lease ; and the remainder of that expenditure shall be apportioned to what remains undisposed of.

Exclusion of premiums taxed under Schedule A etc.

5.—(1) Where by reference to any premium income tax has become chargeable under section 80 of the Taxes Act on any amount, that amount out of the premium shall be excluded from the consideration brought into account in the computation under Chapter II of Part II of this Act of a gain accruing on the disposal for which the premium is consideration except where the consideration is taken into account in the denominator of the fraction by reference to which an apportionment is made under section 35 of this Act (part disposals).

(2) Where by reference to any premium in respect of a sub-lease granted out of a lease the duration of which (that is of the lease) does not, at the time of granting the lease, exceed fifty years, income tax has become chargeable under section 80 of the Taxes Act on any amount that amount shall be deducted from any gain accruing on the disposal for which the premium is consideration as computed in accordance with the provisions of this Act apart from this sub-paragraph, but not so as to convert the gain into a loss, or to increase any loss.

(3) Where income tax has become chargeable under section 82 of the Taxes Act (sale of land with right of re-conveyance) on any amount a sum of that amount shall be excluded from the consideration brought into account in the computation under Chapter II of Part II of this Act of a gain accruing on the disposal of the estate or interest in respect of which income tax becomes so chargeable, except where the consideration is taken into account in

the denominator of the fraction by reference to which an apportion- SCH. 3
ment is made under section 35 of this Act:

Provided that if what is disposed of is the remainder of a lease
or a sub-lease out of a lease the duration of which does not exceed
fifty years the preceding provisions of this sub-paragraph shall not
apply but the said amount shall be deducted from any gain accruing
on the disposal as computed in accordance with the provisions of
this Act apart from this sub-paragraph, but not so as to convert
the gain into a loss, or to increase any loss.

(4) References in sub-paragraph (1) and (2) above to a premium
include references to a premium deemed to have been received
under subsection (3) or subsection (4) of section 80 of the Taxes
Act (which correspond to paragraph 3(2) and (3) of this Schedule).

(5) Section 31 of this Act (exclusion of consideration chargeable to
tax on income) shall not be taken as authorising the exclusion of
any amount from the consideration for a disposal of assets taken
into account in the computation under Chapter II of Part II of this
Act by reference to any amount chargeable to tax under Part III
of the Taxes Act.

6.—(1) If under section 83(2) of the Taxes Act (allowance where,
by the grant of a sub-lease, a lessee has converted a capital amount
into a right to income) a person is to be treated as paying additional
rent in consequence of having granted a sub-lease, the amount of
any loss accruing to him on the disposal by way of the grant of
the sub-lease shall be reduced by the total amount of rent which
he is thereby treated as paying over the term of the sub-lease (and
without regard to whether relief is thereby effectively given over
the term of the sub-lease), but not so as to convert the loss into
a gain, or to increase any gain.

(2) Nothing in section 31 of this Act shall be taken as applying
in relation to any amount on which tax is paid under section 81 of
the Taxes Act (charge on assignment of lease granted at undervalue).

(3) If any adjustment is made under section 82(2)(*b*) of the Taxes
Act on a claim under that paragraph, any necessary adjustment shall
be made to give effect to the consequences of the claim on the
operation of this paragraph or paragraph 5 above.

7. If under section 80(2) of the Taxes Act income tax is chargeable
on any amount, as being a premium the payment of which is
deemed to be required by the lease, the person so chargeable shall
be treated for the purposes of the computation of any gain accruing
to him as having incurred at the time the lease was granted expenditure of that amount (in addition to any other expenditure) attributable to the asset under section 32(1)(*b*) of this Act.

Duration of leases

8.—(1) In ascertaining for the purposes of this Act the duration
of a lease of land the following provisions shall have effect.

(2) Where the terms of the lease include provision for the determination of the lease by notice given by the landlord, the lease

SCH. 3   shall not be treated as granted for a term longer than one ending at the earliest date on which it could be determined by notice given by the landlord.

(3) Where any of the terms of the lease (whether relating to forfeiture or to any other matter) or any other circumstances render it unlikely that the lease will continue beyond a date falling before the expiration of the term of the lease, the lease shall not be treated as having been granted for a term longer than one ending on that date.

(4) Sub-paragraph (3) applies in particular where the lease provides for the rent to go up after a given date, or for the tenant's obligations to become in any other respect more onerous after a given date, but includes provision for the determination of the lease on that date by notice given by the tenant, and those provisions render it unlikely that the lease will continue beyond that date.

(5) Where the terms of the lease include provision for the extension of the lease beyond a given date by notice given by the tenant this paragraph shall apply as if the term of the lease extended for as long as it could be extended by the tenant, but subject to any right of the landlord by notice to determine the lease.

(6) It is hereby declared that the question what is the duration of a lease is to be decided, in relation to the grant or any disposal of the lease, by reference to the facts which were known or ascertainable at the time when the lease was acquired or created.

Leases of property other than land

9.—(1) Paragraphs 2, 3, 4 and 8 of this Schedule shall apply in relation to leases of property other than land as they apply to leases of land, but subject to any necessary modifications.

(2) Where by reference to any capital sum within the meaning of section 492 of the Taxes Act (leases of assets other than land) any person has been charged to income tax on any amount, that amount out of the capital sum shall be deducted from any gain accruing on the disposal for which that capital sum is consideration, as computed in accordance with the provisions of this Act apart from this sub-paragraph, but not so as to convert the gain into a loss, or increase any loss.

(3) In the case of a lease of a wasting asset which is movable property the lease shall be assumed to terminate not later than the end of the life of the wasting asset.

Interpretation

10.—(1) In this Act, unless the context otherwise requires " lease "—

(a) in relation to land, includes an underlease, sublease or any tenancy or licence, and any agreement for a lease, underlease, sublease or tenancy or licence and, in the case of land outside the United Kingdom, any interest corresponding to a lease as so defined, (*b*) in relation to any description of property other than land, means any kind of agreement or arrangement under which payments are made for the use of, or otherwise in respect of, property,

and ." lessor ", " lessee " and " rent " shall be construed accordingly.

(2) In this Schedule " premium " includes any like sum, whether payable to the intermediate or a superior landlord, and for the purposes of this Schedule any sum (other than rent) paid on or in connection with the granting of a tenancy shall be presumed to have been paid by way of premium except in so far as other sufficient consideration for the payment is shown to have been given.

(3) In the application of this Schedule to Scotland " premium " includes in particular a grassum payable to any landlord or intermediate landlord on the creation of a sublease.

SCHEDULE 4

RELIEF FOR GIFTS OF BUSINESS ASSETS

PART I

AGRICULTURAL PROPERTY AND SETTLED PROPERTY

Agricultural property

1.—(1) This paragraph applies where—

(*a*) there is a disposal of an asset which is, or is an interest in, agricultural property within the meaning of Schedule 8 to the Finance Act 1975 (capital transfer tax relief for agri- 1975 c. cultural property), and

(*b*) apart from this paragraph, the disposal would not fall within section 126(1)(*a*) of this Act by reason only that the agricultural property is not used for the purposes of a trade carried on as mentioned in that paragraph.

(2) Where this paragraph applies, section 126(1) of this Act shall apply in relation to the disposal if the circumstances are such that a reduction in respect of the asset—

(*a*) is made under Schedule 8 to the Finance Act 1975 in relation to a chargeable transfer taking place on the occasion of the disposal, or

(*b*) would be so made if there were a chargeable transfer on that occasion and a claim were duly made under that Schedule.

Settled property

2.—(1) If a trustee is deemed, by virtue of section 54(1) or 55(1) of this Act (settled property), to have disposed of, and immediately reacquired—

(*a*) an asset which is, or is an interest in, an asset used for the purposes of a trade, profession or vocation carried on by the trustee or by a relevant beneficiary, or

(b) shares or securities of a trading company as to which not not less than 25 per cent. of the voting rights are exercisable by the trustee at the time of the disposal and reacquisition, subsection (3) of section 126 of this Act shall apply in relation to the disposal if a claim for relief under that section is made by the trustee.

(2) Where subsection (3) of the said section 126 applies by virtue of sub-paragraph (1) above—

(a) a reference to the trustee shall be substituted for the reference in paragraph (a) of that subsection to the transferor and for the reference in paragraph (b) thereof to the transferee, and

(b) subsection (6) of that section shall not apply.

(3) In paragraph (a) of sub-paragraph (1) above, " relevant beneficiary " means—

(a) where the disposal is deemed to occur by virtue of section 54(1) of this Act, a beneficiary who had an interest in possession in the settled property immediately before the disposal ; and

(b) where the disposal is deemed to occur by virtue of section 55(1) of this Act on the termination of a life interest in possession, the beneficiary whose interest it was.

3.—(1) This paragraph applies where—

(a) there is, by virtue of section 54(1) or 55(1) of this Act (settled property), a disposal of an asset which is, or is an interest in, agricultural property within the meaning of Schedule 8 to the Finance Act 1975, and

(b) apart from this paragraph, the disposal would not fall within paragraph (a) of paragraph 2(1) above by reason only that the agricultural property is not used for the purposes of a trade as mentioned in the said paragraph (a).

(2) Where this paragraph applies, paragraph 2(1) above shall apply in relation to the disposal if the circumstances are such that a reduction in respect of the asset—

(a) is made under Schedule 8 to the Finance Act 1975 in relation to a chargeable transfer taking place on the occasion of the disposal, or

(b) would be so made if there were a chargeable transfer on that occasion and a claim were duly made under that Schedule.

PART II

REDUCTIONS IN HELD-OVER GAIN

Application and interpretation

4.—(1) The provisions of this Part of this Schedule apply in cases where a claim for relief is made under section 126 of this Act.

(2) In this Part of this Schedule—

(a) " the principal provision " means section 126(1) of this Act, or, as the case may require, sub-paragraph (1) of paragraph 2 above,

(b) " shares " includes securities,

(c) " the transferor " and " the transferee " have the same meaning as in section 126 of this Act, except that, in a case where paragraph 2 above applies, each of those expressions refers to the trustee mentioned in that paragraph, and

(d) " unrelieved gain ", in relation to a disposal, has the same meaning as in section 126(6) of this Act.

(3) Any reference in this Part of this Schedule to a disposal of an asset is a reference to a disposal which falls within paragraph (a) of the principal provision and any reference to a disposal of shares is a reference to a disposal which falls within paragraph (b) of that provision.

(4) In relation to a disposal of an asset or of shares, any reference in the following provisions of this Part of this Schedule to the held-over gain is a reference to the held-over gain on that disposal as determined under subsection (5) or, as the case may be, subsection (6) of section 126 of this Act (taking account, where paragraph 2 above applies, of sub-paragraph (2)(b) of that paragraph).

Reductions peculiar to disposals of assets

5. If, in the case of a disposal of an asset, the asset was not used for the purposes of the trade, profession or vocation referred to in paragraph (a) of the principal provision throughout the period of its ownership by the transferor, the amount of the held-over gain shall be reduced by multiplying it by the fraction of which the denominator is the number of days in that period of ownership and the numerator is the number of days in that period during which the asset was so used.

6. If, in the case of a disposal of an asset, the asset is a building or structure and, over the period of its ownership by the transferor or any substantial part of that period, part of the building or structure was, and part was not, used for the purposes of the trade, profession or vocation referred to in paragraph (a) of the principal provision, there shall be determined the fraction of the unrelieved gain on the disposal which it is just and reasonable to apportion to the part of the asset which was so used, and the amount of the held-over gain (as reduced, if appropriate, under paragraph 5 above) shall be reduced by multiplying it by that fraction.

Reduction peculiar to disposal of shares

7.—(1) If, in the case of a disposal of shares, the chargeable assets of the company whose shares are disposed of include assets which are not business assets, the amount of the held-over gain shall be reduced by multiplying it by the fraction of which the denominator is the market value of the whole of the company's chargeable assets on the date of the disposal and the numerator is the market value of the company's chargeable business assets on that date.

SCH. 4   (2) For the purpose of this paragraph—

(*a*) an asset is a business asset in relation to a company if it is or is an interest in an asset used for the purposes of a trade, profession or vocation carried on by the company, and

(*b*) an asset is a chargeable asset in relation to a company at any time if, on a disposal of it at that time, a chargeable gain would accrue to the company.

Reduction where gain partly relieved by retirement relief

8.—(1) If, in the case of a disposal of an asset—

(*a*) the disposal is of a chargeable business asset and is comprised in a disposal of the whole or part of a business in respect of gains accruing on which the transferor is entitled to relief under section 124 of this Act (transfer of business on retirement), and

(*b*) apart from this paragraph, the held-over gain on the disposal (as reduced, where appropriate, under the preceding provisions of this Part of this Schedule) would exceed the amount of the chargeable gain which, apart from section 126 of this Act, would accrue on the disposal.

the amount of that held-over gain shall be reduced by the amount of the excess.

(2) In sub-paragraph (1) above " chargeable business asset " has the same meaning as in section 124 of this Act.

(3) If, in the case of a disposal of shares,—

(*a*) the disposal is or forms part of a disposal of shares in respect of the gains accruing on which the transferor is entitled to relief under section 124 of this Act, and

(*b*) apart from this paragraph, the held-over gain on the disposal (as reduced, where appropriate, under paragraph 7 above) would exceed an amount equal to the relevant proportion of the chargeable gain which, apart from section 126 of this Act, would accrue on the disposal,

the amount of that held-over gain shall be reduced by the amount of the excess.

(4) In sub-paragraph (3) above " the relevant proportion ", in relation to a disposal falling within paragraph (*a*) of that sub-paragraph, means the proportion determined under subsection (5)(*b*) of section 124 of this Act in relation to the aggregate sum of the gains which accrue on that disposal.

SCHEDULE 5

Assets Held on 6th April 1965

Part I

Quoted Securities

Deemed acquisition at 6th April 1965 value

1.—(1) This paragraph applies—

    (*a*) to shares and securities which on 6th April 1965 have quoted market values on a recognised stock exchange in the United Kingdom or elsewhere, or which have had such quoted market values at any time in the period of six years ending on 6th April 1965, and

    (*b*) to rights of unit holders in any unit trust scheme the prices of which are published regularly by the managers of the scheme.

(2) For the purposes of this Act it shall be assumed, wherever relevant, that any assets to which this paragraph applies were sold by the owner, and immediately re-acquired by him, at their market value on 6th April 1965.

(3) This paragraph shall not apply in relation to a disposal of shares or securities of a company by a person to whom those shares or securities were issued as an employee either of the company or of some other person on terms which restrict his rights to dispose of them.

Restriction of gain or loss by reference to actual cost

2.—(1) Subject to the rights of election conferred by paragraphs 4 to 7 below, paragraph 1(2) above shall not apply in relation to a disposal of assets—

    (*a*) if on the assumption in paragraph 1(2) a gain would accrue on that disposal to the person making the disposal and either a smaller gain or a loss would so accrue (computed in accordance with Chapter II of Part II) if paragraph 1(2) did not apply, or

    (*b*) if on the assumption in paragraph 1(2) a loss would so accrue and either a smaller loss or a gain would accrue if paragraph 1(2) did not apply,

and accordingly the amount of the gain or loss accruing on the disposal shall be computed without regard to the preceding provisions of this Schedule except that in a case where this sub-paragraph would otherwise substitute a loss for a gain or a gain for a loss it shall be assumed, in relation to the disposal, that the relevant assets were sold by the owner, and immediately re-acquired by him, for a consideration such that, on the disposal, neither a gain nor a loss accrued to the person making the disposal.

(2) For the purpose of—

    (*a*) identifying shares or securities held on 6th April 1965 with shares or securities previously acquired, and

(*b*) identifying the shares or securities held on that date with
          shares or securities subsequently disposed of, and distin-
          guishing them from shares or securities acquired subse-
          quently,

so far as that identification is needed for the purposes of sub-
paragraph (1) above, and so far as the shares or securities are of
the same class, shares or securities acquired at an earlier time shall
be deemed to be disposed of before shares or securities acquired
at a later time.

(3) Sub-paragraph (2) above has effect subject to section 66 of
this Act (disposal on or before day of acquisition).

Exclusion of pooling

3.—(1) Subject to the rights of election conferred by paragraphs
4 to 7 below, section 65 of this Act (pooling of shares and other
assets) shall not apply to quoted securities held on 6th April 1965.

(2) Where—

(*a*) a disposal was made out of quoted securities before 20th
     March 1968 (that is to say before the date on which the
     provisions re-enacted in sub-paragraph (1) above took
     effect), and

(*b*) by virtue of paragraph 2 of Schedule 7 to the Finance Act
          1965 (re-enacted as section 65 of this Act) some of the
          quoted securities out of which the disposal was made were
          acquired before 6th April 1965, and some later

then in computing the gain accruing on any disposal of quoted
securities the question of what remained undisposed of on the
earlier disposal shall be decided on the footing that sub-paragraph
(1) above had effect as respects that earlier disposal.

(3) The rules of identification in paragraph 2(2) above shall apply
for the purposes of this paragraph as they apply for the purposes of
the said paragraph 2.

Election for pooling

4.—(1) If a person so elects, quoted securities covered by the
election shall be excluded from paragraphs 2 and 3 above (so that
neither paragraph 1(2) above nor section 65 of this Act is excluded
by those paragraphs as respects those securities).

(2) An election made by any person under this paragraph shall
be as respects all disposals made by him at any time, including
disposals made before the election but after 19th March 1968—

(*a*) of quoted securities of kinds other than fixed-interest securi-
     ties and preference shares, or

(*b*) of fixed-interest securities and preference shares,

and references to the quoted securities covered by an election shall
be construed accordingly.

Any person may make both of the elections.

(3) An election under this paragraph shall not cover quoted securities which the holder acquired on a disposal after 19th March 1968 in relation to which either of the following enactments (which secure that neither a gain nor a loss accrues on the disposal) applies, that is—

(*a*) section 44 of this Act (disposals between husband and wife),

(*b*) section 273(1) of the Taxes Act (disposals within a group of companies),

but this paragraph shall apply to the quoted securities so held if the person making the original disposal (that is to say the wife or husband of the holder, or the other member of the group of companies) makes an election covering quoted securities of the kind in question.

For the purpose of identifying quoted securities disposed of by the holder with quoted securities acquired by him on a disposal in relation to which either of the said enactments applies, so far as they are of the same class, quoted securities acquired at an earlier time shall be deemed to be disposed of before quoted securities acquired at a later time.

(4) For the avoidance of doubt it is hereby declared—

(*a*) that where a person makes an election under this paragraph as respects quoted securities which he holds in one capacity, that election does not cover quoted securities which he holds in another capacity, and

(*b*) that an election under this paragraph is irrevocable.

(5) An election under this paragraph shall be made by notice in writing to the inspector not later than the expiration of two years from the end of the year of assessment or accounting period of a company in which the first relevant disposal is made, or such further time as the Board may allow.

(6) Subject to paragraph 5 below, in this paragraph the "first relevant disposal", in relation to each of the elections referred to in sub-paragraph (2) of this paragraph, means the first disposal after 19th March 1968 by the person making the election of quoted securities of the kind covered by that election.

(7) All such adjustments shall be made, whether by way of discharge or repayment of tax, or the making of assessments or otherwise, as are required to give effect to an election under this paragraph.

Election by principal company of group

5.—(1) In the case of companies which at the relevant time are members of a group of companies—

(*a*) an election under paragraph 4 above by the company which at that time is the principal company of the group shall have effect also as an election by any other company which at that time is a member of the group, and

(*b*) no election under that paragraph may be made by any other company which at that time is a member of the group.

(2) In this paragraph " the relevant time ", in relation to a group of companies, and in relation to each of the elections referred to in paragraph 4(2) above, is the first occasion after 19th March 1968 when any company which is then a member of a group disposes of quoted securities of a kind covered by that election, and for the purposes of paragraph 4(5) above that occasion is, in relation to the group, " the first relevant disposal ".

(3) This paragraph shall not apply in relation to quoted securities of either kind referred to in paragraph 4(2) above which are owned by a company which, in some period after 19th March 1968 and before the relevant time, was not a member of the group if in that period it had made an election under paragraph 4 above in relation to securities of that kind (or was treated by virtue of this paragraph, in relation to another group, as having done so), or had made a disposal of quoted securities of that kind and did not make an election within the time limited by paragraph 4(5) above.

(4) This paragraph shall apply notwithstanding that a company ceases to be a member of the group at any time after the relevant time.

(5) In this paragraph " company " and " group " shall be construed in accordance with subsections (1) and (2) of section 272 of the Taxes Act.

Pooling at value on 6th April 1965 : exchange of securities etc.

6.—(1) Where a person who has made only one of the elections under paragraph 4 above disposes of quoted securities which, in accordance with Chapter II of Part IV of this Act, are to be regarded as being or forming part of a new holding, the election shall apply according to the nature of the quoted securities disposed of, notwithstanding that under the said Chapter the new holding is to be regarded as the same asset as the original holding and that the election would apply differently to the original holding.

(2) Where the election does not cover the disposal out of the new holding, but does cover quoted securities of the kind comprised in the original holding, then in computing the gain accruing on the disposal out of the new holding (in accordance with paragraph 3 above) the question of what remained undisposed of on any disposal out of the original holding shall be decided on the footing that paragraph 3 above applied to that earlier disposal.

(3) In the case converse to that in sub-paragraph (2) above (that is to say where the election covers the disposal out of the new holding, but does not cover quoted securities of the kind comprised in the original holding) the question of how much of the new holding derives from quoted securities held on 6th April 1965, and how much derives from other quoted securities, shall be decided as it is decided for the purposes of paragraph 3 above.

Underwriters

7. No election under paragraph 4 above shall cover quoted securities comprised in any underwriter's premiums trust fund, or premiums trust fund deposits, or personal reserves, being securities comprised in funds to which section 142 of this Act applies.

Interpretation of paragraphs 3 to 7

8.—(1) In paragraphs 3 to 7 above—

" quoted securities " means assets to which paragraph 1 above applies,

" fixed interest security " means any security as defined by section 82 of this Act,

" preference share " means any share the holder whereof has a right to a dividend at a fixed rate, but has no other right to share in the profits of the company.

(2) If and so far as the question whether at any particular time a share was a preference share depends on the rate of dividends payable on or before 5th April 1973, the reference in the definition of " preference share " in sub-paragraph (1) above to a dividend at a fixed rate includes a dividend at a rate fluctuating in accordance with the standard rate of income tax.

PART II

LAND REFLECTING DEVELOPMENT VALUE

Valuation at 6th April 1965

9.—(1) This paragraph shall apply in relation to a disposal of an asset which is an interest in land situated in the United Kingdom—

(a) if, but for this paragraph, the expenditure allowable as a deduction in computing under Chapter II of Part II of this Act the gain accruing on the disposal would include any expenditure incurred before 6th April 1965, and

(b) if the consideration for the asset acquired on the disposal exceeds the current use value of the asset at the time of the disposal, or if any material development of the land has been carried out after 17th December 1973 since the person making the disposal acquired the asset.

(2) For the purposes of this Act, including Chapter II of Part II, it shall be assumed in relation to the disposal and, if it is a part disposal, in relation to any subsequent diposal of the asset which is an interest in land situated in the United Kingdom that that asset was sold by the person making the disposal, and immediately re-acquired by him, at its market value on 6th April 1965.

(3) Sub-paragraph (2) above shall apply also in relation to any prior part disposal of the asset and, if tax has been charged, or relief allowed, by reference to that part disposal on a different

footing, all such adjustments shall be made, whether by way of assessment or discharge or repayment of tax, as are required to give effect to the provisions of this sub-paragraph.

(4) Sub-paragraph (2) above shall not apply in relation to a disposal of assets—

> (a) if on the assumption in that sub-paragraph a gain would accrue on that disposal to the person making the disposal and either a smaller gain or a loss would so accrue (computed in accordance with the provisions of Chapter II of Part II of this Act) if the said sub-paragraph (2) did not apply, or
>
> (b) if on the assumption in the said sub-paragraph (2) a loss would so accrue and either a smaller loss or a gain would accrue if the said sub-paragraph (2) did not apply,

and accordingly the amount of the gain or loss accruing on the disposal shall be computed without regard to the provisions of this Schedule except that in a case where this sub-paragraph would otherwise substitute a loss for a gain or a gain for a loss it shall be assumed, in relation to the disposal, that the relevant assets were sold by the owner, and immediately re-acquired by him, for a consideration such that, on the disposal, neither a gain nor a loss accrued to the person making the disposal.

(5) For the purposes of this paragraph—

1974 c. 30.
> (a) " interest in land " has the meaning given by section 44(1) of the Finance Act 1974,
>
> (b) " material development " has the meaning given by paragraph 6 of Schedule 3 to the Finance Act 1974,
>
> (c) the current use value of an interest in land shall be computed in accordance with Part I of the said Schedule 3, but so that, in relation to any material development which was begun before 18th December 1973, sub-paragraph (2) of paragraph 1 of that Schedule (definition of current use value) shall have effect as if the words from " other than " to the end of the sub-paragraph (which allow for the completion of duly authorised material development already begun) were omitted,
>
> (d) paragraph 9 of the said Schedule 3 (date when material development is begun) shall apply as it applies for the purposes of that Schedule, and
>
> (e) paragraph 14 of the said Schedule 3 (meaning of material development " carried out after " a particular date) shall apply as it applies for the purposes of paragraphs 11 to 13 of that Schedule.

Allowance for betterment levy

10. Paragraph 9(1) above has effect subject to paragraph 21(2) of Schedule 6 to this Act (valuation at 6th April 1965 on a claim under that paragraph.

PART III

OTHER ASSETS

*Apportionment by reference to straightline growth of gain or loss
over period of ownership*

11.—(1) This paragraph applies subject to Parts I and II of this
Schedule.

(2) On the disposal of assets by a person whose period of ownership began before 6th April 1965 only so much of any gain accruing
on the disposal as is under this paragraph to be apportioned to the
period beginning with 6th April 1965 shall be a chargeable gain.

(3) Subject to the following provisions of this Schedule, the gain
shall be assumed to have grown at a uniform rate from nothing at
the beginning of the period of ownership to its full amount at the
time of the disposal so that, calling the part of that period before
6th April 1965, P, and the time beginning with 6th April 1965 and
ending with the time of the disposal T, the fraction of the gain which

is a chargeable gain is $\dfrac{T}{P+T}$.

(4) If any of the expenditure which is allowable as a deduction
in the computation under Chapter II of Part II of this Act of the
gain is within section 32(1)(*b*) of this Act—

- (*a*) the gain shall be attributed to the expenditure, if any, allowable under paragraph (*a*) of the said secion 32(1) as one
item of expenditure, and to the respective items of expenditure under the said section 32(1)(*b*) in proportion to the
respective amounts of those items of expenditure,

- (*b*) sub-paragraph (3) of this paragraph shall apply to the part
of the gain attributed to the expenditure under the said
section 32(1)(*a*),

- (*c*) each part of the gain attributed to the items of expenditure
under the said section 32(1)(*b*) shall be assumed to have
grown at a uniform rate from nothing at the time when
the relevant item of expenditure was first reflected in the
value of the asset to the full amount of that part of the
gain at the time of the disposal,

so that, calling the respective proportions of the gain E(0), E(1),
E(2) and so on (so that they add up to unity) and calling the respective periods from the times when the items under the said section
32(1)(*b*) were reflected in the value of the asset to 5th April 1965
P(1), P(2) and so on, and employing also the abbreviations in sub-
paragraph (3) above, the fraction of the gain which is a chargeable

gain is $E(0) \dfrac{T}{P+T} + E(1) \dfrac{T}{P(1)+T} + E(2) \dfrac{T}{P(2)+T}$ and so on.

(5) In a case within sub-paragraph (4) above where there is no
initial expenditure (that is no expenditure under section 32(1)(*a*) of
this Act) or that initial expenditure is, compared with any item of

expenditure under section 32(1)(*b*), disproportionately small having regard to the value of the asset immediately before the subsequent item of expenditure was incurred, the part of the gain which is not attributable to the enhancement of the value of the asset due to any item of expenditure under the said section 32(1)(*b*) shall be deemed to be attributed to expenditure incurred at the beginning of the period of ownership and allowable under section 32(1)(*a*), and the part or parts of the gain attributable to expenditure under section 32(1)(*b*) shall be reduced accordingly.

(6) The beginning of the period over which a gain, or a part of a gain, is, under sub-paragraphs (3) and (4) above, to be treated as growing shall not be earlier than 6th April 1945, and this sub-paragraph shall have effect notwithstanding any provision in this Schedule or elsewhere in this Act.

(7) If in pursuance of section 35 of this Act (part disposals) an asset's market value at a date before 6th April 1965 is to be ascertained sub-paragraphs (3) to (5) above shall have effect as if that asset had been on that date sold by the owner, and immediately re-acquired by him, at that market value.

(8) If in pursuance of section 35 of this Act an asset's market value at a date on or after 6th April 1965 is to be ascertained sub-paragraphs (3) to (5) above shall have effect as if—

    (*a*) the asset on that date had been sold by the owner, and immediately re-acquired by him, at that market value, and

    (*b*) accordingly, the computation of any gain on a subsequent disposal of that asset shall be computed—

        (i) by apportioning in accordance with this paragraph the gain or loss over a period ending on the said date (the date of the part disposal), and

        (ii) by bringing into account the entire gain or loss over the period from the date of the part disposal to the date of subsequent disposal.

(9) For the purposes of this paragraph the period of ownership of an asset shall, where under section 36 of this Act (assets derived from other assets) account is to be taken of expenditure in respect of an asset from which the asset disposed of was derived, or where it would so apply if there were any relevant expenditure in respect of that other asset, include the period of ownership of that other asset.

(10) If under this paragraph part only of a gain is a chargeable gain, the fraction in 102(2) of this Act (private residences: amount of relief) shall be applied to that part, instead of to the whole of the gain.

Election for valuation at 6th April 1965

12.—(1) If the person making a disposal so elects paragraph 11 of this Schedule shall not apply in relation to that disposal and it shall be assumed, both for the purposes of computing under Chapter II of Part II of this Act the gain accruing to that person on the disposal, and for all other purposes both in relation to that person and other persons, that the assets disposed of, and any assets of which account is to be taken in relation to the disposal under section 36 of this Act, being assets which were in the ownership of the said person on 6th April 1965, were on that date sold, and immediately re-acquired, by him at their market value on the said 6th April 1965.

(2) Sub-paragraph (1) above shall not apply in relation to a disposal of assets if on the assumption in that sub-paragraph a loss would accrue on that disposal to the person making the disposal and either a smaller loss or a gain would accrue if the said sub-paragraph (1) did not apply, but in a case where this sub-paragraph would otherwise substitute a gain for a loss it shall be assumed, in relation to the disposal, that the relevant assets were sold by the owner, and immediately re-acquired by him, for a consideration such that, on the disposal, neither a gain nor a loss accrued to the person making the disposal.

The displacement of sub-paragraph (1) above by this sub-paragraph shall not be taken as bringing paragraph 11 above into operation.

(3) An election under this paragraph shall be made by notice in writing to the inspector given within two years from the end of the year of assessment or accounting period of a company in which the disposal is made or such further time as the Board may by notice in writing allow.

(4) For the avoidance of doubt it is hereby declared that an election under this paragraph is irrevocable.

(5) An election may not be made under this paragraph as respects, or in relation to, an asset the market value of which at a date on or after 6th April 1965, and before the date of the disposal to which the election relates, is to be ascertained in pursuance of section 35 of this Act (part disposals).

Unquoted shares, commodities, etc.

13.—(1) This paragraph has effect as respects shares held by any person on 6th April 1965 other than shares which are to be treated under this Act as if disposed of and immediately re-acquired by him on that date.

(2) Section 65 of this Act (pooling of shares and other assets) shall not apply in relation to the shares while that person continues to hold them and, in particular, shall not apply in relation to a disposal of the shares by him.

(3) For the purpose of—
  (a) identifying the shares so held on 6th April 1965 with shares previously acquired, and
  (b) identifying the shares so held on that date with shares subsequently disposed of, and distinguishing them from shares acquired subsequently,
so far as the shares are of the same class shares bought at an earlier time shall be deemed to have been disposed of before shares bought at a later time.

(4) Sub-paragraph (3) above has effect subject to section 66 of this Act (disposal on or before day of acquisition).

(5) Shares shall not be treated for the purposes of this paragraph as being of the same class unless if dealt with on a recognised stock exchange in the United Kingdom or elsewhere they would be so treated, but shall be treated in accordance with this paragraph notwithstanding that they are identified in a different way by a disposal or by the transfer or delivery giving effect to it.

(6) This paragraph, without sub-paragraph (5), shall apply in relation to any assets, other than shares, which are of a nature to be dealt with without identifying the particular assets disposed of or acquired.

Reorganisation of share capital, conversion of securities, etc.

14.—(1) For the purposes of this Act, including Chapter II of Part II, it shall be assumed that any shares or securities held by a person on 6th April 1965 (identified in accordance with paragraph 13 above) which, in accordance with Chapter II of Part IV of this Act, are to be regarded as being or forming part of a new holding were sold and immediately re-acquired by him on 6th April 1965 at their market value on that date.

(2) If, at any time after 5th April 1965, a person comes to have, in accordance with the said Chapter II of Part IV, a new holding sub-paragraphs (3) to (5) of paragraph 11 above shall have effect as if—

> (a) the new holding had at that time been sold by the owner, and immediately re-acquired by him, at its market value at that time, and

> (b) accordingly, the amount of any gain on a disposal of the new holding or any part of it shall be computed—

>> (i) by apportioning in accordance with paragraph 11 above the gain or loss over a period ending at the said time, and

>> (ii) by bringing into account the entire gain or loss over the period from that time to the date of the disposal.

(3) This paragraph shall not apply in relation to a reorganisation of a company's share capital if the new holding differs only from the original shares in being a different number, whether greater or less, of shares of the same class as the original shares.

PART IV

MISCELLANEOUS

Capital allowances

15. If under any provision in this Schedule it is to be assumed that any asset was on 6th April 1965 sold by the owner, and immediately re-acquired by him, sections 34 and 39 of this Act

(restriction of losses by reference to capital allowances, and wasting assets qualifying for capital allowances) shall apply in relation to any capital allowance or renewals allowance made in respect of the expenditure actually incurred by the owner in providing the asset, and so made for the year 1965-66 or for any subsequent year of assessment, as if it were made in respect of the expenditure which, on the said assumption, was incurred by him in re-acquiring the asset on 7th April 1965.

Assets transferred to close companies

16.—(1) This paragraph has effect where—

    (*a*) at any time, including a time before 7th April 1965, any of the persons having control of a close company, or any person who is connected with a person having control of a close company, has transferred assets to the company, and

    (*b*) paragraph 11 above applies in relation to a disposal by one of the persons having control of the company of shares or securities in the company, or in relation to a disposal by a person having, up to the time of disposal, a substantial holding of shares or securities in the company, being in either case a disposal after the transfer of the assets.

(2) So far as the gain accruing to the said person on the disposal of the shares is attributable to a profit on the assets so transferred, the period over which the gain is to be treated under paragraph 11 above as growing at a uniform rate shall begin with the time when the assets were transferred to the company, and accordingly a part of a gain attributable to a profit on assets transferred on or after 6th April 1965 shall all be a chargeable gain.

(3) This paragraph shall not apply where a loss, and not a gain, accrues on the disposal.

Husbands and wives

17. Where section 44 of this Act is applied in relation to a disposal of an asset by a man to his wife, or by a man's wife to him, then in relation to a subsequent disposal of the asset (not within section 44) the one making the disposal shall be treated for the purposes of this Schedule as if the other's acquisition or provision of the asset had been his or her acquisition or provision of it.

Compensation and insurance money

18. Where section 21(4)(*a*) of this Act applies to exclude a gain which, in consequence of this Schedule, is not all chargeable gain, the amount of the reduction to be made under section 21(4)(*b*) (corresponding reduction in allowable expenditure in respect of new asset) shall be the amount of the chargeable gain and not the whole amount of the gain ; and in section 21(5)(*b*) of this Act (corresponding reduction in allowable expenditure in respect of the new asset where part only of the consideration in respect of the old asset has been applied as such expenditure) for the reference to the amount by which the gain is reduced under section 21(5)(*a*) there shall be substituted a reference to the amount by which the chargeable gain is proportionately reduced under the said section 21(5)(*a*).

SCHEDULE 6

TRANSITORY

PART I

VALUATION

Preliminary

1. This Part of this Schedule has effect in cases where the market value of an asset or any part of it at a time before the commencement of this Act is material to the computation of a gain under this Act, and in those cases—

> (*a*) section 150 of this Act (which is the same as paragraph 2 below with the amendments in paragraph 4) shall not apply,

> (*b*) section 152 of this Act shall only apply to the extent specified in paragraphs 5 to 8 below,

(but sections 151 and 153 of this Act shall apply in those cases as in later cases).

Original rules

2.—(1) "Market value" in relation to any assets means the price which those assets might reasonably be expected to fetch on a sale in the open market.

(2) In estimating the market value of any assets no reduction shall be made in the estimate on account of the estimate being made on the assumption that the whole of the assets is to be placed on the market at one and the same time:

Provided that where capital gains tax is chargeable, or an allowable loss accrues, in consequence of a death before 31st March 1971 and the market value of any property on the date of death taken into account for the purposes of that tax or loss has been depreciated by reason of the death the estimate of the market value shall take that depreciation into account.

(3) The market value of shares or securities quoted on the London Stock Exchange shall, except where in consequence of special circumstances prices so quoted are by themselves not a proper measure of market value, be as follows—

> (*a*) the lower of the two prices shown in the quotations for the shares or securities in the Stock Exchange Official Daily List on the relevant date plus one-quarter of the difference between those two figures, or

> (*b*) halfway between the highest and lowest prices at which bargains, other than bargains done at special prices, were recorded in the shares or securities for the relevant date,

choosing the amount under paragraph (*a*) if less than that under paragraph (*b*), or if no such bargains were recorded for the relevant

date, and choosing the amount under paragraph (*b*) if less than that
under paragraph (*a*):

Provided that—

    (i) this sub-paragraph shall not apply to shares or securities for which some other stock exchange in the United Kingdom affords a more active market, and

    (ii) if the London Stock Exchange is closed on the relevant date the market value shall be ascertained by reference to the latest previous date or earliest subsequent date on which it is open, whichever affords the lower market value.

(4) " Market value " in relation to any rights of unit holders in any unit trust scheme the buying and selling prices of which are published regularly by the managers of the scheme shall mean an amount equal to the buying price (that is the lower price) so published on the relevant date, or if none were published on that date, on the latest date before.

(5) In relation to an asset of a kind the sale of which is subject to restrictions imposed under the Exchange Control Act 1947 such 1947 c. 14. that part of what is paid by the purchaser is not retainable by the seller the market value, as arrived at under sub-paragraph (1), (3) or (4) above, shall be subject to such adjustment as is appropriate having regard to the difference between the amount payable by a purchaser and the amount receivable by a seller.

(6) This paragraph has effect subject to the following provisions of this Part of this Schedule.

Value of quoted securities on 6th April 1965

3.—(1) For the purpose of ascertaining the market value of any shares or securities in accordance with paragraph 1(2) of Schedule 5 to this Act, paragraph 2 above shall have effect subject to the provisions of this paragraph.

(2) Sub-paragraph (3)(*a*) of that paragraph shall have effect as if for the words, " one-quarter " there were substituted the words " one-half ", and as between the amount under paragraph (*a*) and the amount under paragraph (*b*) of that sub-paragraph the higher, and not the lower, amount shall be chosen.

(3) Sub-paragraph (4) of that paragraph shall have effect as if for the reference to an amount equal to the buying price there were substituted a reference to an amount halfway between the buying and selling prices.

(4) Where the market value of any shares or securities not within the said sub-paragraph (3) falls to be ascertained by reference to a pair of prices quoted on a stock exchange, an adjustment shall be made so as to increase the market value by an amount corresponding to that by which any market value is increased under sub-paragraph (2) above.

Part I   R

References to Stock Exchange on or after 25th March 1973

4. Except in relation to anything done before 25th March 1973, paragraph 2(3) above shall have effect subject to the following amendments—

> (*a*) for the words " quoted on the London Stock Exchange " there shall be substituted the words " listed in The Stock Exchange Daily Official List " and for the words " so quoted " the words " quoted in that List " ;
>
> (*b*) for the words " the Stock Exchange Official Daily List " there shall be substituted the words " The Stock Exchange Daily Official List " ;
>
> (*c*) for the words " some other stock exchange in the United Kingdom affords a more active market " there shall be substituted the words " The Stock Exchange provides a more active market elsewhere than on the London trading floor " ; and
>
> (*d*) for the words " if the London Stock Exchange is closed " there shall be substituted the words " if the London trading floor is closed ".

Unquoted shares and securities: application of section 152 to acquisitions before commencement of this Act

5. Paragraphs 6 to 8 below shall have effect with respect to the application of section 152 of this Act, and in those paragraphs " asset " means an asset to which that section applies.

6. Subject to paragraphs 7 and 8 below, if the market value of an asset or any part of it at the time of its acquisition is material to the computation of any chargeable gain under this Act then, notwithstanding that the acquisition may have occurred before 6th July 1973 (the date on which the provision re-enacted in section 152 of this Act first came into operation as respects disposals) or that the market value of the asset at the time of its acquisition may have been fixed for the purposes of a contemporaneous disposal, section 152 of this Act shall apply for the purposes of the determination of the market value of the asset or, as the case may be, that part of it at the time of its acquisition.

Unquoted shares or securities: acquisition on death

7.—(1) This paragraph applies if, in a case where the market value of an asset at the time of its acquisition is material as mentioned in paragraph 6 above,—

> (*a*) the acquisition took place on the occasion of a death occurring after 30th March 1971 and before 6th July 1973, and
>
> (*b*) by virtue of paragraph 9 below, the principal value of the asset for the purposes of estate duty on that death would, apart from this paragraph, be taken to be the market value of the asset at the date of the death for the purposes of this Act.

(2) If the principal value referred to in sub-paragraph (1)(*b*) above
falls to be determined as mentioned in section 55 of the Finance Act
1940 or section 15 of the Finance (No. 2) Act (Northern Ireland) 1946
(certain controlling shareholdings to be valued on an assets basis),
nothing in section 152 of this Act shall affect the operation of
paragraph 9 below for the purpose of determining the market value
of the asset at the date of the death.

(3) If sub-paragraph (2) above does not apply, paragraph 9 below
shall not apply as mentioned in sub-paragraph (1)(*b*) above and the
market value of the asset on its acquisition at the date of the death
shall be determined in accordance with paragraphs 2 and 6 above.

Unquoted shares or securities : prior part disposal

8.—(1) In any case where—

  (*a*) before 6th July 1973 there has been a part disposal of an
  asset to which section 152 of this Act applies (in this
  paragraph referred to as " the earlier disposal "), and

  (*b*) by virtue of any enactment, the acquisition of the asset or any
  part of it was deemed to be for a consideration equal to its
  market value, and

  (*c*) on or after 6th July 1973 there is a disposal (including a
  part disposal) of the property which remained undisposed
  of immediately before that date (in this paragraph referred
  to as " the later disposal "),

sub-paragraph (2) below shall apply in computing any chargeable
gain accruing on the later disposal.

(2) Where this sub-paragraph applies, the apportionment made by
virtue of paragraph 7 of Schedule 6 to the Finance Act 1965
(corresponding to section 35 of this Act) on the occasion of the
earlier disposal shall be recalculated on the basis that section 152(3)
of this Act was in force at the time, and applied for the purposes, of
the determination of—

  (*a*) the market value referred to in sub-paragraph (1)(*b*) above,
  and

  (*b*) the market value of the property which remained undisposed
  of after the earlier disposal, and

  (*c*) if the consideration for the earlier disposal was, by virtue
  of any enactment, deemed to be equal to the market value
  of the property disposed of, that market value.

Value determined for estate duty

9.—(1) Where estate duty (including estate duty leviable under the
law of Northern Ireland) is chargeable in respect of any property
passing on a death after 30th March 1971 and the principal value
of an asset forming part of that property has been ascertained
(whether in any proceedings or otherwise) for the purposes of that
duty, the principal value so ascertained shall, subject to paragraph
7(3) above, be taken for the purposes of this Act to be the market
value of that asset at the date of the death.

R2

SCH. 6
1968 c. 44.
1968 c. 17 (N.I.).

(2) Where the principal value has been reduced under section 35 of the Finance Act 1968 or section 1 of the Finance Act (Northern Ireland) 1968 (tapering relief for gifts inter vivos etc.), the reference in sub-paragraph (1) above to the principal value as ascertained for the purposes of estate duty is a reference to that value as so ascertained before the reduction.

PART II

ASSETS ACQUIRED BEFORE COMMENCEMENT

Events before commencement

10.—(1) The substitution of this Act for the corresponding enactments repealed by this Act shall not alter the effect of any provision enacted before this Act (whether or not there is a corresponding provision in this Act) so far as it determines whether and to what extent events in, or expenditure incurred in, or other amounts referable to, a period earlier than the chargeable periods to which this Act applies may be taken into account for any tax purposes in a chargeable period to which this Act applies.

(2) Without prejudice to sub-paragraph (1) above, the repeals made by this Act shall not affect—

1971 c. 68.

(*a*) the enactments specified in Part V of Schedule 14 to the Finance Act 1971 (charge on death) so far as their operation before repeal falls to be taken into account in chargeable periods to which this Act applies,

1965 c. 25.

(*b*) the application of the enactments repealed by this Act to events before 6th April 1965 in accordance with paragraph 31 of Schedule 6 to the Finance Act 1965.

(3) This paragraph has no application to the law relating to the determination of the market value of assets (which is stated for all relevant times and occasions in Part I of this Schedule, with Part VIII of this Act).

PART III

OTHER TRANSITORY PROVISIONS

Value-shifting

11. Section 26 of this Act applies only where the reduction in value mentioned in subsection (1) of that section (or, in a case within subsection (8) of that section, the reduction or increase in value) is after 29th March 1977.

Assets acquired on disposal chargeable under Case VII of Schedule D

12.—(1) In this paragraph references to a disposal chargeable under Case VII are references to cases where the acquisition and disposal was in circumstances that the gain accruing on it was chargeable under Case VII of Schedule D, or where it would have been so chargeable if there were a gain so accruing.

(2) The amount or value of the consideration for the acquisition   SCH. 6
of an asset by the person acquiring it on a disposal chargeable
under Case VII shall not under any provision of this Act be deemed
to be an amount greater than the amount taken into account as
consideration on that disposal for the purposes of Case VII.

(3) Any apportionment of consideration or expenditure falling to
be made in relation to a disposal chargeable under Case VII in
accordance with section 164(4) of the Taxes Act, and in particular
in a case where section 164(6) of that Act (enhancement of value of
land by acquisition of adjoining land) applied, shall be followed for
the purposes of this Act both in relation to a disposal of the
assets acquired on the disposal chargeable under Case VII and,
where the disposal chargeable under Case VII was a part disposal, in relation to a disposal of what remains undisposed of.

(4) Sub-paragraph (3) above has effect notwithstanding section
43(4) of this Act (general provisions for apportionment).

Unrelieved Case VII losses

13. Where no relief from income tax (for a year earlier than
1971-72) has been given in respect of a loss or part of a loss allowable under Case VII of Schedule D the loss or part shall, notwithstanding that the loss accrued before that year, be an allowable
loss for the purposes of capital gains tax, but subject to any restrictions imposed by section 62 of this Act (transactions between
connected persons).

Dispositions before 27th March 1974 which attract capital transfer tax

14. Paragraphs 15 and 16 below have effect in respect of dispositions before 27th March 1974 where the disponer dies before
27th March 1981.

Gifts subject to capital transfer tax on death

15.—(1) Where the value of any asset comprised in a gift inter
vivos is by virtue of section 22(5) of the Finance Act 1975 included 1975 c. 7.
in the value of the estate of any person for the purposes of capital
transfer tax, and at the time of that person's death the asset—

    (*a*) is owned by the donee, or

    (*b*) is property settled by the gift or property which for the
        purposes of section 38 of the Finance Act 1957 would by 1957 c. 49.
        virtue of subsection (9) thereof be treated as property
        settled by the gift,

then, subject to sub-paragraph (2) below, the asset shall for the purposes of this Act be deemed to be disposed of and immediately
re-acquired at that time by the donee or trustee for a consideration
equal to the value so included ; but no chargeable gain shall accrue
on the disposal.

(2) Where the value so included is reduced by virtue of section 35
of the Finance Act 1968, the appropriate portion only of the asset 1968 c. 44.
shall be deemed to be so disposed of and re-acquired ; and for this

R3

purpose the appropriate portion is the reduced value so included divided by the value before the reduction.

Life interest terminated on death on which capital transfer tax is chargeable

16. Where a life interest within the meaning of section 55 of this Act in settled property is terminated by the death of a person on whose death capital transfer tax is chargeable under section 22 of
1975 c. 7. the Finance Act 1975 and, under subsection (5) of that section, a value falls to be included in respect of the settled property, then—

> (a) if that value is the principal value of the property, section 56 of this Act shall apply as if that person had been entitled to the life interest at his death, and

> (b) if that value is a value reduced by any percentage under
1969 c. 32.   paragraph 3 of Part II of Schedule 17 to the Finance Act 1969, any chargeable gain or allowable loss accruing on the disposal deemed to be made under section 54(1) or 55(1) of this Act shall be reduced by the complementary percentage, that is to say the percentage found by subtracting the first-mentioned percentage from one hundred per cent.

Devaluation of sterling : securities acquired with borrowed foreign currency

17.—(1) This paragraph applies where, in pursuance of permis-
1947 c. 14. sion granted under the Exchange Control Act 1947, currency other than sterling was borrowed before 19th November 1967 for the purpose of investing in foreign securities (and had not been repaid before that date), and it was a condition of the permission—

> (a) that repayment of the borrowed currency should be made from the proceeds of the sale in foreign currency of the foreign securities so acquired or out of investment currency, and

> (b) that the foreign securities so acquired should be kept in separate accounts to distinguish them from others in the same ownership,

and securities held in such a separate account on 19th November 1967 are in this paragraph referred to as " designated securities ".

(2) In computing the gain accruing to the borrower on the disposal of any designated securities or on the disposal of any currency or amount standing in a bank account on 19th November 1967 and representing the loan the sums allowable as a deduction under section 32(1)(a) of this Act shall be increased by multiplying by seven sixths :

Provided that the total amount of the increases so made in computing all gains (and losses) which are referable to any one loan (made before 19th November 1967) shall not exceed one sixth of the sterling parity value of that loan at the time it was made.

(3) Section 65 of this Act (rules for identification: pooling) shall apply separately in relation to any designated securities held in a

particular account until such time as a disposal takes place on the occurrence of which the proviso to sub-paragraph (2) above operates to limit the increases which would otherwise be made under that sub-paragraph in allowable deductions.

(4) In this paragraph and paragraph 18 below " foreign securities " means securities expressed in a currency other than sterling, or shares having a nominal value expressed in a currency other than sterling, or the dividends on which are payable in a currency other than sterling.

Devaluation of sterling : foreign insurance funds

18.—(1) The sums allowable as a deduction under section 32(1)(a) of this Act in computing any gains to which this paragraph applies shall be increased by multiplying by seven-sixths.

(2) This paragraph applies to gains accruing—

(a) to any underwriting member of Lloyd's or to any other approved association of underwriters, or

(b) to any company engaged in the business of marine protection and indemnity insurance on a mutual basis,

on the disposal by that person after 18th November 1967 of any foreign securities which on that date formed part of a trust fund—

(i) established by that person in any country or territory outside the United Kingdom, and

(ii) representing premiums received in the course of that person's business, and

(iii) wholly or mainly used for the purpose of meeting liabilities arising in that country or territory in respect of that business.

Gilt-edged securities past redemption date

19. So far as material for the purposes of this or any other Act, the definition of " gilt-edged securities " in Schedule 2 to this Act shall include any securities which were specified securities for the purposes of section 41 of the Finance Act 1969, and the redemption date of which fell before 1st January 1979. 1969 c. 32.

Reorganisation of share capital, conversion of securities, etc.

20.—(1) Chapter II of Part IV of this Act has effect subject to the provisions of this paragraph.

(2) The substitution of the said Chapter II for the enactments repealed by this Act shall not alter the law applicable to any reorganisation or reduction of share capital, conversion of securities or company amalgamation taking place before the commencement of this Act.

(3) Sub-paragraph (2) above applies in particular to the law determining whether or not any assets arising on an event mentioned in

that sub-paragraph are to be treated as the same asset as the original holding of shares, securities or other assets.

(4) Notwithstanding the preceding provisions of this paragraph, section 84 of this Act (compensation stock) shall apply where the compulsory acquisition took place after 6th April 1976, but before the commencement of this Act, as well as where it took place after the commencement of this Act.

Land: allowance for betterment levy

21.—(1) Where betterment levy charged in the case of any land in respect of an act or event falling within Case B or Case C or, if it was the renewal, extension or variation of a tenancy, Case F—

    (*a*) has been paid, and

    (*b*) has not been allowed as a deduction in computing the profits or gains or losses of a trade for the purposes of Case I of Schedule D;

then, if the person by whom the levy was paid disposes of the land or any part of it and so claims, the following provisions of this paragraph shall have effect for the purpose of applying Chapter II of Part II of, and Schedule 5 to, this Act to the disposal.

(2) Paragraph 9 of Schedule 5 to this Act (sales of land reflecting development value) shall apply where the condition stated in sub-paragraph (1)(*a*) thereof is satisfied, notwithstanding that the condition stated in sub-paragraph (1)(*b*) thereof is not satisfied.

(3) Subject to the following provisions of this paragraph, there shall be ascertained the excess, if any, of—

    (*a*) the net development value ascertained for the purposes of the levy, over

    (*b*) the increment specified in sub-paragraph (6) below;

and the amount of the excess shall be treated as an amount allowable under section 32(1)(*b*) of this Act.

(4) Where the act or event in respect of which the levy was charged was a part disposal of the land, the said section 32 shall apply as if the part disposal had not taken place and sub-paragraph (5) below shall apply in lieu of sub-paragraph (3) above.

(5) The amount or value of the consideration for the disposal shall be treated as increased by the amount of any premium or like sum paid in respect of the part disposal, and there shall be ascertained the excess, if any, of—

    (*a*) the aggregate specified in sub-paragraph (7) below, over

    (*b*) the increment specified in sub-paragraph (6) below;

and the amount of the excess shall be treated as an amount allowable under section 32(1)(*b*) of this Act.

(6) The increment referred to in sub-paragraphs (3)(*b*) and (5)(*b*) above is the excess, if any, of—

    (*a*) the amount or value of the consideration brought into account under section 32(1)(*a*) of this Act, over

    (*b*) the base value ascertained for the purposes of the levy.

(7) The aggregate referred to in sub-paragraph (5)(*a*) above is the   Sch. 6
aggregate of—

  (*a*) the net development value ascertained for the purposes of
        the levy, and

  (*b*) the amount of any premium or like sum paid in respect of
        the part disposal, in so far as charged to tax under Schedule
        A (or, as the case may be, Case VIII of Schedule D), and

  (*c*) the chargeable gain accruing on the part disposal.

(8) Where betterment levy in respect of more than one act or
event has been charged and paid as mentioned in sub-paragraph (1)
above sub-paragraphs (2) to (7) above shall apply without modifications in relation to the betterment levy in respect of the first of them ;
but in relation to the other or others sub-paragraph (3) or, as the
case may be, (5) above shall have effect as if the amounts to be
treated thereunder as allowable under section 32(1)(*b*) of this Act
were the net development value specified in sub-paragraph (3)(*a*) or,
as the case may be, the aggregate referred to in sub-paragraph (5)(*a*)
of this paragraph.

(9) Where the disposal is of part only of the land sub-paragraphs
(2) to (8) above shall have effect subject to the appropriate apportionments.

(10) References in this paragraph to a premium include any sum
payable as mentioned in subsection (3) or (4) of section 80 of the
Taxes Act (sums payable in lieu of rent or as consideration for the
surrender of lease or for variation or waiver of term) and, in relation
to Scotland, a grassum.

Replacement of business assets

22.—(1) Sections 115 to 121 of this Act (which are substituted for
section 33 of the Finance Act 1965 as amended by subsequent 1965 c. 25.
enactments) have effect subject to the provisions of this paragraph.

(2) The substitution of those sections for the enactments repealed
by this Act shall not alter the effect of those repealed enactments so
far as they apply where the acquisition of, or of the interest in, the
new assets (but not the disposal of, or of the interest in, the old
assets) was before the commencement of this Act.

(3) Where the said section 33 of the Finance Act 1965 applied on
the acquisition, before 23rd July 1970, of, or of an interest in, any
new assets and the adjustment required to be made under subsection
(1)(*a*) or subsection (2)(*a*) of that section was, by virtue of paragraph
9(5) of Schedule 14 to the Finance Act 1967 (allowance for develop- 1967 c. 54.
ment value), required to be computed as mentioned therein, any
adjustment required to be made under section 115(1)(*b*), or 116(1)(*b*),
of this Act shall also be so computed, notwithstanding the repeals
made by the Finance Act 1971 (restoring development value).   1971 c. 68.

Transfer of business to a company

23. Section 123 of this Act shall have effect as if after subsection (4) there were inserted as subsection (4A)—

"(4A) If any development gains within the meaning of Part III of the Finance Act 1974 accrue to the transferor in respect of his disposal of the assets included in the business, then for the purposes of subsection (4) above B (that is, the value of the whole of the consideration received by the transferor in exchange for the business) shall be taken to be what it would be if the value of the consideration other than shares so received by him were less by an amount equal to those gains".

Works of art etc.

24. The repeals made by this Act do not affect the continued operation of sections 31 and 32 of the Finance Act 1965, in the form in which they were before 13th March 1975, in relation to estate duty in respect of deaths occurring before that date.

Disposal before acquisition

25. The substitution of this Act for the corresponding enactments repealed by this Act shall not alter the effect of any provision enacted before this Act (whether or not there is a corresponding provision in this Act) so far as it relates to an asset which —

    (a) was disposed of before being acquired, and

    (b) was disposed of before the commencement of this Act.

Estate duty

26. Nothing in the repeals made by this Act shall affect any enactment as it applies to the determination of any principal value for the purposes of estate duty.

Income and corporation tax : premiums on leases

27. The repeal by this Act of section 116(3) of the Finance Act 1972 shall not affect its application by paragraph 3 of Schedule 13 to that Act.

Validity of subordinate legislation

28. So far as this Act re-enacts any provision contained in a statutory instrument made in exercise of powers conferred by any Act, it shall be without prejudice to the validity of that provision, and any question as to its validity shall be determined as if the re-enacted provision were contained in a statutory instrument made under those powers.

Saving for Part II of this Schedule

29. The provisions of this Part of this Schedule are without prejudice to the generality of Part II of this Schedule.

SCHEDULE 7

CONSEQUENTIAL AMENDMENTS

Taxes Management Act 1970 (*c.* 9)

1.—(1) The Taxes Management Act 1970 shall be amended as follows.

(2) In section 12(2) for paragraph (*a*) substitute—

" (*a*) any assets exempted by the following provisions of the Capital Gains Tax Act 1979, namely—

(i) section 19(4) (rights to winnings from pool betting, lotteries or games with prizes),

(ii) section 71 (government non-marketable securities),

(iii) section 130, 131 or 133 (passenger vehicles, decorations for valour or gallant conduct and foreign currency for personal expenditure) ".

(3) In section 28(1) for " section 41 " (in both places) substitute " section 15 ", for " section 42 " (in both places) substitute " section 17 ", and for " Finance Act 1965 " substitute " Capital Gains Tax Act 1979 ".

Income and Corporation Taxes Act 1970 (*c.* 10)

2.—(1) The Taxes Act shall be amended as follows.

(2) In section 270(3) for the words from " disposal " to the end of the subsection substitute—

" disposal, and the asset consists of specified securities, the company acquiring the asset shall be treated for the purposes of sections 67 to 70 of the Capital Gains Tax Act 1979 as acquiring it at the time when the other acquired it."

(3) At the end of section 270 (in place of the subsection (6) inserted by paragraph 12 of Schedule 10 to the Finance Act 1971) insert—

" (6) In this section " specified securities " means securities which are gilt-edged securities as defined by Schedule 2 to the Capital Gains Tax Act 1979."

(4) In section 279(1)(*a*) after " 1965 " insert " but before 20th April 1977 ".

Finance Act 1974 (*c.* 30)

3. For paragraph 18(6) of Schedule 3 to the Finance Act 1974 substitute—

" (6) The following provisions of the Capital Gains Tax Act 1979 shall, with any necessary modifications, apply for the purposes of this paragraph as they apply for the purposes of section 115 of that Act, namely—

(*a*) subsections (3) to (8) of the said section 115,

(*b*) section 119,

(*c*) section 121."

4. For paragraph 19 of Schedule 3 to the Finance Act 1974 substitute—

"19.—(1) Paragraph 18 above shall have effect subject to the provisions of this paragraph, in which—

(a) the "tax reduction" means the reduction in the income tax or corporation tax to which the person carrying on the trade is chargeable which is made under subparagraph (3) of the said paragraph 18 in connection with a disposal of an asset (called "asset No. 1");

(b) the "expenditure reduction" means the related amount by which under sub-paragraph (4) of that paragraph, and apart from the provisions of this paragraph, the expenditure allowable in respect of another asset (called "asset No. 2") is reduced;

(c) any reference to an expenditure reduction of any amount being carried forward to any asset is a reference to a reduction of that amount in expenditure allowable in respect of that asset.

(2) If asset No. 2 is a depreciating asset, the expenditure reduction shall not be carried forward, but—

(a) when the claimant disposes of asset No. 2, or

(b) when he ceases to use asset No. 2 for the purposes of a trade carried on by him, or

(c) on the expiration of a period of ten years beginning with the acquisition of asset No. 2,

whichever event comes first, an amount equal to the tax reduction may be assessed to tax and recovered accordingly.

Any assessment to income tax or corporation tax under this paragraph shall be made under Case VI of Schedule D.

(3) If, in the circumstances specified in sub-paragraph (4) below, the claimant acquires an asset (called "asset No. 3") which is not a depreciating asset, and so claims under paragraph 18 above—

(a) the expenditure reduction shall be carried forward to asset No. 3, and

(b) the claim which applies to asset No. 2 shall be treated as withdrawn (so that sub-paragraph (2) above does not apply).

(4) The circumstances are that asset No. 3 is acquired not later than the occurrence of whichever of the events mentioned in sub-paragraph (2) above comes first and, assuming—

(a) that the consideration for asset No. 1 was applied in acquiring asset No. 3, and

(b) that the time between the disposal of asset No. 1 and the acquisition of asset No. 3 was within the time limited by section 115(3) of the Capital Gains Tax Act 1979 as applied by paragraph 18(6) above, the whole amount of the expenditure reduction could be carried forward from asset No. 1 to asset No. 3 ; and the claim under sub-paragraph (3) above shall be accepted as if those assumptions were true.

(5) For the purposes of this paragraph an asset is a depreciating asset at any time if—

> (a) at that time it is a wasting asset as defined in section 37(1) of the Capital Gains Tax Act 1979, or
>
> (b) within the period of ten years beginning at that time it will become a wasting asset (so defined).

(6) This paragraph shall be construed as one with paragraph 18 above."

Finance (No. 2) Act 1975 (*c.* 45)

5. For paragraph 2(2) of Schedule 8 to the Finance (No. 2) Act 1975 substitute—

> " (2) Section 150(3) of the Capital Gains Tax Act 1979 (market value of shares or securities listed in The Stock Exchange Daily Official List) shall apply for the purposes of this paragraph as it applies for the purposes of that Act."

Development Land Tax Act 1976 (*c.* 24)

6.—(1) Paragraph 5 of Schedule 6 to the Development Land Tax Act 1976 shall be amended as follows.

(2) In sub-paragraph (1)(*a*)—

> (a) for " section 33 of the Finance Act 1965 " substitute " sections 115 to 121 of the Capital Gains Tax Act 1979 ", and
>
> (b) for " applies " substitute " apply ".

(3) In sub-paragraph (2) for " section 33 of the Finance Act 1965 " substitute " sections 115 to 121 of the Capital Gains Tax Act 1979 ".

(4) In sub-paragraph (4)—

> (a) for " section 33 of the Finance Act 1965 has effect subject to the provisions of paragraph 16 of Schedule 19 to the Finance Act 1969 " substitute " sections 115 and 116 of the Capital Gains Tax Act 1979 have effect subject to the provisions of section 117 of that Act ", and
>
> (b) for " sub-paragraph (2) of that paragraph accrues in accordance with that sub-paragraph " substitute " subsection (2) of of the said section 117 accrues in accordance with that subsection ".

(5) In sub-paragraph (4)(*a*) for " that sub-paragraph " substitute " subsection (2) of the said section 117 ".

(6) In sub-paragraph (4)(*b*) for " sub-paragraph (3) of that paragraph " substitute " subsection (3) of the said section 117 ".

(7) In sub-paragraph (6)—

    (*a*) for " section 33 of the Finance Act 1965 " substitute " sections 115 to 121 of the Capital Gains Tax Act 1979 ", and

    (*b*) for " paragraph 16 of Schedule 19 to the Finance Act 1969 " substitute " section 117 of that Act ".

Finance Act 1976 (*c.40*)

7. For section 54(5) of the Finance Act 1976 substitute—

" (5) Subsection (6) of section 84 of the Capital Gains Tax Act 1979 (gilt-edged securities not issued until after the date when shares are compulsorily acquired) shall apply in relation to this section as it applies in relation to that section, and in this section—

    " gilt-edged securities " has the meaning given by Schedule 2 to that Act ;

    " shares " includes securities within the meaning of section 82 of that Act."

Translation of references to Part III of Finance Act 1965

8. In the enactments specified in the Table below substitute " the Capital Gains Tax Act 1979 " (or " The Capital Gains Tax Act 1979 " if at the beginning of a sentence)—

    (*a*) in the contexts in Part I of the Table, for " Part III of the Finance Act 1965 ",

    (*b*) in the contexts in Part II of the Table, for " Part III of the Finance Act 1965 ", together with the words " (chargeable gains) " or " (capital gains) " or " (capital gains tax) " or " (tax on chargeable gains) " as the case may be.

TABLE
Part I

1. In the Taxes Management Act 1970 (c.9)
    section 11(1)(*b*)
    section 47(1)
    section 57(1)(*a*)
    section 111(1)
    section 118(1), in the definitions of " chargeable gain " and of " the Taxes Acts "
    section 119(4).

2. In the Income and Corporation Taxes Act 1970 (c.10)
    section 265(4)
    section 268(2)
    section 268A(2)
    section 273(1)
    section 278(3)
    section 279(2)
    section 352(7)
    section 526(5), in the definition of " chargeable gain "
    section 540(2).

3. In the Finance Act 1970 (c.24)
    section 29(1)(*b*)
    Schedule 6 paragraph 9.

4. In the Finance Act 1972 (c.41)
   Schedule 12, Part VII, in the definition of " market value " in paragraph 6.

5. In the Finance Act 1973 (c.51)
   section 38(3)
   section 59(3)(*c*).

6. In the Finance Act 1974 (c.30)
   section 40(3)(*a*)
   section 45(1)
   section 57(3)(*c*)
   Schedule 3 paragraph 18(4)
   Schedule 9 paragraph 2(3)
   Schedule 9 paragraph 17.

7. In the Finance Act 1975 (c.7)
   section 51(4)
   Schedule 10 paragraph 4(1).

8. In the Development Land Tax Act 1976 (c.24)
   section 47(1), in the definition of " chargeable gain ".

9. In the Finance Act 1976 (c.40)
   section 67(11)(*d*)
   section 132(3)(*c*).

10. In the Finance Act 1977 (c.36)
    section 42(1) (see also entry above for section 268A(2) of the Taxes Act)
    section 45(3).

Part II

References to Part III of Finance Act 1965 followed by Descriptive Words

1. Section 74(2) of the Post Office Act 1969 (c.48).

2. Section 27(1) of the Taxes Management Act 1970 (c.9).

3. In the Income and Corporation Taxes Act 1970 (c. 10)
   section 321(1)(*a*)
   section 525(2).

4. In the Finance Act 1970 (c.24)
   Schedule 3 paragraph 8(1)
   Schedule 6 paragraph 3(2)(*b*).

5. Paragraph 15 of Schedule 9 to the Finance Act 1974 (c.30).

6. In the Development Land Tax Act 1976 (c.24)
   section 5(6)(*b*)
   section 12(5)(*c*)
   Schedule 8 paragraph 57(1)(*b*).

Translation of references to enactments repealed and re-enacted

9. In the enactments specified in column 1 of the following Table for the words in column 2 substitute the words in column 3, adding, except as otherwise indicated, " of the Capital Gains Tax Act 1979 " (but in all cases saying " to " instead of " of " if the substituted words refer to a Schedule rather than a section).

TABLE

Taxes Management Act 1970 (c. 9)

Enactment amended	Words to be replaced	Corresponding provision of this Act
In the Taxes Management Act 1970 section		
12(2)(b)	section 30(6).	section 128(6) (without adding more words).
25(9)	subsections (1) and (8) of section 45 of the Finance Act 1965.	sections 64, 93 and 155(1).
28(2) ...	section 45(1) of the Finance Act 1965. subsections (1) and (8) of that section.	section 51. sections 64, 93 and 155(1) of that Act (without adding more words).

Income and Corporation Taxes Act 1970 (c. 10)

Enactment amended	Words to be replaced	Corresponding provision of this Act
In the Income and Corporation Taxes Act 1970 section		
186(12)(a) ...	paragraph 4(1)(a) of Schedule 6 to the Finance Act 1965.	section 32(1)(a).
246(2)(b) ...	Part III of the Finance Act 1965.	section 12.
265(3)(a) ...	paragraph 5(2) of Schedule 6 to the Finance Act 1965.	section 33(2).
266(5) ...	paragraph 3 of Schedule 7 to the Finance Act 1965.	section 72(5)(b).
267(1) ...	Part II of Schedule 6 to the Finance Act 1965.	Schedule 5.
267(3) ...	subsection (1) or subsection (2) of section 38 of the Finance Act 1965.	section 96 or 97.
267(3A) ...	Subsections (4) to (7) of section 40 of the Finance Act 1977.	Subsections (2) to (5) of section 88.
	subsection (3)(b).	subsection (1) (without adding more words).
269(1)(a) ...	paragraph 4 of Schedule 6 to the Finance Act 1965.	section 32.
269(1) ...	paragraph 4.	section 32 (without adding more words).
270(4)(a) ...	section 41 of the Finance Act 1969.	section 67.
270(5)(b) ...	section 41 of the Finance Act 1969.	section 67.
273(2) ...	Schedule 7 to the Finance Act 1965.	section 72.
	paragraph 3 of that Schedule.	that section (without adding more words).
274(1) and (2) ...	paragraph 1 of Schedule 7 to the Finance Act 1965.	section 122.

Enactment amended	*Words to be replaced*	*Corresponding provision of this Act*
275(1)	paragraph 6 of Schedule 6 to the Finance Act 1965.	section 34.
275(2) ...	Part II of Schedule 6 to the Finance Act 1965.	Schedule 5.
276(1) ...	section 33 of the Finance Act 1965.	sections 115 to 121.
276(2) ...	Paragraph 16(2) of Schedule 19 to the Finance Act 1969.	Section 117(2).
	paragraph 16(2).	section 117(2) (without adding more words).
278(4)(b) ...	section 33 of the Finance Act 1965.	sections 115 to 121.
279(6) ...	paragraph 6 or paragraph 7 of Schedule 7 to the Finance Act 1965.	section 85 or section 86.
279(7) ...	paragraph 7 of the said Schedule 7.	section 86.
280(8) ...	section 23(4) of the Finance Act 1965.	section 22(2).
305(2) ...	paragraph 2(1) of Schedule 6 to the Finance Act 1965.	section 31(1).
352(7) ...	Part II of Schedule 6.	Schedule 5 (without adding more words).
359(4) ...	subsections (1) and (8) of section 45 of the Finance Act 1965.	sections 64, 93 and 155(1).
360(2) ...	section 35 of the Finance Act 1965.	section 145.
474(2) ...	Part III of the Finance Act 1965.	section 72(5)(b).
488(9) ...	section 29 of the Finance Act 1965.	sections 101 to 105.
	paragraph 2 of Schedule 12 to the Finance Act 1968.	section 103(3) of that Act (without adding more words).
489(11) ...	paragraph 1 of Schedule 7 to the Finance Act 1965.	section 122.
489(12) ...	paragraphs 2 and 5 of Schedule 6 to the Finance Act 1965.	sections 31 and 33.

Finance Act 1970 (c. 24)

In the Finance Act 1970 Schedule 3 paragraph 8(1)	Part II of Schedule 6.	Schedule 5 (without adding more words).

Finance Act 1972 (c. 41)

In the Finance Act 1972 section 79(9)	paragraph 4(1)(a) of Schedule 6 to the Finance Act 1965.	section 32(1)(a).
Schedule 12 Part VII paragraph 6 in the definition of "market value".	section 44.	section 150 (without adding more words).

Enactment amended	Words to be replaced	Corresponding provision of this Act
	Finance Act 1973 (c. 51)	
In the Finance Act 1973		
Schedule 16		
paragraph 5	paragraph 2 or 5 of Schedule 6 to the Finance Act 1965.	section 31 or 33
paragraph 7	specified securities within the meaning of section 41 of the Finance Act 1969.	gilt-edged securities as defined in Schedule 2.
	Finance Act 1974 (c. 30)	
In the Finance Act 1974		
section		
26(2)(a)	section 20(3) of the Finance Act 1965.	section 3.
30(1)	paragraph 5 of Schedule 7 to the Finance Act 1965.	section 82.
38(3)(a) ...	paragraph 4(1)(a) and (b) of Schedule 6 to the Finance Act 1965.	section 32(1)(a) and (b).
39(4)(a) ...	section 45(7)(b) of the Finance Act 1965.	section 60(b).
41(6) ...	section 45(8) of the Finance Act 1965.	section 93.
41(13) ...	paragraph 3 of Schedule 7 to the Finance Act 1965.	section 72.
42(4)(a) ...	paragraph 13(1) of Schedule 7 to the Finance Act 1965.	section 58(1).
42(4) (after paragraphs (a) and (b)).	paragraph 13(1) (twice).	section 58(1) (without adding more words).
42(5) ...	paragraph 13(2) of Schedule 7 to the Finance Act 1965.	section 58(2).
42(5)(a) ...	section 25(3) of the Finance Act 1965.	section 54(1).
42(5)(b) ...	section 42 of the Finance Act 1965.	section 17.
42(6) ...	section 42 (three times).	section 17 (without adding more words).
42(7) ...	Schedule 6 to the Finance Act 1965.	Chapter II of Part II.
43(2)	section 4(1)(a) of that Schedule.	section 32(1)(a).
44(1) (definition of "securities") ...	section 38(2) of the Finance Act 1965.	section 97.
	paragraph 5 of Schedule 7 to the Finance Act 1965.	section 82.
44(1) (definition of "shares")	section 45(1) of the Finance Act 1965.	section 64(1).

Enactment amended		Words to be replaced	Corresponding provision of this Act
Schedule 3			
paragraph 2(3) ...	...	paragraph 7(2) of Schedule 6 to the Finance Act 1965.	subsection (2) of section 35.
		paragraph 7(4) of that Schedule.	subsection (4) of that section (without adding more words).
			Chapter II of Part II of that Act (without adding more words).
		that Schedule.	
paragraph 2(4) ...	...	paragraph 4(1)(a) and (b) of the said Schedule 6.	section 32(1)(a) and (b).
		that Schedule.	Chapter II of Part II of that Act (without adding more words).
paragraph 2(7) ...	...	paragraph 4(1)(a) and (b) of Schedule 6 to the Finance Act 1965.	section 32(1)(a) and (b).
		Schedule 8.	Schedule 3 (without adding more words).
paragraph 3 ...	...	subsection (3) of section 22 of the Finance Act 1965.	subsection (1) of section 20.
paragraph 5(2) ...	...	paragraph 4(1)(a) and (b) of Schedule 6 to the Finance Act 1965.	section 32(1)(a) and (b).
		Schedule 8.	Schedule 3 (without adding more words).
		the said Schedule 6.	Chapter II of Part II of that Act (without adding more words).
paragraph 11(5)(b) ...	...	paragraph 4(1)(b) of Schedule 6 to the Finance Act 1965.	section 32(1)(b).
paragraph 12(1) ...	...	Schedule 8 to the Finance Act 1965.	Schedule 3.
		paragraph 4(1)(b) of Schedule 6 to the Finance Act 1965.	section 32(1)(b) of that Act (without adding more words).
Cross-heading before paragraph 15.		paragraph 23(4) of Schedule 6 to the Finance Act 1965.	paragraph 9(4) of Schedule 5.
paragraph 15 ...	...	paragraph 23 of Schedule 6 to the Finance Act 1965.	paragraph 9 of Schedule 5.
		Part II of that Schedule.	the said Schedule 5 (without adding more words).
paragraph 16(1) ...	...	section 33 of the Finance Act 1965.	sections 115 to 121 (changing "applies" to "apply").
		the said section 33.	those sections (without adding more words).

Enactment amended	*Words to be replaced*	*Corresponding provision of this Act*
paragraph 17	subsection (1)(b) or (2)(b) of section 33 of the Finance Act 1965.	section 115(1)(b) or 116(1)(b).
	Part III of that Act.	that Act (without adding more words).
	subsection (1)(b) or (2)(b).	section 115(1)(b) or 116(1)(b) (without adding more words).
paragraph 18(1)(a) ...	subsection (6) of section 33 of the Finance Act 1965.	section 118 (with section 119).
paragraph 18(7) ...	Part III of the Finance Act 1965 providing generally for apportionments.	section 43(4).
paragraph 18(8) ...	section 33(6) of the Finance Act 1965.	section 118.
	paragraph (b).	paragraph 2 (without adding more words).
	paragraph (a).	paragraph 1 (without adding more words).
paragraph 20(1) ...	paragraph 6 of Schedule 7 to the Finance Act 1965.	section 85.
paragraph 20(2)	paragraph 6.	section 85 (without adding more words).
paragraph 21	paragraph 6.	section 85 (without adding more words).
	subsection (3) of section 29 of the Finance Act 1965.	subsection (2) of section 102.
paragraph 22(1) ...	section 34 of the Finance Act 1965.	section 124.
paragraph 22(2) ...	section 34.	section 124 (without adding more words).
paragraph 22(3) ...	subsection (1) of the said section 34.	the said section 124 (without adding more words).
	subsection (2) or (3).	subsection (4) or (5) (without adding more words).
paragraph 22(5) ...	Subsection (5) of the said section 34.	Subsection (7) of the said section 124 (without adding more words).
	subsection (2) or (3).	subsection (4) or (5) (without adding more words).
paragraph 22(6) ...	section 34.	section 124 (without adding more words).
	subsection (4).	subsection (6) (without adding more words).
	the said subsection (1).	that section 124 (without adding more words).
paragraph 22(7) ...	section 34.	section 124 (without adding more words).
paragraph 23	paragraph 2(1) of Schedule 6 to the Finance Act 1965.	section 31(1).

Enactment amended	Words to be replaced	Corresponding provision of this Act
Schedule 6		
paragraph 2	section 20(2) of the Finance Act 1965.	section 12.
Cross-heading before paragraph 6.	paragraph 23(4) of Schedule 6 to the Finance Act 1965.	paragraph 9(4) of Schedule 5.
paragraph 6	paragraph 23 of Schedule 6 to the Finance Act 1965.	paragraph 9 of Schedule 5.
	Part II of that Schedule.	the said Schedule 5 (without adding more words).
paragraph 7 ...	subsection (3) of section 29 of the Finance Act 1965.	section 102(2).
paragraph 9(1) ...	paragraph 2(1) of Schedule 6 to the Finance Act 1965.	section 31(1).
Schedule 8		
paragraph 1 ...	Subsections (1) and (2) of section 20 of the Finance Act 1965.	Sections 2 and 12.
paragraph 2 ...	Section 41 of the Finance Act 1965.	Section 15.
paragraph 3 ...	Section 42 of the Finance Act 1965.	Section 17.
	section 20(4) of this Act.	section 4(1) above (without adding more words).
paragraph 4 ...	section 33 of the Finance Act 1965.	sections 115 to 121 (substituting " apply " for " applies ").
	that section.	those sections (without adding more words).
	the said section 33 in its application.	those sections in their application (without adding more words).
paragraph 5 ...	Schedule 6 to the Finance Act 1965.	Chapter II of Part II.
	paragraph 4(1)(b) of the said Schedule 6.	section 32(1)(b) of that Act (without adding more words).
paragraph 7(1) ...	paragraph 15 of Schedule 19 to the Finance Act 1969.	section 123.
	said paragraph 15.	said section 123 (without adding more words).
paragraph 7(2)(b)(ii) ...	sub-paragraph (4) of the said paragraph 15.	subsection (4) of the said section 123 (without adding more words).
	that sub-paragraph.	that subsection (without adding more words).
paragraph 7(5) ...	Schedule 6 to the Finance Act 1965.	Chapter II of Part II.
paragraph 7(6) ...	paragraph 4(1)(a) and (b) of the said Schedule 6.	section 32(1)(a) and (b).
	that Schedule.	Chapter II of Part II of that Act (without adding more words).

Enactment amended	Words to be replaced	Corresponding provision of this Act
Schedule 9		
paragraph 14(4)	Schedule 6 to the Finance Act 1965.	Chapter II of Part II.
paragraph 14(5)	paragraph 4(1)(a) and (b) of the said Schedule 6.	section 32(1)(a) and (b).
	that Schedule.	Chapter II of Part II of that Act (without adding more words).
paragraph 14(6)	Paragraph 14 of Schedule 6 to the Finance Act 1965.	Section 40.
paragraph 15	paragraph 2 of Schedule 6 to that Act.	section 31 of that Act (without adding more words).
	that Schedule.	Chapter II of Part II of that Act (without adding more words).
paragraph 16(1)	Schedule 8 to the Finance Act 1965.	Schedule 3.
paragraph 16(2)	Schedule 6 to the Finance Act 1965.	Chapter II of Part II.
	paragraph 4(1) of that Schedule.	section 32(1) of that Act (without adding more words).
	paragraph 7 of that Schedule.	section 35 of that Act (without adding more words).
	that Schedule.	the said Chapter II (without adding more words).
paragraph 16(4)	Schedule 8 to the Finance Act 1965.	Schedule 3.
paragraph 18	Schedule 8 to the Finance Act 1965.	Schedule 3.
	paragraph 4(1)(b) of Schedule 6 to the Finance Act 1965.	section 32(1)(b) of that Act (without adding more words).
Schedule 10		
paragraph 1(a)	section 25(9) of, and paragraph 19 of Schedule 7 to, the Finance Act 1965.	sections 52(4) and 59.
paragraph 2	paragraph 14 of Schedule 6 to the Finance Act 1965 and paragraph 4 of Schedule 10 to that Act and section 57 of the Finance (No. 2) Act 1975.	sections 8 and 40.
paragraph 5(2)(a)	sections 41 and 42 of the Finance Act 1965.	sections 15 and 17.

Finance Act 1975 (c. 7)

Enactment amended	Words to be replaced	Corresponding provision of this Act
In the Finance Act 1975		
section 51(4)	paragraph 21 of Schedule 7 to.	section 63 of (without adding more words).
	that paragraph.	that section (without adding more words).

Enactment amended	Words to be replaced	Corresponding provision of this Act
Schedule 10		
paragraph 4(1)(*b*) ...	paragraph 19 of Schedule 7 to.	section 59 of (without adding more words).
paragraph 27(1) ...	paragraph 4 of Schedule 7 to the Finance Act 1965.	section 78.
paragraph 27(1)(*a*) ...	that paragraph, or reduction of the share capital of a company.	section 77(1) of that Act (without adding more words).
paragraph 27(1)(*b*) ...	paragraph 5 of that Schedule.	section 82 of that Act (without adding more words).
paragraph 27(1)(*c*) ...	paragraph 6 of that Schedule.	section 85 of that Act (without adding more words).
paragraph 27(1)(*d*) ...	paragraph 7 of that Schedule.	section 86 of that Act (without adding more words).
paragraph 27(1) (at end) ...	paragraph 4 of that Schedule applies by virtue of section 45(8) of the Finance Act 1965.	the said section 78 applies by virtue of section 93.
paragraph 27(2) ...	paragraph 4 of the said Schedule 7.	section 77(1).
paragraph 29(1) ...	section 26 of the Finance Act 1965.	section 153.
paragraph 34(2) ...	Schedule 8 to the Finance Act 1965.	Schedule 3.

Finance (No. 2) Act 1975 (c. 45)

Enactment amended	Words to be replaced	Corresponding provision of this Act
In the Finance (No. 2) Act 1975 section		
42(10) ...	section 22(2)(*b*) of the Finance Act 1965.	section 19(2)(*b*).
58(8) ...	paragraph 4 of Schedule 6 to the Finance Act 1965.	section 32.
	sub-paragraph (1)(*c*) of that paragraph.	subsection (1)(*c*) of that section (without adding more words).
	sub-paragraph (1)(*a*) and (*b*) of that paragraph.	subsection (1)(*a*) and (*b*) of that section (without adding more words).
58(9) ...	sub-paragraph (1) of paragraph 6 of Schedule 10 to the Finance Act 1971.	section 66(1).
	sub-paragraph (2) of that paragraph.	subsection (2) of the said section 66 (without adding more words).
	under sub-paragraph (1).	under subsection (1) (without adding more words).
58(12) ...	paragraph 5 of Schedule 7 to the Finance Act 1965.	section 82.
	specified securities within the meaning of section 41 of the Finance Act 1969.	gilt-edged securities as defined in Schedule 2 to that Act (without adding more words).
Schedule 8		
paragraph 2(3) ...	section 51 of the Finance Act 1973.	section 152.

Enactment amended		Words to be replaced	Corresponding provision of this Act
In the Development Land Tax Act 1976		*Development Land Tax Act 1976 (c. 24)*	
Schedule 6			
paragraph 1(5)(a)	...	section 34 of the Finance Act 1965.	section 124 or 125.
paragraph 1(5)(b)	...	section 38(2).	section 97 (without adding more words).
paragraph 2(2) ...	...	section 24(1) of the Finance Act 1965.	section 49(1).
paragraph 3(2) ...	...	Schedule 8 to the Finance Act 1965.	Schedule 3.
paragraph 3(10)	...	sub-paragraph (1) or sub-paragraph (4) of paragraph 5 of Schedule 8 to the Finance Act 1965.	paragraph 5(1) or (3) of Schedule 3.
paragraph 4(1)(a)	...	Schedule 8 to the Finance Act 1965. Schedule 6 to.	Schedule 3. Chapter II of Part II of (without adding more words).
paragraph 4(4)(a)	...	Schedule 8 to the Finance Act 1965.	Schedule 3.
Schedule 8			
paragraph 52(1)(c)	...	the words from " Part III " to " 1969 ".	the Capital Gains Tax Act 1979, section 123 of that Act (without adding more words).
In the Finance Act 1976		*Finance Act 1976 (c. 40)*	
section			
54(3)(a) ...	...	section 53(3) above.	section 84(3).
54(3)(b) ...	...	section 33 of the Finance Act 1965. that section.	sections 115 to 121. section 118 of that Act (without adding more words).
67(11)(d)	...	section 44.	section 150 (without adding more words).
67(13) ...	...	paragraph 4(1)(a) of Schedule 6 to the Finance Act 1965.	section 32(1)(a).
82(2) ...	...	section 31 of the Finance Act 1965.	section 147.
Schedule 10			
paragraph 4(5) ...	...	paragraphs 4 to 7 of Schedule 7 to the Finance Act 1965.	sections 77 to 86.
Schedule 12			
paragraph 4(1) ...	...	paragraph 4 of Schedule 7 to the Finance Act 1965.	section 78.
		section 53 of this Act.	section 84 of that Act (without adding more words).

Enactment amended	Words to be replaced	Corresponding provision of this Act
paragraph 4(1)(*a*) ...	that paragraph, or reduction of the share capital of a company.	section 77(1) of that Act (without adding more words).
paragraph 4(1)(*b*) ...	paragraph 5 of that Schedule.	section 82 of that Act (without adding more words).
paragraph 4(1)(*c*) ...	paragraph 6 of that Schedule.	section 85 of that Act (without adding more words).
paragraph 4(1)(*d*) ...	paragraph 7 of that Schedule.	section 86 of that Act (without adding more words).
paragraph 4(1) (at end) ...	paragraph 4 of that Schedule applies by virtue of section 45(8) of the Finance Act 1965.	the said section 78 applies by virtue of section 93.
paragraph 4(2) ...	the said paragraph 4.	section 77(1).
paragraph 7(2) ...	Schedule 8 to the Finance Act 1965.	Schedule 3.
Schedule 13 ...	(see amendment in this Table of Finance Act 1975 Schedule 10 paragraph 34(2)).	—

Finance Act 1977 (c. 36)

In the Finance Act 1977 section

41(1) ...	(see amendment in this Table of section 267(3A) of the Income and Corporation Taxes Act 1970).	—
46(2)(*a*) ...	paragraph 4, 5, 6 or 7 of Schedule 7 to the Finance Act 1965.	sections 77 to 86.
46(2)(*b*) ...	section 53 of the Finance Act 1976.	section 84 of that Act (without adding more words).
46(6) ...	paragraph 5 of Schedule 7 to the said Act of 1965.	section 82.
	the words from "section 45(8)" to "Finance Act 1971".	section 86(7), 93 or 139 of that Act (without adding more words).
46(7) ...	paragraph 6 or 7 of Schedule 7 to the said Act of 1965.	section 85 or 86.
	section 40(2) above.	section 87(1) of that Act (without adding more words).

Enactment amended	Words to be replaced	Corresponding provision of this Act
	Finance Act 1978 (c. 42)	
In the Finance Act 1978 section		
54(2)(a)	paragraph 4 of Schedule 7 to the Finance Act 1965.	section 77(1)(b).
57(1)	paragraph 4 of Schedule 7 of the Finance Act 1965.	section 77(1)(b).
57(7)	Part III of the Finance Act 1965.	Chapter II of Part IV.
61(1), in the definition of " market value ".	Part III of the Finance Act 1965 (capital gains tax).	Part VIII.
61(3)(b)	paragraph 3 of Schedule 7 to the Finance Act 1965.	section 72(5)(b).
64(5)	(see amendment in this Table of Finance Act 1976 Schedule 10 paragraph 4(5)).	—

SCHEDULE 8

REPEALS

Chapter	Short title	Extent of repeal
1965 c. 25.	Finance Act 1965.	Part III, except section 45(12). Section 94. Schedules 6 to 9. Schedule 10, except paragraph 15.
1966 c. 18.	Finance Act 1966.	Section 43. Schedule 10.
1967 c. 54.	Finance Act 1967.	Section 32. Section 35. Section 37. Section 45(3)(*h*). Schedule 13.
1968 c. 44.	Finance Act 1968.	Section 32. Section 34. Section 61(5). Schedules 11 and 12.
1969 c. 32.	Finance Act 1969.	Sections 41 and 42. Section 61(3)(*e*). Schedules 18 and 19.
1970 c. 9.	Taxes Management Act 1970.	Section 47(4). In section 57(3)(*c*) the words " or under any provision in the Finance Act 1965 ".

1970 c. 10.	Income and Corporation Taxes Act 1970.	In Schedule 15—
		    paragraphs 6 and 7;
		    in Part I of the Table in paragraph 11 the entries amending the Finance Act 1965;
		    in Part II of that Table the entries amending—
		        the Finance Act 1965 (except section 93),
		        the Finance Act 1967,
		        the Finance Act 1968,
		        Schedules 18 and 19 to the Finance Act 1969;
		    paragraph 12(1).

1970 c. 24.	Finance Act 1970.	In section 28(1) the words from " section 41 " to " 1969 and of ".
1971 c. 68.	Finance Act 1971.	Section 55, except subsection (5). Section 56. Sections 58 to 60. In section 69(3) the words from " Part IV " to the end of the subsection. In Schedule 3 paragraph 10. In Schedule 6 paragraph 91. In Schedule 8 paragraph 16(1). Schedule 9, except paragraph 4. Schedule 10. Schedule 12.

Chapter	Short title	Extent of repeal
1972 c. 41.	Finance Act 1972.	Sections 112 to 119. In section 124(2) the words " or gains " before paragraph (*a*), and in paragraph (*a*) the words " or gains " (in three places) and the words " or section 40(1) of the Finance Act 1965.". Section 134(3)(*c*). In Schedule 24 paragraphs 1 and 2.
1973 c. 51.	Finance Act 1973.	Section 37. Section 51. In section 54(1) the words " capital gains tax ". In Schedule 16 paragraph 15. Schedule 20. In Schedule 21 paragraph 4.
1974 c. 30.	Finance Act 1974.	Section 8(8). Sections 31 to 33. Section 48. In section 57(3)(*b*) the words from " and so far " to the end of the paragraph. In Schedule 8 paragraph 6.
1975 c. 7.	Finance Act 1975.	Section 53. In Schedule 12 paragraphs 12, 13 and 17.
1975 c. 45.	Finance (No. 2) Act 1975.	Section 44(4). Section 57. Sections 59 to 64. In section 75(3)(*c*) the words from " and so far " to the end of the paragraph. In Schedule 8 paragraph 5.
1976 c. 40.	Finance Act 1976.	Sections 52 and 53. Sections 55 and 56. In Schedule 11 paragraphs 1 and 6.
1977 c. 36.	Finance Act 1977.	Section 40. Section 43. In section 59(3)(*c*) the words from " and, so far " to the end of the paragraph.
1978 c. 42.	Finance Act 1978.	Section 44. In section 45 subsections (1) to (4), and in subsection (6) the words from " and subsections (2) " to the end of the sub-section. Sections 46 to 52. In section 80(3)(*c*) the words from " and so far " to the end of the paragraph. Schedules 7 and 8. In Schedule 11 paragraph 2.

Statutory instruments

Serial No.	Title	Extent of repeal
S.I. 1970/173.	Capital Gains Tax (Exempt Gilt-edged Securities) Order 1970.	The whole order.
S.I. 1970/1741.	Capital Gains Tax (Exempt Gilt-edged Securities) (No. 2) Order 1970.	The whole order.
S.I. 1971/793.	Capital Gains Tax (Exempt Gilt-edged Securities) Order 1971.	The whole order.
S.I. 1971/1366.	Capital Gains Tax (Exempt Gilt-edged Securities) (No. 2) Order 1971.	The whole order.
S.I. 1971/1786.	Capital Gains Tax (Exempt Gilt-edged Securities) (No. 3) Order 1971.	The whole order.
S.I. 1972/244.	Capital Gains Tax (Exempt Gilt-edged Securities) Order 1972.	The whole order.
S.I. 1972/1015.	Capital Gains Tax (Exempt Gilt-edged Securities) (No. 2) Order 1972.	The whole order.
S.I. 1973/241.	Capital Gains Tax (Exempt Gilt-edged Securities) Order 1973.	The whole order.
S.I. 1973/716.	Capital Gains Tax (Exempt Gilt-edged Securities) (No. 2) Order 1973.	The whole order.
S.I. 1973/1769.	Capital Gains Tax (Exempt Gilt-edged Securities) (No. 3) Order 1973.	The whole order.
S.I. 1974/693.	Capital Gains Tax (Exempt Gilt-edged Securities) Order 1974.	The whole order.
S.I. 1974/1071.	Capital Gains Tax (Exempt Gilt-edged Securities) (No. 2) Order 1974.	The whole order.
S.I. 1974/1907.	Capital Gains Tax (Exempt Gilt-edged Securities) (No. 3) Order 1974.	The whole order.
S.I. 1975/354.	Capital Gains Tax (Exempt Gilt-edged Securities) Order 1975.	The whole order.
S.I. 1975/1129.	Capital Gains Tax (Exempt Gilt-edged Securities) (No. 2) Order 1975.	The whole order.
S.I. 1975/1757.	Capital Gains Tax (Exempt Gilt-edged Securities) (No. 3) Order 1975.	The whole order.
S.I. 1976/698.	Capital Gains Tax (Exempt Gilt-edged Securities) (No. 1) Order 1976.	The whole order.
S.I. 1976/1859.	Capital Gains Tax (Exempt Gilt-edged Securities) (No. 2) Order 1976.	The whole order.
S.I. 1977/347.	Capital Gains Tax (Exempt Gilt-edged Securities) (No. 1) Order 1977.	The whole order.
S.I. 1977/919.	Capital Gains Tax (Exempt Gilt-edged Securities) (No. 2) Order 1977.	The whole order.

Serial No.	Title	Extent of repeal
S.I. 1977/1136.	Capital Gains Tax (Exempt Gilt-edged Securities) (No. 3) Order 1977.	The whole order.
S.I. 1977/1614.	Capital Gains Tax (Exempt Gilt-edged Securities) (No. 4) Order 1977.	The whole order.
S.I. 1978/141.	Capital Gains Tax (Exempt Gilt-edged Securities) (No. 1) Order 1978.	The whole order.
S.I. 1978/1312.	Capital Gains Tax (Exempt Gilt-edged Securities) (No. 2) Grder 1978.	The whole order.
S.I. 1978/1838.	Capital Gains Tax (Exempt Gilt-edged Securities) (No. 3) Order 1978.	The whole order.

House of Commons (Redistribution of Seats) Act 1979

1979 CHAPTER 15

An Act to increase the number of constituencies in Northern Ireland required by rule 1 in Schedule 2 to the House of Commons (Redistribution of Seats) Act 1949.   [22nd March 1979]

BE IT ENACTED by the Queen's most Excellent Majesty, by and with the advice and consent of the Lords Spiritual and Temporal, and Commons, in this present Parliament assembled, and by the authority of the same, as follows:—

1.—(1) In rule 1 of the rules for the redistribution of seats set out in Schedule 2 to the House of Commons (Redistribution of Seats) Act 1949 (referred to below in this section as "the principal Act") for the figure "12" (the required number of constituencies for Northern Ireland) there shall be substituted the words "Not greater than 18 or less than 16".

Increase of number of constituencies in Northern Ireland.
1949 c. 66.

(2) Notwithstanding subsection (1) above, in discharging their functions under section 2 of the principal Act, the Boundary Commission for Northern Ireland shall read rule 1 as if it required the number of constituencies in Northern Ireland to be 17, unless it appears to the Commission that Northern Ireland should for the time being be divided into 16 or (as the case may be) into 18 constituencies.

(3) In framing their first report after the passing of this Act under section 2(1) of the principal Act, the Boundary Commission for Northern Ireland shall read rule 5 of those rules (under which

the electorate of a constituency is to be brought as near the electoral quota as is practicable having regard to the other rules) in accordance with the definitions given in subsection (4) below instead of in accordance with rule 7 of those rules.

(4) In rule 5 as it applies by virtue of subsection (3) above—

(*a*) " electoral quota " shall mean a number obtained by dividing the aggregate electorate (as defined in paragraph (*b*) below) of all the constituencies in Northern Ireland by 17; and

(*b*) " electorate " shall mean, in relation to any constituency, the number of persons whose names appear on the register of parliamentary electors in force for the constituency at the passing of this Act under the Representation of the People Acts.

1973 c. 36.

(5) For subsections (5) and (6) of section 28 of the Northern Ireland Constitution Act 1973 (effect of Orders in Council under the principal Act on elections to the Northern Ireland Assembly) there shall be substituted the following subsections—

" (5) An Order in Council under the said Act of 1949 for giving effect, with or without modifications, to the recommendations contained in a report or supplementary report of the Boundary Commission for Northern Ireland may make amendments consequential on giving effect to those recommendations in section 1(1) of and in the Schedule to the said Act of 1973.

(6) The coming into force of any such Order in Council shall not affect any election to the Assembly before the next general election to the Assembly or affect the constitution of the Assembly then in being."

(6) In framing their first supplementary report after the passing of this Act under section 28 (supplementary reports with respect to the number of members to be returned to the Northern Ireland Assembly by each constituency in Northern Ireland), the Boundary Commission for Northern Ireland shall read subsection (3) of that section (which requires the ratio of the electorate of each constituency to the number of members to be returned by that constituency to be as far as practicable the same in every constituency) as if the electorate were defined by reference to the passing of this Act instead of by reference to the enumeration date.

Citation.

2. This Act may be cited as the House of Commons (Redistribution of Seats) Act 1979, and shall be included among the Acts which may be cited as the Representation of the People Acts, and this Act and the House of Commons (Redistribution of Seats) Acts 1949 and 1958 may be cited together as the House of Commons (Redistribution of Seats) Acts 1949 to 1979.

Criminal Evidence Act 1979

1979 CHAPTER 16

An Act to amend paragraph (*f*)(iii) of the proviso to section 1 of the Criminal Evidence Act 1898 and corresponding enactments extending to Scotland and Northern Ireland. [22nd March 1979]

BE IT ENACTED by the Queen's most Excellent Majesty, by and with the advice and consent of the Lords Spiritual and Temporal, and Commons, in this present Parliament assembled, and by the authority of the same, as follows:—

1.—(1) In paragraph (*f*)(iii) of the proviso to each of the following enactments, that is to say, section 1 of the Criminal Evidence Act 1898, sections 141 and 346 of the Criminal Procedure (Scotland) Act 1975 and section 1 of the Criminal Evidence Act (Northern Ireland) 1923 (under which an accused person who has given evidence against another person charged with the same offence may be cross-examined about his previous convictions and his bad character), for the words " with the same offence " there shall be substituted the words " in the same proceedings ".

Amendment of section 1 of Criminal Evidence Act 1898, etc., and transitional provision.

(2) Notwithstanding subsection (1) above, a person charged with any offence who, before the coming into force of this Act, has given evidence against any other person charged in the same proceedings shall not by reason of that fact be asked or required to answer any question which he could not have been asked and required to answer but for that subsection.

2.—(1) This Act may be cited as the Criminal Evidence Act 1979.

Short title and commencement.

(2) This Act shall come into force at the end of the period of one month beginning with the date on which it is passed.

Criminal Evidence Act 1979

1979 CHAPTER 16

An Act to amend paragraph 1(f)(iii) of the proviso to section 1 of the Criminal Evidence Act 1898 and a provision making similar amendments to Scotland and Northern Ireland. [22nd March 1979]

BE it enacted by the Queen's most Excellent Majesty, by and with the advice and consent of the Lords Spiritual and Temporal, and Commons, in this present Parliament assembled, and by the authority of the same, as follows:—

Vaccine Damage Payments Act 1979

1979 CHAPTER 17

An Act to provide for payments to be made out of public funds in cases where severe disablement occurs as a result of vaccination against certain diseases or of contact with a person who has been vaccinated against any of those diseases; to make provision in connection with similar payments made before the passing of this Act; and for purposes connected therewith. [22nd March 1979]

BE IT ENACTED by the Queen's most Excellent Majesty, by and with the advice and consent of the Lords Spiritual and Temporal, and Commons, in this present Parliament assembled, and by the authority of the same, as follows:—

1.—(1) If, on consideration of a claim, the Secretary of State is satisfied— _Payments to persons severely disabled by vaccination._

    (a) that a person is, or was immediately before his death, severely disabled as a result of vaccination against any of the diseases to which this Act applies ; and

    (b) that the conditions of entitlement which are applicable in accordance with section 2 below are fulfilled,

he shall in accordance with this Act make a payment of £10,000 to or for the benefit of that person or to his personal representatives.

(2) The diseases to which this Act applies are—

    (a) diphtheria,

    (b) tetanus,

S 2

(c) whooping cough,

(d) poliomyelitis,

(e) measles,

(f) rubella,

(g) tuberculosis,

(h) smallpox, and

(i) any other disease which is specified by the Secretary of State for the purposes of this Act by order made by statutory instrument.

(3) Subject to section 2(3) below, this Act has effect with respect to a person who is severely disabled as a result of a vaccination given to his mother before he was born as if the vaccination had been given directly to him and, in such circumstances as may be prescribed by regulations under this Act, this Act has effect with respect to a person who is severely disabled as a result of contracting a disease through contact with a third person who was vaccinated against it as if the vaccination had been given to him and the disablement resulted from it.

(4) For the purposes of this Act, a person is severely disabled if he suffers disablement to the extent of 80 per cent. or more, assessed as for the purposes of section 57 of the Social Security Act 1975 or the Social Security (Northern Ireland) Act 1975 (disablement gratuity and pension).

1975 c. 14.
1975 c. 15.

(5) A statutory instrument under subsection (2)(i) above shall be subject to annulment in pursuance of a resolution of either House of Parliament.

Conditions of entitlement.

2.—(1) Subject to the provisions of this section, the conditions of entitlement referred to in section 1(1)(b) above are—

(a) that the vaccination in question was carried out—

(i) in the United Kingdom or the Isle of Man, and

(ii) on or after 5th July 1948, and

(iii) in the case of vaccination against smallpox, before 1st August 1971;

(b) except in the case of vaccination against poliomyelitis or rubella, that the vaccination was carried out either at a time when the person to whom it was given was under the age of eighteen or at the time of an outbreak within the United Kingdom or the Isle of Man of the disease against which the vaccination was given; and

(c) that the disabled person was over the age of two on the date when the claim was made or, if he died before that date, that he died after 9th May 1978 and was over the age of two when he died.

(2) An order under section 1(2)(*i*) above specifying a disease for the purposes of this Act may provide that, in relation to vaccination against that disease, the conditions of entitlement specified in subsection (1) above shall have effect subject to such modifications as may be specified in the order.

(3) In a case where this Act has effect by virtue of section 1(3) above, the reference in subsection (1)(*b*) above to the person to whom a vaccination was given is a reference to the person to whom it was actually given and not to the disabled person.

(4) With respect to claims made after such date as may be specified in the order and relating to vaccination against such disease as may be so specified, the Secretary of State may by order made by statutory instrument—

   (*a*) provide that, in such circumstances as may be specified in the order, one or more of the conditions of entitlement appropriate to vaccination against that disease need not be fulfilled ; or

   (*b*) add to the conditions of entitlement which are appropriate to vaccination against that disease, either generally or in such circumstances as may be specified in the order.

(5) Regulations under this Act shall specify the cases in which vaccinations given outside the United Kingdom and the Isle of Man to persons defined in the regulations as serving members of Her Majesty's forces or members of their families are to be treated for the purposes of this Act as carried out in England.

(6) The Secretary of State shall not make an order containing any provision made by virtue of paragraph (*b*) of subsection (4) above unless a draft of the order has been laid before Parliament and approved by a resolution of each House ; and a statutory instrument by which any other order is made under that subsection shall be subject to annulment in pursuance of a resolution of either House of Parliament.

3.—(1) Any reference in this Act, other than section 7, to a claim is a reference to a claim for a payment under section 1(1) above which is made— Determination of claims.

   (*a*) by or on behalf of the disabled person concerned or, as the case may be, by his personal representatives ; and

   (*b*) in the manner prescribed by regulations under this Act ; and

   (*c*) within the period of six years beginning on the latest of the following dates, namely, the date of the vaccination to which the claim relates, the date on which the disabled person attained the age of two and 9th May 1978 ;

and, in relation to a claim, any reference to the claimant is a reference to the person by whom the claim was made and any reference to the disabled person is a reference to the person in respect of whose disablement a payment under subsection (1) above is claimed to be payable.

(2) As soon as practicable after he has received a claim, the Secretary of State shall give notice in writing to the claimant of his determination whether he is satisfied that a payment is due under section 1(1) above to or for the benefit of the disabled person or to his personal representatives.

(3) If the Secretary of State is not satisfied that a payment is due as mentioned in subsection (2) above, the notice in writing under that subsection shall state the grounds on which he is not so satisfied.

(4) If, in the case of any claim, the Secretary of State—

    (a) is satisfied that the conditions of entitlement which are applicable in accordance with section 2 above are fulfilled, but

    (b) is not satisfied that the disabled person is or, where he has died, was immediately before his death severely disabled as a result of vaccination against any of the diseases to which this Act applies,

the notice in writing under subsection (2) above shall inform the claimant that, if an application for review is made to the Secretary of State, the matters referred to in paragraph (b) above will be reviewed by an independent medical tribunal in accordance with section 4 below.

(5) If in any case a person is severely disabled, the question whether his severe disablement results from vaccination against any of the diseases to which this Act applies shall be determined for the purposes of this Act on the balance of probability.

Review of extent of disablement and causation by independent tribunals.

4.—(1) Regulations under this Act shall make provision for independent medical tribunals to determine matters referred to them under this section, and such regulations may make provision with respect to—

    (a) the terms of appointment of the persons who are to serve on the tribunals;

    (b) the procedure to be followed for the determination of matters referred to the tribunals;

    (c) the summoning of persons to attend to give evidence or produce documents before the tribunals and the administration of oaths to such persons.

(2) Where an application for review is made to the Secretary of State as mentioned in section 3(4) above, then, subject to sub-

section (3) below, the Secretary of State shall refer to a tribunal under this section—

    (*a*) the question of the extent of the disablement suffered by the disabled person ;

    (*b*) the question whether he is or, as the case may be, was immediately before his death disabled as a result of the vaccination to which the claim relates ; and

    (*c*) the question whether, if he is or was so disabled, the extent of his disability is or was such as to amount to severe disablement.

(3) The Secretary of State may refer to differently constituted tribunals the questions in paragraphs (*a*) to (*c*) of subsection (2) above, and the Secretary of State need not refer to a tribunal any of those questions if—

    (*a*) he and the claimant are not in dispute with respect to it ; or

    (*b*) the decision of a tribunal on another of those questions is such that the disabled person cannot be or, as the case may be, could not immediately before his death have been severely disabled as a result of the vaccination to which the claim relates.

(4) For the purposes of this Act, the decision of a tribunal on a question referred to them under this section shall be conclusive except in so far as it falls to be reconsidered by virtue of section 5 below.

5.—(1) Subject to subsection (2) below, the Secretary of State may reconsider a determination that a payment should not be made under section 1(1) above on the ground— Reconsideration of determinations and recovery of payments in certain cases.

    (*a*) that there has been a material change of circumstances since the determination was made, or

    (*b*) that the determination was made in ignorance of, or was based on a mistake as to, some material fact,

and the Secretary of State may, on the ground set out in paragraph (*b*) above, reconsider a determination that such a payment should be made.

(2) Regulations under this Act shall prescribe the manner and the period in which—

    (*a*) an application may be made to the Secretary of State for his reconsideration of a determination ; and

    (*b*) the Secretary of State may of his own motion institute such a reconsideration.

(3) The Secretary of State shall give notice in writing of his decision on a reconsideration under this section to the person who was the claimant in relation to the claim which gave rise to the determination which has been reconsidered and also, where the disabled person is alive and was not the claimant, to him ; and the provisions of subsections (3) to (5) of section 3 and section 4 above shall apply as if—

> (a) the notice under this subsection were a notice under section 3(2) above ; and
>
> (b) any reference in those provisions to the claimant were a reference to the person who was the claimant in relation to the claim which gave rise to the determination which has been reconsidered.

(4) If, whether fraudulently or otherwise, any person misrepresents or fails to disclose any material fact and in consequence of the misrepresentation or failure a payment is made under section 1(1) above, the person to whom the payment was made shall be liable to repay the amount of that payment to the Secretary of State unless he can show that the misrepresentation or failure occurred without his connivance or consent.

(5) Except as provided by subsection (4) above, no payment under section 1(1) above shall be recoverable by virtue of a reconsideration of a determination under this section.

Payments to or for the benefit of disabled persons.

6.—(1) Where a payment under section 1(1) above falls to be made in respect of a disabled person who is over eighteen and capable of managing his own affairs, the payment shall be made to him.

(2) Where such a payment falls to be made in respect of a disabled person who has died, the payment shall be made to his personal representatives.

(3) Where such a payment falls to be made in respect of any other disabled person, the payment shall be made for his benefit by paying it to such trustees as the Secretary of State may appoint to be held by them upon such trusts or, in Scotland, for such purposes and upon such conditions as may be declared by the Secretary of State.

(4) The making of a claim for, or the receipt of, a payment under section 1(1) above does not prejudice the right of any person to institute or carry on proceedings in respect of disablement suffered as a result of vaccination against any disease to which this Act applies ; but in any civil proceedings brought in respect of disablement resulting from vaccination against such a

disease, the court shall treat a payment made to or in respect of the disabled person concerned under section 1(1) above as paid on account of any damages which the court awards in respect of such disablement.

7.—(1) Any reference in this section to an extra-statutory Payments, payment is a reference to a payment of £10,000 made by the claims etc. Secretary of State to or in respect of a disabled person after made prior 9th May 1978 and before the passing of this Act pursuant to a to the Act. non-statutory scheme of payments for severe vaccine damage.

(2) No such claim as is referred to in section 3(1) above shall be entertained if an extra-statutory payment has been made to or for the benefit of the disabled person or his personal representatives.

(3) For the purposes of section 5 above, a determination that an extra-statutory payment should be made shall be treated as a determination that a payment should be made under section 1(1) above ; and in relation to the reconsideration of such a determination references in subsection (3) of section 5 above to the person who was the claimant in relation to the determination which has been reconsidered shall be construed as references to the person who made the claim for the extra-statutory payment.

(4) Subsections (4) and (5) of section 5 above and section 6(4) above shall apply in relation to an extra-statutory payment as they apply in relation to a payment made under section 1(1) above.

(5) For the purposes of this Act (other than this section) regulations under this Act may—

(*a*) treat claims which were made in connection with the scheme referred to in subsection (1) above and which have not been disposed of at the commencement of this Act as claims falling within section 3(1) above ; and

(*b*) treat information and other evidence furnished and other things done before the commencement of this Act in connection with any such claim as is referred to in paragraph (*a*) above as furnished or done in connection with a claim falling within section 3(1) above.

8.—(1) Any reference in the preceding provisions of this Act Regulations. to regulations under this Act is a reference to regulations made by the Secretary of State.

(2) Any power of the Secretary of State under this Act to make regulations—

(*a*) shall be exercisable by statutory instrument which shall be subject to annulment in pursuance of a resolution of either House of Parliament ; and (*b*) includes power to make such incidental or supplementary provision as appears to the Secretary of State to be appropriate.

    (3) Regulations made by the Secretary of State may contain provision—

    (*a*) with respect to the information and other evidence to be furnished in connection with a claim ;

    (*b*) requiring disabled persons to undergo medical examination before their claims are determined or for the purposes of a reconsideration under section 5 above ;

    (*c*) restricting the disclosure of medical evidence and advice tendered in connection with a claim or a reconsideration under section 5 above ; and

    (*d*) conferring functions on the tribunals constituted under section 4 above with respect to the matters referred to in paragraphs (*a*) to (*c*) above.

Fraudulent statements etc.

    9.—(1) Any person who, for the purpose of obtaining any payment under this Act, whether for himself or some other person,—

    (*a*) knowingly makes any false statement or representation, or

    (*b*) produces or furnishes or causes or knowingly allows to be produced or furnished any document or information which he knows to be false in a material particular,

shall be liable on summary conviction to a fine not exceeding £1,000.

    (2) In the application of subsection (1) above to the Isle of Man, for the words following " liable " there shall be substituted the words " on summary conviction, within the meaning of the Interpretation Act 1976 (an Act of Tynwald), to a fine of £400 and on conviction on information to a fine ".

Scotland.
1978 c. 51.

    10.—(1) In the Scotland Act 1978, at the end of Part III of Schedule 10 (matters dealt with by certain enactments to be included, to the extent specified, in the groups of devolved matters) there shall be added the following entry :—

| " The Vaccine Damage Payments Act 1979 | Included, except for the matters dealt with in section 2(5)." |

    (2) For the purpose of the following provisions of the Scotland Act 1978, this Act shall be deemed to have been passed before the passing of that Act, namely,—

    (*a*) section 21(2) (executive powers) ;

    (*b*) subsections (1) and (2) of section 22 (subordinate instruments) ;

(c) section 60 (modification of enactments providing for payments out of moneys provided by Parliament etc.); and

(d) section 82 (construction and amendment of existing enactments).

11.—(1) In Schedule 2 to the Wales Act 1978 (enactments Wales. under which, except as provided in the second column thereof, 1978 c. 52. functions of Ministers of the Crown are exercisable as regards Wales by the Welsh Assembly) at the end of Part VI (health and social services) there shall be added the following entry:—

"The Vaccine Damage Payments Act 1979	The power to make regulations under section 2(5) and, so far as it relates to any regulations made under that section, the power conferred by section 8(2)(b)."

(2) For the purpose of the following provisions of the Wales Act 1978, this Act shall be deemed to have been passed before the passing of that Act, namely,—

(a) section 55 (modification of enactments providing for payments out of moneys provided by Parliament etc.);

(b) section 74 (construction of references to Ministers); and

(c) subsections (2) and (3) of section 77 (amendment of existing enactments).

12.—(1) The Secretary of State shall pay to persons appointed Financial to serve on tribunals under section 4 of this Act such remunera- provisions. tion and such travelling and other allowances as he may, with the consent of the Minister for the Civil Service, determine.

(2) The Secretary of State shall pay such fees as he considers appropriate to medical practitioners, as defined in Schedule 20 to the Social Security Act 1975, who provide information or 1975 c. 14. other evidence in connection with claims.

(3) The Secretary of State shall pay such travelling and other allowances as he may determine—

(a) to persons required under this Act to undergo medical examinations;

(b) to persons required to attend before tribunals under section 4 above; and

(c) in circumstances where he considers it appropriate, to any person who accompanies a disabled person to such a medical examination or tribunal.

(4) There shall be paid out of moneys provided by Parliament—

(*a*) any expenditure incurred by the Secretary of State in making payments under section 1(1) above ;

(*b*) any expenditure incurred by the Secretary of State by virtue of subsections (1) to (3) above ; and

(*c*) any increase in the administrative expenses of the Secretary of State attributable to this Act.

(5) Any sums repaid to the Secretary of State by virtue of section 5(4) above shall be paid into the Consolidated Fund.

Short title
and extent.

13.—(1) This Act may be cited as the Vaccine Damage Payments Act 1979.

(2) This Act extends to Northern Ireland and the Isle of Man.

Social Security Act 1979

1979 CHAPTER 18

An Act to amend the law relating to social security.

[22nd March 1979]

BE IT ENACTED by the Queen's most Excellent Majesty, by and with the advice and consent of the Lords Spiritual and Temporal, and Commons, in this present Parliament assembled, and by the authority of the same, as follows:—

Interpretation

1. In this Act—

"the principal Act" means the Social Security Act 1975; 1975 c. 14.

"the Pensions Act" means the Social Security Pensions 1975 c. 60. Act 1975;

"the Act of 1976" means the Supplementary Benefits Act 1976 c. 71. 1976;

"the Act of 1977" means the Social Security (Miscellaneous 1977 c. 5. Provisions) Act 1977.

Interpretation.

Allowances and pensions

2.—(1) Section 35 of the principal Act is amended as follows. Attendance

(2) In subsection (2)(*b*) for the words "immediately preceded" there are substituted the words "preceded immediately, or within such period as may be prescribed,".

(3) After subsection (2) there is inserted the following subsection—

"(2A) For the purposes of subsection (2) above a person who suffers from renal failure and is undergoing such form of treatment as may be prescribed shall, in such circumstances as may be prescribed, be deemed to satisfy or to be likely to satisfy one or both of those conditions.".

Attendance allowance.

(4) In subsection (3), for the words " preceding 6 months " there are substituted the words " period of 6 months mentioned in subsection (2)(*b*) above ".

(5) In subsection (4)(*a*), for the words " mentioned in subsection (2)(*b*) above " and " there mentioned " there are substituted, respectively, the words " immediately preceding the period for which the allowance is payable " and " mentioned in subsection (2)(*b*) above " and after the words " that period " there are inserted the words " of 6 months ".

(6) After subsection (5) there is inserted the following subsection—

" (5A) Regulations may provide that, in such circumstances and for such purposes as may be prescribed, a person who is, or is treated under the regulations as, undergoing treatment for renal failure in a hospital or other similar institution otherwise than as an in-patient shall be deemed not to satisfy or to be unlikely to satisfy one or both of the conditions mentioned in subsection (1)(*a*) and (*b*) above.".

Mobility allowance.   3.—(1) Section 37A of the principal Act is amended as follows.

(2) In subsection (4) (increase in rate of mobility allowance) for the words " and such other matters as he thinks relevant " there are substituted the words " any changes in taxation which directly affect the cost of motoring for persons in receipt of mobility allowance and such other matters as he thinks relevant ; and he shall lay before Parliament a statement setting out his conclusion and the reasons therefor as soon as is reasonably practicable.".

(3) In subsection (5) (periods for which mobility allowance is not payable)—

(*a*) in paragraph (*a*) (allowance not payable to a person for any period in which he is under the age of 5 or over pensionable age) for the words " pensionable age " there are substituted the words " the age of 75 "; and

(*b*) the following paragraph is inserted after paragraph (*a*)—

" (*aa*) in respect of a period in which he is over the age of 65 but under the age of 75 unless either—

(i) he had been entitled to a mobility allowance in respect of a period ending immediately before the date on which he attained the age of 65 ; or

(ii) he would have been so entitled but for paragraph (*b*) below and a claim for the allowance by or in respect of him is made before the date on which he attained the age of 66 ; ".

(4) The following subsections are inserted after subsection (6)—

" (6A) Regulations may provide that this section shall have effect in relation to prescribed categories of persons in respect of whom certificates issued in pursuance of regulations made under section 13 of the Social Security (Miscellaneous Provisions) Act 1977 (mobility allowance for person eligible for invalid carriage) are in force as if, in subsection (5), the words " or over the age of 75 " and paragraph (*aa*) were omitted.

(6B) Where, before the coming into force of this subsection, a person has been awarded a mobility allowance for a specified period ending with the date on which he will attain pensionable age, that award shall have effect as if it referred instead to a period ending with the date on which he will attain the age of 75 years.".

(5) Where an application for a certificate under the Mobility S.I. 1977/1229. Allowance (Vehicle Scheme Beneficiaries) Regulations 1977 was refused before the commencement of the Mobility Allowance S.I. 1978/743. (Vehicle Scheme Beneficiaries) Amendment Regulations 1978 any question whether the application was properly refused shall be determined as if that commencement had preceded the refusal.

4.—(1) In section 30 of the principal Act (supplementary Amendment provisions about retirement pensions) the following subsection of provisions is inserted at the end— relating to earnings after

" (6) The Secretary of State may by order— retirement age.

(*a*) substitute for the period of 5 years mentioned in section 27(5) of this Act and subsection (1) above a shorter period ; and

(*b*) substitute for the ages of 65 and 70 mentioned in sections 26(1) and (3), 36(5), 37(6) and 79(2)(*a*) of this Act and subsection (3) above such lower ages as are appropriate in consequence of any provision made by virtue of paragraph (*a*) above.".

(2) In section 167 of the principal Act (Parliamentary control of orders and regulations)—

(*a*) in subsection (1) the following paragraph is inserted after paragraph (*b*)—

" (*c*) no order shall be made under section 30(6), " ; and

(*b*) in subsection (3) after the words " section 17(3) " there is inserted " 30(6),".

(3) In Part II of Schedule 15 to the principal Act (regulations not requiring prior submission to National Insurance Advisory Committee) the following paragraph is inserted after paragraph 17—

" 17A. Regulations contained in a statutory instrument which states that it contains only provisions in consequence of an order under section 30(6) of this Act.".

Amendment of principal Act, Pensions Act and Act of 1977.

5.—(1) The provisions of the principal Act, the Pensions Act and the Act of 1977 specified in Part I of Schedule 1 to this Act shall have effect subject to the amendments there specified (miscellaneous amendments of provisions relating to retirement and invalidity pensions).

(2) The provisions of the principal Act and the Pensions Act specified in Part II of Schedule 1 to this Act shall have effect subject to the amendments there specified (modification of certain provisions in relation to events occurring before 6th April 1979).

Appeals and reviews, etc.

Appeals from and to Supplementary Benefit Appeal Tribunals.

6.—(1) After section 15 of the Act of 1976 (appeals from Supplementary Benefits Commission) there is inserted the following section—

"Appeals from Appeal Tribunal.

15A.—(1) The Secretary of State may by rules make provision for any party to proceedings before an Appeal Tribunal (whether under this or any other Act) to appeal to a National Insurance Commissioner against a decision of the tribunal.

(2) Rules under this section may, in particular, make provision—

(*a*) as to the cases and circumstances in which, and the conditions subject to which, appeals may be made, including provision either generally or in relation to specified classes of case for appeals—

(i) to be confined to points of law ;

(ii) to be made only with leave ;

(*b*) as to the manner in which, and the time within which, appeals are to be brought and (where appropriate) applications are to be made for leave to appeal ;

(*c*) as to the procedure to be followed on appeals ;

(*d*) as to the payment by the Secretary of State to persons attending proceedings before a Commissioner of travelling and other allowances (including compensation for loss of remunerative time).

(3) The power to make provision as to procedure under subsection (2)(*c*) above includes power to make provision as to the representation of one person in any proceedings by another person.

(4) Rules under this section may provide for a Commissioner hearing an appeal—

(*a*) to give any decision which might have been given by the tribunal;

(*b*) to refer the case to another tribunal, with directions;

(*c*) to dispose of the appeal in such other manner as may be specified;

and in any case where directions are given to a tribunal in accordance with rules under this section the tribunal shall proceed accordingly.

(5) In this section " National Insurance Commissioner " has the same meaning as in the Social Security Act 1975 and includes a Tribunal of Commissioners under section 116 of that Act."

(2) For Schedule 4 to the Act of 1976 (constitution, jurisdiction and proceedings of appeal tribunals) there is substituted the Schedule set out in Schedule 2 to this Act.

(3) In section 14(2) of the Act of 1976 (power to make regulations) after paragraph (*e*) there is inserted the following paragraph—

" (*ee*) for suspending the payment of supplementary benefit pending the determination of questions; and ".

7. In section 86 of the principal Act (set-off of overpayments) the following subsection is substituted for subsection (2)— Incompatible benefits.

" (2) Where on review or appeal a decision awarding or refusing a person benefit is revised, or is reversed or varied, but he retains any sums paid either in pursuance of the original decision or of any other decision awarding him benefit and those sums would not have been payable if the decision on the review or appeal had been given in the first instance, then, except in so far as regulations otherwise provide,—

(*a*) where the decision on the review or appeal reverses a decision refusing the person benefit, the decision on the review or appeal shall direct that those sums shall be treated as having been paid on account of that benefit (except to the extent that they exceed the amount of that benefit);

(*b*) in any other case, any subsequent decision awarding the person other benefit, being a benefit to which a right to any of those sums would by virtue of any such provision as is mentioned in subsection (1) above have disentitled him, shall direct that those sums shall be treated as having been paid on account of the other benefit (except to the extent that they exceed the amount of that other benefit).".

Repayment of benefit.

8. After subsection (2) of section 119 of the principal Act there is inserted the following subsection—

" (2A) Where, in pursuance of a decision, an amount of benefit was paid which would not have been paid if the facts established for the purpose of any subsequent decision by an insurance officer, local tribunal or Commissioner had been known and—

(*a*) the subsequent decision is given in relation to the same benefit but is not given on an appeal against or a review of the earlier decision; and

(*b*) the circumstances are not such as to enable the earlier decision to be reviewed;

the subsequent decision shall require repayment of that amount (except so much of it as is directed by the decision to be treated as having been properly paid) unless it is shown to the satisfaction of the insurance officer, tribunal or Commissioner that in the obtaining and receipt of the benefit the beneficiary, and any person acting for him, has throughout used due care and diligence to avoid over-payment.".

Qualification of National Insurance Commissioners in Great Britain and Northern Ireland.

1975 c. 15.

9.—(1) In section 97(3) of the principal Act, after the word " barristers " there is inserted the word " solicitors ".

(2) In section 97(3) of the Social Security (Northern Ireland) Act 1975 after the word " barristers " there are inserted the words " or solicitors ".

Increases in rates etc.

Revaluation of earnings factors.

10.—(1) Section 21 of the Pensions Act (revaluation of earnings factors) is amended as follows.

(2) In subsection (2) (review of general level of earnings and of changes in that level) for the words " since the last review "

there are substituted the words " since the end of the period taken into account for the last review ".

(3) For subsection (3) (increase of earnings factors) there is substituted the following subsection—

" (3) If on any such review the Secretary of State concludes, having regard to earlier orders under this section, that earnings factors for any previous tax year (not being earlier than 1978-79) have not, during the period taken into account for that review, maintained their value in relation to the general level of earnings, he shall prepare and lay before each House of Parliament the draft of an order directing that those earnings factors shall, for the purpose of any such calculation as is mentioned in subsection (1) above, be increased by such percentage of their amount, apart from earlier orders under this section, as he thinks necessary to make up that fall in their value together with other falls in their value which had been made up by such earlier orders.".

(4) For subsection (7) (provisions as to first review) there is substituted the following subsection—

" (7) The first review under this section shall be in the tax year 1979-80 ; and in relation to that review subsection (2) above shall have effect as if for the reference to the end of the period taken into account for the last review there were substituted a reference to the beginning of the latest twelve-month period for which figures are available at the time the review is carried out.".

11.—(1) In section 59 of the Pensions Act (increase of official pensions), in subsection (5) for the words from " a person " to " by reference " (in the second place where they occur) there is substituted— Increase of official pensions.

" (*a*) a person is entitled to a guaranteed minimum pension when an order under this section comes into force ; and

(*b*) entitlement to that guaranteed minimum pension arises from an employment from which (either directly or by virtue of the payment of a transfer credit under section 38 of this Act) entitlement to the official pension also arises ;

the amount by reference ".

(2) In subsection (7) of section 59, in the definition of " base period ", for the words from " the first " to the end there are

substituted the words " 13th November 1978 (date of the relevant order under section 124 of the principal Act, increasing rates of benefit) ; ".

(3) At the end of section 59 there is inserted the following subsection—

" (8) Where, for the purposes of this section, it is necessary to calculate the number of complete months in any period an incomplete month shall be treated as a complete month if it consists of at least 16 days.".

(4) After section 59 there is inserted the following section—

" Modification of effect of section 59(5).

59A.—(1) This section applies where the amount by reference to which an increase in an official pension is to be calculated would, but for the provisions of this section, be reduced under section 59(5) of this Act by an amount equal to the rate of a guaranteed minimum pension.

(2) The Minister for the Civil Service may direct that in such cases or classes of case as may be specified in the direction—

(*a*) no such reduction shall be made ; or

(*b*) the reduction shall be of an amount less than the rate of the guaranteed minimum pension ;

and in any case to which such a direction applies the increase shall, in respect of such period or periods as may be specified in the direction, be calculated in accordance with the direction, notwithstanding section 59(5).

(3) A direction under this section may provide that where it has applied in any case and ceases to apply in that case, the rate of the official pension for any period following the date on which the direction ceases to apply shall, in such circumstances as may be specified in the direction, be calculated as if the direction had never applied.

(4) A direction under this section may provide that the rate of an official pension shall, in such circumstances as may be specified in the direction, be calculated as if the direction had been in force at all times during such period as may be so specified.

(5) A direction made under subsection (2) above may be varied or revoked by a subsequent direction.".

12. The following section is inserted in the principal Act after section 126—

"Up-rating of increments in guaranteed minimum pensions.

126A.—(1) The Secretary of State shall in each tax year review the sums which are payable—

> (*a*) by virtue of section 35(6) of the Pensions Act (increments in guaranteed minimum pension where retirement is postponed), including such sums which are payable by virtue of section 36(3) of that Act, to a person who is also entitled to a Category A or Category B retirement pension (in this section referred to as a " beneficiary ") ; and
>
> (*b*) by virtue of this section to a beneficiary as part of his Category A or Category B retirement pension ;

for the purpose of determining whether those sums have retained their value in relation to the general level of prices (estimated in such manner as the Secretary of State thinks fit) obtaining in Great Britain.

(2) If the Secretary of State concludes that those sums have not retained their value he shall prepare and lay before Parliament the draft of an order increasing the beneficiary's Category A or Category B retirement pension at least by an amount equal to the percentage of the aggregate of the sums under review by which in the opinion of the Secretary of State that aggregate amount would have to be increased in order to restore its value.

(3) If the draft order is approved by resolution of each House of Parliament the Secretary of State shall make the order in the form of the draft.

(4) Section 126 above (supplementary provisions as to up-rating orders) shall have effect as if—

> (*a*) the reference therein to section 125 above included a reference to this section ;
>
> (*b*) the references to subsection (3) of that section included references to subsection (2) of this section ; and
>
> (*c*) the reference to an up-rating order included a reference to an order under this section.

(5) Where sums are payable to a person by virtue of section 35(6) of the Pensions Act (including such sums payable by virtue of section 36(3) of that

Act) during a period ending with the date on which he became entitled to a Category A or Category B retirement pension, then, for the purpose of determining the amount of his Category A or Category B retirement pension, orders made under this section during that period shall be deemed to have come into force (consecutively in the order in which they were made) on the date on which he became entitled to that pension.".

Miscellaneous

Maternity grant and death grant.
13. The Secretary of State shall in the tax year 1978-79 and each subsequent tax year review the sums specified in Part II of Schedule 4 to the principal Act for the purpose of determining whether those sums have retained their value in relation to the general level of earnings or prices obtaining in Great Britain.

Adjustment of secondary Class 1 contributions for exceptions to redundancy provisions.
14.—(1) The following subsection is inserted at the end of section 4 of the principal Act—

" (7) Regulations may provide for reducing secondary Class 1 contributions which are payable in respect of persons to whom section 81 (redundancy payments) of the Employment Protection (Consolidation) Act 1978 does not apply by virtue of section 144(2), 145 or 149 of that Act."

(2) In section 134 of the principal Act (destination of contributions) the following words are inserted at the end of subsection (6) (power to modify section) " and in relation to any contributions which are reduced under section 4(7) of this Act ".

Overlap with benefits under legislation of other member States.
15.—(1) The following subsections are inserted at the end of section 85 of the principal Act (overlapping benefits)—

" (4) Regulations may provide for adjusting benefit payable to or in respect of any person where there is payable in his case any such benefit as is described in subsection (5) below.

(5) Subsection (4) above applies to any benefit payable under the legislation of any member State other than the United Kingdom which is payable to or in respect of—

(*a*) the person referred to in that subsection ;

(*b*) that person's wife or husband ;

(*c*) any child or adult dependant of that person ; or

(*d*) the wife or husband of any adult dependant of that person.".

(2) In Part II of Schedule 15 to the principal Act (regulations not requiring prior submission to National Insurance Advisory

Committee) the following paragraph is inserted after paragraph 12—

> " 12A. Regulations under section 85(4) of this Act (overlap with benefits under legislation of other member States).".

(3) The following section is inserted in the Child Benefit Act 1975 c. 61. 1975 after section 4—

" Overlap with benefits under legislation of other member States.

    4A. Regulations may provide for adjusting child benefit payable in respect of any child in respect of whom any benefit is payable under the legislation of any member State other than the United Kingdom.".

16. For the purposes of the Criminal Evidence Act 1965 as Criminal it applies in relation to proceedings for any offence which is proceedings. connected with— 1965 c. 20.

    (*a*) the obtaining or receipt of any benefit under the Family 1970 c. 55. Income Supplements Act 1970, the Industrial Injuries 1975 c. 16. and Diseases (Old Cases) Act 1975, the Child Benefit Act 1975, the principal Act or the Act of 1976 ; or

    (*b*) the failure to pay any Class 1 or Class 2 contribution (within the meaning of Part I of the principal Act),

" business " shall include the activities of the Secretary of State.

17. Section 139(1) of the principal Act (reference of proposed Reference of regulations to the National Insurance Advisory Committee) shall regulations not apply in relation to regulations— to National Insurance

    (*a*) made under section 119 of the principal Act (effect of Advisory adjudication on payment and recovery) by virtue of Committee. paragraph 9 of Schedule 3 to this Act ;

    (*b*) made by virtue of section 14 of this Act ; or

    (*c*) made under paragraph 4(*a*) of Schedule 1 to the principal Act (calculation and adjustment of amounts) in relation to contributions reduced under section 4(7) of that Act ;

and made within 6 months of the passing of this Act.

18. The following section is inserted in the Pensions Act after Treatment of section 60 :— insignificant amounts.

" Treatment of insignificant amounts.

    60A. Where an amount is required to be calculated in accordance with the provisions of sections 6(3), 35(4) and (6) and 36(3) of, and paragraphs 2(3) and 4A of Schedule 1 to, this Act and, apart from this section, the amount so calculated is less than $\frac{1}{2}$p, then, notwithstanding any other provision of this Act, that amount shall be taken to be zero, and other amounts so calculated shall be rounded to the nearest whole penny, taking ½p as nearest to the next whole penny above ".

Enactment of same provisions for Northern Ireland.

1974 c. 28.

19. An Order in Council under paragraph 1(1)(*b*) of Schedule 1 to the Northern Ireland Act 1974 (legislation for Northern Ireland in the interim period) which contains a statement that it operates only so far as to make for Northern Ireland provision corresponding to provisions contained in this Act—

(*a*) shall not be subject to paragraph 1(4) and (5) of that Schedule (affirmative resolution of both Houses of Parliament), but

(*b*) shall be subject to annulment by resolution of either House.

Financial provisions.

20.—(1) There shall be paid out of money provided by Parliament any increase attributable to any of the provisions of this Act in sums so payable under any other Act.

1978 c. 51.

(2) Section 60(1) of the Scotland Act 1978 (modification of enactments authorising payments out of money provided by Parliament etc.) shall have effect as if subsection (1) above were contained in an Act passed before that Act.

(3) As respects any increase attributable to this Act in the expenses which under subsection (3)(*a*) of section 135 of the principal Act are to be paid out of money provided by Parliament, subsection (1) above is without prejudice to the provision made by subsection (5) of that section for reimbursement out of the National Insurance Fund.

Short title, etc.

21.—(1) This Act may be cited as the Social Security Act 1979, and this Act, the principal Act, the Pensions Act and the Act of 1977 may be cited together as the Social Security Acts 1975 to 1979.

(2) Section 3(3) of this Act shall not come into force in relation to women who on the passing of this Act have attained the age of 60 but not the age of 65 until such day as the Secretary of State may by order made by statutory instrument appoint ; and different days may be so appointed in relation to women of different ages.

An order under this subsection shall be laid before Parliament after being made.

(3) Sections 11 and 12 of, and paragraphs 2 to 22 of Schedule 1 and paragraphs 5, 6, 7, 11, 14 to 20, 22, 23, and 29(*a*) and (*b*) of Schedule 3 to, this Act shall not come into force until 6th April 1979.

(4) The Acts and instruments mentioned in Schedule 3 to this Act shall have effect subject to the minor and consequential amendments specified in that Schedule.

(5) Sections 9(2) and 19 of, and paragraphs 3 and 12 of Schedule 3 to, this Act, and this section so far as it applies for the purposes of those provisions, extend to Northern Ireland but the other provisions of this Act do not.

SCHEDULES

SCHEDULE 1

AMENDMENT OF PRINCIPAL ACT, PENSIONS ACT AND ACT OF 1977

PART I

MISCELLANEOUS AMENDMENTS OF PROVISIONS RELATING TO RETIREMENT AND INVALIDITY PENSIONS

Principal Act

1. In section 15(4) of the principal Act (disregard of certain amounts in calculating amount of pension by reference to which certain invalidity pensions are calculated) there are inserted after paragraph (*b*) the words " and

> (*c*) if he is also entitled to an invalidity allowance, any increase under section 28(7) or 29(8) of this Act (increase in Category A and B retirement pensions by amount equal to invalidity allowance).".

2. In section 39(1)(*c*)(ii) of the principal Act (certain increases to be disregarded in determining entitlement to Category D retirement pension) after the word " disregarding " there are inserted the words " any additional component, any increase so far as attributable to any additional component or to any increase in a guaranteed minimum pension, any graduated retirement benefit and ".

3. In paragraph 5 of Schedule 3 to the principal Act (contribution conditions for retirement pensions etc.), for sub-paragraphs (6) and (7) (which provide for the second condition to be deemed to be satisfied in certain circumstances) there is substituted the following sub-paragraph—

> " (6) The second condition shall be deemed to be satisfied notwithstanding that paragraphs (*a*) and (*b*) of sub-paragraph (3) above are not complied with as respects each of the requisite number of years if—
>
> > (*a*) those paragraphs are complied with as respects at least half that number of years (or at least 20 of them, if that is less than half) ; and
> >
> > (*b*) in each of the other years the contributor concerned was, within the meaning of regulations, precluded from regular employment by responsibilities at home.".

Pensions Act

4. In section 8(1) of the Pensions Act (provision for Category B retirement pension for a widower in certain circumstances) the following paragraph is substituted for paragraph (*c*)—

> " (*c*) before her death she satisfied the contribution conditions specified in paragraph 5 of Part I of Schedule 3 to the principal Act.".

5. In section 20(1) of the Pensions Act (use of former spouse's contributions), after the words " those conditions " there are inserted the words " (but only in respect of any claim for a Category A retirement pension) ".

6. In paragraph 4 of Schedule 1 to the Pensions Act (deferred retirement) there is inserted, after sub-paragraph (2), the following sub-paragraph—

" (3) Where—

(*a*) there is a period between the death of the former spouse and the date on which the surviving spouse becomes entitled to a Category A or Category B retirement pension, and

(*b*) one or more orders have come into force under section 124 of the principal Act (increases in rates of benefit) during that period,

the amount of the increase to which the surviving spouse is entitled under this paragraph shall be determined as if the order or orders had come into force before the beginning of that period.".

7. In the said Schedule 1, the following paragraph is inserted after paragraph 4—

" 4A.—(1) Where a woman is entitled to a Category A or Category B retirement pension and—

(*a*) she has had a husband and he has died, and she was married to him when he died ; and

(*b*) the husband either—

(i) was entitled to a guaranteed minimum pension with an increase under section 35(6) of this Act ; or

(ii) would have been so entitled if he had retired on the date of his death,

the rate of her pension shall be increased by an amount equal to the sum of the following amounts, that is to say, an amount equal to one-half of that increase ; the appropriate amount ; and an amount equal to any increase to which he had been entitled under this paragraph.

(2) Where a man is entitled to a Category A or Category B retirement pension and—

(*a*) he has had a wife and she has died, and he was married to her when she died ; and

(*b*) he was over pensionable age when she died ; and

(*c*) the wife either—

(i) was entitled to a guaranteed minimum pension with an increase under section 35(6) of this Act ; or

(ii) would have been so entitled if she had retired on the date of her death,

the rate of his pension shall be increased by an amount equal to the sum of the following amounts, that is to say, an amount equal to that increase ; the appropriate amount ; and an amount equal to any increase to which she had been entitled under this paragraph.

(3) The " appropriate amount " means either—

(*a*) the amount by which the deceased person's Category A or Category B retirement pension had been increased under section 126A of the principal Act (up-rating of increments in guaranteed minimum pensions), or

(*b*) the amount by which his Category A or Category B retirement pension would have been so increased had he died immediately before his surviving spouse became entitled to a Category A or Category B retirement pension,

whichever is the greater.".

Act of 1977

8. In section 4(1) of the Act of 1977 (provision for payment of Category D retirement pension and Category A or Category B retirement pension at the same time) for the words " a Category D retirement pension " there are substituted the words " a Category C or Category D retirement pension ".

Part II

Modification of Certain Provisions in Relation to Events Occurring Before 6th April 1979

9. Expressions used in this Part of this Schedule and in the principal Act shall have the same meaning in this Part as they have in that Act.

Principal Act

10. In section 16 (rates at which invalidity allowance is payable)—

(*a*) the following paragraphs are substituted for paragraphs (*a*) and (*b*) of subsection (2)—

" (*a*) at the higher rate specified in relation thereto in Schedule 4, Part I, if—

(i) the qualifying date fell before 5th July 1948 ; or

(ii) on the qualifying date the beneficiary was under the age of 35 ; or

(iii) on the qualifying date the beneficiary was under the age of 40 and had not attained pensionable age before 6th April 1979 ;

(*b*) at the middle rate so specified if paragraph (*a*) above does not apply and either—

(i) on the qualifying date the beneficiary was under the age of 45 ; or

(ii) on the qualifying date the beneficiary was under the age of 50 and had not attained pensionable age before 6th April 1979 ;" ; and

(b) the following subsection is inserted after subsection (2)—

" (2A) No payment shall be made by virtue of subsection (2)(a)(iii) or (b)(ii) above in respect of any period before 6th April 1979.".

11. Section 28(2) (entitlement of married woman to Category A retirement pension) shall, notwithstanding its repeal by section 19(4) of and Schedule 5 to the Pensions Act, continue to apply in relation to any woman who attained pensionable age before 6th April 1979.

12. In section 59 (increase of unemployability supplement) the following words are inserted at the end of subsection (1)—

" Provided that no payment shall be made by virtue of heads (aa) or (bb) of that paragraph in respect of any period before 6th April 1979.".

13. In paragraph 5 of Part V of Schedule 4 (weekly rates of the increase in unemployability supplement)—

(a) after paragraph (a) there is inserted the following paragraph—

" (aa) if head (a) above does not apply and on the qualifying date the beneficiary was under the age of 40 and he had not attained pensionable age before 6th April 1979 ...   .   £4·15."

(b) in paragraph (b) for the words " head (a) above does " there are substituted the words " heads (a) and (aa) above do " ;

(c) for paragraph (c) there are substituted the following paragraphs—

" (bb) if heads (a), (aa) and (b) above do not apply and on the qualifying date the beneficiary was under the age of 50 and had not attained pensionable age before 6th April 1979   ...   .   £2·60 ;

(c) in any other case   ...   .   £1·30 ".

Pensions Act

14. Section 8(1) (Category B retirement pension for widower) shall not apply in any case where the death of the wife occurred before 6th April 1979.

15. Section 9 (special provision for surviving spouses) shall not apply in any case where the death of the wife or husband (as the case may be) occurred before 6th April 1979 and the surviving spouse had attained pensionable age before that date.

16. Section 10 (special provision for married women) shall not apply in any case where both the husband and the wife attained pensionable age before 6th April 1979.

17. Section 15 (invalidity pension for widows) shall not apply in relation to a widow unless she ceased to be entitled to a widow's allowance or a widowed mother's allowance after 5th April 1979.

18. Section 16 (invalidity pension for widowers) shall not apply in any case where the wife died before 6th April 1979.

19. Section 17 (which is superseded by paragraphs 10 and 13 above) is hereby repealed.

20. Section 20 (use of former spouse's contributions) shall not apply in relation to any person who attained pensionable age before 6th April 1979 if the termination of his marriage (or, if he had been married more than once, his last marriage) also occurred before that date.

21. In paragraph 2(2)(b) of Schedule 1 (which defines " period of deferment " for the purpose of enabling an increase of pension to be paid where retirement is deferred) for the words from " in relation to " to the end there are substituted the words—

> " (i) in relation to any person who attains pension-able age after 5th April 1979, means the period beginning with the date on which he attains that age and ending with the day before that of his retirement ;
>
> (ii) in relation to any person who reaches pension-able age before 6th April 1979, means the period beginning with that date and ending with the day before the date of his retirement.".

22. In paragraph 4 of Schedule 1 (increase of pension where pensioner's deceased spouse had deferred his retirement) the following sub-paragraph is inserted at the end—

> " (4) The preceding provisions of this paragraph shall not apply in any case where the deceased spouse died before 6th April 1979 and the widow or widower attained pensionable age before that date.".

Section 6(2).

SCHEDULE 2

SCHEDULE INSERTED IN ACT OF 1976 IN SUBSTITUTION FOR SCHEDULE 4

SCHEDULE 4

CONSTITUTION, JURISDICTION AND PROCEEDINGS OF APPEAL TRIBUNALS

1. Every tribunal shall consist of—

(a) one member drawn from a panel of persons appearing to the Secretary of State to have knowledge or experience of con-ditions in the area to which the panel relates and of the problems of people living on low incomes ;

(b) one member drawn from a panel of persons appearing to the Secretary of State to represent work-people ; and

(c) a person drawn from those selected by the Secretary of State to act as chairmen of the tribunals.

2. Panels of the kinds mentioned in paragraph 1 above shall be constituted by the Secretary of State for the whole of Great Britain and each panel shall relate to such area as he thinks fit, and be composed of such persons as he sees fit to appoint.

3. Before appointing members to either of the panels, the Secretary of State may take into consideration recommendations from such organisations or persons as he considers appropriate.

4. A tribunal shall have jurisdiction in respect of the area to which the panels from whose members it is constituted relate.

5. So far as is practicable—

  (*a*) each member of a panel shall be summoned in turn to serve on a tribunal ;

  (*b*) where several persons are selected to act as chairmen for a particular area they shall be invited in turn to preside over a tribunal ;

  (*c*) at least one of the members of the tribunal shall be of the same sex as the claimant.

6. The Secretary of State shall pay to the chairman of a tribunal such remuneration, and to any member thereof such travelling and other allowances (including compensation for the loss of remunerative time), as he may, with the consent of the Minister for the Civil Service, determine.

7.—(1) The Secretary of State shall assign to serve the tribunals having jurisdiction in respect of each area a clerk and such other officers and servants and shall pay them such salaries or fees and such allowances as he may, with the consent of the Minister for the Civil Service, determine.

(2) Before assigning a clerk under this paragraph the Secretary of State shall, if one or more Senior Chairmen have been appointed under paragraph 11 below, consult him or such one of them as he considers appropriate.

(3) The Secretary of State shall consider any representations made to him by a Senior Chairman as to the desirability of terminating the assignment of a clerk and shall take such action, if any, as he considers appropriate.

8. A person appointed to act as a member of a panel shall hold and vacate office in accordance with the terms of his appointment.

9.—(1) The Secretary of State may make rules—

  (*a*) as to the procedure of tribunals and the procedure in connection with the bringing of matters before a tribunal, and as to the time within which matters may be brought before tribunals ;

  (*b*) as to the payment by the Secretary of State to persons attending proceedings before tribunals of travelling and other allowances (including compensation for loss of remunerative time) ;

    (*c*) for authorising proceedings notwithstanding that the members of the tribunal are not all present.

(2) The power to make rules as to procedure under this paragraph includes power to make provision as to the representation of one person in any proceedings by another person.

(3) In any case where proceedings take place in accordance with rules made under sub-paragraph (1)(*c*) above the tribunal shall, notwithstanding anything in this Act, be deemed to be properly constituted, and the chairman shall have a second or casting vote.

10. Notwithstanding the preceding provisions of this Schedule—

    (*a*) a tribunal shall have jurisdiction in respect of such area as the Secretary of State may direct ; and

    (*b*) the chairman and other members may, if the Secretary of State so directs, be drawn from among those selected or appointed in relation to different areas.

Senior Chairmen

11.—(1) The Lord Chancellor may, after consultation with the Lord Advocate, appoint persons who are barristers, advocates or solicitors of not less than 7 years' standing to act in relation to the tribunals as Senior Chairmen.

(2) A person appointed under this paragraph to act as a Senior Chairman shall have such functions in relation to the tribunals, including the function of acting as chairman of a tribunal, as the Secretary of State may from time to time assign to him.

(3) Section 7 of the Tribunals and Inquiries Act 1971 (chairmen of certain tribunals) and paragraph 5(*b*) above shall not apply in relation to a Senior Chairman acting as chairman of a tribunal by virtue of sub-paragraph (2) above.

(4) A Senior Chairman shall hold and vacate office in accordance with the terms of his appointment.

(5) The Secretary of State may pay, or make such payments towards the provision of, such remuneration, pensions, allowances or gratuities to or in respect of Senior Chairmen or any of them as, with the consent of the Minister for the Civil Service, he may determine.

(6) Senior Chairmen shall have such officers and staff as the Secretary of State may, with the consent of the Minister for the Civil Service as to numbers and as to remuneration and other terms and conditions of service, see fit to appoint.

SCHEDULE 3

Minor and Consequential Amendments

The Family Income Supplements Act 1970 (c.55)

1. In section 7(2) of the Family Income Supplements Act 1970 (appeals to Appeal Tribunals), for the words " be final " there are

substituted the words " subject to section 15A of the Supplementary Benefits Act 1976 (appeal from Appeal Tribunals) be final.

Nothing in this subsection shall make a finding of fact or other determination embodied in or necessary to a decision, or on which it is based, conclusive for the purpose of a further decision.".

2. In section 10(2)(*h*) of that Act (review of determinations by the Supplementary Benefits Commission and Appeal Tribunals), at the end there are inserted the words " or by a National Insurance Commissioner or Tribunal of Commissioners by virtue of rules under section 15A of the Supplementary Benefits Act 1976 ".

THE SOCIAL SECURITY ACT 1973 (c.38)

3. In section 68(1) of the Social Security Act 1973 (reference of proposed regulations to the Occupational Pensions Board) for the words from " (other than " to " passing of this Act) " there are substituted the words " (other than regulations made for the purpose only of consolidating other regulations revoked thereby) ".

THE SOCIAL SECURITY ACT 1975 (c.14)

4. In section 4(6) of the principal Act (Class 1 contributions), after the words " regulations under " there are inserted the words " subsection (7) or ".

5. In section 13(5) of the principal Act (calculation of earnings factors) after the words " any tax year " there are inserted the words " (including earnings factors as increased by any order under section 21 of the Pensions Act).".

6. In section 14(6) of the principal Act (disregard of certain increases in computing unemployment and sickness benefit) after paragraph (*a*) there is inserted the following paragraph—

" (*aa*) any increase under section 126A of this Act ; ".

7. In section 15(4) of the principal Act (disregard of certain increases in computing invalidity pension) after paragraph (*a*) there is inserted the following paragraph—

" (*aa*) any increase under section 126A of this Act ; and ".

8. In section 110(1) of the principal Act (review of decision of medical board or medical appeal tribunal) for the words from " in consequence of " to the end there are substituted the words " in ignorance of a material fact or was based on a mistake as to a material fact ".

9. In section 119 of the principal Act—

(*a*) in subsection (3)(*b*), there are inserted at the end the words " or out of a requirement to repay any amount by virtue of subsection (2A) above " ;

(*b*) in subsection (4)—

(i) in paragraph (*c*) for the words " subsections (1) and (2) " there are substituted the words " subsections (1) to (2A) " ;

(ii) in paragraph (*cc*) (inserted by Schedule 4 to the Pensions Act) the words " by way of a mobility allowance " are hereby repealed ; and

(iii) in paragraph (*d*) after the words " subsection (1) " there are inserted the words " or (2A) ".

10. In paragraph 8 of Schedule 3 to the principal Act (satisfaction of contribution conditions) the following sub-paragraph is substituted for sub-paragraph (3)—

" (3) For the purposes of satisfaction by the contributor concerned of paragraph (*b*) of the first contribution condition for unemployment benefit, sickness benefit, a maternity grant or a maternity allowance, or of paragraph (*b*) of the contribution condition for a widow's allowance, all earnings factors derived from his contributions of a relevant class actually paid by him before the relevant time may be aggregated and that aggregate sum shall be treated as his earnings factor for the last complete year before the beginning of the benefit year in which the relevant time falls."

11. In paragraph 9 of Part I of Schedule 4 to the principal Act (as amended by paragraph 62 of Schedule 4 to the Pensions Act) for the words " £6·90 " there are substituted the words " £11·70 ".

The House of Commons Disqualification Act 1975 (c.24)

12. In Part III of Schedule 1 to the House of Commons Disqualification Act 1975 (offices the holders of which are disqualified) at the end of the entry beginning " Chairman of an Appeal Tribunal " there are inserted the words " or Senior Chairman in relation to such a tribunal ".

The Social Security Pensions Act 1975 (c.60)

13. In sections 6(3) and 35(4) of the Pensions Act the words from " and rounding " to the end are hereby repealed.

14. In section 6(4) of the Pensions Act (increase of earnings factors) for the words " any order or orders that have come into force under section 21 below " there are substituted the words " the last order under section 21 below to come into force ".

15. In section 11 of the Pensions Act (application of earnings rule) after the words " the additional component " there are inserted the words ", of any increase so far as attributable to any additional component or to any increase in a guaranteed minimum pension ".

16. In section 23(1)(*c*) of the Pensions Act (up-rating of certain increases under Schedule 1) after the words " such pensions " there are inserted the words " or to increases in guaranteed minimum pensions ".

17. In section 34(6) of the Pensions Act (increase of earnings) for the words " any order or orders coming into force under section 21 above " there are substituted the words " the last order under section 21 above to come into force ".

18. In section 35 of the Pensions Act (earner's guaranteed minimum)—

   (*a*) in subsection (5) (increase of earnings factors) for the words " any order or orders that have come into force under section 21 above " there are substituted the words " the last order under section 21 above to come into force " ;

   (*b*) in subsection (7) (early retirement) for the words " any order or orders that come into force under the said section 21 " there are substituted the words " the last order under the said section 21 to come into force ".

19. In section 37(3) of the Pensions Act (earner's salary as factor of widow's pension) for the words " any order or orders coming into force under section 21 above " there are substituted the words " the last order under section 21 above to come into force ".

20. In section 59(7) of the Pensions Act, after the words " this section " (in the two places where they occur after the definition of " lump sum ") there are inserted in each case the words " and section 59A of this Act ".

21. In section 61(2) of the Pensions Act (reference of proposed regulations to the Occupational Pensions Board) for the words from " to be made " to " passing of this Act " there are substituted the words " made for the purpose only of consolidating other regulations revoked thereby ".

22. In sections 66(2) and 68(3)(*a*) of the Pensions Act, for the words " section 59 " there are, in each case, substituted the words " sections 59 and 59A ".

23. In paragraph 4 of Schedule 1 to the Pensions Act (deferred retirement) at the end of both sub-paragraph (1) and sub-paragraph (2) there are inserted the words " under this Schedule apart from paragraph 4A.".

The Supplementary Benefits Act 1976 (c.71)

24. In section 2(1) of the Act of 1976 (determination of benefit, subject to provisions of section 15 as to appeals) for the words " section 15 " there are substituted the words " sections 15 and 15A ".

25. In section 14(2)(*d*) of the Act of 1976 (review of determinations), at the end there are inserted the words " or by a National Insurance Commissioner or Tribunal of Commissioners by virtue of rules under section 15A of this Act ".

26. In section 15 of the Act of 1976 (appeals to Appeal Tribunals), in subsection (3) the words from "and any" to the end are omitted and at the end there is inserted the following subsection:—

"(4) Subject to section 15A of this Act, any determination of an Appeal Tribunal shall be final ; but nothing in this section shall make any finding of fact or other determination embodied in or necessary to a decision, or on which it is based, conclusive for the purpose of any further decision.".

27. In section 33 of the Act of 1976 (rules and regulations) the following subsection is inserted after subsection (1)—

"(1A) Rules and regulations under this Act may make different provision for different classes of case and otherwise for different circumstances.".

28. In paragraph 8 of Schedule 2 to the Act of 1976 (increase of amount of award on appeal), in sub-paragraph (a) after the words "section 15" there are inserted the words "or 15A".

THE SOCIAL SECURITY (MISCELLANEOUS PROVISIONS) ACT 1977
(c.5)

29. In the Act of 1977—

(a) section 3(3) to (5),

(b) section 5(2), and

(c) section 13(2),

are hereby repealed.

THE EMPLOYMENT PROTECTION (CONSOLIDATION) ACT 1978 (c.44)

30. In section 132 of the Employment Protection (Consolidation) Act 1978—

(a) in subsection (3)(e) for the words "and (3)" there are substituted the words "to (4)" ; and

(b) in subsection (4)(a) for the words "and (2)" there are substituted the words "(2) and (2A)".

THE SUPPLEMENTARY BENEFIT (APPEAL TRIBUNAL) RULES 1971
(S.I. No. 680)

31. Rule 2 of the Supplementary Benefit (Appeal Tribunal) Rules 1971 (tenure of office of members of Appeal Tribunals) is hereby revoked.

THE MOBILITY ALLOWANCE (VEHICLE SCHEME BENEFICIARIES)
REGULATIONS 1977 (S.I. No. 1229)

32. In Regulation 6 of the Mobility Allowance (Vehicle Scheme Beneficiaries) Regulations 1977 the following paragraph is substituted for paragraph (a)—

"(a) section 37A(5) of the principal Act shall have effect as though the words "or over the age of 75" and paragraph (aa) were omitted ; ".

Administration of Justice (Emergency Provisions) (Scotland) Act 1979

1979 CHAPTER 19

An Act to provide for emergency arrangements for the administration of justice in Scotland; to suspend in part the operation of section 17 of the Stamp Act 1891; and for connected purposes.   [22nd March 1979]

BE IT ENACTED by the Queen's most Excellent Majesty, by and with the advice and consent of the Lords Spiritual and Temporal, and Commons, in this present Parliament assembled, and by the authority of the same, as follows:—

1.—(1) This Act shall cease to be in force one month after the date prescribed by the Secretary of State by order made by statutory instrument; and the period from 23rd February 1979 until the prescribed date is in this Act referred to as "the emergency period". Duration and effect of Act.

(2) This Act shall have effect, and shall be deemed always to have had effect, in relation to the whole of the emergency period.

2. Subject to sections 3 and 4 of this Act, where, by reference to any time-limit or period of time, the time, or the latest time, when for any purpose anything requires to be done in relation to legal proceedings, civil or criminal (including the institution of such proceedings), occurs during the emergency period, that thing may be done at any time which is not later than one month after the expiry of the emergency period. Extension of time limits, etc.

T 3

Period of
detention of
unconvicted
prisoners.
1975 c. 21.

3. Nothing in section 2 of this Act shall affect section 101 of the Criminal Procedure (Scotland) Act 1975 (prevention of delay in trials) but, in computing the period of 110 days for the purposes of that section, no account shall be taken of any period of detention of an accused person since committal until liberated in due course of law, being a period of detention which occurred during the emergency period.

Prosecution of
offences and
criminal diets.

4.—(1) For the avoidance of doubt, any power to cite accused persons and witnesses to a criminal diet shall be exercisable during the emergency period notwithstanding that any ordinary sitting of the court has been suspended.

(2) Any criminal diet, which is due to be held on a date during the emergency period and which is not called or duly adjourned or continued, shall be deemed to be adjourned, as if the accused person had failed to appear, to such date as the court may determine on an application by the prosecutor (which application need not be intimated to the accused person) made at any time which is not later than one month after the expiry of the emergency period, and such date shall be intimated to the accused person not less than seven days before it occurs.

Arrangements
for court
proceedings
during
emergency
period.

5.—(1) Without prejudice to any existing powers, a judge of any court may do anything during the emergency period in relation to legal proceedings, civil or criminal (including the institution of such proceedings), which could be done by the clerk of court, sheriff clerk or other officer of court, and in any particular case may with the consent of the Secretary of State authorise any person to do any such thing in relation to such proceedings.

(2) During the emergency period, a copy of any document lodged in court in connection with legal proceedings (civil or criminal) may be accepted by the court in lieu of the original; and any such copy shall be taken to be a true copy unless the contrary is proved.

(3) Any failure or omission of a judge or other person doing anything by virtue of subsection (1) above, in relation to the keeping of any record of proceedings, shall not invalidate the proceedings.

Partial
suspension of
operation of
s. 17 of Stamp
Act 1891, etc.
1891 c. 39.

6. Section 17 of the Stamp Act 1891 (penalty for enrolling, etc., instrument not duly stamped) shall not have effect in relation to the Keeper of the Registers of Scotland while this Act is in force; and a deed recorded or registered in conformity with this section shall, notwithstanding section 14 of that Act, be available for any purpose provided that the deed is duly stamped within three months of its recording or registering, as the case may be, or such later time as the Commissioners of Inland Revenue may allow.

7.—(1) This Act may be cited as the Administration of Justice Stort title
(Emergency Provisions) (Scotland) Act 1979. and extent.

(2) This Act shall extend to Scotland only.

Consolidated Fund Act 1979

1979 CHAPTER 20

An Act to apply certain sums out of the Consolidated
Fund to the service of the years ending on 31st March
1978 and 1979.   [22nd March 1979]

Most Gracious Sovereign,

WE, Your Majesty's most dutiful and loyal subjects, the
Commons of the United Kingdom in Parliament
assembled, towards making good the supply which
we have cheerfully granted to Your Majesty in this Session of
Parliament, have resolved to grant unto Your Majesty the sums
hereinafter mentioned; and do therefore most humbly beseech
Your Majesty that it may be enacted, and be it enacted by the
Queen's most Excellent Majesty, by and with the advice and
consent of the Lords Spiritual and Temporal, and Commons, in
this present Parliament assembled, and by the authority of the
same, as follows:—

Issue out of the
Consolidated
Fund for the
year ending
31st March
1978.

1. The Treasury may issue out of the Consolidated Fund of
the United Kingdom and apply towards making good the supply
granted to Her Majesty for the service of the year ending on
31st March 1978 the sum of £29,504,147·67.

Issue out of the
Consolidated
Fund for the
year ending
31st March
1979.

2. The Treasury may issue out of the Consolidated Fund of
the United Kingdom and apply towards making good the supply
granted to Her Majesty for the service of the year ending on
31st March 1979 the sum of £577,727,000.

Short title.

3. This Act may be cited as the Consolidated Fund Act 1979.

Forestry Act 1979

1979 CHAPTER 21

An Act to re-state the power of the Forestry Commissioners to make grants and loans; and to provide for the metrication of enactments relating to forestry and forest lands. [29th March 1979]

BE IT ENACTED by the Queen's most Excellent Majesty, by and with the advice and consent of the Lords Spiritual and Temporal, and Commons, in this present Parliament assembled, and by the authority of the same, as follows:—

1.—(1) The Forestry Commissioners may, with Treasury approval, make grants and loans to owners and lessees of land for and in connection with the use and management of the land for forestry purposes. *Finance for forestry.*

(2) Any such grant or loan shall be made out of the Forestry Fund and be on such terms and conditions as the Commissioners think fit.

2.—(1) The Forestry Act 1967 is amended as shown in Schedule 1 to this Act (the amendments being to substitute metric units of measurement throughout the Act). *Metrication of measurements.* *1967 c. 10.*

(2) The Forestry Commissioners may by regulations amend enactments to which this subsection applies so as to substitute—

> (*a*) for any reference to a number of acres, a reference to a number of hectares;

> (*b*) for any reference to a number of feet, a reference to a number of metres; and

> (*c*) for any requirement that plans be made on the scale of 3 chains to an inch, a requirement that they be made on the scale of 1 : 2,500;

and for this purpose " number " includes a number less than unity.

(3) Subsection (2) applies to any enactment contained in an Act (whether public general, local or private) relating to particular forest lands in England and Wales.

(4) Before making any such regulations, the Commissioners shall consult such persons and organisations as appear to them to be representative of interests likely to be affected.

(5) The regulations—

(*a*) may contain such incidental, supplementary and consequential provisions (if any) as the Commissioners consider expedient; and

(*b*) shall be made by statutory instrument subject to annulment by resolution of either House of Parliament.

Citation, etc.
1967 c. 10.

3.—(1) This Act may be cited as the Forestry Act 1979; and the Forestry Act 1967 and this Act may be cited together as the Forestry Acts 1967 and 1979.

(2) The Forestry Act 1967 is repealed to the extent specified in Schedule 2 to this Act.

(3) This Act comes into force at the expiration of two months from the date on which it is passed.

(4) This Act does not extend to Northern Ireland.

SCHEDULES

SCHEDULE 1

METRICATION OF 1967 ACT

In section 9 (requirement of felling licence; exemptions from that requirement)—

> in subsection (2)(*a*), for " 3 inches " and " 6 inches " substitute respectively " 8 centimetres " and " 15 centimetres ";
>
> in subsection (3)(*a*), for " 4 inches " substitute " 10 centimetres ";
>
> in subsection (3)(*b*), for " 825 cubic feet " and " 150 cubic feet ", substitute respectively " 30 cubic metres " and " 5·5 cubic metres ";
>
> in subsection (5)(*a*), for " 3 inches " and " 4 inches ", substitute respectively " 8 centimetres " and " 10 centimetres ", and for " 825 cubic feet " and " 150 cubic feet " substitute respectively " 30 cubic metres " and " 5·5 cubic metres ";
>
> in subsection (5)(*b*) for " 6 inches " substitute " 15 centimetres ";
>
> in subsection (5)(*c*) for " 825 cubic feet " and " 150 cubic feet " substitute respectively " 30 cubic metres " and " 5·5 cubic metres "; and
>
> in subsection (6) for " five feet " substitute " 1·3 metres ".

In section 43(1) (satisfaction of contingent liability to Crown Estate), for " five acres " substitute " 2 hectares ".

SCHEDULE 2

REPEALS IN 1967 ACT

Section 4.

In section 9(6), the words from " and references to the cubic content " onwards.

Confirmation to Small Estates (Scotland) Act 1979

1979 CHAPTER 22

An Act to amend the law relating to confirmation to small estates in Scotland; and for connected purposes.
[29th March 1979]

BE IT ENACTED by the Queen's most Excellent Majesty, by and with the advice and consent of the Lords Spiritual and Temporal, and Commons, in this present Parliament assembled, and by the authority of the same, as follows:—

Confirmation to small estate.

1875 c. 41.

1.—(1) In the Intestates Widows and Children (Scotland) Act 1875—

(*a*) in section 3 (confirmation to small intestate estate)—

(i) for the words " the net estate of an intestate is of a value less than one thousand pounds, and his gross estate is of a value less than three thousand pounds, his widow or any one or more of his children, or in the case of an intestate widow any one or more of her children," there shall be substituted the words " the whole estate of an intestate is of a value not exceeding £10,000 an applicant for confirmation thereto "; and

(ii) for the words " without the payment of any fee therefor save as is provided in Schedule C annexed to this Act " there shall be substituted the words " on payment of the requisite fee ";

(*b*) in section 5 (commissary clerk to be satisfied as to value of estate), for the words " either of the values " there shall be substituted the words " the value ";

(*c*) in section 7 (acts of sederunt), the words " ; but the total amount to be charged to applicants shall not in any case exceed the sums mentioned in Schedule C annexed to this Act " shall cease to have effect;

(*d*) in Schedule A (form of inventory and relative oath) for the words " 150*l*. " there shall be substituted the words " £10,000 ";

(*e*) in Schedule B (form of confirmation) for the words " 150*l*. " there shall be substituted the words " £10,000 "; and

(*f*) Schedule C (fees) shall cease to have effect.

(2) In the Small Testate Estates (Scotland) Act 1876—

1876 c. 24.

(*a*) in section 3 (confirmation to small testate estate)—

(i) for the words " the net estate of a testate is of a value less than one thousand pounds, and his gross estate is of a value less than three thousand pounds the executor of such testate " there shall be substituted the words " the whole estate of a testate is of a value not exceeding £10,000 an applicant for confirmation thereto "; and

(ii) for the words " without the payment of any fee therefor save as is provided in Schedule C annexed to this Act " there shall be substituted the words " on payment of the requisite fee ";

(*b*) in section 5 (commissary clerk to be satisfied as to value of estate) for the words " either of the values " there shall be substituted the words " the value ";

(*c*) in section 7 (procedure and fees) the words " ; but the total amount to be charged to executors shall not in any case exceed the sums mentioned in Schedule C annexed to this Act " shall cease to have effect;

(*d*) in Schedule A (form of inventory and relative oath) for the words " 150*l*. " there shall be substituted the words £10,000 "; and

(*e*) Schedule C (fees) shall cease to have effect.

(3) The Secretary of State may by order made by statutory instrument amend the provisions mentioned in subsections (1)(*a*), (*d*) and (*e*) or (2)(*a*) and (*d*) above to alter the limit of value at or below which confirmation may be expeded under the said Act of 1875 or 1876 (as the case may be).

(4) An order under subsection (3) above shall be subject to annulment in pursuance of a resolution of either House of Parliament.

Repeals.

2. The enactments mentioned in the Schedule to this Act are hereby repealed to the extent specified in the third column of that Schedule.

Short title, extent, construction and commencement.

3.—(1) This Act may be cited as the Confirmation to Small Estates (Scotland) Act 1979 and extends to Scotland only.

(2) This Act, except this section, shall come into force on such date as the Secretary of State may by order made by statutory instrument appoint.

1978 c. 51.

(3) For the purposes of sections 21, 22 and 82(1) of the Scotland Act 1978 (which provide, respectively, for the exercise of executive powers, the making of subordinate legislation and construction) this Act shall be deemed to be an enactment passed before the passing of that Act.

SCHEDULE

REPEALS

Chapter	Short Title	Extent of Repeal
38 & 39 Vict. c. 41.	The Intestates Widows and Children (Scotland) Act 1875.	In section 7 the words " ; but the total amount to be charged to applicants shall not in any case exceed the sums mentioned in Schedule C annexed to this Act ". Schedule C.
39 & 40 Vict. c. 24.	The Small Testate Estates (Scotland) Act 1876.	In section 7, the words " ; but the total amount to be charged to executors shall not in any case exceed the sums mentioned in Schedule C annexed to this Act ". Schedule C.
44 & 45 Vict. c. 12.	The Customs and Inland Revenue Act 1881.	Section 34.
9 & 10 Eliz. 2. c. 37.	The Small Estates (Representation) Act 1961.	The whole Act.

Public Health Laboratory Service Act 1979

1979 CHAPTER 23

An Act to extend the powers conferred by section 5(2)(*c*) of the National Health Service Act 1977 and to amend certain provisions of that Act relating to the Public Health Laboratory Service Board.   [29th March 1979]

BE IT ENACTED by the Queen's most Excellent Majesty, by and with the advice and consent of the Lords Spiritual and Temporal, and Commons, in this present Parliament assembled, and by the authority of the same, as follows:—

Extension of public health laboratory service.

1977 c. 49.

1.—(1) In section 5 of the National Health Service Act 1977 (miscellaneous services) in paragraph (*c*) of subsection (2) (provision of a microbiological service for the control of the spread of infectious diseases) for the words following " diseases " there shall be substituted " and carry on such other activities as in his opinion can conveniently be carried on in conjunction with that service".

(2) After that subsection there shall be inserted—

" (2A) Charges may be made for services or materials supplied by virtue of paragraph (*c*) of subsection (2) above; and the powers conferred by that paragraph may be exercised both for the purposes of the health service and for other purposes.".

(3) In subsection (4) of that section (functions of Public Health Laboratory Service Board) for the words from " administration " to the end there shall be substituted " powers conferred by paragraph (*c*) of subsection (2) above as the Secretary of State may determine ".

(4) In Schedule 3 to that Act (constitution etc. of Public Health Laboratory Service Board) in paragraph 2 for the words from " the public " to the end there shall be substituted " its functions ".

2. In paragraph 12 of Schedule 3 to that Act (payment of travelling and other allowances) for the words from " travelling " to the end there shall be substituted " remuneration and allowances, and may make such provision for the payment of pensions, gratuities or allowances to or in respect of persons who have ceased to be members of the Board, as the Secretary of State may with the approval of the Minister for the Civil Service determine ". Payments in respect of membership of Public Health Laboratory Service Board and its committees.

3.—(1) This Act may be cited as the Public Health Laboratory Service Act 1979. Short title and extent.

(2) This Act does not extend to Scotland or Northern Ireland.

Appropriation Act 1979

1979 CHAPTER 24

An Act to appropriate the supplies granted in this Session of Parliament. [4th April 1979]

Most Gracious Sovereign,

WE, Your Majesty's most dutiful and loyal subjects the Commons of the United Kingdom in Parliament assembled, towards making good the supply which we have cheerfully granted to Your Majesty in this Session of Parliament, have resolved to grant unto Your Majesty the sum hereinafter mentioned; and do therefore most humbly beseech Your Majesty that it may be enacted, and be it enacted by the Queen's Most Excellent Majesty, by and with the advice and consent of the Lords Spiritual and Temporal, and Commons, in this present Parliament assembled, and by the authority of the same, as follows:—

1. All sums granted by the Acts mentioned in Schedule (A) annexed to this Act out of the Consolidated Fund towards making good the supply granted to Her Majesty amounting, as appears by the said schedule, in the aggregate, to the sum of £23,344,270,047·67 are appropriated, and shall be deemed to have been appropriated as from the date of the passing of the Acts mentioned in the said Schedule (A), for the services and purposes expressed in Schedule (B) annexed hereto.

Appropriation of sums voted for supply services.

The abstract of schedules and schedules annexed hereto, with the notes (if any) to such schedules, shall be deemed to be part of this Act in the same manner as if they had been contained in the body thereof.

1891 c. 24.

In addition to the said sums granted out of the Consolidated Fund, there may be applied out of any money directed, under section 2 of the Public Accounts and Charges Act 1891, to be applied as appropriations in aid of the grants for the services and purposes specified in Schedule (B) annexed hereto the sums respectively set forth in the last column of such parts of the said schedule as relate to the year ended 31st March 1979.

Short title.

2. This Act may be cited as the Appropriation Act 1979.

ABSTRACT

OF

SCHEDULES (A) and (B) to which this Act refers

SCHEDULE (A)

Section 1.

Grants out of the Consolidated Fund   –   £23,344,270,047·67

SCHEDULE (B)—APPROPRIATION OF GRANTS

Section 1.

	Supply Grants	Appropriations in Aid
	£	£
1977–78 and 1978–79		
Part 1. Defence (Excesses), 1977–78	24,497,963·99	—
Part 2. Civil (Excesses), 1977–78	5,006,183·68	478·72
Part 3. Defence (Supplementary), 1978–79	389,669,000·00	*−49,037,000·00
Part 4. Civil Departments (Supplementary), 1978–79	2,296,720,000·00	127,304,139·00
	£2,715,893,147·67	£78,267,617·72

* Deficit.

SCHEDULE (B)—Appropriation of Grants—*continued*

	Supply Grants not exceeding
	£
1979–80	
Part 5. Defence, Class I - - - - -	3,155,066,000·00
Part 6. Civil, Class II - - - -	494,907,000·00
Part 7. Civil, Class III - - - -	276,876,000·00
Part 8. Civil, Class IV - - - -	1,379,040,000·00
Part 9. Civil, Class V - - - -	442,000,000·00
Part 10. Civil, Class VI - - - -	571,424,000·00
Part 11. Civil, Class VII - - - -	1,152,683,000·00
Part 12. Civil, Class VIII - - - -	142,223,000·00
Part 13. Civil, Class IX - - - -	629,465,000·00
Part 14. Civil, Class X - - - -	777,935,000·00
Part 15. Civil, Class XI - - - -	3,200,688,000·00
Part 16. Civil, Class XII - - - -	2,565,029,000·00
Part 17. Civil, Class XIII - - - -	508,901,400·00
Part 18. Civil, Class XIIIA - - -	2,726,000·00
Part 19. Civil, Class XIV - - - -	570,885,000·00
Part 20. Civil, Class XV - - - -	266,296,000·00
Part 21. Civil, Class XVII - - -	4,492,232,500·00
TOTAL, DEFENCE AND CIVIL - - -	£20,628,376,900·00
GRAND TOTAL - - - - - -	£23,344,270,047·67

SCHEDULE (A)

GRANTS OUT OF THE CONSOLIDATED FUND

£

For the service of the year ended 31st March
1978—
    Under Act 1979 c. 20   ...   .   29,504,147·67

For the service of the year ended 31st March
1979—
    Under Act 1978 c. 59   ...   .   2,108,662,000·00
    Under Act 1979 c. 20   ...   .   577,727,000·00

For the service of the year ending on 31st March
1980—
    Under Act 1978 c. 59   ...   .   20,628,376,900·00

        TOTAL   ...   .   £23,344,270,047·67

SCHEDULE (B)—PART 1

DEFENCE (EXCESSES), 1977–78

SUMS granted, and sums which may be applied as appropriations in aid in addition thereto, to make good excesses on certain grants for Defence Services for the year ended 31st March 1978, viz.:—

	Supply Grants	Surplus receipts available to be applied as Appropriations in Aid
	£	£
Vote		
CLASS I		
10. DEFENCE PROCUREMENT: AIR SYSTEMS - - - -	13,946,068·81	—
11. DEFENCE ACCOMMODATION SERVICES, &c. - - - -	10,551,895·18	—
TOTAL, DEFENCE (EXCESSES), 1977–78 - - -£	24,497,963·99	—

SCHEDULE (B)—PART 2

CIVIL (EXCESSES), 1977–78

SUMS granted, and sums which may be applied as appropriations in aid in addition thereto, to make good excesses on certain grants for Civil Services for the year ended 31st March 1978, viz.:—

	Supply Grants	Surplus receipts available to be applied as Appropriations in Aid
	£	£
Vote		
CLASS III		
2. AGRICULTURAL SUPPORT (DEPARTMENT OF AGRICULTURE AND FISHERIES FOR SCOTLAND)	1,639,566·75	478·72
CLASS IV		
5. INDUSTRIAL INNOVATION: AEROSPACE - - - - -	3,293,544·88	—
CLASS VIII		
3. ENVIRONMENTAL RESEARCH -	73,072·05	—
TOTAL, CIVIL (EXCESSES), 1977–78 - - -£	5,006,183·68	478·72

SCHEDULE (B)—PART 3

DEFENCE (SUPPLEMENTARY), 1978–79

SCHEDULE OF SUPPLEMENTARY SUMS granted, and of the sums which may be applied as appropriations in aid in addition thereto, to defray the charges for the Defence Services herein particularly mentioned for the year ended 31st March 1979, viz.:—

	Supply Grants	Appropriations in Aid
CLASS I	£	£
Vote		
1. For expenditure by the Ministry of Defence on pay, allowances &c of the Royal Navy, the Royal Marines, the Royal Naval Reserve, the Royal Fleet Reserve and Cadet Forces, &c	4,401,000	1,300,000
2. For expenditure by the Ministry of Defence on pay, allowances &c of the Army, the Regular Reserve, the Territorial and Army Volunteer Reserve, the Ulster Defence Regiment and Cadet Forces - - - -	6,000,000	1,800,000
3. For expenditure by the Ministry of Defence on pay, allowances &c of the Royal Air Force, RAF Reserves, Royal Auxiliary Air Force and Cadet Forces - - - - - -	14,338,000	*−637,000
4. For expenditure by the Ministry of Defence on retired pay, pensions &c and related non-recurrent payments and for the Royal Hospital, Chelsea	25,480,000	220,000
5. For expenditure by the Ministry of Defence on movements; certain stores; supplies and services; plant and machinery; charter and contract repair of ships; certain research; lands and buildings; sundry grants; payments abroad including contributions and subscriptions to international organisations; and grants in aid -	24,570,000	21,911,000
6. For expenditure by the Ministry of Defence on pay &c of Defence Ministers and of certain civilian staff employed by the Ministry of Defence	41,623,000	3,233,000

* Deficit.

	Supply Grants	Appropria-tions in Aid
	£	£
CLASS I—*continued*		
Vote		
7. For expenditure by the Procurement Executive of the Ministry of Defence in operating its Headquarters and Establishments and for its other common services, for research &c by contract, for certain contingent liabilities, and for sundry other Procurement Executive services including those on repayment terms to non-Exchequer customers, and in respect of a commercial company - -	38,250,000	*—1,315,000
8. For expenditure by the Ministry of Defence on development by contract, production, repair &c and purchases for sale abroad of sea systems, and associated equipment and for a grant	1,000	—
10. For expenditure by the Ministry of Defence on development by contract, production, repair &c and purchases for sale abroad of air systems and associated equipment - - -	185,393,000	*—68,334,000
11. For expenditure including loans by the Property Services Agency of the Department of the Environment on public building work and certain accommodation services &c for defence purposes - - - -	36,612,000	*—8,500,000
12. For operating the Royal Dockyards and for the repair of ships by contract including work undertaken on repayment terms for Exchequer and non-Exchequer customers - - -	13,001,000	1,285,000
TOTAL, DEFENCE (SUPPLEMENTARY), 1978–79 - - - - -£	389,669,000	*—49,037,000

* Deficit.

SCHEDULE (B)—PART 4

CIVIL DEPARTMENTS (SUPPLEMENTARY), 1978–79

SCHEDULE OF SUPPLEMENTARY SUMS granted, and of the sums which may be applied as appropriations in aid in addition thereto, to defray the charges for the Civil Services herein particularly mentioned for the year ended 31st March 1979, viz.:—

	Supply Grants	Appropria-tions in Aid
	£	£
CLASS II		
Vote		
1. For expenditure by the Foreign and Commonwealth Office on the salaries and expenses of Her Majesty's Diplomatic Service and sundry other services and loans - - - -	750,000	6,850,000
3. For expenditure by the Foreign and Commonwealth Office on official information services, promotion of cultural and information exchanges and external broadcasting and for grants in aid of the British Broadcasting Corporation and the British Council - - - - -	4,028,000	60,000
4. For expenditure by the Foreign and Commonwealth Office on subscriptions, &c, to certain international organisations, military aid, certain grants in aid and sundry other grants and services - - - - -	16,095,000	821,480
5. For a grant in aid of the Commonwealth War Graves Commission and certain other expenses - - - -	431,000	—
6. For Her Majesty's foreign and other secret services - - - -	1,000,000	—
7. For expenditure by the Ministry of Overseas Development on the official United Kingdom aid programme and certain aid administration expenses, for certain subscriptions to International Organisations, for certain payments under the Commonwealth Scholarship and Fellowship Plan and assistance to the Crown Agents and Millbank Technical Services, including grants in aid - - - -	4,455,000	*—*1,517,789*

* Deficit.

	Supply Grants	Appropria- tions in Aid
	£	£

CLASS II—*continued*

Vote

8. For expenditure by the Ministry of Overseas Development on adminis- tration - - - - - - | 307,000 | — |

9. For expenditure by the Ministry of Overseas Development on pensions and supplements to pensions in respect of overseas service, the Cotton Research Corporation and for sundry services and expenses - - | 1,000 | — |

CLASS III

1. For expenditure by the Ministry of Agriculture, Fisheries and Food in England and Wales on price guaran- tees, production grants and subsidies, grants and loans for capital and other improvements, support for agriculture in special areas and certain other services; and, for certain of these services, elsewhere in the United Kingdom - - - - - | 34,919,000 | *—670,000 |

2. For expenditure by the Department of Agriculture and Fisheries for Scotland on price guarantees, production grants and subsidies, grants and loans for capital and other improvements, support for agriculture in special areas and certain other services - - | 1,364,000 | *—281,000 |

3. For expenditure by the Intervention Board for Agricultural Produce on carrying out the obligations of the United Kingdom under the Common Agricultural Policy of the European Economic Community in connection with arrangements for import and export, support for certain agricul- tural and other products including fish, assistance to producers, and arrangements for food aid; and for certain other services - - - | 2,000 | 14,482,100 |

* Deficit

	Supply Grants	Appropriations in Aid
	£	£
CLASS III—*continued*		
Vote		
4. For expenditure by the Ministry of Agriculture, Fisheries and Food on educational, advisory, research and development services, livestock services and pest control, food services and assistance to marketing and processing, including grants in aid -	6,799,000	486,000
5. For expenditure by the Welsh Office on price guarantees, production grants and subsidies, grants and loans for capital and other improvements, support for agriculture in special areas, livestock services and pest control, assistance to marketing and processing, land management and smallholdings, land drainage, assistance to the fishing industry and certain other services	265,000	*—551,000
6. For expenditure by the Department of Agriculture and Fisheries for Scotland on educational, advisory, research and development services, livestock services and pest control, assistance to marketing and processing, administration, land management and land settlement, the Royal Botanic and associated Gardens, assistance to crofters and certain other services, including grants in aid	1,220,000	654,000
7. For expenditure by the Ministry of Agriculture, Fisheries and Food on central administration including land management and smallholdings, Royal Botanic Gardens, land drainage and flood protection and certain other services including subscriptions to certain international organisations	3,648,000	371,000
8. For expenditure by the Ministry of Agriculture, Fisheries and Food on assistance to the fishing industry, research and development, administration, protective and other services including a grant in aid and subscriptions to certain international organisations	622,000	60,000
10. For a grant in aid of the Forestry Fund	3,679,000	—

* Deficit.

	Supply Grants	Appropriations in Aid
	£	£
CLASS IV		
Vote		
1. For expenditure by the Department of Industry on regional development grants, provision of land and buildings, selective assistance to industry in assisted areas, assistance for publicity and certain other services, including grants in aid - - -	1,000	*−4,800,000
2. For expenditure by the Department of Industry on the Research Establishments of the Department, the Computer Aided Design Centre and on contracts, grants and other support for industrial research and development including loans and grants in aid	2,000	—
4. For the expenditure by the Department of Industry on civil aerospace research and development, the support of development and production of civil aircraft and associated equipment, provision for British Aerospace, contributions to international organisations, loans, the purchase of certain assets of companies and sundry other items - - - - - -	113,983,000	*−11,306,000
5. For the expenditure by the United Kingdom Atomic Energy Authority and the Department of Energy in connection with nuclear energy and related research and development, including the purchase of nuclear materials, subscriptions and contributions to international organisations and projects, grants in aid, loans, guarantees, the purchase of shares &c, and for sundry other services -	7,788,000	7,500,000
6. For expenditure by the Department of Industry on selective assistance to industry and certain other services, and support for the Steel Industry -	2,000	—
7. For expenditure by the Department of Industry on support for the shipbuilding industry and investment grants - - - - - -	1,000	—

* Deficit.

	Supply Grants	Appropria- tions in Aid
	£	£

CLASS IV—*continued*

Vote

8. For expenditure by the Department of Energy in connection with the energy industries, including related research and development, selective assistance to industry, the nationalised industries, oil storage, financial assistance to certain classes of energy consumers, energy conservation and certain other services including grants in aid and an international subscription - -   128,901,000   2,190,000

9. For expenditure by the Department of Trade on promotion of tourism, export promotion, trade co-operation, protection of innovation, regulation of trading practices, central and miscellaneous services and certain other services including grants in aid and international subscriptions - -   1,000   —

10. For expenditure by the Export Credits Guarantee Department in connection with export credits guarantees including an international subscription, payments to minimise loss under guarantees, special guarantees, refinancing and financing arrangements made for facilitating trade with other countries and assistance towards the cost of financing export credits, the purchase of securities, overseas investment insurance and cost escalation guarantees - - - -   103,952,000   18,818,000

11. For expenditure by the Office of Fair Trading - - - - -   1,000   68,450

12. For the salaries and expenses of the Registry of Friendly Societies - -   273,000   *—75,000

* Deficit.

	Supply Grants	Appropria- tions in Aid
	£	£

CLASS IV—*continued*

Vote

13. For expenditure by the Department of Employment on grants in aid to the Manpower Services Commission, the Health and Safety Commission and the Advisory, Conciliation and Arbitration Service; on the Royal Commission on the Distribution of Income and Wealth; on the National Dock Labour Board; on agency payments including those made on behalf of the European Economic Community; on an international subscription and on other services including those for the labour market, industrial relations and seriously disabled people and on residual payments of regional employment premiums and selective employment payments - - - - -

| | 1,000 | *−1,000,000 |

14. For the expenditure of the Department of Industry on central and miscellaneous services, on those common services shared with the Departments of Trade and Prices and Consumer Protection, on payments for arbitration tribunals, on international subscriptions and on Post Office civil defence - - - - -

| | 2,442,000 | 271,000 |

15. For expenditure by the Scottish Economic Planning Department on grants in aid to the Scottish Development Agency and to the Highlands and Islands Development Board; on selective assistance to industry; on the promotion of tourism, on financial assistance to nationalised industries and certain classes of energy consumers; on the Manpower Services Commission in Scotland; on employment services in Scotland; on state owned harbours, and on sundry other services in connection with trade and industry - - - - -

| | 2,000 | 668,303 |

* Deficit.

	Supply Grants	Appropriations in Aid
	£	£

CLASS IV—*continued*

Vote

16. For expenditure by the Welsh Office on selective assistance to industry in assisted areas, special assistance for rural and highland areas, on the Welsh Development Agency, the promotion of tourism, on the Manpower Services Commission and certain other services including grants in aid   **2,000**   **—**

17. For expenditure by the Department of Prices and Consumer Protection on prices, consumer protection, standards and central and miscellaneous services, including a grant in aid to the Price Commission, other grants in aid, international subscriptions and remanet expenditure on food subsidies   **770,000**   **58,000**

CLASS VI

1. For expenditure by the Department of Transport on roads and certain associated services including lorry areas, lighting and road safety, and certain grants   -   -   -   -   **1,000**   **—**

2. For expenditure by the Department of Transport on support to nationalised transport industries, assistance to local transport, ports, research, services in connection with a Channel Tunnel and certain other transport services, including international subscriptions   -   -   -   -   **11,536,000**   **—**

3. For expenditure by the Scottish Development Department on roads and certain associated services, including lighting and road safety, on assistance to local transport, on support for transport services in the Highlands and Islands, piers and harbours and on certain other transport services and grants -   -   -   -   -   -   **11,173,000**   **345,000**

5. For expenditure by the Department of Trade on services connected with shipping including a grant in aid and an international subscription   -   -   **4,569,000**   **129,000**

	Supply Grants	Appropria-tions in Aid
	£	£

CLASS VI—*continued*

Vote

6. For expenditure by the Department of Trade on civil aviation services including a grant in aid of the Civil Aviation Authority and international subscriptions   -   -   - | 1,000 | —

7. For expenditure by the Department of Transport on central and other administration and certain other services   -   -   -   -   - | 1,000,000 | 1,793,000

CLASS VII

1. For expenditure by the Department of the Environment on subsidies, the option mortgage scheme, improvements, grants to housing associations and the housing corporation, the rent officer service and sundry other housing services   -   -   -   - | 166,300,000 | —

4. For expenditure by the Welsh Office on subsidies, the option mortgage scheme, improvements, grants to housing associations, the rent officer service and sundry other housing services   -   -   -   -   - | 3,143,000 | —

CLASS VIII

1. For expenditure by the Department of the Environment on water supply and sewerage, including a grant in aid, town and country planning (including compensation), recreation and other environmental services including grants in aid and international sub-scriptions, the urban programme, on a grant in aid to the Development Fund, and on sundry other services including loans   -   -   -   - | 6,524,000 | 49,000

	Supply Grants	Appropriations in Aid
	£	£

CLASS VIII—*continued*

Vote

2. For expenditure by the Department of the Environment on Royal Palaces, Royal Parks, historic buildings and ancient monuments, on certain public buildings and accommodation services, including grants in aid, and a grant to the Architectural Heritage Fund - - - - - -   5,001,000   583,000

3. For expenditure by the Department of the Environment on research, including grants in aid and an international subscription - - - - -   1,932,000   403,000

4. For expenditure by the Scottish Development Department in connection with water supply, sewerage, land drainage and flood protection, town and country planning (including compensation), recreation, Royal Parks, historic buildings and ancient monuments, acquisition of land, domestic rate relief, urban programme and other environmental services including a grant in aid - - - -   300,000   830,990

5. For expenditure by the Welsh Office in connection with water supply, sewerage, town and country planning (including compensation), recreation, historic buildings and ancient monuments, the urban programme, and other environmental services including safety measures, on grants for rate rebates and domestic rate relief and on sundry other services including grants in aid - - - - -   1,510,000   64,385

6. For expenditure by the Department of the Environment on central administration and certain other services -   1,173,000   1,618,000

CLASS IX

1. For expenditure by the Lord Chancellor's Department on court services, the Law Commission and certain other legal services - - -   3,460,000   1,460,000

	Supply Grants	Appropria- tions in Aid
	£	£

CLASS IX—*continued*

Vote

2. For expenditure by the Scottish Courts Administration on court services, the Scottish Law Commission and certain other legal services, including a grant in aid   -   -   -   -   -   - | 1,000 | 345,000

3. For grants to the Legal Aid Fund and to Law Centres -   -   -   -   - | 887,000 | —

4. For expenditure by the Departments of the Director of Public Prosecutions, the Law Officers and the Treasury Solicitor on Crown prosecutions and other legal services and on legal services for Government Departments | 340,000 | 9,000

5. For expenditure by the Queen's and Lord Treasurer's Remembrancer on Crown prosecutions, legal services for Government Departments and certain other legal services   -   -   - | 337,000 | 5,000

6. For expenditure by the Home Office on court services, Crown prosecutions, legal aid and other services related to crime, including a grant in aid   - | 6,665,000 | 754,000

7. For expenditure by the Home Office on prisons, probation, after-care and other services for the treatment of offenders, including a grant in aid   - | 34,266,000 | *—683,000*

8. For expenditure by the Home Office on police, fire, control of immigration and nationality and of gaming, and other protective services, including grants in aid and an international subscription -   -   -   -   - | 16,647,000 | 551,010

9. For expenditure by the Home Office on civil defence -   -   -   -   - | 257,000 | —

10. For expenditure by the Ministry of Agriculture, Fisheries and Food on emergency food services and strategic reserves   -   -   -   - | 359,000 | 31,000

11. For expenditure by the Home Office on community relations, assistance to- wards certain voluntary services, including grants in aid and certain other services   -   -   -   - | 5,551,000 | 2,281,000

* Deficit.

U3

	Supply Grants	Appropria- tions in Aid
	£	£
CLASS IX—*continued*		
Vote		
12. For expenditure by the Home Office on central administration and certain other services including expenses of the Referendum on the European Economic Community - - -	945,000	*−666,000
13. For expenditure by the Scottish Home and Health Department on legal aid, services related to crime, prisons, other services for the treatment of offenders, police, fire services, civil defence and certain other services, including a grant in aid - - -	5,755,000	*−746,000
CLASS X		
1. For expenditure by the Department of Education and Science on schools, the University Grants Committee, universities and certain other institutions, further education, teacher training and student awards, including grants in aid and a subscription to an international organisation - -	16,061,000	98,000
2. For expenditure by the Scottish Education Department on schools, including certain grants to local authorities, higher and further education, libraries, miscellaneous educational services, including compensation payments for redundant staff at colleges of education, research and administration, sport, and certain grants in aid -	9,524,000	—
3. For grants in aid to the British Library and certain other institutions - -	10,000	—
4. For the expenditure of the National Library of Scotland, including a purchase grant in aid - - -	71,000	—
5. For expenditure by the Welsh Office on schools, higher and further education, grants in aid of the National Library of Wales and the National Museum of Wales, student awards, miscellaneous educational services, research and administration and other arts - - - - -	1,093,000	192,000

* Deficit.

	Supply Grants	Appropriations in Aid
	£	£
CLASS X—*continued*		
Vote		
6. For expenditure by the Department of Education and Science on miscellaneous educational services, research and administration, including grants in aid and international subscriptions and compensation payments to redundant direct grant school teachers and staff at Colleges of Education - -	2,000	509,000
7. For a grant in aid of the Agricultural Research Council - - - -	2,554,000	—
8. For grants in aid of the Medical Research Council including subscriptions to certain international organisations - - - - - -	2,789,000	—
9. For a grant in aid of the Natural Environment Research Council -	2,185,000	—
10. For grants in aid of the Science Research Council including subscriptions to certain international organisations -	7,389,000	64,000
11. For grants in aid of the Social Science Research Council - - - -	200,000	—
12. For the expenditure of the British Museum (Natural History), including a purchase grant in aid - - -	332,000	—
13. For a grant in aid of the Royal Society	5,000	—
14. For the expenditure of the British Museum including a purchase grant in aid - - - - - -	670,000	—
15. For the expenditure of the Science Museum including purchase grants in aid - - - - - -	183,000	—
16. For the expenditure of the Victoria and Albert Museum including purchase grants in aid - - - - -	299,000	—.
17. For the expenditure of the Imperial War Museum including a purchase grant in aid - - - - - -	131,000	—
18. For the expenditure of the National Gallery, including a purchase grant in aid - - - - - -	143,000	- -

	Supply Grants	Appropriations in Aid
	£	£

CLASS X—*continued*

Vote

19. For the expenditure of the National Maritime Museum, including a purchase grant in aid - - - - | 25,000 | —

21. For the expenditure of the Tate Gallery including purchase grants in aid - | 493,000 | —

23. For the expenditure of the National Gallery of Scotland, the Scottish National Gallery of Modern Art, the Scottish National Portrait Gallery and the Department of Prints and Drawings, including purchase grants in aid - - - - - - | 73,000 | —

25. For expenditure by the Scottish Education Department on the Royal Scottish Museum and certain grants for the arts including purchase grants in aid - - - - - - | 489,000 | —

26. For grants in aid to the Arts Council and certain other institutions and for other grants for the Arts - - | 1,582,000 | —

CLASS XI

1. For expenditure by the Department of Health and Social Security on the provision of services under the National Health Service in England, on other health and personal social services including certain services in relation to the United Kingdom, and on research, services for the disabled, welfare food and certain other services; including grants in aid, international subscriptions and grants under section 8 of the Industry Act 1972 - - - - - - | 272,839,000 | 44,006,980

2. For expenditure by the Scottish Home and Health Department on the provision of services under the National Health Service in Scotland, on other health services and on research, services for the disabled, welfare food and certain other services - - | 70,280,000 | 3,036,980

	Supply Grants	Appropria-tions in Aid
	£	£

CLASS XI—*continued*

Vote
4. For expenditure by the Welsh Office on the provision of services under the National Health Service in Wales, on other health and personal social services, and on research, services for the disabled, welfare food and certain other services including a grant in aid

	39,015,000	1,742,000

CLASS XII

1. For sums payable out of the Consolidated Fund to the National Insurance Fund - - - - - -

	85,000,000	—

2. For expenditure by the Department of Health and Social Security on pensions, &c, for disablement or death arising out of war or service in the Armed Forces after 2 September 1939 and on certain associated services, on attendance allowances, invalid care allowance, old persons' retirement pensions, non-contributory invalidity pensions, lump sum payments for pensioners, and mobility allowance, &c - - - - -

	101,000,000	—

5. For expenditure by the Department of Health and Social Security on administration and certain other services including an international subscription

	20,750,000	15,300,000

CLASS XIII

1. For the expenditure of the House of Lords - - - - - -

	325,000	3,000

2. For the expenditure of the House of Commons, including a grant in aid -

	2,768,000	*—4,000

4. For expenditure by the Treasury on the management of the economy, exchange control and U.K. coinage and certain other services including grants in aid to certain Parliamentary bodies and others - - - - -

	4,077,000	100,000

5. For the expenditure of the Department of the Comptroller and Auditor General, including an international subscription - - - - -

	100,000	110,000

* Deficit.

	Supply Grants	Appropria-tions in Aid
	£	£

CLASS XIII—*continued*

Vote

	Supply Grants	Appropria-tions in Aid
6. For expenditure by the Customs and Excise Department including the expenses of Value Added Tax Tribunals and an international subscription -	12,065,000	715,000
7. For the expenditure of the Inland Revenue Department - - -	26,498,000	337,000
8. For expenditure by the Department of Transport in connection with driver and motor vehicle registration and licensing and the collection of revenue and certain ex-gratia payments - - - - -	3,400,000	400,000
10. For the expenditure of the Public Works Loan Commission - - - -	1,000	9,000
11. For the expenditure of the Department for National Savings - - -	1,167,000	1,114,000
12. For the expenditure by the Civil Service Department on the central management of the civil service, on Royal Commissions, Committees, special enquiries, the Office of the Parliamentary Counsel, and certain other services, including grants in aid to the Government Hospitality Fund and other bodies - - - - -	531,000	70,000
14. For the expenditure of the Scottish Record Office and on certain other services including a grant in aid -	33,000	21,250
15. For the expenditure of the Office of Population Censuses and Surveys, including a grant in aid - - -	288,000	203,000
17. For the expenditure of the Land Registry - - - - -	1,000	1,990,000
18. For the expenditure of the Department of the Registers of Scotland - -	1,000	189,000
19. For the expenditure of the Charity Commission for England and Wales -	30,000	—
20. For expenditure by the Ordnance Survey on the survey of Great Britain and other mapping services - - -	1,000	943,000

	Supply Grants	Appropriations in Aid
	£	£

CLASS XIII—*continued*

Vote

21. For the expenditure of the Cabinet Office and subscriptions to international organisations - - - | 398,000 | 4,400

22. For expenditure by the Scottish Office on central administration, certain preliminary expenses of devolution and certain other services - - - | 1,891,000 | 45,000

24. For expenditure by the Home Office on grants to the British Broadcasting Corporation for home broadcasting, and civil defence, central administration, wireless telegraphy and sundry other services - - - - | 14,725,000 | 222,100

25. For the expenditure of the Office of the Parliamentary Commissioner for Administration and the Health Service Commissioners for England, Scotland and Wales - - - - - | 5,000 | —

26. For the expenditure of the Office of the Public Trustee - - - - | 1,000 | 129,000

CLASS XIV

1. For expenditure by the Property Services Agency of the Department of the Environment on public building work and accommodation services, &c, for civil purposes in the United Kingdom, transport services and sundry other services - - - - - | 9,000,000 | 177,000

2. For expenditure by Her Majesty's Stationery Office on the procurement and production of stationery and printing, on publishing, and on certain other services - - - - | 7,873,000 | 3,056,000

4. For expenditure by the Central Office of Information on home and overseas publicity - - - - - | 1,810,000 | 2,716,000

5. For expenditure by the Assistant Paymaster General on the superannuation of civil servants, pensions &c, in respect of former members of the Royal Irish Constabulary and other pensions and non-recurrent payments; and for certain other services - - | 8,250,000 | 5,000,000

	Supply Grants	Appropria-tions in Aid
	£	£
CLASS XIV—*continued*		
Vote		
7. For the expenditure of the Department of the Government Actuary - -	1,000	11,000
9. For expenditure by the Paymaster General's Office - - - - -	87,000	19,000
CLASS XV		
1. For expenditure by the Ministry of Agriculture, Fisheries and Food on certain services in Northern Ireland, including price guarantees, production grants and subsidies, grants and loans for capital and other improvements, support for agriculture in special areas, food services and assistance to marketing, land management, special assistance to agriculture in Northern Ireland, assistance to the fishing industry and administration by the Department of Agriculture for Northern Ireland - - - -	2,991,000	*—*171,000*
2. For expenditure by the Northern Ireland Office on court services, Crown prosecutions, legal aid, forensic science service, other services related to crime, compensation for criminal injuries, prisons, probation and aftercare, young offenders, police, home defence, central and miscellaneous services, accommodation services and legal services for Government departments including grants in aid - -	18,480,000	*—*108,000*
3. For expenditure by the Northern Ireland Office on the Supreme Court of Judicature and Court of Criminal Appeal of Northern Ireland and on certain other legal services in Northern Ireland - - - -	44,000	50,500
4. For expenditure by the Northern Ireland Office on election expenses, central administration, transfers to the Northern Ireland Consolidated Fund, including a grant in aid, and accommodation services - - - -	180,000,000	21,000

* Deficit.

	Supply Grants	Appropriations in Aid
	£	£
CLASS XVII		
Vote		
1. For rate support grants and compensation for loss of rates to local authorities in England and Wales, for National Parks supplementary grants to County Councils and for rate rebate and domestic rate relief grants to local authorities in England -	534,888,000	—
2. For supplementary grants for transport purposes to County Councils and the Greater London Council - -	24,500,000	—
3. For rate support grants, equalisation grants and rate rebates grants to local authorities in Scotland - - -	77,900,000	—
5. For the expenditure by the Scottish Home and Health Department on superannuation allowances and gratuities, &c, in respect of teachers, and the widows and dependants of deceased teachers - - -	1,000	734,000
8. For payment of pensions, &c, to persons who contributed to the United Kingdom Atomic Energy Authority's Superannuation Schemes and other related expenditure - -	2,000	1,935,000
10. For the salaries and expenses of the Crown Estate Office - -	60,000	—
TOTAL, CIVIL DEPARTMENTS (SUPPLEMENTARY), 1978–79 -£	2,296,720,000	127,304,139

SCHEDULE (B)—PART 5

DEFENCE—CLASS I

SCHEDULE OF SUMS granted, on account, towards defraying the charges of the several Defence Services herein particularly mentioned, which will come in course of payment during the year ending on 31st March 1980, viz.:—

	Sums not exceeding
	£
Vote	
1. For expenditure by the Ministry of Defence on pay, allowances &c of the Armed Forces and their Reserves and Cadet Forces &c; pay &c of Defence Ministers and of certain civilian staff employed by the Ministry of Defence; on movements; certain stores; supplies and services; plant and machinery; charter and contract repair of ships; certain research; lands and buildings; sundry grants; payments abroad including contributions and subscriptions to international organisations; and grants in aid -	1,386,307,000
2. For expenditure by the Procurement Executive of the Ministry of Defence in operating its Headquarters and Establishments and for its other common services, for research &c by contract; for development by contract, production, repair &c and purchases for sale abroad of sea systems, land systems, air systems and associated equipment; for reservation of capacity in Royal Ordnance Factories; for certain contingent liabilities, and for sundry other Procurement Executive services including those on repayment terms to non-Exchequer customers - - -	1,311,689,000
3. For expenditure by the Ministry of Defence on retired pay, pensions &c and related non-recurrent payments and for the Royal Hospital, Chelsea -	182,428,000
4. For expenditure including loans by the Property Services Agency of the Department of the Environment on public building work and certain accommodation services &c for defence purposes - - - - - - -	153,508,000
5. For operating the Royal Dockyards and for the repair of ships by contract including work undertaken on repayment terms for Exchequer and non-Exchequer customers - - - -	121,134,000
TOTAL, DEFENCE, CLASS I - - - -£	3,155,066,000

SCHEDULE (B)—PART 6

CIVIL—CLASS II

SCHEDULE OF SUMS granted, on account, towards defraying the charges of the several Civil Services herein particularly mentioned, which will come in course of payment during the year ending on 31st March 1980, viz.:—

	Sums not exceeding
	£
Vote	
1. For expenditure by the Foreign and Commonwealth Office on the salaries and expenses of Her Majesty's Diplomatic Service and sundry other services and loans - - - - - -	58,453,000
2. For expenditure by the Property Services Agency of the Department of the Environment on public building work and accommodation services &c for civil purposes overseas - - - - -	11,363,000
3. For expenditure by the Foreign and Commonwealth Office on grants in aid of the British Broadcasting Corporation for external broadcasting and monitoring services - - - - -	13,432,000
4. For expenditure by the Foreign and Commonwealth Office on a grant in aid of the British Council -	10,949,000
5. For expenditure by the Foreign and Commonwealth Office on official information services, military aid, certain grants in aid and sundry other grants and services - - - - - - -	3,610,000
6. For expenditure by the Foreign and Commonwealth Office on grants and subscriptions, &c, to certain international organisations, a grant in aid, special payments and assistance, military aid, and sundry other grants and services - - - -	20,000,000
7. For a grant in aid of the Commonwealth War Graves Commission and certain other expenses -	2,745,000
8. For Her Majesty's foreign and other secret services -	14,625,000
9. For expenditure by the Ministry of Overseas Development on pensions and superannuation payments &c in respect of overseas service, pensions in respect of service with the Cotton Research Corporation and sundry other services and expenses - - - - - -	26,404,000

	Sums not exceeding
	£
CLASS II—*continued* Vote	
10. For expenditure by the Ministry of Overseas Development on the official United Kingdom aid programme including pensions and allowances in respect of overseas service, for grants in aid and certain subscriptions to International Organisations and certain payments under the Commonwealth Scholarship and Fellowship Plan - -	328,190,000
11. For expenditure by the Ministry of Overseas Development on administration - - -	5,136,000
TOTAL, CIVIL, CLASS II - - - - -£	494,907,000

SCHEDULE (B)—PART 7

CIVIL—CLASS III

SCHEDULE OF SUMS granted, on account, towards defraying the charges of the several Civil Services herein particularly mentioned, which will come in course of payment during the year ending on 31st March 1980, viz.:—

	Sums not exceeding
	£
Vote	
1. For expenditure by the Intervention Board for Agricultural Produce on carrying out the obligations of the United Kingdom under the Common Agricultural Policy of the European Economic Community in connection with arrangements for import and export, support for certain agricultural and other products including fish, assistance to producers, and arrangements for food aid; and for certain other services - - - -	32,975,000
2. For expenditure by the Ministry of Agriculture, Fisheries and Food in England on price guarantees, production grants and subsidies, grants and loans for capital and other improvements, support for agriculture in special areas, animal health and support services, land drainage and flood protection and certain other services; and, for certain of these services, elsewhere in the United Kingdom - - - - - - -	110,576,000
3. For expenditure by the Department of Agriculture and Fisheries for Scotland on price guarantees, production grants and subsidies, grants and loans for capital and other improvements, support for agriculture in special areas and certain other services including services relating to livestock diseases - - - - - - -	25,455,000
4. For expenditure by the Welsh Office on price guarantees, production grants and subsidies, grants and loans for capital and other improvements, support for agriculture in special areas, pest control, assistance to marketing and processing, animal health and support services, land management and smallholdings, land drainage, assistance to the fishing industry, protective and other services to the fishing industry and certain other services - - - - - -	11,601,000

SCHEDULE (B)—Part 7—*continued*

	Sums not exceeding
	£
Vote	
5. For expenditure by the Ministry of Agriculture, Fisheries and Food on educational, advisory, research and development services, livestock services and pest control, food services and assistance to marketing and processing, land management and smallholdings, emergency and strategic food services, some central and other services, including grants in aid and subscriptions to certain international organisations - - - - -	21,364,000
6. For expenditure by the Department of Agriculture and Fisheries for Scotland on educational, advisory, research and development services, livestock services and pest control, assistance to marketing and processing, administration, land management and land settlement, the Royal Botanic and associated Gardens, assistance to crofters, assistance to the Scottish fishing industry and the United Kingdom herring industry, research and development and protective and certain other services, including grants in aid -	14,789,000
7. For expenditure by the Intervention Board for Agricultural Produce on central administration and miscellaneous services - - - -	3,500,000
8. For expenditure by the Ministry of Agriculture, Fisheries and Food on assistance to the fishing industry, research and development, protective and other services including a grant in aid and subscriptions to certain international organisations - - - - - - - -	6,259,000
9. For a grant in aid of the Forestry Fund - -	14,009,000
10. For expenditure by the Ministry of Agriculture, Fisheries and Food on departmental administration - - - - - - - -	36,348,000
Total, Civil, Class III - - - -£	276,876,000

SCHEDULE (B)—Part 8

CIVIL—Class IV

Schedule of Sums granted, on account, towards defraying the charges of the several Civil Services herein particularly mentioned, which will come in course of payment during the year ending on 31st March 1980, viz.:—

	Sums not exceeding
	£
Vote	
1. For expenditure by the Department of Industry on regional development grants, selective assistance to industry, certain other services including the provision of public dividend capital to the National Enterprise Board; and on investment grants - - - - - - - -	400,000,000
2. For expenditure by the Department of Industry on provision of land and buildings, assistance for publicity, and other support services including grants in aid - - - - - - -	11,891,000
3. For expenditure by the Department of Energy in connection with the energy industries, including selective assistance to industry and the nationalised industries, financial assistance to certain classes of energy consumers and certain other services	47,270,000
4. For expenditure by the Department of Trade on promotion of tourism, export promotion, trade co-operation, protection of innovation, regulation of trading practices, central and miscellaneous services and certain other services including grants in aid and international subscriptions - - - - - - -	27,073,000
5. For expenditure by the Welsh Office on selective assistance to industry in assisted areas, special assistance for rural and highland areas, on the Welsh Development Agency, the promotion of tourism and certain other services including grants in aid - - - - - - -	26,168,000
6. For expenditure by the Scottish Economic Planning Department on grants in aid to the Scottish Development Agency and to the Highlands and Islands Development Board; on selective assistance to industry; on the promotion of tourism; on financial assistance to nationalised industries and certain classes of energy consumers; on employment services in Scotland; on state owned harbours, and on sundry other services in connection with trade and industry -	55,468,000

SCHEDULE (B)—PART 8—*continued*

	Sums not exceeding
	£

Vote

7. For expenditure by the Department of Industry on the Department's Research Establishments; Industrial Research and Development and other support; General Research and Development; on Aircraft and Aeroengines and associated equipment; National and International Space Technology Programmes; loans, grants in aid, international subscriptions and a grant to the National Research Development Corporation - 50,183,000

8. For expenditure by the Department of Energy in connection with the energy industries including related research and development, the nationalised industries, energy conservation, oil storage, and certain other services including grants in aid and an international subscription - - - 20,254,000

9. For expenditure by the United Kingdom Atomic Energy Authority and the Department of Energy in connection with nuclear energy and related research and development, including the purchase of nuclear materials, subscriptions and contributions to international organisations and projects, grants in aid, loans, guarantees, and for sundry other services - - - - - 56,875,000

10. For expenditure by the Department of Industry on support for the aerospace and shipbuilding industries, including loans, grants, and the purchase of assets, and assistance to redundant steel workers - - - - - - - 40,464,000

11. For expenditure by the Export Credits Guarantee Department on administration - - - 5,000,000

12. For expenditure by the Export Credits Guarantee Department in connection with export credits guarantees including an international subscription, special guarantees, refinancing and financing arrangements made for facilitating trade with other countries and assistance towards the cost of financing export credits, the purchase of securities, overseas investment insurance and cost escalation guarantees - - - - 80,000,000

13. For expenditure by the Department of Prices and Consumer Protection on prices, consumer protection, standards and central and miscellaneous services, including a grant in aid to the Price Commission, other grants in aid, international subscriptions and remanet expenditure on food subsidies - - - - - - - 9,315,000

SCHEDULE (B)—Part 8—*continued*

	Sums not exceeding
	£

Vote

14. For expenditure by the Registry of Friendly Societies — 208,000

15. For expenditure by the Office of Fair Trading — 273,000

16. For expenditure by the Department of Employment on general labour market services, on services for seriously disabled people and on an international subscription - - - - - - - 50,000,000

17. For expenditure by the Department of Employment on demand determined measures to promote and preserve employment opportunities, on the National Dock Labour Board and on residual payments of regional employment premiums and selective employment payments - - - 131,657,000

18. For expenditure by the Department of Employment on a grant in aid to the Advisory, Conciliation and Arbitration Service - - - - - 4,500,000

19. For expenditure by the Department of Employment on a grant aid to the Manpower Services Commission - - - - - - - 247,000,000

20. For expenditure by the Welsh Office on the Manpower Services Commission - - - - 17,400,000

21. For expenditure by the Scottish Economic Planning Department on Manpower Services Commission activities in Scotland - - - - - 34,000,000

22. For expenditure by the Department of Employment on the administration of benefit services, on central and miscellaneous services and on the Royal Commission on the Distribution of Income and Wealth - - - - - - - 27,000,000

23. For expenditure by the Department of Industry on central and miscellaneous services, on those common services shared with the Departments of Trade and of Prices and Consumer Protection, on services provided by the Ministry of Defence (Procurement Executive) Headquarters, on international subscriptions and on Post Office Civil Defence - - - - - - - 12,541,000

24. For expenditure by the Department of Energy on salaries and other services - - - - 3,500,000

SCHEDULE (B)—Part 8—*continued*

	Sums not exceeding
	£
Vote	
25. For expenditure by the Department of Employment as a grant in aid to the Health and Safety Commission - - - - - - -	21,000,000
Total, Civil, Class IV - - - -£	1,379,040,000

SCHEDULE (B)—Part 9

CIVIL—Class V

SCHEDULE OF SUMS granted, on account, towards defraying the charges of the several Civil Services herein particularly mentioned, which will come in course of payment during the year ending on 31st March 1980, viz.:—

	Sums not exceeding
	£
Vote	
1. For Government Investment in British Aerospace and the British Steel Corporation - - -	432,000,000
2. For Government Investment in the British Airways Board - - - - - - - -	10,000,000
TOTAL, CIVIL, CLASS V - - - -£	442,000,000

SCHEDULE (B)—PART 10

CIVIL—CLASS VI

SCHEDULE OF SUMS granted, on account, towards defraying the charges of the several Civil Services herein particularly mentioned, which will come in course of payment during the year ending on 31st March 1980, viz.:—

	Sums not exceeding
	£
Vote	
1. For expenditure by the Scottish Development Department on roads and certain associated services, including lighting and road safety, on assistance to local transport, on support for transport services in the Highland and Islands, piers and harbours and on certain other transport services and grants - - - - - -	43,852,000
2. For expenditure by the Welsh Office on roads and certain associated services including lorry areas, lighting and road safety, and on assistance to public surface transport, and certain grants -	33,188,000
3. For expenditure by the Department of Transport on roads and certain associated services including lorry areas, lighting and road safety, and certain grants - - - - - - - -	155,000,000
4. For expenditure by the Department of Transport on support to nationalised transport industries, assistance to local transport, research and certain other transport services, including civil defence and international subscriptions - - - -	35,928,000
5. For expenditure by the Department of Transport on support to nationalised transport industries and assistance to ports - - - - - -	280,000,000
6. For expenditure by the Department of Trade on services connected with shipping and civil aviation including grants in aid to the Civil Aviation Authority and the Merchant Navy Welfare Board, and international subscriptions - - - -	15,000,000
7. For expenditure by the Department of Transport on central and other administration, certain licensing and testing schemes and certain other services -	8,456,000
TOTAL, CIVIL, CLASS VI - - - -£	571,424,000

SCHEDULE (B)—PART 11

CIVIL—CLASS VII

SCHEDULE OF SUMS granted, on account, towards defraying the charges of the several Civil Services herein particularly mentioned, which will come in course of payment during the year ending on 31st March 1980, viz.:—

	Sums not exceeding
	£
Vote	
1. For expenditure by the Scottish Development Department on subsidies, the option mortgage scheme, improvements and investment, rent registration, capital grants to housing associations, a grant in aid and sundry other housing services - - - - - - -	95,000,000
2. For expenditure by the Department of the Environment on subsidies, the option mortgage scheme, improvements and investment, grants to housing associations and the Housing Corporation and sundry other housing services - - - -	990,121,000
3. For expenditure by the Welsh Office on subsidies, the option mortgage scheme, improvements, investment, grants to housing associations, and sundry other housing services - - - -	53,657,000
4. For expenditure by the Scottish Economic Planning Department on grants to New Town Development Corporations in connection with housing and other services - - - - - -	13,905,000
TOTAL, CIVIL, CLASS VII - - - -£	1,152,683,000

SCHEDULE (B)—PART 12

CIVIL—CLASS VIII

SCHEDULE OF SUMS granted, on account, towards defraying the charges of the several Civil Services herein particularly mentioned, which will come in course of payment during the year ending on 31st March 1980, viz.:—

	Sums not exceeding
	£
Vote	
1. For expenditure by the Department of the Environment on assistance to the construction industry, other water supply, conservation and sewerage, local authority and other environmental services including recreation - - - - -	10,232,000
2. For expenditure by the Scottish Development Department in connection with water supply, sewerage, land drainage and flood protection, town and country planning (including compensation), recreation, Royal Parks, historic buildings and ancient monuments, acquisition of land, domestic rate relief, urban programme and other environmental services including a grant in aid	11,156,000
3. For expenditure by the Welsh Office in connection with water supply, sewerage, town and country planning (including compensation), recreation, historic buildings and ancient monuments, other environmental services including safety measures, community land grants, on grants for rate rebates and on sundry other services including civil defence and a grant in aid - - -	6,398,000
4. For expenditure by the Department of the Environment on other environmental services including grants in aid and international subscriptions, on grants in aid to the British Waterways Board and Development Fund, on bridgeworks, and on maintaining Civil Defence water supply and sewerage equipment - - - - -	24,477,000
5. For expenditure by the Department of the Environment on town and country planning (including compensation), derelict land, community land and other local services - - - - -	9,551,000
6. For expenditure by the Department of the Environment on Royal Palaces, Royal Parks, historic buildings and ancient monuments, on certain public buildings and accommodation services, including grants in aid and a grant to the Architectural Heritage Fund - - - - -	17,360,000

SCHEDULE (B)—PART 12—*continued*

	Sums not exceeding
	£
Vote	
7. For expenditure by the Department of the Environment on central and housing administration, research, including grants in aid and an international subscription, and certain other services	37,085,000
8. For expenditure by the Department of the Environment on the urban programme - - -	25,964,000
TOTAL, CIVIL, CLASS VIII - - - -£	142,223,000

SCHEDULE (B)—PART 13

CIVIL—CLASS IX

SCHEDULE OF SUMS granted, on account, towards defraying the charges
of the several Civil Services herein particularly mentioned,
which will come in course of payment during the year ending on
31st March 1980, viz.:—

	Sums not exceeding
	£
Vote	
1. For expenditure by the Lord Chancellor's Department on court services, the Law Commission, Legal Aid administration and certain other legal services - - - - - - -	10,938,000
2. For expenditure by the Scottish Courts Administration on court services, the Scottish Law Commission and certain other legal services, including a grant in aid - - - - -	582,000
3. For expenditure by the Home Office on court services, Crown prosecutions, legal aid and other services related to crime, including a grant in aid	49,885,000
4. For expenditure by the Departments of the Director of Public Prosecutions, and the Treasury Solicitor on Crown prosecutions and other legal services -	1,504,000
5. For expenditure by the Queen's and Lord Treasurer's Remembrancer on Crown prosecutions, legal services for Government Departments and certain other legal services - - - -	623,000
6. For grants to the Legal Aid Fund, to Law Centres and for expenditure by the Lord Chancellor's Department on court services - - - -	31,183,000
7. For expenditure by the Scottish Home and Health Department on legal aid (excluding administration) and certain services relating to crime, treatment of offenders, police and fire services superannuation and police and civil defence grants - - - - - - - -	30,102,000
8. For expenditure by the Scottish Home and Health Department on legal aid administration, prisons, and on fire services, police and civil defence (excluding grants and superannuation) and certain other services including a grant in aid - -	12,153,000
9. For expenditure by the Home Office on prisons, probation, after-care and other services for the treatment of offenders, including a grant in aid	124,912,000

SCHEDULE (B)—PART 13—*continued*

	Sums not exceeding
	£
Vote	
10. For expenditure by the Home Office on police, fire, control of immigration and nationality and of gaming, and other protective services, including grants in aid and an international subscription -	330,200,000
11. For expenditure by the Home Office on civil defence	3,590,000
12. For expenditure by the Home Office on community relations, assistance towards certain voluntary services, including grants in aid and certain other services -	23,500,000
13. For expenditure by the Departments of the Director of Public Prosecutions, the Law Officers and the Treasury Solicitor on central and miscellaneous services -	2,009,000
14. For expenditure by the Queen's and Lord Treasurer's Remembrancer on central and miscellaneous services -	1,699,000
15. For expenditure by the Home Office on central administration and certain other services including expenses of the Referendum on the European Economic Community - - - -	6,585,000
TOTAL, CIVIL, CLASS IX - - - -£	629,465,000

SCHEDULE (B)—PART 14

CIVIL—CLASS X

SCHEDULE OF SUMS granted, on account, towards defraying the charges of the several Civil Services herein particularly mentioned, which will come in course of payment during the year ending on 31st March 1980, viz.:—

	Sums not exceeding
	£
Vote	
1. For expenditure by the Department of Education and Science on schools, further education and teacher training - - - - - -	18,287,000
2. For expenditure by the Scottish Education Department on schools, and certain grants to local authorities, higher and further education, libraries, miscellaneous educational services including compensation payments for redundant staff at colleges of education, research and administration, the Royal Scottish Museum, certain grants for the arts, including purchase grants in aid, sport and other grants in aid - - - -	23,292,000
3. For expenditure by the Welsh Office on schools, higher and further education, grants in aid of the National Library of Wales and the National Museum of Wales, student awards, miscellaneous educational services, and other arts - - -	4,098,000
4. For expenditure by the Department of Education and Science on universities and certain other institutions, including grants in aid and a subscription to an international organisation - -	339,068,000
5. For expenditure by the Department of Education and Science on grants for higher and further education - - - - - - -	8,626,000
6. For expenditure by the Department of Education and Science on further education, teacher training, miscellaneous educational services and research, including grants in aid and international subscriptions - - - - - -	30,531,000
7. For expenditure by the Department of Education and Science on student awards and compensation payments to redundant direct grant school teachers and staff at Colleges of Education -	143,165,000
8. For expenditure by the Scottish Education Department on awards to students receiving higher and further education - - - - - -	30,794,000

SCHEDULE (B)—PART 14—*continued*

	Sums not exceeding
	£
Vote	
9. For grants in aid to the British Library and certain other institutions - - - - - -	11,051,000
10. For expenditure by the National Library of Scotland, including a purchase grant in aid - - -	506,000
11. For expenditure by the Department of Education and Science and the University Grants Committee on administration - - - -	8,085,000
12. For a grant in aid of the Agricultural Research Council - - - - - - -	10,688,000
13. For grants in aid of the Medical Research Council including subscriptions to certain international organisations - - - - - -	19,930,000
14. For a grant in aid of the Natural Environment Research Council - - - - - -	13,458,000
15. For grants in aid of the Science Research Council including subscriptions to certain international organisations - - - - - -	65,664,000
16. For grants in aid of the Social Science Research Council - - - - - - -	7,005,000
17. For the expenditure of the British Museum (Natural History), including a purchase grant in aid -	1,951,000
18. For a grant in aid of the Royal Society - -	1,076,000
19. For the expenditure of the British Museum including a purchase grant in aid - - - -	2,840,000
20. For the expenditure of the Science Museum including purchase grants in aid - - - -	1,622,000
21. For the expenditure of the Victoria and Albert Museum including purchase grants in aid - -	2,978,000
22. For the expenditure of the Imperial War Museum including a purchase grant in aid - - -	948,000
23. For the expenditure of the National Gallery, including a purchase grant in aid - - -	2,381,000
24. For the expenditure of the National Maritime Museum, including a purchase grant in aid -	976,000
25. For the expenditure of the National Portrait Gallery including a purchase grant in aid - -	522,000

SCHEDULE (B)—Part 14—*continued*

	Sums not exceeding
	£
Vote	
26. For the expenditure of the Tate Gallery including a purchase grant in aid - - - - -	1,451,000
27. For the expenditure of the Wallace Collection -	166,000
28. For the expenditure of the National Gallery of Scotland, the Scottish National Gallery of Modern Art, the Scottish National Portrait Gallery and the Department of Prints and Drawings, including purchase grants in aid -	808,000
29. For the expenditure of the National Museum of Antiquities of Scotland, including a purchase grant in aid - - - - - - - -	219,000
30. For grants in aid to the Arts Council and certain other institutions and for other grants for the Arts	25,749,000
Total, Civil, Class X - - - -£	777,935,000

SCHEDULE (B)—PART 15

CIVIL—CLASS XI

SCHEDULE OF SUMS granted, on account, towards defraying the charges of the several Civil Services herein particularly mentioned, which will come in course of payment during the year ending on 31st March 1980, viz.:—

	Sums not exceeding
	£
Vote	
1. For expenditure by the Department of Health and Social Security on the provision of services under the National Health Service in England, on other health and personal social services including certain services in relation to the United Kingdom, and on research, services for the disabled and certain other services; including grants in aid and international subscriptions - - -	2,150,000,000
2. For expenditure by the Department of Health and Social Security on the provision of services under the National Health Service in England, on other health and personal social services, on welfare food and certain other services including grants under section 8 of the Industry Act 1972 - -	570,000,000
3. For expenditure by the Welsh Office on the provision of services under the National Health Service in Wales, on other health and personal social services, and on research, services for the disabled, welfare food and certain other services	148,017,000
4. For expenditure by the Scottish Home and Health Department on the provision of services under the National Health Service in Scotland, on other health services and on research, services for the disabled, welfare food and certain other services	329,111,000
5. For expenditure by the Scottish Education Department in connection with social work - -	3,560,000
TOTAL, CIVIL, CLASS XI - - - -£	3,200,688,000

SCHEDULE (B)—PART 16

CIVIL—CLASS XII

SCHEDULE OF SUMS granted, on account, towards defraying the charges of the several Civil Services herein particularly mentioned, which will come in course of payment during the year ending on 31st March 1980, viz.:—

	Sums not exceeding
	£
Vote	
1. For expenditure by the Department of Health and Social Security on pensions, &c, for disablement or death arising out of war or service in the Armed Forces after 2 September 1939 and on certain associated services, on attendance allowances, invalid care allowance, old persons' retirement pensions, non-contributory invalidity pensions, lump sum payments for pensioners, and mobility allowance, &c - - - -	318,991,000
2. For expenditure by the Department of Health and Social Security on supplementary pensions and allowances and repayments to Local Authorities	983,250,000
3. For expenditure by the Department of Health and Social Security on child benefit and family income supplements - - - - - - -	1,135,000,000
4. For expenditure by the Department of Health and Social Security on administration and certain other services including an international subscription - - - - - - -	127,788,000
TOTAL, CIVIL, CLASS XII - - - -£	2,565,029,000

SCHEDULE (B)—PART 17

CIVIL—CLASS XIII

SCHEDULE OF SUMS granted, on account, towards defraying the charges of the several Civil Services herein particularly mentioned, which will come in course of payment during the year ending on 31st March 1980, viz.:—

	Sums not exceeding
	£
Vote	
1. For the expenditure of the House of Lords - -	1,291,000
2. For the expenditure of the House of Commons on members' salaries, allowances, pensions, &c, financial assistance to opposition parties and a grant in aid - - - - - - -	5,451,000
3. For the expenditure of the Department of Her Majesty's Most Honourable Privy Council -	135,000
4. For expenditure by the Treasury on the management of the economy, and for certain other services including grants in aid to certain Parliamentary bodies and others - - - -	5,369,000
5. For expenditure by the Customs and Excise Department including the expenses of Value Added Tax Tribunals and an international subscription - - - - - - -	62,000,000
6. For the expenditure of the Inland Revenue Department - - - - - - -	157,050,000
7. For expenditure by the Department of Transport in connection with driver and motor vehicle registration and licensing and the collection of revenue - - - - - - -	19,521,000
8. For the expenditure of the Inland Revenue Department on life assurance premium relief - -	4,000,000
9. For the expenditure of the Department of the Comptroller and Auditor General, including an international subscription - - - -	1,688,000
10. For the expenditure of the National Debt Office and Pensions Commutation Board - - -	100
11. For the expenditure of the Public Works Loan Commission - - - - - - -	100
12. For the expenditure of the Department for National Savings - - - - - - -	15,394,000

X2

SCHEDULE (B)—PART 17—*continued*

	Sums not exceeding
	£
Vote	
13. For expenditure by the Treasury on exchange control - - - - - - - -	5,817,000
14. For expenditure by the Treasury in connection with the manufacture and distribution of coinage for use in the United Kingdom - - - -	5,186,000
15. For the expenditure by the Civil Service Department on the central management of the civil service, on Royal Commissions, Committees, special enquiries, the Office of the Parliamentary Counsel, and certain other services, including grants in aid to the Government Hospitality Fund and other bodies - - - - - - - -	9,907,000
16. For the expenditure of the Public Record Office -	764,000
17. For the expenditure of the Scottish Record Office and on certain other services including a grant in aid - - - - - - - -	196,000
18. For the expenditure of the Office of Population Censuses and Surveys, including a grant in aid -	4,269,000
19. For the expenditure of the Department of the Registrar General of Births, Deaths and Marriages in Scotland - - - - - - -	622,000
20. For the expenditure of the Land Registry - -	11,326,000
21. For the expenditure of the Department of the Registers of Scotland - - - - -	100
22. For the expenditure of the Charity Commission for England and Wales - - - - -	775,000
23. For expenditure by the Ordnance Survey on the survey of Great Britain and other mapping services - - - - - - -	4,985,000
24. For the expenditure of the Cabinet Office and contributions to international organisations -	1,931,000
25. For expenditure by the Scottish Office on central administration, certain expenses of devolution and certain other services - - - -	19,208,000
26. For the expenditure by the Welsh Office on central administration, the Rent Officer Service and certain preliminary expenses of devolution -	7,962,000

SCHEDULE (B)—PART 17—*continued*

	Sums not exceeding
	£
Vote	
27. For expenditure by the Home Office on grants to the British Broadcasting Corporation for home broadcasting, and civil defence, central administration, wireless telegraphy and sundry other services -	163,597,000
28. For the expenditure of the Office of the Parliamentary Commissioner for Administration and the Health Service Commissioners for England, Scotland and Wales - - - - -	312,000
29. For the expenditure of the office of the Public Trustee - - - - - - - -	100
30. For charges in connection with land purchases in Northern Ireland, and the expenses of management of guaranteed stocks and bonds issued for the purpose of Irish land purchases - - -	140,000
31. For transitional payments to certain charities -	5,000
TOTAL, CIVIL, CLASS XIII - - - -£	508,901,400

SCHEDULE (B)—PART 18

CIVIL—CLASS XIIIA

SCHEDULE OF SUM granted, on account, towards defraying the charges of the several Civil Services herein particularly mentioned, which will come in course of payment during the year ending on 31st March 1980, viz.:—

	Sum not exceeding
	£
Vote	
1. For the expenditure of the House of Commons Commission - - - - - - -	2,726,000
TOTAL, CIVIL, CLASS XIIIA - - - -£	2,726,000

SCHEDULE (B)—PART 19

CIVIL—CLASS XIV

SCHEDULE OF SUMS granted, on account, towards defraying the charges of the several Civil Services herein particularly mentioned, which will come in course of payment during the year ending on 31st March 1980, viz.:—

	Sums not exceeding
	£
Vote	
1. For expenditure including loans by the Property Services Agency of the Department of the Environment on public building work and accommodation services, &c, for civil purposes in the United Kingdom, transport services and sundry other services - - - - -	146,753,000
2. For expenditure by the Property Services Agency of the Department of the Environment on administration and certain other services - - -	47,677,000
3. For expenditure by Her Majesty's Stationery Office on the procurement and production of stationery and printing, on publishing, and on certain other services - - - - - - -	39,868,000
4. For expenditure by the Central Computer Agency (Civil Service Department) in connection with computers and general telecommunications including an international subscription - -	23,636,000
5. For expenditure by the Central Office of Information on home and overseas publicity - - -	12,358,000
6. For expenditure by the Paymaster General's Office on the superannuation of civil servants, pensions, &c, in respect of former members of the Royal Irish Constabulary and other pensions and non-recurrent payments; and for certain other services	202,010,000
7. For rates and contributions in lieu of rates paid by the Rating of Government Property Department in respect of property occupied by the Crown and premises occupied by representatives of Commonwealth and foreign countries and international organisations - - - - - -	96,000,000
For the expenditure of the Department of the Government Actuary - - - - -	123,000
9. For the expenditure of the Civil Service Catering Organisation (Civil Service Department) in connection with the provision of catering services -	516,000

X4

SCHEDULE (B)—PART 19—*continued*

	Sums not exceeding
	£
Vote	
10. For expenditure by the Paymaster General's Office	1,944,000
TOTAL, CIVIL, CLASS XIV - - - -£	570,885,000

SCHEDULE (B)—PART 20

CIVIL—CLASS XV

SCHEDULE OF SUMS granted, on account, towards defraying the charges of the several Civil Services herein particularly mentioned, which will come in course of payment during the year ending on 31st March 1980, viz.:—

	Sums not exceeding
	£
Vote	
1. For expenditure by the Ministry of Agriculture, Fisheries and Food on certain services in Northern Ireland, including price guarantees, production grants and subsidies, grants and loans for capital and other improvements, support for agriculture in special areas, land management, assistance to the fishing industry and administration by the Department of Agriculture for Northern Ireland - - - - - -	11,615,000
2. For expenditure by the Northern Ireland Office on legal services for Government departments, Crown prosecutions, legal aid, forensic science service, other services related to crime, compensation for criminal injuries, prisons, probation and after-care, young offenders, police, home defence, central and miscellaneous services, accommodation services and certain grants in aid - -	80,811,000
3. For expenditure by the Northern Ireland Court Service Administration on Court Services, certain other legal services and Accommodation Services	1,281,000
4. For expenditure by the Northern Ireland Office on election expenses, central administration and accommodation services - - - - -	1,589,000
5. For expenditure by the Northern Ireland Office on a grant in aid of the Northern Ireland Consolidated Fund and other transfers - - -	171,000,000
TOTAL, CIVIL, CLASS XV - - - -£	266,296,000

SCHEDULE (B)—PART 21

CIVIL—CLASS XVII

SCHEDULE OF SUMS granted, on account, towards defraying the charges of the several Civil Services herein particularly mentioned, which will come in course of payment during the year ending on 31st March 1980, viz.:—

	Sums not exceeding
	£
Vote	
1. For rate support grants to local authorities in England and Wales and for National Parks supplementary grants to County Councils - -	2,936,025,000
2. For rate support grants in Scotland - - -	476,000,000
3. For rate rebate and domestic rate relief grants to local authorities in England and for additional rate support grants and payments of compensation for loss of rates to local authorities in England and Wales - - - - -	69,180,000
4. For rate rebates grants to local authorities in Scotland - - - - - - -	11,500,000
5. For sums payable out of the Consolidated Fund to the National Insurance Fund - - - -	850,950,000
6. For expenditure by the Department of Education and Science on superannuation allowances and gratuities, &c, in respect of teachers, and the widows, children and dependants of deceased teachers - - - - - - -	100
7. For the expenditure by the Scottish Home and Health Department on superannuation allowances and gratuities, &c, in respect of teachers, and the widows and dependants of deceased teachers -	100
8. For expenditure by the Department of Health and Social Security on pensions, allowances, gratuities, &c, to or in respect of persons engaged in health services or in other approved employment -	100
9. For expenditure by the Scottish Home and Health Department on pensions, allowances, gratuities, &c, to or in respect of persons engaged in health services or in other approved employment -	100
10. For the salaries and expenses of the Crown Estate Office - - - - - - - -	327,000

SCHEDULE (B)—PART 21—*continued*

	Sums not exceeding
	£
Vote	
11. For transitional relief under the Finance Acts 1965 and 1972, for companies with an overseas source of trading income - - - - - -	2,000,000
12. For payment of pensions, &c, to persons who contributed to the United Kingdom Atomic Energy Authority's Superannuation Schemes and other related expenditure - - - - -	100
13. For payment to the Trustees of the Post Office Pensions Fund in respect of former civil servants	22,500,000
14. For supplementary grants for transport purposes to County Councils and the Greater London Council - - - - - - -	123,750,000
TOTAL, CIVIL, CLASS XVII - - - -£	4,492,232,500

Finance Act 1979

1979 CHAPTER 25

An Act to continue income tax and corporation tax at the existing rates; to increase the main personal reliefs from income tax; to withdraw child tax allowances; and to continue the limit on relief for interest imposed by paragraph 5 of Schedule 1 to the Finance Act 1974.   [4th April 1979]

Most Gracious Sovereign,

WE, Your Majesty's most dutiful and loyal subjects, the Commons of the United Kingdom in Parliament assembled, towards raising the necessary supplies to defray Your Majesty's public expenses, and making an addition to the public revenue, have freely and voluntarily resolved to give and grant unto Your Majesty the several duties hereinafter mentioned; and do therefore most humbly beseech Your Majesty that it may be enacted, and be it enacted by the Queen's most Excellent Majesty, by and with the advice and consent of the Lords Spiritual and Temporal, and Commons, in this present Parliament assembled, and by the authority of the same, as follows:—

Income tax.

1.—(1) Income tax for the year 1979–80 shall be charged at the same rates as for the year 1978–79.

1970 c. 10.

(2) In section 8 of the Income and Corporation Taxes Act 1970 (personal reliefs)—

(a) in subsection (1)(a) (married) for " £1,535 " there shall be substituted " £1,675 ";

(*b*) in subsection (1)(*b*) (single) and (2) (wife's earned income relief) for " £985 " there shall be substituted " £1,075 ";

(*c*) in subsection (1A) (age allowance) for " £2,075 " and " £1,300 " there shall be substituted " £2,265 " and " £1,420 " respectively;

(*d*) in subsection (1B) (income limit for age allowance) for " £4,000 " there shall be substituted " £4,400 ";

and in section 14(2) and (3) of that Act (additional relief for widows and others in respect of children) for " £550 " there shall be substituted " £600 ".

(3) Neither subsection (2) above nor section 22(2) or (3) of the Finance Act 1977 shall require any change to be made in the 1977 c. 36. amounts deductible or repayable under section 204 of the said Act of 1970 (pay as you earn) before 1st August 1979.

(4) No relief shall be given under section 10 of the said Act of 1970 (child tax allowances) for the year 1979–80 or any subsequent year of assessment except in the case of a child to whom section 25 or 26 of the said Act of 1977 applies.

(5) In paragraph 5(1) of Schedule 1 to the Finance Act 1974 1974 c. 30. (limit on relief for interest on certain loans for the purchase or improvement of land) the references to £25,000 shall have effect for the year 1979–80 as well as for previous years of assessment.

2.—(1) Corporation tax shall be charged for the financial year Corporation 1978 at the same rate as for the financial year 1977; and the tax. small companies rate and the fraction mentioned in section 95(2) of the Finance Act 1972 (marginal relief for small companies) 1972 c. 41. shall also be the same for the financial year 1978 as for the financial year 1977.

(2) The rate of advance corporation tax for the financial year 1979 shall be the same as for the financial year 1978.

3. This Act may be cited as the Finance Act 1979.   Short title.

Legal Aid Act 1979

1979 CHAPTER 26

An Act to amend certain enactments relating to legal aid and legal advice and assistance.   [4th April 1979]

BE IT ENACTED by the Queen's most Excellent Majesty, by and with the advice and consent of the Lords Spiritual and Temporal, and Commons, in this present Parliament assembled, and by the authority of the same, as follows:—

PART I

PROVISIONS FOR ENGLAND AND WALES

Extension of assistance to representation in proceedings.

1974 c. 4.

1.—(1) In section 2 (scope of advice and assistance) of the Legal Aid Act 1974 (in this Act referred to as "the Act of 1974 ")—

    (*a*) in subsection (1) for the words "the following provisions of this section" there shall be substituted the words "subsection (2) and section 2A below"; and

    (*b*) subsections (3) and (4) and, in subsection (6), the words from "and" onwards shall be omitted.

(2) After that section there shall be inserted the following section—

"Representation in proceedings.

2A.—(1) In this Part of this Act 'assistance by way of representation' means any assistance given to a person by taking on his behalf any step in the institution or conduct of any proceedings before a court or tribunal, or of any proceedings in connection with a statutory inquiry, whether by representing him in those proceedings or by otherwise taking any step on his behalf (as distinct from assisting him in taking such a step on his own behalf).

(2) Without prejudice to section 2(2) above and subject to any prescribed exceptions, section 1 above

does not apply to any assistance by way of representation unless it is approved by an appropriate
authority in accordance with regulations made for
the purposes of this section ; and regulations so made
may make different provision for different cases or
classes of cases.

(3) Regulations may—

    (*a*) describe the proceedings in relation to which
assistance by way of representation may be
approved by reference to the court, tribunal
or statutory inquiry, to the issues involved,
to the capacity in which the person requiring the assistance is concerned, or in any
other way ;

    (*b*) specify, in relation to any proceedings so
described, the assistance by way of representation which may be approved ; and

    (*c*) preclude the giving of approval in the case
of persons who would not be eligible for
assistance if paragraph (*a*) of section 1(1)
above were omitted or for the weekly sum
specified in that paragraph there were substituted such lower weekly sum as may be
prescribed.

(4) Regulations may also make provision—

    (*a*) as to which committees, courts, tribunals or
other persons or bodies of persons are to
be appropriate authorities ;

    (*b*) as to the procedure to be followed in apply-
ing for approval, the criteria for determining whether approval should be given and
the conditions which should or may be
imposed ; and

    (*c*) as to the circumstances in which approval
may be withdrawn and the effect of its
withdrawal.

(5) Where a person receives any assistance by
way of representation in any civil proceedings before
a court or any proceedings before a tribunal, then,
except in so far as regulations otherwise provide,
his liability by virtue of an order for costs made
against him with respect to the proceedings shall
not exceed the amount (if any) which is a reasonable
one for him to pay having regard to all the circumstances, including the means of all the parties and
their conduct in connection with the dispute ; and
regulations shall make provision as to the court,

tribunal or person by whom that amount is to be determined and the extent to which any determination of that amount is to be final.

(6) For the purposes of any inquiry under subsection (5) above as to the means of a person against whom an order for costs has been made, his dwelling house and household furniture and the tools and implements of his trade shall be left out of account except in such cases and to such extent as may be prescribed, and except as so prescribed they shall, in all parts of the United Kingdom, be protected from seizure in execution to enforce the order.

(7) In this section 'statutory inquiry' has the meaning assigned to it by section 19(1) of the Tribunals and Inquiries Act 1971."

(3) In section 7 of the Act of 1974 (scope of legal aid)—

(*a*) in subsection (5) the words from "and may also" onwards shall be omitted; and

(*b*) after that subsection there shall be inserted the following subsection—

"(5A) A person may be refused legal aid if, in the particular circumstances of the case, it appears—

(*a*) unreasonable that he should receive it; or

(*b*) more appropriate that he should receive assistance by way of representation;

and regulations may prescribe the criteria for determining any question arising under paragraph (*b*) above."

(4) In section 13 of the Act of 1974 (power to award costs out of legal aid fund) after subsection (6) there shall be inserted the following subsection—

"(7) References in this section and section 14 below to legal aid include references to assistance by way of representation."

(5) In section 25 of the Act of 1974 (interpretation of Part I) after the definitions of "advice" and "assistance" there shall be inserted the following definition—

"'assistance by way of representation' has the meaning assigned to it by section 2A(1) above;"."

Financial limits on prospective cost of advice and assistance.

2. In section 3(2) of the Act of 1974 (financial limit on prospective cost of advice and assistance) for the words from "such larger sum" onwards there shall be substituted the words "such other sum as may be prescribed; and regulations made for the purposes of this subsection may prescribe different sums for different cases or classes of cases".

3. In section 4 of the Act of 1974 (contributions from persons receiving advice or assistance)—

PART I
Contributions
from persons
receiving
advice or
assistance.

    (*a*) in subsection (2) for the words from "such amount" onwards there shall be substituted the words "such amount as may be prescribed ; and regulations made for the purposes of this subsection may prescribe different maximum payments for different amounts of disposable income and for different cases or classes of cases " ;

    (*b*) subsection (3) shall be omitted ; and

    (*c*) in subsection (4) for the words " any sum specified in subsection (2) or (3) " there shall be substituted the words " the sum specified in subsection (2) ".

4.—(1) For section 9(1) of the Act of 1974 (contributions from persons receiving legal aid) there shall be substituted the following subsection—

    " (1) Where a person receives legal aid in connection with any proceedings, his contribution to the legal aid fund in respect of those proceedings may include—

        (*a*) if his disposable income exceeds £1,500 a year, a contribution in respect of income not greater than one quarter of the excess or such other proportion of the excess or such amount as may be prescribed by regulations ; and

        (*b*) if his disposal capital exceeds £1,200, a contribution in respect of capital not greater than the excess or such lesser amount as may be so prescribed ;

and regulations made for the purposes of this subsection may make different provision for different amounts of disposable income or disposable capital and for different cases or classes of cases."

(2) In section 20(8) of that Act (regulations not to come into force unless or until approved by a resolution of each House of Parliament) for " 9(2) " there shall be substituted " 9(1) or (2) ".

5.—(1) For section 9(9) of the Act of 1974 (charge on property recovered for persons receiving legal aid) there shall be substituted the following subsections—

Charge on
property
recovered
for persons
receiving
legal aid.

    " (9) In this section references to the net liability of the legal aid fund on any person's account in relation to any proceedings are references to the aggregate amount of—

        (*a*) the sums paid or payable out of that fund on his account in respect of those proceedings to any solicitor or counsel ; and (*b*) if he has received any advice or assistance in connection with those proceedings or any matter to which those proceedings relate, any sums paid or payable out of that fund in respect of that advice or assistance to any solicitor,

being sums not recouped to that fund by sums which are recovered by virtue of an order or agreement for costs made in his favour with respect to those proceedings, or by virtue of any right of his to be indemnified against expenses incurred by him in connection with those proceedings.

(10) Where the solicitor acting for a person is a solicitor employed by the Law Society in employment to which section 16 below applies, references in subsection (9) above to sums payable out of the legal aid fund include references to sums which would have been so payable if the solicitor had not been so employed."

(2) Section 24(6) of that Act (which is superseded by this section) shall cease to have effect.

PART II

PROVISIONS FOR SCOTLAND

Extension of assistance to representation in proceedings.
1972 c. 50.

6.—(1) In section 2 (scope of advice and assistance) of the Legal Advice and Assistance Act 1972 (in this Act referred to as " the Act of 1972 ")—

(*a*) in subsection (1) for the words " the following provisions of this section " there shall be substituted the words " subsection (2) of this section and section 2A of this Act " ;

(*b*) subsections (3) and (4) shall be omitted ;

(*c*) for subsection (5) there shall be substituted the following subsection—

" (5) In the application of this section to Scotland, in subsection (2), for paragraphs (*a*) and (*b*) there shall be substituted the words ' at a time when he is receiving legal aid for the purposes of those proceedings '." ; and

(*d*) subsection (6) shall be omitted.

(2) After that section there shall be inserted the following section—

" Representation in proceedings.

2A.—(1) In this Part of this Act ' assistance by way of representation' means any assistance given to a person by taking on his behalf any step in the institution or conduct of any proceedings before a court or tribunal, or of any proceedings in connection with a statutory inquiry, whether by representing him in those proceedings or by otherwise taking any step on his behalf (as distinct from assisting him in taking such a step on his own behalf).

(2) Without prejudice to section 2(2) of this Act and subject to any prescribed exceptions, section 1 of this Act does not apply to any assistance by way of representation unless it is approved by an appropriate authority in accordance with regulations made for the purposes of this section; and regulations so made may make different provision for different cases or classes of cases.

(3) Regulations may—

    (*a*) describe the proceedings in relation to which assistance by way of representation may be approved by reference to the court, tribunal or statutory inquiry, to the issues involved, to the capacity in which the person requiring the assistance is concerned, or in any other way;

    (*b*) specify, in relation to any proceedings so described, the assistance by way of representation which may be approved; and

    (*c*) preclude the giving of approval in the case of persons who would not be eligible for assistance if paragraph (*a*) of section 1 of this Act were omitted or for the weekly sum specified in that paragraph there were substituted such lower weekly sum as may be prescribed.

(4) Regulations may also make provision—

    (*a*) as to which committees, courts, tribunals or other persons or bodies of persons are to be appropriate authorities;

    (*b*) as to the procedure to be followed in applying for approval, the criteria for determining whether approval should be given and the conditions which should or may be imposed; and

    (*c*) as to the circumstances in which approval may be withdrawn and the effect of its withdrawal.

(5) Where a person receives any assistance by way of representation in any civil proceedings before a court or any proceedings before a tribunal, then, except in so far as regulations otherwise provide, his liability by virtue of an order for expenses made against him with respect to the proceedings shall not exceed the amount (if any) which is a reasonable one

for him to pay having regard to all the circumstances, including the means of all the parties and their conduct in connection with the dispute ; and regulations shall make provision as to the court, tribunal or person by whom that amount is to be determined and the extent to which any determination of that amount is to be final.

(6) For the purposes of any inquiry under subsection (5) of this section as to the means of a person against whom an order for expenses has been made, his dwelling house, wearing apparel and household furniture and the tools and implements of his trade shall be left out of account except in such cases and to such extent as may be prescribed, and except as so prescribed they shall, in all parts of the United Kingdom, be protected from diligence or any corresponding process in the execution of the award.

(7) In this section ' statutory inquiry' has the meaning assigned to it by section 19(1) of the Tribunals and Inquiries Act 1971."

1967 c. 43.

(3) In section 1 (scope of legal aid) of the Legal Aid (Scotland) Act 1967 (in this Act referred to as " the Act of 1967 ")—

(a) in subsection (6) the words from "and may also " onwards shall be omitted ; and

(b) after subsection (6A) there shall be inserted the following subsection—

" (6B) A person may be refused legal aid if, in the particular circumstances of the case, it appears—

(a) unreasonable that he should receive it ; or

(b) more appropriate that he should receive assistance by way of representation ;

and regulations may prescribe the criteria for determining any question arising under paragraph (b) of this subsection."

(4) In section 13 of the Act of 1967 (power to award expenses out of legal aid fund) after subsection (6) there shall be inserted the following subsection—

" (7) References in this section and section 14 of this Act to legal aid include references to assistance by way of representation."

(5) In section 20 of the Act of 1967 (interpretation and construction) before the definition of the expression " Law Society " there shall be inserted the following definition—

" the expression ' assistance by way of representation ' has the meaning assigned to it by section 2A(1) of the Legal Advice and Assistance Act 1972 ; ".

7.—In section 3(2) of the Act of 1972 (financial limit on prospective cost of advice and assistance) for the words from "such larger sum" onwards there shall be substituted the words "such other sum as may be prescribed ; and regulations made for the purposes of this subsection may prescribe different sums for different cases or classes of cases ". Part II
Financial
limits on
prospective
cost of
advice and
assistance.

8.—(1) In section 4 of the Act of 1972 (contributions from persons receiving advice or assistance)— Contributions
from persons
receiving
advice or
assistance.

> (*a*) in subsection (2) for the words from "such amount" onwards there shall be substituted the words "such amount as may be prescribed ; and regulations made for the purposes of this subsection may prescribe different maximum payments for different amounts of disposable income and for different cases or classes of cases " ;

> (*b*) subsection (3) shall be omitted ; and

> (*c*) in subsection (4) for the words "any sum specified in subsection (2) of this section or in Schedule 1 to this Act" there shall be substituted the words "the sum specified in subsection (2) of this section ".

(2) Schedule 1 to the Act of 1972 (clients' contributions) shall be omitted.

9. For section 3(1) of the Act of 1967 (contributions from persons receiving legal aid) there shall be substituted the following subsection— Contributions
from persons
receiving
legal aid.

> " (1) A person's contribution to the legal aid fund in respect of any proceedings may include—

>> (*a*) if his disposable income exceeds £1,500 a year, a contribution in respect of income not greater than one quarter of the excess or such other proportion of the excess or such amount as may be prescribed by regulations ; and

>> (*b*) if his disposable capital exceeds £1,200, a contribution in respect of capital not greater than the excess or such lesser amount as may be so prescribed ;

> and regulations made for the purposes of this subsection may make different provision for different amounts of disposable income or disposable capital and for different cases or classes of cases."

PART II

Payments out of property recovered for persons receiving legal aid.

10.—(1) For section 3(7) of the Act of 1967 (payments out of property recovered for persons receiving legal aid) there shall be substituted the following subsections—

" (7) In this section references to the net liability of the legal aid fund on any person's account in relation to any proceedings are references to the aggregate amount of—

(a) the sums paid or payable out of that fund on his account in respect of those proceedings to any solicitor ; and

(b) if he has received any advice or assistance in connection with those proceedings or any matter to which those proceedings relate, any sums paid or payable out of that fund in respect of that advice or assistance to any solicitor,

being sums not recouped to that fund by sums which are recovered by virtue of an order or agreement for expenses made in his favour with respect to those proceedings, or by virtue of any right of his to be indemnified against expenses incurred by him in connection with those proceedings.

(8) Where the solicitor acting for a person is a solicitor employed by the Law Society in accordance with Part II of the Legal Advice and Assistance Act 1972, references in subsection (7) of this section to sums payable out of the legal aid fund include references to sums which would have been so payable if the solicitor had not been so employed."

(2) Section 17(5) of the Act of 1967 (which is superseded by this section) shall cease to have effect.

PART III

GENERAL

Financial provisions.

11. There shall be defrayed out of moneys provided by Parliament any increase attributable to this Act in the sums payable out of moneys so provided under the Act of 1974 or the Act of 1967.

Interpretation, etc.

12.—(1) In this Act—

" the Act of 1967 " means the Legal Aid (Scotland) Act 1967 ;

1967 c. 43.
1972 c. 50.

" the Act of 1972 " means the Legal Advice and Assistance Act 1972 ;

1974 c. 4.

" the Act of 1974 " means the Legal Aid Act 1974.

1978 c. 51.

(2) This Act shall be treated for the purposes of the Scotland Act 1978 as if it had been passed before that Act.

13.—(1) The enactments mentioned in Schedule 1 to this Act shall have effect subject to the amendments specified in that Schedule.

PART III

Minor amendments and repeals.

(2) The enactments mentioned in Schedule 2 to this Act are hereby repealed to the extent specified in the third column of that Schedule.

14.—(1) This Act may be cited as the Legal Aid Act 1979.

Citation, commence- ment and extent.

(2) This Act may be cited together with the Act of 1974 as the Legal Aid Acts 1974 and 1979 and may be cited together with the Act of 1967 and the Act of 1972 as the Legal Aid and Advice (Scotland) Acts 1967 to 1979.

(3) This Act shall come into force—

    (*a*) in relation to England and Wales, on such date as the Lord Chancellor may by order made by statutory instrument appoint ; and

    (*b*) in relation to Scotland, on such date as the Secretary of State may by order made by statutory instrument appoint ;

and different dates may be so appointed for different provisions or different purposes.

(4) An order under subsection (3) above may make such transitional provision as appears to the Lord Chancellor or, as the case may be, the Secretary of State to be necessary or expedient in connection with the provisions thereby brought into force.

(5) This Act, except—

    (*a*) section 1(2) so far as it relates to section 2A(6) of the Act of 1974 ;

    (*b*) section 6(2) so far as it relates to section 2A(6) of the Act of 1972 ; and

    (*c*) paragraphs 8 and 19 of Schedule 1,

does not extend to Northern Ireland.

SCHEDULES

SCHEDULE 1

Minor Amendments

The Legal Aid (Scotland) Act 1967

1. In section 2(1) of the Legal Aid (Scotland) Act 1967 (financial conditions of legal aid) and in the proviso thereto for the word " larger ", wherever it occurs, there shall be substituted the word " other ".

2. In section 4(5) of that Act (provision for applying the rules in Schedule 1 to the Supplementary Benefits Act 1976)—

    (*a*) for the word " shall ", in the first place where it occurs, there shall be substituted the word " may ";

    (*b*) the words " there shall be observed " shall be omitted; and

    (*c*) for the words from " except that " onwards there shall be substituted the words " shall be observed to such extent as may be prescribed ".

3. In section 18 of that Act (offences)—

    (*a*) in subsections (1) and (2) for the words " one hundred pounds " there shall be substituted " £500 "; and

    (*b*) in proviso (i) to subsection (2) after the word " any " there shall be inserted the words " committee, court, tribunal or other ".

4. In section 20 of that Act (interpretation) in the definition of " person " after the word " unincorporate " there shall be inserted the words " which is not concerned in a representative, fiduciary or official capacity ".

The Legal Advice and Assistance Act 1972

5. In section 1 of the Legal Advice and Assistance Act 1972 (variation of limits of disposable income and disposable capital) for the word " larger ", wherever it occurs, there shall be substituted the word " other ".

6. In section 3(5) of that Act (meaning of " regulations ") for the words " as so extended " there shall be inserted the words " as extended from time to time ".

7. In section 11(1) of that Act (meaning of " prescribed ") for the words " as so extended " there shall be substituted the words " as extended from time to time ".

8. In section 14(5) of that Act (Act not to form part of the Law of Northern Ireland) after the word " Except " there shall be inserted the words " for section 2A(6) and except ".

The Legal Aid Act 1974

9. In section 1(2) of the Legal Aid Act 1974 (variation of limits on disposable income and disposable capital) the words " not less than £20 " and " not less than £125 " shall be omitted.

10. In section 2(2)(*b*) of that Act (section 1 not to apply if there is a legal aid order) after the words " criminal proceedings " there shall be inserted the words " or any proceedings mentioned in sub-section (3), (6) or (6A) of section 28 below ".

11. In section 5(3)(*a*) of that Act (first charge for benefit of solicitor on any costs or property recovered) the words " or expenses " shall be omitted.

12. In section 6(2) of that Act (variation of limits on disposable income and disposable capital) the words " not less than £700 " and " not less than £500 " shall be omitted.

13. In section 9(2) of that Act (variation of amounts of free dispos-able income and free disposable capital) the words " not less than £250 " and " not less than £125 " shall be omitted.

14. In section 11(6) of that Act (provision for applying the rules in Schedule 1 to the Supplementary Benefits Act 1976)—

    (*a*) for the word " shall ", in the first place where it occurs, there shall be substituted the word " may " ;

    (*b*) the words " there shall be observed " shall be omitted ; and

    (*c*) for the words from " except that " onwards there shall be substituted the words " shall be observed to such extent as may be prescribed ".

15. In section 21(1) of that Act (advisory committee) after the word " and ", in the first place where it occurs, there shall be inserted the words " to make to him recommendations on such matters so relating as they consider appropriate ; and the Lord Chancellor ".

16. In section 22 of that Act (secrecy)—

    (*a*) in subsection (1) in paragraph (*a*) after the word " any " there shall be inserted the words " committee, court, tribunal or other " ; and

    (*b*) in subsection (3) for " £100 " there shall be substituted " £500 ".

17. In section 23(1) of that Act (proceedings for misrepresentation etc.) for " £100 " there shall be substituted " £500 ".

18. In section 25 of that Act (interpretation of Part I) in the definition of " person " after the word " unincorporate " there shall be inserted the words " which is not concerned in a representative, fiduciary or official capacity ".

19. In section 43(5) of that Act (Act not to extend to Scotland or Northern Ireland) after the word " Act " there shall be inserted the words " (except sections 2A(6) and 8(4)) ".

20. In Schedule 1 to that Act (proceedings for which legal aid may be given under Part I) paragraph 1(*b*) shall be omitted.

SCHEDULE 2

REPEALS

Chapter	Short title	Extent of repeal
1967 c. 43.	The Legal Aid (Scotland) Act 1967.	In section 1(6) the words from " and may also " onwards. In section 4(5) the words " there shall be observed ". Section 17(5).
1972 c. 50.	The Legal Advice and Assistance Act 1972.	In section 2, subsections (3), (4) and (6), Section 4(3). Schedule 1. In Schedule 2, the entry relating to section 3(7) of the Legal Aid (Scotland) Act 1967.
1974 c. 4.	The Legal Aid Act 1974.	In section 1(2) the words " not less than £20 " and " not less than £125 ". In section 2, subsections (3) and (4) and, in subsection (6), the words from " and " onwards. Section 4(3). In section 5(3)(*a*) the words " or expenses ". In section 6(2) the words " not less than £700 " and " not less than £500 ". In section 7(5) the words from " and may also " onwards. In section 9(2) the words " not less than £250 " and " not less than £125 ". In section 11(6) the words " there shall be observed ". Section 24(6). In Schedule 1, paragraph 1(*b*).

Kiribati Act 1979

1979 CHAPTER 27

An Act to make provision for and in connection with the attainment by the Gilbert Islands of fully responsible status as a Republic within the Commonwealth under the name of Kiribati.   [19th June 1979]

BE IT ENACTED by the Queen's most Excellent Majesty, by and with the advice and consent of the Lords Spiritual and Temporal, and Commons, in this present Parliament assembled, and by the authority of the same, as follows:—

1.—(1) On and after 12th July 1979 (in this Act referred to as " Independence Day ") Her Majesty's Government in the United Kingdom shall have no responsibility for the government of Kiribati. *Independence for Kiribati.*

(2) No Act of the Parliament of the United Kingdom passed on or after Independence Day shall extend, or be deemed to extend, to Kiribati as part of its law.

2. Her Majesty may by Order in Council (which shall be laid before Parliament after being made) make provision for the constitution of Kiribati as a Republic on Independence Day. *Power to provide for constitution of Kiribati as Republic.*

3.—(1) Subject to the following provisions of this Act, all law to which this section applies, whether being a rule of law or a provision of an Act of Parliament or of any other enactment or instrument whatsoever, which is in force on Independence Day, or, having been passed or made before that day, comes into force thereafter, shall, unless and until provision to the contrary is made by Parliament or some other authority *Operation of existing law.*

having power in that behalf, have the same operation in relation to Kiribati and persons and things belonging to or connected with Kiribati, as it would have had apart from this subsection if there had been no change in the status of Kiribati.

(2) This section applies to law of, or any part of, the United Kingdom, the Channel Islands and the Isle of Man and, in relation only to any enactment of the Parliament of the United Kingdom or any Order in Council made by virtue of any such enactment whereby any such enactment applies in relation to Kiribati, to law of any other country or territory to which that enactment or Order extends.

(3) Subsection (1) above shall not apply in relation to section 9 of the British Nationality Act 1948 as set out in Appendix C to Schedule 1 to the Immigration Act 1971.

1948 c. 56.
1971 c. 77.

(4) On and after Independence Day the provisions specified in the Schedule to this Act shall have effect subject to the amendments there specified.

(5) Subsection (4) above, and the Schedule to this Act, shall not extend to Kiribati as part of its law.

Consequential modifications of British Nationality Acts.

4.—(1) On and after Independence Day the British Nationality Acts 1948 to 1965 shall have effect as if in section 1(3) of the 1948 Act (Commonwealth countries having separate citizenship) there were added at the end the words " and Kiribati ".

(2) Except as provided by section 5 below, any person who immediately before Independence Day is a citizen of the United Kingdom and Colonies shall on that day cease to be such a citizen if he becomes on that day a citizen of Kiribati.

(3) Except as provided by section 5 below, a person who immediately before Independence Day is a citizen of the United Kingdom and Colonies and—

> (a) who was born, or whose father was born, in Kiribati, or, in the case of a woman, who became a citizen of the United Kingdom and Colonies by reason of her marriage to a man who was born, or whose father was born, in Kiribati ; and
>
> (b) who on Independence Day does not become a citizen of Kiribati ;

shall on Independence Day cease to be a citizen of the United Kingdom and Colonies if he is then a citizen of some other country.

(4) Section 6(2) of the 1948 Act (registration as citizens of the United Kingdom and Colonies of women who have been married to such citizens) shall not apply to a woman by virtue of her

marriage to a person who on Independence Day ceases to be such a citizen under subsection (2) or (3) above or who would have done so if living on that day.

(5) In accordance with section 3(3) of the West Indies Act 1967 c. 4. 1967, it is hereby declared that this and the following section extend to all associated states.

5.—(1) A person shall not cease to be a citizen of the United Retention of Kingdom and Colonies under section 4(2) or (3) above if he, his citizenship of father or his father's father— the United Kingdom and

(a) was born in the United Kingdom or a relevant territory; Colonies in or certain cases.

(b) is or was a person naturalised in the United Kingdom and Colonies by virtue of a certificate of naturalisation granted in the United Kingdom or a relevant territory; or

(c) was, in the United Kingdom or a relevant territory, registered as a citizen of the United Kingdom and Colonies, or was so registered by a High Commissioner exercising functions under section 8(2) or 12(7) of the 1948 Act; or

(d) became a British subject by reason of the annexation of any territory included in a relevant territory;

or if his father or his father's father would, if living immediately before the commencement of the 1948 Act, have become a person naturalised in the United Kingdom and Colonies under section 32(6) of that Act (previous local naturalisation in a colony or protectorate) by virtue of having enjoyed the privileges of naturalisation in a relevant territory.

(2) In subsection (1) above " relevant territory " means any territory which on Independence Day is a colony or an associated state, other than any territory which on that day is not a colony for the purposes of the 1948 Act as then in force (and accordingly does not include Kiribati).

(3) Subsection (1)(c) above shall not apply to a woman by virtue of her registration as a citizen of the United Kingdom and Colonies if that registration was effected under section 6(2) of the 1948 Act (registration as citizens of the United Kingdom and Colonies of women who have been married to such citizens).

(4) A woman who is a citizen of the United Kingdom and Colonies, and is the wife of such a citizen, shall not herself cease to be such a citizen under section 4(2) or (3) above unless her husband does so.

(5) Part III of the 1948 Act (supplementary provisions) as in force from time to time, except section 23 (legitimated children), shall have effect for the purposes of this section as if this section were included in that Act.

(6) A person born out of wedlock and legitimated (within the meaning of section 23(2) of the 1948 Act) by the subsequent marriage of his parents shall be treated, for the purpose of determining whether he has by virtue of this Act ceased to be a citizen of the United Kingdom and Colonies, as if he had been born legitimate.

Appeals to the Privy Council.

6.—(1) Her Majesty may by Order in Council confer on the Judicial Committee of the Privy Council such jurisdiction and powers as may be appropriate in cases in which provision is made by the law of Kiribati for appeals to the Committee from courts of Kiribati.

(2) An Order in Council under this section may contain such incidental and supplemental provisions as appear to Her Majesty to be expedient.

(3) Any such Order in Council may contain such transitional provisions as appear to Her Majesty to be expedient—

(*a*) in relation to appeals in which the records have been registered in the Office of the Judicial Committee on or before Independence Day ; and

(*b*) in relation to petitions for leave to appeal filed in that Office on or before that date.

1833 c. 41.

(4) Except so far as otherwise provided by or in accordance with an Order in Council under this section, and subject to such modifications as may be so provided, the Judicial Committee Act 1833 shall have effect in relation to appeals in respect of which jurisdiction is conferred under this section as it has effect in relation to appeals to Her Majesty in Council.

(5) An Order in Council under this section shall be laid before Parliament after being made.

Interpretation.

7.—(1) In this Act, and in any amendment made by this Act in any other enactment, " Kiribati " means the territories which immediately before Independence Day constitute the colony of the Gilbert Islands.

1948 c. 56.

(2) In this Act, " the 1948 Act " means the British Nationality Act 1948.

Short title.

8. This Act may be cited as the Kiribati Act 1979.

SCHEDULE

Section 3.

CONSEQUENTIAL AMENDMENTS

Diplomatic immunities

1. In section 1(5) of the Diplomatic Immunities (Conferences with 1961 c. 11.
Commonwealth Countries and Republic of Ireland) Act 1961, before
the word " and " in the last place where it occurs there shall be
inserted the word " Kiribati ".

The Services

2. The expression " colony " in the Army Act 1955, the Air Force 1955 c. 18.
Act 1955 and the Naval Discipline Act 1957 shall not include 1955 c. 19.
Kiribati ; and in the definitions of " Commonwealth force " in section 1957 c. 53.
225(1) and 223(1) respectively of those Acts of 1955, and in the
definition of " Commonwealth country " in section 135(1) of that
Act of 1957, at the end there shall be added the words " or Kiribati ".

Visiting forces

3. In the Visiting Forces (British Commonwealth) Act 1933, section 1933 c. 6.
4 (attachment and mutual powers of command) shall apply in relation
to forces raised in Kiribati as it applies to forces raised in Dominions
within the meaning of the Statute of Westminster 1931.   1931 c. 4
(22 & 23 Geo. 5.).

4. In the Visiting Forces Act 1952—   1952 c. 67.

   (*a*) in section 1(1)(*a*) (countries to which the Act applies) at
   the end there shall be added the words " Kiribati or " ;

   (*b*) in section 10(1)(*a*), the expression " colony " shall not
   include Kiribati ;

and, until express provision with respect to Kiribati is made by an
Order in Council under section 8 of that Act (application to visiting
forces of law relating to home forces), any such Order for the time
being in force shall be deemed to apply to visiting forces of Kiribati.

Ships and aircraft

5. In section 427(2) of the Merchant Shipping Act 1894, as set 1894 c. 60.
out in section 2 of the Merchant Shipping (Safety Convention) Act 1949 c. 43.
1949, before the words " or in any " there shall be inserted the
words " or Kiribati ".

6. In the Whaling Industry (Regulation) Act 1934, the expression 1934 c. 49.
" British ship to which this Act applies " shall not include a British
ship registered in Kiribati.

7. Kiribati shall not be a relevant overseas territory for the
purposes of sections 21(2) and 22(3) of the Civil Aviation Act 1971. 1971 c. 75.

Colonial stock

1877 c. 59. 8. Section 20 of the Colonial Stock Act 1877 (which relates to the jurisdiction of courts in the United Kingdom as to colonial stock) shall, in its application to stock of Kiribati, have effect as if for the second paragraph there were substituted—

" (2) Any person claiming to be interested in colonial stock to which this Act applies, or in any dividend thereon, may institute civil proceedings in the United Kingdom against the registrar in relation to that stock or dividend.

(3) Notwithstanding anything in the foregoing provisions of this section, the registrar shall not by virtue of an order made by any court in the United Kingdom in any such proceedings as are referred to in this section be liable to make any payment otherwise than out of moneys in his possession in the United Kingdom as registrar."

Commonwealth Institute

1925 ch. xvii.
1958 c. 16. 9. In section 8(2) of the Imperial Institute Act 1925, as amended by the Commonwealth Institute Act 1958, (power to vary the provisions of the said Act of 1925 if an agreement for the purpose is made with the governments of certain territories which for the time being are contributing towards the expenses of the Commonwealth Institute) at the end there shall be added the words " and Kiribati ".

INDEX

TO THE

PUBLIC GENERAL ACTS

AND

GENERAL SYNOD MEASURES 1979

A

ANCIENT MONUMENTS AND ARCHAEOLOGICAL AREAS ACT: c. 46   II, p. 1147

PART 1

ANCIENT MONUMENTS

Protection of scheduled monuments

B

C

PART VI

PROPERTY: FURTHER PROVISIONS

Replacement of business assets

Stock in trade

Transfer of business to a company

Transfer of business on retirement

Gifts of business assets

Movable property

Other property

PART VII

OTHER PROVISIONS

Insurance

Superannuation funds, annuities and annual payments

Other exemptions and reliefs

Registration as a credit union

§ 1. Registration under the Industrial and Provident Societies Act 1965, II, p. 757.
   2. Supplementary and transitional provisions as to registration, II, p. 759.
   3. Use of name " credit union ", etc., II, p. 760.

Rules and membership

4 and schedule 1.   Rules, II, pp. 760, 782.
   5. Membership and voting rights, II, p. 761.
   6. Minimum and maximum number of members, II, p. 761.

Operation of credit union

   7. Shares, II, p. 763.
   8. General prohibition on deposit-taking, II, p. 763.
   9. Deposits by persons too young to be members, II, p. 764.
  10. Power to borrow money, II, p. 765.
  11. Loans, II, p. 765.
  12. Power to hold land for limited purposes, II, p. 766.
  13. Investments, II, p. 767.
  14. Computation and application of profits, II, p. 768.

Insurance and other arrangements

  15. Insurance against fraud or other dishonesty, II, p. 769.
  16. Guarantee funds, II, p. 770.

Powers of registrar

  17. Power to require information, II, p. 771.
  18. Power to appoint inspector and call meeting, II, p. 771.
19 and schedule 2.   Power to suspend operations of credit union, II, pp. 772, 783.
  20. Cancellation or suspension of registration and petition for winding up, II, p. 773.

Amalgamations, transfers of engagements and conversions

  21. Amalgamations and transfers of engagements, II, p. 773.
  22. No conversion of credit union into company, etc., II, p. 774.
  23. Conversion of company into credit union, II, p. 774.

Part IX

Control of Excise Licence Trades and Revenue Traders

Excise licences—general provisions

General provisions as to entries of premises, etc.

General provisions as to revenue traders

Part X

Duties and Drawbacks—General Provisions

General provisions relating to imported goods

General provisions relating to charge of duty on and delivery of goods

Drawback, allowances, duties, etc.—general

Part XI

Detention of Persons, Forfeiture and Legal Proceedings

Detention of persons

Part XII

General and Miscellaneous

General powers, etc.

D

E

ENTRY. Powers of, under—

Alcoholic Liquor Duties Act (c. 4, ss. 25(6), 53(5), 79, 83)

I, pp. 184, 201, 214, 216

Ancient Monuments and Archaeological Areas Act (c. 46, ss. 5, 6, 13(5), 15(4), 26, 38–40, 43, 44, 54) II, pp. 1152, 1161, 1163, 1173, 1181, 1186, 1195

Customs and Excise Management Act (c. 2, ss. 33, 84(5), 112, 113, 161, 162)

I, pp. 28, 64, 80, 109, 110

Electricity (Scotland) Act (c. 11, s. 13) ...   .   I, p. 293
Estate Agents Act (c. 38, s. 11) ...   .   II, p. 906
Merchant Shipping Act (c. 39, s. 27(1)) ...   .   II, p. 966
Wages Councils Act (c. 12, s. 22(3))   ...   .   I, p. 349
Weights and Measures Act (c. 45, sch. 2, paras. 1–3) ...   ...   II, p. 1123

ESTATE AGENTS ACT: c. 38 ...   .   II, p. 895

Application of Act
§ 1. Estate agency work, II, p. 895.
   2. Interests in land, II, p. 896.

Orders by Director General of Fair Trading
   3 and schedule 1. Orders prohibiting unfit persons from doing estate agency work, II, pp. 897, 929.
   4. Warning orders, II, p. 899.
   5 and schedule 2. Supplementary provisions as to orders under sections 3 and 4, II, pp. 900, 930.
   6 and schedule 2. Revocation and variation of orders under sections 3 and 4, II, pp. 901, 930.
   7. Appeals, II, p. 902.
   8 and schedule 2. Register of orders etc., II, pp. 903, 930.

Information, entry and inspection
   9. Information for the Director, II, p. 904.
  10. Restriction on disclosure of information, II, p. 905.
  11. Powers of entry and inspection, II, p. 906.

Clients' money and accounts
  12. Meaning of " clients' money " etc., II, p. 908.
  13. Clients' money held on trust or as agent, II, p. 909.
  14. Keeping of client accounts, II, p. 909.
  15. Interest on clients' money, II, p. 911.
  16. Insurance cover for clients' money, II, p. 912.
  17. Exemptions from section 16, II, p. 914.

Regulation of other aspects of estate agency work
  18. Information to clients of prospective liabilities, II, p. 915.
  19. Regulation of pre-contract deposits outside Scotland, II, p. 917.

Supervision, enforcement, publicity etc.
  20. Prohibition of pre-contract deposits in Scotland, II, p. 917.
  21. Transactions in which an estate agent has a personal interest, II, p. 918.
  22. Standards of competence, II, p. 919.
  23. Bankrupts not to engage in estate agency work, II, p. 920.
  24. Supervision by Council on Tribunals, II, p. 920.
  25. General duties of Director, II, p. 921.
  26. Enforcement authorities, II, p. 921.
  27. Obstruction and personation of authorised officers, II, p. 922.

Supplementary
  28. General provisions as to offences, II, p. 923.
  29. Service of notices etc., II, p. 923.
  30. Orders and regulations, II, p. 924.

F

FORESTRY ACT: c. 21... ... ...   I, p. 585

> § 1. Finance for forestry, I, p. 585.
> 2 and schedule 1. Metrication of measurements, I, pp. 585, 587.
> 3 and schedule 2. Citation, etc., I, pp. 586, 587.
>
> Schedule 1. Metrication of 1967 Act, I, p. 587.
> Schedule 2. Repeals in 1967 Act, I, p. 587.

G

GIBRALTAR. Application to, under Pensioners' Payments and Social Security
Act (c. 48, s. 2(3)) ... ...   II, p. 1248

H

HIGH COURT. *See also* ARBITRATION ACT (c. 42); CHARGING ORDERS ACT
(c. 53). Appeal or application to, under—
Ancient Monuments and Archaeological Areas Act (c. 46, ss. 35(10), 55)
II, pp. 1178, 1195
Banking Act (c. 37, s. 13) ... ...   II, p. 836
Customs and Excise Management Act (c. 2, s. 127, sch. 3, para. 8)
I, pp. 88, 124
Estate Agents Act (c. 38, s. 7(4)) ... ...   II, p. 902
Justices of the Peace Act (c. 55, s. 48) ... ...   II, p. 1379
Merchant Shipping Act (c. 39, sch. 4, Pt. II, para. 11)   ...   II, p. 1018
Nurses, Midwives and Health Visitors Act (c. 36, s. 13)   ...   II, p. 798

HIGH COURT IN NORTHERN IRELAND. Appeals or application to, under—
Banking Act (c. 37, s. 13) ... ...   II, p. 836
Estate Agents Act (c. 38, s. 7(4)) ... ...   II, p. 902
Merchant Shipping Act (c. 39, sch. 4, Pt. II, para. 11)   ...   II, p. 1018
Nurses, Midwives and Health Visitors Act (c. 36, s. 13)   ...   II, p. 798

HISTORIC BUILDINGS. *See* ANCIENT MONUMENTS AND ARCHAEOLOGICAL AREAS
ACT (c. 46).

HOUSE OF COMMONS. *See also* HOUSE OF COMMONS (REDISTRIBUTION OF SEATS)
ACT (c. 15); PARLIAMENT. Disqualification of membership under—
Merchant Shipping Act (c. 39, s. 1(6)) ... ...   II, p. 936
Nurses, Midwives and Health Visitors Act (c. 36, sch. 1 para. 5, sch. 2
para. 5) ... ...   II, pp. 806, 808
Public Lending Right Act (c. 10, sch. para. 4) ... ...   I, p. 285
Social Security Act (c. 18, sch. 3 para. 12) ... ...   I, p. 578

HOUSE OF COMMONS (REDISTRIBUTION OF SEATS) ACT: c. 15 ...   I, p. 543

> § 1. Increase of number of constituencies in Northern Ireland, I, p. 543.
> 2. Citation, I, p. 544.

I

ISLE OF MAN ACT: c. 58   ...   .   II, p. 1407

ISLES OF SCILLY.   Application to, under—

J

JUSTICES OF THE PEACE ACT: c. 55 ...   .   II, p. 1349

PART I

GENERAL

Areas and commissions of the peace

K

L

PART 1

REGISTRATION OF INTEREST IN LAND

PART II

INDEMNITY IN RESPECT OF REGISTERED INTERESTS IN LAND

PART III

SIMPLIFICATION AND EFFECT OF DEEDS

PART IV

MISCELLANEOUS AND GENERAL

M

N

The Central Council

§ 1 and schedule 1.　Constitution of Central Council, II, pp. 789, 805.
　2.　Functions of Council, II, p. 790.
　3.　Standing committees of Council, II, p. 790.
　4.　The Midwifery Committee, II, p. 791.

The National Boards and their relationship
to the Central Council

　5 and schedule 2.　Constitution of National Boards, II, pp. 792, 807.
　6.　Functions of Boards, II, p. 793.
　7.　Standing committees of Boards, II, p. 793.
　8.　Joint committees of Council and Boards, II, p. 794.
　9.　Local training committees, II, p. 795.

Registration

　10.　The professional register, II, p. 795.
　11.　Admission to register, II, p. 796.
　12 and schedule 3.　Removal from, and restoration to, register, II, pp. 797, 809.
　13.　Appeals, II, p. 798.
　14.　False claim of professional qualification, II, p. 798.

Miscellaneous provisions about midwifery

　15.　Rules as to midwifery practice, II, p. 799.
　16.　Local supervision of midwifery practice, II, p. 799.

O

OIL. *See* EXCISE DUTIES (SURCHARGES OR REBATES) ACT (c. 8); HYDROCARBON
OIL DUTIES ACT (c. 5).

P

PARLIAMENT. *See also* HOUSE OF COMMONS (REDISTRIBUTION OF SEATS) ACT
(c. 15); REPRESENTATION OF THE PEOPLE ACT (c. 40).

Orders, regulations, reports etc. to be laid before Parliament under—

Ancient Monuments and Archaeological Areas Act (c. 46, s. 23)
II, p. 1172

Banking Act (c. 37, s. 4(4))   ...   .   II, p. 828
Crown Agents Act (c. 43, ss. 9(2), 11(3), 21(2)(4), 22(7), sch. 5 para. 20(3))
II, pp. 1063, 1071, 1073, 1091
Customs and Excise Duties (General Reliefs) Act (c. 3, s. 16, sch. 2 para. 5)
I, pp. 158, 162
Electricity (Scotland) Act (c. 11, ss. 24(5), 25(5)(6), 30(4))
I, pp. 299, 300, 303
European Assembly (Pay and Pensions) Act (c. 50, s. 4(5))   II, p. 1257
Isle of Man Act (c. 58, s. 2(5))   ...   .   II, p. 1409
Kiribati Act (c. 27, ss. 2, 6(5)) ...   .   I, pp. 667, 670
Merchant Shipping Act (c. 39, ss. 5, 6(4), 49(5))   II, pp. 939, 941, 989
Nurses, Midwives and Health Visitors Act (c. 36, s. 20(6))...   II, p. 801
Public Lending Right Act (c. 10, ss. 2(6), 3(1)(2)(8))   I, pp. 281, 282
Social Security Act (c. 18, ss. 3(2), 10(3), 21(2))   I, pp. 558, 563, 568
Southern Rhodesia Act (c. 52, s. 1(3))   ...   .   II, p. 1303
Zimbabwe Act (c. 60, s. 1(3)) ...   .   II, p. 1425

Orders, regulations, reports etc. to be laid before the House of Commons
under—

Customs and Excise Duties (General Reliefs) Act (c. 3, s. 17(4)) I, p. 158
Matches and Mechanical Lighters Duties Act (c. 6, s. 5(3))   I, p. 260
Tobacco Products Duty Act (c. 7, ss. 1(4), 6(3))   ...   I, pp. 266, 268

Resolution of each House of Parliament required for approval of orders, regulations etc. under—

Resolution of House of Commons required for approval of orders, regulations etc. under—

PENSIONERS' PAYMENTS AND SOCIAL SECURITY ACT: c. 48 ... II, p. 1245

Lump sum payments to pensioners

PENSIONS. *See also* EUROPEAN ASSEMBLY (PAY AND PENSIONS) ACT (c. 50); PENSIONERS' PAYMENTS AND SOCIAL SECURITY ACT (c. 48); SOCIAL SECURITY ACT (c. 18). Provisions for, under—

W

5J